Administrating Kinship: Marriage Impediments and Dispensation Policies in the 18th and 19th Centuries

Legal History Library

VOLUME 63

The titles published in this series are listed at *brill.com/lhl*

Administrating Kinship: Marriage Impediments and Dispensation Policies in the 18th and 19th Centuries

By

Margareth Lanzinger

BRILL | NIJHOFF

LEIDEN | BOSTON

Published with the support of Austrian Science Fund (FWF): PUB 643-G.

Originally published as Verwaltete Verwandtschaft. Eheverbote, kirchliche und staatliche Dispenspraxis im 18. und 19 by Böhlau in 2015.
The text was translated from Germany by Christopher Roth and copyedited by Christine Brooks.

Der Wissenschaftsfonds.

Cover illustration: Diözesanarchiv Brixen, Konsistorialakten 1848, Fasc. 5a, Römische Dispenden, no. 16

The Library of Congress Cataloging-in-Publication Data is available online at https://catalog.loc.gov
LC record available at https://lccn.loc.gov/2023003158

Typeface for the Latin, Greek, and Cyrillic scripts: "Brill". See and download: brill.com/brill-typeface.

ISSN 1874-1793
ISBN 978-90-04-43107-2 (hardback)
ISBN 978-90-04-53987-7 (e-book)

This book is printed on acid-free paper and produced in a sustainable manner.

Contents

Preface to the English Edition

This book has a long history. It began as a *Habilitation* thesis at the University of Vienna. The aim was to investigate kin marriages in light of changing dispensation policies with a focus on the procedural diversity of dispensation practice within a transregional context while also relating such marriages to logics of domestic organisation. The research was conducted as part of a three-year Hertha Firnberg Fellowship (2005–2007) and a subsequent, likewise three-year Elise Richter Fellowship (2008–2011), financed by the Austrian Science Fund (FWF). I would therefore first like to acknowledge my debt of gratitude to this funding body and to these grant programmes' dedicated employees. This is also the place to express my thanks to the University of Vienna's Department of History, where both projects were institutionally situated and thus anchored in a collegial atmosphere with very good working conditions. During this period, I was able to share my passion for the research fields of kinship and kin marriage in a productive way with Edith Saurer (1942–2011). I would also like to extend my warmest thanks to Jon Mathieu for his constructive and critical commentaries on this work. And finally, I owe great thanks in myriad ways to Claudia Ulbrich.

Two one-month research stays at the Max Planck Institute for European Legal History – now the Max Planck Institute for Legal History and Legal Theory – in Frankfurt in 2009 and 2010 not only afforded me access to outstanding library holdings, especially concerning canon law, but also provided me with an ideal atmosphere for concentrated work. And later on, the period that I spent as a guest lecturer and a visiting professor at the Department of History (Historisches Seminar) of Leibniz University Hannover made it possible for me to complete this book. I have to thank Michaela Hohkamp for this opportunity that turned up at precisely the right time.

The archives used for this research project revealed exceptionally rich source material. For their friendly welcomes and the support they provided me in researching this topic, I extend thanks to their heads and their employees: to Eduard Scheiber of the diocesan archives in Brixen, Albert Fischer of the diocesan archives in Chur and Michael Fliri of the diocesan archives in Feldkirch, as well as to the employees of the diocesan archives in Salzburg, the diocesan archives in Trento, the Tyrolean State Archives in Innsbruck, the State Archives of Bolzano, the State Archives of Trento, the State Archives of Vorarlberg in Bregenz and the Austrian State Archives (Haus-, Hof- und Staatsarchiv and Allgemeines Verwaltungsarchiv) in Vienna.

In thinking about just how to go about investigating this topic, I was able to call upon a multitude of impulses and ideas from the field of historical kinship studies – which in recent years have seen grow continually broader in terms of publications, topics and participating historians – and from exchange with colleagues on the topic itself as well as regarding theoretical and methodical approaches. An important role was played by the discussions that took place at international events such as the Social Science History Conferences and at working group meetings and workshops, as part of which I had opportunities to present individual aspects of this work. Here, I would like to mention above all the working groups: Haus im Kontext – Kommunikation und Lebenswelt (House in Context – Communication and Spheres of Life), Historische Demographie (Historical Demography), Geschlechtergeschichte der Frühen Neuzeit (Early Modern Gender History) and the Irseer Arbeitskreis für vorindustrielle Wirtschafts- und Sozialgeschichte (Irsee Working Group on Preindustrial Economic and Social History). Additionally, numerous events outside of such organisational structures as well as university research colloquia provided further stimulating forums.

Involvement in research networks also opened up opportunities for both theoretical and substantive work. In this context, I would like to give explicit mention to the international research network Gender Differences in the History of European Legal Cultures, the research association of the Leibniz project "Kinship in the Premodern Era. Institutions and Forms of Thought of Intergenerational Transfer" (Verwandtschaft in der Vormoderne. Institutionen und Denkformen intergenerationeller Übertragung) headed by Bernhard Jussen in Frankfurt, the COFIN programme on the History of the Family (Storia della famiglia. Constanti e varianti in una prospettiva europea secoli XV–XX) that was coordinated by Silvana Seidel Menchi in Pisa from 2006 to 2008 and the COST Action A-34 "Gender and Well-Being: Work, Family and Public Policies", coordinated by Cristina Borderias of the Universidad de Barcelona. Of special value in terms of deeper conceptual questions and problems, moreover, were two discussion groups – one with Ernst Langthaler and Annemarie Steidl in Vienna, and the other with Michaela Hohkamp, Kirsten Rüther and Simon Teuscher in various places.

Funding from the FWF made possible the 2015 release of this book's German-language edition both in print and as an open access publication. The decision to publish an English-language edition of this book came thanks to its character as a basic empirical study that employs a broad range of perspectives to offer new insights into the kin marriage phenomenon. This is the first study to have examined and interrelated the logics surrounding kin marriages during the late eighteenth and nineteenth centuries from the perspectives of administration, canon and civil law and the state. The period at issue here is widely viewed as having been the decisive phase during which this phenomenon enjoyed broad societal presence, above all in various public discourses. Comparing how marriage projects involving close consanguineous and affinal kin were administrated by the Church in the four neighbouring dioceses of Brixen, Chur, Salzburg and Trento shows that these dioceses acted in starkly differing ways. Furthermore, this book analyses highly revealing marriage dispensation requests and thus source material that is altogether quite extensive and exceptionally rich. Such analysis serves to make visible the arguments, strategies and logics of those couples who were affected by the marriage impediment of close consanguineous and/or affinal kinship. With this, the present publication opens up an abundance of new perspectives – on church power and associated ambivalences, on Josephinism including its contradictions and the difficulties encountered by its implementation in parts of the Habsburg monarchy and on marriage concepts and emotions, matters of household organisation and the attitude toward stepmothers. In this way, the present study's findings shed new light on the long transition from the early modern period to the nineteenth and twentieth centuries, thereby making important contributions to various fields of research.

It hence remains for me to once again thank the Austrian Science Fund for supporting this volume's English translation and enabling its release as a printed and open-access publication as well as the University of Vienna and its Faculty of Historical and Cultural Studies for their provision of funds and grants for translation and proofreading. And finally, sincere thanks are due above all to Christopher Roth for his thoughtful translation and resolution of the numerous associated challenges as well as Christine Brocks for her meticulous final proofreading.

Vienna, September 2022

Figures, Maps, Tables and Graph

Figures

Maps

Tables

Graph

CHAPTER 1

Introduction

> Thus all social action is seen to be
> the result of an individual's constant
> negotiation, manipulation, choices
> and decisions in the face
> of a normative reality which,
> though pervasive, nevertheless offers
> many possibilities of personal
> interpretations and freedoms.[1]

In recent years, the field of historical kinship studies has taken on sharper contours as well as a greater measure of diversity and nuance. Various aspects and forms, meanings and chronologies of kinship practice have been and still are being discussed, contributing to the change of conventional conceptions of history that were championed during the nineteenth and twentieth centuries under the banner of progress and modernisation. Significant here is the finding that kinship,[2] though repeatedly 'disappeared' from the history of modern Europe, did indeed retain its efficacity in the modern era as a structure of ordering and orientation, as knowledge formation and as a category that gave rise to inclusion and exclusion. It follows that kinship can no longer be

1 Giovanni Levi, "On Microhistory", in *New Perspectives on Historical Writing*, ed. Peter Burke (Cambridge, 1991), pp. 93–113, 94.

2 "Kinship has been said to have been in decline at almost every moment during Western history." David Warren Sabean and Simon Teuscher, "Kinship in Europe: A New Approach to Long-Term Development", in *Kinship in Europe: Approaches to Long-Term Development, 1300–1900*, ed. David Warren Sabean, Simon Teuscher and Jon Mathieu (New York/Oxford, 2007), pp. 1–32, 1. An overview of research on this topic is provided in a review of this volume by François-Joseph Ruggiu, "Histoire de la parenté ou anthropologie historique de la parenté? Autour de Kinship in Europe", *Annales de Démographie Historique* 1 (2010), 223–256. On "narratives of decline" see also Simon Teuscher, "Verwandtschaft in der Vormoderne: Zur politischen Karriere eines Beziehungskonzepts", in *Die Ahnenprobe in der Vormoderne. Selektion – Initiation – Repräsentation*, ed. Elizabeth Harding and Michael Hecht (Münster, 2011), pp. 85–106.

 | DOI:10.1163/9789004539877_002

regarded as an "archaic organisational principle".[3] This notion was much rather an inheritance from nineteenth-century sociologists, philosophers and intellectuals that effectively obscured the view. For "the first thing", writes a critical Carola Lipp, that they "expelled" from the ranks of socially and politically relevant categories in their definition of modernity was "the concept of kinship".[4]

By contrast, newer research regards kinship as a "historical factor *sui generis*",[5] as a significant principle structuring social relationships – relationships between and within generations as well as between men and women. Whether or not these relationships were sustained by a special attention economy and by loyalty must be verified in each individual case, however, for kinship simultaneously represented a social realm of competition, dispute and conflict.[6] Particularly in recent years, historians and representatives of other disciplines have produced numerous studies on how kin relations manifested themselves in different places and periods.[7] Still, a great many questions remain open.

3 Jon Mathieu, "Verwandtschaft als historischer Faktor. Schweizer Fallstudien und Trends, 1500–1900", *Historische Anthropologie* 10, 2 (2002), pp. 225–244, 225.

4 Carola Lipp, "Verwandtschaft – ein negiertes Element in der politischen Kultur des 19. Jahrhunderts", *Historische Zeitschrift* 283 (2006), pp. 31–77, 31, 34.

5 Jon Mathieu, "'Ein Cousin an jeder Zaunlücke': Überlegungen zum Wandel von Verwandtschaft und ländlicher Gemeinde, 1700–1900", in *Politiken der Verwandtschaft: Beziehungsnetze, Geschlecht und Recht*, ed. Margareth Lanzinger and Edith Saurer (Göttingen, 2007), pp. 55–71, 59; Mathieu, "Verwandtschaft als historischer Faktor". Ida Fazio also opposes a primarily reactive view of kinship as "defence or protection" in processes of social change. Her desire is to liberate both kinship and the market from the antagonistic relationship implied by this view. Ida Fazio, "Parentela e mercato nell'isola di Stromboli nel XIX secolo", in *Famiglie. Circolazione di beni, circuiti di affetti in età moderna*, ed. Renata Ago and Benedetta Borello (Rome, 2008), pp. 141–181, 141.

6 See Detlef Berghorn, *Verwandtschaft als Streitzusammenhang. Eine Fall-Geschichte in Beziehungen im hohen Adel des Alten Reiches, 16. bis 19. Jahrhundert* (Vienna/Cologne, 2021).

7 A selection of these would be: Eva Labouvie and Ramona Myrrhe (eds.), *Familienbande – Familienschande. Geschlechterverhältnisse in Familie und Verwandtschaft* (Cologne/Weimar/Vienna, 2007); Lanzinger/Saurer, *Politiken der Verwandtschaft*; Johannes Pflegerl and Christine Geserick, *Kinship and Social Security in Austria. A Social History for the 20th Century* (Innsbruck, 2007); Sabean/Teuscher/Mathieu, *Kinship in Europe*; Johannes F.K. Schmidt et al. (eds.), *Freundschaft und Verwandtschaft. Zur Unterscheidung und Verflechtung zweier Beziehungssysteme* (Constance, 2007); Andreas Holzem and Ines Weber (eds.), *Ehe – Familie – Verwandtschaft: Vergesellschaftung in Religion und sozialer Lebenswelt* (Paderborn, 2008); Gerhard Lubich, *Verwandtsein. Lesarten einer politisch-sozialen Beziehung im Frühmittelalter* (Cologne/Weimar/Vienna, 2008); Heidi Rosenbaum and Elisabeth Timm, *Private Netzwerke im Wohlfahrtsstaat: Familie, Verwandtschaft und soziale Sicherheit im Deutschland des 20. Jahrhunderts* (Constance, 2008). See also the special issues of *Traverse* 3 (1996), "Starke Bande. Verwandtschaft, Arbeit und Geschlecht", ed. Frédéric Sardet and Marianne Stubenvoll; of *L'Homme. Z.F.G.* 13, 1 (2002), "Die Liebe der Geschwister", ed. Karin Hausen and Regina Schulte; of *Historical Social Research* 30, 3 (2005), "Siblings – Parents – Grandparants",

Research desiderata here include deeper investigation of the increase in the number of kin marriages[8] that can be observed from the middle or, at the latest, by the end of the eighteenth century in various European contexts – a trend that was to continue into the twentieth century. Marriages between close blood and affinal kin must be accorded a considerable degree of importance in modern history – not only with an eye to the figuration of gender relations and intergenerational relations but also in connection with the formation of alliances, of social milieus and hence of a society's very foundations. It is with this phenomenon, which would appear at first glance to have been widely prevalent, that this study begins – with the intent of arriving at a nuanced impression.

On the basis of the belief that man and woman became 'one flesh' via the union of their bodies, affinity was subject to prohibitions on marriage that ran parallel to the ones pertaining to kinship by blood.[9] In the Catholic context, such restrictions – which extended four generations back – remained valid and efficacious over a very long period of time, from the beginning of the thirteenth

---

ed. Georg Fertig; of *Berliner Blätter. Ethnographische und ethnologische Beiträge* 42 (2007), "Verwandtschaft machen. Reproduktionsmedizin und Adoption in Deutschland und der Türkei", ed. Michi Knecht et al.; and of *WerkstattGeschichte* 46 (2007) "Tanten", ed. Michaela Hohkamp.

8 Cf. André Burguière, "'Cher Cousin': Les usages matrimoniaux de la parenté proche dans la France du 18e siècle", *Annales Histoire, Sciences Sociales* 52, 6 (1997), 1339–1360; Gérard Delille, *Famille et propriété dans le Royaume de Naples, XV–XIXe siècle* (Rome/Paris, 1985), pp. 369–370; Jean-Marie Gouesse, "Mariages de proches parents (XVIe–XXe siècle). Esquisse d'une conjuncture", in *Le modèle familial Européen. Normes, déviances, contrôle du pouvoir. Actes des séminaires organisés par l'École française de Rome et l'Università di Roma* (Rome, 1986), pp. 31–61; Jean-Marie Gouesse, "Parenté, famille et mariage en Normandie aux XVIIe et XVIIIe siècles", *Annales ESC* 27, 4–5 (1972), 1139–1154; Mathieu, Verwandtschaft als historischer Faktor, pp. 238–242; David Warren Sabean, *Kinship in Neckarhausen, 1700–1870* (Cambridge, 1998), pp. 217–237; 274–292; 379–396; Edith Saurer, "Stiefmütter und Stiefsöhne. Endogamieverbote zwischen kanonischem und zivilem Recht am Beispiel Österreichs (1790–1850)", in *Frauen in der Geschichte des Rechts. Von der Frühen Neuzeit bis zur Gegenwart*, ed. Ute Gerhard (Munich, 1997), pp. 345–366; Marion Trévisi, "Le mariage entre parents à La Roche-Guyon (Vexin français) au XVIIIe siècle: une étude de la perception du lien de parenté dans le cas des mariages avec dispense", in *Eheschließungen im Europa des 18. und 19. Jahrhunderts: Muster und Strategien*, ed. Christophe Duhamelle and Jürgen Schlumbohm (Göttingen, 2003), pp. 241–265.

9 Cf. Margareth Lanzinger, "'Und werden sein die zwey ein Fleisch'. Das Eheverbot der Schwägerschaft", *Mitteilungen des Instituts für Wissenschaft und Kunst* 1–2 (2006), 36–42. On 'blood' and 'flesh' in the sense of bodily substances that serve as metaphors for kinship bonds cf. Anita Guerreau-Jalabert, "Flesh and Blood in Medieval Language about Kinship", in *Blood & Kinship: Matter for Metaphor from Ancient Rome to the Present*, ed. Christopher H. Johnson et al. (New York/Oxford, 2013), pp. 61–82.

century all the way to the beginning of the twentieth century. Overcoming these marriage prohibitions required a so-called dispensation. The procedure associated with procuring a dispensation depended on the type and proximity of kinship at issue and changed over the centuries. During the period of time concerned here, decisions on dispensation requests in close degrees were usually made by the papal authorities in Rome. The late eighteenth and nineteenth centuries were by no means an easy time for prospective couples who were related closely by blood or affinity. Moreover, the granting and refusal of dispensations gave rise to much debate: at inns and in village gossip as well as in the English Parliament, in tracts by jurists, theologians, physicians and heredity theorists, and in dramas and fictional prose. Throughout the nineteenth century, the subject of kin marriages proved fit to agitate and preoccupy individuals and institutions in all kinds of ways.

Just how contentious this topic was, in particular from the late eighteenth century onward, becomes apparent in the associated discourse populated by theological, legal, medical and scientific positions. Representatives of confessions and states, scholars and practitioners of scientific disciplines held divergent views. And from the perspective of the dioceses studied here, those of Brixen, Chur, Salzburg and Trento, the logics of the church and state bureaucracies and authorities responsible for dispensation policy and practice were sources of repeated controversy. The period of time covered here thus witnessed a battle for definitional power regarding the sensibility and extent of marriage prohibitions, the perception of incest and the 'danger' associated with kin marriages. Analysing this phenomenon in its diverse discursive and conceptual, legal and political, administrative and bureaucratic, as well as familial and household-organisational contexts is the objective of this book. These contexts, in a way that is closely interwoven, lead us through numerous stations ranging from the local parish house and town hall to the Roman Curia and the Imperial Court Chancellery in Vienna.

David Sabean has argued that pressure 'from below' caused all European states to make a de facto transition to a liberal dispensation policy or in fact do away altogether with the prohibitions on consanguine and affinal marriage from the mid-eighteenth century onward.[10] This presupposes the jurisdiction of a liberal state in this material. In Austria, however, the period in question

10 David Warren Sabean, "Kinship and Class Dynamics in Nineteenth-Century Europe", in *Kinship in Europe*, Sabean/Teuscher/Mathieu, pp. 301–313, 310–311; Sabean/Teuscher, "Kinship in Europe", p. 21: "From around the middle of the eighteenth century, pushed from below, the older prohibitions became subject to pro forma dispensations or were abrogated altogether."

reveals only "liberal interludes":[11] during the Josephinism of the 1780s and the era of liberal government between 1867 and 1878. Even if here, as well, the laws of the state did attempt to break the Catholic Church's lock on the granting of dispensations from the 1770s onward, the Church remained involved to varying extents throughout the entire nineteenth century. It even functioned as the primary actor in dioceses such as that of Brixen. The more liberal provisions regarding kin marriage adopted by Prussia, France and Great Britain contrasted with legal frameworks in other territories where the Church managed to retain its normative power largely intact.

Dispensation was no mere formality. This is shown by numerous rejected requests, but also by the uncertainty associated with the administrative procedures as well as by the detours and strategies to which affected couples repeatedly resorted in order to reach their goal. One crucial prerequisite for success that became evident over the course of this research was tenacity: refusal to give up a marriage project as well as perseverance even after receiving signals that it was hopeless and encountering ever-new obstacles. Viewed in the context of dispensation practice, tenacity was a significant social resource that can also be read as an element of a certain political culture.

In the 1770s, a political power struggle arose in Austria that revolved around staking out the extent of marriage prohibitions and incest taboos as well as the matter of jurisdiction when it came to the procedures involved in dispensation-granting. State intervention in dispensation-related matters caused the administration of kinship to take on conflicting and converging forms as it entered a new phase: Church and state now competed for definitional authority over marriage prohibitions and the handling of dispensatory power. The way in which kin marriages were dealt with was quite generally characterised by the unconsummated separation of Church and state where matters of marriage were concerned.[12] While France implemented this

---

11 On this term see Karl Vocelka, *Geschichte Österreichs. Kultur – Gesellschaft – Politik*, 3rd ed. (Munich, 2002), p. 216. See also the contributions by Pieter M. Judson, "Early Liberalism in Austrian Society", in *Der deutsche und österreichische Liberalismus: Geschichts- und politikwissenschaftliche Perspektiven im Vergleich*, ed. Helmut Reinalter and Harm Klueting (Innsbruck, 2010), pp. 105–120; Alfred Ableitinger, "Die historische Entwicklung des Liberalismus in Österreich im 19. und beginnenden 20. Jahrhundert", in ibid., pp. 121–147; Helmut Reinalter, "Liberalismus und Kirche in Österreich im 19. Jahrhundert", in ibid., pp. 149–160.

12 At the beginning of the period under examination, the integration of Austria's territories into a unified state was still far from having been accomplished – but it was this period in particular during which massive processes of centralisation were initiated. At that time, 'state' as an entity (*der Staat*) and as an adjective (*staatlich*) was a term denoting a position that was simultaneously opposite and separate from the Church.

separation in 1792 with its policy of mandatory civil marriage, the situation in Austria featured a back-and-forth in terms of competencies that would drag on for decades. For closely related would-be spouses, this not only entailed laborious and obstacle-strewn administrative processes but also fundamental dependence on the Church's mercy, a consequence that was far more severe in a socio-political sense. After all, there existed no legal claim whatsoever to a dispensation.[13] These circumstances gave rise to a melange of conflicting interests that proceeded to determine the actions taken by members of the state and church administrative hierarchies. Ernst Hanisch has stated that the "long shadow of the state" was responsible for the underdeveloped collective consciousness of civil society in Austria.[14] But at least on the regional level and from the perspective of the nineteenth century, the persistence of the Church's long arm surely made a no less powerful contribution as an underlying factor.[15]

This study's spatial scope encompasses four dioceses that occupied a contiguous area now situated in Austria, Italy and Switzerland (see Map 1). The differences between them should provide insights into the spectrum of dispensation practices and the structured repertoires of action associated therewith.[16] The Diocese of Brixen encompassed the northern parts of historical Tyrol and hence an area whose Catholicism was pronouncedly political and ultramontane in character.[17] The nineteenth century saw the addition of Vorarlberg, a region where industrialisation set in early.[18] The neighbouring Swiss Diocese of Chur, by way of contrast, represented a confessionally mixed area. Salzburg – just like the ecclesiastical territories of Brixen and Trent – was

---

13 Angela Groppi identifies the same logic in her study on institutional care for the destitute elderly in Rome as typically Catholic. This, she writes, was based on the idea that the benefactor – there, as here, the Catholic Church – earned gratitude on the part of those benefited that would not have had to be shown an institution if there had existed a legal claim to said benefits. Angela Groppi, *Il welfare prima del welfare. Assistenza alla vecchiaia e solidarietà tra generazioni a Roma in età moderna* (Rome, 2010), p. 70.

14 Ernst Hanisch, *Der lange Schatten des Staates. Österreichische Gesellschaftsgeschichte im 20. Jahrhundert*, 1890–1990 (Vienna, 1994).

15 On the influence of the clergy especially in Tyrol cf. Helmut Alexander, "Zur regionalen Herkunft des Priesternachwuchses der Diözese Brixen im 19. Jahrhundert", *Histoire des Alpes / Storia delle Alpi / Geschichte der Alpen* 3 (1998), 309–325.

16 On this concept cf. Gadi Algazi, "Kulturkult und die Rekonstruktion von Handlungsrepertoires", *L'Homme. Z.F.G.* 11, 1 (2000), 105–119.

17 For a general impression see Josef Fontana, *Der Kulturkampf in Tirol, 1861–1892* (Bolzano, 1978); Gustav Pfeifer and Josef Nössing (eds.), *Kulturkampf in Tirol und in den Nachbarländern: Akten des Internationalen Kolloquiums des Tiroler Geschichtsvereins (Sektion Bozen) im Kolpinghaus Bozen, 9. November 2012* (Innsbruck, 2013).

18 Cf. Hubert Weitensfelder, *Industrie-Provinz. Vorarlberg in der Frühindustrialisierung 1740–1870* (Frankfurt a. M./New York, 2001).

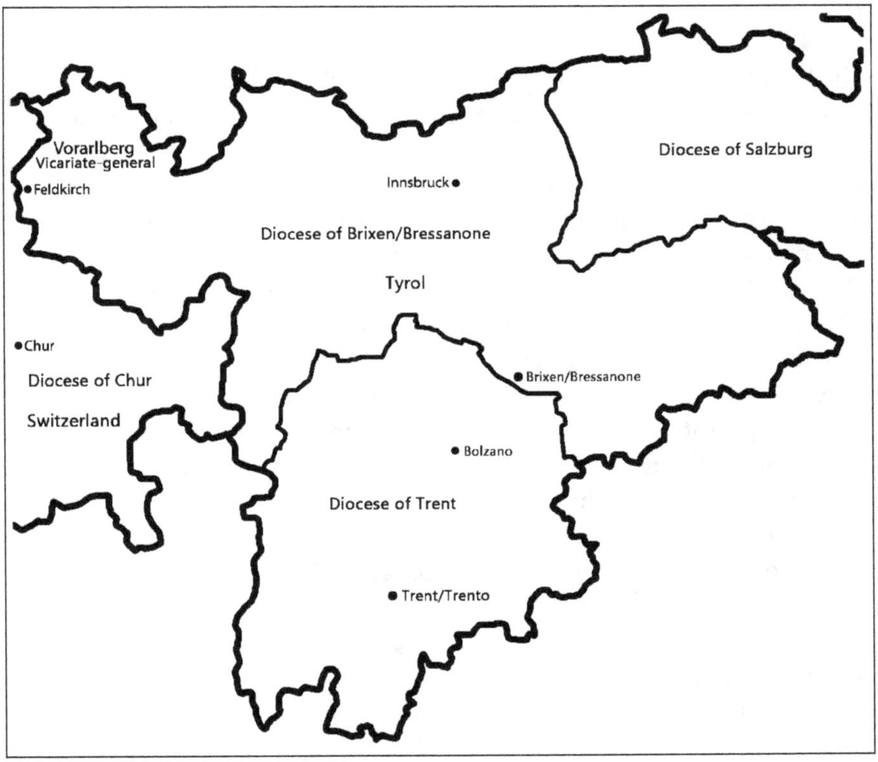

MAP 1 The Dioceses of Brixen, Chur, Salzburg and Trento after 1818
SOURCE: DIGITISED BY MARIO MOSSER FROM THE ORIGINAL IN: ERWIN GATZ (ED.), *DIE BISTÜMER DER DEUTSCHSPRACHIGEN LÄNDER VON DER SÄKULARISATION BIS ZUR GEGENWART* (FREIBURG, 2005), MAP 2: NEUUMSCHREIBUNG DER BISTÜMER IN TIROL UND VORARLBERG. DIE BISTUMSEINTEILUNG TIROLS UND VORARLBERGS SEIT 1818.

secularised as a former ecclesiastical territory in 1803 and only permanently integrated into the Habsburg Monarchy in 1816, following a multi-year interlude of Bavarian and French rule. Furthermore, Salzburg's Prince-Archbishop Count Hieronymus von Colloredo – in contrast to the Prince-Bishops of Brixen – had been an adherent of enlightened Josephine policies during the late eighteenth century. The Diocese of Trento, for its part, was responsible for the southern parts of historical Tyrol. This not only included Italian-speaking areas but also parts of present-day South Tyrol.[19]

19 The parishes in the lower Vinschgau and in the Sarn, Fassa and lower Eisack valleys were appended to the Diocese of Trento in the nineteenth century. The Adige or Etsch Valley with its towns of Meran and Bozen already belonged to it.

1 Kinship and Kin Marriage

The broad notion of kinship prevalent during the Middle Ages and the early modern period narrowed markedly as time went on. While the definition of kinship provided by the mid-eighteenth-century *Zedlers Universallexikon* had included diverse social relations such as guild or university colleagues, thereby encompassing all members of such institutions,[20] such definitions proceeded to shrink in a way not unlike that of the shrinking piece of shagreen in Balzac's *The Wild Ass's Skin*.[21] In the normatively Catholic context, however, it still did encompass blood relations and affinal kin all the way out to the fourth degree – which reached back four generations to common great-great-grandparents – as well as an extended network including godparents, godchildren and their parents as spiritual kin.[22] The rules to this effect remained unchanged from 1215 to 1917 and thus over an impressively long period of 700 years. The notion of kinship according to the ecclesiastical and civil laws that underlay marriage prohibitions was defined independently of whether such kinship was lived or activated and updated in certain situations – and was therefore something of which the kin in question were conscious. All that mattered here were genealogically reconstructable degrees of blood and affinal kinship. The issue of who was counted among one's kin in everyday life from a personal perspective, however – for example, when deciding whom to invite to a wedding or inform about a death in the family – could involve an entirely different logic.

Individual disciplines and 'national' academic cultures have researched and debated kinship with varying intensity.[23] Modern-era German-language

20 Article: "Verwandt", in *Johann Heinrich Zedlers Grosses vollständiges Universallexicon aller Wissenschaften und Künste…*, vol. 48 (Leipzig/Halle, 1746), col. 141–146. On this see also the broad-based concept of 'fründe' – meaning 'friends', but also a synonym for 'relatives' – in the study by Simon Teuscher, *Bekannte – Klienten – Verwandte. Soziabilität und Politik in der Stadt Bern um 1500* (Cologne/Weimar/Vienna, 1998).

21 This is the metaphor used by Gérard Delille: "Comme un peau de chagrin, l'aire de la parenté s'est restrainte de manière décisive et brutale." Delille, *Famille et propriété*, p. 365. With reference to the mid-twentieth century in the USA and the "urban middle class areas of society", Talcott Parsons spoke of the "isolated conjugal family". Talcott Parsons, "The Kinship System of the Contemporary United States", *American Anthropologist, New Series* 45, 1 (1943), 22–38, 27, 29–32.

22 Cf. Guido Alfani and Vincent Gourdon (eds.), *Spiritual Kinship in Europe, 1500–1900* (Basingstoke, 2012); Guido Alfani, *Fathers and Godfathers. Spiritual Kinship in Early Modern Italy* (Aldershot, 2009 [2006]); Bernhard Jussen, *Spiritual Kinship as Social Practice. Godparenthood and Adoption in the Early Middle Ages* (London/Newark, 2000).

23 A broad overview is provided by Leonore Davidoff, *Thicker than Water. Siblings and Their Relations, 1780–1920* (Oxford, 2012), pp. 14–28. In the context of research on kinship pertaining to the Middle Ages, Bernhard Jussen compares German-language approaches and

and Anglo-Saxon historiography were relatively late in taking up the theme of kinship in the sense of a politically, socially and economically efficacious organisational structure. It was the influence of anthropological approaches that first sparked greater interest during the 1980s, primarily in the field of social history. A pioneering work that opened up new research perspectives was the 1984 volume on emotions and material interests edited by Hans Medick and David Sabean.[24] Major impulses also came from Italian micro-history, above all from Giovanni Levi's study *L'eredità immateriale – Inheriting Power –*, which was published in German translation in 1986 and in an English translation in 1988.[25] At first, these and other impulses did not result in a systematic or continually expanding, independent field of historiographic research.[26] The past two a half decades, however, have not only led to a considerable increase in the number of related publications but also to projects and events that, taken together, now do indeed allow us to speak of a field of historical kinship studies.[27]

---

concepts with French ones and points out the differences: Bernhard Jussen, "Perspektiven der Verwandtschaftsforschung fünfundzwanzig Jahre nach Jack Goodys 'Entwicklung von Ehe und Familie in Europa'", in *Die Familie in der Gesellschaft des Mittelalters*, ed. Karl-Heinz Spieß (Ostfildern, 2009), pp. 275–324. On varying emphases see also Margareth Lanzinger and Edith Saurer, "Politiken der Verwandtschaft. Einleitung", in *Politiken der Verwandtschaft*, ed. Saurer/Lanzinger, pp. 7–22; Margareth Lanzinger, "Parenté et genre: des mariages par alliance", in *Genre, femmes, histoire en Europe. France, Italie, Espagne, Autriche*, ed. Anna Bellavitis and Nicole Edelman (Paris, 2011), pp. 233–253, 233–239.

24 Hans Medick and David Warren Sabean (eds.), *Emotionen und materielle Interessen. Sozialanthropologische und historische Beiträge zur Familienforschung* (Göttingen, 1984).

25 Giovanni Levi, *Inheriting Power: The Story of an Exorcist* (Chicago, 1988 [1985]). In this volume, the author makes visible the multifarious reciprocities among kin involved in the pricing of land upon its sale and purchase. In transactions between kin, the sums – in contrast to what one might expect – were comparatively higher than among non-kin. This can be explained by how such transactions were used to provide remuneration for various kinds of work and other services as well as to settle existing debts or loans. The result was a social price, that is a price that was not oriented primarily toward the size and quality of the land but rather played a role in social relationships.

26 On this cf. the statement by Andrejs Plakans that retained its validity beyond the 1980s in: *Kinship in the Past. Anthropology of European Family Life, 1500–1900* (Oxford, 1984), pp. VI–IX, VII.

27 To name just a few: the project funded by the European Union's Sixth Framework Programme involving German and Austrian sociologists, historians, European ethnologists, et al. "Kinship and Social Security" (KASS), with an emphasis on the twentieth century, which was based in Halle; the Leibniz Project by Bernhard Jussen with an emphasis on kinship: "Institutionen und Denkformen intergenerationaler Übertragung" – Institutions and Patterns of Thought of Intergenerational Transference – at the University of Frankfurt; the kinship panels organised by David Warren Sabean and colleagues as part of the European Social Science History Conferences "Politics of Kinship" in The

Kinship's being more or less newly 'discovered' as a phenomenon can be explained by two paradigm shifts. The first pivotal change consisted in the revision of a widely held view according to which kinship disappeared as a socially relevant factor. One hypothesis to this effect had been that it was already the rise of Christianity in Latin Europe that, in contrast to how it was in other societies, had noticeably weakened kinship as a social institution from late antiquity onward.[28] Another influential assumption was that the growing significance and elaboration of the state had diminished the power of kinship bonds. And finally, as has already been critically questioned above, it was held that the modern era's expansion of economic markets and industrialisation, individualisation and societies' increasingly meritocratic character had ultimately rendered kin relations unimportant.

1970s and 1980s Anglo-Saxon and German-language research on the history of the family concentrated primarily on households. It thus broadened the overall perspective compared with a strictly genealogical family concept by centring on the social family, which encompassed everyone living within a household: married couples, children, grandparents, widows and widowers, servants, apprentices, journeymen, single aunts, foster children and others.[29] At the same time, however, it tended to remain focused on households as such along with their inner organisation.[30] Early critiques of the employed

---

Hague (2002), "Sibling Relations" in Berlin (2004), "International Families" in Amsterdam (2006), and "Construction of Blood" in Lisbon (2008), as well as the volumes to which they gave rise. Last but not least, I would like to mention my own research project on the topic "The Role of Wealth in Defining and Constituting Kinship Spaces from 16th to the 18th Century", funded by the Austrian Science Fund FWF (P29394-G28 2016–2020, P33348-G28 2020–2023), which is in its second phase.

28 On this cf. Michael Mitterauer, *Warum Europa? Mittelalterliche Grundlagen eines Sonderwegs* (Munich, 2003), pp. 70–108; Bernhard Jussen, "Erbe und Verwandtschaft. Kulturen der Übertragung im Mittelalter", in *Erbe. Übertragungskonzepte zwischen Natur und Kultur*, ed. Stefan Willer, Sigrid Weigel and Bernhard Jussen (Frankfurt a. M., 2013), pp. 37–64.

29 For critical voices cf. Sandro Guzzi-Heeb, "Von der Familien- zur Verwandtschaftsgeschichte: Der mikrohistorische Blick. Geschichte von Verwandten im Walliser Dorf Vouvry zwischen 1750 und 1850", *Historical Social Research* 30, 3 (2005), 107–129; David Warren Sabean, "Reflections on Microhistory", in *Transnationale Geschichte. Themen, Tendenzen und Theorien*, ed. Gunilla Budde, Sebastian Conrad and Oliver Janz (Göttingen, 2006), pp. 275–289; and from even earlier Heidi Rosenbaum, *Formen der Familie: Untersuchungen zum Zusammenhang von Familienverhältnissen, Sozialstruktur und sozialem Wandel in der deutschen Gesellschaft des 19. Jahrhunderts*, 5th ed. (Frankfurt a. M., 1990 [1982]), p. 26.

30 For classic examples see Peter Laslett, "Family and Household as Work Group and Kin Group: Areas of Traditional Europe Compared", in *Family Forms in Historic Europe*, ed. Richard Wall, Jean Robin and Peter Laslett (Cambridge, 1993), pp. 513–563; Peter Laslett,

classification by household type due to its formalistic character came above all from Italy and France.[31] This criticism concerned first and foremost the reduction of analysis to the persons present within the household, an approach that was said to entail the neglect of more extensive relational networks. Alongside relationships with neighbours, friends and occupational colleagues, such networks included above all relationships with relatives who did not live beneath the same roof.[32] The disregard for such relatives can thus be seen as the flipside of viewing the nuclear family in a positive light – as an indicator of modernity that also bore connotations of economic and social progress.[33] The nuclear family functioned as a paradigmatic representation of liberation from the "forced bonds" of kinship, which – to follow this highly schematic narrative – was first made possible by the idea of marriage for love and the "the dismantling of strict sex-role divisions", based on "the rejection of traditional, community-imposed forms in interpersonal matters".[34]

"Introduction: the History of the Family", in *Household and Family in Past Time*, ed. Peter Laslett and Richard Wall (Cambridge, 1972), pp. 1–89, 31, 41–42; Michael Mitterauer and Reinhard Sieder, "The Developmental Process of Domestic Groups: Problems of Reconstruction and Possibilities of Interpretation", *Journal of Family History* 4 (1979), 257–284.

31 Cf. Edoardo Grendi, "A proposito di 'famiglia e communità': questo fascicolo di Quaderni storici", *Quaderni storici* 33 (1976), 881–891, 882; Françoise Zonabend, "Verwandtschaft in der anthropologischen Forschung Frankreichs", in *Deutsche Volkskunde – Französische Ethnologie – Zwei Standortbestimmungen*, ed. Isac Chiva and Utz Jeggle (Frankfurt a. M., 1987), pp. 178–193. One must also mention here the relativisation undertaken by Lutz Berkner that resulted in a new orientation with a focus on life courses. He pointed out that the registered household configurations were all momentary snapshots that could change quickly due to factors such as generational breaks, etc. Lutz K. Berkner, "The Stem Family and the Developmental Cycle of the Peasant Household. An Eighteenth-Century Austrian Example", *American Historical Review* 77 (1972), 398–418.

32 Very critical of this view is Naomi Tadmor, *Family and Friends in Eighteenth-Century England: Household. Kinship, and Patronage* (Cambridge, 2001), pp. 107–117. On a relational network that extended far beyond a single household that becomes visible in the context of a supplication following a fire and defined itself in large part via provided support cf. the essay by Guzzi-Heeb, "Von der Familien- zur Verwandtschaftsgeschichte".

33 Cf. Jane C. Schneider and Peter T. Schneider, *Festival of the Poor. Fertility Decline & the Ideology of Class in Sicily, 1860–1980* (Tucson, 1996), p. 47; John Hajnal, "European Marriage Patterns in Perspective", in *Population in History. Essays in Historical Demography*, ed. D.V. Glass and D.E.C. Eversley (London, 1965), pp. 101–143. For a critical assessment see Hans Medick, "Zwischen Mythos und Realität – die historische Erforschung der Familie", in *Die Zukunft der Familie*, ed. Susanne Mayer and Dietmar Schulte (Munich, 2007), pp. 37–55.

34 Edward Shorter, *The Making of the Modern Family* (London, 1976), pp. 15–16. Cf. also Parsons, "The Kinship System", 31–38.

In the 1990s, however, relatives gradually began commanding a stronger presence on the historiographic stage: Jürgen Schlumbohm, in his 1994 study on life courses, families and farms, analysed various kin relationships in the contexts of households and inheritance in the parish of Belm in the Prince-Bishopric of Osnabrück. He did so with an eye to the question of whether kinship ties contributed to a possible lessening of social differences or, in fact, to their exacerbation.[35] David Sabean, in his study *Kinship in Neckarhausen*, revealed an intensification of solidarity among kin – namely as a phenomenon that went hand-in-hand with societal changes that unfolded during the nineteenth century.[36] To be sure, Western societies tended to be characterised by a great deal of openness and flexibility in the ways in which kinship was organised.[37] An open and flexible form that did not entail the ex ante coupling of expectations, obligations and claims ranging beyond one's close circle of kin to certain relational positions may have contributed to how kinship, in contrast to how it was in societies structured in a strictly patrilineal manner, for instance, stood less clearly in the foreground. For this reason, kinship's presence and power need to be investigated in a targeted manner.

A second paradigm shift and impulse for historical scholarship came from social anthropology, which advocates the "rediscovery" and "revival of kinship studies".[38] The catalyst for this was the abandonment of a priori definitions of what kinship had meant and what circle of persons it had encompassed in a given society at a given point in time. David Schneider's book *A Critique of the Study of Kinship*, published in 1984, plunged especially American anthropological kinship studies into a crisis.[39] In the wake of the realisation that communities from around the world under study by the discipline were being squeezed into readymade kinship-concepts oriented on the Western societies from which the researchers came, the idea was at first to do entirely without kinship schemes. But what initially followed as an alternative was merely a dissatisfying relativism. A way out of this dilemma and a new approach were opened up by shifting the perspective away from the definitional question of

35 Jürgen Schlumbohm, *Lebensläufe, Familien, Höfe: Die Bauern und Heuerleute des Osnabrückischen Kirchspiels Belm in proto-industrieller Zeit, 1650–1860* (Göttingen, 1994).

36 Sabean, *Kinship in Neckarhausen*, p. 458. This investigation ranges far beyond the household: kin assumed the most varied functions including as godparents, as guarantors, as witnesses, etc. Alongside this, a clearly visible rise in marriages between first cousins as well as second cousins was ascertained.

37 Cf. Mitterauer, *Warum Europa*, pp. 70–108.

38 Peter P. Schweitzer, "Introduction", in *Dividends of Kinship. Meanings and Uses of Social Relatedness*, ed. Peter P. Schweitzer (London/New York, 2000), pp. 1–32, 1–2.

39 David M. Schneider, *A Critique of the Study of Kinship* (Ann Arbor, 1984).

what kinship *is* and towards the question of "what is done through kinship", a question that "refers to material, symbolic and emotional gains that can be secured through cultural constructs of relatedness".[40] What is more, this new orientation – which one might term "after nature"[41] – proved open to categories of difference, predominantly with respect to gender and ethnicity.[42]

In a comparable manner, newer historiographic approaches focus on kinship's social construction and structuring power as well as on kinship as a context of action.[43] Such work has shown that kin by no means disappeared from 'modern' lives. Kin did, in fact, continue to be – and were increasingly – present and involved in the most varied social contexts: in connection with migration, in the search for employment and the procurement of employment for others, in making loans, in the transferral of property and wealth, in business relations, in nominations to political posts, in forms of sociability and domestic organisation, in caregiving work, in difficult life situations, as godparents and not least as marriage partners.[44]

---

40 Cf. Schweitzer, "Introduction", pp. 1–2.

41 To quote the title of a book by Marilyn Strathern, *After Nature: English Kinship in the Late Twentieth Century* (Cambridge, 1992); on this see also Janet Carsten, *After Kinship* (Cambridge, 2004); Janet Carsten, "Introduction: Cultures of Relatedness", in *Cultures of Relatedness. New Approaches to the Study of Kinship*, ed. Janet Carsten (Cambridge, 2000), pp. 1–36; Mary Jo Maynes et al., "Introduction: Toward a Comparative History of Gender, Kinship and Power", in *Gender, Kinship, Power. A Comparative and Interdisciplinary History*, ed. Mary Jo Maynes et al. (New York/London, 1996), pp. 1–23, 1. See also her more recent book Marilyn Strathern, *Relations. An Anthropological Account* (Durham/London, 2020).

42 It was above all Sylvia Yanagisako who contributed to the revitalisation of kinship studies in this sense "by introducing issues of ethnicity and gender to the discourse". Schweitzer, "Introduction", p. 4. Sylvia J. Yanagisako and Jane F. Collier, "Toward a Unified Analysis of Gender and Kinship", in *Gender and Kinship. Towards a Unified Analysis*, ed. Yanagisako/Collier (Stanford, 1987), pp. 14–50.

43 See Benedetta Borello and Margareth Lanzinger, "Introduction", *Quaderni storici* 165, 3 (2020), special issue on "Open Kinship", 629–641.

44 As a selection in addition to the publications already mentioned cf. Andreas Hansert, *Geburtsaristokratie in Frankfurt am Main. Geschichte des reichsstädtischen Patriziats* (Vienna/Cologne/Weimar, 2014); Tamara K. Hareven, *Families, History and Social Change. Life-Course and Cross-Cultural Perspectives* (Boulder, 2000); Elisabeth Joris and Heidi Witzig, *Brave Frauen, aufmüpfige Weiber. Wie sich die Industrialisierung auf Alltag und Lebenszusammenhänge von Frauen auswirkte*, 1820–1940 (Zurich, 1992), pp. 239–271; Carola Lipp, "Kinship Networks, Local Government, and Elections in a Town in Southwest Germany, 1800–1850", *Journal of Family History* 30, 4 (2005), 347–365; Tadmor, *Family and Friends*, 278; Annemarie Steidl, "Verwandtschaft und Freundschaft als soziale Netzwerke transatlantischer MigrantInnen in der Spätphase der Habsburgermonarchie", in *Politiken der Verwandtschaft*, ed. Lanzinger/Saurer, pp. 117–144; Migration and kinship is currently an important topic in various global contexts.

Interconnections have been ascertained between the increase in the number of kin marriages during the second half of the eighteenth century and diverse social changes that were occurring on the threshold between the early modern and modern periods. For one thing, these changes had a mobilising effect, for example on processes of state formation, public administration's expansion and the economy's capitalisation. They also went hand in hand with new concepts of love and marriage based on intimacy and familiarity.[45] Above all in the bourgeois milieu, kin endogamy came along with social homogamy and thus also closed the circle of inheritances, capital and other resources. What is more, the stage for marriage project initiation was set not least by well-developed forms of sociability among equals.[46] Sunday get-togethers between blood relatives and affinal kin to take walks, have coffee or perhaps hold an evening soirée served as controlled environments in which to select the 'right' future spouse in terms of socioeconomic and sociocultural criteria. They also represented social capital in the form of newly made or refreshed contacts as well as information exchanged. Elisabeth Joris and Heidi Witzig conducted research back in the early 1990s that revealed the feminisation of the activity of maintaining kin relations as a structural pattern.[47] Elisabeth Joris has shown for the context of the Swiss bourgeoisie that women frequently acted as go-betweens.[48] And finally, economic fundamentals still remained an important criterion in partner selection.[49]

---

45 Cf. Saurer, "Stiefmütter und Stiefsöhne"; Ramón A. Gutierrez, *Cuando Jesús llegó, las madres del maís se fueron. Matrimonio, sexualidad y poder en Nuevo México, 1500–1846* (Mexico, 1993).

46 Cf. Christopher H. Johnson, "Siblinghood and the Emotional Dimensions of the New Kinship System, 1800–1850: A French Example", in *Sibling Relations & the Transformation of European Kinship 1300–1900*, ed. Christopher H. Johnson and David Warren Sabean (New York/Oxford, 2011), pp. 189–220, 208–210; Margareth Lanzinger, "Spouses and the Competition for Wealth", in *The Routledge History of the Domestic Sphere in Europe Sixteenth to Nineteenth Century*, ed. Joachim Eibach and Margareth Lanzinger (London, 2020), pp. 61–78; Joachim Eibach, *Fragile Familien. Ehe und häusliche Lebenswelt in der bürgerlichen Moderne* (Berlin/Boston 2022).

47 Joris/Witzig, *Brave Frauen, aufmüpfige Weiber*, especially chapter v.

48 Elisabeth Joris, "Kinship and Gender: Property, Enterprise, and Politics", in *Kinship in Europe*, ed. Sabean/Teuscher/Mathieu, pp. 231–257. Sandro Guzzi-Heeb is another who accords an important role to women in connection with maintaining kin relations and the marriage projects that resulted therefrom. Sandro Guzzi-Heeb, *Donne, uomini, parentela. Casati alpini nell'Europa preindustriale, 1650–1850* (Turin, 2007), pp. 335–336.

49 Cf. Davidoff, *Thicker than Water*, pp. 60–64; 235–238. During the nineteenth century, financial questions were openly discussed prior to weddings. Relevant studies ascertain a concern among both parties for security via a marriage among equals that existed all across the various social milieus. On this see Peter Borscheid, "Geld und Liebe. Zu den Auswirkungen des Romantischen auf die Partnerwahl im 19. Jahrhundert", in *Ehe, Liebe,*

A classic marriage configuration of this era was that of two cousins. The preceding paradigm of intensified relationships between siblings has received a great deal of attention in the historical kinship studies of recent years. In this regard, Christopher H. Johnson speaks of a "sibling archipelago".[50] This re-positioning of siblings – and, accordingly, of cousins – touched off a process, he states, resulting in kinship becoming more horizontal.[51] Up to now, the ascertainment of a connection between intensified sibling relations and the frequency of cousin marriages has come mainly from studies on bourgeois milieus. Before this backdrop, researching kin marriages across a broad swath of social milieus and adding further nuance to the contexts of such unions is a gap that this book attempts to fill.

Existing research has associated marriages between close kin with economic advantageousness[52] – such as the objective of combining property or keeping it whole in rural areas and agrarian milieus. Especially for areas where it was customary to divide property such as lots, meadows, fields, etc. among children as heirs, it would hence seem reasonable to assume the existence of efforts to acquire the 'missing' parts of sensible economic units by way of accordingly advantageous marital unions.

Tod. Zum Wandel der Familie, der Geschlechts- und Generationsbeziehungen in der Neuzeit, ed. Peter Borscheid and Hans J. Teuteberg (Münster, 1983), pp. 112–134, especially 122–134.

50 Christopher H. Johnson, "Das 'Geschwister Archipel': Bruder-Schwester-Liebe und Klassenformation im Frankreich des 19. Jahrhundert", *L'Homme. Z.F.G.* 13, 1 (2002), 50–67; Christopher H. Johnson, "Siblinghood and the Emotional Dimensions", p. 213; Christopher H. Johnson, *Becoming Bourgeois. Love, Kinship, and Power in Provincial France, 1670–1880* (Ithaca/London, 2015).

51 Cf. Sabean/Teuscher, "Kinship in Europe", pp. 16–24.

52 In his study *The Development of the Family and Marriage in Europe*, published in 1983, Jack Goody developed a thesis according to which the reason for the wide-ranging marriage prohibitions among kin during the Middle Ages was mainly the Catholic Church's interest in the accumulation of property. Jochen Martin voiced criticism of this assumption, pointing out things such as how Goody has equated law with actual practice and used legal foundations to make assumptions about levels of action. Furthermore, Martin pointed out that, "due to his broad-based comparison", Goody had conceived of canon law as a "uniform monolith" and thus as too hermetic. Jochen Martin, "Zur Anthropologie von Heiratsregeln und Besitzübertragung. 10 Jahre nach den Goody-Thesen", *Historische Anthropologie* 1, 1 (1993), 149–162, 150. Highly critical and extensive arguments against Goody's view are also made by Lloyd Bonfield, "Canon Law and Family Law in Medieval Western Christendom", *Continuity and Change* 6, 3 (1991), 361–374; Margareth Lanzinger, "Verwandtenheirat – ein 'aristokratisches' Ehemodell? Debatten um die Goody-Thesen und Dispenspraxis Ende des 18. Jahrhunderts", in *Beziehungen, Vernetzungen, Konflikte. Perspektiven Historischer Verwandtschaftsforschung*, ed. Christine Fertig and Margareth Lanzinger (Vienna/Cologne/Weimar, 2016), pp. 143–166.

The Diocese of Brixen, on which this study focuses, was intersected by a dividing line in terms of prevailing inheritance practices: in its eastern half, property was generally succeeded to as a whole, while the western part of Tyrol as well as Vorarlberg generally featured partible inheritance of land.[53] It was one of this study's hypotheses that the number of dispensation requests could be expected to be higher in the diocese's western half with partible inheritance of land. In terms of quantitative findings, this assumption held true – at least at first glance. However, close examination of these dispensation requests caused the initially assumed link with partible inheritance of land to recede. Instead, it became increasingly apparent that political culture as well as the inner logics of household and familial organisation played a highly significant role, along with a snowball effect of sorts touched off by the knowledge and hope that receiving a dispensation might be possible.

2 Confessional Distinctions

In the mid-nineteenth century, Johann Kutschker – a Catholic theologist who wrote on marital law – ascertained: "What most commonly stands in the way of a marriage's validity is the impediment of kinship."[54] At that point, society had already been experiencing a successively greater presence of kin marriages for several decades, particularly in terms of marriage projects between *close* kin. Up to the end of the *Ancien Régime*, such unions had tended to be reserved for the high nobility. The *Decretum Tametsi* issued by the Council of Trent in 1563 had mandated that absolutely no dispensations were to be granted for marriages

53 See Rudolf Palme, "Die Entwicklung des Erbrechtes im ländlichen Bereich", in *Südtiroler Erbhöfe. Menschen und Geschichten* ed. Paul Rösch (Bolzano, 1994), pp. 25–37; Paul Rösch, "Lebensläufe und Schicksale. Auswirkungen von zwei unterschiedlichen Erbsitten in Tirol", in ibid., pp. 61–70. On the effects of "the feudal agrarian structure of large farms" and "the communal small-farming structure" on farm sizes cf. Jon Mathieu, *History of the Alps, 1500–1900. Environment, Development, and Society* (Morgantown, 2009 [2001]), pp. 135–160, quote 136; cf. also Jon Mathieu, "Von der verstreuten Familie zum 'Ganzen Haus': Sozialgeschichtliche Übergänge im schweizerisch-österreichischen Alpenraum des 17. bis 19. Jahrhundert", in *Der Vinschgau und seine Nachbarräume*, Vorträge des landeskundlichen Symposiums Schloß Goldrain 27. bis 30. Juni 1991, ed. Rainer Loose (Bolzano, 1993), pp. 245–255, 246–247; Pier Paolo Viazzo, *Upland Communities. Environment, Population and Social Structure in the Alps since the Sixteenth Century* (Cambridge, 1989).

54 Johann Kutschker, *Das Eherecht der katholischen Kirche nach seiner Theorie und Praxis mit besonderer Berücksichtigung der in Österreich zu Recht bestehenden Gesetze*, vol. 3 (Vienna, 1856). He quotes canonists extensively, above all Tomás Sánchez.

between kin, with exceptions permitted only in rare cases, for specific reasons and out of mercy.[55] In keeping with this norm, dispensations in the second degree – that is, those for first cousins – remained confined to the high nobility and to unions deemed to be in the public interest. In the more distant third and fourth degrees, however, the granting of dispensations was relatively common during the sixteenth and seventeenth centuries.[56] And over the course of the eighteenth century's second half, the ranks of those who desired to marry a cousin or sister-in-law – that means, in close degrees – grew increasingly larger and gradually came to encompass all social milieus. Nobles still continued to occupy a privileged position. Prospective spouses from wealthy families that had made contributions to the Church – in the form of endowments or donations, for instance – had significantly better cards as well, as did those who could boast connections to higher ecclesiastical and civil officials. Altogether, though, the submitted requests were spread rather broadly throughout society, a fact that might be taken to indicate a certain 'democratisation' of kin marriages. It was thus that, come the nineteenth century, such unions were no longer a primarily aristocratic and bourgeois phenomenon.

---

55 Decretum Tametsi, Sessio 24, Caput 5: "In contrahendis matrimoniis vel nulla omnino detur dispensatio, vel raro, idque ex causa, & gratia concedatur." Cr. *Il sacro concilio di Trento con le notizie più precise riguardante la sua intimazione a ciascuna delle sessioni. Nuova traduzione italiana col testo latino a fronte* (Venice, 1822), p. 284.

56 See Raul Merzario, *Il paese stretto. Strategie matrimoniali nella diocesi di Como, secoli XVI–XVIII* (Turin, 1981), pp. 54–55: Merzario analysed 493 dispensations from the period between 1564 and 1630, that is from the period following the Council of Trent: 74.43 per cent of them were dispensations in the fourth degree while 19.47 per cent were in the third and fourth unequal degrees, 6.29 per cent were in the third degree and 0.81 per cent were in the second and third unequal degrees. This last group consisted exclusively of dispensations for affinal kin. A similar impression can be gleaned from the evaluation of the two parishes in the Vallouise Valley in the Département Hautes-Alpes that Michel Prost conducted – albeit only for cases of consanguine marriage: during the period between 1674 and 1729, nearly 70 per cent of the granted dispensations were in the fourth degree, while the dispensations from the period between 1730 and 1789 were distributed more heavily amongst the various degrees beginning with the second and third unequal degrees. The fourth degrees still accounted for 33.3 per cent of the dispensations in Vigneaux and 42.5 per cent in Vallouise. A question that always exists here, however, regards the extent to which such records are complete and reliable. See Michel Prost, "Evolution comparée de l'apparentement dans les deux paroisses de la vallée de Valloiuse en Briançonnais. XVIIe et XVIIIe siècles", in *Le choix du conjoint. Premiers entretiens de la Société de Démographie Historique, Paris 15–16 novembre 1996*, ed. Guy Brunet, Antoinette Fauve-Chamoux and Michel Oris (Villeurbanne, 1998), pp. 151–166. See also Jutta Sperling, "Marriage at the Time of the Council of Trent (1560–70): Clandestine Marriages, Kinship Prohibitions and Dowry Exchange in European Comparison", *Journal of Early Modern History* 8, 1–2 (2004), 67–108, 85–88.

In numerous Protestant territories, marriage projects in close degrees of blood and affinal kinship were easier to realise during this period.[57] In contrast to the centrally decreed Catholic policy, the prohibited degrees in the Protestant and Reformed churches were not uniform in their extent and changed more than once over the course of the modern period.[58] This also meant that the number of prohibited degrees was, in many cases, reduced earlier than in the Catholic context. Back in the early phase of the Reformation, in Zwingli's Zurich, marriages between first cousins had been permitted to take place with no further ado.[59] But this liberal policy did not endure,[60] with a new line subsequently being drawn at the third degree.[61] The reasons for this reversal of policy were said to be "the negative reaction and attendant pressure of the populace"[62] as well as regulatory and moral interests: it was "in part out of a concern for the reduction of offence and abomination" that support for the retention of marriage prohibitions had been expressed.[63] The stricter handling of such matters in neighbouring regions likely also played a role.[64] The extent to which changes to marriage prohibitions' scope and incest's

---

57 See Sabean, *Kinship in Neckarhausen*, pp. 428–436; David Warren Sabean, "Kinship and Prohibited Marriages in Baroque Germany: Divergent Strategies among Jewish and Christian Populations", *Leo Baeck Institute Yearbook* 47 (2002), 91–103; in the case of cousin marriages, this also applies to the Anglican sphere, see Nancy Fix Anderson, "Cousin Marriage in Victorian England", *Journal of Family History* 11, 3 (1986), 285–301; Adam Kuper, *Incest & Influence. The Private Life of Bourgeois England* (Cambridge, Mass./London, 2009); as an example of evidently unproblematic marriages in close degrees of affinity, see Takashi Iida, "Wiederheiraten und Verwandtschaftsnetze auf dem unteilbaren Hof: Bauern, Büdner und Einlieger des brandenburgischen Amtes Alt-Ruppin im 18. Jahrhundert", in *Eheschließungen im Europa*, ed. Duhamelle/Schlumbohm, pp. 125–155.

58 In Geneva, the prohibition of marriages between cousins was abolished as early as 1713; in Zurich, it fell during the 1850s, with this liberalisation being expanded to cover all of Switzerland in 1874. Mathieu, "Verwandtschaft als historischer Faktor", p. 237. On further regulations see Jon Matthieu, "Kin Marriages. Trends and Interpretations from the Swiss Example", in *Kinship in Europe*, ed. Sabean/Teuscher/Matthieu, pp. 211–230, pp. 213–216. In Prussia, the prohibition of marriage between affinal kin was already abolished in 1740. Cf. Claudia Jarzebowski, *Inzest. Verwandtschaft und Sexualität im 18. Jahrhundert* (Cologne/Weimar/Vienna, 2005), p. 113.

59 See Mathieu, "Verwandtschaft als historischer Faktor", p. 235.

60 See Jürg-Christian Hürlimann, *Die Eheschließungsverbote zwischen Verwandten und Verschwägerten* (Bern, 1987), p. 60; Max Thomas Safley, "Canon Law and Swiss Reform: Legal Theory and Practice in the Marital Courts of Zurich, Basel, and St. Gall", in *Canon Law in Protestant Lands*, ed. Richard H. Helmholz (Berlin, 1992), pp. 187–201, p. 198.

61 See Mathieu, "Verwandtschaft als historischer Faktor", p. 235.

62 Mathieu, "Verwandtschaft als historischer Faktor", p. 235.

63 Quoted in Susanna Burghartz, *Zeiten der Reinheit. Orte der Unzucht. Ehe und Sexualität in Basel während der Frühen Neuzeit* (Paderborn, 1999), p. 79.

64 See Safley, "Canon Law", pp. 187–201.

definition in terms of degrees of kinship served to express confessional differentiation from the Reformation period onward has yet to be investigated in a systematic manner.[65]

As Zwingli's initiative showed, actual practice alternated between liberalisation and renewed restraint. And also in other spatial and confessional contexts, both of these tendencies were likewise manifested in widely varying ways all the way down to the level of courts of law and municipalities. Immanuel Weber was one who commented on the accordingly great degree of confusion inherent in this situation in a 1714 text addressed to students. In this pamphlet he ascertained that "a near-immeasurable number of tracts has been sent out into the world" regarding which degrees were permissible or prohibited and the ways in which degrees "must be calculated in all possible lines" as well as on the so-called *arbores Consanguinitatis & affinitatis*. And yet "the matter has grown so confused on account of various opinions among those who see to its interpretation that one can make out hardly any means by which to cope with said confusion".[66] Protestant rules did, on the whole, tend to be more liberal than those that applied in the Catholic world. However, the remaining prohibited degrees were, here and there, observed all the more strictly in that they were regarded as absolute, with no allowance for possible dispensation.[67] Concrete dispensation practice likewise exhibited clear differences in comparison with the Catholic context. After all, the 'purchase' of dispensations had been among the practices criticised by Protestant reformers.[68]

---

65 On this see also Isabel V. Hull, *Sexuality, State, and Civil Society in Germany, 1700–1815* (Ithaca/London, 1996), especially chapters 1 and 2.

66 *Immanuel Weber, J.U.D. Prof. Publ. Ordin. eröffnet der studierenden Jugend zu Giessen ein Collegium Theoretico-Practicum über die nothwendige und nützliche Lehre von zugelassenen und verbotenen Graden im Heyrathen* (Giessen, 1714), p. 3.

67 Anne-Lise Head-König makes reference to a restrictive approach in the Swiss Protestant context: she writes that permission to marry was granted but rarely in some places, for which reason couples related by blood or by affinity who wished to marry sometimes moved abroad or to cantons with more liberal rules. Anne-Lise Head-König, "Forced Marriages and Forbidden Marriages in Switzerland: State Control of the Formation of Marriages in Catholic and Protestant Cantons in the Eighteenth and Nineteenth Centuries", *Continuity and Change* 8 (1993), 441–465, 455–456. Jürgen Schlumbohm highlights the case of the widowed Marie Elisabeth Middendorf, who sought to marry her brother-in-law. The Protestant consistory in Osnabrück, however, had declared such unions to be "entirely forbidden", for which reason dispensation requests to this effect were to be rejected. It was thanks only to a special dispensation granted by the king that the couple was ultimately able to marry in 1814. Schlumbohm, *Lebensläufe, Familien, Höfe*, pp. 454–455.

68 See Safley, "Canon Law", p. 189; Siegrid Westphal, "Kirchenzucht als Ehe- und Sittenzucht. Die Auswirkungen von lutherischer Konfessionalisierung auf das Geschlechterverhältnis",

Throughout the early modern period as well as during the period covered by this study, canon law remained unrevised – including with regard to the subject matter addressed here. But even just the rising number of dispensations that were being granted in close degrees of blood and affinal kinship does indeed suggest that within this rigid normative framework actual practice was subject to change. The papal positions on dispensation-granting alternated over the course of the nineteenth century with certain relaxations being followed by new instances of tightening. Moreover, practices in different dioceses varied quite a bit despite the centralistic leadership structure of the Catholic Church, for the clerics responsible for handling dispensation requests at the various hierarchical levels – parish priests, deans, vicars general and bishops – held differing opinions and acted accordingly. As a consequence, the willingness to handle dispensation requests as well as the modes of processing and endorsing them encountered by supplicants differed considerably – both over time and synchronously between and within dioceses.[69]

3 Administrating Kinship

The political, administrative and institutional aspects of kin marriage have so far received little attention from historians specialised in the modern period.[70] To approach this topic via the administration of kinship is rewarding as it provides insights into processes that integrated the state and the Church, as well as the state and its individual regions.[71] The transition from a world organised based on estates to a citizen-led modern society was by no means a linear

---

in *'In Christo ist weder man noch weyb'. Frauen in der Zeit der Reformation und der katholischen Reform*, ed. Anne Conrad (Münster, 1999), pp. 152–171, p. 156.

69 Edith Saurer, in her comparison of marriage dispensation practices in Lower Austria and Venice in the early nineteenth century, accordingly points out how, despite identical legal situations in terms of both civil and criminal law as well as church rules, "differing political, legal, societal, and cultural traditions" brought forth "differing norms and practices in terms of relationships between kin". Edith Saurer, "Formen von Verwandtschaft und Liebe – Traditionen und Brüche. Venetien und Niederösterreich im frühen 19. Jahrhundert", in *Politiken der Verwandtschaft*, ed. Lanzinger/Saurer, pp. 255–271, pp. 256–257.

70 An exception here is the study based on a sample of mid-nineteenth-century dispensation requests from the city of Rome by Margherita Pelaja, "Marriage by Exception: Marriage Dispensations and Ecclesiastical Policies in Nineteenth-Century Rome", *Journal of Modern Italian Studies* 1, 2 (1996), 223–244.

71 On the concept of the region as a social space that needs to be concretely defined on an individual basis see Axel Flügel, "Der Ort der Regionalgeschichte in der neuzeitlichen Geschichte", in *Kultur und Staat in der Provinz. Perspektiven und Erträge der Regionalgeschichte*, ed. Stefan Brakensiek et al. (Bielefeld, 1992), pp. 1–28; Stefan Brakensiek and Axel

one. In the contexts analysed here, the 'enlightened' state was rather unable to position itself successfully vis-à-vis the Church by way of legal innovations meant to ease administrative processes, since these in fact entailed a number of complications. Ultimately, therefore, church and state logics and legal situations found themselves locked in a fairly irreconcilable conflict in this regard, embodying two centres of power with their own respective bureaucracies and claims to comprehensive validity.

As a rule, administration aims to achieve order. To administrate is to possess definitional, organisational and decision-making power in clearly defined substantive areas and to wield this power in accordance with certain criteria via structured processes. Administration is closely intertwined with politics: with the territorial enforcement of rule, with the formation of the state, with the implementation of reforms and with political ideas.[72] But even so, the administrators[73] – those representing either the Church or the state – created their own spheres of action rather than functioning merely as marionette-like implementers of prepared scripts.[74] The role played by them must be viewed as multifaceted – for they were, as Karin Gottschalk has written of local officials, "mediators and at the same time protagonists and addressees".[75] The positions they assumed in a given decision-making process cannot be deduced on the basis of occupational socialisations and official functions alone, for personal characteristics could also come into play. Their respective stances hence

---

Flügel (eds.), *Regionalgeschichte in Europa. Methoden und Erträge der Forschung zum 16. bis 19. Jahrhundert* (Paderborn, 2000).

72 On this see also Peter Becker, "Sprachvollzug: Kommunikation und Verwaltung", in *Sprachvollzug im Amt. Kommunikation und Verwaltung im Europa des 19. und 20. Jahrhunderts*, ed. Peter Becker (Bielefeld, 2011), pp. 9–42.

73 The protagonists of administration appear here in their contexts of action. However, it would be impossible to reconstruct individual biographies or the profiles of individual offices as part of the present work. On this topic see Michaela Hohkamp, *Herrschaft in der Herrschaft. Die vorderösterreichische Obervogtei Triberg von 1737–1780* (Göttingen, 1998); Joachim Eibach, *Der Staat vor Ort. Amtmänner und Bürger im 19. Jahrhundert am Beispiel Badens* (Frankfurt a. M., 1994); Rüdiger von Krosigk, *Bürger in die Verwaltung! Bürokratiekritik und Bürgerbeteiligung in Baden. Zur Geschichte moderner Staatlichkeit im Deutschland des 19. Jahrhunderts* (Bielefeld, 2010).

74 On this see the study by Waltraud Heindl, *Gehorsame Rebellen. Bürokratie und Beamte in Österreich 1780 bis 1848* (Vienna/Cologne/Graz, 1991); Waltraud Heindl, *Josephinische Mandarine. Bürokratie und Beamte in Österreich* (Vienna/Cologne/Weimar, 2013).

75 Karin Gottschalk, "Herrschaftsvermittlung als kultureller Transfer? Lokalverwaltung und Verwaltungskultur in der Landgrafschaft Hessen-Kassel im 18. Jahrhundert", in *Kultureller Austausch. Bilanz und Perspektiven der Frühneuzeitforschung*, ed. Michael North (Cologne/Weimar/Vienna, 2009), pp. 175–191, p. 188.

embodied an integrative component of the administrative machinery, which itself consisted of a network of protagonists.

Administration also requires institutions. Institutions can be conceived of quite generally as rules,[76] as societally anchored structures of ordering and orientation. The implementation of rules and concepts of order in the social realm requires representatives who, in the places and times concerned here, operated as part of administrative apparatuses from which they derived their legitimacy with regard to the matters at hand. Viewed historically, bureaucracies represented relational configurations and fields of action embodied by male actors. What makes administrative fields of action and relational configurations different from informal ones are their surrounding frames of reference. These are defined via authority, legitimacy and certain competencies while also being based on a superordinate – territorial, state, ecclesiastical – context of rule.

Officials interacted internally – both within their own institutions as well as with subordinate and superordinate authorities – and also with the outside world, dealing with people's enquiries and requests, supplications and complaints as representatives of the institutions that they served. This study shows how ecclesiastical and civil officials' spheres of action were entangled at various hierarchical levels with those of couples closely related by blood and by affinity. Their interactions were characterised by various power imbalances.[77] They took place in a range of forms including spoken communication or written documents as well as in person or via intermediaries. Rules – arrangements, conventions, decrees, statutes, laws, etc. – structured interaction and communication as well as the sequenced steps in administrative processes. And although the existing systems of rules and their administration had been established for the long term, they did not remain unchanged. New circumstances

---

76 This is the concept of institution employed by Douglas C. North in his *Institutions, Institutional Change and Economic Performance* (Cambridge, 1990), p. 3: "Institutions are the rules of the game in a society or, more formally, are the humanly devised constraints that shape human interaction." It is useful here even without employing his institutional economics approach. For a critical view that deals especially with the distinction between institutions and organisations that North's concept entails see Thomas Edeling, "Organisationen als Institutionen", in *Neuer Institutionalismus. Zur soziologischen Erklärung von Organisation, Moral und Vertrauen*, ed. Andrea Maurer and Michael Schmidt (Frankfurt a. M., 2002), pp. 219–235, 220–225.

77 In the early 1990s, Alf Lüdtke has already pointed out the necessity of a perspective that trains its sights on these various spaces of interaction. He coined the term of the "ambiguity of being ruled". Alf Lüdtke, "Einleitung. Herrschaft als soziale Praxis", in *Herrschaft als soziale Praxis. Historische und sozial-anthropologische Studien*, ed. Alf Lüdtke (Göttingen, 1991), pp. 9–63, p. 13.

of power and rule, new legal situations and institutional contexts had to be taken into account by both the administrators and the administrated – and, irrespective of all this, adaptations always had to be made when implementing norms and procedures in actual practice. Asking as to appropriations and reinterpretations, ambiguities and incoherencies has been an aspect of historical scholarship for some time now.[78] Therefore, administrating is to be understood as a process, with administration as such embodying a space of communication. New research perspectives, which have come to feature a decided focus on administrative culture in recent years, also highlight the construct-like character of the "organisation and ordering of social reality".[79] This organisation and ordering played out within the framework of specific institutional processes that differed considerably between the neighbouring dioceses of Brixen, Chur, Salzburg and Trento and in turn materialised as fairly heterogenous archival holdings.

Local and regional, ecclesiastical and state spaces of interaction were closely intertwined with one another. And as Francesca Trivellato has emphasised, the path leading beyond the local cannot be conceived of as a series of hierarchically ordered concentric circles that expand from small to large.[80] The object here is much rather, as Bruno Latour's actor-network theory illustrates, to reconstruct the "continuous connections leading from one local interaction to the other places, times, and agencies"[81] – agencies that, in turn, engaged in actions and interactions of their own. The central mission of accordingly conceived research is to make visible the "path" that connects the individual places, the respective "local sites", with one another. For every action is locally situated and can therefore only ever be understood in a localised manner; and since its further networking starts from the local, the reconstruction of such

---

78 Levi, "On Microhistory".

79 Stefan Haas, *Die Kultur der Verwaltung. Die Umsetzung der preußischen Reformen 1800–1848* (Frankfurt a. M./New York, 2005), p. 12. Luhmann is taken as a point of reference in the volume by Barbara Stolberg-Rilinger and André Krischer (eds.), *Herstellung und Darstellung von Entscheidungen. Verfahren, Verwalten und Verhandeln in der Vormoderne* (Berlin, 2010), especially in the introduction by Barbara Stolberg-Rilinger, pp. 9–31.

80 Francesca Trivellato, "Is There a Future for Italian Microhistory in the Age of Global History?", *California Italian Studies* 2, 1 (2011), at http://escholarship.org/uc/item/0z94n9hq (last access May 2022) [without page numbers, p. 15].

81 Bruno Latour, *Reassembling the Social. An Introduction to Actor-Network-Theory* (Oxford, 2005), p. 173. Latour's "actant" concept is based on the notion that objects, structural characteristics, corporate bodies, loose aggregates, etc. have the power to make a difference. It therefore serves to identify the interaction between human actors and things in networks of action. Actants challenge – and sometimes even force – actors to react, to take action. Ibid., p. 54.

networking can likewise only ever start from the local. In such networks of connections and interactions, which ran via "long chains of actors", there occurred processes of translation and transformation.[82] For historians, a problem that does present itself here is the often fragmentary preservation of sources. As a result, such connections and configurations cannot always be discovered and (re-)constructed in their entirety. However, the fundamental and primary point here is to conceptualise interactions as a network within a space. In this way, the social – which, to again quote Latour, is not a given but "flashes only briefly, just at the fleeting moment" as social ties – is to be retraced. "It's traceable only when it's being modified."[83] Capturing such moments of change requires deeper analysis of the source materials and an empirically saturated form of portrayal.

On the long and arduous paths taken by the dispensation requests of couples closely related by blood or affinity, the 'transaction cost' for each connection leading from one station to the next must also be taken into account.[84] It was not only the financial resources and time required for dispensation proceedings that came into play here, but above all the transformations underwent by things said and written. On the journey through the numerous official channels within the sequence of involved entities, negotiations and recommendations, such transformations could manifest themselves as addenda and explanations, interpretations and sharpenings of focus, summaries, emphases and omissions, or the attachment of additional documents, all of which could alter the content – embellishing it, dramatising it or drastically reducing it and shifting the trajectory of argumentation.[85]

4 Sources in Context

The study draws upon source material that is largely of three types. First, treatises on contemporary canon and civil law along with medically and scientifically inspired treatises shed light on the field of discourse. Second, late eighteenth-century written correspondence between state and church authorities concerning dispensations makes it possible to retrace the consequences of Josephine innovations including the irritations and uncertainties to which they gave rise. And finally, nineteenth-century dispensation requests by couples

82 Latour, *Reassembling the Social*, p. 173.
83 Ibid., p. 159.
84 Ibid., p. 180.
85 Ibid., pp. 183–190.

who were closely related by blood or affinity allow us to deduce such couples' logics as well as the logics followed by ecclesiastical and secular institutions involved in these matters. In contrast to sweeping quantitative studies or those that concentrate on individual families, this study takes the respective diocesan levels – and thus a socially nuanced space covering a fairly large region – as its field of investigation. Quantitative findings are linked here with qualitative ones as well as contextualised politically, legally and administratively.

In some dioceses, such as in Brixen, dispensation requests travelled through the entire church hierarchy: they were first submitted to a local parish priest or curate and continued on to the appropriate dean, who headed a deanery consisting of several parishes. The next step was the bishop and/or diocesan consistory – although in some cases, such as in Vorarlberg, a vicar general was positioned in between – and subsequently the Apostolic Dataria or Penitentiaria, the two competent papal authorities in Rome where dispensations were concerned, or – in exceptional cases – to the Apostolic Nunciature in Vienna. Beginning in the 1780s, various Austrian civil authorities also became involved in such proceedings: provincial governments, district offices (*Kreisämter*) and regional courts (*Landgerichte*), the Imperial Court Chancellery in Vienna, the Austrian Imperial-Royal agents in Rome, and – with the nineteenth-century introduction of the requirement of political marriage consent – the municipalities. It was the protagonists inhabiting this space of interaction and communication who authored the documents evaluated here as sources, and it is these documents' contexts of production that allow their content to be understood.

Strictly speaking, dispensation requests were petitions of grace whose documented history reaches far back.[86] The purpose and aim of such a petition was to obtain the benefit of a specific instrument of mercy, a dispensation, that would lift a marriage impediment being deemed to be present. The second chapter of this study begins with an introduction to the logic underlying both the act of dispensation as such and the linkage of the realm of kinship defined in marriage prohibitions with notions of incest. New concepts of love and marriage that emerged around 1800 proceeded to break through these incest boundaries and marriage prohibitions. In terms of the rhetorical strategies employed in the requests' authorship, achieving a certain balance between economic requirements and the social or emotional aspects of a planned marriage

86 Cf. Andreas Würgler, "Bitten und Begehren. Suppliken und Gravamina in der deutschsprachigen Frühneuzeitforschung", in *Bittschriften und Gravamina. Politik, Verwaltung und Justiz in Europa, 14.–18. Jahrhundert*, ed. Cecilia Nubola and Andreas Würgler (Berlin, 2005), pp. 17–52, 27.

appears to have been an undertaking that was particularly sensitive. However, there was room for manoeuvre when it came to justifying sexual transgressions on the basis of passion. It was during precisely this period that the discourses regarding prohibitions on kin marriage began featuring increasingly more voices. At the end of the eighteenth century – a delicate moment in the history of power politics – writings on canon and secular law began appearing with particular frequency. At the same time, an intensified debate among physiologists, physicians, heredity theorists and ethnologically and anthropologically interested parties emerged, which will be systematised in this second chapter.

Theories about health dangers stemming from marriages between close blood relatives, with 'degeneration' as their consequence, informed the relevant tracts. With heredity being a virulent topic during the nineteenth century, it came to figure prominently in the kin marriage discourse. Theological concepts and the Church's definitional power thus experienced competition not only from secular law but also from those natural science fields that were pursuing heredity as a topic – fields that, at least in theory, could also have represented a source of support.[87] The sciences' concentration on blood kinship represented a problem, however, for this perspective did not concern itself with the parallel prohibitions on marriages between affinal kin that had been constructed on the theological side. The focus on 'blood' as the kinship-generating substance attracted a counterpart in dispensation requests' talk of 'common blood' and 'blood bonds' as guarantors of trustworthiness and reliability. And with its delineation between the 'that of the other' and 'that of one's own', one strand of this discourse and its associated concepts would ultimately lead to argumentations underpinned by racism.

Since the High Middle Ages, the authority to grant dispensations had been the domain of the popes, who, as a rule, held on to this authority in the close degrees throughout the early modern period while successively delegating decisions on cases involving more distant degrees to the bishops. The Josephine Marriage Patent of 1783 formally obligated the bishops to grant dispensations in close degrees on their own authority. Moreover, the Marriage Patent reduced the number of degrees for which a dispensation was needed. The routes via which to obtain a dispensation, previously rather diverse, had already been limited and centralised by ordinances issued by Empress Maria Theresia. Furthermore, all communications with Rome had become subject to state control via the now obligatory *placet* of the provincial government as

87 For an overview cf. Staffan Müller-Wille and Hans-Jörg Rheinberger (eds.), *Heredity Produced. At the Crossroads of Biology, Politics, and Culture, 1500–1870* (Cambridge, Mass./London, 2007).

the ruler's representative. The interventions under Joseph II threw the existing dispensation-granting procedures into disarray and also resulted in their periodic blockage. The way how clerics in the diocesan consistories and parishes, civil officials employed by the provincial governments, district offices and regional courts, and not least the related couples themselves adapted to and dealt with the legal and political changes as well as the associated uncertainty and more than a few nasty predicaments is the topic of this study's third chapter.

The streams of official correspondence that converged at the offices of the provincial governments – for the region studied here first and foremost the *Gubernium*[88] in Innsbruck – during the eighteenth century's final decades can shed light on the divergent logics of church and state representatives. In this situation, charged as it was by power struggles, conflicts and controlling measures, reprimands and calls to order gave rise to their own social spaces.[89] Those couples – from the most varied social milieus by this point – who turned to the proper institutions with their dispensation requests were the ones who suffered in this competition-charged atmosphere. Some of them ultimately ended up taking matters into their own hands. Viewed in a broader context, however, the power struggle revolved around eliminating the involvement of Rome – including the nunciature in Vienna as its representative – as a 'foreign' jurisdiction on state territory. The resulting conflicts, which dragged on into the early nineteenth century, bring to light significant social and political processes that decisively influenced the relationship between the state, the Church and society. The interest here is not so much in the success or failure of a particular Josephine reform but rather in the varieties and limitations of power that can be discerned.

---

88 The institution of the *Gubernium*, the provincial government, had been set up in 1763, in a form that would persist until the mid-nineteenth century, as part of an initial major centralisation measure designed to ease intervention in the affairs of the individual provinces. The *Gubernium* was succeeded later on by the *Statthalterei* (prefecture). Directly subordinate to the *Gubernium* were the *Kreisämter* (district offices), which had already been established in 1754.

89 The concept of social space employed here is oriented on the communication-focused theory of Rudolf Schlögl, albeit expanded by relationships and interactions. On this cf. Rudolf Schlögl, "Kommunikation und Vergesellschaftung unter Anwesenden. Formen des Sozialen und ihre Transformation in der Frühen Neuzeit", *Geschichte und Gesellschaft* 34, 2 (2008), 155–224; cf. also Jörg Döring and Tristan Thielmann, "Einleitung: Was lesen wir im Raume? Der *Spatial Turn* und das geheime Wissen der Geographen", in *Spatial Turn. Das Raumparadigma in den Kultur- und Sozialwissenschaften*, ed. Döring/Thielmann (Bielefeld, 2008), pp. 7–45.

Wars, secularisation and territorial reordering marked the initial years of the nineteenth century, and these events caused dispensation-related matters to fade into the background until the early 1820s. Political and diocesan borders were redrawn, and relevant documentary material from this period is scant for the region under study. Marriage dispensation-related conflicts between state and Church that had been prominent during the late eighteenth century did not ultimately end up being reignited at a comparable level of fierceness and irreconcilability. Depending on the state of play between the Church and the political realm in a given diocese, the one side or the other was finally in possession of more competencies – with the necessary cooperation being fairly quick to take on largely routine forms. The Concordat of Vienna (1855) saw the Church in Austria regain supreme authority over matters of marriage and thus also over marriage dispensations. The Church celebrated this step as a "departure from Josephine state churchdom" and a "liberation".[90] As a result, during the mid-nineteenth century procedures necessary to obtain a papal dispensation were simplified by eliminating the previously mandatory requirement to obtain approval from one's provincial government. In return, Rome compensated by instituting tougher policies of a strongly moralising character.

The fourth chapter describes the practical steps involved in applying for a dispensation and provides a closer introduction to the sources analysed thereafter. The four dioceses of Brixen, Chur, Salzburg and Trento were distinct from one another not only in terms of their church politics and differing confessional and social situations but also with regard to administrative procedures and fundamental attitudes in connection with dispensation requests. Thus, the nineteenth-century material that has come down to us likewise exhibits major differences. The sources mainly consist of requests for dispensations in close degrees of blood and affinal kinship that are either held as their own collections – such as at the diocesan archives of Brixen, Salzburg and to some extent also in Chur – or can partly be found among district office records at the state archives of Bolzano and Trento. Since it was, as a rule, the papal authorities in Rome that were responsible for granting such dispensations, records of this type are referred to as "papal" or "Roman marriage dispensations". In order to investigate certain specific questions, these dispensation records are complemented by various dispensation registers in the diocesan archives, the records of the Imperial-Royal Agency in Rome – which acted as a mediator on behalf of the Austrian state – now held at the *Haus-, Hof-, und Staatsarchiv* of the Austrian State Archives in Vienna, the later *Gubernium* (*jüngeres Gubernium*)

90 Reinalter, "Liberalismus und Kirche", p. 156.

holdings in Innsbruck for the civil law aspects of dispensation-granting and material from the Vorarlberg State Archives.

The focus on Roman dispensations is owed, above all, to the fact that requests in the more distant third and fourth degrees, as they are known from the research and as became evident from a spot-check of the Diocese of Brixen's materials, provide little in the way of substantive information. The reasons for dispensation contained in such requests are stereotypically formulated and almost never include more detailed descriptions of concrete life situations. Most importantly, however, their procurement was organised in a fairly simple manner: in such cases, the bishops possessed dispensatory authority, which they in turn – as is documented for the Diocese of Brixen during the 1850s – delegated to the deans at the next lower level of the hierarchy. The Roman dispensation records are vastly richer and more diverse in terms of their extent and substance. Alongside letters, penned for the most part by clergymen, containing exhaustive situational portrayals, the protocols from the questioning of the two witnesses, the bride and the bridegroom – the so-called matrimonial examinations that were customary in the Diocese of Brixen – are of particular analytical value, for which reason the main focus is on these materials. Furthermore, the holdings in question are ordered in a systematic and chronological way, which allowed a database to be compiled that contains a wealth of information covering a good thirty years (from 1831 to 1864) and basic data for the following decades up to 1890.[91] The matrimonial examinations enable us to discern the couples' social positioning; their knowledge about their relatedness was queried, and all those who were questioned had to justify the proposed marriage. Also revealed are the techniques that helped ascertain whether an impediment to marriage – in the sense of blood or affinal kinship close enough to require a dispensation – existed as well as these techniques' limitations. And finally, a certain phase of the period under study saw local clerics also required to submit their evaluation of how a planned marriage would be perceived by the public. It is thus that no single one of the nearly 2,150 dispensation requests preserved from the period between 1831 and 1890 sounds quite like any other.

The documents to be found in the dispensation records tell of family crises, existential worries and emotional dramas – and since they were produced within the administrative apparatus, they lead far beyond the domestic sphere. At the same time, the uncircumventable bureaucratic pathways with their various legal frameworks opened up a vast space of strategic communication. After all, the church- and state-stipulated logics according to which dispensation

91 On this see the section on organisation of the material in the Appendix.

requests had to be argued were not necessarily compatible with the cares and hardships of those women and men who submitted them. What is more, the dispensation policies pursued by civil servants, bishops and popes – and thus the criteria governing what would be recognised as a reason for dispensation – changed repeatedly during the period under study. Therefore, the fourth chapter not only analyses the various obstacles strewing the way to a dispensation but also justificational logics and ambivalences.

Compared with the information sent on to Rome by the diocesan consistories, the dispensation records held by the diocesan archives – especially those in Brixen and Salzburg – are significantly more extensive and dense in terms of the information they contain. The papal offices received no more than a strongly formalised version composed in Latin, typically accompanied by a letter of endorsement addressed to an intermediary situated there. In these 'concentrates', which employed highly stereotypical reasons as justification, very little remained of the real-life contexts, the local clerics' portrayals and the tribulations of the affected women and men. They represent the conclusion of an extensive process of communication that played out between church and state representatives, the couple and the couple's witnesses over the course of weeks and months.

Up to now, attention has been paid mainly to successful dispensation requests – those that led to kin marriages ultimately being concluded. But priests, deans, vicars and bishops could also refuse to forward dispensation requests to the next higher authority if they deemed there to be little chance of success. Provincial governments and the papal offices in Rome, for their part, could likewise respond in the negative. Failure, above all in close degrees, is therefore an integral aspect of the history of kin marriages. Even so, numerous couples remained adamant about their desire to marry and refused to give up hope that they would eventually be able to have the marriage impediments that stood in their way lifted after all. They would submit one, two, three further requests, frequently over a period of years, and some made even more attempts.

Viewed broadly, it is marriages between blood relatives, between first-degree cousins, that predominate in a great many of the societies that have been researched to date and thus also in the research landscape.[92] But in other

92 Cf. for example Burguière, "'Cher Cousin'"; Francisco García González, "La historia de la familia en el interior castellano. Estado de la cuestión y esbozo bibliográfico, ss. XVI–XIX", in *La historia de la familia en la Península Ibérica. Balance regional y perspectivas*, ed. Francisco García González (Cuenca, 2008), pp. 277–329, 294–296; Mathieu, "Ein Cousin an jeder Zaunlücke"; Raul Merzario, "Land, Kinship and Consanguineous Marriage in Italy from the Seventeenth to the Nineteenth Century", *Journal of Family*

places, such as the region studied here, marriages between men and women who were closely related by affinity could be just as numerous.[93] As previously mentioned, canon law as well as the civil law based thereupon included both blood kinship and affinal kinship in the scope of their respective marriage prohibitions. Affinity, as a particularly prominent phenomenon in this research context that was also paid much attention in the contemporaneous British debate, is therefore the subject of this study's fifth chapter. In the 1830s and 1840s, during the reign of Pope Gregory XVI, unions between close affinal kin met with a papal policy of extreme resistance and were near-impossible to realise. The proceedings around some dispensation requests during this period took dramatic turns, bearing witness to the power of the Church but also, repeatedly, to the power of those who persisted in their marriage projects and set out on unconventional paths. In this difficult situation, a crucial role was played by mediation and endorsements – forms of assistance that were accessible particularly to those who possessed the appropriate contacts and opportunities. Moreover, such forms of intercession had to be cleared with the Austrian Imperial-Royal Agency in Rome, the institution officially charged with handling such matters. In 1846, the ascent of Pius IX opened up a chance for those who lacked prominent networks or were less creative in devising counterstrategies to receive a dispensation after all. It is hence with particular clarity that a look at these two decades allows us to perceive the implications of shifting papal dispensation policies.

At the same time, the requests in close degrees of affinity allow specific logics of spatial and social proximity to become visible. Among affine marriage projects, the most important configuration by far was that of a widower and his sister-in-law. In marrying a sister of his deceased wife, the widower would be taking to bride an aunt of his children – a person who had often already spent years living and working together with them in the same household. It was a situation in which the consequences of a rejected dispensation request were all the more tragic. For in such a case, a concubinage clause was triggered that mandated the two adults' separation. So, for a brother- and sister-in-law living beneath the same roof, every such request entailed a risk. Such a step

History 15 (1990), 529–546; Raul Merzario, "Terra, parentela e matrimoni consanguinei in Italia, secoli XVII–XIX", in *Storia della famiglia italiana 1750–1950*, ed. Marzio Barbagli and David I. Kertzer (Bologna, 1992), pp. 253–272; Sabean, *Kinship in Neckarhausen*, especially the chapter "Consanguinty in modern Europe", pp. 428–448.

93 A balanced ratio between consanguineous and affinal unions was also ascertained by Saurer, "Stiefmütter und Stiefsöhne", pp. 358–359; and for Brittany, Martine Segalen ascertained high rates of marriage between affinal kin. Martine Segalen, *Fifteen Generations of Bretons. Kinship and Society in Lower Brittany 1720–1980* (Cambridge, 2007), pp. 95–103.

therefore had to be weighed against the implications of unmarried cohabitation, be they in terms of one's own respectability or of the attitudes present in one's social sphere.

Consanguine unions are the topic of the sixth and final chapter. Opinions regarding potentially negative health consequences had long since entered circulation by way of legal commentaries as well as via medical tracts and church circulars. And yet, couples in the region under study who were considering marriage to close blood relatives only began having to reckon with limitations on dispensation-granting towards the close of the nineteenth century. These new limitations affected first-degree cousins. Such unions, just like those in close degrees of affinity, were to be found in various social milieus – from inhabitants of remote, mountainous places, where the local conditions and *angustia loci*, the narrowness of the place, could be employed as arguments, to wealthy bourgeois families. Among the latter, such marriage projects did indeed have to do with preserving and compounding wealth and prestige. However, the diversity of situative aspects and contexts that becomes visible in these couple configurations cannot be associated with specific economic interests in an all-too-mechanistic way. Hardly any large accumulations of such unions within individual kin groups can be made out in the dispensation records that were studied save for one exception: that of the Metzler family from Schwarzenberg in the Bregenz Forest. In this family, one generation witnessed a clustering of cousin marriages that will be discussed in its own section.

In the Diocese of Brixen's Vorarlberg deaneries, cousins had to reckon with both objections to and rejections of their requests as early as the mid-1860s. This more severe stance was owed to the installation of Joseph Feßler as auxiliary bishop at the vicariate general in Feldkirch. Just a few years later, however, Feßler was transferred to a new post. Even in the superordinate consistory of the Prince-Bishop in Brixen, which was in general comparatively rigid in its handling of dispensation matters, Feßler's morally motivated and almost doggedly pursued battle against such unions found little support. Nearly two decades later, Feldkirch's vicar general Simon Aichner reacted to the oft-lamented increase in kin marriages. He initiated an enquiry regarding the consequences of marriages concluded on the basis of papal dispensations. This investigation was conducted in keeping with canon law's normative view, which entailed no distinction between consanguineous and affine unions. Aichner's enquiry was followed by the next wave of refusals to grant dispensations requested by cousins – this time with broader support, including from Brixen and Rome.

Amidst the tightening seen in certain aspects of dispensation policy during this period, prospective couples living in Austrian dioceses did receive some support in the form of the 'emergency civil marriage' (*Notzivilehe*) introduced as part of the 1868 May Laws. As the dispensation proceedings following its introduction show, this newly created option meant that the church authorities invested with dispensatory power could, to a certain extent, be blackmailed. It had therefore now become a question of what was worse – of whether the clergy held civil marriages or marriages between close kin to be the greater evil. Initially, it would appear that everything was done to prevent a civil marriage. This is, at least, what is indicated by the case of the physician and long-time Dornbirn mayor Johann Georg Waibl and Aurelia Waibl, who were uncle and niece. This exceptional configuration represented the closest possible degree of blood kinship for which a dispensation could be granted. It particularly highlights both the broad variety of actions taken by church representatives and the room for manoeuvre that supplicants could strategically exploit. In another such instance, an identically configured couple whose request had been categorically rejected by the Bishop of Linz found a sympathetic ear in Salzburg and received their desired dispensation without much further ado. A final look at the figures concerning dispensations granted in the Diocese of Brixen helps clearly discern the degree to which the constant complaints about the increase in kin marriages were justified. Even so, we should bear in mind the problematic aspects of numerical comparison in this context.

Viewed from the perspective of dispensation practice and dispensation policy, the history of prohibitions on marriage between kin appears not to have proceeded in a linear fashion towards successively more liberal handling. Instead, it is characterised by vicissitudes as well as considerable confessional and regional differences all the way into the early twentieth century. Analysing these makes it possible to not only explore various criteria for the choice of partner but also central debates during a long period of transition to more liberal laws and a more scientific worldview, power struggles between Church and state, the divergent logics adhered to by church and state administrations and not least the power of perseverance. This study therefore takes a first-ever systematic look at dispensation practice in four dioceses and employs crossing perspectives[94] in its linkage of the elaborate administrative and procedural paths of the Church and the state with logics of domestic and familial organisation.

94 On the concept of 'crossing' and *histoire croissèe* see the introduction in Natalie Zemon Davis, *Trickster Travels. A Sixteenth-Century Muslim Between Worlds* (New York, 2006), pp. 3–13; Michael Werner and Bénédicte Zimmermann, "Vergleich, Transfer, Verflechtung. Der Ansatz der *histoire croisée* und die Herausforderung des Transnationalen", *Geschichte und Gesellschaft* 28 (2002), 607–636.

CHAPTER 2

Concepts and Discourses

Just who was considered to be among one's kin – whether close, distant or indeed at all – was not a given. This much rather depended on conventions that were subject to change and defined differently in different places and times as well as in accordance with cultural, legal and social contexts. It is therefore necessary to determine who was considered kin in which situation within a specific research context. Over the course of the centuries, the extent to which prohibitions on kin marriage applied proved variable – with even the methods used to count the degrees that determined kinship's closeness diverging. Marriage prohibitions were inseparably connected with notions of incest. But even so, there did exist the possibility of overriding such prohibitions by means of a dispensation. This 'mercy' was, in principle, meant to be an exception – but as the number of requests increased, the number of granted dispensations likewise rose. Throughout the nineteenth century, popes and bishops voiced repeated admonishments to handle this matter with more stringency. The fear was that the numerous exceptions being granted would completely hollow out the marriage prohibitions that were in place – which would have not only weakened the underlying norm but also the ecclesiastical power that championed it. Despite all their efforts, however, it appears that this process was not to be stopped.

Early modern criminal law had likewise oriented itself on the association of marriage prohibitions among blood and affinal kin with notions of incest. The legal situation shifted during the period studied here as the categories of persons with whom sexual relations were considered punishable were reduced. This was probably of a certain relevance as the backdrop to an increasing dissolution of taboos on previously unthinkable couple configurations, for which men and women now began requesting dispensations. Parallel to this, the Josephine Marriage Patent of 1783 limited the number of prohibited degrees of kinship in the civil law context, even if to a far lesser extent than did the General State Laws for the Prussian States (*Allgemeines Landrecht*) of 1794 or the French Civil Code of 1804. In these changes, Edith Saurer perceived a "process of kinship's deconstruction": "the acceptance of canonical and civil marriage prohibitions had nearly vanished", having been superseded by a "love-based logic of closeness".[1] It is therefore necessary to query the power of love in dispensation practice and the ways in which this power was

1 Saurer, "Stiefmütter und Stiefsöhne", pp. 365–366.

communicated – because fundamentally, it must be assumed that the talk of love in our source material cannot be separated from the perceptions represented by canon law.[2]

The upheavals of this period injected an exceptional degree of liveliness into the debates concerning whether prohibitions of kin marriage made sense. Canon law, which had for centuries defined the Catholic world's prerequisites for marriage, was characterised as 'foreign' law in conjunction with efforts to establish state churches and became subject to competition in the form of civil law. The backdrop of the discussions was hence the question as to the separation of Church and state. Secular-minded jurists felt compelled to justify the reduction of marriage prohibitions' scope while representatives of church law felt compelled to defend maintaining the status quo. And finally, the discourses initiated by physiologists, physicians, heredity theorists and other natural scientists regarding the dangers and general harmfulness of unions between close blood relatives became increasingly present. A comprehensive investigation of the participants in this debate, their positions and the resulting argumentative patterns and bricolages would indeed merit its very own study. Here, we will feature a number of conspicuous voices and employ their statements in order to elucidate the important argumentative strands. Moreover, the channels of mediation between the learned discourse and church representatives, both local and regional, will be explored by reconstructing networks of communication and reception.

1 Marriage Prohibitions: Extent and Counting Methods

Marriage prohibitions arose on the basis of the incest rules from the Old Testament books of Leviticus and Deuteronomy.[3] During the initial centuries of early Christendom, these rules – formulated only for individual couple configurations in the aforementioned books – were developed further and successively added to.[4] This resulted in identical marriage prohibitions being imposed on men and women in the Christian context.[5] These marriage prohibitions, formulated along the incest boundary, ultimately extended to the

2 Cf. also Saurer, "Formen von Verwandtschaft und Liebe", pp. 265–266.

3 Cf. Michael Mitterauer, "Christianity and Endogamy", *Continuity and Change* 6, 3 (1991), 295–333, and Gérard Delille, *L'economia di Dio. Famiglia e mercato tra cristianesimo, ebraismo, islam* (Rome, 2013), pp. 31–38.

4 On this process cf. Michael M. Sheehan, "The European Family and Canon Law", *Continuity and Change* 6, 3 (1991), 347–360.

5 See Margareth Lanzinger, "The Relativity of Kinship and Gender-Specific Logics in the Context of Marriage Dispensations in the Nineteenth-Century Alps (Diocese of Brixen)",

hardly reconstructible seventh degree of kinship. In 1215, at the Fourth Lateran Council, Pope Innocent III limited their extent to the fourth degree.[6] According to the canonical method of counting, this encompassed all relatives who shared one of a person's sixteen great-great-grandmothers or grandfathers. Catholics were subject to this norm until the Codex Iuris Canonici, the Code of Canon Law, took effect just over 700 years later in 1917, bringing with it a further reduction in the extent of marriage prohibitions. Partial drafts of this document had been produced and submitted to the church authorities for deliberation beginning in 1912. There was no public debate on the matter, with all those involved sworn to the strictest secrecy.[7]

Genre & Histoire 21, 1 (2018), 1–19, online since 1 September 2018, connection on 3 October 2018, http://journals.openedition.org/genrehistoire/3036 (last access: May 2022).

6 Cf. Mitterauer, "Christianity and Endogamy"; Goody, *The Development of the Family*. The rules governing proof of nobility likewise typically extended to this degree or thereabouts. Cf. Josef Matzerath, "Die Einführung der Ahnenprobe in der kursächsischen Ritterschaft in der zweiten Hälfte des 17. Jahrhunderts", in *Die Ahnenprobe in der Vormoderne*, ed. Harding/Hecht, pp. 233–245. Matzerath quotes a rule according to which a distinction was made between *stiftsfähige* knights with access to positions in cathedral chapters, who needed "to document 16 proper forebears" by means of a proof of nobility, and those who could not document an "impeccable lineage" extending "back to the third and fourth generations" (ibid., 236). On the corresponding rules for the Rhenish Imperial Knighthood cf. Christophe Duhamelle, *L'heritage collectif. La noblesse d'Église rhenane, 17e–18e siècles* (Paris, 1998); Christophe Duhamelle, "The Making of Stability. Kinship, Church and Power among the Rhenish Imperial Knighthood, Seventeenth and Eighteenth Century", in *Kinship in Europe*, ed. Sabean/Teuscher/Mathieu, pp. 125–144. According to Duhamelle's findings, "a candidate had to show that every ancestor, man or woman, for four or five generations, had been a member not only of an old noble family, but also of a *stiftsfähige* family, i.e. one where a member had previously been elected as a canon" (The Making of Stability, p. 127); Sylvia Schraut, "'Die Ehen werden in dem Himmel gemacht'. Ehe- und Liebeskonzepte der katholischen Reichsritterschaft im 17. und 18. Jahrhundert", in *Tugend, Vernunft und Gefühl: Geschlechterdiskurse der Aufklärung und weiblichen Lebenswelten*, ed. Claudia Opitz, Ulrike Weckel and Elke Kleinau (Münster, 2000), pp. 15–32; Sylvia Schraut, "'Doch das bei weitem schwierigste Ehehindernis ist das der Verwandtschaft': Verbotene Ehe zwischen Inzest Tabu und dem Gedeihen der Adelsfamilie (Deutsches Reich 17./18. Jh.)", https://www.unibw.de/geschichte/prof/neu/pers/schraut/downloads/a11b_schraut-ger.pdf (last access: May 2022); Sylvia Schraut, *Das Haus Schönborn – eine Familienbiographie. Katholischer Reichsadel 1640–1840* (Paderborn, 2005); Sylvia Schraut, "Familie ist mehr als die Summe ihrer Mitglieder – Verwandtschaftsbeziehungen katholischen stiftsfähigen Reichsadels", *WerkstattGeschichte* 46 (2007), 13–24.

7 Cf. Ulrich Stutz, *Der Geist des Codex juris canonici. Eine Einführung in das auf Geheiß Papst Pius X. verfaßte und von Papst Benedikt XV. erlassene Gesetzbuch der katholischen Kirche* (Stuttgart, 1918), p. 21. The predecessor to the 1917 code was the Corpus Iuris Canonici, a collection of laws reorganised at the initiative of Pius X beginning in 1904 and consisting of multiple books. On this cf. Christina Deutsch, *Ehegerichtsbarkeit im Bistum Regensburg, 1480–1538* (Cologne/Weimar/Vienna, 2005), pp. 29–31.

The Codex Iuris Canonici of 1917[8] eliminated the necessity of obtaining a dispensation in the fourth degree of blood kinship as well as in the third and fourth degrees of affinity, and it also limited the impediments to marriage associated with godparenthood.[9] 1983 saw an amended version of the Codex Iuris Canonici eliminate further marriage prohibitions, with marriages between brother and sister-in-law as well as between two cousins also being permitted by the Church. Prohibited to this day are unions between stepparents and stepchildren – which are, however, now possible under civil law in Germany, Austria and Switzerland.[10]

Eighteenth-century civil law codes took up a variety of confessionally and politically tinged stances regarding marriage prohibitions' extent: the Codex Maximilianeus Bavaricus civilis, the Bavarian civil code of 1756, adhered to the marriage prohibitions defined by canon law.[11] The 1794 General State Laws for the Prussian States, on the other hand, forbade only marriages between blood relatives in a straight line of descent as well as between siblings, between stepparents and stepchildren and between parents-in-law and children-in-law. "In all other degrees of blood kinship and affinity", it stated, "marriage is permitted and requires no dispensation". Only in the case of marriage to an aunt or to another female relative in an ascending line, "who is older in years", was state permission required.[12] The gender-specifically one-sided formulation of this

8 Codex Iuris Canonici, 1917, can. 1076, §§1, 2, 3; can. 1077, can. 1079, http://www.codex-iuris-canonici.de/ (last access: April 2022).

9 Godparenthood, the conception of which developed as a form of spiritual kinship over the course of the Middle Ages, entailed a whole series of marriage prohibitions: these applied to the baptised and confirmed and their godmothers and godfathers as well as to the parents of the baptised and confirmed. On this cf. Anita Guerreau-Jalabert, "*Spiritus* et *Caritas*. Le baptême dans la société médiévale", in *La parenté spirituelle*, ed. Françoise Héritier-Augé and Elisabeth Copet-Rougier (Paris, 1995), pp. 133–203; Alfani, *Fathers and Godfathers*.

10 A table containing an overview of the marriage prohibitions that applied to blood and adoptive kin as well as affinal kin in individual European countries during the 1980s is provided in Hürlimann, *Die Eheschließungsverbote*, pp. 140–141. Since then, however, further liberalisations have been enacted.

11 *Das Bayerische Landrecht vom Jahre 1756 in seiner heutigen Geltung*, ed. by Max Danzer (Munich, 1894), part 1, chap. 6, § 9: "Marriage is impermissible 1. Among blood kin in the ascending and descending line, as far as this may extend, as well as in the collateral line out to and including the fourth degree calculated in accordance with ecclesiastical law." Point two applies to spiritual kinship, while point three details prohibitions applying to adoptees and their foster parents. And finally, "4. Between in-laws out to the fourth degree of affinity, and in cases of affinity due to extramarital copulation out to and including the second degree according to the calculating method of religious law."

12 *Allgemeines Landrecht für die Preußischen Staaten*, 1794, zweiter Teil, erster Titel, §§ 3 to 5, § 7 and § 8.

rule was grounded in the tradition of *respectus parentelae*, the respect to be shown older relatives, which was limited here to the configuration of nephew and aunt and did not apply to that of niece and uncle. By comparison, the Josephine Marriage Patent of 1783 took up an intermediate position in that it reduced the extent of marriage prohibitions from four degrees to two. Hence, just like church rules, civil rules also exhibited pronounced differences. At the same time, they did still interrelate with church rules valid in each case.

Marriage prohibitions according to civil and church law addressed kinship by blood and kinship by affinity to differing extents. Blood kinship is undoubtedly the object of greater interest among researchers, especially in cases where the focus is on biological and medical aspects. However, any notion of kinship – as "a way of conceptualising social relationships" – is historically, culturally and legally contingent.[13] For this reason, distinguishing between biological kinship based on descent and other forms such as affinity generated by marriage or godparenthood – the latter of which has frequently been characterised as ritual, fictitious or metaphorical[14] – is implausible from a theoretical perspective, as Bernhard Jussen has indeed emphasised. In the ecclesiastical norm, which was well known all the way down to the smallest village on account of the marriage prohibitions that it entailed, all three forms of relatedness were conceptualised as kinship and must hence be recognised as such. This entails that the "relationship between biology and kinship" must much rather be "a *subject* of kinship research" and not "a *premise*".[15] In this spirit, kinship can be understood as a type of knowledge formation that features various components in various contexts and is constituted according to differing logics.

A number of conspicuous events led to existing matrimonial law being discussed – with quite some attention given to matters of marriage impediments, kin marriage and dispensations. A multitude of handbooks, instructional texts, commentaries and tracts appeared from the late eighteenth century onward, written from secular and ecclesiastical standpoints as well as from intermediatory perspectives between the two. These events included state interventions in matrimonial law, in particular the definition of marriage as a civil contract in the Josephine Marriage Patent of 1783, whose fundamental

13 Bernhard Jussen, "Künstliche und natürliche Verwandtschaft? Biologismen in den kulturwissenschaftlichen Konzepten von Verwandtschaft", in *Das Individuum und die Seinen. Individualität in der okzidentalen und der russischen Kultur in Mittelalter und Früher Neuzeit*, ed. Yuri L. Bessmertny and Otto Gerhard Oexle (Göttingen, 2001), pp. 40–58, 40. Opposition to the biologisation of kinship has also been voiced by Yanagisako/Collier, *Towards a Unified Analysis.*

14 Cf. Jussen, *Spiritual Kinship as Social Practice.*

15 Jussen, "Künstliche und natürliche Verwandtschaft", p. 42.

provisions were carried over into the Austrian Civil Code of 1811. Other factors were the liberalisation of criminal law's rules concerning incest as well as, in particular, the strengthening of the Catholic Church's authority relating to marriage in Austria with the Concordat of 1855.[16] In these decades, marked by increasing competition between the Church and the state regarding definitional power over marriage, it seems to have been important to recognise an author's standpoint at first glance: it was to this effect that authors declared themselves on the title pages of their works. Even towards the close of the nineteenth century, this page of Wolfgang Dannerbauer's *Praktisches Geschäftsbuch für den Curat-Clerus Oesterreichs* (Practical Manual for Austria's Curates) lists ordinariates and consistories the author claimed had "endorsed" his manual, among which were the Dioceses of Salzburg and Trento.[17] Moreover, the fact that this was difficult terrain can be seen not least in the fact that two Latin-language university textbooks on canon law, those by Georg Rechberger and Matthias Dannermayer, were placed on the *Index Librorum Prohibitorum* – the List of Prohibited Books – in January 1820. These bans, tantamount to a "manifesto against state law-making in Austria", were also of symbolic significance.[18]

Up to the mid-nineteenth century, a somewhat greater share of the works published on the topic were situated in the context of civil law, whereas the canon law context saw numerous books published beginning in the mid-1850s. The authors usually went beyond simple portrayal of the current legal situation, also striving to justify it – including with rationales that addressed marriage impediments' sensibility and purpose. In this way, their writings provide insights into the construction of marriage prohibitions, blood kinship and affinal kinship. The authors made heavy use of arguments that were common at that time, copying from each other more or less verbatim or slightly rephrased and sometimes also supplementing them with further ones.[19] It was not only representatives of canon law who defended marriage prohibitions; writers

---

16 See *Reichsgesetzblatt, RGBl* (official government gazette of the Austrian Monarchy), 195.

17 Wolfgang Dannerbauer, *Praktisches Geschäftsbuch für den Curat-Clerus Oesterreichs* (Vienna, 1893).

18 Ferdinand Maaß, *Der Josephinismus. Quellen zu seiner Geschichte in Österreich 1760–1850. Amtliche Dokumente aus dem Haus-, Hof- und Staatsarchiv und dem Allgemeinen Verwaltungsarchiv in Wien sowie dem Archivio Segreto Vaticano in Rom*, vol. 5: *Lockerung und Aufhebung des Josephinismus 1820–1850* (Vienna, 1961), chap. 3: Der Kampf um das Lehrbuch des Kirchenrechts (*1820–1837*), pp. 51–73, 51. The prohibited books in question were *Enchiridion juris ecclesiastici austriaci* by Georg Rechberger and *Institutiones historiae ecclesiasticae* by Matthias Dannermayer.

19 There were also various authors who took up particularist stances. A noteworthy example would be Joseph Valentin Eybel, *Nichts Mehreres von Ehedispensen als was Religion, Recht, Nutzen, Klugheit und Pflicht fordert* (Wahrheitsthal, 1782).

hailing from the realm of civil law were in fact quite willing to second them, at least where close degrees were concerned. In general, dissenting voices – like that of Jacques Bertillon, who turned against the Catholic discourse and portrayed consanguine marriages in a positive light – were rare.[20]

The divergences between canon and state law formed the backdrop to this broad discourse on the extent of marriage prohibitions, their classification and the method of counting kinship degrees. The church context classified consanguinity by so-called canonical degrees.[21] In this system, siblings formed a single unit; they were related in the first degree and represented the first generation. Their children – first cousins –, as the next generation, were related in the second degree. The third and fourth degrees were determined in an analogous fashion. The degrees of kinship followed the generational steps away from the initial couple, in keeping with the motto: "Tot sunt gradus, quot sunt generationes". Degrees of affinity were determined in the same way, corresponding to the respective degrees of blood kinship that connected the deceased spouse with the prospective new bride or groom. The civil degree system differed, focusing on the number of conceptions that lay in between: while two cousins were related in the second degree according to canon law, they were fourth-degree relatives according to the civil system. Since the source material for this study is derived primarily from ecclesiastical records, the degrees indicated here are those of the canonical system unless specified otherwise.

A prospective couple's ability to receive a dispensation depended on how close their degree of kinship was. Unions between ascendents and descendants, meaning blood kin in a straight line of descent such as grandparents, parents and children were up for debate neither on the ecclesiastical nor on the civil side. The "quite controversial but, in truth, quite pointless question" of whether this marriage impediment extended only to the fourth degree did indeed get asked here and there.[22] From the Church's perspective, such impediments were a matter of divine law (*ius divinum*) that, in principle, applied ad infinitum in the spirit of a sexual taboo that was said to exist among all

---

20 Jacques Bertillon, article "Mariage", in: *Dictionnaire encyclopédique des sciences médicales*, series 2, vol. 5 (Paris, 1874), pp. 7–83, especially 61–62. For this reference, I thank Domenico Rizzo.

21 On this cf. for example Nikolaus Knopp, *Vollständiges katholisches Eherecht. Mit besonderer Rücksicht auf die practische Seelsorge*, 4th ed. (Regensburg, 1873), p. 158; Goody, *The Development of the Family*, pp. 151–156.

22 Theodor Pachmann, *Lehrbuch des Kirchenrechtes mit Berücksichtigung der auf die kirchlichen Verhältnisse Bezug nehmenden österreichischen Gesetze und Verordnungen*, vol. 2/1 (Vienna, 1851), p. 265, note 4.

"civilised", "educated peoples" and to be based on a "natural abhorrence"[23] conceived of as more or less inscribed into the human body. Thomas Dolliner, a representative of civil law, did not seek an explanation of this in some sort of "natural" predisposition but rather emphasised the irreconcilability of sexuality's inherent familiarity with respect: he wrote that such unions were "morally impermissible because the mutual familiarity between spouses" would seem to "contradict the reverence that progeny owe their progenitors".[24] For such configurations, dispensations could not be requested.

Two further types of very close union, though unaffected by divine law, were likewise ineligible for dispensation due to their closeness. The first type was unions between siblings, who were related in the first collateral degree; the second type was between a stepparent and stepchild, who were related in the first degree of affinity in the direct line. Among blood and affinal kin who were less close, a distinction was made between close and more distant degrees. From the Church's standpoint, the pope was competent to dispense in the former while bishops could grant dispensations in the latter. Just how far close degrees under the pope's direct purview extended depended on the authority granted by Rome to each bishop upon his assumption of office. In the dioceses studied here, the line of demarcation between episcopal and papal competency ran just within or just outside the second and third unequal degree during the nineteenth century. Such intermediate degrees arose due to generational shifts. Among blood kin, the second and third unequal degree existed when a man married his cousin's daughter or, conversely, when a woman married her cousin's son (see Fig. 1). Thomas Dolliner, commentator of the Austrian General Civil Code, argued in favour of the civil degree system not least because it facilitated "far more specific" definition of relatedness in unequal degrees. After all, the rule "[a]s many degrees as conceptions" made it possible to express unequal degrees using a single number.[25]

Unions between uncle and niece were quite rare and controversial. In the canonical system, this represented consanguinity in the first and second unequal degree. For one thing, this configuration – being adjacent to the first degree – came close to the direct line of descent, between father and daughter. Furthermore, *respectus parentelae* – a special relationship based on respect and reverence – was said to exist with a father's or mother's brother as well as

---

23 Knopp, *Vollständiges katholisches Eherecht*, p. 200; cf. also Heinrich Brandhuber von Etschfeld, *Über Dispensation und Dispensationsrecht nach katholischem Kirchenrecht* (Leipzig/Vienna, 1888), pp. 19–24.

24 Thomas Dolliner, *Handbuch des in Oesterreich geltenden Eherechts* (Vienna/Triest, 1813), p. 181.

25 Dolliner, *Handbuch*, pp. 179–180.

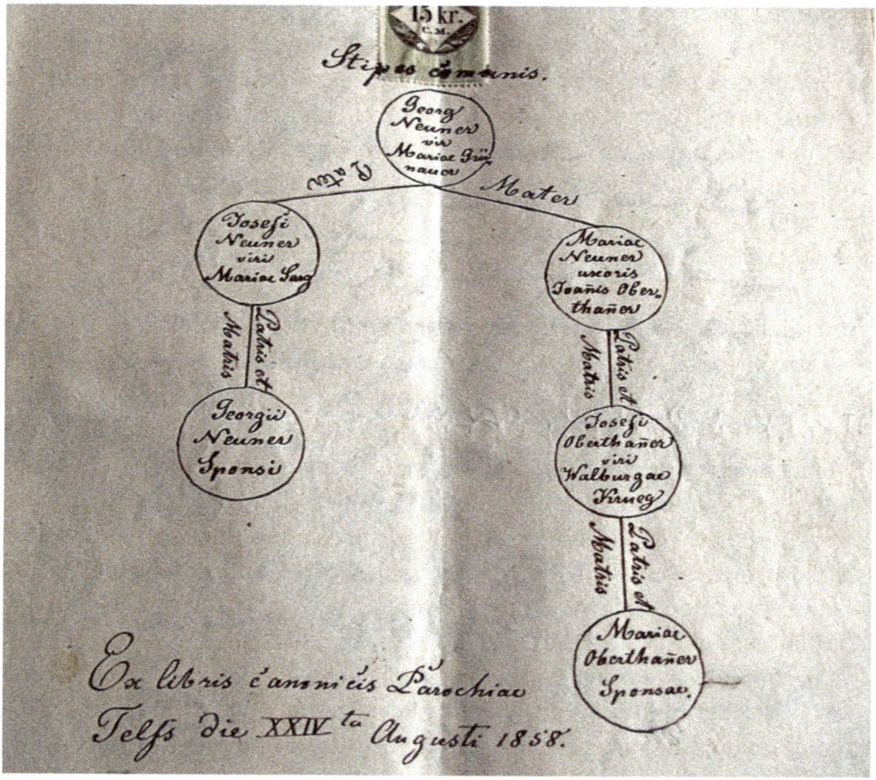

FIGURE 1 The second and third unequal degree of consanguinity: family tree from the dispensation request submitted by Georg Neuner and Maria Oberthaner of Telfs
SOURCE: DIÖZESANARCHIV BRIXEN, KONSISTORIALAKTEN 1858, FASC. 5A, RÖMISCHE DISPENSEN, NO. 30.

with a father's or mother's sister, and such a relationship was held to be incompatible with a sexual one.[26]

Among affinal kin, in contrast to blood kin, a union in the first collateral degree – namely, between brother- and sister-in-law – was indeed eligible for a dispensation. And since divorce with the possibility of remarriage was prohibited in the Catholic context, marriages between in-laws always involved at

26 The authors who mention this include Franz Stapf and Carl Egger, *Vollständiger Pastoralunterricht über die Ehe, oder über das gesetz- und pflichtmäßige Verhalten des Pfarrers vor – bei und nach der ehelichen Trauung, nach den Grundsätzen des katholischen Kirchenrechts, mit steter Rücksicht auf Civilgesetze*, 6th ed. (Frankfurt a. M., 1839), p. 235. This mention is not in the original edition, however, which may indicate that dispensation requests for this configuration had begun to appear more frequently than before.

least one widowed partner:[27] in the first degree of affinity, this could be a widower marrying a sister of his deceased wife, a widow marrying a brother of her deceased husband, or – something that is extremely rare in the dispensation records – a widower marrying his likewise-widowed sister-in-law. An affinal marriage in the first and second unequal degree was one in which the bride or groom was a niece or nephew of the deceased spouse, while an affinal marriage in the second degree was to a cousin of the deceased spouse.

Alongside affinal kinship based on a marital union, there was also "dishonourable affinal kinship" or *affinitas ex copula illicita*, which likewise represented an impediment to marriage. It arose from premarital sexual contact between the groom and a sister, niece or cousin of the bride or between the bride and a brother, cousin or nephew of the groom.[28] This marriage impediment arising from illicit sexual contact was also metaphorically referred to as being from "an illicit bed", *ex thoro illicito*. The basis for this was the canon law concept of affinity as derived from Corinthians (1 Corinthians 6:16), where it is linked not with marriage but with sexual intercourse: *Affinitas est personarum proximitas proveniens ex coitu*. As the enumeration of potential persons involved clearly suggests, the need to obtain a dispensation for this type of affinity extended not to the fourth degree but only to the second. Some theologians felt a need to explain this limitation to the second degree: "The church policy exists not out of leniency towards debauchery, but in order to keep this impediment from growing too widespread on account of the secrecy and frequency of sins of the flesh, in which case it would endanger the freedom to marry".[29] The Marriage Patent of 1783 did not incorporate this impediment to marriage,[30] nor did the Josephine Code of 1786 or the Austrian Civil Code of 1811.[31] From the perspective of the Church, however, the obligation to obtain a dispensation in such a case continued to exist.[32]

---

27 An exception here was affinity generated by premarital sexual contact (*affinitas ex copula illicita*).

28 This rule is attributed to St. Paul (1 Corinthians 6:16): "What? know ye not that he which is joined to an harlot is one body? for two, saith he, shall be one flesh". – *qui adhaeret meretrici una caro efficitur cum ea.*

29 Stapf/Egger, *Vollständiger Pastoralunterricht*, p. 267.

30 Entschließung vom 13. April 1783, in *Sammlung der Kaiserlich-Königlichen Landesfürstlichen Gesetze und Verordnungen in Publico-Ecclesiasticis vom Jahre 1782 bis 1783*, part 2 (Vienna, 1784), p. 67. This resolution emphasised that "the recently enacted marriage contract laws would apply only to those impediments stemming from a valid marriage".

31 Saurer, "Stiefmütter und Stiefsöhne", p. 355.

32 The state held that "Reverend Ordinaries remain free to decide" to turn to the Apostolic Penitentiary "on behalf of the parties in such cases". Edict of 10 July 1783, *Sammlung in Publico-Ecclesiasticis vom Jahre 1782 bis 1783*, p. 90.

In the dioceses of Brixen and Salzburg,[33] dispensation requests of this type are documented throughout the entire nineteenth century.[34] In the analysis for Brixen, such requests in fact amounted to seven per cent of all cases. Their total came to 152 of 2,142, with quite a few of them also concerning further marriage impediments that related to consanguinity or affinity. In the majority of these cases, totalling 82 couples, the impediment involved a prior relationship with a brother of the groom or sister of the bride, followed by prior relationships with cousins in 47 cases. The distribution over time shows that their number increased markedly beginning in the 1860s as compared to the previous three decades. The zenith was reached during the final five years from which the data was analysed: a full 29 such requests were made between 1885 and 1889 – meaning that 20 per cent were made during this period alone. For this, two conceivable explanations would suggest themselves: either this period witnessed an actual increase in sexual contacts among close social relations. Or the clerics – in the pre-wedding religious examinations that were mandatory in these decades, with their more severe policies regarding morality – were that much more insistent in their questioning with regard to previous sexual encounters with close relations of the bride or groom.

The altered significance of kinship in the wake of an increased number of marriages between close kin has been controversially discussed in recent years, with two hypotheses in play. Gérard Delille holds that a contraction of kinship took place. He points out that during the High Middle Ages as well as in the early modern period and at least up to the eighteenth century, distant kin who lay beyond the fourth canonical degree – and thus outside the reach of Catholic marriage prohibitions – were deliberately and systematically used for marriage alliances. But from the eighteenth century, he argues, such unions gave way to an increasing number of marriages between close kin. His conclusion is hence that the circle of kin selected for marriage grew smaller, with kinship's overall significance having been consequently reduced.[35] David Sabean, on the other

---

33 Cf. for example Archiv der Erzdiözese Salzburg (AES), Kasten 22/34, Ehedispensen I. u. II. Grades 1813–1880. Therein, one finds 50 files concerning papal dispensations in the first and second degrees of affinity *ex copula illicita*. Further holdings there extend all the way to 1920.

34 In individual cases where *copula illicita* joined blood kinship to form a double impediment to marriage, the former was actually considered more serious. Cf. for example DIÖAB, Konsistorialakten 1867, Fasc. 22a, Römische Dispensen, no. 39.

35 Gérard Delille, "Parenté et alliance en Europe occidentale. Un essai d'interprétation Générale", *L'Homme. Z.F.G.* 193 (2010), 75–135; Gérard Delille, "Position und Rolle von Frauen im europäischen System der Heiratsallianzen", in *Politiken der Verwandtschaft*, ed. Lanzinger/Saurer, pp. 227–254; Gérard Delille, "Kinship, Marriage, and Politics", in *Kinship in Europe*, ed. Sabean/Teuscher/Mathieu, pp. 163–183.

hand, interprets the increasing presence of close kin – including in the context of marriages – as signifying an increase in kinship's significance.[36] The issue underlying these different positions is ultimately that of what "significance" means in connection with kinship and kin marriage. In order to resolve this apparent contradiction, it seems sensible to draw a distinction between kinship as it was experienced socially and kinship as a notion laden with taboos. In the nineteenth and twentieth centuries, kin did not lose their significance in terms of social presence and interaction. However, the significance of the notions of incest that were connected with kinship most probably did wane markedly. The dissipation of taboos on prohibited degrees of consanguinity and affinity as well as the increase in marriages between close kin went hand in hand with changes in dispensation practice. At the same time, the fundamental character of marriage dispensations remained unchanged.

2 Mercy and Punishment

Dispensations were a class of legal instruments that constituted an important component of canon law logic.[37] The specific character of dispensations – including those used as a means of lifting impediments to marriage – lies in the fact that they could only be requested. It follows that even in the modern era, there was no legal right or entitlement to a dispensation. There also existed no channel to appeal a decision in the event a request was rejected. The only option for unsuccessful supplicants was to resubmit their requests. In the understanding of the Church, a dispensation continued to be what it had been for centuries: a form of mercy that could be granted or denied in response to a supplication.[38]

36 Sabean, *Kinship in Neckarhausen*; Sabean/Teuscher, "Kinship in Europe".

37 On the concept of the dispensation in this context and its distinction from other legal instruments cf. Brandhuber von Etschfeld, *Über Dispensation und Dispensationsrecht*, pp. 1–19; on the history of dispensations from the perspective of canon law cf. Eduardo Baura, *La dispensa canonica dalla legge* (Milan, 1997); from the perspective of German state law, for which "dispensatory authority, which lay in part with the pope and in part with the bishops in Catholic canon law, [was] of no significance" cf. Julius Steinitz, *Dispensationsbegriff und Dispensationsgewalt auf dem Gebiet des deutschen Staatsrechts* (Wroclaw, 1901); cf. also Arturo Carlo Jemolo, *Il matrimonio nel diritto canonico. Dal Concilio di Trento al Codice del 1917* (Bologna, 1993), pp. 245–260.

38 "A bishop's refusal to grant a dispensation can never cause him to face legal proceedings, for this is an act of mercy; however, every person does have recourse [here meaning renewed supplication in Rome, M.L.] to the head of the church". Article: "Ehedispense"

Generally speaking, a dispensation grants an exemption from a law in the presence of certain prerequisites.[39] The legal discourse devoted broad discussion to one explanation of the concept that appears repeatedly in the writings of Thomas Aquinas: "dispensatio est iuris relaxatio"[40] – a dispensation is a relaxation of the law. It was meant to "compensate for hardships that laws formulated for the masses can entail in individual cases". In doing so, it eliminated "the obligatory force of a legal tenet" without "replacing the norm thus set aside with a new norm".[41] Dispensations were used for a wide range of matters,[42] and one large area where they were employed was that of marriage. A marriage dispensation could override the impediments to marriage represented by the spiritual kinship engendered via godparenthood (*cognatio spiritualis*), a difference in religious confession (*disparitas cultus*) and adultery (*impedimentum criminis*). A dispensation *publicae honestatis* was necessary if an earlier promise of marriage with a first-degree relative of the bride or groom had been dissolved. Couples also had to request a dispensation in the following cases: a. The three obligatory banns of marriage – public announcements of the planned union – could not be announced on account of time constraints or other reasons. b. A marriage was to take place in the "forbidden period" – *tempore vetito* – of Lent or Advent during which sexual abstinence was mandated. c. A marriage was to take place somewhere other than in the competent parish or if a person desired to marry despite having taken a vow of chastity.

According to the corresponding entry in an 1886 encyclopaedia of Catholic theology, a marriage dispensation was defined as follows: "A marriage dispensation consists in the lifting of an impediment to marriage by the legally competent church leader in a specific case."[43] It is probably no coincidence that in

---

in *Lexikon für Theologie und Kirche*, ed. Michael Buchberger, 2nd ed. (Freiburg i. Br., 1931), col. 174–181, 178.

39 Cf. Margherita Pelaja and Lucetta Scaraffia, *Due in una carne. Chiesa e sessualità nella storia* (Rome/Bari, 2008), pp. 140–148.

40 On this, as well as on dispensations' exceptional character, cf. Luca Bianchi, "'Cotidiana miracula', comune corso della natura e dispense al diritto matrimoniale: il miracolo fra Agostino e Tommaso d'Aquino", *Quaderni storici* 131 (2009), 313–328, 320.

41 Klaus Mörsdorf, *Lehrbuch des Kirchenrechts auf Grund des Codex Iuris Canonici*, vol. 1: Einleitung, Allgemeiner Teil und Personenrecht, 9th ed. (Munich/Paderborn/Vienna, 1959), p. 174.

42 Dispensations were also granted to read books on the *Index librorum prohibitorum* (the Index of Forbidden Books), to be exempted from the commitment to fast if required to eat meat for health reasons and to lift the "stigma of illegitimate birth" (also referred to as "irregularity") that was necessary when joining the clergy.

43 Article: "Ehedispense", in *Wetzer und Welte's Kirchenlexikon oder Encyklopädie der katholischen Theologie und ihrer Hilfswissenschaften*, vol. 4, ed. Joseph Hergenröther and Franz Kaulen, 2nd ed. (Freiburg i. Br., 1886), col. 174–181, 174.

this very general explanation, some points remain vague. From the late eighteenth century, competence in dispensation matters had been a major bone of contention even within the Church itself. Who was considered the "legally competent church leader" in terms of church hierarchy, place and the matter at hand? In which cases could what impediment to marriage be lifted? What counted as an impediment to marriage? All these questions grew more complicated. The formal definition that the above-quoted encyclopaedia article provides is also paradigmatic of the highly legalistic emphasis brought to bear by those who engaged in the discourse on this topic. The actual practice of dispensation-granting, on the other hand, has so far remained comparatively obscure.

While Rome was Catholicism's dispensation-granting centre, nowhere near all marriage projects between close kin made it there to be decided upon. Numerous rejections issued by diocesan consistories cut that journey short. What is more, local clerics and deans were required to attempt to dissuade related dispensation-seekers from pursuing their marriage projects further. Cases in which supplicants desisted already in this first phase are rarely documented in the source material. But from the perspective of the Church, only a granted dispensation provided protection from the sin of incest in kinship configurations for which one was required.

Church and state prohibitions on marriage between blood and affinal kin adhered to a logic that was formal and arithmetical in character. They were based on genealogy, on degrees of kinship determined via specific methods of counting. A sexual relationship within one of the four prohibited degrees of blood or affinal kinship was viewed as having crossed the boundary to incest.[44] Incest was hence defined quite broadly in this context, and every infringement upon a sexual prohibition of this sort represented the violation of a norm. It amounted to *copula incestuosa*, rendered in German as *Blutschande* – literally "disgrace of the blood".[45] *Incestus* means, among other things, "tainted" and "impure".[46] The fear of impurity, of being tainted or polluted, had become increasingly present in the theological and canonistic literature over the course of the seventeenth century. This was underlined by a Christian worldview according to which sinful acts by a single person would bring divine

---

44 Concerning the Middle Ages cf. Ludwig Schmugge, *Ehen vor Gericht. Paare der Renaissance vor dem Papst* (Berlin, 2008), pp. 58–61; Karl Ubl, *Inzestverbot und Gesetzgebung. Die Konstruktion eines Verbrechens, 300–1100* (Berlin/New York, 2008).

45 On the topic of incest cf. David Warren Sabean, "Inzestdiskurse vom Barock bis zur Romantik", *L'Homme. Z.F.G.* 13, 1 (2002), 7–28; Jutta Eming, Claudia Jarzebowski and Claudia Ulbrich (eds.), *Historische Inzestdiskurse. Interdisziplinäre Zugänge* (Königstein/Taunus, 2003); Jarzebowski, *Inzest*.

46 More generally on this topic cf. Burghartz, *Zeiten der Reinheit*.

punishment down upon all. Hence incest, once committed, was thought to be capable of bringing about the ruin of an entire city or country.[47] Peter Burschel has shown the significance of purity as an early modern cultural code, as a mark of distinction and as an obsession.[48]

A piece of writing published anonymously in 1557 describes to its Saxon audience the disastrous anticipated consequences of limiting marriage prohibitions only to the second degree of kinship. Its closing passage more or less implores all of Christendom to avert any possible punishment while at the same time conjuring up a classic punishment scenario: "That he may have a pure Christian conscience, and also avoid bringing upon himself the wrath and severe punishment of God Almighty and worldly authorities, indeed not defile, bring misery and need upon land and people on account of such sins, as the holy scriptures show us with terrifying examples of the unwavering severity of God's punishment of incest and debauchery as testified to by the punishment of the Great Flood and his divine retribution visited upon the cities of Sodom and Gomorrah and upon the Sichinites, where the debauchery of one man caused an entire city to be deprecated and destroyed."[49]

Incest was a criminal offence. And even if early modern criminal law was based on canon law and hence employed a broad definition of incest, the prescribed punishments were graduated according to how closely the involved parties were related. In the *Constitutio Criminalis Theresiana* or Maria-Theresian Criminal Code of 1768, which was already considered obsolete when it took effect, the crime concerned here was known as "incest" (*Blutschand*) and defined by way of marriage prohibitions:[50] "Incest is committed between those persons who are so closely related by blood or affinity that they cannot marry each other."[51] The *Constitutio Theresiana* prescribed three possible

---

47 Vgl. Sabean, "Inzestdiskurse", p. 10.

48 Peter Burschel, *Die Erfindung der Reinheit. Eine andere Geschichte der Frühen Neuzeit* (Göttingen, 2014).

49 *Die Ehe wirdt vornemlich / von wegen der Blutfreuntschafft / Darnach auch von wegen der Schwegerschaft / wie folgend zusehen / verboten* [Marriage is Mainly / Prohibited / In Cases of Blood Kinship / And also in Cases of Affinity / As Shall Be Shown in the Following], Dresden, 1557, without page numbers, in the concluding section of this tract.

50 The *Constitutio Criminalis Carolina* (1532) contains a section (§ 117) entitled "Unchaste with Close Relations", which refers to affinal relations: stepdaughters, daughters-in-law and stepmothers are specified. In cases involving these as well as other affinal relations, the punishment was to correspond to the written, established and enforced imperial laws and be administered upon consultation with "competent jurisprudents". The *Carolina* was applied in a way that was subsidiary to territorial laws.

51 *Constitutio Criminalis Theresiana*, Art. 75, § 1, online at http://www.archive.org/details/ConstitutioCriminalisTheresiana-1768 (last access: April 2022).

degrees of penalty.[52] The most severe penalty – death by the sword – was reserved for cases of incest between blood relatives in the ascending and descending line between grandparents, parents, children, grandchildren, etc. A milder sentence – "severe corporal punishment" and banishment from the court district – applied to incest between siblings, cousins, uncles and nieces or aunts and nephews, brother- and sister-in-law, father-in-law and daughter-in-law, stepfather and stepdaughter and stepmother and stepson. And finally, for incest in more distant degrees of kinship up to and including the fourth degree, the penalty was not defined in detail, but it was stipulated that it should be more severe than for people guilty of "common commingling" (*gemeine Vermischung*).

The *Josephinisches Strafgesetzbuch*, the Josephine Penal Code, Patent of 13 January 1787 for all Lands of the Monarchy, which stood out above all for its abolishment of the death penalty, replaced the *Constitutio Theresiana* after only a few years. It does not contain an incest paragraph. At the end of the same year, however, an imperial court decree on the matter was announced in the individual Austrian lands between 8 and 29 November 1787: the "crime of incest" was, "where it becomes known and scandal ensues, to be treated and punishable as a political crime". A "political crime" (*politisches Verbrechen*) was distinct from other crimes in that, among other things, it did not fall within the competence of "criminal judges", with punishment coming instead "only from the state authorities". In the court decree referred to here, incest was defined as "commingling" between kin in the ascending and descending line as well as with "spouses of parents, children or siblings" – that is, with stepparents,

---

52 These provisions were based to a large extent on the provincial court ordinances of Upper Austria (Erzherzogtum Österreich ob der Enns) of 1675 and those of Lower Austria (Erzherzogtum Österreich unter der Enns) of 1656. On this cf. Ernst C. Hellbling, *Grundlegende Strafrechtsquellen der österreichischen Erbländer vom Beginn der Neuzeit bis zur Theresiana. Ein Beitrag zur Geschichte des Strafrechts in Österreich*, ed. Ilse Reiter (Vienna/Cologne/Weimar, 1996), pp. 122–123; Susanne Hehenberger, "Inzest oder 'Hurerey'? Inzest in der gerichtlichen Praxis des 18. Jahrhunderts. Eine Untersuchung am Beispiel Oberösterreichs", in *Historische Inzestdiskurse*, ed. Eming/Jarzebowski/Ulbrich, pp. 189–213, 192 and note 8; Jarzebowski, *Inzest*. Claudia Jarzebowski makes a theme of both dispensable relationships and relationships that were incestuous in a narrower sense, thereby addressing the matter of which argumentative patterns – from economics to emotion and on to power, dependency and violence as well as their gender-specific characteristics – were accorded more weight. The criminal punishment of wildly varying forms of incest increasingly came to be viewed as a problem, since it put sexual assaults on dependents on an equal footing with relationships such as between a widower and his sister-in-law who had merely not been granted a dispensation to marry. On this cf. Patrizia Guarnieri, "Inzest als 'öffentliches Ärgernis'. Gesetzeslage und Moralvorstellungen im vereinten Italien", *L'Homme. Z.F.G.* 13, 1 (2002), 68–94.

children-in-law and brothers- or sisters-in-law. The punishment was to be one degree more severe than for adultery if the case involved a blood relative or a relative in the ascending or descending line. In the collateral lines, however, the punishment was to be equal to that for adultery. For adultery, the Josephine Penal Code (Part 2, § 46) prescribed "correction by flagellation or a term of imprisonment made more severe by fasting". And with that, analogue to the Austrian state's liberalisation of marriage prohibitions and dispensation-granting practices, the circle of those persons who could be brought before a judge for illicit sexual relations was sharply reduced relative to the old rules, as was the severity of the prescribed punishments.[53]

This liberalisation of criminal law most probably helped weaken the broad notions and stigmas associated with incest. In this respect, it interacted with the spread of the kin marriage phenomenon and the radical breaking of taboos in terms of marriage projects that can be observed from the end of the eighteenth century onward. But even so, the Catholic Church continued to use its power to banish sexuality, love and passion from the realm of social proximity constituted by blood and affinal kinship.

3 Love and Passion

The question of the effects and formative power of emotions as "historical assets"[54] has been en vogue for quite some time now,[55] with several decades having passed since Lucien Febvre urged historical scholarship not to shirk

---

53 1803 saw a new penal code take effect in Austria that was proclaimed anew in a version amended by supplementary material and reforms in 1852 and only replaced in 1975. In the 1803 version, "incest" was included under the heading of "rape and other cases of incest" and referred to relatives in the ascending and descending line. *Gesetzbuch über Verbrechen* (Vienna, 1803), § 113. The 1852 version made a distinction between "incest", once again involving relatives in the ascending and descending line (§ 131), and "fornication between blood and affinal kin" (§ 501). Siblings and the "marital companions" of parents, children and siblings were all part of this group of persons. Imperial Patent of 27 May 1852, effective 1 September 1852.

54 Ute Frevert, "Angst vor Gefühlen? Die Geschichtsmächtigkeit von Emotionen im 20. Jahrhundert", in *Perspektiven der Gesellschaftsgeschichte*, ed. Paul Nolte et al. (Munich, 2000), pp. 95–111, 106; Edith Saurer, *Liebe und Arbeit. Geschlechterbeziehungen im 19. und 20. Jahrhundert*, ed. by Margareth Lanzinger (Vienna/Cologne/Weimar, 2014); Ute Frevert, *Gefühle in der Geschichte* (Göttingen, 2021).

55 An extensive overview of the relevant research is provided by Bettina Hitzer, "Emotionengeschichte – ein Anfang mit Folgen", *H-Soz-u-Kult* 23 November 2011, http://hsozkult.geschichte.hu-berlin.de/forum/2011-11-001 (last access: May 2022).

from this perhaps indeed "infinitely difficult task".[56] However, much still remains to be done on this topic. More recent research has striven to arrive at a nuanced perspective that incorporates criticism both of boldly simplistic ascriptions and of notions undergirded by a reverent belief in progress.[57] An approach thus conceived fundamentally precludes all-too-dichotomous perspectives. This goes above all for the narrative in which "affective modernity" is juxtaposed with an "affectless, cold premodernity", with the result that the latter is portrayed "in light of oppressed, reduced and indeed inferior emotionality".[58]

A broad range of emotions finds expression in dispensation records – emotions on the part of those women and men who applied for dispensations, of their relatives, neighbours and acquaintances and of witnesses and clerics who spoke about them. Time and time again, love and passion were at issue. They also spoke of fear, joy, sadness, shame, impatience, trepidation and despair, of the "gloom" (*Schwermuth*) that threatened to set in or of medically confirmed melancholy. And sometimes there were threats of suicide in the event of a rejected request. Gender history has identified the concept of romantic love propagated by intellectuals at the transition from the eighteenth to the nineteenth centuries as being an ambivalent one. Such love did indeed ignore situational constraints and reject socio-economic partner selection barriers, instead raising the demand that marriage and family should be based on love and compatibility of disposition. And in this radical form, love could function as "a subversive force counter to the legal and moral order of estates-based society" because it "asserted individual sovereignty, individual choice of

---

56 Lucien Febvre, "Sensibilität und Geschichte. Zugänge zum Gefühlsleben früherer Epochen", in: *Schrift und Materie der Geschichte. Vorschläge zur systematischen Aneignung historischer Prozesse*, M. Bloch, F. Braudel, L. Febvre et al., ed. Claudia Honegger (Frankfurt a. M., 1977), pp. 313–334, 323. In full: "It goes without saying that reconstituting the emotional life [*la vie affective*] of an era is a task that is both extremely seductive and terribly difficult, but one that the historian has no right to desert".

57 Cf. for example Anthony Giddens, *The Transformation of Intimacy. Sexuality, Love and Eroticism in Modern Societies* (Cambridge, 1992).

58 Anne-Charlott Trepp, "Gefühl oder kulturelle Konstruktion? Überlegungen zur Geschichte der Emotionen", *Querelles. Jahrbuch für Frauenforschung* 7 (2002), 86–103, 88. The criticism here is aimed at the classics Philippe Ariès, *Centuries of Childhood. A Social History of Family Life* (New York, 1962 [1960]); Shorter, *The Making of the Modern Family*; Lawrence Stone, *The Family, Sex and Marriage in England 1500–1800* (London, 1977); regarding these two works cf. also Alan MacFarlane, "Review Essay", *History and Theory* 18 (1979), 103–126, 106–107. On the alterity of cultures of emotion in the Middle Ages and the early modern period cf. Ingrid Casten, Gesa Stedman and Margarete Zimmermann, "Einleitung: Lucien Febvre und die Folgen. Zu einer Geschichte der Gefühle und ihrer Erforschung", *Querelles. Jahrbuch für Frauenforschung* 7 (2002), 9–25, 17.

partner and individual passion over collective demands".[59] Such a postulate was tantamount to an assault on the social order. At the same time, relationships continued to be characterised by hierarchy and inequality between the sexes as an integral part of the romantically patterned couple concept.

Above all, we must differentiate between notions and discourses and what could actually be lived out by men and women. The real-life practice of 'romantic love' first emerged as an experiment in bourgeois and intellectual circles. But it was an experiment that shone far beyond, offering a basis for the criticism of marriage as well as for alternative societal models, and it can still be viewed as a guiding principle of couple relationships today. Even so, questions of wealth as well as practical criteria did continue to be of influence when it came to choosing a spouse.[60] Hans Medick and David Sabean asserted as early as the 1980s that economic considerations and emotional proximity should not be juxtaposed with one another as incompatible but much rather thought of in combination.[61] And in the historical research of recent years, the search has therefore no longer been – as it indeed still quite classically was in the works of Lawrence Stone and Edward Shorter – for the origins of marriage based on romantic love and the "modern family".[62] Instead, the more current questions concern representations of emotions that were specific to each period. The focus here is on relative emphases, overlaps and simultaneities between various notions and expectations as well as the forms in which they were expressed.[63]

---

59 Cornelia Koppetsch, "Liebesökonomie. Ambivalenzen moderner Paarbeziehungen", *Westend. Neue Zeitschrift für Sozialforschung* 2, 1 (2005), 96–107, 98.

60 Cf. Borscheid, "Geld und Liebe", 124–134; Ute Frevert, "Ehe und Leidenschaft im 19. und 20. Jahrhundert", in *Geschlechterverhältnis und Sexualität*, ed. Christof Gestrich (Berlin, 1997), pp. 119–133.

61 Hans Medick and David Sabean, "Emotionen und materielle Interessen in Familie und Verwandtschaft: Überlegungen zu neuen Wegen und Bereichen einer historischen und sozialanthropologischen Familienforschung", in *Emotionen und materielle Interessen*, ed. Medick/Sabean, pp. 27–54. Emotional and material interests could also be integrated via Pierre Bourdieu's broadly laid out concept of capital as "accumulated labour" in material as well as "embodied" forms, since it includes the forging of relationships and the upholding of networks of acquaintances and kin. Pierre Bourdieu, "The Forms of Capital", in *Handbook of Theory and Research for the Sociology of Education*, ed. John G. Richardson (Westport, 1986), pp. 241–258, 241.

62 Stone's view was that marriage for love originated in the Puritan emotional culture of the English educated middle class in the seventeenth century. Shorter, on the other hand, viewed capitalist wage labour, which made men and women independent of their parents where choosing partners was concerned, as a prerequisite for this since they could also hardly have founded their existences upon inherited wealth. Shorter, *The Making of the Modern Family*; Stone, *The Family, Sex and Marriage*.

63 Cf. for example Guzzi-Heeb, *Donne, uomini, parentela*, pp. 329–345. Among other things, he points out that romantic passion and arranged marriages were but two models among countless possible variants of love (ibid., 332).

In the dispensation records of the Diocese of Brixen, love and passion are spoken of mainly in the questioning with witnesses and with the prospective bride and groom as part of the so-called matrimonial examinations as well as in letters of supplication. The statements in matrimonial examinations were made under oath,[64] and protocolled by members of the clergy. The letters of supplication were likewise – with few exceptions – put to paper by church representatives. In this light, the assertions regarding emotional states that one encounters here and there cannot be considered 'authentic'. Furthermore, the context of their performance was characterised by authority and hierarchy as well as behavioural expectations appropriate to the couples' status. What one encounters in the matrimonial examinations and letters of supplication are therefore representations of feelings conveyed as part of filtered communication. As dispensation requests followed highly specific logics, the relationship between portrayal and the specific medium of portrayal needs to be viewed as central.[65] Regarding positive emotions, one must first consider that the matrimonial examinations' question-and-answer format entailed that affectivities were or indeed had to be verbalised that might not otherwise have been explicated in verbal form.[66] But particularly in the context of courtship, 'signals' ritualised in the context of everyday life[67] could stand in for linguistic codes of love.[68] Furthermore, the statements in such examinations were protocolled in

64 Adriano Prosperi speaks of "valore magico", the magical value of an oath. Adriano Prosperi, "Fede, giuramento, inquisizione", in *Glaube und Eid. Treueformeln, Glaubensbekenntnisse und Sozialdisziplinierung zwischen Mittelalter und Neuzeit*, ed. Paolo Prodi (Oldenburg, 1993), pp. 157–171, 158–159.

65 Cf. Claudia Benthien, Anne Flaig and Ingrid Kasten, "Einleitung", in *Emotionalität. Zur Geschichte der Gefühle*, ed. Benthien/Flaig/Kasten (Cologne/Weimar/Vienna, 2000), pp. 7–20, 9.

66 Francesca Cancian pointed out many years ago that concentration on the linguistic level leads to a feminisation of love in that it causes other forms of expression, such as the provision of support or assistance by men, to be overlooked. Francesca M. Cancian, "The Feminization of Love", *Signs. Journal for Women in Culture and Society* 11, 4 (1986), 692–708.

67 For a classic treatment of codes cf. Niklas Luhmann, *Love as Passion. The Codification of Intimacy* (Cambridge/Mass., 1987 [1982]).

68 On the interdependence of linguistic articulation, emotion, and prevailing values cf. Trepp, "Gefühl oder kulturelle Konstruktion", p. 89. Eva Illouz shows this using the example of nineteenth-century novels: courtship did not involve talk of feelings. "The readers, like the characters in the novels, pick up feelings and intentions from subtle changes of facial expression and not from words that would be capable of lending these feelings direct expression." Eva Illouz, "Vermarktung der Leidenschaft: Bedeutungswandel der Liebe im Kapitalismus", *Westend. Neue Zeitschrift für Sozialforschung* 2, 1 (2005), 80–95, 80. Ritualised forms included night courting (*Fensterln*) as well as a certain practice of giving and receiving. If a woman did not return a gift that she had received from an admirer within a certain time, this – as Beatrice Moring has shown for Finland – was

writing – certainly more in general terms than verbatim, as a rule. In the process of this protocolling, the statements were also adapted to conform to the vocabularies and linguistic styles of the examining cleric and the person serving as secretary – and hence also to their worldviews. This was necessary due to the specific requirements that such a request had to fulfil, above all in terms of the presence of specific church-recognised grounds for dispensation. In this respect, it was always something of a 'translation' – much like what has been discussed in the research on court and inquisition records.[69] Finally, the terms with which these protagonists operated – "acquaintance" (*Bekanntschaft*), "affection" (*Neigung*), "love" (*Liebe*), "passion" (*Leidenschaft*) – should not be unquestioningly imbued with the notions of our own era. In part, they serve to express nuances, intensities and colourations for which present-day parlance hardly offers any equivalents.[70]

The most important factor in shaping a matrimonial examination's formulation consisted in the requirements that had to be fulfilled because it was part of a supplication. And in the Diocese of Brixen, the tendency was for couples who were closely related by blood or affinity to reach this stage of proceedings only if the competent clergymen supported their request and desired to assist them in eliciting a positive response. It was therefore not only within these clerics' purview and responsibility but also in their interest to shape the couples' supplications around the reasons for dispensation which would be required in the further proceedings so that they were most likely to be successful. The interviewees probably also said things that differed from what was recorded in writing. In cases where some aspects are very present while others make no appearance at all – where, for example, much is written about

---

taken as a sign of her consent to the relationship. Beatrice Moring, "Land, Labour, and Love: Household Arrangements in Nineteenth Century Eastern Finland – Cultural Heritage or Socio-Economic Structure?", *The History of the Family* 4, 2 (1999), 159–184, 175. On this cf. also the chapter "Eheanbahnung und Ehewerbung" in Siegrid Westphal, Inken Schmidt-Voges and Anette Baumann, *Venus und Vulcanus. Ehen und ihre Konflikte in der Frühen Neuzeit* (Munich, 2011), pp. 32–50.

69 Carlo Ginzburg, referring to inquisition records, speaks of a "barrier" that these seem to form, thereby obscuring from view the ideas held by the accused. Carlo Ginzburg, *The Cheese and the Worms. The Cosmos of a Sixteenth-Century Miller* (Baltimore, 1980 [1976]), p. xix. On the discussion of this issue as it pertains to court documents cf. for example the position of Michaela Hohkamp, who points out that court records reflect ruling practice. Hohkamp, *Herrschaft in der Herrschaft*, pp. 23–24; cf. also Andrea Griesebner, *Konkurrierende Wahrheiten. Malefizprozesse vor dem Landgericht Perchtoldsdorf im 18. Jahrhundert* (Vienna/Cologne/Weimar, 2000), especially chap. v.

70 On the problem of the linguistic blurring of emotions both in the research and in primary sources cf. Casten/Stedman/Zimmermann, "Einleitung", p. 12.

"household matters" and "provision" without a single word lost on love –, this should not lead us to conclude that the union was 'devoid of feeling' and a pure marriage of convenience. The recording of such protocols involved a process of selection and emphasis along with expedient weighting. And yet, the consistory in Brixen would frequently still deem the results insufficient for the initiation of the next steps.

Ramón A. Gutierrez evaluated dispensation requests from the Spanish colony of Nuevo México covering an extended period of time. For the late eighteenth century, he ascertained couples no longer mentioned religiously motivated reasons common in earlier times such as salvation of their souls or the fulfilment of obligations, but rather love and desire. He interprets this as a result from the emergence of the concept of romantic love – which, by 1800, had come to be viewed as sufficient justification for the choice of a certain groom or a certain bride. His source material contains the term *voluntad* – which the author equates to *deseo*, meaning yearning or desire – for the first time in a marriage register from 1798. Here, José García from Albuquerque declares his desire to marry María Lopez, "por la creciente voluntad que nos tenemos mutuamente uno y otra" – on account of the growing desire that each of them had for the other.[71] If a declaration of this sort was sufficient, then one must assume a milder form of dispensation practice – a Romanic model?[72] Of the extant dispensation records of the Diocese of Brixen from 1831 onward, which were subjected to content analysis for the initial subsequent 33 years, nearly two thirds contain no explicit expressions of love. This is likely due in part to the logics of the respective administrative procedures and how the associated types of text were fabricated and thus to considerations of what rhetoric and linguistic strategies the authors of these requests thought would be effective.

71 Gutierrez, *Cuando Jesús llegó*, p. 390; see also Ramón A. Gutierrez, "Honor Ideology, Marriage Negotiation, and Class-Gender Domination in New Mexico, 1690–1846", *Latin American Perspectives* 12, 1 (1985), 81–104, 100–101.

72 The picture that Edith Saurer paints of Venetian dispensation practice would suggest as much, whereas in Mexico the colonial context may have further reinforced more liberal handling of the matter. Saurer points out the lower number of rejections in Venice than in Lower Austria and views this in connection with the greater involvement of parish priests in the individual dispensation cases. These priests would also themselves appear as witnesses and frequently even provided financial support. She also ascertains that in one dramatic case of violent separation, the Bishop of Belluno ultimately recognised "the power of emotions, their inescapability" – a finding that could hardly be applied to the consistory of the prince-bishop in Brixen. Saurer, "Formen von Verwandtschaft und Liebe", pp. 263–264 (quote 264).

If a request spoke of long-standing acquaintance and great familiarity, however, this could serve as a transition to a reason for dispensation that had long been efficacious: *conversatio suspecta* (suspect familiarity) and the associated "perils" of *conversatio falsa* (forbidden familiarity), which suggested "co-mingling" and "sins of the flesh" and even a suspected or existing pregnancy. Such passages could be and indeed were strategically employed especially in cases where a second matrimonial examination following a rejected dispensation request exhibits. This shows a clear shift in the line of argumentation compared with the first version. It thus repeatedly occurred that the first version would emphasise the bride and the groom's respectability and impeccable moral conduct, arguing the necessity of the planned marriage on the basis of the prospective couple's economic and general life situations. The second version, in contrast, would devote far less attention to economic and everyday matters and instead highlight all-too-familiar relations, an all-too-great degree of love, a possible pregnancy and the 'public scandal' that threatened to erupt. Even then, however, there was no guarantee that the desired success would be achieved.

All this clearly identifies the two poles between which dispensation requests oscillated: either the total absence of expressions of emotion or featuring such expressions in a clearly strategic way, referring to a *causa laesa* fit to elicit a 'public scandal'. In between, however, lies a broad palette of variants and forms with mentions of love being worked into these matrimonial examinations. As the answer given by the 39-year-old Anton Hackl to explain the reasons for his planned marriage to Elisabeth Reheis, the following terse passage is recorded: "Affectio cordis, aetas Sponsi [*sic*], he can find none who is as well-suited to his household economy as this one."[73] It would be difficult to find a clearer example than this Latin version of "heartfelt affection" when it comes to demonstrating the gulf between the protagonists' perspective and the process of protocolling – a gulf that must always be kept in mind.

In the testimony of the likewise 39-year-old widower Johann Lösch, the love he felt for his bride Anna Grabherr was patched in between the lines after the fact: "I have already begun my 40th year and am forced to remarry since I own a property that, though small, makes for much worry, [and since] I have four children of whom the eldest is 11 and the youngest is 4 years old. I wish to give the children a Christian upbringing, for which I need a person who is neither too young nor too old, who knows how to run my household, and in particular who is concerned with raising the children in a Christian way, characteristics that I, as a widower, must pay the utmost heed and that only in my

73 DIÖAB, Konsistorialakten 1835, Fasc. 5a, Römische Dispensen, no. 12.

hoped-for bride" – interjected here above the line: "whom I love very much" – "do I believe to have found".[74] Here, the portrayal of the situation primarily emphasises the necessity of entering into a further marriage along with laying out what would be required of the bride. And even so, it apparently was indeed important – from the perspective of the groom? The dean? Or the person who produced the protocol? – to mention love. The consistory in Brixen repeatedly criticised requests that betrayed obvious economic motivations, especially in cases where property- and wealth-related interests associated with the desired marriage were all-too-clearly visible. Emotional components could therefore serve as a counterweight of sorts while simultaneously underlining the mutual consent that Catholic norms stipulated as a prerequisite for marriage.[75]

In these portrayals, the feelings of "respect", "friendship" and "affection" were often owed to the personal characteristics of the desired spouse.[76] Such sentiments were held to be a solid foundation of a marriage in accordance with the early modern, Christian-influenced ideal of marriage. This is often found in the dispensation records from the first half of the nineteenth century: "[F]urthermore, he knows this person and harbours special affection for her on account of her industriousness and cleverness".[77] Or in the words of the Innsbruck merchant Karl Mörz: "[I]t was she who, with her modesty, preserved peace and harmony in the family, organising and running the entire household with wise domesticity. She has constantly been and still is a tireless provider of care and a great benefit to us all. It is precisely these rare qualities and no others that draw me to her and upon which I seek to build my future serenity and happiness".[78]

The frequently emphasised characteristics of prospective brides also included moral and religious qualities: they were to be "moral", "honest", "good", to use the terminology of that day, alongside possessing practical life skills and, depending on the context, various other work-related skills. With only a few exceptions, attributions like hard-working, busy, industrious, homely, efficient, frugal, clever, etc. were employed situationally in characterisations of both brides *and* grooms rather than being divided between women and men

---

74 DIÖAB, Konsistorialakten 1840, Fasc. 5a, Römische Dispensen, no. 25.

75 For a general treatment of this cf. Daniela Lombardi, *Matrimoni di antico regime* (Bologna, 2001); Silvana Seidel, "Menchi, Percorsi variegati, percorsi obbligati. Elogio del matrimonio pre-tridentino", in *Matrimoni in dubbio. Unioni controverse e nozze clandestine in Italia dal XIV al XVIII secolo*, ed. Silvana Seidel Menchi and Diego Quaglioni (Bologna, 2001), pp. 17–60.

76 DIÖAB, Konsistorialakten 1841, Fasc. 5a, Römische Dispensen, no. 13.

77 DIÖAB, Konsistorialakten 1832, Fasc. 5a, Römische Dispensen, no. 4.

78 Ibid., no. 5.

in a gender-specific, polarising way. But "sober", referring to alcohol consumption, was indeed male-connoted while "peaceable" tended to be attributed to women.[79] It is especially those requests made by bourgeois couples described as educated, wealthy and from commensurate family backgrounds that, in a nearly prototypical way, feature the romantic ideal of consonance in terms of temperament and mindset. Conceptually, however, this cannot be clearly characterised as a defining attribute of modernity, since it was indeed already present in the early modern period.[80]

There are also, however, numerous requests that contain admissions of having clearly stepped over the line – as evidenced by the matrimonial examination of Ignaz Natter and Maria Katharina Kauffmann, who were related by affinity: "For some time, our coexistence had been innocent, irreproachable; but unnoticed to us, we eventually grew familiar with each other due to our frequent interactions, with our mutual love likewise growing over time. Sinful wishes and desires were awakened in us – though at first we recoiled in horror when such thoughts emerged, encouraging each other to steadfastly resist the temptation to sin. But alas, being weak people, we eventually did give into temptation. After which the dam had been broken, with innocent love being replaced by carnal love, and ever since that time we have regrettably fallen deeper and deeper, now finding ourselves in an abyss from which we are incapable of escape; for we have, and we hardly dare to admit it, engaged frequently in carnal sin for the past three months."[81] The talk here is of "temptation", "falling" and an "abyss" of sinful occurrences – and the couple's words would seem quite pathos-laden, departing somewhat from the style of writing that was otherwise typical. But other dispensation records from this period also contain such passages, formulated in ways that remind of a novel of manners rather than an official protocol. A systematic survey showed that all of these documents originated in the Bregenz Forest deanery during the deanship of

---

79 On this polarisation cf. Karin Hausen, "Family and Role-Division. The Polarization of Sexual Stereotypes in the Nineteenth Century. An Aspect of Dissociation of Work and Family Life", in *Social History of the Family in Nineteenth and Twentieth Centuries Germany*, ed. Richard J. Evans and W.R. Lee (London, 1981), pp. 51–83.

80 On bourgeois notions of love and marriage cf. Rebekka Habermas, *Frauen und Männer des Bürgertums. Eine Familiengeschichte, 1750–1850* (Göttingen, 2000); Anne-Charlott Trepp, *Sanfte Männlichkeit und selbständige Weiblichkeit. Frauen und Männer im Hamburger Bürgertum zwischen 1770 und 1840* (Göttingen, 1996). Attention has been called to such notions of consonance in early modern marital contexts by Kristina Bake, *Spiegel einer Christlichen und friedsamen Haußhaltung. Die Ehe in der populären Druckgraphik des 16. und 17. Jahrhunderts* (Wiesbaden, 2013).

81 DIÖAB, Konsistorialakten 1831, Fasc. 5a, Römische Dispensen, no. 17.

Johann Baptist Sinz. This indicates that styles of portrayal could be tied to a specific person even in primarily administrative (con)texts.

Despite the involved processes of filtering, translation and insertion, these statements are by no means without value. After all, how situations were spoken of was not divorced from real-life situations, experiences and observations. They grew out of notions and perceptions, out of the textures of their times, and were based on at least partially intersubjective shared understandings with regard to content and meaning. How something was communicated was interlaced with horizons of thought shaped in part by normative notions.

Distinct from love is passion. In the Catholic mind, passion was negatively connoted and represented a poor basis for a marriage, particularly if the marriage was concluded out of "pure passion" (*nimia passione*). As far as the prevailing norm was concerned, marriage was for the conception and raising of offspring as well as for the provision of mutual support and assistance. Its crucial value was constancy. Passion, on the other hand, was regarded as something ephemeral and perilous, an open door to "disorderly love", "carnal commingling" and "sin". In line with this normative concept, statements in dispensation requests would sometimes explicitly deny the presence of passion in order to emphasise the solid and hence 'correct' feelings acceptable to the Church upon which a marriage was to be built. It was thus that a civil servant at the district office in Imst began his exhaustive justification in support of the dispensation request of Johann Schöpf and Maria Auerin, the latest in a series of attempts made by this couple over a period of several years, in an October 1797 communication to the Court Commission on Spiritual Affairs in Vienna: "The fact that the aforementioned unwaveringly insists upon his choice of Maria Auerin and only her as his spouse is due not to excessive passion but to substantial motivations that he discusses at great length in his letter of supplication."[82]

In the bourgeois milieu, ideas about emotional control and general self-control may have also played a role.[83] All too excessive expressions of emotion may have contradicted the self- and class understandings of bourgeois men or the clerics who protocolled their statements. In a likewise highly detailed communication from the deanery office of St. Johann in Tyrol, the dean paradigmatically attested that Kitzbühel's Imperial-Royal District Captain Franz

82 Tiroler Landesarchiv (TLA) Innsbruck, Jüngeres Gubernium, Hauptgruppe 64 Ehesachen, 1797–1798, Fasc. 314, 1797, no. 136.

83 On this cf. Martina Kessel, "Das Trauma der Affektkontrolle. Zur Sehnsucht nach Gefühlen im 19. Jahrhundert", in *Emotionalität*, ed. Benthien/Flaig/Kasten, pp. 156–177, 157–158.

Joseph Blitzburg[84] – who had applied for a dispensation to marry "Miss Julie von Lutteroti", resident in the Diocese of Brixen and the cousin of his deceased wife – had approached the selection of his desired spouse on an ideal motivational basis: "In the selection of his bride, this noble and Christian-minded man was guided not by earthly or sensual motives but rather solely by the upstanding wish to acquire for his beloved children a virtuous mother and for himself a life companion gifted with sterling qualities of the spirit and the heart."[85]

When a couple was forced to acknowledge that there had already been sexual contact between them, passion – much like "human weakness" and frivolousness – was a justification that was considered acceptable by the Church. Temptation and opportunity could lure even the most upstanding prospective couple into a 'misstep'. 'Weak flesh' was immanent to Catholic thinking as a quasi-anthropological constant. And in the moral assessment of couples, a line of demarcation ran between those who had 'fallen' in an exceptional situation but were fundamentally 'upstanding' and those who led thoroughly 'dissolute' lives. For this reason, the complex of 'all-too-great' love and of passion likewise fails to fit into the master narrative of the history of emotions as a history of increasing control – which has also been criticised elsewhere[86] – as overpowering feelings could indeed befall anyone.

Countless writings of the *Admonitions for Young Lads and Ladies* variety were authored in response to this ubiquitous 'peril'. In one such work, a tract authored by a "country parish priest from the Diocese of Brixen", a section headed by "In particular, have a care when associating […]" contains the following admonition after "[…] with persons of the other sex": "But you, young ladies, should pay special heed to what Saint Bernard so urgently commended to his sister Humbelina: 'My dear sister in Jesus Christ! No man, be he old or young, should associate with you closely and frequently, even if he is a righteous and holy man. Familiarity alone has led to the downfall of those who were impervious to lust, for the opportunity to sin is often the very thing that awakens the idea and desire to do so in the first place.'" The author continues: "And when one least suspects, its [vice's, M.L.] flame rages so fiercely that

84 The deaneries of St. Johann in Tyrol and Kitzbühel belonged to the Diocese of Salzburg.

85 DIÖAB, Konsistorialakten 1853, Fasc. 5a, Römische Dispensen, no. 13. He is described as, among other things, an "outstandingly exemplary civil servant" who conscientiously fulfilled his religious obligations and was commensurately industrious and selfless when acting in his official capacity, for which reason the state "is to be sincerely congratulated on its employment of such a civil servant".

86 Criticism in this regard has arisen above all from the perspective of mediaeval studies, cf. Barbara H. Rosenwein, "Controlling Paradigms", in *Anger's Past. The Social Uses of an Emotion in the Middle Ages*, ed. Barbara H. Rosenwein (Ithaca/London, 1998), pp. 233–247.

one ends up respecting neither kinship nor friendship, neither fearing God nor cherishing honour, and even disparaging life and the punishments of hell."[87] Such lessons were meant to warn of the peril of lust that constantly lurked in familiar situations and spared not even kinfolk – but they also provide confirmation of precisely this phenomenon.

Feelings are socially shaped and must hence always be analysed in the context of social practices.[88] Many couples had already had a 'long acquaintance' before applying for a dispensation and/or before their application had been put to paper. At that time, the term 'acquaintance' (*Bekanntschaft*) denoted a highly familiar and thus significantly more intense relationship than what is associated with the term today. The durations of such acquaintances are occasionally specified in greater detail, with some having existed for five, ten and even fifteen years. Johann Haspinger and Maria Jud from the deanery of Bruneck had, as the first witness in their matrimonial examination indicated, maintained an "acquaintance" with each other ten years prior, giving rise to "various rumours in the community". Later on, their acquaintance had ended since they had thought it "impossible, on account of being related by blood" for them to receive "forbearance [a dispensation]". The witness went on to say that five months prior, their acquaintance had arisen "anew".[89] The "acquaintance" of Johann Unterberger, the 60-year-old owner of a small holding, with the 37-year-old day labourer Maria Winkler had already been running for 15 years. They had two children together and continued to "live in sin". The dean reported: "[B]oth of them seem incapable of separation".[90] A 14-year acquaintance united the salt miner Mathias Schmid and Anna Schmid, whose father was likewise a salt miner and also a smallholder. He was 58 and she was 45. As children of two fathers who were stepbrothers, they were cousins. Eleven years before, a child had been born that had died after just over a year. And they had recently purchased a small property together, for, as the bride put it: "clerics and layfolk told me that we would eventually be able to marry".[91] Joint purchases of property by related couples in the run-up to dispensation

87 *Ermahnungen an Jünglinge und Jungfrauen, auch an Menschen jeden Alters und Standes von einem Landpfarrer der Diözese Brixen* [*Admonitions for Young Lads and Ladies, also for People of Any Age or Estate*, by a Rural Parish Priest from the Diocese of Brixen], 6th ed. (Brixen, 1900), pp. 183–184.

88 Cf. Frevert, "Angst vor Gefühlen", p. 97; Medick/Sabean, "Emotionen und materielle Interessen in Familie und Verwandtschaft".

89 DIÖAB, Konsistorialakten 1840, Fasc. 5a, Römische Dispensen, no. 24.

90 DIÖAB, Konsistorialakten 1841, Fasc. 5a, Römische Dispensen, no. 2 as well as ibid., 1840, Fasc. 5b, Ehedispensen in occultis, no. 3; this is where the dean's first enquiry is filed.

91 DIÖAB, Konsistorialakten 1858, Fasc. 5a, Römische Dispensen, no. 27.

proceedings numbered among those strategies, frequently lamented by clergymen. Supplicants hoped to increase the ease or certainty of receiving a dispensation to marry through this strategy.

Finally, scenarios of this type bring to light various situations of action – such as when Joseph Strasser of Kartitsch in East Tyrol recounted: "[I] would frequently also visit my only beloved at night, such that people took note of it. I am incapable of ever giving her up, have completely taken her into my heart although I have often attempted to renounce her; it is on her that my entire happiness depends".[92] Urban Zingerle, for his part, told of walks together with and nocturnal visits to his intended bride.[93] Sometimes, women and men would deliberately attempt to put special distance between themselves, only to end up bridging said distance when the "flames of love" could not be quenched.[94] In order to avoid "sinning" further, Elizabeth Hörburger from Riefensberg in the Bregenz Forest deanery moved to a neighbouring community. "[T]he only thing was that she was incapable of even praying properly and thought of the supplicant day and night", the protocol records her as having admitted, and she also had to acknowledge "that even during this time, they came together in sin".[95] Emotional proximity is most often expressed in portrayals of everyday situations where support was provided. Lorenz Nessler assisted his widowed bride Susanna Nessler financially with money that he had earned "abroad", and he worked for her "as often as she needed a worker or farmhand". He was, "moreover, in the widow's house every day, since the two were neighbours".[96]

Though concepts of marriage have changed over the centuries, there are clear continuities between the early modern and modern periods. A central aspect of the transition from the eighteenth to the nineteenth century was a discursive and projective redefinition of the relationship between love and economy sparked by criticism of materially motivated marriages of convenience. However, paying no heed whatsoever to economic considerations or status-related interests was a feasible option for only a very few. This is by no means to negate the power of emotional bonds. The representations of love in the dispensation records exhibit all manner of different facets, both in their linguistic expression and in how they manifested in certain action situations. And normative concepts of marriage and love, whether adhered to or transgressed against, functioned as frameworks in which the rhetoric of

---

92 DIÖAB, Konsistorialakten 1831, Fasc. 5a, Römische Dispensen, no. 4.

93 Cf. DIÖAB, Konsistorialakten 1832, Fasc. 5a, Römische Dispensen, no. 15.

94 DIÖAB, Konsistorialakten 1833, Fasc. 5a, Römische Dispensen, no. 21.

95 DIÖAB, Konsistorialakten 1831, Fasc. 5a, Römische Dispensen, no. 18.

96 DIÖAB, Konsistorialakten 1832, Fasc. 5a, Römische Dispensen, no. 3.

dispensation requests was deployed – rhetoric that must be contextualised in terms of its specific communicational situation.

4 Socio-political and Moral Arguments

During the late eighteenth and early nineteenth centuries, numerous countries witnessed the negotiation of a "new order of things within the state", including the norms associated with marriage impediments. In 1811, the faculty of law at the Royal Bavarian University of Landshut challenge its candidates with a prize question on the matter, namely: "Which canonical marriage impediments should be retained, defined in more detail or abolished?"[97] The intent was to spur on work towards redefining the relationship between the Church and the state in this realm. The debates of this period generally revolved around the sense and purpose of marriage prohibitions within the degrees of kinship that were fundamentally dispensable. And initially, there were two main lines of reasoning that authors schooled in civil or canon law employed to justify upholding bans on marriage between consanguineous and affinal kin: one was socio-political, the other moral in nature.[98]

Socially relevant justifications frequently referred back to Saint Augustine.[99] The marriage prohibitions that were in place entailed that blood relatives were "forced to seek out marital unions with strange families, to the supreme advantage of the social order", as Thomas Dolliner wrote in 1813.[100] The objective was to employ "the great significance of the family in order to combat egoism", explained Johann Friedrich Schulte, one of nineteenth-century Germany's

97 *Welche canonische Ehehindernisse sollen beibehalten werden, oder näher bestimmt, oder aufgehoben werden? Eine Preisschrift vom Jahre 1811* (Nuremberg, 1859).

98 Extensive discussion of grounds for such marriage prohibitions can be found in Karl August Moriz Schlegel, *Kritische und systematische Darstellung der verbotenen Grade der Verwandtschaft und Schwägerschaft, bey Heurathen, nach dem Mosaischen Gesetze, dem Römischen und Canonischen Rechte, und den Protestantischen Kirchenordnungen …* (Hannover, 1802), pp. 525–581.

99 Augustinus, De Civitate Dei, Liber XV, Cap. 16: "Habita est enim ratio rectissima caritatis, ut homines, quibus esset utilis atque honesta concordia, diversarum necessitudinum vinculis necterentur, nec unus in uno multas haberet, sed singulae spargerentur in singulos ac sic ad socialem vitam diligentius conligandam plurimae plurimos obtinerent. Pater quippe et socer duarum sunt necessitudinum nomina. Ut ergo alium quisque habeat patrem, alium socerum, numerosius se caritas porrigit". http://www.hs-augsburg.de/~harsch/Chronologia/Lspost05/Augustinus/aug_cd15.html#16 (last access: May 2022).

100 Dolliner, *Handbuch*, p. 181.

foremost professors of canon law, in 1857.[101] Various commentators referred to arguments of this type as "political grounds": "the desire to further propagate ties of friendship, mutual assistance, and especially the sharing of wealth".[102] The Austrian moral theologian Johann Kutschker explicitly took up Augustine's emphasis on unselfish love (*caritas*), writing that Augustine regarded intermarriage between kin "as impermissible because it isolates families and selfishly restricts love to one's close circle of relatives".[103] Moreover, an 1864 article published in the diocesan circular *Brixner Diözesan-Blatt* documents how such theological arguments trickled down to the 'provincial' level, putting it quite similarly: in marriages within a pre-existing family circle, the article held, "familial egoism" would prevail, for which reason this "narrow-heartedness of familial love" had to be opened up via the introduction of ever new members to the family circle. This would then spread the existing *caritas* to others.[104]

A more statist attitude can be discerned in the words of Carl Christian Sattler, who held doctorates in both legal systems and published his Austrian marital law handbook *Handbuch des österreichischen Ehe-Rechts* from a secular perspective in 1804: "For nothing is more propitious to the social unification of multiple families than when members of the same family who share blood or affinal kinship in certain degrees are prohibited from marrying and must therefore seek refuge with other families, from which they choose a spouse. This transforms hitherto individually existing families into larger ones, bringing more distant elements of the state closer to one another on the basis of common family interests and hence more closely connecting the individual members of a state's society at large. The state itself experiences the most beneficial consequences from such merging of families."[105] The emphasis in the Church's argumentation did, albeit not always, tend to be situated differently than in the field of civil law, as Theodor Pachmann, a civil servant in the rank of Imperial-Royal Counsellor but also a canon law expert, summarized concisely in an instructional text. He ascribed to the Church ideal-typical values and to the state an interest in the broader distribution of wealth within society: the

101 Johann Friedrich Schulte, *Erläuterung des Gesetzes über die Ehen der Katholiken im Kaiserthume Oesterreich vom 8. Oktober 1856 und des kaiserlichen Patentes dazu nebst Darlegung und Begründung der Bestimmungen des Kirchengesetzes* (Prague, 1857), p. 65.

102 Stapf/Egger, *Vollständiger Pastoralunterricht*, p. 237.

103 Kutschker, *Das Eherecht der katholischen Kirche*, vol. 3, p. 308.

104 "Casus x: Ehen zwischen Blutsverwandten", *Brixner Diözesan-Blatt* 8 (1864), 130–140, 131–132.

105 Carl Christian Sattler, *Handbuch des österreichischen Ehe-Rechts nach den darüber erlassenen Gesetzen und Verordnungen, und mit Bemerkungen der Abweichungen des bürgerlichen Gesetzbuchs für Westgalizien. In schematischer Ordnung bearbeitet* (Vienna, 1804), pp. 117–118.

marriage impediment of kinship, he wrote, was intended by the Church "to combat selfishness [...], promote peace and spread love, while secular legislation has additionally sought to better distribute wealth".[106]

The second argument in favour of marriage prohibitions brought "decency" within the family and its circle of relatives into play as a "moral" rationale: the barrier of marriage prohibitions, tantamount to "foiling all hopes of future marriage", was said to protect kin from the "early debauchery that would otherwise be a near-unavoidable consequence of their highly familiar interaction day in and day out".[107] Johann Kutschker, arguing from an ecclesiastical standpoint, held that marriages among close kin, "if they occur commonly, poison family life, into the associations of which they introduce sensual desire and suspicion of the same".[108] Nikolaus Knopp, likewise a representative of canon law, viewed "the reproduction of the human species by way of identical blood" as being "contrary to nature"[109] and deemed marriage prohibitions to be "the strongest bulwark against the abuse of that close sort of relationship to which common flesh and blood between persons of the opposite sex and of the same family quite naturally" gave rise.[110] In pastoral practice, the moral argument appears to have been mainly employed. Joseph Stadelmann, for example, who headed the Deanery of Bregenz in Vorarlberg, reported that he had turned away a couple who had requested a dispensation and, to his mind, were driven merely by "selfish infatuation", by "introducing them to the significance of the law with respect to morality".[111] It is remarkable to see how the positions taken by both state-oriented and church-oriented authors were, at their core, near-identical. During this period, though, the former had in mind marriage prohibitions extending to the second degree while the latter meant marriage prohibitions extending to the fourth degree.

The prohibitions of marriage between affinal kin were more in need of a rationale than were those affecting blood kin. Nikolaus Knopp's above-quoted formulation pertaining to "common flesh and blood" conveyed canon law's postulated equation of affinity and consanguinity in terms of the respective marriage prohibitions' range and weight. This approach was also upheld by

---

106 Pachmann, *Lehrbuch des Kirchenrechtes*, vol. 2/1, p. 264.

107 Dolliner, *Handbuch*, p. 181. In connection with this argument, which was taken up by numerous contemporary authors, there are many references to the writings of Johann David Michaelis from the second half of the eighteenth century.

108 Kutschker, *Das Eherecht der katholischen Kirche*, vol. 3, p. 305; the same passage can also be found in Dannerbauer, *Praktisches Geschäftsbuch*, p. 168.

109 Knopp, *Vollständiges katholisches Eherecht*, p. 200.

110 Ibid., p. 151.

111 DIÖAB, Konsistorialakten 1832, Fasc. 5c, Verschiedenes über Ehesachen, no. 1.

Austria's civil legislation. Between persons descended from each other or "from the same ancestors", there was said to exist "a certain unity of the blood",[112] while the "sexual commingling" of man and woman was considered to result in a "unity of the flesh" – *una caro*.[113] On this, the Gospel of Saint Mark states: "And they twain shall be one flesh" (Mark 10:8).[114] In accordance with this conception, affinity was thought to be just as intrinsic to the body as was blood kinship. The Church's interpretation also attributed intellectual and spiritual dimensions to this oneness, which represented a problem in the case of interconfessional unions.[115] Mediaeval and early modern discourses had focused on the commingling of body fluids, of male and female seed. This had been the basis for the idea of 'one flesh' as a rationale for the marriage impediment of affinity in the writings of Thomas Aquinas: "vir et mulier efficiuntur in carnali copula una caro per commixtionem seminum".[116] Over a long stretch of European medical history, male seed was thought of as a "transformation of blood", as a "foam of the blood" – an idea that can be documented all the way from antiquity to the eighteenth century.[117] Galen, however, had reconceived

112 Nikolaus Knopp, *Vollständiges katholisches Eherecht. Mit besonderer Rücksicht auf die practische Seelsorge*, 2nd ed. (Regensburg, 1854), p. 152, 202.

113 The concept of 'one flesh' is also still formulated in the latest version of the Codex Iuris Canonici (promulgated in 1983), in Book 4, Title VII, Canon 1061 § 1, which addresses the procreation of offspring as the purpose of marriage, "to which marriage is ordered by its nature and by which the spouses become one flesh".

114 Birgit Klein traces the notion of *una caro* back to Adam's words: "bone of my bones, flesh of my flesh" (Genesis 2:23). Birgit Klein, "Allein nach dem 'Gesetz Mosis'? – Inzestdiskurse über jüdische Heiratspraxis in der Frühen Neuzeit", in *Historische Inzestdiskurse*, ed. Eming/Jarzebowski/Ulbrich, pp. 86–115, 95. Lanzinger, "Und werden sein die zwey ein Fleisch".

115 On this cf. Dagmar Freist, "'One Body, Two Confessions': Mixed Marriages in Germany", in *Gender in Early Modern German History*, ed. Ulinka Rublack (Cambridge, 2002), pp. 275–304; Dagmar Freist, *Glaube – Liebe – Zwietracht. Religiös-konfessionell gemischte Ehen in der Frühen Neuzeit* (Berlin/Boston, 2017). This topic is likewise addressed by Cecilia Cristellon, "Due fedi in un corpo. Matrimoni misti fra delicta carnis, scandalo, seduzione e sacramento nell'Europa di età moderna", *Quaderni storici* 145 (2014), 41–70; Cecilia Cristellon, "'Unstable and Weak-Minded' or a Missionary? Catholic Women in Mixed Marriages (1563–1798)", in *Gender Difference in European Legal Cultures. Historical Perspectives. Festschrift für Heide Wunder*, ed. Karin Gottschalk (Stuttgart, 2013), pp. 83–93.

116 Thomas Aquinas, Scriptum super Sententiis, lib. 4 d. 41 q. 1 a. 1 qc. 4 ad 2, http://www.corpusthomisticum.org/snp4037.html (last access: May 2022). Regarding later discourses cf. Sabean, "Inzestdiskurse", pp. 14–15; Leonore Davidoff, "'Eins sein zu zweit'. Geschwisterinzest in der englischen Mittelschicht des späten 18. und frühen 19. Jahrhunderts", *L'Homme. Z.F.G.* 13, 1 (2002), 29–49, 32.

117 Gianna Pomata, "Vollkommen oder verdorben? Der männliche Samen im frühneuzeitlichen Europa", *L'Homme. Z.F.G.* 6, 2 (1995), 59–85, 61–70.

the haematogenous theory of reproduction and ascribed roles in the physical formation of the embryo to both the male and the female seed, thus rejecting the Aristotelian "polarisation of paternal and maternal movements as form versus material".[118]

The notion of 'one flesh' also made the relatives of a couple's one member into relatives of its other member. It followed that consanguineous and affinal kin would be equally subject to the corresponding marriage prohibitions. Marrying the sister of one's deceased wife – sororate marriage – was first condemned in the Christian context at the Synod of Elvira in 307, while marrying the brother of one's deceased husband – levirate marriage – was first condemned at the Synod of Neo-Caesarea, which took place between 314 and 325.[119] A sexual act between affinal kin, just like one between close blood relatives, was considered "disgrace of the blood" (*Blutschande*) or *copula incestuosa*. It hence seems little wonder that prohibitions of affinal marriage, defined in this way, were called into question during the nineteenth century – not least due to the rise of diverse research fields that gave birth to the various natural sciences and also led to the dissemination and popularisation of new findings relating to heredity. The interest of physiologists, physicians and natural scientists centred on blood kinship, causing 'unity of the flesh' as a basis for the prohibition of affinal marriage to be relegated to the realm of purely theological construction. Carl Christian Sattler, on the basis of his decidedly secular position, took precisely this view regarding affinity's supposed incestuousness and proclaimed it a "*fiction* that those persons who commingle their flesh become one flesh through this intimate association".[120]

Dispensation requests also make visible points of fracture between personal perceptions of affinity and institutional norms and taboos that had apparently ceased to be comprehensible. Affected couples or their intermediaries repeatedly showed little understanding for the marriage impediment of affinity. Johann Fuchs, a widower from Namlos in the Deanery of Breitenwang in western Tyrol, was related to his prospective bride in the second and third unequal degree of affinity as well as in the third and fourth unequal degree of consanguinity. A witness questioned during the dispensation proceedings argued that their blood kinship was "so distant" that it was not even known to anybody, and as for the more weighty marriage impediment in this case, he was of the

118 Pomata, "Vollkommen oder verdorben", pp. 67–68.

119 Vgl. Mitterauer, "Christianity and Endogamy", p. 299; Françoise Héritier, *Two Sisters and Their Mother. The Anthropology of Incest* (New York, 1999), especially pp. 7–125.

120 Sattler, *Handbuch des österreichischen Ehe-Rechts*, p. 111, with reference to 1 Cor. 6; emphasis added.

opinion that "folk" did not understand what the problem was with affinity. Therefore, no one in the community had suspected that this couple would need a dispensation from the Church.[121] Regarding the dispensation request of Joseph Bell and Agatha Ender, who were likewise related by marriage in the second and third unequal degree, the parish priest of Götzis in the Deanery of Feldkirch wrote the following lapidary statement in his assessment – a standard requirement during these years – of whether the marriage project he had before him would cause a sensation in the community: "This marriage would not raise much of a stir in the community since this couple's relatedness is known to hardly anyone and because our people generally do not view more distant kin relationships as something worth mentioning".[122]

It was above all couples related by marriage who, in matrimonial examinations, answered the standard question of whether they had known of an existing marriage impediment by saying that it had only been discovered by their priest. In 1841, Martin Tschurtschenthaler stated the following: "I do not believe myself capable of marrying any other than Maria, no one is so dear to me, I had promised her that we would marry and had not suspected that this kinship would be so touchy a matter".[123] This was likewise a dispensation request in the second degree of affinity, for a marriage to the cousin of his deceased wife. In certain cases, the supplicants claimed to have been unaware of the obligation to obtain a dispensation. A bride who was related to her groom in the second degree of affinity answered: "It was only now that we heard we need a dispensation; for we believed that only blood relations needed one."[124] Even if the statements protocolled in these requests are characterised by justificatory rhetoric and must always be viewed as strategic communication, it is conspicuous how these types of answers tend to crop up in affinal configurations. A revealing case in this respect is that of Joseph Steinlechner and Ursula Schwaniger from the Deanery of Schwaz. They married in February 1862 after having received a dispensation in the third degree of consanguinity. Alongside this, however, they were also related in the second degree of affinity – a fact that had initially been overlooked. One week later, it became necessary to request a dispensation from Rome after the fact to "revalidate" the marriage, which effectively entailed concluding it anew.[125]

Offensive questioning of the impediment of affinity, though rare in dispensation requests, did occur in isolated cases: the widower Wilhelm von

121 DIÖAB, Konsistorialakten 1859, Fasc. 5a, Römische Dispensen, no. 9.
122 DIÖAB, Konsistorialakten 1862, Fasc. 5a, Römische Dispensen, no. 12.
123 DIÖAB, Konsistorialakten 1841, Fasc. 5a, Römische Dispensen, no. 22.
124 DIÖAB, Konsistorialakten 1831, Fasc. 5a, Römische Dispensen, no. 17.
125 DIÖAB, Konsistorialakten 1862, Fasc. 22a, Römische Dispensen, no. 10.

Guggenberg from Welsberg in the Puster Valley, a financially well-off innkeeper, miller and landowner who was also a municipal councillor at that time as well as the father of two small children, and his sister-in-law Carolina Offer, the daughter of a merchant from near the Brenner Pass, sent a several-page letter of supplication to their local curate in December 1863, explaining the reasons for their marriage project in detail. Towards the end of this letter, in point six, its author weighed consanguinity and affinity against each other and opined: "They allow themselves, however, to point out that though this strict interpretation is indeed appropriate regarding the impediment of *consanguinity*, due to the associated disadvantageous religious and moral as well as social consequences", while any "effect of an impediment of affinity, both in general and especially in the present case, would weigh significantly less by comparison", regardless from which "point of view one" one looks at the matter.[126]

In informing the prince-episcopal ordinariate in Brixen of Guggenberg's renewed attempt, the local curate identified this letter as a "long-winded request, without a doubt stylised by a lawyer" who was, "however, unknown" to him. Such fundamental relativisation of affinity's weight represented quite a daring line of argumentation in the context of supplication and mercy. However, this fact cannot be viewed independently of the prospective couple's social status. And by turning the matter over to a "lawyer", they simultaneously shifted responsibility away from themselves, transferring it to a third party whose profession was generally viewed as suspect by the consistory in Brixen. At any rate, the horror once evoked by the incestuous character of such relationships does seem to have faded by that time. And here and there, even local clerics were wont to note that a less-than-particularly-close case of affinity was "viewed among our people as not being related at all".[127]

Even in handbooks loyal to the Church, the view that consanguinity and affinity were indeed not equivalent shines through, albeit followed by the more or less obligatory defence of the prohibition of affinal marriage. Nikolaus Knopp, for example, in his treatment of Catholic marital law that appeared in several editions beginning in the mid-1850s, presupposed a civilised and natural sort of sense with regard to consanguinity: "the revulsion towards sexual commingling with one's own blood that is innate to every human being who has not become entirely bestial".[128] Regarding affinity, on the other hand, he

126 DIÖAB, Konsistorialakten 1864, Fasc. 22a, Römische Dispensen, no. 9, emphasis underlined in the original.

127 DIÖAB, Konsistorialakten 1861, Fasc. 22a, Römische Dispensen, no. 16. This request was in the second and third unequal degree of affinity.

128 In various cases, discussion was also devoted to the question of whether this revulsion was innate or a product of upbringing. Cf. Heinrich Spöndlin, *Ueber das Eheverboth wegen Verwandtschaft und das Verbrechen des Incestes* (Zurich, 1844), p. 8.

argued for the "moral necessity" of this marriage impediment as the "only dam capable of holding back the approaching maelstrom of the most holy familial bond's appalling abuse".[129] The Church, as this shows, did not "enjoy" the great benefit of the aforementioned natural revulsion with regard to affinity. Thus, he also ascribed to this marriage impediment – above all in the configuration of brother- and sister-in-law – "far greater significance" in terms of morality due to the especially close relationships that he held to exist between in-laws.[130]

In commentaries on civil law, the material addressing this point reveals ambivalent attitudes, with various arguments being mixed together. Nikolaus Knopp spoke of affinity's "natural bond, *vinculum naturale*" being the "factual basis of this marriage impediment" in canon law.[131] In contrast, precisely this notion of a "natural" marriage impediment was rejected by authors who championed an enlightened Josephine position. Theodor Pachmann, for example, wrote: "Affinity, however, is surely by no means a *natural* marriage impediment".[132] Kinship, or – as he more precisely defines in a footnote – "consanguinitas as such is connection via shared blood by way of generation", which is to say: by way of procreation.[133] Some representatives of civil law went even further and torpedoed the very moral cornerstone of marriage prohibitions – including not only prohibitions of affinal marriage but also those that pertained to marriages between cousins. In the mid-nineteenth century, Thomas Dolliner's opinion was as follows: "Reason does not, in fact, allow one to deduce any convincing grounds for a natural immorality of marriages between collateral blood relatives or between persons related by affinity."[134]

---

129 Knopp, *Vollständiges katholisches Eherecht*, p. 201.

130 Ibid., p. 201.

131 Ibid., p. 226.

132 Theodor Pachmann, *Lehrbuch des Kirchenrechtes mit Berücksichtigung der auf die kirchlichen Verhältnisse Bezug nehmenden österreichischen Gesetze und Verordnungen*, vol. 2/1, zweite verbesserte und vermehrte Auflage (Vienna, 1853), pp. 277–278; emphasis letter-spaced in the original.

133 Theodor Pachmann, *Lehrbuch des Kirchenrechtes mit Berücksichtigung der auf die kirchlichen Verhältnisse Bezug nehmenden österreichischen Gesetze und Verordnungen*, vol. 2, dritte ganz umgearbeitete Auflage (Vienna, 1865), p. 282.

134 Also with the following justification: "Those [marriage prohibitions] that one sought to derive from so-called *Respectu parentelae*, that is the reverence that a niece should owe her uncle and a nephew should owe his aunt" had, he said, already been "sufficiently refuted" by a certain Michaelis in his book on Mosaic law – even if Michaelis's reasoning, thought Dolliner, did not make sense. Thomas Dolliner, *Handbuch des oesterreichischen Eherechts, ausführliche Erläuterung des zweiten Hauptstückes des bürgerlichen Gesetzbuches von § 44–77*: Neue Ausgabe, vol. 1, 2nd ed. (Vienna, 1848), p. 100. The arguments that Dolliner quotes here, which had not yet appeared in his work's 1813 edition,

Immorality, he continues, must only be feared if youth have "been brought up without having being taught any firm moral principles". Even so, he closed by saying that there were good reasons "to forbid such marriage in the interest of ensuring morality within families".[135] In the 1813 edition of his work, on the other hand, he had remarked that "the same reasons that speak against marriages between close blood relations" also speak – "though not with the same force" – against marriages between close affinal kin insofar as their affinity is based on marriage.[136] These arguments illustrate how various positions wavered over time.

During this period, such assessments were quite obviously in a state of flux. Even representatives of civil law were genuinely struggling to arrive at justifications. One reason for this is that even in the Josephine era, when the power struggle with the Church was carried out quite openly, the directive was issued to make every effort to avoid any all too obvious contradictions and "*Collissionen*" between canon and civil law that might give rise to irritation. Nevertheless, such contradictions did arise. This was ultimately owed to the fact that the 1783 Marriage Patent defined marriage as a "civil contract"[137] but refrained from introducing civil marriage as such. In other words, it had stopped halfway, leaving the conclusion of marriages – and hence control and power over the prerequisites necessary to have a marriage concluded – to representatives of the Church.

The 1830s saw affinity – or, more precisely, the question as to whether marriages between widowers and the sisters of their deceased wives should be allowed – become the topic of a broad discussion in Victorian England that was to remain virulent for decades. Parliament repeatedly debated the Marriage with a Deceased Wife's Sister Bill from 1842 onwards, and the conflicts surrounding it dragged on until 1907.[138] In 1847, a royal commission was

can be found in §§ 104, 105, and 107 of Johann David Michaelis, *Abhandlung von den Ehegesetzen Mosis, welche die Heyrathen in die nahe Freundschaft untersagen*, zweite und vermehrte Auflage (Frankfurt a.M./Leipzig, 1786). Michaelis advocated only regarding those configurations specifically mentioned in the Bible as prohibited, and not the ones that had been equated therewith later on.

135 Dolliner, *Handbuch des oesterreichischen Eherechts*, p. 102.

136 Dolliner, *Handbuch*, p. 208.

137 This formulation refers to marriage's legal consequences, for which civil courts were to be responsible in the future.

138 Cf. Nancy F. Anderson, "The 'Marriage with a Deceased Wife's Sister Bill' Controversy: Incest Anxiety and the Defense of Family Purity in Victorian England", *Journal of British Studies* 21, 2 (1982), 67–86, 68; Sybil Wolfram, *In-Laws and Outlaws: Kinship and Marriage in England* (London/Sydney, 1987), pp. 30–40.

established in order to assess the legal situation and its effects.[139] The hotly contested debate over this bill was accompanied by newspaper headlines such as "A Burning Question! A National Wrong!".[140] It is of interest in this context because it built upon fears of incest starting from the topic of affinity and exhibited lines of argumentation comparable to those being employed in German-speaking lands.

The catalyst for England's intense engagement with this question was Lord Lyndhurst's Act of 1835.[141] Its primary purpose was to eliminate an element of legal uncertainty arising from a rule established by Henry VIII in 1533.[142] According to that rule, a marriage within the prohibited degrees of kinship could be annulled by an ecclesiastical court at any point in time during the lifetimes of the marital partners. This resulted in uncertainties not only for the affected couples but above all for their children – regarding both the legitimacy of their birth and recognition of their inheritance claims. Ample evidence suggests parishes did not apply strict scrutiny in the interest of avoiding such marriages. What is more, couples could sidestep any existing knowledge concerning prohibited degrees by getting married in larger neighbouring parishes, where they would encounter no administrative problems.[143] Such marriages did, however, represent a certain risk – particularly in tense situations relating to family and inheritance politics. This primarily involved marital unions between sister- and brother-in-law, since cousin marriages were not

---

139 Cf. Anderson, "The Marriage", p. 68. See, for example, the commission's initial reports *First Report of the Commissioners Appointed to Inquire into the State and Operation of the Law of Marriage, As Relating to the Prohibited Degrees of Affinity, and to Marriages Solemnized Abroad or in the British Colonies* (London, 1848), printed Series of British Parliamentary Papers, Reports from Commissioners, vol. XXVIII, session 18 November 1847–5 September 1848, Law of Marriage, 973; Edward B. Pusey, *Marriage with a Deceased Wife's Sister Prohibited by Holy Scripture as Understood by the Church for 1500 Years. Evidence given Before the Commission Appointed to Inquire into the State and Operation of the Law of Marriage as Relating to the Prohibited Degrees of Affinity* (Oxford, 1849). This report favours a ban on such marriages and supports its position using the 'one flesh' construction.

140 Margaret Morganroth Gullette, "The Puzzling Case of the Deceased Wife's Sister: Nineteenth-Century England Deals with a Second-Chance Plot", *Representations* 31, 2 (1990), 142–166, 146.

141 Anderson, "The Marriage", p. 67; Davidoff, *Thicker than Water*, pp. 216–217; Polly Morris, "Incest or Survival Strategy? Plebeian Marriage within the Prohibited Degrees in Somerset, 1730–1835", *Journal of the History of Sexuality* 2, 2 (1991), 235–265, 237.

142 On this cf. Wolfram, *In-Laws*, p. 23.

143 Cf. Morris, "Incest or Survival Strategy", pp. 239–240, 256.

subject to any prohibitions.[144] Lord Chancellor Lyndhurst therefore introduced a bill that proposed to limit the period during which annulment was possible to two years. The impetus for this was a marriage between a brother- and a sister-in-law involving the 7th Duke of Beaufort, where the intent was to ensure succession to rank and inheritance by the Duke's son.

A reworked version of this bill, which Parliament passed fairly swiftly and without much discussion, ultimately declared all marriages concluded between brothers- and sisters-in-law up to 31 August 1835 to be valid. However, all unions concluded thereafter that fell within the prohibited degrees of consanguinity or affinity were to be considered invalid.[145] Many assumed that marriage with the sister of one's deceased wife was soon to be removed from the realm of prohibited degrees, why they had involved themselves but little with this matter.[146] However, it ultimately took until 1907 for such a rule to be realised with the Deceased Wife's Sister's Marriage Act. Margaret Morganroth Gullette sums this up as follows: "The source of a controversy that was to last seventy-two years and cause so much misery was in some sense an accident."[147] And it was only in 1921 that the reverse configuration, marriage with a brother of one's deceased husband, was likewise made legal.[148]

For the interim decades, researchers assume that thousands of middle- and upper-class couples who commanded the necessary means and information had themselves married in other countries less strict in terms of marriage prohibitions: in German territories, in Danish-ruled Altona or in the notorious Scottish community of Gretna Green.[149] If they returned to Britain, however, they ran the risk of seeing their marriages annulled.[150] Affected couples therefore had a great interest in the elimination of this marriage prohibition and proceeded to play a decisive role in keeping debate on the issue alive. This also went for those who had married within the prohibited degrees in England

144 On this, Polly Morris writes: "The marriage of affines could have served to preserve or consolidate property, but, unlike the perfectly legal unions of first cousins, affinal marriages were vulnerable to legal attack by disgruntled heirs." Morris, "Incest or Survival Strategy", p. 248.

145 It included no explicit mention, however, of exactly which degrees were prohibited. Cf. Gullette, "The Puzzling Case", p. 151. She comments: "It was a blank unless a reader thought he knew which degrees were prohibited and by whom." On the altogether somewhat confusing British legal situation cf. Wolfram, *In-Laws*, pp. 21–30.

146 Cf. Anderson, "The Marriage", p. 67.

147 Gullette, "The Puzzling Case", p. 152.

148 Cf. Anderson, "The Marriage", pp. 84–85.

149 Cf. Gullette, "The Puzzling Case", pp. 149–150.

150 Cf. Anderson, "The Marriage", p. 68, 73, 80–81.

itself after 1835. An 1847 commission report on this specific matter put the number of marriages in the forbidden degrees in five English districts at 1,364 – of which 90 per cent were between widower and sister-in-law.[151]

Viewed from the Anglican standpoint, a bill that would permit marriage in the first degree of affinity represented state encroachment on church authority and power. But neither the opposition, "spearheaded by defenders of the Anglican establishment", nor reservations about such changes on fundamentally conservative grounds are sufficient, writes Nancy F. Anderson, to fully explain the duration and intensity of this conflict – considering that there were also Liberals who opposed the lifting of this provision. The key factor, she continues, was much rather such affinal unions' association with incest.[152] The basis of this notion was social and spatial proximity: the situation of the single sister living beneath the same roof as the married sister and her husband. Cousin marriages, she points out by way of contrast, did not evoke associations with incest during this period, since cousins were not viewed as having previously shared the same "isolated emotional intimacy".[153]

The fear that the possibility of such marriages could introduce sexuality into the family circle dominated the discussion. Nancy Anderson quotes statements taken from an early report by the appointed royal commission, which was repeatedly called upon to clarify the legal practice from 1847 onward. These statements seamlessly took up the morally-charged line of argument that has been outlined here for German-speaking lands: this marriage prohibition was viewed as a *cordon sanitaire* protecting the "dignity and purity" of family life – and it was said that should it be eliminated, a "flaming torch of sensual and inordinate desire would fill the sanctuary with smoke" and "transform a consecrated Church into a menagerie of wild beasts".[154] Moreover, the prohibition of marriage within close degrees of affinity was viewed as also being a bulwark against incestuous consanguine relationships among close kin.[155]

Anderson sees this situation of alarm with regard to close affinal kin as having been framed particularly by the intensification of family and especially

151 See the section "Appendix to the Evidence", in *First Report of the Commissioners Appointed to Inquire*, 140; cf. also Gullette, "The Puzzling Case", pp. 143–144.

152 Anderson, "The Marriage", pp. 68–69.

153 Ibid., pp. 74, 77.

154 The 1850s and 1860s also saw reference made to Leviticus 18:16 – to a sentence that, in the German Catholic *Einheitsübersetzung*, literally reads: "You must not expose the private parts of your brother's wife, for they are your brother's private parts." The King James version reads: "Thou shalt not uncover the nakedness of thy brother's wife: it is thy brother's nakedness." Cf. Anderson, "The Marriage", p. 77.

155 Cf. Morris, "Incest or Survival Strategy", p. 237, Anderson, "The Marriage", pp. 80–81.

sibling relationships. While other studies have considered cousin marriages a consequence of a special degree of emotional proximity between collateral kin,[156] the focus in the British discussion at that time was on the single sister who lived in the same household as her married sister. This proximity and that to her brother-in-law made the sister-in-law a figure who carried incestuous connotations. In literary works, the equation of sister-in-law and sister found plastic expression that, in English, comes through more clearly than in other languages due to the formulation "sister-in-law" itself. At the same time, the British discussion likewise included the voices of those who found it problematic that the *horror naturalis* commonly associated with consanguine sexual relationships and generally regarded as fundamentally sensible carried no weight in the realm of affinity.[157] Therefore, the prohibition on marrying sisters-in-law was viewed "as a bulwark, a line of defence against the threatening onslaught of unrestrained incest. Without this fortification, family purity would be corrupted by even more blatant incestuous demands than that of marriage with a wife's sister", concludes Nancy Anderson, alluding to the intimisation of the brother-sister relationship.[158] It should be noted that the debate around abolishing the prohibition of marriage between widowers and their sisters-in-law was "a battle between men", as Margaret Morganroth Gullette has ascertained.[159]

5 Physiological and Medical Discourses

Over the course of the nineteenth century, the socio-political and moral arguments against kin marriage were joined by a third line of reasoning that was physiologically and medically founded. It first impacted the civil law discourse before eventually also affecting the discourse within the Church. Its initial scattered and brief appearances were aimed at manifestations of 'degeneration'. The fear of degeneration and hereditary illnesses was receiving broad academic and social attention beyond the specific context of kin marriages.[160] During the nineteenth century, degeneration was linked to heredity and reduced to

---

156 Cf. Christopher H. Johnson and David Warren Sabean, "Introduction. From Siblingship to Siblinghood: Kinship in the Shaping of European Society (1300–1900)", in *Sibling Relations*, ed. Johnson/Sabean, pp. 1–28.

157 Anderson, "The Marriage", p. 76.

158 Ibid. p. 81.

159 Gullette, "The Puzzling Case", p. 146.

160 Cf. Philipp Sarasin, *Reizbare Maschinen. Eine Geschichte des Körpers 1765–1914* (Frankfurt a. M., 2001), 433–451; Peter Weingart, Jürgen Kroll and Kurt Bayertz, *Rasse, Blut und*

pathological manifestations of a physical nature.[161] In handbooks and journal articles published from the mid-nineteenth century onward, this argument was increasingly employed in connection with consanguine marriage.[162] It is conspicuous, however, that the discussions of dangers to health caused by kin marriages were echoed only relatively late in the dispensation records.

Associating consanguine marriages with dangers to the health of the resulting progeny was nothing new. Michael Mitterauer, for instance, refers to the eighth-century Nestorian patriarch Ishoʿbokht, who wrote negatively of the consequences stemming from marriages with close relations frequently entered into by Zoroastrian Persians – marriages that were said to have also included religiously motivated unions between siblings as well as between parents and children.[163] In this context, he referred to the children's physical constitution: "their limbs, eyes, hands and feet", he stated, "show a weakness, and their skin is of various colours". He viewed this as God's judgement of such "filthy unions".[164] It must not be forgotten, however, that divergent concepts of incest, corresponding rules and prohibitions and criticism thereof frequently served as marks of differentiation from 'others' and should hence be regarded as elements of demarcational rhetoric. A defining phenomenon for the period beginning in the late eighteenth century and continuing into the nineteenth century was the intensification of the discourse on marriage prohibitions and on the 'danger' of consanguine marriages, not least as a consequence of hypotheses advanced by natural scientists and physicians along with their philosophical and anthropological underpinnings.[165] Various media took up

---

Gene. Geschichte der Eugenik und Rassenhygiene in Deutschland (Frankfurt a. M., 1992), pp. 42–50.

161 "From the mid-eighteenth to the mid-nineteenth century, the term changed its meaning considerably, from an evil inflicted by luxury and civilization, to a natural tendency of pathological decline", writes Laure Cartron on this topic. Laure Cartron, "Degeneration and 'Alienism' in Early Nineteenth-Century France", in *Heredity Produced*, ed. Müller-Wille/Rheinberger, pp. 155–174, 156.

162 Cf. also Sabean, *Kinship in Neckarhausen*, p. 428.

163 Michael Mitterauer, "Kontrastierende Heiratsregeln. Traditionen des Orients und Europas im interkulturellen Vergleich", *Historische Sozialkunde* 41, 2 (2011), 4–16, 8.

164 Edward Sachau, *Syrische Rechtsbücher*, vol. 3 (Berlin, 1907), p. 35, quoted in Michael Mitterauer, "Customs of the Magicians", in *Sexual Knowledge, Sexual Science: The History of Attitudes to Sexuality*, ed. Roy Porter and Mikulaš Teich (Cambridge, 1994), pp. 231–250, 237.

165 As an example of this cf. Georg Simmel, "Die Verwandtenehe", *Vossische Zeitung* (Berlin), Sonntagsbeilage no. 22/23 (3 and 10 June 1894). In the article entitled "Das Verbot der Ehen zwischen Verwandten", *Der Katholik. Zeitschrift für katholische Wissenschaft und kirchliches Leben* 43, 1 (1863), 143–160 (discussed in greater detail below), statistical findings on concentrations of physical and mental defects as consequences of consanguine marriages were reported and included comparisons with China, where the author's argument held that hardly any deaf-mutes existed since kin marriage was entirely forbidden.

this topic and popularised it, and it likewise circulated in media published by the Church.

Indications of the increasing discourse on degeneration and endangerment can be gleaned from a look at various editions of commentaries and handbooks on marital law. In the first edition (1813) of the marital law handbook authored by Thomas Dolliner, there is no references whatsoever to possible health consequences of consanguine marriages. In its later editions of 1835 and 1848, however, Dollinger wrote of a danger of "degeneration" in cases where marriages "had long occurred exclusively between relatives".[166] Theodor Pachmann began his 1853 textbook's section on marriage prohibitions by referring to the "natural law of procreation"[167] as a reason for kin marriage prohibitions without going into greater detail. In the revised version of 1865, he wrote of the "experience of unmistakable degeneration" that would preclude such marriages.[168] By this point, the theme of "degeneration" had been set;[169] it proceeded to circulate and also impacted the diocesan level as the moral argument had been joined by a "physical" one.

In 1858, Prince-Bishop Vinzenz Gasser wrote the following in the diocesan circular that he had himself founded, the *Brixner Diözesan-Blatt*: "To my great dismay, the marriage requests in those degrees of consanguinity and affinity that only the Apostolic See can dispense are becoming absolutely rampant in this diocese. The rampancy of such marriages undoubtedly entails numerous morally detrimental consequences. They are even associated with physical disadvantages. Madhouses bear witness to the fact that idiocy and insanity not infrequently inhabit children born to such blood-related parents. I therefore renew the regulations decreed by my predecessors and admonish our most reverend priests to undertake everything in their power to fend off such marriage requests."[170] In the quoted passage, the prince-bishop wrote only regarding dangers to the health of children of "blood-related parents", leaving out the matter of affinity. This was by no means typical among high-ranking

---

166 Thomas Dolliner, *Ausführliche Erläuterung des zweyten Hauptstückes des allgemeinen bürger(lichen) Gesetzbuches von § 44–77* (Vienna, 1835), p. 208, and in the same formulation, Dolliner, *Handbuch des oesterreichischen Eherechts*, p. 208. Cf. also Saurer, "Stiefmütter und Stiefsöhne", p. 353.

167 Pachmann, *Lehrbuch des Kirchenrechtes*, vol. 2/1, 1853, p. 270.

168 Ibid., vol. 2, 1865, p. 285.

169 In his *Commentar zum allgemeinen österreichischen bürgerlichen Gesetzbuch*, Moritz von Stubenrauch referred to Theodor Pachmann. Cf. Moritz von Stubenrauch, *Commentar zum allgemeinen österreichischen bürgerlichen Gesetzbuche sammt den dazu erflossenen Nachtrags-Verordnungen*, vol. 1 (Vienna, 1864), p. 146.

170 "Verordnung über einige bei Eheschließungen zu befolgende Punkte", *Brixner Diözesan-Blatt* 2 (1858), 15–17, 16–17. Vincenz Gasser, who had been invested as bishop in 1856, founded the *Brixner Diözesan-Blatt* in 1857.

representatives of the Catholic Church during the nineteenth century's second half.

In 1863, the periodical *Der Katholik* published a lengthy, anonymous article on "The Prohibition of Marriage between Kinfolk" that provides an extensive look at the state of the discussion at that time.[171] *Der Katholik*, which had first appeared in Mainz in 1821, was intended for the entire German-speaking world. It marked the beginning of a type of Catholic publishing that defined itself not just confessionally but also as a "spiritual movement" – with the motto, "united with Rome and loyal to the Church" (*romverbunden und kirchentreu*) – and for a long time represented the leading religious and church political publication.[172] In this light, its positions as well as the authors and works it quoted can be viewed as paradigmatic of the frame of reference for the Catholic debate in German-speaking lands.

In its introduction, this article proceeded to interweave morality and nature – and hence theology and research on nature:[173] it stated that disregarding moral imperatives, including non-observance of prohibitions on marriages between close kin, would be "punished and avenged in the physical realm" since God was also the creator of nature. Altogether, the presentation of nature-based justifications for marriage prohibitions took up far more space than the social and moral argumentation sketched out above – which can perhaps be read as a clear sign that the focus of the discussion was increasingly shifting in this direction.

The article situates its theme within a long line of tradition. It states that Pope Gregory the Great (590–604) pointed out how marriages between kin were frequently childless.[174] And in more recent times, it holds that "the closer

171 Original title: "Das Verbot der Ehen zwischen Verwandten".

172 Rudolf Pesch, *Die kirchlich-politische Presse der Katholiken in der Rheinprovinz vor 1848* (Mainz, 1966), p. 141; Michael Schmolke, *Die schlechte Presse. Katholiken und Publizistik zwischen 'Katholik' und 'Publik', 1821–1968* (Münster, 1971), p. 13, 40.

173 Especially religious groups not belonging to the established denominations, but not only these, viewed research on natural laws as a "task of the greatest importance", these being signs of the divine permeation of the world. In this context, natural scientists were said to fulfil the "decisive intermediary function". Andreas W. Daum, *Wissenschaftspopularisierung im 19. Jahrhundert. Bürgerliche Kultur, naturwissenschaftliche Bildung und die deutsche Öffentlichkeit, 1848–1914* (Munich, 1998), pp. 200–201.

174 He did so in response to Augustine, as Beda reports in the *Historia ecclesiastica gentis Angelorum*, holding that unions between cousins did not produce any offspring: "Quaedam terrena lex in Romana republica permittit, ut sive fratris et sororis, sive duorum fratrum germanorum, seu duarum sororum filius et filia misceantur. Sed experimento didicimus, ex tali conjugio sobolem non posse succrescere". c. 2 § 5 C. xxxv. qu. 5, quoted in Hermann Eichborn, *Das Ehehinderniß der Blutsverwandtschaft nach kanonischem*

observation of nature and careful examination of its laws now allow one to recognise that in nature's various kingdoms, procreation within the same family contributes to the weakening, degeneration, and crippling of its progeny". The author, like others, uses comparisons with animals as a reference and proof. He cites an English physiologist having emphasised how it is a "noteworthy law in the animal kingdom that sexual unions between individuals of the same blood contribute decisively to the deterioration of the race".[175] This is applied to human beings: the author reasons that even if the resulting effects may sometimes not be especially conspicuous, such that one might perhaps be led to believe that nature's law did not apply here, one must not be deceived. It still holds true, he maintains, for natural laws never make exceptions. A "conspicuous defect" in parents, he writes, will be manifested in the worst possible way in their children. "So even if there do exist countries where princes marry their nieces and where marriages between cousins are concluded without a second thought", it is known by "every knowledgeable physiologist that this is diametrically opposed to the laws of nature".[176]

Two authors whose works are deemed compatible with the Catholic worldview are likewise at the centre of this article's considerations: the one is Joseph de Maistre, a philosopher, author and diplomat in service to the Kingdom of Sardinia, who was regarded as ultramontane Catholic and "anti-modern". In his book about the papacy, published in Lyon in 1819, he spoke out against phenomena including what he regarded as all-too-frequently permitted kin marriage among noble families.[177] One reason for this was that he vehemently advocated papal authority's limitation to spiritual matters, to a realm divorced from political interests and power. The other was the French physician Francis Devay, whose book *Du danger des mariages consanguines sous le rapport sanitaire* – which addressed the dangers to health arising from consanguine marriage – was published in 1857 and again, in a second and expanded edition,

Rechte. In seiner geschichtlichen Entwicklung aus den Quellen bearbeitet und übersichtlich dargestellt (Wrozlaw, 1872), p. 8.

175 "Das Verbot der Ehen zwischen Verwandten", p. 152.

176 The reference here is to: George Combe, *The Constitution of Man Considered in Relation to External Objects* (Edinburgh/London, 1828) with numerous further editions. Combe writes here about notions of heredity, which he considers to be closely linked to morality, character, etc.

177 Joseph de Maistre, *Du pape* (Lyon, 1819). Regarding his person cf. Martin Burckhardt, "Das Ungeheuer der Vernunft. Joseph de Maistre zur Einführung", in Joseph de Maistre, *Vom Papst. Ausgewählte Texte* (Berlin, 2007), pp. 7–39; Carolina Armenteros and Richard A. Lebrun, "Introduction", in *Joseph du Maistre and his European Readers*, ed. Carolina Armenteros and Richard A. Lebrun (Leiden/Boston, 2011), pp. 1–15.

in 1862.[178] Of interest here are above all the associations proposed by these two authors. Joseph de Maistre was among those who drew parallels to the plant and animal kingdoms. He came to the conclusion that the material order of animals should serve as our teachers: "Dans l'ordre matériel les animaux sont nos maîtres."[179] A reference to horse-breeding backs up his argument in a way that is as concrete as it is vivid: "Through what regrettable delusion can a man who wastes a gigantic sum of money to do something like mating an Arabian stallion with a Norman mare still proceed to take a bride of his own blood without the slightest demur?" This would beg the question, he continued, as to whether the pope had the right to "dispense from physical laws".[180]

Francis Devay, in his book, likewise assumes that consanguine marriages are "contraires à la nature" – contrary to nature.[181] He emphasises the oneness of "hygiène physique" and "hygiène morale", from which he then transitions to discuss "hygiène matrimoniale". Infertility as a consequence of kin marriage as well as hereditary and other diseases are discussed in this work, and Devay comes to the conclusion that consanguine marriages should, strictly speaking, be viewed "as an offence against public hygiene" – "comme une infraction à l'hygiène publique" – and would hence require attention from lawgivers.[182] The legal situation in France, however, was different. The Code civil of 1804 only forbade marriages between consanguine and affinal kin related in a direct line – that is, between ascendants and descendants as well as between step-parents and stepchildren (§ 163), collaterally between siblings, between affinal kin in the same degree (§ 162), and between uncle and niece as well as aunt and nephew (§ 163). Marriages between cousins, therefore, faced no civil law obstacles.

---

178 Francis Devay, *Du danger des mariages consanguines sous le rapport sanitaire*, 2nd ed. (Paris, 1862 [1857]).

179 De Maistre, *Du pape*, p. 278.

180 The quoted wording is based on the German translation used in the *Der Katholik* article discussed here. "Das Verbot der Ehen zwischen Verwandten", p. 158. The original can be found in de Maistre, *Du pape*, p. 278: "Par quel aveuglement déplorable l'homme qui dépensera une somme énorme pour unir, par exemple, le cheval d'Arabie à la cavale normande, se donnera-t-il néanmoins sans la moindre difficulté une épouse de son sang? [...] Le Souverain Pontife auroit-il par hasard le droit de dispenser des lois physiques?" George Combe likewise employed a comparison with horse breeding: "Yet we every day see very sensible people, who are anxiously attentive to preserve or improve the breed of their horses, tainting the blood of their children, and entailing on them not only the most loathsome diseases of the body, but madness, folly, and the most unworthy dispositions." George Combe, *The Constitution of Man and Its Relation to External Objects*, 8th ed. (Edinburgh/London/Dublin, 1847), pp. 189–190.

181 Devay, *Du danger*, p. 1.

182 Ibid., pp. XIV, XVII, 67.

A final interesting reference made by the 1863 article in *Der Katholik* is to a saying that was meant to sum up the disadvantageous consequences attributed to kin marriage: "No heirs, or ruination, or an untimely death". – "Keine Erben, oder Verderben, oder früh sterben".[183] The German wording's catchy, rhyming quality quite obviously had its intended effect. In the following year, 1864, the *Brixner Diözesan-Blatt* referred to this article in a didactic pastoral case study authored in Latin. "Casus x" concerned a closely related couple who had received – or, according to church logic, had "fraudulently obtained" – a dispensation on the basis of false claims. The saying "keine Erben, Verderben, oder früh sterben" is included in a related comment as a warning and a mnemonic of sorts.[184] In the parishes of the Diocese of Brixen, the *Diözesan-Blatt* was required reading for clergymen – and in dispensation proceedings, repeated reference was made to the instructions printed here. It is therefore fair to assume broad regional reception. The saying was even employed in an 1866 dispensation request from precisely this diocese: a prospective couple, reported a local clergyman, refused to give up on its marriage project in hopes that God, should they receive a dispensation from the Church, would "refrain from punishment such as: untimely death or ruination or no heir".[185] It was thus that arguments and discourses made the rounds.

In an echo of Devay's statements, the classic consequences of marriages between close kin were said to include not only specific pathologies such as deaf-mutism, blindness, disorders of the skin and organic anomalies ranging all the way to monstrosities and mental impairment, but also infertility, premature births and elevated rates of infant mortality. Charles Darwin, who was married to his cousin Emma Wedgewood and part of a network of cousin marriages both vertically and horizontally, himself examined the potential harms resulting from such unions. His interest in the topic was motivated not least by personal worries.[186] He pushed to find proof for the hypotheses in circulation at that time and advocated – albeit unsuccessfully – for the inclusion of a question as to whether married couples were related to each another in the English census of 1871: "In England and many parts of Europe the marriages of cousins are objected to from their supposed injurious consequences; but this belief rests on no direct evidence." He also asked his neighbour and ally

183 This saying is also known in a longer version: "He who desires ruination, untimely death, and to remain without heirs must take a wife from his own family". "Wer will verderben, früh sterben, und bleiben ohne Erben, der muss eine Frau in der Familie sich werben".

184 Casus x, 130ff as well as 132, note 1.

185 DIÖAB, Konsistorialakten 1866, Fasc. 22a, Römische Dispensen, no. 7.

186 Kuper, *Incest & Influence*, pp. 84–85; on this cousin marriage network cf. also Davidoff, *Thicker than Water*, pp. 225–227.

John Lubbock, a member of Parliament, to present his proposal there. To this end, he authored a paper where he argued: "If the census recorded cousin marriages it could be established whether they were less fertile than the average. Later it might also be possible to find out, whether or not consanguineous marriages lead to deafness, and dumbness, blindness, &c."[187] Parliament rejected Lubbock's proposal for being "too sensitive and awkward", since its implementation would "stigmatise" the numerous existing cousin marriages.[188]

From a medical and scientific standpoint, attention was focused exclusively on marriage configurations involving close blood relatives. The Church, on the other hand, felt obligated to continue defending and enforcing marriage prohibitions in close degrees of affinity – and it did so in its own way. Theres Waldner and Christian Bodner, the couple who had submitted the above-mentioned request that cited the saying on untimely death, ruination and a lack of heirs, were not blood relatives but rather related by marriage in the second and third unequal degree. So at least in some cases, it appears, Church and clergy did seamlessly transfer the physiological and medical discourses on shared blood and descent to kinship by marriage. During the nineteenth century's second half, therefore, affinal relationships were not exempt from the concerns regarding health dangers that had generally begun to appear more frequently in the correspondence surrounding marriage dispensation requests.

In some mid-1870s dispensation requests from the Diocese of Salzburg, one sees the 'physiological' grounds for marriage prohibitions explicitly applied to affine couples: in response to a request by the widower Paul Kraihamer, who wished to marry his sister-in-law Victoria Wuppinger, the diocesan consistory expressed "serious concerns" regarding the proliferation of such marriages, which were "held to be highly inadvisable for physiological reasons".[189] In the case of another affine couple, Rupert Schragl and Maria Schweinberger, the consistory complained of "the growing prevalence of unions in such close degrees that are not only disapproved of by the Church but also from the standpoint of physiology being characterised by physicians themselves as harmful".[190] In the Diocese of Brixen, a clergyman approved an affine marriage in 1895 with reference to the already advanced age of the bride, being of the opinion that "the damaging consequences with regard to progeny, etc., etc. that would speak

187 Charles Darwin to Lubbock, 17 July 1870, in Frances Darwin (ed.), *The Life and Letters of Charles Darwin*, vol. 3 (London, 1887), p. 129, quoted in Kuper, *Incest & Influence*, pp. 94–96, quotes p. 95.

188 Anderson, "The Marriage", p. 84; Davidoff, *Thicker than Water*, p. 241. On cousin marriage, which had been legalised by Henry VIII cf. Anderson, "Cousin Marriage".

189 AES, Kasten 22/39, Päpstliche Ehe-Dispensen 1868–1877, 1876, no. 10.

190 Ibid., no. 14.

against such a union must surely not be feared in this case due to *supra superquadultam aetatem sponsae*".[191] After all, she would presumably have no more children. The doubts, expressed here and there in dispensation requests, as to whether the prohibition of affine marriages was justified at all were met by representatives of the Church with silence. Deigning to discuss the matter would have been tantamount to an admission that one could indeed question affinity's incestuous character. An 1883 survey conducted in the Vicariate-General of Feldkirch, which belonged to the Diocese of Brixen, fits into this impression of a communicative strategy that sought to use silence or generic terms to paper over the fact that the concepts to legitimise marriage prohibitions stood in part on shaky ground. Its objective was to ascertain "the effects of marriages concluded on the basis of Roman dispensations" in Vorarlberg's deaneries[192] – marriages that also included those between affinal kin.

The interest of medical and natural science researchers in heredity and 'degeneration' could, in principle, have supported the efforts of the Catholic Church to prevent marriages between close kin to the most thorough possible extent. Physicians and natural scientists, after all, held views that provided additional arguments to this effect and were thus, in this specific area, working *in favour of* the Church – in contrast to their confrontational relationship with the Church regarding certain other theories that developed in the natural sciences during that period. What is more, their biological arguments disarmed the appeals to reason by those state-oriented legal scholars who were interested in easing the conclusion of marriages between kin. The problem for the Church was that the natural scientists' and physicians' arguments pertained entirely to consanguine unions. This would have ultimately rendered obsolete the impediment of affinity – and with it the centuries-old position of equating affinity and consanguinity where incest was concerned. Thus, with regard to upholding prohibitions of affinal marriage, the Church became subject to a certain degree of pressure over the course of the nineteenth century.

In terms of the discourse, it seemed as if affinity was indeed being said by the Church to possess some sort of physical character. However, this may also simply have been a strategy of communication that sought to obfuscate the distinction between consanguine and affine marriages and hence render the discourse on the various dangers of the former transferable to affinity, fitting the medical and natural science discourse into the Church's own interpretive

191 DIÖAB, Konsistorialakten 1895, Fasc. 22a, Römische Dispensen, no. 20.

192 Archiv der Diözese Feldkirch (ADF), Generalvikariat Matrimonialia (GA), Karton Ehesachen V, 1877–1885, Römische Dispensen III, 1883, Erhebung über die Auswirkungen der mit Römischer Dispens geschlossenen Ehen. On this see chapter six.

framework. This ambivalent situation could provide an explanation for why church representatives only reluctantly took up the discourse on the dangers of marriages between close blood relatives in the context of dispensation requests and the reasons given for their rejection. Thus, the 'physiological' argument was harnessed in order to more or less biologise the prohibitions of affine marriage while cousin marriage continued to be opposed on primarily moral and ethical grounds all the way into the 1880s.

6 From 'Common' and 'Strange Blood' to Racialisation

The increase in discursive physiological arguments from the mid-nineteenth century brought with it a stronger emphasis on 'common blood' in contrast to 'strange blood', a term with various connotations depending on the context. In dispensation requests made by widowers seeking to marry their sisters-in-law as well as requests pertaining to consanguine marriage projects, an ever greater role in the argumentation was being played by the 'common blood' or 'blood ties' via which the bride was said to be connected to her nephews and nieces as their aunt or to the children of the widower as a close relative. 'Common blood' was understood as being synonymous with a special kind of closeness and familiarity, with dependability and a feeling of responsibility, and ultimately as a guarantor of good, selfless childcare and childrearing.

The widower Franz Fessler, a master baker in Bregenz, had six children, including a "crippled boy" who required "loving and patient care". Such care, went the reasoning he employed in support of his marriage to Katharina Reichard, a cousin of his deceased wife, could "only be hoped for from a Christian-minded, virtuous and – thanks to her blood ties – all the more close female person".[193] Jakob Bertsch from Nenzing in the Vorarlberg deanery of Sonnenberg, who had three children with the youngest being just one-and-a-half years old, intended to marry his sister-in-law Eva Jutz. In their matrimonial examination, Christian Selb, the second witness who was questioned, mentioned as one of his arguments in favour of the marriage that he assumed "the groom desires to marry this sister-in-law of his because he has three children from his first marriage and therefore considers a blood relative to be better and more suitable".[194] Johann Michael Dörler, an Imperial-Royal Chancery clerk at the district office in Bregenz, was likewise a widower and had four children. When he submitted his initial request for a dispensation to marry his sister-in-law Paulina Hilbe, his

193 DIÖAB, Konsistorialakten 1851, Fasc. 5a, Römische Dispensen, no. 24.

194 DIÖAB, Konsistorialakten 1858, Fasc. 5a, Römische Dispensen, no. 38.

children were aged between just under one month and eight years. Following the rejection of this request, he addressed a four-page letter of supplication to the Vicariate-General of Feldkirch in July 1865 in which he stated his reasons anew. He explained, among other things, that his request for a dispensation was "in no way based on any dishonest motives", it being "much rather" owed to "the worries of a fearful father who desires to avoid endangering the existence and future of his poor children and to give them a mother who is already partial to them and loves them on account of their blood ties".[195] In contrast to such a portrayal, the 'strange' was negatively connoted, implicitly and often also in a way that was quite explicit – classically in the figure of the strange stepmother, who was hence cast in an evil light.[196]

In nineteenth-century writings on heredity, blood initially represented just one of various elements that were said to have a certain effect on the transference of positive and negative characteristics to offspring.[197] Organs, the brain, muscles, one's way of living, morals and character and other things represented further elements that were also deemed relevant.[198] The reception of theories from medicine and the natural sciences saw this broad range of factors successively reduced. At the same time, the perception of blood in the discourse around marriage prohibitions shifted toward a more strongly biological understanding.[199] The distinction between 'common' and 'strange blood' drove

195 DIÖAB, Konsistorialakten 1865, Fasc. 22a, Römische Dispensen, no. 12. Another supplicant, the aforementioned Wilhelm von Guggenberg, argued in favour of the second marriage with his sister-in-law by stating that "a truly caring stepmother, experience has shown, can hardly be found elsewhere then among one's closest relatives". DIÖAB, Konsistorialakten 1864, Fasc. 22a, Römische Dispensen, no. 8.

196 On this cf. also chapter five.

197 On historical concepts of blood, which were characterised by "humoral-pathological theories of conception" beginning with Aristotle and into the nineteenth century until blood lost its significance as a generative substance with the establishment of the "cellular pathological paradigm" in the mid-nineteenth century before 're-conquering' this status with the rise of serology and blood group research at the end of the nineteenth century, cf. Myriam Spörri, "Moderne Blutsverwandtschaften. Die 'Blutprobe' und die Biologisierung der Vaterschaft in der Weimarer Republik", *L'Homme. Z.F.G.* 21, 2 (2010), 33–49, especially 35–41.

198 On the "production of heritability" as an episteme and knowledge formation as well as a biological concept cf. Staffan Müller-Wille and Hans-Jörg Rheinberger, "Heredity – The Formation of an Epistemic Space", in *Heredity Produced*, ed. Müller-Wille/Rheinberger, pp. 3–34.

199 Recent research indicates that blood became a significant substance of relatedness and superseded a more strongly flesh-oriented way of thinking at the transition from the Middle Ages to the early modern period. Guerreau-Jalabert, *Flesh and Blood*, p. 75; for a foundational look at the conception of bodily substances and relatedness in the late Middle Ages and the early modern period cf. Simon Teuscher, "Flesh and Blood in the

these notions forward, and to proponents of exogamous marriage, 'strange' – meaning unrelated – blood was positively connoted: admitting new members into a family was, as already mentioned, a focus in arguments that defended kinship-related marriage impediments.

The Bremen-based jurisprudent Heinrich Spöndlin even held a given society's creative potential to be dependent upon "fresh mixtures of blood": "The lack of original people that so severely afflicts our era is due just as much to the lack of fresh mixtures of blood as it is to an excessive uniformity of upbringing, that all-too-broadly similar *acquired* hereditary nature".[200] Starting from this distinction, Spöndlin opposed the prohibition of marriage between affinal kin since one could not speak of a "detrimental concentration of the these hereditary natures" in such cases. What is more, "if the widower takes the sister of his wife and the widow takes the brother of his husband as a spouse", the second marriage would have "the same hereditary natures as the first", hence allowing children and parents to get along "far better": "The sister of the mother will more easily learn to love her nephews and nieces as children then a strange person would be able, and a brother will be more capable of becoming a father to his brother's children than would a third person due to their possession of his own hereditary nature."[201] While "hereditary nature" functions here as an equivalent for commonality, the aforementioned "prize question" of 1811 contrasts the terms "isolation" (*Absonderung*), meaning closed circles resulting from intermarriage among kin, and "mixing" (*Vermischung*): "This isolation, however, would necessarily be detrimental to physical and intellectual culture just as it would also be to the populace, while mixing within the citizenry spreads physical and mental strength and power and encourages procreation."[202] Even so, the anonymous author

---

Treatises on the *Arbor Consanguinitatis* (Thirteenth to Sixteenth Century)", in *Blood & Kinship*, ed. Johnson et al., pp. 83–104.

200 Spöndlin, *Ueber das Eheverboth*, pp. 82–83; emphasis letterspaced in the original. His argument regarding "acquired hereditary nature" refers to step-relationships and other relationships not regarded as consanguine to which he ascribes a similar kinship character: "If the suggested expansion of prohibitions in the case of full kinship is based on and hence justified by physical and psychological inheritance, then the absent reason of physical and innate psychological relatedness is replaced by the binding and uniting power of marriage and the significance of family in the case of half-, step- or chosen kinship, and just as the congenital hereditary nature embodies the marriage impediment in the former case, in the latter case it is the one that is *acquired through upbringing*, which constitutes kinship every bit as much as blood does." Ibid., p. 82.

201 Spöndlin, *Ueber das Eheverboth*, pp. 93–94.

202 *Welche canonische Ehehindernisse*, p. 69.

does advocate "by all means" permitting marriages between cousins a few pages later.[203]

An antagonist here was embodied by the 'others'. The legal scholar Hermann Eichborn, for example, referred to the "numerous examples of degenerate tribes that avoided mixing their own with strange blood" in his 1872 portrayal of the "marriage impediment of consanguinity as defined by canon law".[204] Eichborn effected distance here from an example not to be emulated via a diffuse mode of ethnicisation and exoticisation, in which said example was projected onto unspecified far-off 'tribes' as well as via the attribute of 'degeneracy' (*Entartung*). This – during this period and in this context – must be read as an equivalent of the term 'degeneration' (*Degeneration*).

Alongside this, there also existed a notion of 'common blood' in various concentrations, running more or less from high percentages to trace amounts. This was regarded as a consequence of its successive dilution via the repeated new 'mixings' that would occur over the course of generations. This was how Theodor Pachmann justified both the state's reduction of prohibited degrees and the civil method of counting degrees of kinship, which was based on the number of successful procreative acts in between. He assumed that kinship's "inherent connection" would "not be present everywhere in equal intensity", for "[e]ach successive conception results in a renewed mixing of blood and hence weakens blood's commonality".[205]

Decades prior, in the 1813 edition of his *Handbuch des in Oesterreich geltenden Eherechts*, Thomas Dolliner had discussed marriage prohibitions in degrees ranging out to the fourth. In doing so, he made reference to the justification provided by Pope Innocent III at the Fourth Lateran Council of 1215: Dolliner held that Innocent had perceived there to be a correlation between the four forbidden degrees and the four humours (*humores*).[206] At that time,

203 Ibid., p. 72. As a justification for the sensibleness of such a marriage prohibition in earlier times, he refers to *patria potestas*, paternal authority, which – in a legal sense – also extended to already married sons. This, he holds, had made it more probable that such sons would to live in their fathers' households together with other married siblings. This marriage prohibition – as it was applied to siblings and here also extended to cousins – had therefore been about "moral purity" in a context of spatial proximity. But now, he holds, patriarchal authority is no longer possessed of such "efficacy", for which reason he deems this marriage prohibition to be obsolete.

204 Eichborn, *Das Ehehinderniß der Blutsverwandtschaft*, p. 8.

205 Pachmann, *Lehrbuch des Kirchenrechtes*, vol. 2/1, 1851, p. 266.

206 "Quaternarius vero numerus bene congruit prohibitioni conjugii corporalis [...] quia quatuor sunt humores in corpore, qui constant ex quatuor elementis", in: Emil Friedberg and Ludwig Richter (eds.), *Corpus Iuris Canonici. Editio Lipsiensis secunda*, part 2: *Decretalium Collectionis* (Graz, 1955) [unaltered reprint of the edition published in Leipzig in 1879],

the objective had been to justify narrowing down the realm of prohibited degrees from seven to four. The underlying problem was that marriage prohibitions beyond the fourth degree of consanguinity and/or affinity could not be considered and duly complied with without great effort.[207] The same justification was employed by legal scholars arguing in the Josephine style 570 years later when the issue was paring back marriage prohibitions to the second canonical degree. Pope Innocent's recourse to the *humores* struck Dolliner as a reason that "sounds quite strange". Dolliner himself set more store in the idea that "degeneracy" (*Unarten*) would cease to be an issue further out than four generations. In this regard, he referred to the *Lehrbuch des Naturrechts als einer Philosophie des positiven Rechts*, a textbook on natural law as a philosophy of positive law by Gustav Ritter von Hugo – specifically to a passage from the chapter on "Juridical Anthropology".[208]

In order to explain what he meant by "degeneracy" (*Unarten*), Dolliner quoted the associated footnote from the abovementioned work by Hugo in a slightly modified form: "It is observed by naturalists that he who is descended from a negro, be it even only in the fourth degree, will necessarily still have something negro-like about him. In farther degrees, however, such characteristics disappear entirely."[209] In Hugo's original version, the latter sentence reads as follows: "He who is related in the fifth or greater degrees, however, can indeed be a full European."[210] With this, a thread had been spun from the prohibition of kin marriage to theories of heredity whose proofs were sought in their transferral to non-European societies, leading to the racialisation of arguments such as this one. In late nineteenth- and early twentieth-century Brazil, the

---

Dekretalien Gregor IX., Buch 4, Tit. 14, Cap. 8, Sp. 704. One also finds a quotation of this passage (with "matrimonii" in place of "conjugii") in Dolliner, *Handbuch*, p. 182. On the opinion prevalent at the council cf. also Paul B. Pixton, *The German Episcopacy and the Implementation of the Decrees of the Fourth Lateran-Council 1216–1245: Watchmen on the Tower* (Leiden/New York/Cologne, 1995).

207 Conc. Lateran IV, can. 50: "Prohibitio copulae conjugalis quartum consanguinitatis et affinitatis gradum non excedat, quoniam in ulterioribus gradibus non potest absque gravi dispendio hujusmodi prohibitio generaliter observari". Quoted in Stapf/Egger, *Vollständiger Pastoralunterricht*, p. 235.

208 Gustav Ritter von Hugo, *Lehrbuch des Naturrechts als einer Philosophie des positiven Rechts*, 2. umgearb. Versuch (Berlin, 1799).

209 Dolliner, *Handbuch*, p. 182; in reference to Gustav Ritter von Hugo, *Lehrbuch des Naturrechts als einer Philosophie des positiven Rechts*, 2. umgearb. Versuch (Berlin, 1799), § 64, 78 (the corresponding footnote is marked with three asterisks). The passage "it is observed by naturalists" is an addition by Dolliner and not present in the original.

210 Hugo, *Lehrbuch des Naturrechts*, p. 78. See for a brief overview of concepts of blood purification and commingling Myriam Spörri, *Reines und gemischtes Blut. Zur Kulturgeschichte der Blutgruppenforschung, 1900–1933* (Bielefeld, 2013), pp. 25–40.

idea of gradual 'purification' over the course of generations leading to eventual whiteness was widespread both as a myth and a political programme known as *branqueamento racial*: if *mestizos* would mate solely with whites, the idea went, they would grow ever-whiter, with Brazil ultimately becoming a white nation.[211] This policy was founded on blood, and its colour – black, indigenous or white – was the criterion by which its success was measured.[212]

Such myths and programmatic notions anticipate how the conceptions of 'common' and 'strange' blood developed as the twentieth century dawned. In this regard, Brigitta Hauser-Schäublin has ascertained: "The notion of race as it was employed in National Socialism would be unthinkable without the idea of common and strange blood."[213] This path had already been charted for decades,[214] though its continuation – which led to genocide – need not have been. Blood, in the context of racial anthropology, served as a means to identify "races"[215] and hence became a "racial characteristic". The route led via "racial hygiene" and hereditary biology-based understandings to the concept of race that National Socialism employed.[216] Piero Camporesi speaks of a "rediscovery of blood as a driving force of history in the twentieth century" that "turned in a negative direction" resulting "in a barbarous return to violence".[217] One could

211 Cf. Giralda Seyferth, "Colonização, imigração e a questão racial no Brasil", *Revista USP* 53 (2002), 117–149, https://www.revistas.usp.br/revusp/article/view/33192/35930 (last access: May 2022). For this reference, I thank Sol Glik.

212 Seyferth, "Colonização, imigração e a questão racial", pp. 136–147.

213 Brigitta Hauser-Schäublin, "Blutsverwandtschaft", in *Mythen des Blutes*, ed. Christina von Braun and Christoph Wulf (Frankfurt a. M./New York, 2007), pp. 171–183, 173.

214 The 1860s witnessed the emergence of eugenics, evolutionary theory and the principles of Mendelian inheritance. Eugenics began with Francis Galton, whose essay "Hereditary Talent and Character" was published in 1865. In Germany, eugenics emerged only later on, in the 1890s, cf. Weingart/Kroll/Bayertz, *Rasse, Blut*, pp. 36–37. Charles Darwin's *On the Origin of Species* was published in 1859, and Mendel's theory of heredity was presented in 1865; the latter, however, reached a broader audience only at the beginning of the twentieth century.

215 As in the writings of Gustav Schwalbe, cf. Weingart/Kroll/Bayertz, *Rasse, Blut*, p. 180. The recourse to blood in the context of a racial anthropology-based approach is referred to here as a "new idea".

216 It was thus that the article "Die Verwandtenehen in der Erzdiözese Wien" [Kin Marriages in the Archdiocese of Vienna] by the paediatrician Herbert Orel, who was himself forced to flee Austria in 1938, was published in a journal whose title translates as *Archive for Racial and Social Biology including Racial and Social Hygiene: Archiv für Rassen- und Gesellschaftsbiologie einschließlich Rassen- und Gesellschaftshygiene* 26 (1932), 249–278. For this reference, I thank Peter Melichar.

217 Piero Camporesi, *Das Blut. Symbolik und Magie* (Vienna, 2004), p. 29 (engl. *Juice of Life: The Symbolic and Magic Significance of Blood* (New York, 1995)). The introduction from which the quote is taken has not been translated into English.

indeed draw waves representing blood's presence. A similar phenomenon is the severe segregatory policy aimed at baptised Jews and Muslims and their offspring in Spain from the fifteenth century onward on the basis of the notion of *limpieza de sangre*, purity of the blood, to which they did not conform.[218]

British authors who defended cousin marriages in the 1870s, even if their starting point was a different one, ended up settling on what was fundamentally the same line of reasoning. Their argument was that it was 'natural' to desire to marry someone who exhibited commonalities with oneself, with 'commonalities' understood here not via metaphors of blood but – at first glance, at least – socio-culturally. At second glance, however, this view featured racist underpinnings: if one assumes the existence of a natural horror towards kin marriage, then one can also assume an equally generalised and far better-founded aversion to marriage with 'foreigners'. These 'foreigners', in a way that was inseparable from the colonial context, were defined by the factor of colour: "God made white men, and God made black men, but the Devil made half-castes." Nancy Anderson has thus hypothesised that in nineteenth-century Great Britain "anxiety about miscegenation" could trump fears related to incest.[219] And via a series of linkages, discursive strands focused on 'familiar' and 'foreign' blood spread into colonial contexts and merged with racist arguments of exclusion.

•••

One objective of this second chapter has been to introduce the fundamental logics behind the institution of dispensation as well as significant contexts of dispensation practice as it changed: alongside the fundamental character of dispensations as acts of mercy, a decisive role in proceedings that occurred during the period under study was played by the range of marriage prohibitions established in various ways by church and civil authorities along with the associated underlying notions. Also important was the trend toward relaxation of criminal laws pertaining to a realm of incest that, in parallel with the extent of marriage prohibitions, was quite broadly conceived. This chapter has also aimed to shed light on relevant period-specific filters of discourse, relating these to findings from the analysed archival material. The question regarding how love

---

218 Max Sebastián Hering Torres, *Rassismus in der Vormoderne. Die 'Reinheit des Blutes' im Spanien der Frühen Neuzeit* (Frankfurt a. M./New York, 2006); cf. also Burschel, *Die Erfindung der Reinheit*, especially section VII: "Gutes Blut, böses Blut".

219 Anderson, "The Marriage", p. 84. The author quotes from the article "Kin, The Marriage of the Near", published in *Westminster Review* CIV (1875), 147–155.

and passion were spoken of proved challenging in a methodical sense. Signs of a more strongly present love-concept centred on familiar intimacy and similarity of character most certainly can be found in the dispensation requests, but we find equal emphasis placed upon that quality of constancy that was considered essential in early modern marriages as well as good character traits. The codes could vary according to the social milieu, but particularly in bourgeois circles they would also often appear closely interwoven with one another or couched in period-specific terms – such as 'acquaintance' – that were connoted differently than they are today. At the same time, it proved important to think about levels of action as well as talk of love from the standpoint of the logic adhered to by those who authored the sources. Doing so allowed elements of strategic communication to become visible. Identifying such elements is essential when it comes to interpreting this material and understanding the administrative processes as a whole. Moreover, such a multiperspective approach underscores the diversity of notions that characterised the arena of love during the nineteenth century.

From the end of the eighteenth century onward, various discourses were distributed quite broadly in terms of their support of or opposition to either extended and intensified or limited marriage prohibitions. On several points, such as the validity of the taboo of incest between parents, children and siblings or the endorsement of exogamous unions, there existed far-reaching agreement – albeit based on differing lines of argumentation. 'Decency' represented a significant foundation upon which the considerations of both canon law and civil law-oriented authors played out. Hygiene, analogies to the animal world and heredity-related hypotheses, on the other hand, dominate the arguments in writings with an eye to medical and natural research. And clear lines of demarcation can be seen in the attitude towards affinity as a marriage impediment, which England – with the Marriage with a Deceased Wife's Sister Bill of 1835 – saw become a focal point of public debate almost simultaneously with the increased restrictiveness of papal dispensation policy beginning in the 1830s. As we can recognise frequently in dispensation requests, clergymen – including those on the local and regional levels – found it increasingly difficult to justify their stance.

Positions rooted in physiology, medical science and heredity theory began to solidify towards the end of the eighteenth century. They influenced how marriage prohibitions were dealt with in the contexts of both civil and canon law, where the discourse on 'degeneration' became a factor – at first more broadly in tracts and treatises than in actual dispensation proceedings. The views put forth by physicians and representatives of the nascent natural sciences were well suited to reinforcing the Church's position regarding the prohibition of marriage between consanguineous relatives – for the pope, as Joseph de Maistre nonchalantly remarked, did not have the power to dispense from natural laws. However, such arguments' limitation to consanguineous unions eliminated affinity entirely from the spectrum of relevance, an effect that the Catholic Church must have found intolerable despite the obvious brittleness of the prohibitions pertaining to marriage between affinal kin by that point in time. Its reaction spoke volumes: when faced with questions and scrutiny, church representatives responded with silence. An attempt to defend marriage prohibitions between affinal kin would have proven that they *could*, fundamentally, be called into question, and it appears to have been precisely this impression that they wanted to avoid. At the same time, however, there were individual cases where clergymen summarily applied warnings about possible health hazards of consanguine marriage projects to affinal ones in explaining their rejection or approval of dispensation requests.

While champions of marriage prohibitions railed against the "narrow-heartedness of familial love", it was precisely prospective couples related by marriage – above all in configurations where a widower desired to marry his sister-in-law, who was simultaneously the aunt of his children – who argued with reference to a number of positive connotations and expectations associated with their 'common blood'. The emphasis on and high regard for 'common blood' simultaneously entails outward demarcation vis-à-vis 'strange blood'. This way of thinking brought about a strand of discourse that would grow more powerful in the late-nineteenth century and eventually culminate in colonial and National Socialist racism.

CHAPTER 3

Church and State in Competition

> Hacia Roma caminan
> dos pelegrinos,
> a que los case el Papa,
> mamita,
> porque son primos,
> niña bonita,
> porque son primos,
> niña.[1]

∵

A young couple pilgrimages to Rome in order to be wed by the pope. For, as the Spanish folk song goes on to explain, they are *primos* – first cousins. In the subsequent verses, they do indeed arrive at the Apostolic Palace and enter its audience chamber. The pope asks their names and ages, where they are from and whether they have sinned. All they have done is kissed – and soon after, the wedding bells ring. In this song's telling, close kinship seems not to have represented a serious impediment: the pope apparently exempted them from it with no major bureaucratic obstacles. The great effort here lay much rather in the pilgrimage that they had undertaken, spurred on by the hope of achieving their objective more easily and quickly through the papal offices in Rome than they could have if mediated by their parish, their diocese or third parties. The prospects of being granted dispensations and other mercies directly in Rome were indeed good, and commensurate expectations existed from the Middle Ages into the nineteenth century.[2] The most important institution in

1 From *Los pelegrinitos*, Spanish folksong, as transcribed by Federico García Lorca. I thank Fernanda Alfieri for pointing this out to me.

2 An example of this beyond the purely ecclesiastical context would be the so-called Roman marriages due to the economic obstacles that marriage projects faced on the municipal level, obstacles circumvented in this way particularly by couples from Tyrolean territory during the eighteenth and nineteenth centuries. Cf. Margareth Lanzinger, "La scelta del coniuge. Fra amore romantico e matrimoni proibiti", *Storicamente* 6 (2010), http://www.storica

this respect was the Apostolic Penitentiary, which was viewed as the place where one could best and most quickly obtain divine mercy: "quo citius et melius misericordiam Dei consequerentur".[3]

In Austria, canon law had represented the definitive standard governing how kin marriage was dealt with all the way into the early 1780s. The relevant administrative competencies and decision-making power lay with the Church, which thus held a practical monopoly over the granting of marriage dispensations. But from this point onward, new regulations pertaining to marriage-related matters enacted by the secular authorities caused the situation to fundamentally change. For the Church, such regulations entailed a deep-reaching intrusion into its domain.[4] Initial ordinances and decrees had already begun limiting church power over marriage during the late 1770s. That period had also seen it become nearly impossible for related couples to travel to Rome in order to obtain a dispensation and marry – above all because such travel had been made illegal. The only way of turning to turn to Rome that now remained was through the diocesan consistories, and doing so required provincial government permission.

This marked the onset of a phase that, at least in parts of Austria, was to prove turbulent. The process by which 'modern' statehood developed during the period under study is hence not one that can be viewed solely from the perspective of a "'dualistic' tension between the state and society or between 'state administration and self-administration'"[5] – for the Church, as a third protagonist, played a role that was not insignificant.[6] Dispensation matters were one of several realms in which the Josephine era's power struggle between the

mente.org/07_dossier/famiglia/scelta_del_coniuge.htm (last access: May 2022); Margareth Lanzinger, "Landlessness and Marriage Restrictions: Tyrol and Vorarlberg in the Eighteenth and Nineteenth Centuries", in *Landless Households in Rural Europe 1600–1900*, ed. Christine Fertig, Richard Paping and Henry French (Suffolk, 2022). pp. 243–269.

3 Filippo Tamburini, "Le dispense matrimoniali come fonte storica nei documenti della Penitenzieria apostolica (sec. XIII–XVI)", in *Le modèle familial Européen. Normes, déviances, contrôle du pouvoir*. Actes des séminaires organisés par l'École française de Rome et l'Università di Roma (Rome, 1986), pp. 9–30, 9.

4 On the fundamental characteristics of marriage's "subjugation" to theological and state priorities cf. Dieter Schwab, "Der Zugriff von Staat und Kirche auf die Ehe – eine historische Reflexion", in *Rechtsgeschichte mit internationalen Perspektiven. Festschrift für Wilhelm Brauneder zum 65. Geburtstag*, ed. Gerald Kohl, Christian Neschwara and Thomas Simon (Vienna, 2008), pp. 615–633.

5 Krosigk, *Bürger in die Verwaltung*, p. 11.

6 On areas of conflict between Church, state and society during this period cf. Karl-Egon Lönne, *Politischer Katholizismus im 19. und 20. Jahrhundert* (Frankfurt a. M., 1986), chapter 2.

pope and the emperor played out.[7] Bureaucratic procedures changed, with civil administrative bodies now also becoming involved. Political authorities on the provincial level, in this case the provincial government in Innsbruck, served as hubs of communication between diocesan ordinariates, district offices (*Kreisämter*) as the "mainsprings of the overall political machinery"[8] and the office at the imperial court in Vienna known as the *Hofstelle*. Lawgivers' efforts to standardise as many procedures as possible[9] gave rise to that many more questions in actual practice. These were to be clarified via a "system of enquiries at court in cases of doubt". This can be viewed as an expression of both the growing "omnipotence of the ruler" and a belief in the inadequacy of lower-level administrative bodies that implemented policy.[10] The overall bureaucratic burden grew apace.

In his volume on the history of Austrian marital law, Adalbert Theodor Michel commented trenchantly on the confusing situation during these years: "The most interesting chapter in the history of marital law during the period under discussion here is that of the imperial-royal ordinances regarding

---

7 Concerning Josephinism, the following are a few recently published volumes that cover the current state of research as well as the various concepts while also containing references to a range of further literature: Peter Hersche, *Muße und Verschwendung. Europäische Gesellschaft und Kultur* (Freiburg i. Breisgau et al., 2006) and Wolfgang Schmale, Renate Zedinger and Jean Mondot (eds.), *Josephinismus – eine Bilanz / Échecs et réussites du Joséphisme* (Bochum, 2008), with overviews by Helmut Reinalter, "Josephinismus als Aufgeklärter Absolutismus – ein Forschungsproblem? Gesellschaftlicher Strukturwandel und theresianisch-josephinische Reformen", in ibid., 19–33; Christoph Gnant, "Der Josephinismus und das Heilige Römische Reich. 'Territorialer Etatismus' und josephinische Reichspolitik", in ibid., 35–51. On the climate that arose with the onset of Empress Maria Theresia's reforms cf. for example Umberto Dell'Orto, *La nunziatura a Vienna di Giuseppe Garampi 1776–1785* (Città del Vaticano, 1995), pp. 14–42.

8 Joseph Kropatschek, *Oestreichs Staatsverfassung, vereinbart mit den zusammengezogenen bestehenden Gesetzten* [...], vol. 1 (Vienna, 1794), quoted in Reinhard Stauber, *Der Zentralstaat an seinen Grenzen. Administrative Integration, Herrschaftswechsel und politische Kultur im südlichen Alpenraum 1750–1820* (Göttingen, 2001), p. 237. The right of codetermination, emphasised by Stauber, that the district captains (*Kreishauptmänner*) enjoyed in the administrative realm particularly when it came to handling individual cases, can be largely confirmed from the standpoint of dispensation-related matters. Here, as well, their reports and recommendations were often forwarded by the Innsbruck government to Vienna "entirely unaltered or with but a few comments added". Ibid., pp. 240–241. On bureaucracy cf. also Peter G.M. Dickson, "Monarchy and Bureaucracy in Late Eighteenth-Century Austria", *The English Historical Review* 110, 436 (1995), 323–367.

9 Altogether, Dickson specifies the figure of just under 5,400 decrees issued between 1781 and 1795. The lion's share, at 1,263, pertained to spiritual matters. Cf. Dickson, "Monarchy and Bureaucracy", p. 354.

10 Gernot Kocher, "Die Rechtsreformen Joseph II.", in *Josephinismus als Aufgeklärter Absolutismus*, ed. Helmut Reinalter (Vienna, 2008), pp. 125–161, 128.

marriage dispensations. These consisted mostly of half-measures and were not always generally announced; they sought to avoid conflicts with the Church and reconcile diametrically opposed principles; they quite naturally failed to achieve this end but did indeed damage esteem for the legal framework itself, for whose amendment or removal there was a lack of courage. This material is, moreover, difficult to navigate."[11]

Heuristically, such a period of upheaval offers insights into the 'production of the social'. When procedures depart from the routine and competition arises between interests and views, protagonists justify, explain and above all experiment. It follows that in the situation at issue here, violations of the declared regime were bound to occur. This chapter can hence also be read in light of the question as to the Josephine reforms' implementation and actual practice. Despite the numerous publications on this era, there are still under-researched aspects, in particular with respect to the reactions of affected parties.[12]

1 The *placetum regium* – A 'formalité si humiliante pour l'Eglise'

As a matter of principle, Rome was the competent authority where marriage dispensations in the close degrees of consanguinity and affinity were concerned. During the early modern period, a dispensation could be obtained in several ways. From the vantage point of the early nineteenth century, Thomas Dolliner characterised this "first epoch" – perhaps a bit too generously – as one that had offered numerous courses of action from which to choose: "It was typical to permit neither the secular authorities nor the bishop to know anything about the matter. He who required a marriage impediment to be lifted either went to Rome himself, sent someone there in his stead or turned to the papal nuncio or another Roman agent and obtained a dispensation in that way. He could then, upon presenting this dispensation, be married by a priest."[13] During the final decades of the eighteenth century, however, couples who were closely related by blood or affinity no longer enjoyed these options. The question of by whom a dispensation had to be granted had become a bone

11 Adalbert Theodor Michel, *Beiträge zur Geschichte des österreichischen Eherechtes* (Graz, 1870), p. 59.

12 On this cf. Hersche, *Muße und Verschwendung*, vol. 2, pp. 1013–1015; for Germany during this period cf. Hull, *Sexuality, State, and Civil Society*.

13 Thomas Dolliner, "Erläuterung des 83. § des bürgerlichen Gesetzbuches über die Ehe-Dispensen", in *Materialien für Gesetzkunde und Rechtspflege in den Oesterreichischen Erbstaaten*, ed. Carl Joseph Pratobevera (Vienna, 1815), pp. 56–99, 57.

of contention in the competition between ecclesiastical and secular power.[14] It began with 'recourse' to Rome being made generally – and thus also where dispensations were concerned – subject to state control: this now required the *placetum regium*, a writ of permission to turn to the Roman Curia issued by the competent provincial government.

In her ordinance of 27 September 1777, Empress Maria Theresia declared it "forbidden and a severely punishable offense for any and all persons to travel personally to Rome on account of a dispensation case in marriage situations *without provincial government permission*".[15] Both laypeople and clergy were thus prohibited from "dealing directly with Rome".[16] Prior to the submission of a given dispensation request to Rome, the *placetum regium* had to be obtained from the competent provincial government. This policy was justified in an ordinance of 11 May 1782 with reference to the rules laid down by the Council of Trent. It provided that dispensation in the close degrees was to "take place but seldomly" and, moreover, only for a select group of people. On this basis, the 1782 ordinance – which was representative of Joseph II's self-understanding – concluded that "such motivations, however", could "be scrutinised and assessed with greatest assurance by the authorities of the state alone". Therefore, all those who desired to request a dispensation in the close degrees were from then on to *first* "effectuate" permission from the provincial government and only then turn to the competent bishop.[17]

In the eyes of the Church, this was perceived as a "formalité si humiliante" – an extremely humiliating formality that representatives of the clergy found neither necessary nor sensible. It was "absolument superflue", absolutely superfluous and ultimately dangerous, an enslavement of the Church. With these words the Archbishop-Elector of Trier, Clemens Wenceslaus of Saxony,

14 On this cf. also Margareth Lanzinger, "Staatliches und kirchliches Recht in Konkurrenz. Verwandtenenehen und Dispenspraxis im Tirol des ausgehenden 18. Jahrhunderts", *Geschichte und Region / Storia e Regione* 20, 2 (2011), 73–91.

15 "Verordnung vom 27. September 1777", in *Sammlung der Kaiserlich-Königlichen Landesfürstlichen Gesetze und Verordnungen in Publico-Ecclesiasticis vom Jahre 1767 bis Ende 1782* (Vienna, 1782), pp. 104–105, 104; emphasis added. On this see also Johannes Mühlsteiger, *Der Geist des Josephinischen Eherechtes* (Vienna/Munich,1967), pp. 43–47.

16 Michel, *Beiträge zur Geschichte*, p. 8. Cf. also Christian Steeb and Birgit Strimitzer, "Österreichs diplomatische Vertretung am Heiligen Stuhl im Spiegel der k. (u.) k. Vatikanpolitik im 19. Jahrhundert", in *Österreich und der Heilige Stuhl im 19. und 20. Jahrhundert*, ed. Hans Paarhammer and Alfred Rinnerthaler (Frankfurt a. M. et al., 2002), pp. 35–63.

17 "Verordnung vom 11. Mai 1782", in *Sammlung in Publico-Ecclesiasticis vom Jahre 1767 bis Ende 1782*, pp. 203–205, 204. On the Tridentine equivalent see Jemolo, *Il matrimonio*, p. 64.

presented his view on the matter in written correspondence with his "cousin"[18] Joseph II. This written exchange was published in 1782.[19] Joseph II's brief and concise argument for his position was that he needed to be informed of decisions being made by the Vatican so that he would be in a position to influence them.[20] The *placetum regium* was to remain a mandatory in connection with Roman dispensation requests until the mid-nineteenth century. Obtaining it was, for the most part, a formality – albeit one laden with great symbolic significance.

This step towards stringent provincial political control also entailed the centralisation of dispensation-granting policy overall.[21] Since the Middle Ages, setting out for Rome on account of various matters and even from quite far off had been common practice not only in Spain but also in German-speaking lands, above all in the context of penal and expiatory pilgrimages.[22] Hans Hochenegg points to the common letters of indulgence "with numerous attached seal impressions of Roman cardinals" that pilgrims to Rome procured there for parish churches and brotherhoods in Tyrol.[23] And it was surely also the case that some couples chose to travel directly to Rome on account of marital and dispensation-related business. At any rate, one of the arguments

18 Clemens Wenceslaus of Saxony was a son of Archduchess Maria Josepha, a daughter of Emperor Joseph I.

19 Österreichisches Staatsarchiv (ÖSTA), Haus-, Hof- und Staatsarchiv (HHStA), Rom Varia 1778–1784, K. 58, Ins. 2. Correspondence entre S. Maj. L'Emperéur Joseph II. et S.A.R. L'Electeur de Tréve touchant les édits impériaux en matiere de religion (Philadelphia, 1782), pp. 4–5.

20 ÖSTA, HHStA, Rom Varia 1778–1784, K. 58, Ins. 2. Correspondence entre S. Maj. L'Emperéur, p. 18: "Quant au *Placitum regium* il m'a paru, que quand le Chef (comme Elle l'apelle,) visible de l'Eglise, fait émaner quelqu'ordre du Vatican aux fideles de mes Etats, leur Chef, très palpable & réel comme moi, en doit être instruit & y influer pour quelque chose." The *placetum regium* is assumed to have originated from the principle formulated in medieval canon law as "Quod omnes tangit debet ab omnibus approbari", from which it follows that the assent of those who hold secular power, as representatives of the people, is necessary in order that decisions by the Church be considered binding. Cf. Rudolf Pranzl, "Das Verhältnis von Staat und Kirche/Religion im theresianisch-josephinischen Zeitalter", in *Josephinismus als Aufgeklärter Absolutismus*, ed. Reinalter, pp. 17–52, 35.

21 This is a point where control and centralisation undeniably converge. Helmut Reinalter perceives the question of control as being in the foreground "in the battle for the supremacy of state power over that of the Church". Reinalter, "Josephinismus als Aufgeklärter Absolutismus – ein Forschungsproblem", p. 23.

22 Cf. Louis Carlen, "Straf- und Sühnewallfahrten nach Rom", in *Recht und Geschichte. Festschrift Hermann Baltl zum 70. Geburtstag*, ed. Helfried Valentinitsch (Graz, 1988), pp. 131–153.

23 Hans Hochenegg, "Wallfahrten über die Landesgrenzen. Ein Beitrag zur religiösen Volkskunde", *Tiroler Heimat* 12 (1948), 7–23, 10.

in favour of intervening in such matters was that it could "not possibly be of no concern to the state if its citizens" had to "undertake arduous journeys to distant lands at great cost and with all manner of detours in order to request the necessary dispensation".[24] Less direct channels had likewise seen frequent use. For instance, supplications also reached the Roman Curia via so-called procurators. Ludwig Schmugge puts the number of supplications from across the Catholic world that reached the Apostolic Penitentiary and were registered by the scribes there between 1455 and 1492 at an impressive 114,480. 6,387 of them originated from the territory of the Holy Roman Empire.[25] A circular of the Diocese of Brixen sent out to its secular and regular clergy[26] on 3 November 1777 instructed that dispensations not obtained via the diocesan ordinariate were henceforth no longer to be accepted. This piece of writing was directed "primarily" to the "superiors of their orders".[27] Alongside papal envoys and ordinariates, it was primarily monastic orders to whom special papal authorities were delegated during the early modern period. Even so, it would seem that they were invested with few, if any, competencies relevant to marriage dispensations excepting in the context of missions.[28] For this reason, it is fair to assume that they acted above all as intermediaries.

As research conducted by Marina D'Amelia has shown, however, obtaining a dispensation directly in Rome was not exactly easy. The Apostolic Datary, in particular, demonstrated no interest in reducing the degree of uncertainty or striving for more standardised procedures. It was much rather the case, she writes, that information on the rules of play and on the financial outlays that were actually necessary beyond the chancery fees, which were accessible as printed lists, was lacking. According to D'Amelia, the entire complex

---

24 *Ernst Valentin Schwaigers rechtliche Abhandlung von dem Rechte und der Pflicht der Bischöfe in allen Fällen zu dispensiren da der Landesfürst die Dispensreserven abschaffet. Nebst angehängten Lehrsätzen aus der gesammten Rechtsgelehrsamkeit* (Vienna, 1784), pp. 62–63.

25 Schmugge, *Ehen vor Gericht*, p. 15.

26 The distinction between secular and regular clergy lies in the former's territorial localisation and administration of the sacraments, for which reason they performed a public function similar to the one assumed by registrars later on. The latter included members of orders subject only to the authority of their abbots and the rules of their orders and abbeys. That is why they were "extra- or a-territorial" in actual practice and called upon to assume responsibilities such as missioning. Cf. Elena Brambilla, *La giustizia intollerante. Inquisizione e tribunali confessionali in Europa, secoli IV–XVIII* (Rome, 2006), pp. 21–22.

27 Copy of the circular of 3 November 1777, TLA Innsbruck, Jüngeres Gubernium, Gubernialratsprotokolle, Ecclesiastica, Fasc. 212, 1783 (Jan.–Feb.), Ein- und Auslauf, vol. 2, no. 42.

28 On this cf. Leo Mergentheim, *Die Quinquennalfakultäten pro foro externo. Ihre Entstehung und Einführung in deutschen Bistümern*, vol. 2 (Stuttgart, 1908 [reprint Amsterdam, 1965]), pp. 3–38.

surrounding the granting of mercies ultimately had the appearance of one big labyrinth. This notwithstanding, it was common knowledge among Catholics that the pope possessed the authority to grant mercy in countless matters. And in order to actually obtain such mercy, one needed agents and intermediaries on location. Such persons might live there and have access to the Datary, or be sent to Rome for this specific purpose. Rivers of bribe money flowed, and it repeatedly occurred that dispensation briefs were forged.[29] Marina D'Amelia looks at the sixteenth and seventeenth centuries, but we may assume that the situation she depicted most probably remained somewhat valid thereafter as well. And before this backdrop, standardised procedures – with the diocesan bureaucracies as the main protagonists – that saved supplicants the trip to Rome may indeed have delivered a certain degree of relief. However, this centralisation also entailed that closely related couples' marriage projects had now become entirely dependent upon the willingness of local and regional clergymen, the competent diocesan consistory and provincial government as well as the Court Chancellery in Vienna to support their dispensation requests.

Despite all the changes that were made, it proved impossible to fully eliminate unauthorised journeys to Rome. Those who dared to go this route could, however, expect to face punitive measures. Joseph Schuster and Maria Nockerin from the court district of Altrasen in the Puster Valley, who were cousins, had "gone personally to Rome" in 1785 in order to receive a dispensation, "following effectuation of which" they had themselves married on the spot. Once returned home, the couple was arrested and "placed in separate and solitary but quite moderate confinement". The provincial government in Innsbruck was made aware of this incident and, in turn, informed the Court Chancellery (*Hofkanzlei*) in Vienna. In April 1785, the Court Chancellery confirmed the legality of the action taken against the couple and instructed the provincial government to also forward the Roman marriage certificate "without delay" for its inspection. This evidently failed to occur, for there followed in July of the same year a renewed demand to send a report including the "certificate of the coupling that actually occurred in Rome" and to do so "without any delay", since the couple would have to be confined until a decision had been made at the highest level. This decision was then issued in August 1785: his Majesty had "mercifully deigned, this time, to permit the civil contract[30]

29 Marina D'Amelia, "Agenti e intermediari tra negozi curiali e merci false (Roma tra Cinque e Seicento)", *Quaderni storici* 124 (2007), 43–78, 44–46.

30 The definition of marriage as a 'civil contract' is the core element of the Josephine Marriage Patent of 1783, which did not institute civil marriage as such but did serve as a document from which the legal prerequisites for and consequences of marriage were

between Joseph Schuster and Maria Nockerin to be revalidated, on which basis the two may be united by their proper priest". The wedding therefore had to be repeated even though this couple had been married in Saint Peter's Basilica, the absolute centre of the Catholic world – but not by the couple's own priest – as the Marriage Patent of 1783 prescribed – and without the secular procedure of the obligatory three banns of marriage.[31] As punishment for their "travel outside the country without permission from the authorities", the couple was obligated to perform public service – albeit only for six weeks, in light of their prior confinement – which had to be completed before they could be "re-coupled".[32]

In the 1820s, the civil authorities in Innsbruck issued an explicit call for deaneries to monitor their people. The context was the so-called jubilee, the holy year declared every quarter-century, during which an extraordinary indulgence could be obtained. Such a year gave cause for many Catholics to make the pilgrimage to Rome – and, in doing so, to get other things done as well. "Priests from a neighbouring diocese" had allowed themselves to be enticed into "giving a peasant who was pilgrimaging to Rome letters and supplications addressed to the Holy See for the purpose of requesting spiritual authorities and the extension thereof, dispensations, etc.". For this reason, the Imperial-Royal Provincial Presidium had ordered that the Diocese of Brixen admonish its clergy, "on the occasion of this year's jubilee in Rome, to refrain from using this association with the Holy See in a way that runs counter to the hierarchy in general or to Austrian church law in particular". The diocesan consistory deemed this worry to be unfounded. Moreover, it held that publication of "such a general admonishment" would only awaken "the temptation to bypass proper channels". It therefore decided that its deans should "be called upon to appropriately monitor this matter in complete secrecy".[33]

The civil authorities became active not only at the beginning of dispensation proceedings but also upon the arrival of a dispensation brief from Rome. An ordinance dated 26 March 1781 stipulates that "since all bulls, briefs or other ordinances issued by the Holy See may relate to the *statum publicum*, we deem it necessary that their content always be submitted to us following their issue but prior to their further promulgation for the purpose of granting

derived, these being the sole domain of the state from this point onward. The obligatory banns of marriage were hence also among those things that were now subject to civil law.

31 Marriage Patent of 1783, §§ 29 and 31.

32 TLA Innsbruck, Jüngeres Gubernium, Geistliche Sachen, Fasc. 434, 1785, Akten und Protokolle, file no. 6.596, no. 1.072; file no. 10.895, no. 1.731; file no. 12.086, no. 1.902 ½.

33 ADF, GA, Ehesachen I, 1820–1850, 1825, Fasc. 58.

our provincial government *Placiti Regii* or *Exequatur*".[34] This ordinance specified the provincial governments as the competent bodies. Accordingly, dispensations – issued in the form of papal briefs – were to first be transmitted by the diocesan ordinariates to the competent provincial governments. Here, they had to be endorsed with the word *exequatur*, "be it executed", before the weddings thus permitted could go forward. The provincial government's own dispensation was issued in the process. This civil dispensation was required because the Marriage Patent forbade marriages between blood and affinal relatives within the second degree, hence representing an instance of civil prohibition that likewise needed to be lifted.

Bishops, however, repeatedly acted according to their own judgement. And in such cases, the tone in which the proper procedures were explained to them and insisted upon was quite firm. It was not only the clergymen of the consistory in Brixen, faithful to Rome, who proved unruly; likewise loath to submit to the various and sundry legal reforms were bishops whose dioceses lay only partly on Austrian territory during the late eighteenth century.[35] The government in Innsbruck repeatedly received orders from Vienna to forward instructions on such matters. In a letter of 12 May 1804, for example, the Court Chancellery called the Bishop of Augsburg to order with regard to dispensation briefs: "Since no use of a Roman document may be made prior to the request and issuance of the *placetum regium*, the *Gubernium* is to demand from the Augsburg ordinariate the papal dispensation brief in the original, most importantly, as well as to issue the *placetum regium* in the usual form insofar as the content of said brief does not contradict provincial laws. It is only once this has occurred that the ordinariate may act upon the authorisation contained in the dispensation issued to it by the Holy See and the government may grant permission to the specified bridal couple for the valid conclusion of their civil marriage contract."[36]

The directives regarding the appropriate procedures changed relatively soon, in the context of the dispute over bishops' authority to dispense and the intended independence from Rome where marriage dispensations were concerned. Since the bishops did not accede to these directives without further ado, it was first necessary to obtain written commitments from them that

---

34 Ordinance of 26 March 1781, in *Sammlung in Publico-Ecclesiasticis vom Jahre 1767 bis Ende 1782*, pp. 124–125, 124.

35 The affected areas included parts of the dioceses of Augsburg, Chur, Constance and St. Gallen. A map showing these areas can be found in Josef Gelmi, *Geschichte der Kirche in Tirol. Nord-, Ost- und Südtirol* (Innsbruck/Vienna/Bolzano, 2001), p. 235.

36 TLA Innsbruck, Jüngeres Gubernium, Hauptgruppe 64 Ehesachen, 1804, Fasc. no. 318, no. 66.

they would dispense on their own authority. Therefore, bridal couples had to supply a declaration by the bishop to this effect along with their dispensation requests. If this had been done, the provincial government was authorised to grant them permission to marry. Each year in October, which marked the conclusion of the "military year", an index of the granted marriage dispensations was to be sent to Vienna.[37] Five years later, however, a new set of rules went into effect that marked a return to centralism. Now, "in cases where the bishops dispense on the authority of their own office, the *placetum* for an episcopal dispensation" was "no longer to be issued by the provincial government, but always to be requested from this *Directorio*".[38] The reference here was to the Court Chancellery in Vienna, which evidently desired to exercise control itself and thus once again had to be informed and consulted prior to the granting of dispensations. In the intervening years, in particular immediately following promulgation of the Marriage Patent of 1783, it was therefore civil authorities that evaluated whether couples were worthy of dispensation. As a result, special standards were brought to bear.

2 State Dispensation Policy under the Banner of 'the Common Good'

In order for a marriage between close blood or affinal kin to go forward, the prospective couple not only needed to submit a dispensation request – which had to go through a lengthy administrative process – but also to sufficiently justify a marriage project such as their own. On the side of the Church, there existed a catalogue of officially recognised reasons: the so-called canonical reasons for dispensation.[39] But as a consequence of the Josephine reforms, the early 1780s saw the insertion of the civil authorities as a mandatory first stop where consanguineous and affinal kin also had to "indicate their motivations". According to an ordinance of 11 May 1782, the provincial government was to evaluate whether these were of "sufficient weight" and either endorse the request or, if the stated motivations were insufficient, summarily reject it in the interest of avoiding "pointless paperwork".[40]

---

37 Court decree of 8 February 1790, TLA Innsbruck, Jüngeres Gubernium, Hauptgruppe 57 Placetum Regium, 1790–1793, Fasc. no. 1.622, 1790, no. 7.

38 TLA Innsbruck, Jüngeres Gubernium, Hauptgruppe 64 Ehesachen, 1794–1795, Fasc. no. 312, 1795, no. 17. Letter of the Imperial Court Chancellery in Vienna to the Upper Austrian Gubernium dated 2 January 1795.

39 On this see chapter four.

40 Ordinance of 11 May 1782, in *Sammlung in Publico-Ecclesiasticis vom Jahre 1767 bis Ende 1782*, pp. 203–205, 204.

The reasons listed in the ordinance and now accepted by the state in connection with a marriage dispensation were not new. For, interestingly enough, these reasons were modelled after the Church's requirements as they referred to the corresponding rules laid down by the Council of Trent, albeit in reverse order: dispensations were to be "granted but rarely, and if so, due to publicam causam & inter magnos Principes" – when in the public interest and among great princes.[41] The sixteenth-century view had been that kin marriages should serve above all to afford nobles and others of high station marriages of an appropriate status. However, the state ordinance at issue here was promulgated during an era in which more and more prospective couples from the most varied social backgrounds were requesting dispensations. Before this backdrop, the 'enlightened' state's recourse to decisions by the Council of Trent does seem anachronistic. In order to justify these new secular powers, the Josephine ordinance further stressed that such "motivations and the truth of the underlying claims" could "be scrutinised with the greatest degree of assurance by the authorities of the state alone".

In the wake of the Marriage Patent's introduction in 1783, the authorities in Innsbruck responsible for such evaluations included the Upper Austrian Fiscal Office,[42] which then forwarded them to the *Gubernium*. In this initial phase, the supplicant couples were evaluated rather strictly in terms of their worthiness of dispensation. In keeping with the quoted ordinance, the only reasons recognised in actual practice were "public utility" and high social status. At the beginning of February 1783, the dispensation certificate permitting Cajetan Zignoli from Sacco in the Diocese of Trento to marry his sister-in-law arrived in Innsbruck. The internal report of the Fiscal Office explained that Zignoli had "applied for this dispensation two years before, at which time it was permissible to effectuate such dispensations in Rome", but had only been granted it following the Marriage Patent's issuance. In view of this situation, the office recommended granting the *placetum regium* – but not without pointing out that if Cajetan Zignoli had applied to take recourse to Rome now, his application

41 The public interest, or common good, was also a topic in canon law, albeit more as a theoretical foundation than in concrete dispensation practice: Brandhuber von Etschfeld, referring to the canonist Florens in *Über Dispensation und Dispensationsrecht*, pp. 66–67, specified three "reasons upon which a dispensation should be based": *misericordia* or *charitas*, *utilitas*, and *necessitas*, quoted in Florens Franciscus, *De dispensationibus ecclesiasticis praefatio in apieriendis juris scholis publice habita* (Parisiis, 1648), p. 17; on this cf. also Baura, *La dispensa canonica*, pp. 66–67; Jemolo, *Il matrimonio*, p. 64.

42 During this period, Upper Austria – *Austria superior* – was an administrative unit comprised of Tyrol, Further Austria – Austria's possessions in south-western Germany (Vorderösterreich) – and Vorarlberg.

"would have been summarily refused". After all, this dispensation was "neither for persons of high estate" nor was it foreseeable "how public utility would be served by it".[43] It was with this same justification that, in May 1783, the request by Anton Rungger, a court usher in Neumarkt who desired to marry a niece of his deceased wife, was rejected "since it involves neither persons of high estate nor public utility".[44] For a time, things were to continue in this way.[45]

In the first edition of his handbook on Austrian marital law (1813), Thomas Dolliner criticised church marriage prohibitions by arguing that these subjected "the innate freedom of the subjects to marry according to their preferences" to limitations that were unnecessary, "without utility and without reasonable cause". At the same time, they also – to the detriment of the state – exacerbated the difficulty of achieving "marital unions in smaller communities where nearly all families tend to be closely or distantly related with each other, particularly in remote valleys with little contact with the rest of the country into which outsiders are rarely pleased to marry".[46] Dolliner probably had in mind the obligation to obtain a dispensation in the third and fourth degree, which had been eliminated by that point in civil law. But where the first and second degree were concerned, the civil servants of the *Gubernium* did not necessarily have this clientele in mind. It was apparent that civil authorities had difficulty with the fact that marriage projects in close degrees were now arising increasingly often in less wealthy circles, among women and men from the agrarian, trade and commercial milieus, and not only from towns but also in villages and valleys.

The documentation from these initial years following the Marriage Patent's introduction is rather vague on how it was organised. Beginning around 1786,

---

43 TLA Innsbruck, Jüngeres Gubernium, Gubernialratsprotokolle, Ecclesiastica, Fasc. 212, 1783 (Jan.–Feb.), Ein- und Auslauf, vol. 6, no. 251. Just how convoluted the decision-making pathways during this period were is documented by the entries in TLA Innsbruck, Protokolle der Geistlichen Commissions-Sachen vom 21. Februar 1782 bis 19. Februar 1783, Kommissions Protokoll in Ecclesiasticis vom 8. Januar 1783, no. 14, vom 12. Februar 1783, unnumbered TLA Innsbruck, Protocolla in Geistlichen Co[mmissi]ons-Sachen vom 19. Februar bis Ende Dezember 1783, Kommissions Protokoll in Geistlichen Sachen vom 16. April 1783, no. 531.

44 TLA Innsbruck, Jüngeres Gubernium, Gubernialratsprotokolle, Ecclesiastica, Fasc. 213, 1783 (March–July), Ein- und Auslauf, vol. 7, no. 964.

45 Cf. also the request, likewise rejected in light of the ordinance of May 1782, of Anton Schächtle from the dominion of Sonnenberg in Vorarlberg, who desired to marry his cousin Theresia Schächtlin: requests in the second degree, "wherever no obvious utility is present and no persons of high estate are involved", were "only to be summarily refused". TLA Innsbruck, Hofregistratur, Älteres Gubernium, Reihe L, Publica, Politica, 1783, Fasc. 220, Pos. 29–32, Ein- und Auslauf, Pos. 31, Ehebewilligungen, no. 993.

46 Dolliner, *Handbuch*, p. 188.

"persons of high estate" – at least as an explicit reference – faded into the background, but estates as categories of social stratification did remain present in people's minds. The district office in Bruneck, when asked to evaluate the marriage project of the peasant Jakob Mutschlechner and his cousin Agnes Harrasserin in 1798, was loath to support the granting of a dispensation, arguing instead that "among the peasantry", this was inadvisable both on general principles and "due to the great sensation" to which it would give rise.[47] The notion that certain marriage configurations should remain reserved for those of higher standing would seem to have persisted as one of those inconsistencies that were paradigmatic of this era. This was a fundamental contradiction of so-called enlightened absolutism, which was not only personified by the monarch but had also come to permeate various state bureaucracies.[48]

Beginning in the mid-1780s, the question of whether *evidens ratio boni publici* was present – namely whether the planned marriage would promote the "general well-being of the state"[49] – came into focus, providing a basis for the evaluations issued by the Fiscal Office and the *Gubernium*'s Commission on Spiritual Affairs.[50] The district offices endorsed and supported dispensation requests, emphasising their worthiness of consideration and forbearance. Exactly what was meant by the "general well-being of the state", however, remained rather diffuse. This was contrasted with mere "private benefit" – which was grounds

---

47 TLA Innsbruck, Jüngeres Gubernium, Hauptgruppe 64, Ehesachen, Fasc. 314, 1798, no. 156.

48 On this cf. Reinalter, "Josephinismus als Aufgeklärter Absolutismus – ein Forschungsproblem", p. 30. With regard to the abovementioned contradiction, he writes: "While the Enlightenment exhibited an at least incipient tendency towards overcoming estatist structures, absolutism was based on estatist structures and persisted in conserving them." This finding of a certain ambivalence holds true here, even if the term 'absolutism' needs to be viewed in a critical light. On this see the classic work Reinhard Blänkner, *'Absolutismus'. Eine begriffsgeschichtliche Studie zur politischen Theorie und zur Geschichtswissenschaft in Deutschland, 1830–1870*, 2nd ed. (Frankfurt a. M. et al., 2011).

49 This – "das Gemeine Wohl des Staates" – is how the Latin expression was rendered in German in one dispensation request. TLA Innsbruck, Jüngeres Gubernium, Hauptgruppe 57 Placetum Regium, 1786–1789, Fasc. no. 1.621, 1786, no. 8.

50 In the context of Joseph II's dissolution of numerous monasteries, a Commission on Spiritual Affairs had been established on the basis of a Court Chamber decree of 31 January 1782 that, "under the chairmanship of the head of the provincial government and including the chamber representatives and advisers" as well as two committees of prelates or clergymen, was to meet once a week – or twice, if needed – and send its protocols to the Imperial-Royal Court Chamber. The topics covered by these protocols diversified rather quickly and came to encompass a wide range of spiritual matters including enquiries regarding dispensations. Later on, beginning in 1786, the reports on dispensation-related matters were filed and archived separately. TLA Innsbruck, Protokolle der Geistlichen Commissions-Sachen vom 21. Februar 1782 bis 19. Februar 1783, initial entry in this volume.

for a request's denial.[51] In some cases, the benefit that might accrue to the state was at least implied. The request of the seal office controller Johann Peter von Tausch, for instance, was endorsed because a fortune of 8,000 gulden might otherwise "leave the country": were his bride to remain unmarried and die without issue, this sum would go to her relatives in Bavaria. Even so, the Office of the Chamber Procurator in Innsbruck deemed the stated grounds – which also included the fact that the groom was a widower and had a small child – to be insufficient. As a result, it forwarded the matter to the Court Chancellery in Vienna in a very extensive report. Included was a certificate from the city judge in Klausen confirming the mentioned sum of money. The Court Chancellery in Vienna instructed that this request was "only to be rejected".[52]

Better luck was had by Joseph Anton Rist of Heimenkirch, which belonged to the Further Austrian domain of Bregenz-Hohenegg that was to pass to Bavaria in the nineteenth century. He desired to marry his uncle's widow Theresia Dempflin. Like his deceased uncle, who had lived in Wengen in the southern German Allgäu region, Rist worked in the carrying trade and thus possessed similar occupational experience. It was therefore also to be expected that the widow would be "a housewife exceptionally well suited to his line of business". More importantly, however, she possessed a fortune of 10,000 gulden, which their marriage would "bring into Austrian territory, thereby augmenting the amount of domestic taxable wealth". Furthermore, "the carriage of his uncle would also be brought into the country along with the widow" and added to his own. "Through this expansion of commercial transport, the nourishment of the subjects in Vorarlberg would be improved whilst toll proceeds would rise". But if the widow were to marry elsewhere, it was to be feared that the "useful carriage trade would easily veer off of domestic roads, crossing the border and continuing on through the Holy Roman Empire". The Court Chancellery subsequently ordered that Joseph Anton Rist "present a clear declaration" by the ordinariate that it would dispense on its own authority.[53] This was one of the few positively evaluated requests from these years that were also accepted

51 Evaluation of 17 July 1786, prepared by Johann de Lama and addressed to the provincial government, TLA Innsbruck, Jüngeres Gubernium, Hauptgruppe 57 Placetum Regium, 1786–1789, Fasc. no. 1.621, 1786, no. 8.

52 Ibid., 1788, no. 1. Johann Peter von Tausch did not give up: in 1790, he made a renewed attempt. This time, after initially being confronted with the declaration that the bishop in Brixen would not dispense on his own authority, he received permission from Vienna to apply in Rome. TLA Innsbruck, Jüngeres Gubernium, Hauptgruppe 57 Placetum Regium, 1790–1793, Fasc. no. 1.622, 1790, no. 17 and no. 21.

53 TLA Innsbruck, Jüngeres Gubernium, Hauptgruppe 57 Placetum Regium, 1786–1789, Fasc. no. 1.621, 1789, no. 18.

in Vienna. Among them is a further request whose success – in light of the social status of the supplicants, Count Felix von Spaur and Countess Mariana von Kuen Bellasi – will hardly have been a mere coincidence.[54]

It was in vain, on the other hand, when prospective couples from other social milieus attempted to make explicit arguments with reference to the common good in their letters of supplication. Anton Firler, a farmhand who desired to marry his uncle's widow, wrote that the two would unite capital worth 3,000 gulden and thus be able to ensure the "well-being" of her five fatherless children. He claimed to have also acquired all of the necessary farming and viticultural knowledge. Regarding his diligence and industriousness, he invoked "his spiritual and worldly superiors" as witnesses. And finally, he referred to his good upbringing and closed with the following: "For all of the reasons mentioned above, the undersigned entertains the pleasant notion that even consideration of the common good will support this most humble request; in that, among other things, this is about maintaining certain plots of land in a fruitful state, as well as about raising several children to become useful citizens of the world." The district office in Bozen sent this request to Innsbruck along with the brief comment that it was doing so based "on great mercy alone". And in Innsbruck, despite the explicit reference to the "common good" and "useful citizens of the world", it was rejected on account of its featuring "no sufficient grounds for support".[55]

The master red tanner Anton Wopfner, who sought to marry the widow of his deceased brother, suffered a similar fate. According to a report by the Commission adviser, he justified his intent as follows: "because, 1st of all, he has now been handed the leatherworking and -selling business of his deceased brother as well as the widow and her two underage children to care for and raise; 2nd of all, the widow is very experienced in the leather trade and thus

---

54 Ibid., no. 40. The following "motivations" are mentioned in their request: "1st, because neither commands a large income, for which reason the groom would have difficulty obtaining a wealthy bride without having to satisfy great and onerous demands, while the bride, with her very moderate marriage portion, would be very hard-pressed to find a respectable opportunity, and 2nd, on the other hand, this equal union will perhaps give rise to mutual satisfaction and relief, and 3rd, well-run holdings and the other benefits of marriage would flow of their own accord, particularly because, 4th, there is no great difference in age between them and, finally, 5th, because they had believed to have received assurance of being able to obtain a dispensation from their reverend ordinary". Unfortunately, the records from these years do not contain the correspondence with the diocesan ordinariates, for which reason they provide no indication of the courses subsequently taken by the various requests.

55 TLA Innsbruck, Jüngeres Gubernium, Hauptgruppe 57 Placetum Regium, 1786–1789, Fasc. no. 1.621, 1788, no. 4.

essential to him in carrying it forward, and because 3rd of all, were he to marry otherwise, he would have to turn out this woman along with her two underage children and also pay out to them the fatherly inheritance, thereby becoming incapable of continuing this leather business that is so beneficial to the public since he could not possibly continue running it together with this widow in a decent way without being united in marriage due to his already-made declaration of love". His request likewise referred to the "public" – but the evaluators ruled in a similarly terse manner: "Since the present case involves the first degree of affinity, and no evident reason for dispensation in terms of the *actual common good* pertains, the supplicant and his supplication can only be refused in accordance with the existing imperial regulations."[56] For the most part, dispensation requests centred on the ways in which the planned marriages would favour the economic advancement of peasants, tradesmen or small merchants. It would seem that arguments of this type were thought to have the best chances of resulting in success.

It counted just as little when a couple already had a child, as did the affinal couple Johann Jakob Fink and Anna Maria Einslin from Sulzberg: the utility of their "marriage to each other [...] and the conceived child", stated the evaluation, was "precisely not" to be viewed as "such a one that would have an obvious influence on the common good".[57] And the request of the peasant Simon Pacher and Agnes Tschurtschenthalerin, who had two children, evoked an indignant response from the Court Chancellery in Vienna, which instructed the *Gubernium* in Innsbruck to respond to the prospective couple "only in the negative and, in the future, to independently and summarily reject such impermissible supplications, in no case supporting them and thereby fuelling the proliferation of superfluous paperwork".[58]

Beginning in 1790, it was once again the bishops' verdicts that were decisive. If they agreed to dispense on their own authority, the provincial governments had to grant their permission to marry "without further ado". This marked the end of the state's role in evaluating dispensation requests, with the abstract and hardly satisfiable criterion of 'the common good' hence waning in its significance – even if it still would be referred to here and there in recommendations and reports.[59] Overall, the logic of the civil authorities –

56 Ibid., no. 24; emphasis added.

57 Ibid., no. 23.

58 Ibid., no. 29. The vast amounts of written correspondence are a frequent theme. Reinhard Stauber views this "proliferation of written matter" as a "hydra" of Habsburg administration. Stauber, *Der Zentralstaat*, pp. 233–234.

59 The district captain in Bozen, for example, concluded a very lengthy letter of endorsement in June 1795 by mentioning the "interest of the state" and utility: "If one regards this

especially at the higher levels of the provincial government and the Court Chancellery – had been beholden to markedly different considerations than the needs of those men and women who submitted requests. The primacy of economic arguments in the 1780s requests that they evaluated was likely owed to the hope that these would go furthest in satisfying the new state requirements. Such substantive emphases, which can be identified as situational and contextual, make clear yet again how letters of recommendation and supplication did not simply serve to represent real life situations but were indeed oriented toward the presumed expectations of the recipients and accordingly focused on certain aspects.

3 The Extent of Marriage Prohibitions: To the Second or to the Fourth Degree?

The Marriage Patent of 16 January 1783 limited the obligation to apply for a dispensation to marry to the first and second canonical degrees, thus allowing two degrees that were classified as forbidden by canon law.[60] The treatise *Ist es wahr, daß die k. k. Verordnungen in Ehesachen dem Sakramente entgegen stehen – Is It True That the Imperial-Royal Ordinances Pertaining to Marriage Contradict the Sacrament* –, published anonymously in 1785 and attributed to Johann Bernhard Horton (1735–1786), takes up civil law's point of view in its extensive arguments in favour of lifting these religious prohibitions, characterising it as having been imposed by a "foreign power".[61] "The population of the states" and hence "the most important basis of general well-being", it

---

marriage with consideration for the interest of the state, it would appear to be useful on account of its provision of a destitute person with sustenance while also, in light of how the groom is wealthy and the bride poorer, achieving the intended more even distribution of wealth." TLA Innsbruck, Jüngeres Gubernium, Hauptgruppe 64 Ehesachen, 1796, Fasc. no. 313, no. 2.

60 Blood kinship up to and including the second canonical degree encompassed marriages between uncle and niece as well as between aunt and nephew (first and second unequal degree), which were possible only very rarely, as well as between first cousins (second degree). Affine configurations included unions between step-parents and step-children (first lineal degree), which were ineligible for dispensation, as well as with a sister (first degree), a niece (first and second unequal degree) or a cousin (second degree) of a deceased wife or, conversely, with a brother, nephew or cousin of a deceased husband.

61 [Johann Bernhard Horten], *Ist es wahr, daß die k. k. Verordnungen in Ehesachen dem Sakramente entgegen stehen?* (Vienna, 1785), p. 3. This is also referred to in the deliberations of Dolliner, *Handbuch*, p. 188.

holds, depends upon the "encouragement and easing" of marriage.[62] And it is "without need, to no end and out of sheer arbitrariness" that the prohibitions extend "as far as they do". This, it concludes, represents a violation of human freedom. The "impeccable inclinations of the subjects" are limited by force, surreptitiously undermining their happiness.[63] The law, asserts this book's author, saddles one with "the obligation" to seek out all relatives extending to the fourth degree, for "one cannot guard against something if one does not know in advance from what one is to guard oneself".[64]

The author goes on to describe and elaborate upon the difficulties and exertions entailed during this period by the project of researching one's own "forebears" back to one's great-great-grandparents with something almost like relish.[65] This might be easy for "old noble houses", he states, but among the "other classes of subjects" it requires great effort to ascertain the birthplaces and marriage locations of sixty "forebears".[66] "How many journeys must he not undertake, how much time must he not fritter away and how much additional expense must he not incur?"[67] This is necessary, he writes, even just to reconstruct one's blood relatives, with affinal kin being even more difficult if not impossible. The result is "the sad but indeed logical consequence that among so many thousand marriages existing in every state excepting marriages between old noble families, not a single person can enjoy the comfort of reliable assurance".[68] After all, a fraught aspect of marriage prohibitions was that an overlooked marriage impediment would render a marriage null and void. Horton accordingly pointed out how the extent of canon law's marriage impediments resulted in constant incertitude regarding the validity of a marriage while state-imposed laws offered legal assurance.

From now on, marriages between blood and affinal kin in the third and fourth degrees could be concluded unhindered. But this did not actually solve the problem, for the fact that such marriages were still considered invalid by the Church rendered the state's limits on the obligation to procure a dispensation a double-edged sword. The fact that this change would not be simply

---

62 The elimination of marriage impediments was viewed by eighteenth-century population theorists such as Johann Peter Süßmilch as being an urgent priority in the interest of promoting the "felicity of the state". Cf. Josef Ehmer, *Heiratsverhalten, Sozialstruktur, ökonomischer Wandel. England und Mitteleuropa in der Formationsperiode des Kapitalismus* (Göttingen, 1991), pp. 34–36.

63 [Horten], *Ist es wahr*, pp. 133–134.

64 Ibid., p. 135.

65 Ibid., pp. 144–156.

66 Ibid., p. 157.

67 Ibid., p. 161.

68 Ibid., p. 164.

accepted seems to have become evident rather soon. For as early as the version of the Marriage Patent that was printed for distribution to the dioceses, a passage was added at the end that contained an additional, after-the-fact resolution by the court. This resolution left open the option of a church dispensation in the degrees upon which state restrictions had just been removed – an almost immediate partial walk back, as it were. "Parties that, *due to an excessively sensitive conscience*, turn to the bishops for a dispensation in a degree not prohibited by the aforegoing patent should be granted the requested dispensations always and free of charge",[69] the resolution states.

It is difficult to assess the extent to which men and women related in the third and fourth degrees actually did experience inner moral conflict over the prospect of marrying without a dispensation and the number of people who could bring themselves to view these relaxed restrictions as a welcome removal of bureaucratic obstacles. What is documented is that such dispensation requests continued to be submitted[70] – and, above all, that local clergymen applied massive pressure. In Tyrol, church representatives were altogether highly reluctant towards the Josephine reforms and changes. As far as the act of marriage was concerned, they still did have the reins firmly in hand since there was no alternative to a church wedding and thus also no escape from the grasp and influence of the Church in the context of marriage. At the same time, the state also found itself needing to bring its own administrators into line. A court decree of 31 May 1783 made it clear that people who were unhindered by a marriage impediment "must never be instructed to turn to their ordinariate", since they were now free to decide on their own whether they would turn to their bishop.[71]

---

69 Court resolution of 6 March 1783, quoted in Joseph Kropatschek, *Handbuch aller unter der Regierung des Kaisers Joseph II. für die k. k. Erbländer ergangenen Verordnungen und Gesetze in einer sistematischen Verbindung*, vol. 2, 1780–1784 (Vienna, 1785), p. 170. These ordinances and laws are accessible via *Alex – historische Rechts- und Gesetzestexte online*, a portal of the Austrian National Library, at http://alex.onb.ac.at/_in the section "Justizgesetzsammlung", which covers the period of 1780–1848 (last access: May 2022).

70 In April of 1783, for example, two couples – the one consanguineous in the second and third unequal degree, the other related by marriage in the second and third unequal degree – applied to the provincial authorities for the *placetum regium* "to obtain marriage dispensations". They were officially informed that they could "be pleased" in light of the lately "expressed imperial volition" and were "no longer affected by this prohibition on marriage". TLA Innsbruck, Jüngeres Gubernium, Gubernialratsprotokolle, Ecclesiastica, Fasc. 213, 1783 (March–July), Ein- und Auslauf, vol. 4, unnumbered.

71 This decree was intended to convey "knowledge and according procedures". TLA Innsbruck, Protocolla in Geistlichen Co[mmissi]ons-Sachen vom 19. Februar bis Ende Dezember 1783, 18 June 1783, fol. 400.

The obligation to observe this "highest ordinance" was "to be borne in mind". If prospective couples were to complain to the *Gubernium* that "the priest refuses to unite them", the provincial government was to "use such means of compulsion as are necessary to elicit the priest's blessing".[72] A wide range of complaints to this effect were sent by district offices to Innsbruck: in 1792, the Oberinnthal district office reported "that in the court district of Naudersberg and Glurns, couples related by blood or by marriage in the third and fourth degrees are always directed by the priests to obtain dispensations from their vicariate or ordinariate". The district office requested instructions on "how this practice can best be remedied without raising a stir". Its report also indicated that "clerical rule by force is becoming more prevalent": "In the Diocese of Brixen, as far as this district office is aware, every priest has been explicitly delegated the power to dispense in cases involving such kinship."[73] This would mean that the diocesan ordinariate had more or less granted dispensation authorities to its lowest-level clergymen as an emergency measure.

The quoted enquiry addresses a problem that was rather pressing at that time and indeed unsolvable under the new rules: the incompatibility between canon and civil law was to be prevented from becoming all that clear in public, "among the people", and raising an attendant stir – which, considering how things stood, was no simple task. In September 1783, the bishops had accordingly been admonished "to guard most carefully against provoking a collision" with regard to the validity of marriages. They should, at the same time, "refrain from making things difficult for bridal couples or withholding priestly support and eliminate all delays and unpleasantness in administering the sacrament in those cases where the Marriage Patent permits the marriage to be concluded and where, therefore, no legal hindrance exists".[74]

Sebastian Hueber from Innichen was a supplicant who complained to the *Gubernium*. On the occasion of his planned 1794 marriage to Anna Valtiner, with whom he was related in the second and third unequal degree, the "princely episcopal consistory in Brixen foisted upon him a dispensation, granting it at no cost but refusing to afford him a priestly blessing should it be refused". In a very lengthy reply, the priest was guaranteed protection should he wed the couple without a dispensation. At the same time, he was warned of the "conflict between the supreme provincial government and the pastorate" that would be entailed by "episcopal behaviour" counter to "the supreme ordinances". For

---

72 TLA Innsbruck, Protokoll Geistliche Kommission, 1785, part 1, no. 1.022, fos. 123–124.

73 TLA Innsbruck, Jüngeres Gubernium, Hauptgruppe 57 Placetum Regium, 1790–1793, Fasc. no. 1.622, 1792, no. 12.

74 Court decree of 4 September 1783, quoted in Michel, *Beiträge zur Geschichte*, p. 25.

this would "give rise to quite a stir" among "the people", from whom "such collisions" would not remain concealed. This was followed by an appeal for the bishop, "in the future" to adhere to the provincial government's laws, "which are intended for to the good of the people without the slightest reduction of true clerical rights", and to refrain from "contributing to unrest among the people" with his "untimely interspersions and one-sided dispositions".[75]

The explanations demanded of local clergymen who had refused to carry out weddings indicate their continued adherence to the position that the prohibition of marriage in the third and fourth degrees had "at all times been maintained by the Church". For this reason, the priests had been instructed by the bishops "to request dispensation".[76] In practice, they had evidently reinterpreted the aforementioned "may"-passage in the addendum to the Marriage Patent as a "must"-passage. The Imperial-Royal Judge and Warden (*Pfleger*) of Naudersberg commented on this in the style of an enlightened civil servant: "As for the second matter, the clergymen are lost in a dense thicket of confusion, since they are interpreting advice provided by the lawgiver for the timid of soul in an entirely erroneous manner. For the law obligates nobody to turn to the sacred authorities for dispensation; it is much rather the case that the unenlightened have the option of procuring a dispensation from the clergy in order to calm their weak souls, as the law's wording only too clearly indicates. Who, then, would allow themselves to attach to the words *can* and *may* the literal meanings of *should* and *must*?" Such dispensations, he concluded, were accordingly "an unnecessary thing" and retained "only for the timid of soul".[77] The administrator in the office of the judge (*Landrichteramtsverwalter*) of Glurns and Mals, for his part, indicated that the clergymen did not dare wed a couple without a dispensation.[78]

Instructions were subsequently sent to the bishops involved in these cases, those of Brixen and Chur, to "adhere to the existing marriage regulations more precisely than before".[79] This was not to remain the only admonishment in this matter, for the ordinariate in Brixen was unimpressed and continued to accord canon law a superordinate role. A 1798 complaint elicited the following

---

75 TLA Innsbruck, Jüngeres Gubernium, Hauptgruppe 64 Ehesachen, 1794–1795, Fasc. no. 312, 1794, no. 90.

76 TLA Innsbruck, Jüngeres Gubernium, Hauptgruppe 57 Placetum Regium, 1790–1793, Fasc. no. 1.622, 1792, no. 12, letter from the parish priest of Haid, dated 21 February 1792.

77 Ibid., letter from the Imperial-Royal Judge and Warden of Naudersberg, dated 23 February 1792, emphasis underlined in the original.

78 Cf. ibid., letter from the administrator to the judge of Glurns and Mals, dated 8 March 1792.

79 Ibid., reply to the aforementioned notification by the Oberinntal district office, dated 29 March 1792.

terse reaction from the bishop's side: "Whether dispensation in the third degree of blood relation was necessary is something that we, as *Ordinarius*, must ourselves know."[80] But the secular institution of the district office in Schwaz also forwarded a dispensation request – that of master baker Franz Rummler and Anna Schnaggerin – to the *Gubernium*. It then received the lecturing answer that in this case, "as a consequence of the supreme Marriage Patent", no dispensation was necessary, and that the district office would now "know how to act without needing to request further instructions in similar cases in the future".[81]

Divergent positions also existed with regard to the second and third unequal degree according to the canonical counting method. The Church dealt with such intermediate degrees on the basis of the closer degree, thus focusing on the second degree in this configuration. The Marriage Patent, on the other hand, stipulated that the second and third unequal degree should be treated like the third degree and thus as one where no dispensation was necessary.[82] As a result, skirmishes and uncertainty also arose in this regard. The ordinance of 11 May 1782 had mentioned marriage impediments adjacent to the second degree but refrained from demanding that Rome also cede dispensation authority in these cases.[83] And on this basis, the Prince-Bishop of Brixen attempted to continue handling such couple configurations according to church logics and norms.[84] The Bishop of Augsburg was sent instructions to "pose no further obstacles" to the unequal second- and third-degree relatives Simon Maldoner and Ursula Lechleitnerin from Stanzach in the Lech Valley, since this degree was "outside of those marriage impediments that require dispensation by the diocesan consistories". In order to make this request more

80 TLA Innsbruck, Jüngeres Gubernium, Hauptgruppe 64 Ehesachen, 1797–1798, Fasc. no. 314, 1798, no. 14.

81 TLA Innsbruck, Jüngeres Gubernium, Hauptgruppe 57 Placetum Regium, 1786–1789, Fasc. no. 1.621, 1788, no. 19.

82 The Bishop of Brixen obtained assurance regarding the church position from the agent Giorgio Merenda in Rome, who confirmed to him that it was generally agreed that the more distant degree "is pulled towards" the closer one. "In tanto io le dirò, che sembra ad ogni uno insussistente secondo il Gius commune, come in deto foglio Pro-memoria, che il grado più remoto tragga a se il più prossimo. Tutti bensì convengono, che il più prossimo grado trae a se il più remoto, e siccome, quando nel grado terzo concorre il secondo, questo è il più prossimo, cosi il secondo deve tirare a se il terzo perché il più rimoto e con distinto ossequio mi confermo." DIÖAB, Konsistorialcodices Romana, ab anno 1764 inclusive Mense Majo usque ad annum 1861, pp. 151–152, 152.

83 Ordinance of 11 May 1782, in *Sammlung in Publico-Ecclesiasticis vom Jahre 1767 bis Ende 1782*, pp. 203–205, 203–204.

84 Cf. TLA Innsbruck, Protocolla cum Indice in Geistlichen Co[mmissi]ons-Sachen vom ersten Jänner bis Ende Juni 1784, 17 March 1784, fol. 299.

convincing, the bishop was threatened with "the imposition of punitive measures" should he fail to comply.[85]

Given the extent of the diocesan territories subject to the *Gubernium* in Innsbruck and the relative commonness of marriage projects in the third and fourth degrees, rather few complaints actually reached the provincial government. Some grievances probably got stuck at the lower administrative levels. And who were the people who complained? Sebastian Hueber from the market town of Innichen, who had turned with his complaint to the *Gubernium* as quoted above, may well have been representative of this apparently rather small group. He was a merchant from a well-regarded family in his town, and his father, grandfather, brothers and cousins had spent decades and generations performing various functions at the regional court: as court officials, apprentice clerks and scribes. He was hence surrounded by relatives who were quite familiar with law, legal innovations and proceedings.[86]

In April 1791, eight years after the Marriage Patent's introduction, Joseph II's successor Leopold II (1790–1792) had an evaluation performed in reaction to various complaints emanating from the bishops. The resulting report indicated that alongside promises of marriage, dispensations in the prohibited degrees were the area affected by the Marriage Patent that was causing the greatest amount of difficulty. It ascertained that "secular authorities are now actually wielding their exclusive power over this civil contractual matter" and that this exercise of power only extended up to and including the second collateral degree. Despite this ascertainment, there does seem to have been discussion as to whether it made sense to leave things that way. Ultimately, however, the report found it "inadvisable to now once again extend prohibitions to further degrees than are specified in the Marriage Patent, for such inconsistency, as it were, would expose itself, seeming as if born of doubt regarding the legitimacy of exclusive lawgiving authority on this point and hence seeking remediation by bringing secular law into unison with formerly valid canon law; furthermore, such a step would in part serve to provoke nothing but suspicion and unease with regard to marriages concluded in those degrees that had been legally permitted during the intervening eight years; and on the other hand, there is no sufficient reason in and of itself to once again disrupt the existing

85 TLA Innsbruck, Protocolla cum Indice in Geistlichen Co[mmissi]ons-Sachen vom 1. Juli 1785 bis Ende Juni 1786, 12 November 1785, fol. 1819.

86 On this cf. also Margareth Lanzinger, "Von der Macht der Linie zur Gegenseitigkeit Heiratskontrakte in den Südtiroler Gerichten Welsberg und Innichen 1750–1850", in Margareth Lanzinger, Gunda Barth-Scalmani, Ellinor Forster and Gertrude Langer-Ostrawsky, *Aushandeln von Ehe. Heiratsverträge der Neuzeit im europäischen Vergleich*, 2nd ed. (Cologne/Weimar/Vienna, 2015), pp. 205–326, 210–212.

freedom in terms of what is now legally permitted".[87] Changing the rules laid down in the Marriage Patent, this line of argument held, would have served primarily to damage general esteem for civil law and the lawgiver while also giving rise to new uncertainties.

In his history of Austrian marital law, Adalbert Theodor Michel wrote on Tyrol that "there were several cases in which clerical opposition to secular marriage laws made necessary intervention by the highest government bodies and even the emperor himself" – and before providing an example, he ascertained: "Here, however, the resulting intervention was strict. When, namely, the Bishop of Augsburg (1794) forbade a priest to wed a couple related in the 3rd degree touching the 2nd without a dispensation from the Church, the emperor contradicted the opinion of the *Direktorium* – which had requested permission to impose forceful sanctions on the bishop – and commanded that the priest's access to his temporalities be blocked until he had provided his priestly blessing."[88] A court decree of November 1783 had actually mandated that bishops' access to their temporalities – these being the worldly rights and incomes associated with a church office – be blocked if they refused to grant dispensations to those couples who were permitted to marry according to the Marriage Patent.[89] Ascertaining the extent to which this occurred would require a separate investigation.[90]

---

87 ÖSTA, Allgemeines Verwaltungsarchiv (AVA), Alter Cultus, Ehesachen und Taufen, K. 9, 1781–1805, no. 851, fol. 5–5'. This report's final version can be found under the title, "Kolowrat an Leopold II: Über die Zuständigkeit des Staates in Eheangelegenheiten" [Kolowrat to Leopold II: On the Competence of the State in Matters of Marriage], final draft of 26 June 1791, in: Ferdinand Maaß, *Der Josephinismus. Quellen zu seiner Geschichte in Österreich 1760–1850. Amtliche Dokumente aus dem Haus-, Hof- und Staatsarchiv und dem Allgemeinen Verwaltungsarchiv in Vienna*, vol. 4: Der Spätjosephinismus 1790–1820 (Vienna, 1957), pp. 224–230, 227.

88 Michel, *Beiträge zur Geschichte*, pp. 39–40.

89 Cf. TLA Innsbruck, Protocolla in Geistlichen Co[mmissi]ons-Sachen vom 19. Februar bis Ende Dezember 1783, fol. 847, no. 2.678. One finds a reference here to a court decree of 1 November, presented on 12 November. Cf. also the ordinance of 4 September 1781, in: *Sammlung in Publico-Ecclesiasticis vom Jahre 1767 bis Ende 1782*, pp. 132–133, 133.

90 In Michel, *Beiträge zur Geschichte*, pp. 85–88 (here: 85–86), a "Lecture of the Imperial-Royal Directorium" of 18 May 1797 is printed that makes a theme of this question in light of a dispensation that the Viennese "Cardinal-Archbishop" had refused to grant on his own authority due to "timidness of conscience"; this lecture allows us to make out the associated ambivalences. In a man "over 80 years old", it holds, this should not be considered "recalcitrance", since he will have simply found it difficult to depart from "preconceived opinions". In a case of conscience, it continued, "blockage of access to temporalities" would be a "problematic step" – "particularly in our times, where the clergy and their chief overseer deserve that all reasonable measures be taken to spare them in the eyes of the people". Regarding the priest, the "blockage of his incomes would be even

The Josephine Code of 1786 upheld the rules contained in the Marriage Patent. Regarding the case of collateral kin, article 17 of its third part stipulated that the "inability" to marry was to extend no further than "to marriage between brother and sister, then between a brother and the daughter of his brother or sister, as well as between a sister and the son of her brother or sister, and to marriage between the children of siblings". Parallel to this, article 19 lists the marriage prohibitions affecting affinal kin. No reference is made to church dispensations, however, not even in connection with the close degrees.[91] According to article 20, in cases where "very important reasons are present" that would make such a marriage "advisable", it should be "always brought to the attention of the provincial government, whose decisions are to be complied with".[92] In the Marriage Patent of 1783, this passage regarding notification of the provincial government had continued as follows: "and only upon having received permission from the same may a sacred court then be turned to".[93] These divergent formulations once again illustrate how the rule itself had not changed while the associated administrative procedures indeed had within just a few short years.

4 Authorisations to Dispense: Divergent and Conflicting Logics

The move to narrow the scope of the obligation to obtain a dispensation to the second degree weighed less than a further mandate contained in the

---

more inappropriate", since he was merely obeying the command of his superior. He would thereby be induced, "by way of political compulsion, to disobey" his superior, a "precarious collision" that should be "avoided by a wise civil administration in any way possible".

91 Thomas Dolliner writes that this "silence on the part of the law" was out of an intent to "remove the point of reference" that clergymen "had previously had in cases of importunate applications to obtain a spiritual dispensation for abolished canonical marriage impediments". At the same time, there was also an intent to "gradually expunge the memory of these defunct marriage impediments, in this way clearing away the previous fodder for uneasiness of conscience among unknowing bridal couples". Dolliner's assessment of the effect here is sober: he remarks that the third chapter of the Josephine Code had "not been particularly well advertised" to the clergy. "They hence took no note …". Dolliner, "Erläuterung des 83. §", p. 71.

92 Josephine Code or General Civil Code, Patent of 1 November 1786, in *Joseph des Zweyten Römischen Kaysers Gesetze und Verfassungen im Justiz-Fache. Für Böhmen, Mähren, Schlesien, Oesterreich ob und unter der Enns, Steyermark, Kärnthen, Krain, Görz, Gradisca, Triest, Tyrol und die Vorlande. In dem sechsten Jahre seiner Regierung*. Jahrgang von 1786 bis 1786, 2. Fortsetzung 1786 (Vienna, 1817), no. 591, pp. 71–129.

93 Marriage Patent of 1783, § 16. The previously mentioned report for Leopold II (originally dated 30 April 1791) pointed out this inconsistency. ÖSTA, AVA, Alter Cultus, Ehesachen und Taufen, Karton 9, 1781–1805, no. 851, fol. 6; Maaß, *Der Josephinismus*, vol. 4, pp. 224–230, 227.

Marriage Patent: it provided that bishops were to grant dispensations in the close degrees on their own authority, circumventing the papal authorities in Rome. The arguments raised on the secular end were financial in nature: it was pointed out that flows of money to the pope – that is, abroad – were to be eliminated. However, the primary aim behind empowering and obligating the bishops to dispense on their own authority in the close degrees was to reduce the influence of the pope and hence of a "foreign" jurisdiction.[94] Even prior to the Marriage Patent, there had been ordinances pointing in this direction: an ordinance of September 1781 instructed the bishops on the basis of "provincial government power" that they were "from now on to dispense" in matters of marriage "*jure proprio* if reasons are present and, insofar as no impediment stemming from divine or natural law pertains", in all cases of "other canonical impediments" in return for moderate registry fees and "without waiting for a papal or other dispensation". The argument in favour of this held that it was "a matter of immense urgency to the state, for the most imperative reasons, that the bishops suitably employ their God-given powers of office". The "best interest of the state" demanded that bishops "exercise their office alone" in these matters, doing so "free from any foreign influence".[95] An ordinance of May 1782 called upon the bishops to obtain for themselves certain authorities of dispensation for the rest of their lives, authorities that would cover all of Roman dispensation logic's socially stratified categories: for the higher-ranking "nobiles & ditiores" in the prohibited degrees of consanguinity and affinity as well as for the general populace in the usual form "Forma consueta" – meaning in the fourth and third degrees, as this had already been the case "pro Pauperibus", for the "poor".[96] This group encompassed all people who earned a living through their own labour.

In his study, Peter Hersche counts "the state-church relationship, externally relevant questions of jurisdiction and church organisation and the 'abduction of funds' to Rome for taxes and dispensations" as being among those "things that older research, which concentrated on political issues and paid little attention to cultural history, often placed all too far in the foreground". In Catholic states, reformed absolutism battled the Baroque "as a matter of principle, with determination and in all areas" in the interest of achieving the exact opposite of a culture of "leisure and waste", which represented the central target of its

94 Examined from a political and diplomatic perspective in Mühlsteiger, *Der Geist des Josephinischen Eherechtes*, pp. 36–41, 48–73.

95 Ordinance of 4 September 1781, in *Sammlung in Publico-Ecclesiasticis vom Jahre 1767 bis Ende 1782*, pp. 132–133, 132.

96 Ordinance of 11 May 1782, in *Sammlung in Publico-Ecclesiasticis vom Jahre 1767 bis Ende 1782*, pp. 203–205, 203–204.

reform efforts.[97] In this conception, papal dispensations probably fell into the category of "waste". The Church, for its part, likely viewed marriage prohibitions as a norm that it needed to convey not only in terms of content but also in terms of form. After all, the secular demand for episcopal powers of dispensation degraded the significance of marriage prohibitions in the close degrees, putting them practically on a par with the third and fourth degrees. As a result, it made for a simpler procedure. It is fair to assume that this, in the Church's point of view, diminished the weight and implications of the dispensations themselves and hence the prohibition of kin marriage as well as the associated definition of incest. The act of mercy and its exceptional character[98] likewise waned in significance due to this elimination of administrative effort and the associated costs. In the symbolic realm, these elements were critical to the representation of ecclesiastical power and the attendant monopoly on the administration of mercy – and a diocesan ordinariate was hardly in a position to stage something comparable.

Viewing papal dispensations simply in terms of unnecessary effort and wasted money obscures both the cultural dimension of this phenomenon and the significance attributed to marriage prohibitions and hence marriage itself in the logic of those times. The fact that a dispensation could be achieved only with effort and capital outlay – and, even then, was anything but a sure thing – was certainly meant to dissuade and deter people from making such requests.[99] On the other hand, an act of mercy wrung from the hands of this institution was fit to evoke a feeling of eternal gratitude and indebtedness. This, in turn, benefitted the Church in the form of symbolic and material acknowledgement. It thus ultimately had the effect of propping up the system, something that the Church doubtless also intended. To be sure, official justifications surrounding the question of dispensation authority were dominated by legal and political positions on both sides. The legal discussion revolved around matters including the question of whether a provincial government was permitted to

97 Hersche, *Muße und Verschwendung*, vol. 2, p. 977.

98 The state viewed the "power to make an exception" as a power that could not be done without. This is evident in the April 1791 report to Emperor Leopold II mentioned earlier, which held that it would be "salubrious" for absolutely no more provincial government dispensations to be granted in the prohibited degrees in order to accustom "the people that much more to observing the law", although it ultimately refrained from recommending this "since it would be unseemly for the law to be written such that the lawgiver denies himself all power to make an exception". ÖSTA, AVA, Alter Cultus, Ehesachen und Taufen, Karton 9, 1781–1805, no. 851, fol. 7; Maaß, *Der Josephinismus*, vol. 4, pp. 224–230, 227.

99 Cf. Brandhuber von Etschfeld, *Über Dispensation und Dispensationsrecht*, p. 83.

intervene in laws not of its own making.[100] Canon law authorities spoke out unequivocally against this: the laws of the Church, they held, had been decreed by the popes. "Who, then, should have the right to dispense from universally valid church laws if not the pope?"[101]

Within the Church, the rules that specified the couple configurations for which dispensation requests had to be sent to Rome and those for which such requests could be handled by bishops were generally not uniform. Instead they depended on which powers had been delegated by the pope to each individual bishop. Popes had been delegating various dispensatory powers to the bishops since the seventeenth century.[102] In certain territories, the respective authorisations were regularly granted. In German lands, these authorisations were valid for five years each; in the Austrian territories, they were at first granted for periods determined by the Propaganda Fide and thereafter likewise for five years at a time. This is why they were referred to as "quinquennial faculties".[103] The extent of the dispensation authorities delegated to bishops would seem to have depended on multiple factors: on the rank of the bishop[104] and especially on conditions in the diocese – such as being on an island or far from Rome or characterised by a specific situation, as was the case in confessionally mixed territories and in so-called mission areas.

---

100 On this cf. for example a contemporary dissertation that defends provincial governments' right to do so: *Ernst Valentin Schwaigers rechtliche Abhandlung*.

101 Brandhuber von Etschfeld, *Über Dispensation und Dispensationsrecht*, p. 43. This is also emphasised by Johann Kutschker in the fifth volume of his work on marital law, which was published in 1857 – after the Concordat had entered effect. Johann Kutschker, *Das Eherecht der katholischen Kirche nach seiner Theorie und Praxis mit besonderer Berücksichtigung der in Österreich zu Recht bestehenden Gesetze*, vol. 5 (Vienna, 1857), pp. 3–4.

102 Cf. Brandhuber von Etschfeld, *Über Dispensation und Dispensationsrecht*, pp. 53–61; on the dispensation authorities of bishops cf. also Kutschker, *Das Eherecht der katholischen Kirche*, vol. 5, pp. 9–18.

103 Cf. Brandhuber von Etschfeld, *Über Dispensation und Dispensationsrecht*, p. 56; cf. also Kutschker, *Das Eherecht der katholischen Kirche*, vol. 5, pp. 40–70. The German quinquennial faculties can be traced back to the *facultates septemtrionales*, which the Jesuits were granted as 'Counter-Reformatory authorities' for Germany. Bishops' and nuncios' faculties likewise number among their predecessors. Cf. Mergentheim, *Die Quinquennalfakultäten*, p. 28, 31. On the procedure of compiling lists of assigned faculties (*formulae*) for the various dioceses that took place at a congregation that convened in 1634 to make revisions cf. ibid., pp. 68–80 as well as ibid., pp. 83–111 on the *formula* x and the quinquennial text for the German lands.

104 Mergentheim, for example, points out that the seventeenth century saw the Bishop and Cardinal of Augsburg as well as the Bishop and Cardinal of Trento "delegated a pure privilege, containing marriage dispensations, among other things", on account of their "outstanding political position in the Church". Mergentheim, *Die Quinquennalfakultäten*, pp. 85–88.

Chur's Bishop Heinrich von Hewen (1491–1509), for example, was invested with the authority to grant marriage dispensations in the third and fourth degrees of consanguinity and affinity early on. The stated reasons for this were classic: the remote communities nestled in the diocese's mountains and forests, the population's inexperience and lack of knowledge in legal matters and a degree of poverty that made it impossible for them to turn to the Roman Curia. An additional argument was the worry, inseparably linked with the history of marriage prohibitions and dispensations, that men would enter into marriages in the prohibited degrees despite their being forbidden and use these marriages' legal invalidity as an excuse to separate from their brides later on, giving rise to sensation and scandal.[105] Such authorisations usually, as was the case in Chur, included the authority to dispense in the third and fourth degrees – *pro pauperibus*, for the broader populace. Beyond such commonly granted authorities, bishops were also permitted to dispense in cases of the "interruption of communications with the Holy See", that is when a dispensation request could only be sent to the papal authorities with great difficulty or in urgent cases where a delay would entail serious or irreversible harm.[106] Particularly this last point left open a discretionary margin that should not be underestimated – provided there was a will to exploit it.

The special conditions that justified expanded ecclesiastical dispensation authorities included remoteness. A well-known case of this type was Corsica. It was an "abuso gravissimo", a highly serious abuse, as one missionary described the frequently seen practice there of marriages between close relatives as early as the sixteenth century.[107] But it was especially "mission areas", *terrae missionis*, that were equipped with particular rights, rights that extended far back through history, in order to avoid endangering the success of their missionary

105 "In civitate et dyocesi Curiensi et eiusdem dyocesis locis montuosis et silvestribus habitant quamplures rudes et iuris ignari [...] vel propter paupertatem et impossibilitatem ex certis causis accendendum ad curiam romanam aut alias, pocius in sic de facto contractis matrimoniis remanent, quam quod ab eorum uxoribus se separere velint, eciam propter scandala, que exinde subsequerentur [...]." Cf. Copia dispensandi in tercio et quarto gradibus, printed as a supplement in Oskar Vasella, "Untersuchungen über die Bildungsverhältnisse im Bistum Chur mit besonderer Berücksichtigung des Klerus. Vom Ausgang des 13. Jahrhunderts bis um 1530", *Jahresbericht der Historisch-Antiquarischen Gesellschaft von Graubünden* 62 (1932), 1–211, 183–184. Michel, in *Beiträge zur Geschichte*, p. 62, writes that the bishops and archbishops in the "German-Slavic provinces" of Austria possessed "far-reaching *Facultates dispensandi*" and use these "mostly such that the parties had to incur neither noteworthy investments of money and time nor any inconvenience".

106 Brandhuber von Etschfeld, *Über Dispensation und Dispensationsrecht*, p. 62.

107 Adriano Prosperi, *Tribunali della coscienza. Inquisitori, confessori, missionari* (Turin, 1996), p. 656.

work.[108] This also entailed "certain relaxations" with regard to marriage and especially marriage prohibitions associated with consanguinity and affinity.[109] Such relaxations were based on a legal understanding according to which the salvation of souls, *salus animarum*, was the Church's primary aim. Generally applicable rules and principles could therefore be relaxed in order to achieve this objective wherever local conditions made it necessary.

To those who had converted to Catholicism "in the distant districts of the Saracen and heathen lands", the so-called neophytes, a Jesuit faculty of 1549 was applied. It provided which dispensations could be granted for marriages that had already been concluded in the prohibited degrees, albeit not for those that had been concluded against divine law: "in gradibus illicitis non contra ius divinum de iam contractis dispensari posse".[110] In 1563, Pius IV (1559–1565) expanded this exception further: in India and in the Orient as a whole, it was also to be valid for new marriage projects.[111] Alexander VIII (1689–1691) excepted the first degree of consanguinity and affinity from this exemption with an explicit ban. Clement XII (1730–1740) made possible dispensations in the first degree of affinity "ex illicita copula in linea recta", at first only if they fell within the *forum conscientiae* – the realm of conscience.[112] Later on, this authority was expanded to apply generally. The French Capuchins in Brazil,

108 Cf. Mergentheim, *Die Quinquennalfakultäten*, pp. 13–16; Bendetta Albani, *Sposarsi nel nuovo mondo. Politica, dottina e pratiche della concessione di dispense matrimoniali tra la Nuova Spagna e la Santa Sede (1585–1670)*, PhD thesis, Univesità degli Studi di Roma "Tor Vergata", 2008–2009.

109 Otto Mejer, *Die Propaganda, ihre Provinzen und ihr Recht. Mit besonderer Rücksicht auf Deutschland*, part 2 (Göttingen/Leipzig, 1853), p. 560. Gregory XV had founded the Propaganda Fide in 1622 as a congregation responsible for missionary work.

110 Divine law prohibited marriage in the ascending and descending straight line – that is, between parents, children, children's children, etc.

111 Mejer, *Die Propaganda*, p. 560.

112 Canon law distinguishes between a *forum externum* and a *forum internum*. The former relates to that which was brought before an ecclesiastical court or handled according to officially defined administrative procedures but was not subject to secrecy, while the *forum internum*, also called *forum conscientiae*, *forum poenitentiae* or *forum poenitentiale*, was internal to the Church. This is to say that, just like confession, it fell within the realm of conscience and penance and was immune to access by external parties such as state authorities. A detailed discussion of this can be found in Antonio Mostaza, "Forum internum – Forum externum. (En torno a la naturaleza jurídica del fuero interno)", *Revista española de derecho canonico* 23, 65 (1967), 253–331. Cf. also Gabriella Zarri, "Die tridentinische Ehe", in *Das Konzil von Trient und die Moderne*, ed. Paolo Prodi (Berlin, 2001), pp. 343–379, 377–378. She concludes that the secularisation of marriage and hence the post-Tridentine growth of the Church's power over the *forum conscientiae* were interrelated. "Control over conscience lends church authority great power over the institution of marriage". Ibid., p. 378. Adriano Prosperi, as well, discusses overlaps between access to

having found some among the "savages" who had "married entirely without regard to degree prohibitions", were given permission to grant dispensations all the way to the second collateral degree. This authority was also delegated to the Bishop of Québec in 1766. "It is this far that one goes in mission areas", was how Otto Mejer concluded his comments on expanded dispensation authorities. In a footnote, he adds that Breslau (Wrocław), Culm (Chełmno) and Posen (Poznań) had also been granted faculties extending inward to the second degree of consanguinity and to the first and second unequal degree of affinity, "but only in a certain number of cases".[113] During the nineteenth century, such contingents were also possessed by the confessionally mixed diocese of Chur.

According to Matthias Pulte, who has examined the retroactive effects of mission law on generally applicable church law, "the relaxation of marriage prohibitions based on consanguinity and affinity" was "of outstanding significance for the project of spreading the faith" in mission areas.[114] In connection with eased dispensation-granting, mention should be made of faculties that could include the granting of marriage dispensations – usually in certain degrees and in specified numbers – with which legates and nuncios are documented to have been invested since the Middle Ages.[115] Regarding delegated and sub-delegated dispensation authorities, Paolo Ostinelli emphasises "the ramification of the canon law system" and points to the continual relationship between the centre and the periphery.[116] Possible retroactive effects on the centre would also be worth querying. But whatever the case may have been, these parallel structures were targeted for elimination in late eighteenth-century Austria. The dispute concerning nunciatures – and, above all, concerning nunciatures' jurisdiction – as permanent representatives of the Holy See was thus

---

the consciences of the flock and power politics in his chapter entitled "Foro interno, foro esterno". Prosperi, *Tribunali della coscienza*, pp. 476–484.

113 Mejer, *Die Propaganda*, pp. 560–561.

114 Mattias Pulte, *Das Missionsrecht ein Vorreiter des universalen Kirchenrechts. Rechtliche Einflüsse aus den Missionen auf die konziliare und nachkonziliare Gesetzgebung der lateinischen Kirche* (Nettetal, 2006), p. 203.

115 Cf. Schmugge, *Ehen vor Gericht*, pp. 34–35; more general and with references to further literature is Werner Maleczek, "Die päpstlichen Legaten im 14. und 15. Jahrhundert", in *Gesandtschafts- und Botenwesen im spätmittelalterlichen Europa*, ed. Rainer C. Schwinges and Klaus Wriedt (Ostfildern, 2003), pp. 33–86; Paolo Ostinelli, "L'offerta della grazia. Dispense e assoluzioni concesse da vescovi e inviati pontifici in Lombardia nel xv secolo", in *Päpste, Pilger, Pönitentiarie. Festschrift für Ludwig Schmugge zum 65. Geburtstag*, ed. Andreas Meyer, Constanze Rendtel and Maria Wittmer-Butsch (Tübingen, 2004), pp. 531–549.

116 Ostinelli, "L'offerta della grazia", pp. 532–533, 541–544.

part of the conflict over dispensation authorities[117] and had a massive effect on actual dispensation practice.

Part and parcel of the "Nunciature dispute" were conflicts over whether bishops were authorised to dispense in the close degrees or, conversely, this authority constituted a reserved right of the pope. Alongside Joseph II, several German bishops – the Archbishops of Mainz,[118] Cologne and Trier as well as the Archbishop of Salzburg[119] – had taken up this position even earlier on as part of their push for a state church that would be more independent of

117 The complaints against the Curia's claims to authority voiced in 1769 by the bishops of Trier, Mainz and Cologne included criticism of the papal right "to maintain nunciatures in Germany that are equipped with various authorities that interfere with those of the episcopate". They held that the nunciatures should limit themselves to diplomatic representation. And in 1785, when Pius VI established a permanent nunciature in Munich that affected the jurisdictional powers of 17 bishops, there arose the so-called Nunciature dispute in which the Bishops of Mainz and Salzburg played key roles. The emperor intervened in Rome, which reacted "with both surprise and consternation". The demand to eliminate the nunciatures or at least their jurisdiction was also made in the 1786 *Punctation of Ems*. Alfred Stefan Weiß, "'Dem Pabste brach darüber das Herz ...'. Salzburgs Beziehungen zu Rom unter Erzbischof Colloredo – ein gespanntes Verhältnis?", in *Salzburg und der Heilige Stuhl im 19. und 20. Jahrhundert. Festgabe zum 75. Geburtstag von Erzbischof Georg Eder*, ed. Hans Paarhammer and Alfred Rinnerthaler (Frankfurt a. M. et al., 2003), pp. 433–460, 443–453; Burkhard Roberg, "Verkehrung der Fronten? Bartolomeo Pacca und der Nuntiaturstreit 1785–1794", in *Kurie und Politik. Stand und Perspektiven der Nuntiaturforschung*, ed. Alexander Koller (Tübingen, 1998), pp. 376–394; Pierre Blet, *Histoire de la représentation diplomatique du Saint Siège des origines a l'aube du XIXe siècle* (Città del Vaticano, 1982), chapter 20. For a general look at the climate of mind cf. Umberto Dell'Orto, "Die Wiener Nuntiatur im 18. Jahrhundert unter besonderer Berücksichtigung der Nuntiatur von Giuseppe Garampi (1776–1785)", in *Kurie und Politik*, ed. Koller, pp. 175–207.

118 Cf. Georg May, *Die Auseinandersetzungen zwischen den Mainzer Erzbischöfen und dem Heiligen Stuhl um die Dispensbefugnis im 18. Jahrhundert* (Frankfurt a. M. et al., 2007).

119 Salzburg's Archbishop Colloredo became "a driving force behind the German episcopalistic-national church movement". At the Congress of Ems in 1786, it was Salzburg that pushed "most radically for a decidedly episcopalist programme aimed at the rigorous limitation of papal power". The *Punctation* formulated on this occasion regarding church reform, though it "did correspond to the emperor's plans for a state church in many respects", was ultimately not implemented. The emperor's involvement in this matter was only half-hearted, "since he also had to fear condemnation of his efforts towards a state church". Alfred Stefan Weiß, "Josephinismus in Salzburg? Ein Beispiel der kirchlichen Reformtätigkeit", in *Josephinismus – eine Bilanz*, ed. Schmale/Zedinger/Mondot, pp. 93–114, 100–101; cf. also Ludwig Hammermayer, "Die letzte Epoche des Erzstifts Salzburg. Politik und Kirchenpolitik unter Erzbischof Graf Hieronymus Colloredo (1772–1803)", in *Geschichte Salzburgs. Stadt und Land*, vol. II/2, ed. Heinz Dopsch and Hans Spatzenegger (Salzburg, 1988), pp. 453–535, 464–470.

Rome.[120] In support of the dispensation authority that they demanded, they argued based on history[121] and, consistently, in the same vein as the 1788 tract on *Justifying the Actions of the Four German Archbishops Counter to the Impositions of the Roman Court*. This document refers to an "episcopal era" and "pure church discipline in the handling of dispensations". "Just as every bishop has been entrusted by God himself with the governance of his Church in order that he directly exercise spiritual power over his flock; as he knows best the needs of his sheep, knows by which means they can be helped, and has, as it were, everything in view; nothing would be more natural than for the bishops themselves to make exceptions to the law in urgent cases or to dispense, just as they did in the initial centuries of the Christian Church, during which apostolic simplicity and pure church discipline blossomed, where the generally held view was that every matter must be settled in its own diocese or at least in its own province. Such cases were, of course, extremely rare, but there is nonetheless no shortage of examples."

Later on, the tract points out, the bishops had handled dispensation-related matters collectively at their annual synods – which changed nothing about their "original authority to dispense". "The bishops indeed did frequently report important dispensation cases to the pope; but certainly not because they failed to recognise their own authority to dispense and were waiting for

---

120 To summarise the events preceding this: Johann Nikolaus von Hontheim, the Bishop of Trier, had expressed the "desire to give rise to a German national system of church law similar to that of the Gallic Church" in his tract *De statu ecclesiae et legitima potestate Romane Pontificis liber singularis ad reuniendos dissidentes in religione christianos compositus*, which was published under the pseudonym of Justinus Febronius in 1763. The pope's authorities were to be limited to "representation and supervision, admonition and reprimand", which did not include the right to exercise powers of dispensation in dioceses other than his own. A further stage in this conflict, featuring an initial instance of collective action, was represented by the complaints of the imperial church regarding the Curia's claims to power brought forward by representatives of the Rhenish archdioceses of Trier, Mainz and Cologne under von Hontheim's leadership. Weiß, "Dem Pabste brach darüber das Herz", pp. 442–444; cf. also Franz Xaver Seppelt, *Papstgeschichte von den Anfängen bis zur Gegenwart*, 5th ed. (Munich, 1949), p. 276.

121 The same narrative, with reference to the French canonist Louis Thomassin (1619–1695), can also be found towards the end of the nineteenth century in the writings of Brandhuber von Etschfeld, for example, who viewed episcopalism as "merely a product of man's insatiable hubris". Brandhuber von Etschfeld, *Über Dispensation und Dispensationsrecht*, p. 50. His further chronology notes that the centralisation of dispensation law had been completed in thirteenth-century Rome and that the Gallic Church had begun opposing it as early as the sixteenth century (ibid., pp. 28–29). The Belgian canonist Zeger Bernhard van Espen (1646–1728), wrote von Etschfeld, was the first figure outside of France to oppose papal dispensation law. His student was Nikolaus von Hontheim, also known as Febronius (ibid., pp. 37–38).

Rome to do so." These reports much rather represented "a glorious monument to the care and circumspection that bishops brought to bear in dispensing". It was Innocent II (1198–1216), "thoroughly intoxicated with the consummate nature of his papal power", who "snatched" away dispensations for himself, which marked the beginning of dispensation authority's abuse and "a general corruption of morals".[122] This narrative conformed to the tenor of those efforts toward reforming the Church that had been ongoing from the late seventeenth century.[123]

Before this backdrop, the papacy of Pius VI (1775–1799) was marked by severe shocks: due to the French Revolution, secularisation measures and the split in the French Catholic Church that hung like a sword of Damocles over the conflicts within the Holy Roman Empire, due to episcopalist tendencies and not least due to Joseph II himself – with whom the "enlightened ideas had even ascended to the imperial throne". The papal history classic by Franz Xaver Seppelt refers to the pontificate of Pius VI as "the martyrdom of the papacy". Pius VI travelled to Vienna in 1782 with the intent of persuading the emperor to show greater consideration for church interests. While he was received with all due honours, the pope achieved "almost nothing of substance". Seppelt concludes: "The Josephine system was upheld unaltered."[124] Looking at the realm of marriage dispensations, however, this assessment becomes less clear.

Not all late eighteenth-century bishops took up a stance that was decidedly critical of the pope, least of all those who generally pursued Rome-oriented policies. What is more, even those who viewed reforms in a fundamentally positive light had their difficulties implementing secular requirements where dispensations were concerned. This was true of Prince-Bishop Joseph von Spaur

---

122 *Gründliche Entwicklung der Emser Dispens- und Nuntiaturstreitigkeiten zur Rechtfertigung des Verfahrens der vier deutschen Erzbischöfe wider die Anmaßungen des römischen Hofes samt einer Prüfung des Fürstbischöflich speyerischen Antwortschreibens an S.e. Kurfürstliche Gnaden zu Mainz in Betref* [*sic*] *der Emser Punkte* ([n.p.], 1788), pp. 65–67. In the 22 points of the *Punctation of Ems*, the bishops demanded "the independence of episcopal power from papal power, the elimination of exemptions and quinquennial faculties, the elimination of the nunciatures in their entirety or at least in terms of their competing jurisdiction, the bishops' right of disposal over pious foundations, an episcopal right of consent to papal bulls and briefs, and the settlement of church legal proceedings by domestic judges". Weiß, "Dem Pabste brach darüber das Herz", p. 449. On the previous history of papal primacy cf. the recent work Matthias Schrör, *Metropolitangewalt und papstgeschichtliche Wende* (Husum, 2009).

123 On this cf. Hersche, *Muße und Verschwendung*, vol. 2, pp. 952–1012. On the situation of the German Reich Church and the Church in France in the context of secularisation cf. Lönne, *Politischer Katholizismus*, pp. 31–50.

124 Seppelt, *Papstgeschichte*, pp. 276–277.

(1779–1791), for example, who has been characterised as "a decided Josephinist on the bishop's throne in Brixen"[125] and as a Jansenist[126] who, though he rejected the Enlightenment, ultimately did back Josephine measures.[127] In terms of dispensation practice, however, this view must be qualified. Spaur's successor, Karl Franz von Lodron (1791–1828), on the other hand, "notorious" at the Viennese Court Chancellery and at the *Gubernium* in Innsbruck "as a 'papalist' and as 'the Ultramontane'", "neither answered the letters of the provincial government nor complied with court decrees".[128]

The Marriage Patent plunged bishops of Lodron's persuasion, as well as those who were less opposed to Josephinism, into a conflict: as far as internal church logic was concerned, the call to dispense on one's own authority in close degrees would only have been legitimate on the basis of an authorisation granted by the pope. Bishops were therefore caught between two 'masters'. The new requirements also resulted in parallel structures within administrative procedures – and when diocesan consistories explored and tested out detours, civil authorities were forced to react. Last but not least, couples who requested marriage dispensations during this period found themselves in a double-bind between the differing logics of the Church and civil authorities. This situation confronted them with ever new imponderables as the administrative processes were repeatedly changed and adjusted after the fact. During this phase, the granting of dispensations frequently ground to a complete halt. As a consequence, two decades passed during which no routines of obtaining a marriage dispensation developed.

5 No More Dispensations from Rome?

In 1780, Brixen's Prince-Archbishop Joseph von Spaur was granted the right to dispense marriage projects between blood and affinal kin in the third and fourth equal and unequal degrees "cum pauperibus" – for the simple folk – as point three among the faculties delegated to him.[129] That same year, he applied to also be granted dispensatory authorities for the wealthy and the nobility that were mandated in the court decree of 11 May 1782, as he later explained in

125 Paul Rainer, *Die Diözese Brixen im Vormärz. Ein Beitrag zur Kirchengeschichte Tirols 1815–1848*, PhD thesis, University of Vienna, 1968, p. 14; cf. also Dell'Orto, *La nunziatura a Vienna*, p. 26.

126 Cf. Hersche, *Muße und Verschwendung*, vol. 2, p. 955.

127 Cf. Gelmi, *Geschichte der Kirche in Tirol*, pp. 225–229.

128 Rainer, *Die Diözese Brixen*, p. 16.

129 Cf. DIÖAB, Konsistorialcodices Romana, ab anno 1764, fos. 96–101, 97.

a detailed letter to the *Gubernium*.[130] In reaction to the Marriage Patent's entry into force in January 1783, he subsequently charged Giorgio Merenda, the agent in Rome with whom the consistory in Brixen maintained regular contact, with investigating whether it might be possible to have his faculties extended to the second and third unequal degree. In his March 1784 reply, Merenda voiced great scepticism in this regard. He wrote that he had spoken with the competent person, the "officiale deputato", at the Datary. This official had assured Merenda that he had heard nothing to the effect that such faculties had been conferred upon bishops in German territories. Merenda, not yet satisfied by this response, had gone on to enquire with the secretary responsible for the "Brevi ad Principes". This second official, as well, knew nothing of the pope's having granted such authorities to bishops in German-speaking territories. He had told him in confidence that if they were to be granted to one bishop, they would have to be granted to all others. From all this Merenda concluded that such a request would be "dangerous", which is why he had not made it and would also refrain from doing so unless explicitly instructed to.[131] This justificatory rhetoric makes clear the not entirely simple nature of the bishops' position between ecclesiastical and secular mandates. They were caught in the middle, between state and Church. What is more, this period prior to the early nineteenth-century secularisations saw the bishops of Brixen, Trento and Salzburg themselves playing a dual role, serving both as church representatives and territorial princes.

Inspection of the entries in Brixen's dispensation registers beginning in 1780 reveals that initially most dispensations in the second and third unequal degree had been granted by the nunciature in Vienna. From 1784 onward, however, there are only scattered indications of this, and it is fair to assume that the bishop himself saw to it beyond that point in time. These dispensations in the second and third unequal degree were mostly for couples from the territory of

---

130 Cf. TLA Innsbruck, Jüngeres Gubernium, Hauptgruppe 57 Placetum Regium, 1790–1793, Fasc. no. 1.622, 1790, no. 1. Cf. also DIÖAB, Konsistorialcodices Romana, ab anno 1764, pp. 123–129, 125.

131 "Il medesimo m'ha assicurato, che non è al di Lui Notizia, che ad alcuno de Vescovi della Germania sia stata mandata facoltà alcuna di dispensare sopra il grado in 3° quando tocca il Secondo. Non contento di ciò ho parlato con M[onsi]g[no]r Segretario de Brevi ad Principes per sentire dal medesimo se mai ad alcuno de Vescovi di Germania per Breve ad Principes fosse stata mandata dal Papa in dirittura una tal facoltà. Mi assicurò di nò. Il medesimo, con cui ho servitù particolare, in discorso mi disse, che se nostro Signore concede ad uno de Vescovi di Germania tal facoltà, deve indispensabilmente allora concederla a tutti li altri. Da ciò io deduco essere cosa assai pericolosa di fare una tal istanza; e questa io non ho fatta in vista di ciò, ne la farò senza ordine espresso". DIÖAB, Konsistorialcodices Romana, ab anno 1764, pp. 151–152.

the Prince-Bishopric of Brixen, in which church rules still applied rather than the state Marriage Patent.[132] This realm of episcopal jurisdiction is indicated in the dispensation registers next to the names of the concerned couples by the specifying remark: "Territorii Brixinensis".[133] Evidently, the Prince-Bishop of Brixen's authority to dispense had been expanded during this period.

For close degrees, bishops' decisions whether or not to turn to Rome for a dispensation were, for the time being, defined as a matter of conscience under civil law.[134] But this relaxation of the Marriage Patent's rules, which had already started in 1784, posed a problem – namely, that it was coupled with the issuance of a dispensation free of charge. In practice, fulfilment of this demand was impossible.[135] It was hence a point that opened up a further field of conflict. If the civil authorities approved the bishop's "intervening" in Rome, "free of charge" (*unentgeltlich*) was usually underlined for emphasis in the letters of the *Gubernium* and the Court Chancellery. Peter Beykircher, a peasant in Sistrans, had been notified by the ordinariate in Brixen that his dispensation could not be obtained for free. In light of this bleak situation, he appealed – in vain – to "the provincial government's consummate power", on the basis of

---

132 Late eighteenth-century state regulations, including the various provisions of the Marriage Patent, only applied to Austrian subjects – who, during the period under study, included the inhabitants of the Oberinntal, Unterinntal and Wipptal districts, as well as those of Puster Valley, Burggrafenamt and Vinschgau, An Etsch and Eisack and finally An den Welschen Konfinen with its seat in Rovereto. They did not apply to those who resided within the territorial domains of the three ecclesiastical principalities, these being the Prince-Bishoprics of Brixen and Trento and the Prince-Archbishopric of Salzburg.

133 DIÖAB, Dispensationes matrimoniales ab anno 1774 usque ad annum 1794 inclusive, pp. 193–195; ibid., Dispensationes matrimoniales ab anno 1795 usque ad annum 1829 inclusive, 1–3.

134 Cf. TLA Innsbruck, Jüngeres Gubernium, Geistliche Sachen, Fasc. 433, 1784, Akten, no. 1,282 and, almost identically, no. 6,546: "Since, moreover, every bishop is free to dispose over all this himself or have Rome dispose over it, as he sees fit in accordance with his conscience, without His Majesty demanding a reckoning insofar as nothing counter to his declared supreme will be done, […]."

135 Adalbert Theodor Michel, looking back, writes that the "elimination of these 'payments sent abroad'" was suggested, "but dropped at the behest of the *Directorium* on 4 July 1794". Official reports from Count Heržan, the ambassador in Rome, indicate that it had been "by no means established" in the agreement reached between Pius VI and Joseph II in 1782 "that the marriage dispensations still reserved to the pope should simply be issued free of charged by the Apostolic Penitentiary". It was also emphasised, writes Michel, "that the fees sent to Rome from all over Austria, averaged over several years, amounted to the paltry total of just 1,000 scudi annually, while all other Catholic countries sent incomparably greater sums there – with Portugal paying 12,000 scudi and Spain double that amount in just a single month". Michel, *Beiträge zur Geschichte*, p. 39.

which he requested that his "permission to marry" be granted.[136] But as an internal report of the *Gubernium* had noted earlier on in October 1796, such cases permitted no more than a terse conclusion: if the marriage dispensation could not be obtained free of charge in Rome and the bishop was unwilling to grant it on his own authority, the "parties' requests" would have to "be refused".[137]

The Prince-Bishop of Brixen held fast to his position, explaining in a lengthy letter of 1790 how he could "not grant" a dispensation in the second degree "without giving insult to the Holy See".[138] In this, he was not alone. That same year, Vienna once again issued an order to all ordinariates, district offices and the municipal administration of Innsbruck. It provided that bishops were *required* to dispense on their own authority. This came in reaction to a letter from the consistory in Salzburg, which – years after the Marriage Patent's entry into force – had requested clarification regarding the currently valid ordinances.[139] In the dioceses of Trento and Chur, it was likewise the case that neither the Marriage Patent's rules on dispensations nor related court decrees and ordinances were adhered to without further ado.

As a consequence, it was difficult during these years to assess one's chances of being granted a dispensation. The answers from the *Gubernium* in Innsbruck typically amounted to no more than a standardised reply instructing the couple to first ask the competent diocesan ordinariate for its written pledge to grant them their dispensation on its own authority. This pledge, however, was typically withheld. The Prince-Bishop of Brixen's tireless refrain was much rather that it was not in his power to dispense in the first and second degrees. The Bishop of Chur likewise had "qualms about [granting] supplicants dispensations on the authority of his own ordinariate" and requested permission

136 TLA Innsbruck, Jüngeres Gubernium, Hauptgruppe 64 Ehesachen, 1799–1800, Fasc. no. 315, 1798, no. 12.

137 TLA Innsbruck, Jüngeres Gubernium, Hauptgruppe 64 Ehesachen, 1796, Fasc. no. 313, no. 40. Here, the *Gubernium* had sent Brixen the following response: "It cannot be permitted that the parties be financially burdened in the case of marriage dispensations such as requested by Sebastian Tusch. If it, therefore, were impossible to obtain the dispensation from Rome, and the Most Reverend Prince-Bishop of Brixen wished not to use his own power to dispense, as is done by so many other ordinaries without a second thought, the requests of those supplicants who desire dispensation would be refused – as must necessarily occur if an episcopal or a gratuitous Roman dispensation is not granted."

138 TLA Innsbruck, Jüngeres Gubernium, Hauptgruppe 57 Placetum Regium, 1790–1793, Fasc. no. 1.622, 1790, no. 1, report: "Geistliche Sache" [Spiritual Matter] of 25 February 1790. The associated dispensation proceedings for Karl Anton Weller of Sterzing had already been underway for four years.

139 Cf. ibid., no. 7, letter of the Salzburg consistory dated 10 March 1790.

to obtain them in Rome.[140] In a similar vein, the civil authorities in Trento reported that the prince-bishop had "refused to dispense on the authority of his own ordinariate". This prompted the representatives of the district office in Rovereto to laconically conclude: "If a bishop does not know his own episcopal rights and doubts the power to which he is actually entitled in accordance with true canonical principles, then the district office can do nothing but hope that he may be enlightened by God's anointed ones."[141]

Franz von Riccabona, deputy to district captain Anton von Zoller at the district office in Bozen, put the dilemma faced by supplicant couples in a nutshell. In reference to a complaint filed by a couple whose request had been effectively refused through its blockage at the submission stage he wrote: "For they say that if the political authorities, for their part, only act on such dispensation requests once the bishop has granted the church dispensation in advance and on his own authority, and if the bishop, for his part, holds that he has no right to grant this marriage dispensation, the result is that such a marriage dispensation is rendered an impossibility." He concluded that one could hardly "fail to comprehend" such a complaint.[142] In the period that followed, however, dispensations from Trento did indeed turn up – albeit absent the required formulation that they had been granted "on the ordinariate's own authority".[143] Strategies of circumvention were beginning to take hold.

One way of granting a dispensation without giving "insult" to Rome was to have Rome delegate dispensation authorities.[144] This was something the state had by no means intended. The initial responses to this around 1790 were quite strict, but the Court Chancellery in Vienna soon did prove willing to accept this to a certain extent. Thomas Dolliner associated the possibility of delegated papal authority with as early an event as Pius VI's 1782 visit to Vienna, and he characterised it as "regressive" from the standpoint of civil law. Such "regression" had become necessary, he wrote, because the "enforcement" of the state ordinances had faced "unspeakable difficulties stemming from the timidity of the bishops and the prejudices of priests and the people".[145]

140 Ibid., no. 24.

141 TLA Innsbruck, Jüngeres Gubernium, Hauptgruppe 57 Placetum Regium, 1790–1793, Fasc. no. 1.622, 1791, no. 1.

142 TLA Innsbruck, Jüngeres Gubernium, Hauptgruppe 64 Ehesachen, 1796, Fasc. no. 313, no. 2.

143 Cf. TLA Innsbruck, Jüngeres Gubernium, Hauptgruppe 57 Placetum Regium, 1790–1793, Fasc. no. 1.622, 1791, no. 20.

144 On the delegation of dispensatory authority cf. Brandhuber von Etschfeld, *Über Dispensation und Dispensationsrecht*, pp. 53–72.

145 Dolliner, "Erläuterung des 83. §", pp. 60–61.

In the Diocese of Trento, it had initially appeared as if the prince-bishop had begun granting even dispensations in the first degree on his own. However, it turned out that these dispensations had in fact not been granted on his ordinariate's own authority. In two dispensation certificates from 1790, the name of the prince-bishop – Peter Michael Vigilius von Thun-Hohenstein (1776–1800) – was followed by the tell-tale handwritten formulation "tamquam a Sancta Sede delegatus", an expression that the ordinariate – as the district captain in Rovereto noted – had "not included on other such dispensations".[146] The *Gubernium* subsequently withheld the *placetum regium* and filed these dispensation certificates away. At the next opportunity, the Prince-Bishop of Trento declared he was in no case authorised to dispense in the first and second degrees: Johann Clementi and Dorothea Brugnara had complained about this to the "Sacra Maestà" in a 1793 letter of supplication, "but the Prince-Bishop of Trento literally answered that regarding the first and second degree, he been delegated absolutely no authority to grant such dispensations".[147] One year later, in 1794, the prince-bishop again dispensed and – to the *Gubernium's* great consternation – sent the certificate documenting the granted dispensation without having first requested the *Gubernium's* permission to grant it. The *Gubernium* attributed this impropriety to the "supplicant".[148] The problem of steps not being taken in the officially mandated order was to recur frequently during this period.

Maximilian Christoph von Rodt, Prince-Bishop of Constance (1775–1799), employed a different formulation in 1791. He refrained from writing that he had granted the dispensation "ex aucthoritate propria" or "on his own authority", as would have been required, instead – and as the *Gubernium* saw it, *merely* – writing "ex aucthoritate apostolica specialiter sibi delgata", or on the basis of the ecclesiastical power explicitly delegated to him. And with that, the pope was again in play. The *Gubernium*'s Commission on Spiritual Affairs felt compelled to enquire with the Imperial-Royal Court Chancellery in Vienna "as to the matter of several expressions used by His Excellency the Prince-Bishop of

---

146 One of these couples was Anton Girardelli and Maria Gobbi, and the other was Anton Martinelli and Katharina Tonioli; both couples were related in the second degree of consanguinity. TLA Innsbruck, Jüngeres Gubernium, Hauptgruppe 57 Placetum Regium, 1790–1793, Fasc. no. 1.622, 1792, no. 38.

147 Ibid., 1793, no. 26. "Ma il Vescovo Principe di Trento vocalmente rispose, di non tenere per il Grado primo e secondo Delegazione alcuna per emender simile Dispensa". Letter of 3 June 1794 to the district administration office of Rovereto, signed by Trentinaglia. In the rough draft, the final passage reads: "[...] we would be *willing* to process, at this point, supreme dispensations *that may possibly be received*".

148 TLA Innsbruck, Jüngeres Gubernium, Hauptgruppe 64 Ehesachen, 1794–1795, Fasc. no. 312, 1794, no. 28.

Constance in dispensing marriages in the second degree of consanguinity and affinity". Vienna did end up granting its approval of the marriage in this specific case, but it also went on to instruct the Bishop of Constance that dispensations for the purpose of lifting marriage impediments could "also be granted based on the *Authoritate apostolica* received by Your Excellency".[149]

The years that followed witnessed frequent criticism of divergent formulations and, analogously, of divergent actions, for the employed variants clearly indicated that consultations with Rome were taking place.[150] The *Hofstelle* in Vienna had grown wary, to say the least. Together with an order to send a list of dispensation cases to Vienna on a semi-annual basis, the court also instructed that the ordinariates' own dispensation certificates be attached "in order that one might become convinced here, as well, that such documents contain no expressions or clauses that would encroach upon His Imperial Majesty's rights, as has already quite frequently occurred".[151] But this did not eliminate the problem. In 1803, the *Gubernium* found cause to send a dispensation certificate issued in Brixen separately to Vienna for inspection. This time, however, the authorities there – represented by the *Hofstelle* – dismissed such action as overzealousness and pointed out to the *Gubernium* that dispensations granted free of charge no longer needed to be to submitted.[152]

A second strategy aimed at circumventing the Marriage Patent's rules was to organise dispensations via the nunciature in Vienna, which had formerly been responsible for such matters.[153] An extant set of seventeenth-century rules for the Viennese nunciature explains that one of the reasons for so many marriage dispensations to be handled there was "perché in Germania sono facili ad imparentarsi fra di loro" – because in German-speaking lands, it was easier to

149 TLA Innsbruck, Jüngeres Gubernium, Hauptgruppe 57 Placetum Regium, 1790–1793, Fasc. no. 1.622, 1791, no. 22 and 1792, no. 3.

150 TLA Innsbruck, Jüngeres Gubernium, Hauptgruppe 64 Ehesachen, 1794–1795, Fasc. no. 312, 1794, no. 50.

151 TLA Innsbruck, Jüngeres Gubernium, Hauptgruppe 64 Ehesachen, 1796, Fasc. no. 313, no. 86.

152 Cf. TLA Innsbruck, Jüngeres Gubernium, Hauptgruppe 64 Ehesachen, 1803, Fasc. no. 317, no. 122. The prince-bishop had declared that he had "obtained the special authority from Rome to grant this couple the aforementioned dispensation only with exceptional effort".

153 A look at the older Brixen register reveals that the majority of the dispensations not granted by the bishop and above all those touching the second degree had gone via the nunciature in Vienna. Certain dispensations bear the additional remark: "ex commissione ap[osto]l[i]ca romana". Cf. DIÖAB, Registratura Dispensation[um] Matrimonial[ium] inc[o]hoata anno 1690 [until 1730]; ibid., Registratura Dispensation[um] Matrimonial[ium] inc[o]hoata anno 1733 usque ad annum 1752; as well as ibid., Registratura Dispensation[um] Matrimonial[ium] anno 1753 usque ad annum 1768.

become related (by marriage) with one another.[154] The overall circumstances had changed due to the dispute regarding the nunciatures as instances of "foreign" jurisdiction. But despite this difficult situation, the bishops resorted to them once more.[155] Beginning in 1793, the records indicate the repeated granting of dispensations by the nunciature.[156] For it was via the nunciature, according to the consistory in Brixen, that a dispensation could be obtained "in the swiftest and easiest manner".[157] It was not long, however, before objections to this were voiced.[158] It happened that the Prince-Bishop of Brixen submitted two dispensations in the second degree of consanguinity to the *Gubernium* in order to receive its provincial *exequatur*. January 1796 saw the *Gubernium* report that it had, "in the process, noticed that it pleased His Princely Holiness to have such certificates produced by the office of the nunciature in Vienna for a small agency fee". The reaction to this was harsh, for a court decree of the

---

154 Archivio dell'Ufficio delle celebrazioni liturgiche del Sommo Pontefice, vol. 47, Regolamento per la famiglia del nunzio di Vienna, fol. 344, quoted in Alexander Koller, "Nuntienalltag. Überlegungen zur Lebenswelt eines kirchlichen Diplomatenhaushalts im 16. und 17. Jahrhundert", in *Impulse für eine religiöse Alltagsgeschichte des Donau-Alpen-Adria-Raumes*, ed. Rupert Klieber and Hermann Hold (Vienna/Cologne/Weimar, 2005), pp. 95–108, 99. An impression of the extent of dispensation-related activities is also provided by the marriage dispensation registers mentioned in an inventory of the Archive of the Apostolic Nuncio in Vienna compiled by Walter Wagner. Walter Wagner, "Die Bestände des Archivio della Nunziatura Vienna bis 1792", *Römische Historische Mitteilungen* 2 (1957/58), 82–203.

155 On the nunciatory faculties, which had become more important with the establishment of permanent nunciatures beginning in 1513 cf. Mergentheim, *Die Quinquennalfakultäten*, pp. 42–46, regarding marriage dispensations ibid., pp. 95–100.

156 One of the first enquiries came in December 1793 from the "district office of the Welsch Confines"; it pertains to a dispensation in the second degree of affinity. The cause for this enquiry was "that the Reverend Ordinary of Trento has stated that the granting of same lies beyond his power". TLA Innsbruck, Jüngeres Gubernium, Hauptgruppe 57 Placetum Regium, 1790–1793, Fasc. no. 1.622, 1793, no. 32.

157 TLA Innsbruck, Jüngeres Gubernium, Hauptgruppe 64 Ehesachen, 1794–1795, Fasc. no. 312, 1794, no. 3.

158 Corresponding court resolutions were decreed in 1795: the court resolution of 22 May 1795 announced that dispensation briefs were, in the future, "to be granted by Rome directly to the ordinariates and no longer to be decreed by the nunciature, which can no longer be conceded jurisdiction in the Imperial-Royal hereditary lands". By way of a court resolution of 12 June 1795, the Imperial-Royal Privy Court and State Chancellery instructed Cardinal Heržan in Rome to the effect "that all papal briefs, bulls, and other such issuances are no longer to be sent via the Roman nunciature here [in Vienna], but rather directly to the ordinariates", and that in cases of non-compliance – as threatened in the court resolution quoted above – the *Placetum regium* would be refused. Joh[ann] Schwerdling, *Praktische Anwendung aller vom Antritte der Regierung Sr. kaiserl. königl. apostol. Majestät Franz II. bis 1. Jäner 1798 für die gesammten Erbländer in geistlichen Sachen (Publico ecclesiasticis) ergangenen Verordnungen*, 3rd ed. (Krems, 1816), § 189–191, 448 and § 42–43, 37–38.

previous year had explicitly forbidden such intervention by the nunciature. The consistory in Brixen subsequently defended its actions and emphasised how this dispensation's low cost benefitted the couple, particularly because such a dispensation could not have been obtained for free in Rome. This was confirmed by an enclosed letter from the imperial-royal agent there, a man by the name of von Brunati.[159] The suspicion that fees had been charged for dispensations in violation of the directives in force had indeed already been voiced in connection with an earlier request.[160]

The nunciature had offered a simple pathway to a dispensation particularly in cases where a bride was pregnant or a couple already had one or more children – and at first, the consistories were still successful with this argument vis-à-vis the *Hofstelle* in Vienna. But this state of affairs did not last long. In response to the dispensation request submitted by the cousins Michael Bacher and Agnes Tschurtschenthalerin, who already had two children, the *Gubernium* stated in February 1797 that turning to the nunciature in Vienna was "now also forbidden" in such cases.[161]

In a very long letter written that same year, Brixen's bishop adamantly pointed out the advantages of nunciatory dispensations. Likely intuiting that this ban would not be lifted or amended anytime soon and clearly in a state of exasperation, he told the provincial government that in light of the circumstances, it would be best to immediately turn down couples seeking dispensations "so that this excess of fruitless written correspondence with the associated errors, detours, irksomeness and a certain measure of sin and vice can be avoided".[162] Indeed, this evoked the onset of a merciless practice: at the next opportunity, the assessment of a request from the Diocese of Brixen by the Commission on Spiritual Affairs at the Innsbruck *Gubernium* read simply: "Reject, since ordinariate does not dispense". It was signed, as was most of the provincial government's official correspondence during these years, by Government Counsellor (*Gubernialrat*) Josef von Trentinaglia.[163] The situation was evidently coming to

---

159 TLA Innsbruck, Jüngeres Gubernium, Hauptgruppe 64 Ehesachen, 1796, Fasc. no. 313, no. 9.

160 In a relatively laborious dispensation case from the Diocese of Trento, the dispensation document submitted to the *Gubernium* was rejected in part because "everything shows quite unambiguously that the supplicants did not come through the process without having to pay any fees". TLA Innsbruck, Jüngeres Gubernium, Hauptgruppe 64 Ehesachen, 1796, Fasc. no. 313, no. 2.

161 TLA Innsbruck, Jüngeres Gubernium, Hauptgruppe 64 Ehesachen, 1797–1798, Fasc. no. 314, 1797, no. 6. Cf. also ibid., no. 89.

162 Ibid., no. 6.

163 Ibid., no. 8. This request had been submitted by Anton Giner, a 53-year-old "pork butcher" from Innsbruck, and his widowed sister-in-law Elisabeth Suiterin, who had two children.

a head. Once the provincial government in Innsbruck had complained about him in Vienna, the Bishop of Brixen became the direct target of calls to order and threats. He was "so flagrantly" complicating and foiling "the granting of such dispensations", unlike all other "ordinariates in the Province of Tyrol",[164] went the accusation. This was followed by the lament that the provincial government had "no means at its disposal" to force "this ordinariate to make use of the powers associated with its responsibilities (*Berufsbefugnisse*)". As it stood, the *Gubernium* could "only take pity on the parties whose domestic and spiritual well-being are being disturbed by such pretermission".[165]

Early July of 1798 saw the Court Chancellery in Vienna instruct Ferdinand von Bissingen, the Imperial-Royal Provincial Governor in Tyrol, to suggest that the prince-bishop take a more conciliatory stance in the matter of dispensations. Failing which one would "be forced to make the unpleasant assumption" that his refusal had to do merely with the loss of fee revenues.[166] His dispensation-related actions were even subjected to a review, which found that he had "deigned to complacently submit [to the pope] for the purpose of receiving papal dispensations" during the mid-1790s. The author of the report by the provincial government in Innsbruck, echoing the note from Vienna quoted above, threatened to "bring these circumstances to the attention of His Imperial Majesty".[167]

Despite the French occupation of the Papal States in early 1798, the pope's removal,[168] the various military events of the wartime years and the resulting

---

The Bishop of Brixen not only argued that it was not within "our powers" to grant such a dispensation but also that "the motivations of the supplicant" were in this case insufficient to be granted a dispensation "by the Holy See".

164 In a subsequent letter, the Bishop of Brixen's remarks on the matter were that "the behaviour of the same" could "not be [his] standard" because he would have to "take sole responsibility for his actions" while also being "un[willing] to investigate the pathways via which the same have obtained their authority". TLA Innsbruck, Jüngeres Gubernium, Hauptgruppe 64 Ehesachen, 1799–1800, Fasc. no. 315, 1799, no. 45.

165 TLA Innsbruck, Jüngeres Gubernium, Hauptgruppe 64 Ehesachen, 1797–1798, Fasc. no. 314, 1798, no. 12, report of the *Gubernium* to the Imperial-Royal Court Chancellery in Vienna of 13 June 1798.

166 Ibid., letter from Vienna dated 28 June 1798.

167 Ibid.

168 General Berthier had arrived in Rome on 10 February 1798. The city was turned over to him and the Republic proclaimed on 15 February, with Pius VI (1775–1799) being declared deposed. Berthier had been ordered to permit the pope to flee, but the pope refused. Berthier was then commanded to take him away. "Without any preparation, this weak and ill old man [he was 80 years old at the time – M.L.] was placed in a stagecoach and first brought to Siena, then (on 30 May 1798) to the Carthusian monastery near Florence". In 1799, upon the beginning of the War of the Second Coalition, he was ultimately

difficulty in communicating with Rome, the nunciature remained neutralised as an alternative as far as dispensation-granting was concerned. A message from the district office in Bozen in late 1798 to the effect that the Bishop of Brixen had "left over to the papal nunciature in Vienna" the dispensation request of a couple related in the second degree of affinity was immediately followed by an imperial court decree reaffirming the ban on this practice.[169] A letter written in March 1799 indicates that the papal nuncio in Vienna was then "interrogated" by the Court Chancellery. The nuncio indicated that "even in the present times and circumstances, which have forced the head of the Church to vacate his residence in Rome", he had received no general authority from the pope to grant marriage dispensations but had indeed, at the request of several bishops, obtained authorisation "on a case-by-case basis".[170] As a consequence, the Bishop of Brixen was issued the official instruction to turn directly to the pope. He was to present the dispensation brief to the provincial government upon receiving.[171]

All this notwithstanding, nunciatory dispensations continue to show up in the dispensation register of the Diocese of Brixen after 1795. Grouping the communities from which these couples came by the domains in which they were located, a clear trend becomes visible. Initially, the dispensations' destinations were mixed: there was a total of four such dispensations in 1795, including two for couples resident in territories ruled by the bishop and two for couples from territories ruled by the provincial government, of which one was marked with the phrase "cum adscripto placeto regio".[172] In 1796, there were six of them – of which three, in the second and third unequal degree, were for couples from areas ruled by the bishop.[173] The sole nunciatory dispensation from 1797 contained in the records was for a couple from Felthurns, which was on the territory

sent on via Parma, Tortona and Turin, thereafter being carried on a simple litter over Mt. Genèvre to Briançon, Grenoble and Valence, where he died on 29 August 1799. Seppelt, *Papstgeschichte*, p. 279.

169 The dispensation request at issue had been submitted by Michael and Anna Krößs from the court district of Sarnthein, who were related in the second degree of affinity. This couple does not appear in the dispensation register. TLA Innsbruck, Jüngeres Gubernium, Hauptgruppe 64 Ehesachen, 1799–1800, Fasc. no. 315, 1799, no. 30.

170 According to his faculties, however, the nuncio Giuseppe Garampi (1776–1785) was indeed fundamentally permitted to grant dispensations to "poor" couples, who included everyone except the nobility and the wealthy, and to converts in the second degree as well as to all supplicants in the more distant third and the fourth degrees. Dell'Orto, *La nunziatura a Vienna*, p. 51.

171 TLA Innsbruck, Jüngeres Gubernium, Hauptgruppe 64 Ehesachen, 1799–1800, Fasc. no. 315, 1799, no. 45.

172 DIÖAB, Dispensationes matrimoniales ab anno 1795, p. 2, 7, 11–12.

173 Cf. ibid., p. 17, 23–24, 27.

of the Prince-Bishopric of Brixen.[174] 1798 makes a similar impression: from that year, two dispensations were granted by the nunciature for couples from Brixen's territory – from Thurn im Gadertal and from Anras, respectively.[175] For 1799, the register contains no dispensations of this type. 1800 and 1801, on the other hand, feature two nunciatory dispensations each – all for couples from the territory ruled by Brixen (*territorii Brixinensis*).[176] The following years reveal no further nunciatory dispensations. In connection with the practice of resorting to the nunciature, it become clear that actions were taking place in parallel and according to two norms: canon law and civil law. The contents of the register also suggest that the ban on turning to the nunciature would seem to have taken hold from 1797 onward in areas ruled by the province.

With this, the situation grew even more dire. In response to a dispensation request made by residents of the Diocese of Trento, the provincial government in Innsbruck itself responded in 1799 by recommending that the diocese turn to the nunciature.[177] Vienna, however, remained firm. When the Bishop of Augsburg procured a dispensation via the nunciature in Munich for a couple from present-day North Tyrol in 1803, this dispensation was rejected by Vienna with reference to a Court Chancellery decree and a "supreme resolution": "In my states, no papal nuncio may exercise jurisdiction in spiritual or church matters."[178] An internal report (*Relation*) of the Court Chancellery had initially defended this nunciatory dispensation, thus a decision was requested from the emperor. It was during this period that a general "low point of papal diplomacy" was reached. By 1808, there were only two nuncios left in office – in Lisbon and in Vienna.[179]

---

174 Cf. ibid., p. 45.

175 Cf. ibid., pp. 59–60.

176 Ibid., p. 87, 91, 100, 102.

177 "In light of the circumstances, the diocesan ordinariate has been most graciously permitted to itself request papal indulgence for the supplicant couple, which would hardly be obtainable in the present situation were it not to take place via the nuncio in Vienna." TLA Innsbruck, Jüngeres Gubernium, Hauptgruppe 64 Ehesachen, 1799–1800 Fasc. no. 315, 1799, no. 82.

178 TLA Innsbruck, Jüngeres Gubernium, Hauptgruppe 64 Ehesachen, 1803, Fasc. no. 317, no. 132 as well as ÖSTA, AVA, Alter Cultus, Ehesachen und Taufen, K. 9, 1781–1805, no. 18.431. The nunciature in Munich, established in 1785, was vacant between 1800 and 1818, but the papal special envoy Annibale della Genga did exercise rights of papal jurisdiction in 1800, 1803, 1806 and 1807, since he was present in Bavaria in connection with the Imperial Diet in Regensburg and the Concordat negotiations. Cf. Michael F. Feldkamp, "Apostolische Nuntiatur, München", in *Historisches Lexikon Bayerns*, http://www.historisches-lexikon-bayerns.de/artikel/artikel_44502 (last access: May 2022).

179 Fabrizio Rossi, *Der Vatikan. Politik und Organisation*, 5th ed. (Munich, 2005), p. 68. At the Congress of Vienna, nuncios were re-installed and made equal in status to papal legates.

From the perspective of the Church, Nuncio Giuseppe Garampi (1776–1785), whom Dries Vanysacker has characterised as "an enlightened ultramontane",[180] had been stationed in Vienna as a "head" to the entire "body" of the Habsburg Monarchy's secular and regular clergy, as an official to whom – as his secretary wrote – one could turn in all questions of religion, the Church and religious doctrine. His jurisdiction encompassed around 60 dioceses.[181] Garampi regarded the Marriage Patent as the most egregious of all measures implemented by the emperor.[182] His protests against interventions in religious matters and papal competencies, however, had already begun prior to that point. In response, State Chancellor Kaunitz declared him to be an "ambassador of a foreign power", as which he had no right to intervene in reforms that were in planning or already implemented.[183] Garampi's successor Giovanni Battista Caprara (1785–1793), who had previously been the nuncio in Lucerne, has been characterised as reserved. He took pains to maintain relations with the emperor. He was viewed as "Francophile" and also came to be referred to as a "Jacobin Cardinal" later on.[184] He was followed by Luigi Ruffo (1793–1802), whose term of office played out against the backdrop of the wars against France. It was only Antonio Gabriele Severoli (1802–1816), who once again became active in matters of dispensation. Severoli's status as a diplomat had been abolished by the Treaty of Schönbrunn in October 1809, but he had been equipped with exceptional authorities whose exercise in church matters was also recognised by the imperial government.[185]

Altogether, the mid-1790s saw the limitations on action concerning dispensations in close degrees grow increasingly severe, with new or newly popular options being promptly eliminated. In light of this, it is hardly surprising that some bridal couples ended up taking matters into their own hands.

---

180 Dries Vanysacker, *Cardinal Giuseppe Garampi (1725–1792). An Enlightened Ultramonane* (Brussels et al., 1995).

181 Dell'Orto, *La nunziatura a Vienna*, p. 50; cf. also Donato Squicciarini, *Die apostolischen Nuntien in Wien*, 2nd ed. (Vatican City, 2000), p. 48, 225–229.

182 Cf. Dell'Orto, *La nunziatura a Vienna*, p. 467. On the following pages the author also sketches out the reactions of several bishops.

183 Squicciarini, *Die apostolischen Nuntien*, p. 227. On Kaunitz, who is often referred to as the 'father of Josephinism' cf. Hersche, *Muße und Verschwendung*, vol. 2, pp. 983–984.

184 Squicciarini, *Die apostolischen Nuntien*, pp. 230–235.

185 Cf. ibid., pp. 239–242.

6 Arbitrary Acts – and Their Limitations

In July 1798, the Bishop of Brixen sent a dispensation certificate to the *Gubernium* in Innsbruck with a request for provincial government approval. Since this document contained an unusual formulation, it was forwarded to Vienna. While the imperial authorities did grant permission to marry, their response expressed objection to the fact that the dispensation certificate had already been issued without the *Gubernium* first having been asked for permission to turn to Rome. The consistory in Brixen, in responding to this reprimand, stated that they did not feel addressed by it since they had not forwarded this dispensation request to Rome, "it being much rather the parties themselves who found ways to obtain this from His Papal Holiness".[186] The *Gubernium* then ordered the district office in Schwaz to hold the couple, Franz Schober and Maria Lergethbohrerin, to account.[187]

This would indicate that couples were now requesting dispensations from the papal authorities on their own and evidently meeting with success. In 1800, the lawyer Philipp von Wörndle pursued this strategy and obtained a dispensation in the first degree of affinity. Since his dispensation had been granted free of charge, the *placetum regium* was not denied him.[188] Among couples who had taken this sort of action and appear in the records from this point onward, some had made unsuccessful dispensation requests years before. The teacher Johann Schöpf of Niederthei in the Ötz Valley and Maria Auerin, who were cousins and had requested a dispensation for the first time nine years prior, finally – in 1800 – received one from the "Apostolic Penitentiary in Venice",[189] to where the papal bureaucracy had temporarily relocated due to the French occupation of the Papal States.[190] In 1797, the couple had sent a futile ten

186 A note to this effect can be found in the 1798 section of the Brixen dispensation register. The nunciature in Vienna is specified as the issuing authority, immediately followed by the added remark that this dispensation had been procured by the couple themselves: "Ex Nunciatura Viennensi. NB ab ipsis oratoribus hac dispensatio procurata fuit." DIÖAB, Dispensationes matrimoniales ab anno 1795 usque ad annum 1829 inclusive, p. 59.

187 Cf. TLA Innsbruck, Jüngeres Gubernium, Hauptgruppe 64 Ehesachen, 1797–1798, Fasc. no. 314, 1798, no. 130.

188 Cf. TLA Innsbruck, Jüngeres Gubernium, Hauptgruppe 64 Ehesachen, 1799–1800, Fasc. no. 315, 1800, no. 63.

189 Ibid., no. 64.

190 Pius VII (1800–1823) had been elected at a conclave in Venice under Austria's protection. It was on 3 July 1800 that he entered Rome. The Concordat of 15 July 1801 and a papal bull of 29 November 1801 restored "absolute papal power"; bishops who did not consent were removed from office – a measure that Franz Xaver Seppelt interpreted as "a deadly blow

page letter of supplication to the Court Commission on Spiritual Affairs as their sole remaining "resort" in what was a muddled situation. In this letter they portrayed in detail their attempts since 1791 to obtain a dispensation, their oscillation between hope and despair, and all of the imponderables of dispensation practice during these years.[191] Shortly afterwards, three further dispensation certificates from Brixen followed for couples who had likewise previously been turned down.[192] News of the more favourable situation had apparently got round.

Soon, however, restrictions reappeared here, as well. In an 1802 letter to the Prince-Bishop of Brixen, the provincial government stated categorically that Austrian subjects were not permitted to turn directly to Rome for a marriage dispensation.[193] But despite all rebukes, there is evidence from the nineteenth century's initial years indicating that the provincial government continued to be circumvented. Dispensation documents appeared for which permission had never been requested. Vienna reacted with consternation and sent out repeated admonishments to adhere to the official rules.[194] In the case of Christian Berthold and Maria Kreszenz Tschoflin of Dalaas in the Diocese of Chur, the *Gubernium* initially received merely notification by a priest that the two had been granted a dispensation. The dispensation certificate, which the *Gubernium* requested for inspection in July 1801, revealed to have come directly from Rome. It followed the usual declaration that the diocesan consistory was not authorised to refer Austrian subjects to Rome.[195]

In 1802, the district office in Bregenz had given the supplicants Joseph Schneider and Maria Hellböckin of Höchst, who were related in the second degree of affinity, its "sanction" to approach the ecclesiastical authorities for a dispensation even though their request had been rejected by the provincial government due to what had been deemed insufficient justification. When the

---

to Gallicanism", which had been viewed as a danger fit to cause a schism in the Church. Seppelt, *Papstgeschichte*, pp. 280–284, quote 283.

191 Cf. TLA Innsbruck, Jüngeres Gubernium, Hauptgruppe 64 Ehesachen, 1797–1798, Fasc. no. 314, 1797, no. 136.

192 Cf. TLA Innsbruck, Jüngeres Gubernium, Hauptgruppe 64 Ehesachen, 1799–1800, Fasc. no. 315, 1800, no. 73; cf. also ibid., no. 83.

193 Cf. TLA Innsbruck, Jüngeres Gubernium, Hauptgruppe 64 Ehesachen, 1801–1802, Fasc. no. 316, 1802, no. 42.

194 Cf. ibid., no. 96. In the case dealt with in this particular source, an enquiry had been sent to Vienna due to the suspicion "that this dispensation has been obtained by the parties from the papal nuncio to the Imperial-Royal Court, since the *officium spirituale* of Trento [declares] itself to be merely an *Executor deputatus*".

195 Cf. TLA Innsbruck, Jüngeres Gubernium, Hauptgruppe 64 Ehesachen, 1801–1802, Fasc. no. 316, 1801, no. 39.

local priest urged procurement of provincial authorisation following the dispensation's receipt, it became clear that this dispensation had been granted without the involvement of the competent diocesan ordinariate. Rather it came from the papal nuncio who was accredited in Switzerland. In this case, the *Gubernium* recommended that the dispensation "not be heeded". Instead, "the parties" were to be instructed to remain entirely within the officially sanctioned channels.[196] A later report indicated that this couple's detour via the papal nunciature in Switzerland[197] had come about at the initiative of their priest, who had personally contacted the nunciature in this regard. The parish of Höchst was subject to the patronage of the Princely Abbey of St. Gallen, but neither the Prince-Abbot of St. Gallen nor his judicial vicar felt authorised to dispense on their own authority following rejection of the nunciatory dispensation. The district office in Bregenz recommended that the request be forwarded to the ordinariate in Constance.[198] Thus the couple was ultimately able to present their official "ordinariate dispensation of the Prince-Bishopric of Constance" in February 1803.[199]

These individual initiatives and circumventions of the officially sanctioned channels that ended up leaving behind traces in the records were most probably the proverbial tip of the iceberg. Since Austrian marital law and the corresponding rules on dispensations enjoyed only partial validity in the ecclesiastical territories of Brixen, Salzburg and Trento[200] up to their secularisation in 1803, a certain 'dispensation tourism' – not unlike the phenomenon of 'divorce tourism' – may have arisen everywhere close to the borders of these territories, which offered more favourable conditions in terms of required effort and chances of success.[201] After all, it was unquestionably easier during

196 Ibid., 1802, no. 102.

197 Jon Mathieu has shown that the nunciature in Lucerne, established in 1586, approved dispensation requests "almost without exception". Mathieu, "Verwandtschaft als historischer Faktor", p. 241.

198 Cf. TLA Innsbruck, Jüngeres Gubernium, Hauptgruppe 64 Ehesachen, 1801–1802, Fasc. no. 316, 1802, no. 194.

199 TLA Innsbruck, Jüngeres Gubernium, Hauptgruppe 64 Ehesachen, 1803, Fasc. no. 317, no. 48.

200 On measures towards stronger territorial integration of the Prince-Bishopric of Trento during the period at issue here cf. the contribution by Marco Meriggi, "Il principato vescovile dal 1776 alla secolarizzazione", in *Storia del Trentino*, vol. 4: L'età moderna, ed. Marco Bellabarba and Giuseppe Olmi (Bologna, 2002), pp. 127–156. This is to say that there was quite generally a situation of competition over sovereignty that must be considered as part of the context within which marriage dispensation matters were handled.

201 Cf. for example Margarete Grandner and Ulrike Harmat, "Begrenzt verliebt. Gesetzliche Ehehindernisse und die Grenze zwischen Österreich und Ungarn", in *Liebe und*

this period to obtain a dispensation in the ecclesiastical principalities, where the usual routes – via the nunciature or via Rome – were still open. These territories were in part fragmented – the Prince-Bishopric of Brixen, most of all, but also the district containing the border regions known as the Welsch Confines (*Welsche Konfinen*), which meant that the borders to the outside world were numerous and easily crossed.

If a bride and groom were from different legal spheres, they most probably took any available opportunity to exploit such legal plurality, turning to the authority that seemed more promising of success. Problems occurred, however, when authorities from the 'other' side were involved or actively intervened. The district office in Rovereto received a dispensation that had been organised directly in Rome for provincial government approval and justified the actions of the diocesan ordinariate on the basis of the groom's Venetian origins as well as his unfamiliarity with the Austrian legal situation. It proceeded to act as a representative of the bride's interests: "Even though this behaviour by the ordinariate of Trento does not conform to the existing supreme regulations, it is indeed believed that this fact most likely was not known to the couple, since the groom, whose decision it may have been to take recourse to Rome in order to obtain a dispensation, will have been unfamiliar, as a former subject of Venice, with the provincial laws according to which such recourse is forbidden. We hence express our endorsement of the supplicant's request, that it may be granted to her."[202]

Ambiguities at various hierarchical levels, imbroglios between different legal orders, the conflicted standpoint from which the clerics had to fulfil their official duties and villagers' policing of one another: all this came together in the commotion surrounding the – valid or invalid? – marriage of Matthias Margoni and Agnes Casari in 1795. The parochial vicar (*Kooperator*) Johann Jakob Dipauli of Arsio at the Nonsberg, giving the "quaresimale"[203] in a "Tridentine community" during Lent, had been told confidentially ("sub rosa") that "a Tridentine subject" had married "an immediate Austrian subject" to whom he was related in the second degree with only "a preliminary marriage dispensation from the ordinariate". In doing so, "the fact had remained unknown" that, for the bride, this would "eventuate" the obligation to obtain a provincial dispensation. The priest had therefore asked his superiors to obtain this from the civil authorities

---

Widerstand. Ambivalenzen historischer Geschlechterbeziehungen, ed. Ingrid Bauer, Christa Hämmerle and Gabriella Hauch (Vienna/Cologne/Weimar, 2005), pp. 287–304.

202 TLA Innsbruck, Jüngeres Gubernium, Hauptgruppe 64 Ehesachen, 1801–1802, Fasc. no. 316, 1802, no. 170.

203 The sermons that were prescribed during Lent.

after the fact without raising a stir. The regional court in Castelfondo reported this incident to the district office in Bozen, where Dipauli was asked to send the dispensation certificate. Dipauli, however, declared himself incapable of doing so, since he had learned of it "sub sigillo confessionis" – under the seal of confession. In response, the district office had the court in Castelfondo "point out to him the laws in force", according to which said marriage was invalid. They held that it was thus his obligation to investigate the matter despite the seal of confession. And if he were unwilling to do so, he was to move the "parties" to request provincial permission themselves. Otherwise, threatened the district office, they were forced to open an investigation that would "have the nastiest of consequences" for him and the affected spouses. After that, Dipauli sent the district office in Bozen the ordinariate's dispensation along with a report and a request.[204]

The mistake was explained by pointing out that, for one thing, the father of the bride had been unfamiliar with the provincial laws. After all, explicated the *Gubernium* in a report to "His Majesty", the bride's place of residence at the Nonsberg was a "mixed community of Austrian and Tridentine subjects" with houses "belonging partly to the [Tyrolean] province and partly to [episcopal] Tridentine territory". In the latter, a church dispensation sufficed in order to conclude a valid marriage; in the former, provincial government permission was required. In this case, the father of the bride had come under Austrian rule just a few days before her marriage because he had moved from the Tridentine part of the house to provincial jurisdiction.[205] What is more, according to the district office's own report, the marriage had taken place on Tridentine territory where the groom was a resident, and it had been concluded by a local priest who was not required to be familiar with Austrian laws. Ultimately, therefore, the couple had concluded this marriage *bona fide*, in good faith, and hence without the intention of circumventing any administrative steps or legal requirements. The district office once again emphasised the "legal ignorance of this couple" and their relations as well as the "inadvertence" of their infraction and requested that the provincial dispensation be granted after the fact. The final paragraph of the district office's extensive report objected to the opinion – evidently expressed by the regional court in Castelfondo – that a

---

204 TLA Innsbruck, Jüngeres Gubernium, Hauptgruppe 64 Ehesachen, 1794–1795, Fasc. no. 312, 1795, no. 78. Letter from the district office in Bozen dated 15 June 1795.

205 Ibid., letter from the Innsbruck Gubernium to the Imperial Court Chancellery in Vienna dated 26 June 1795.

provincial dispensation would not be necessary since the couple was related in the second and third unequal degree.[206]

In fact, marriage prohibitions according to the Josephine Marriage Patent and legal code extended only to the second degree, as the Court Chancellery confirmed. This case hence required no dispensation at all, as far as the state was concerned – neither from the Church nor from the provincial government. So was all this fuss ultimately pointless? In principle, yes – but from the Viennese standpoint, there was indeed still one point of reproach: the dispensation had been illicitly requested from and granted by the nunciature.[207] The institutional overzealousness exhibited in this case reflects the overall situation, which was characterised by hypervigilance and a considerable degree of uncertainty.

While some eighteenth-century bishops had themselves laid claim to extensive authorities to dispense, others were unwilling to use the powers accorded to them by civil laws to dispense in close degrees on their own. They also proved unwilling to simply adhere to the new state-imposed rules concerning marriage prohibitions among consanguineous and affinal kin. The positions on both sides had hardened after just a few years, with practically no willingness to partake of the logic of their opposites – even if, as the years went by, a certain acceptance of church peculiarities did arise here and there among protagonists on the side of the state. This meant that the rules of the Church remained more or less superordinate to those of civil law. From the standpoint of canonical logic, both of the two major civil reforms – the limitation of the degrees requiring dispensation to the first and second as well as the obligation of the bishops to dispense on their own authority in these remaining close degrees – represented instances of massive state overreach. From this perspective, legitimacy and authority were inseparably linked with Rome, while the episcopalist and state church view attributed legitimacy and authenticity to the model of a decentrally organised territorial Church, conceived of as being similar to the Church of early Christianity. The conflict was over what had to be respected – the rights reserved to the pope or episcopal authorities. It was thus that a bone of contention within the Church itself became intertwined with power political interests of the state.

Actions on the level of the *Gubernium* and, in part, at the district offices were obviously characterised by quite some zeal, but certain district captains also took the side of the couples and repeatedly suggested pragmatic solutions – albeit to little success. The expansion of what Rudolf Pranzl has

206 Ibid., letter from the district office in Bozen dated 15 June 1795.

207 Ibid., letter from the Imperial Court Chancellery in Vienna dated 10 July 1795.

termed "the episcopal sphere of action", a realm that also included dispensation authorities, was certainly meant to make bishops independent of Rome. But the flipside of this, which has become more than clear in this chapter, was that they became all the more dependent on and controllable by state bureaucrats.[208] Moreover, it cannot be said – in view of actual dispensation-granting practice during the final decades of the eighteenth century and the initial years of the nineteenth – that the Marriage Patent's legal reforms had succeeded in easing marriage for couples closely related by blood or by affinity; instead, the opposite was the case.

We should bear in mind that this space of legal and political competition was overshadowed by the problematic eventuality of invalid marriages. For the affected couples this meant a life lived "in sin" according to the standpoint of the Church. In the absence of a dispensation, a marriage between consanguineous or affinal kin out to and including the fourth degree was invalid under canon law, as was an episcopal dispensation in the close degrees without authorisation from the pope. The marriage was invalid from a civil standpoint if the procedures mandated by civil law were not adhered to, including the three obligatory banns of marriage in the couple's community of residence and the requirement that a marriage had to be concluded in the presence of the priest "in whose parish or part thereof the couple resides".[209] An instrument of power that must not be underestimated was how the Church used the notions of conscience, sin and damnation. In his study on divorce, Dirk Blasius points out that "the churches' grip on people's everyday lives and everyday conflicts" was relaxed "only quite gradually", and that the nineteenth century therefore still left the churches with "a power that featured great definitional capacity when it came to shaping societies' internal relationships".[210] Even many years after the Marriage Patent had been decreed, complaints about non-compliance still arose[211] – and some of these would seem to suggest that indifference to it was, in fact, widespread. In 1800, the district office in Bozen complained about the curates of the Diocese of Trento for "concerning themselves" but little with the Marriage Patent's rules.[212]

Not only was the March 1804 promulgation of the Marriage Patent on the territory of the dioceses of Brixen and Trento associated with secularisation, as part of which it took effect in these former prince-bishoprics. It also

208 Pranzl, "Das Verhältnis von Staat und Kirche", p. 36.

209 Marriage Patent of 1783, §§ 31 and 29.

210 Dirk Blasius, *Ehescheidung in Deutschland 1794–1945* (Göttingen, 1987), p. 73.

211 Cf. TLA Innsbruck, Jüngeres Gubernium, Hauptgruppe 64 Ehesachen, 1799–1800, Fasc. no. 315, 1799, no. 173.

212 Ibid., 1800, no. 49.

encountered copiously evident resistance on the part of the Church. The explanation issued along with it read as follows: "Since in the districts of Trento and Brixen breach of promise lawsuits still exist that may result in collisions with the state with regard to dispensations concerning the banns of marriage or other matters that would affect the validity of the marriages themselves, it has been deemed highly necessary to promulgate the supreme Marriage Patent as well as the associated regulations without delay in the districts of Trento and Brixen."[213]

From the perspective of the dispensation practice that existed in the dioceses during the nineteenth century, Joseph II's liberal forays in the realm of civil law must be considered a failure.[214] Everything that he had attempted to abolish or change during the years preceding and following 1783 recurred in the 1820s and 1830s – and hence long before the Concordat of 1855 – as the renewed routine, already present unremarked and unopposed.[215] Bridal couples in the dioceses of Brixen, Chur, Salzburg and Trento submitted dispensation requests in the third and fourth degrees throughout the entire nineteenth century.[216] The requests in the close degrees, for their part, were handled mainly by the church authorities in Rome, and money continued to flow there without further objection. The demand for "congruence between civil and canon marital law" – and hence also the matter of divergences in terms of marriage impediments – remained on the Church's agenda. It was also dealt with

213 TLA Innsbruck, Jüngeres Gubernium, Hauptgruppe 64 Ehesachen, 1804, Fasc. no. 318, no. 63.

214 Cf. more generally on this topic Derek Beales, *Enlightenment and Reform in Eighteenth Century Europe* (London, 2005), especially chapter 11 and 12.

215 It was thus that Michel, in *Beiträge zur Geschichte*, pp. 60–62, ascertained the following with regard to the period after the General Civil Code (the ABGB) had taken effect: "Meanwhile, this matter had come to look different in practice than it had been envisioned when the a.b.G.B. was authored. [...] Regarding dispensations", authorities oriented themselves "once again universally according to the difference between the marriage impediments". Which was to say: "In the case of a purely ecclesiastical marriage impediments, the authorities refrained from all interference, for which reason it was left to the parties to obtain an ecclesiastical dispensation in the interest of their own peace of mind. [...] But if it was, finally, about a marriage impediment that was identically defined in civil and canon law, the dispensation request was always referred by the provincial government to the ordinariate and handled according to the opinions of the latter. [...] And in those cases where an ordinary held a papal dispensation to be necessary, the parties had to obtain such via their diocesan bishop and the appointed imperial-royal agent in Rome."

216 Early nineteenth-century dispensation requests in the third and fourth degrees also occurred in the Venetian Province, while spot checks of individual years for Lower Austria indicate that none were made there in 1820, for instance, and various other years featured only very few. Cf. Saurer, "Formen von Verwandtschaft und Liebe", p. 261, 267.

at the Austrian Conference of Bishops in Vienna in early 1849 and was later included in one of their petitions to the Ministry of the Interior.[217]

From this perspective, but also even just with an eye to dispensation-granting practice during the two decades following introduction of the Josephine Marriage Patent of 1783, the question of the enforcement, implementation and appropriation of law arises.[218] Politics is not a "one-dimensional act or process in which decrees, governance, decisions take place in a top-down manner", but is rather based on a participatory "act of understanding", as Ute Frevert puts it.[219] However, such an act – which, in combination with a certain willingness to accept it, constitutes a prerequisite for implementation – is hardly possible if the notions of the participating protagonists are diametrically opposed to whatever is being ordained and if said ordinances contradict their own logics. Incompatible parallel structures that emerged as a result persisted over decades. The main reason for this was the existence of a specific situation in which canon and civil law represented two opposed and equally institutionalised normative complexes connected with powerful institutions. Both of these two power centres on the same territory were capable of getting their way with regard to their respective, differently constructed marriage prohibitions and divergent understandings of dispensation-granting, enforcing their own respective laws and partially ignoring or circumventing the laws of the opposing side. Individual initiatives, obstinacy and persistence on the part of the clergy kept things in flow despite the countless ordinances, admonitions, rebukes and threats. At times, the Court Chancellery in Vienna worried about provincial government "reputation", viewing it as being under threat of "degradation" when, for instance, it issued a "Court Authorisation for Recourse to Rome", which, however, the diocesan ordinariate subsequently did not put to use.[220] Cases where couples themselves set out in search of possible options

---

217 Erika Weinzierl-Fischer, *Die österreichischen Konkordate von 1855 und 1933* (Vienna, 1960), p. 42.

218 Not only the enactment but also the enforcement of norms is a question of power. Enacting norms is not the same thing as their en*force*ment. Both, however, must be viewed in relation to instances of resistance and possible avenues of circumvention. On this cf. Achim Landwehr, *Policey im Alltag. Die Implementation frühneuzeitlicher Policeyordnungen in Leonberg* (Frankfurt a. M., 2000); Jürgen Schlumbohm, "Gesetze, die nicht durchgesetzt werden – ein Strukturmerkmal des frühneuzeitlichen Staates?", *Geschichte und Gesellschaft* 23 (1997), 647–663.

219 Ute Frevert, "Neue Politikgeschichte: Konzepte und Herausforderungen", in *Neue Politikgeschichte. Perspektiven einer historischen Politikforschung*, ed. Ute Frevert and Heinz-Gerhard Haupt (Frankfurt a. M./New York, 2005), pp. 7–26, 15.

220 ÖSTA, AVA, Alter Cultus, Ehesachen und Taufen, Karton 9, 1781–1805, no. 4.339. This case involved a dispensation request in the first degree of affinity by a couple from the Diocese

and took advantage of them in order to reach their objectives clearly show how agency was present more broadly than just in the various hierarchical levels within the state and church institutions.[221]

When sizeable parts of Tyrol – including the diocesan seat of Brixen and the *Gubernium's* seat of Innsbruck – came under Bavarian rule in 1806, their documents ceased to be routed via the Viennese Court Chancellery. Permission to turn to Rome for a papal dispensation now once again came from Innsbruck – in a way that was quite obligingly automatic. The request of Johann Müller – a smith at the Royal Ironworks in Jenbach – and his sister-in-law Katharina Hußlin, for example, was forwarded by the district office in Schwaz to the *Gubernium*, which in turn forwarded it to the ordinariate in Brixen together with the remark that "should the ordinariate desire to apply for a papal dispensation, provincial authorisation is herewith granted".[222] For the years of 1807 and 1808, the records concerning dispensations handled by the *Gubernium* are sparse. Pope Pius VII was imprisoned in Fontainebleau after having been taken prisoner by Napoleon in 1806. The series contains nothing between 1809 and 1813, followed by only a few requests submitted in 1814. With the end of Bavarian rule[223] and the pope's liberation, "supreme permission to turn to the papal court" was once again required. The exceptional dispensation authorities with which the pope had invested bishops during his period of captivity were "now to expire", as was communicated to authorities including the ordinariate in Brixen and the consistory in Salzburg. This also made it once again necessary to turn to the provincial government for authorisation to turn to Rome. At the same time, it was made known that only Imperial-Royal Agent Andreoli was authorised to conduct this Roman "business".[224]

---

of Trento: Jakob Mayr of Stein am Ritten, a peasant and innkeeper, and his sister-in-law Theresia Gasserin.

221 On the "institutionally anchored concept of power" in political and social history as well as on the concept of power viewed from the perspective of cultural history "as a dynamic and reciprocal occurrence" cf. Achim Landwehr, "Diskurs – Macht – Wissen. Perspektiven einer Kulturgeschichte des Politischen", *Archiv für Kulturgeschichte* 85, 1 (2003), 71–117, 88–89, 110–113.

222 TLA Innsbruck, Jüngeres Gubernium, Hauptgruppe 64 Ehesachen, 1805–1808, Fasc. no. 319, 1807, no. 34.

223 TLA Innsbruck, Jüngeres Gubernium, Hauptgruppe 64 Ehesachen, 1814, Fasc. no. 320, no. 8.481.

224 A corresponding notice from the Imperial-Royal Provisional General Commissariat of 6 August 1814 entitled "Die Behandlung der mit dem Päpstlichen Stuhle anfallenden Geschäfte" [The Handling of Business with the Holy See], which was also sent to the regional courts, can be found in Vorarlberger Landesarchiv (VLA) Bregenz, Landgericht Bezau Akten, box 35, II.49.

The examination of the dispensation registers of the Diocese of Brixen for the years between 1806 and 1814 shows that dispensations in the second and third unequal degree were granted by the bishop, some of them with the note that it had been done *auctoritate ordinaria*. For one couple related by blood in the second and third unequal degree, an April 1809 dispensation includes the explanation that episcopal authority had been exercised due to the difficulty of recourse to Rome.[225] For couple configurations in close degrees, one continues to see the note indicating that Rome had dispensed – *a Sede Apostolica dispensati sunt* – frequently also with a reference to the *placetum regium*.[226] Between three and five such dispensations are recorded for each year. During the first half of 1810, these were also granted by the bishop himself with the explanation that "ex certis causis", for certain reasons, it had been impossible to turn to the Holy See at that time.[227] Only dispensations *ex auctoritate ordinaria* occurred between 1811 and 1814, with Roman dispensations reappearing not before 1815.[228]

•••

This chapter has analysed administrative practice during a particularly conflict-ridden period. It has pointed out how and with what consequences the state involved itself with matters relating to marriage prohibitions and dispensations during the eighteenth century's final decades, breaking into a domain that had previously been administrated solely by the Church. Initial ordinances – promulgated even before the pivotal Marriage Patent of 1783 – aimed to centralise procedures by stipulating that only the consistories of the respective dioceses could forward dispensation requests to Rome. This requirement intended to eliminate all other mediatory channels as well as journeys to Rome by the couples themselves in order to obtain dispensations in person. Such journeys, not uncommon during the early modern period, were certainly onerous and entailed numerous additional hurdles presented by the papal bureaucracy upon arrival. Even so, this option had still represented a sphere of action – one that was now eliminated and/or made a punishable offence if prospective couples attempted to exploit it. At the same time, any 'recourse' to

225 Cf. DIÖAB, Dispensationes matrimoniales ab anno 1795 usque ad annum 1829 inclusive, p. 203, 19 April 1809.

226 Cf. for example ibid., p. 176, 31 January 1807; p. 205, 24 June 1809.

227 Ibid., p. 217, 28 May 1810; p. 219, 20 June 1810.

228 Cf. ibid., p. 270, 20 January 1815. This is the first dispensation to once again come from Rome – bearing the remark: "a Sede Ap[osto]l[i]ca impetrata est dispensatio".

Rome as well as the decisions made there still needed to be approved via issuance of the *placetum regium* by the competent provincial government.

The provisions of the Josephine Marriage Patent had been meant to ease conditions and included both a reduction of the degrees requiring dispensation and authorisation for bishops to dispense in the close degrees of consanguinity and affinity. And yet, they proved enormously difficult to implement in parts of the dioceses of Augsburg, Brixen, Chur, Constance, Salzburg and Trento, which fell within the territory ruled by the *Gubernium* in Innsbruck. For one thing, state authorities had become involved in these proceedings for the first time. This touched off a lengthy, change-ridden process of attributing and negotiating competencies while also giving rise to highly elaborate enquiries and requests for clarification plus other correspondence with the Imperial Court Chancellery in Vienna. On the other hand, the bishops here – in contrast to the proponents of a state church – found themselves embroiled in a massive conflict of loyalties. Despite state demands to the contrary, they attempted by all possible means to continue fulfilling their obligations to the pope and ensure that Rome, as a decision-making instance that Joseph II aimed to nullify to the greatest possible extent where dispensations were concerned, would continue to play a role. The objective of denying the church jurisdiction – synonymous with a 'foreign' jurisdiction – its sphere of action and efficacy on state territory was also and not insignificantly aimed at the apostolic nunciatures, which had been functioning as important and inexpensive points of contact for sensitive and urgent dispensation requests and whose use was henceforth forbidden.

The power struggle between Church and state that left its traces in the records of the Innsbruck *Gubernium* manifested itself in a wide diversity of complaints, in the civil authorities' wavering between indecision, pragmatism and hard decisions, in structurally induced conflicts with village priests and bishops who failed to adhere to the rules, and above all in great unpredictability for prospective couples closely related by blood or by marriage. During this phase, such couples could predict neither how their cases would be decided nor by whom and according to what logic such decisions would effectively be made. This becomes particularly obvious during the years when the provincial governments were primarily responsible for deciding if dispensation requests were sufficiently justified on the basis of whether the proposed unions would serve the 'common good' – a criterion that hardly anyone could fulfil. It is most striking how this criterion conformed to the dispensation rules of the Council of Trent (1545–1563), therefore standing paradigmatically for the half-heartedness of dispensation matters' and marital law's "nationalisation". This also goes for the Marriage Patent as a whole, which legally defined marriage as a civil contract but still left the ability to wed people within the domain of the Church – an arrangement that was one of the more significant factors underlying some difficulties experienced in the implementation of state dispensation rules. If, for instance, priests refused to marry couples related in the third or fourth degree without a dispensation, the alternative of civil marriage simply did not exist. Based on the complaints received by district offices, it is fair to conclude that clerics on the local level employed strategies of circumvention in order to continue fulfilling the obligations regarding dispensation that were entailed by canon law. At the same time, however, members of the clergy were called upon to do their utmost to prevent the contradictions between church and state law from becoming visible – an ultimately impossible tightrope act.

This situation escalated to the point where the processing of dispensation requests came to an almost complete standstill: if a bishop – and the one in Brixen seems to have been particularly tenacious – did not wish to grant dispensations to close-degree couples on his own and simultaneously needed – de facto impossible – assurance from the papal authorities that dispensations would be granted free of charge in order to be permitted to turn to Rome, such requests were effectively blocked and therefore had to be denied. We must assume a certain amount of 'dispensation tourism' since Austrian territory, where the Josephine Marriage Patent was in force, was intermixed with the territories of Brixen and Trento, where canon law held sway. The borders between the various domains occasionally divided communities and, in extreme cases, even individual houses, which made it easy to switch from one domain and hence one legal realm to another. And for the years around the turn of the eighteenth to the nineteenth century, which saw papal offices moved to Venice as a consequence of the Papal States' occupation by the French, the archival material contains traces of couples who had successfully – if, in principle, 'illegally' – applied for dispensations on their own. Viewed altogether, then, a period of over twenty years was characterised by uncertainty on the part of both civil and ecclesiastical administrators as well as supplicants when it came to dispensation practice. Accordingly, this chapter has shown the obstacles and contradictions, implications and limitations of the Josephine reforms pertaining to marriage dispensations in both ecclesiastical and civil administrative practice as well as in terms of their consequences for the affected couples. The state's efforts to simplify the required procedures must be viewed as having ultimately failed. As a result, the state also failed to achieve the potentially related effect of presenting itself in a positive light vis-à-vis ecclesiastical power and dominance.

CHAPTER 4

Procedures, Evidence and Logics

By the 1820s, diocesan borders had been redrawn – and the granting of dispensations once again adhered to regular procedures. One piece of Maria Theresian and Josephine heritage, namely centralisation, continued to be a salient characteristic of nineteenth-century dispensation practice in Austria: all dispensation requests had to be handled by the diocesan consistories.[1] Their number successively rose, and around 1900, Paul Baumgarten ascertained regarding the Roman Curia that "the workload of this authority has increased massively over the past fifty years".[2] The *placetum regium*, introduced in 1782, as well as the *Exequatur* of the dispensation briefs by the *Gubernium* that was necessary prior to a marriage remained part of the mandatory bureaucratic procedures into the 1850s.[3] Save for a few exceptions, the Diocese of Brixen treated this state role as a formality. But in the Diocese of Trento, the situation looked different. Though the massive conflicts of the eighteenth century's final decades did not continue, new problems emerged. The fact that the diocesan consistories were once again turning to Rome concerning requests for dispensations in the

1 This did not always go smoothly: 1842 saw the *Gubernium* in Innsbruck file a report in Vienna concerning the marriage of Johann Leit[n]er and Anna Reiner, who were first-degree cousins, in Rome. Prior to that, the two had submitted "a request for dispensation". "The prince-episcopal ordinariate" – the reference here was to the one in Trento – had declared in a note of August 1841 "that having made extensive, reliable enquiries, it considered the intended marriage too ill-advised in every respect and had also found no tenable canonical reasons to submit to the Holy See in order to obtain the necessary dispensation". The *Gubernium* stated that it had therefore likewise been forced to refuse this request. Regarding this point, the letter refers to a court decree of 6 February 1823, No. 3.342. "But hardly had the two prospective spouses received this official decision than they resolved to realise their plan by travelling to Rome." They had been married there on 7 December 1841. ÖSTA, AVA, Alter Kultus, K. 12, Ehesachen, Taufen, Akatholiken, NÖ, Böhmen, OÖ, Slzb, Stmk, Innerösterr., Vorderösterr., Tirol, 1842, no. 27.282. This couple also receives brief mention in Rainer, *Die Diözese Brixen*, pp. 158–160. They were, however, subject to the Diocese of Trento, as is indicated by the note mentioned in the aforegoing. On this see TLA Innsbruck, Jüngeres Gubernium, Hauptgruppe 64 Ehesachen, 1840–1842, Fasc. no. 323, 1841, no. 20.042. This record contains no additional information.

2 Paul M. Baumgarten, "Die Geschäftsführung an der Kurie", in *Die römische Kurie um 1900. Ausgewählte Aufsätze von Paul M. Baumgarten*, ed. Christoph Weber (Cologne/Vienna, 1986), pp. 90–98, 90.

3 On this cf. Steeb/Strimitzer, "Österreichs diplomatische Vertretung", p. 41.

DOI:10.1163/9789004539877_005

close degrees no longer triggered active opposition by the state. However, the Imperial-Royal Provisional General Commissariat in Innsbruck had notified the regional courts in Vorarlberg – "for information and future observance" – that "His Majesty" had decreed "that any and all influence by the Roman curial authorities that runs counter to the supreme provincial governments' laws and ordinances in His Majesty's own states is always and everywhere to be steadfastly suppressed".[4] The procedure once more primarily followed church norms and logics.[5] Battles of authority between Church and state regarding marital law focused above all on interconfessional marriages, separations of table and bed and – during the final third of the nineteenth century – the "emergency civil marriage" (*Notzivilehe*).

The source material on dispensation requests to be found in diocesan archives differs substantially from diocese to diocese. In terms of density and organisation, it made sense to place the material of the Diocese of Brixen at the centre of further investigation. It is there that the available information concerning dispensation policies, dispensation practice and actions at the various ecclesiastical and state levels as well as on the part of the couples who requested dispensations is densest and most abundant. And because local and supra-local communication and mediation prior to the requests' arrival at the diocesan consistory and the *Gubernium* are also documented there, this material affords insights into various stages of the long bureaucratic processes as well as the logics that characterised dispensation practice. This chapter seeks to investigate knowledge about relatedness and how kin marriages were perceived in village contexts. It also explores several conspicuous aspects that affected the process of dispensation-granting. Occasional attention will also be given to the neighbouring dioceses of Chur, Salzburg and Trento in order

---

4 VLA Bregenz, Landgericht Bezau Akten, box 35, X.48.

5 In July 1836, the suffragan bishop and future archbishop Hermann von Vicari, who held office in Freiburg, wrote to the consistory in Brixen that the "worldly state government" sought to move his ordinariate to grant dispensations in the first and second degrees of affinity and consanguinity on its own authority. The government's arguments "repeatedly" pointed to "the example in the Austrian imperial state", he wrote. He stated that he was familiar with the Josephine ordinances but believed that Emperor Francis had amended the "ordinances that do not conform to the church canons". For this reason, his consistory was requesting "information on current practice in this matter". In its reply, the consistory in Brixen reported "that these marriage dispensation cases are submitted to the Holy See" and that "the Austrian bishops are not required to grant such dispensations *auctoritate ordinaria*". The decades-long power struggle between the Church and the Austrian state concerning this issue went unmentioned. DIÖAB, Konsistorialakten 1836, Fasc. 5c, Verschiedenes über Ehe, no. 7.

to show repertoires of action and the range of modes in which kinship was administrated.[6]

1 Dispensation Records and Dioceses

In Brixen, the dispensation records pertaining to marriage projects in close degrees of consanguinity and affinity preserved in the diocesan archive range from 1831 to 1910. This diocese stands out not only for the central position occupied by clergy and Church in dispensation matters throughout the nineteenth century[7] but also on account of how strict it handled dispensation requests. This affected the extent and content of the material contained in the records,

---

6 In 1830, the Church's "registers of souls" put the number of people living in the Diocese of Brixen at 355,000, of whom around one third lived in Vorarlberg. Towards the end of the nineteenth century, this figure reached 400,000. Salzburg's diocesan schematism indicated a total of 198,448 "souls" in 1831, and that number had grown to 234,723 by 1892. In the Diocese of Trento, 385,046 persons were counted in 1826 and 546,117 in 1892. The Catholic population of the Diocese of Chur numbered 130,000 in 1825. Cf. *Catalogus personarum ecclesiasticarum Dioecesis Brixinensis ad initium anni MCCCCXXXI*, vol. 22 (Brixen, 1831), p. 352. This source contains the Diocese of Brixen's figures for 1829. The Tyrolean portion of the diocese was home to ca. 266,000 inhabitants, while 89,000 lived in Vorarlberg. For the end of the nineteenth century cf. for example *Schematismus der Säcular- und Regular-Geistlichkeit der Diözese Brixen. 1892*, vol. 76 (Brixen, 1892), p. 230. This source puts the population of the diocese's Tyrolean areas at ca. 280,000, with ca. 117,000 said to reside in Vorarlberg; *Personalstand der Säkular- und Regular-Geistlichkeit des Erzbisthums Salzburg nebst dem Lehrpersonal-Stande der deutschen Schulen. In dem Jahre 1831* (Salzburg, 1831), p. 75; *Personalstand der Säcular- und Regulargeistlichkeit des Erzbisthums Salzburg auf das Jahr 1892* (Salzburg, 1892), p. 183; *Clerus et Dioecesis Tridentina exeunte anno MDCCCXXVI* (Trent, 1826), p. 205; *Catalogus Cleri Dioecesis Tridentinae ineunte anno MDCCCXCII* (Trent, 1892), pp. 233–234. In 1892, the Italian-speaking part of the Diocese of Trento was home to 417,174 people while the German-speaking part was home to 128,943. Albert Fischer, "Bistum Chur", in *Die Bistümer der deutschsprachigen Länder*, ed. Gatz, pp. 156–174, 157.

7 The situation in the Diocese of Brixen seems to have been comparable with what Edith Saurer ascertained for the Venetian territory in the early nineteenth century. Cf. Saurer, "Formen von Verwandtschaft und Liebe", pp. 263–267. What is more, both areas also exhibited a comparably high density of clergymen relative to the total population, a fact that has to be viewed not only with respect to their support of couples but also with respect to their ability to exercise control. Saurer writes: "In Venice, there were 132 inhabitants per Catholic clergyman in 1830, whereas the ratio for the entire region of Veneto was 249 to 1; in Vienna, it was 796 to 1, and in Lower Austria as a whole it was 1,197 to 1" (ibid., p. 262). Comparing Austrian territories, Tyrol/Vorarlberg had the highest density of clergymen followed by Salzburg. While the Empire's western half had an average of 1.5 clergymen for every 1,000 inhabitants, Salzburg had 4.7 and Tyrol including Vorarlberg had 5.8. Cf. Norbert Ortmayr, "Späte Heirat. Ursachen und Folgen des alpinen Heiratsmusters", *Zeitgeschichte* 16 (1988/89), 119–134, 129, 132 (table). Helmut Alexander has shown that the "recruiting of pastoral clergy in the Diocese of Brixen

with elaborate portrayals of couples' situations being produced. The comparatively numerous requests that were already rejected at the diocesan level were frequently followed by renewed attempts, often made years later. Nearly 20 per cent of the requests submitted between 1831 and 1864 were by couples whose requests had previously been rejected. The density of information contained in these resubmitted and even more urgently argued writings is all the greater, entailing a particularly rich body of documentation. Moreover, a major strong point of these holdings is that drafts of the correspondence sent by the diocese are included in the corresponding dispensation records up into the 1880s.[8]

Papal dispensations are organised by year and numbered consecutively, in the order in which they arrived at the consistory, on the respective fascicules' cover pages. However, it frequently happened that a request could not be fully processed within the year of its submission. In such cases, the associated correspondence was transferred to the following or a later year and assigned with a new number, for which reason ascertaining the annual number of submitted requests – though it may appear easy at first glance – can in fact be tricky. Last but not least, we can repeatedly find records on interconfessional marriages or dispensations made necessary by adultery. "Faszikel a" with the Roman dispensations is usually joined by two further partial fascicules, namely "b geheime Dispensen", Secret Dispensations, and "c Verschiedenes über Ehe", Miscellany Concerning Marriage. Both the secret dispensations and the colourfully mixed, marriage-related "miscellany" also contain documents on kin marriage.

Obtaining a dispensation in the more distant third or fourth degree rarely entailed any difficulties, but there were isolated occasions where Brixen's consistory reprimanded deans or imposed conditions on supplicants. Such gestures were probably intended to make examples of people while also emphasising that dispensations in the more distant degrees were not to be treated as mere formal acts. As a rule, the authority to dispense in the third and fourth degrees lay with the bishops. In the Diocese of Brixen, however, this authority passed to the deans in the mid-nineteenth century. The instructions sent to the deanery offices in November 1854 explicitly stated that this authority was contingent upon the presence of canonical reasons and that dispensations lacking "proper legal justification" were "invalid". Dispensation was only permitted to "take place following examination of the couple's knowledge of existing marriage impediments". The closer the degree of kinship, the stronger

took place almost exclusively within the diocese itself". Their place of training was the seminary in Brixen. Alexander, "Zur regionalen Herkunft des Priesternachwuchses", p. 314.

8 Later on, this dwindles to only brief and often barely legible annotations. For this reason, 1890 seemed like a point of empirical saturation in this respect.

the reasons needed to be. As a suggestion intended to help deans determine how to proceed, the consistory noted “that the dispenser [should] dispense in the fourth degree not blindly but also not fearfully”.[9] A few years prior, at the 1849 Episcopal Conference of Austria in Vienna, the Austrian bishops expressed themselves to the effect “in Central Europe, the third and fourth degrees of kinship can no longer be enforced as marriage impediments” – for across “nearly the entire empire”, it had “for many long years been customary for forbearance to be granted without difficulties”.[10] The Bishop of Brixen had not attended this meeting in person.[11]

The archived dispensation records in the Archdiocese of Salzburg are organised in an entirely different way than those in Brixen. Salzburg’s holdings are grouped not by year, but in part by specific degrees of consanguinity and affinity. Some of the holdings are also grouped together in a fascicule labelled “Ehedispensen”, marriage dispensations, that contains dispensations of various types from multiple decades: dispensations pertaining to affinity based on premarital sexual contact (*ex copula illicita*) or spiritual kinship (*cognationis spiritualis*), but also various papal dispensations. The records in Salzburg contain both overlaps and gaps, therefore it is difficult to get a good overview. Doing so for the dioceses of Chur[12] and Trento[13] is even more difficult. At the diocesan archive in Chur, it was possible to examine dispensation records from the period between 1827 and 1857. The majority of these records consist of individual letters with attachments such as baptismal certificates, certificates of unmarried status, family trees and certificates of domicile rather than complete documentation of cases’ progress from beginning to end. Dispensations from an extremely broad range of categories are collected within the individual years: dispensations of the banns of marriage, dispensations in order to marry during “forbidden times”, dispensations due to adultery, dispensations due to

---

9 DIÖAB, Konsistorialakten 1854, Fasc. 5c, Verschiedenes über Ehe, no. 14. This “assessment of a highly respected and high-ranking canonist of our time” was characterised as being in conformance with earlier canonists.

10 Michel, *Beiträge zur Geschichte*, p. 67; cf also Saurer, “Stiefmütter und Stiefsöhne”, p. 352.

11 Cf. Peter Leisching, *Die Bischofskonferenz. Beiträge zu ihrer Rechtsgeschichte, mit besonderer Berücksichtigung ihrer Entwicklung in Österreich* (Vienna/Munich, 1963), p. 130.

12 For a general impression on the Diocese of Chur in the nineteenth century cf. Fischer, “Bistum Chur”; Albert Gasser, “Kirche, Staat und Gesellschaft”, in *Handbuch der Bündner Geschichte*, vol. 3: 19. und 20. Jahrhundert, ed. Verein für Bündner Kulturforschung im Auftrag der Regierung des Kantons Graubünden, 2nd ed. (Chur, 2000), pp. 229–247, 232–236.

13 For a general impression on the Diocese of Trento in the nineteenth century cf. Sergio Benvenuti, “Le istituzioni ecclesiastiche”, in *Storia del Trentino*, vol. 5: L’età contemporanea 1803–1918, ed. Maria Garberi and Andrea Leonardi (Bologna, 2000), pp. 275–317.

wide age gaps between the prospective spouses and – not insignificantly – dispensations for kin marriages in distant and close degrees.

Insights into dispensation practice are also afforded by registers, of which Chur possesses several from the nineteenth century, listing various types of dispensations. Quite numerous in this diocese were dispensations for interconfessional marriages (*disparitas cultus* or *mixtae religionis*). In the attached pieces of correspondence, interconfessionality was perceived as a problem much more than marriage between close kin. One also sees a significantly more complex situation than in Brixen and Salzburg due to the diverse modes of obtaining or granting a dispensation that remained possible into the nineteenth century. In the nineteenth-century central registers, which not only contain dispensations from Chur but also from the dioceses of Basel, Constance, Lausanne, Sitten and the Swiss areas of the dioceses of Como and Milan, it turns out that requests from the Swiss dioceses were sent to Rome en masse at more or less regular intervals of one or two months – "*Romam missae fuerunt*". The resulting dispensation briefs returned in a similar manner: "*advenerunt ab urbe*".[14] Up to its elimination in 1873, the nunciature in Lucerne occupied an important position in the forwarding process as well as otherwise.[15] For here, all roads did not lead to Rome.[16] In August 1822 and again in June 1823, for example, Papal Nuncio Ignazio Nasalli had been granted authority to dispense 20 marriages each in the second and third as well as second and fourth unequal degrees of consanguinity and affinity, but not in the second degree itself.[17] In the individual registers, papal dispensations are followed by numerous

---

14 Bischöfliches Archiv Chur (BAC), Dispensationes matrimoniales, ab anno 1816 de Novem[bris] ad mensem Decembris 1818; ibid. Regestum Dispensationum Matrimon[ialium] quae Auctoritate Ap[osto]lica concessae sunt Ab Exc[ellentissi]mo P. Vincentio Macchi Nuntio, Ab Ill[ustrissi]mo P. Aloysio Nevi Internuntio, et ab Exc[ellentissi]mo P. Ignatio ex Comitibus Nasalli Archi-Episcopo Cyri, et Pro Sancta Sede ad Helevtos Nuntio Apostolico 1818–1828; ibid., Register Gizzi, Salzmann, Gizzi, Dispensationes Matrimoniales, 1823–1828. Cf. also BAC, Dispensationes matrimoniales, 1848–1853; and BAC, Dispensationes matrimoniales expeditae ab Ill[ustrissi]mo et R[everendissi]mo D[omi]no Jos[eph] Mar[ia] Bovieri S[anctis] Sedis Negotiorum Gestore, ab initio anni 1854 usque ad initium Decembris 1864. In both registers, the note reads either "*Romam transmissae*" or "*Romam missae*". Giuseppe Maria Bovieri served as nuncio in Switzerland from 1848 to 1854. On this cf. also Mathieu, "Verwandtschaft als historischer Faktor", p. 241.

15 Cf. Mathieu, "Verwandtschaft als historischer Faktor", p. 242.

16 The various routes are depicted in the registers, which are typically divided into multiple sections. Cf. for example BAC, Dispens[ationes] Matrimoniales, Expeditiones Romanae, Curae Animarum, Confirmatio ad Beneficia, 1859–1933. This register contains both Roman and nunciatory dispensations.

17 Cf. the 18 June 1823 letter from the secretary of the Propaganda Fide that, among other things, refers to the authorities that had been delegated in 1822. This is included in the

dispensations granted by the nunciature. However, there were repeated conflicts over authority with individual dioceses.[18]

The broader range of authorities to which one could turn probably came thanks not least to the mixed confessional situation. The Catholic Church was more liberal in its delegation of authority wherever it perceived its flock to be in 'danger'. Particularly relevant in this context were the authorities delegated to the bishop, which also included contingent-like allowances that – much like those of legates and nuncios[19] – encompassed specific numbers of dispensations for specific degrees and situations. If necessary, a bishop could grant these without being required to consult with Rome.[20] A volume labelled as a fee register that covers the years between 1877 and 1892 documents such "dispensation packages" in a section entitled *Dispensationes ex facultates Quinquennalibus et aliis extraordinariis Indultis*.[21] The entry fields are divided into rubrics for the various degrees and made it possible for dispensations to be granted in cases of imminent danger – "*periculum in mora*" – or in urgent cases – "*casus urgentes*".[22] It is likely that consanguineous and affine couples in the Diocese of Chur will have had an altogether easier time obtaining marriage

---

previously cited register *Regestum Dispensationum Matrimon[ialium], 1818–1828*. Ignazio Nasalli (1750–1831), who became the titular Bishop of Cyrrhus (Syria) in 1819, was accredited in Switzerland as nuncio from 1820 to 1826. Cf. Manfred E. Welti, "Das apostolische Gesandtschaftswesen in der Schweiz", in *Schweizerische Kardinäle. Das apostolische Gesandtschaftswesen in der Schweiz. Erzbistümer und Bistümer I*, ed. Albert Bruckner (Bern, 1972), pp. 35–60, 56; Markus Ries, "Nasalli, Ignazio", *Historisches Lexikon der Schweiz* http://www.hls-dhs-dss.ch/textes/d/D26834.php (last access: June 2022).

18 Cf. Mathieu, "Verwandtschaft als historische Faktor", 241; Urban Fink, *Die Luzerner Nuntiatur 1586–1873. Zur Behördengeschichte und Quellenkunde der päpstlichen Diplomatie in der Schweiz* (Lucerne/Stuttgart, 1997), pp. 104, 117, 134.

19 Lucerne's first nuncio Giovanni Battista Santonio, who was stationed there in 1586, is said to have already possessed "extensive dispensatory powers concerning marriage". During the eighteenth century, for which the faculties delegated to the Lucerne nuncios are documented, the granting of marriage dispensations numbered among the basic faculties. Fink, Die *Luzerner Nuntiatur*, pp. 44, 103–104.

20 On the assignment of dispensation contingencies to the Diocese of Chur cf. the body of documents in BAC, 111.02.04, Päpstliche Erlasse, Bestände 19. Jahrhundert.

21 BAC, Dispens[ationes] Matrim[oniales], 1877–1892.

22 Cf. for example BAC, Registrum Dispensationum Matrimonialium quae Auctoritate Apostolica concessae sunt a Rev[erendissi]mo D[omi]no Paschale Gizzi Archiepiscopo Thebarum et ad Helvetos Ap[osto]lico Nuntio, 1839 ad 1841 [1848]. The volumes of this register are in part unpaginated. The section "*Dispensationes in 2°gradu aequali cum facultate extraord[inaria] concessa a Summo Pontifice pro 12 casibus, quando adest periculum in mora*" follows immediately after the entries from the years of 1839 to 1848. Cf. also the section "*casus urgentes*" in BAC, Dispens[ationes] Matrim[oniales], 1877–1892. These cases are positioned following the dispensations in the first and second unequal degree. Many such cases are also documented in BAC, Dispensationes Matrim[oniales] Specialium Facult[atis] Apost[olicae], incipit mense Maji 1892.

dispensations than such couples in the Diocese of Brixen. Concerning many of these numerous requests, however, the only extant evidence consists of their entries in the register.

In the diocesan archive in Trento, the nineteenth-century dispensation records only cover the more distant degrees of kinship. Until the mid-1830s, these included dispensations in the second and third unequal degree.[23] For certain periods of time, there exist registers concerning dispensation fees[24] that provide an overview of the number and closeness of the degrees of kinship at issue, but it is often not indicated whether such kinship was consanguineous or affinal.[25] No materials concerning papal dispensations were found. The documentation held by the Archivio di Stato di Trento and the State Archives of Bolzano indicates that in the Diocese of Trento, the district offices functioned as central nodes of communication during the nineteenth century. They were in contact with the diocesan ordinariate as well as the respective regional courts (*Landgerichte*). The latter submitted their own evaluations of marriage projects and couples, and they also communicated with the *Gubernium* in Innsbruck – to which, judging by the surviving notes and similarly to how things were in Salzburg, extensive documentation was sent. Dispensation requests are contained in the records of the district office in Rovereto that were investigated beginning in the 1820s, but those in Trento only contain dispensation requests from a few years beginning in 1843.[26] The records from the district office in Bozen in the categories of "Spiritual" and/or "Marriage" that were analysed from 1831 onward contain only few dispensation requests, with some years containing none at all. Evidently, such documents were only kept in certain cases.[27] This disparate source situation provides only fragmentary insights

23 Scrutiny with this in mind was devoted to the fascicules Archivio Diocesano Tridentino (ADT), Dispense matrimoniali, Dispense 1830; ibid., Dispense 1831, which also contains dispensations from 1833; ibid., Dispense 1832; ibid., Dispense 1836; ibid., Dispense 1842; ibid., Dispense 1846; ibid., Dispense 1855; the years between 1856 and 1858 are missing.

24 Cf. ADT, Registro delle spese per dispense pontificie dei relativi depositi, dei pagamenti agli agenti, 1823. This lists dispensations up to 1841; the entries regarding various financial transactions run until 1848.

25 This remains open in ADT, Protocolli cancelleria. Indice dall'anno 1842 fino al 1845 inclusive; as well as ibid., Indice Eccl[esiastico] 1846–1849. Here, one finds a list of papal dispensations ordered alphabetically and chronologically according to the grooms' surnames.

26 Archivio di Stato di Trento (ASTn), Capitanato Circolare di Rovereto, busta 90, 1823, Matrimoni; busta 120, 1825, Matrimoni; busta 143, 1827, Matrimoni; busta 156, 1828, Matrimoni. ASTn, Capitanato Circolare di Trento, busta 130, 1843, Ehe; busta 195, 1846, matrimoni; busta 213, 1847, Ehe – matrimoni. For the period around the mid-1850s, there exist no more dispensation records – which may have to do with the abolishment of the obligation to obtain provincial government consent.

27 Archivio di Stato Bolzano / Staatsarchiv Bozen (ASBz / SABo), Kreisamt Bozen, Bündel 331, 1 and 2, 1831, Geistlich, Ehe I; Bündel 332, 1831, Geistlich, Ehe II; Bündel 345, 1832,

into nineteenth-century dispensation practice in the Diocese of Trento. But even so, certain routines and salient issues can still be recognised.

In the Diocese of Trento, in contrast to how things were in Brixen, the nineteenth century saw secular authorities remain far more strongly involved in the administrative procedures associated with dispensation practice. This can be seen in how, not unimportantly, the *Gubernium* in Innsbruck intervened here in a clearer way than it did vis-à-vis the consistory in Brixen. An example is the request of Giovanni S. and Maria C., already submitted multiple times. The *Gubernium* objected to how the ordinariate was proceeding – not only on principle, in view of what it deemed to be an excessively great number of submitted requests overall, but also in terms of substance via criticism of this request's justification, which the *Gubernium* deemed to be too weak, why it rejected this request: "The dispensation requests coming so frequently from the Tridentine districts have moved the *Gubernium* to suspect that the prince-episcopal ordinariate is likely making its own work too easy in such cases."[28] Various subsequent references allow us to conclude that dispensation matters were probably not handled all that strictly here on the diocesan level. A decree by the provincial government addressed the "Italian ordinariates" with the admonishment to exhibit "strict observance" regarding the issuance of marriage dispensations in close degrees of kinship. This decree referred to the Court Chancellery decree of 29 May 1837 that came in reaction to a papal hierography received from the Imperial-Royal embassy in Rome.[29]

One context that may have caused state authorities to assume a central role in dispensation proceedings in the Diocese of Trento was that in Trentino a liberal flavour of Catholicism predominated during the *Vormärz* period. This was very much in contrast to German-speaking Tyrol "where the priests were recruited largely from the peasantry and the secondary schools were led mostly by anti-Josephine and ultramontane regular clergy". According to the findings of Thomas Götz, "openness to the world, trust in education and the sciences and moderate political progressiveness" succeeded in uniting representatives

---

Geistlich, Ehe I; Bündel 346, 1832, Geistlich, Ehe II; Bündel 353, 1833, Geistlich, Ehe I; Bündel 354, 1833, Geistlich, Ehe II; Bündel 373, 1 and 2, 1834, Geistlich, Ehe; Bündel 388, 1 and 2, 1835, Geistlich, Ehe; Bündel 399, 1 and 2, Miscellanea [Though the repertory mentions marriage dispensations, none were found in the fascicule]; Bündel 401, 1 and 2, 1836, Geistlich, Ehe; Bündel 420, 1 and 2, 1837, Geistlich, Ehe; Bündel 426, 1838, Geistlich, Ehe, Schul....; Bündel 430, 1, 1839, Geistlich, Kanzl.

28 Letter from the Gubernium dated 31 July 1824, ASTn, Capitanato Circolare di Rovereto, busta 120 (1825), no. 7.310/702 Matrimoni; Italian version to the regional court in Tione dated 12 August 1824, ibid., no. 14.824/1.617 Ehe. In keeping with the policies of the State Archive in Trento, personal names from its holdings are anonymised here.

29 ASBz / SABo, Kreisamt Bozen, Bündel 420, 1 and 2, 1837, Geistlich, Ehe, no. 120.

of the most varied groups. In Trentino, "the Catholic clergy for a while remained, at least as far as its members with an above-average education were concerned, a prominent exponent of bourgeois culture in the 'provinces'".[30]

Looking at individual dioceses makes clear that their internal organisation varied significantly.[31] But it was not only the degrees of state and church involvement in individual cases and the structuring of procedures that differed; there were also most certainly differences in terms of how the individual bishops proceeded. In addition, dioceses and even their various constituent regions had their own prior ecclesiastical and political histories in which the handling of dispensations had, in some cases, been organised in far simpler ways. The relative stability of bureaucratic procedures from the 1820s and 1830s onward had been preceded by turbulent times, most recently due to the restructuring of the dioceses during the nineteenth century's initial two decades. Borders now ran differently, with some areas having been made part of other dioceses. Such changes had taken place in all four neighbouring dioceses of Brixen, Chur, Salzburg and Trento: the areas south of Brixen that belong to present-day South Tyrol, including Säben, passed to the Diocese of Trento in 1819. Vorarlberg was appended to the Diocese of Brixen,[32] as were areas of present-day East Tyrol that had previously been part of the Diocese of Salzburg, and so on.[33]

---

30 Thomas Götz, *Bürgertum und Liberalismus in Tirol 1840–1873. Zwischen Stadt und 'Region', Staat und Nation* (Cologne, 2001), pp. 102–103. In German-speaking Tyrol, liberals indeed put their stamp on the "historical reality" if not "the image of their country", as Thomas Götz has ascertained. From 1861 and, after a brief interruption, from 1869 onward, Innsbruck had "a liberal mayor, a liberal city council and liberal municipal committees", while Bozen's "liberal municipal administration" stood "uncontested from the dawn of the constitutional era onward" (ibid., p. 14).

31 Ida Fazio, as well, has emphasised that there was no exclusive and monolithic Church, in contrast to the impression that often comes across in cases where the Church is equated with the pope or the Roman Curia. Ida Fazio, "Matrimoni, conflitti, istituzioni giudiziarie: le specificità italiane di un percorso di ricerca", *Rivista storica italiana* 2 (2009), 645–672, 648.

32 On this cf. the document "Abtretung der bisher von den Fürst-Bischöfen in Chur und Constanz im Lande Vorarlberg besessenen Diözesan-Antheilen an den Fürstbischof in Brixen, die Aufstellung eines bischöflichen Vikars für Vorarlberg, und die Einführung des Placetum regium in kirchlichen und geistlichen Dingen 1814, 1815, 1816, 1817", VLA Bregenz, Landgericht Bezau Akten, box 35, X.48.

33 On this cf. Hubert Bastgen, *Die Neuerrichtung der Bistümer in Österreich nach der Säkularisation* (Vienna, 1914), pp. 301–344; Aldo Stella, "I principati vescovili di Trento e Bressanone", in *I Ducati padani Trento e Trieste*, ed. Lino Marini et al. (Turin, 1979), pp. 499–606, especially chapters IV and V; Franz Ortner, "Erzbistum Salzburg", in *Die Bistümer der deutschsprachigen Länder*, ed. Gatz, pp. 638–653, 638–639; Fischer, "Bistum Chur", pp. 156–157; Albert Gasser, "Vom rätischen Fürstbistum zur schweizerischen Diözese",

Particularly in Vorarlberg, the transition period surrounding its transfer to the Diocese of Brixen was protracted and riddled with conflicts. Parishes that had previously been subject to the authority of Chur went unstaffed, and there was a lack of clarity as to who was competent where dispensation was concerned. "Where should the priest, where should the Christian subject now turn?", asked the judge who presided over the regional court in the Montafon. The handling of certain cases could not be delayed, he stated, but the ordinariate in Brixen had declared that it did not consider itself authorised to "intervene" on behalf of those belonging to the Diocese of Chur. As a result, marriage dispensation requests were once again blocked.[34] A report from the regional court in Feldkirch dated 20 June 1815 struck a similar note: "The current state of affairs regarding this matter", it read, was "such that not even de facto" knowledge existed as to "which of those bishops it is who has assumed spiritual stewardship of the parishes in Vorarlberg that were previously subject to the Diocese of Chur". For the Bishop of Brixen was not assuming the handling of "any business" concerning the territory that had belonged to Chur, the letter's author continued, while the Prince-Bishop of Chur did not dare act there publicly as prince-bishop.[35] Moreover, obtaining a dispensation would seem to have become noticeably more difficult upon the region's transfer to the Diocese of Brixen. This is indicated by complaints voiced here and there as late as the 1830s. The Bregenz Forest's dean, Johann Baptist Sinz, portrayed matters as follows: "Back when we *still* belonged *to Constance*, obtaining a marriage dispensation had been *very easy*. It was possible to obtain one in 3 to 4 days using one's own messenger."[36] In terms of church organisation, Vorarlberg had previously been divided between the dioceses of Chur, Constance and Augsburg.[37]

in *Studien zur Geschichte des Bistums Chur, 451–2001*, ed. Michael Durst (Freiburg, 2002), pp. 145–174, 145–147; Mercedes Blaas, *Der letzte Fürstbischof von Chur und sein Klerus in Tirol. Der Tiroler Anteil der Diözese Chur unter Bischof Karl Rudolf von Buol-Schauenstein (1794–1808 und 1815–1816). Ein Beitrag zur Geschichte des Jahres 1809*, PhD thesis, University of Innsbruck, 1983; Elmar Fischer, *Die Seelsorge im Generalvikariat Feldkirch von seiner Gründung bis zum Jahr 1848*, PhD thesis, University of Innsbruck, 1968, pp. 8–11.

34 These complaints appear in a very extensive letter from the Imperial-Royal Provincial Regional Court in the Montafon dated 22 June 1815. VLA Bregenz, Kreisamt 1, box 286, Präsidiale 1814–1848, Fasc. 18b, Akten über die Bischöflich Churischen Dioces-Angelegenheiten, no. 605.

35 VLA Bregenz, Kreisamt 1, box 286, Präsidiale 1814–1848, Fasc. 18b, Akten über die Bischöflich Churischen Dioces-Angelegenheiten, no. 890.

36 DIÖAB, Konsistorialakten 1832, Fasc. 5a, Römische Dispensen, no. 11, emphases in the original are underlined in red, which was probably done in Brixen.

37 Cf. Josef Gelmi, "Bistum Bozen-Brixen (bis 1964: Brixen)", in *Die Bistümer der deutschsprachigen Länder*, ed. Gatz, pp. 141–155, 141; very detailed concerning the facts: Edmund Karlinger and Carl Holböck, *Die Vorarlberger Bistumsfrage. Geschichtliche Entwicklung und kirchenrechtliche Beurteilung* (Graz/Vienna/Cologne, 1963), pp. 149–265.

It was thus that the nineteenth-century Diocese of Brixen came to encompass large areas of present-day North Tyrol (excepting its north-eastern part, which still belongs to the Diocese of Salzburg today), the northern part of present-day South Tyrol (the Puster Valley, the Upper Eisack Valley and the Upper Vinschgau), present-day East Tyrol and Vorarlberg (see Map 2).[38] Beginning in 1820 (and until 1968), Vorarlberg had the status of a vicariate general with its seat in Feldkirch – a concession that Brixen had not made without resistance. The process of political reorganisation that began in 1815 saw the province involuntarily combined with Tyrol under a single *Gubernium*, with the province thus formed becoming a prefecture in 1850. During the nineteenth century, the repeated initiatives by Vorarlberg to obtain independent civil and ecclesiastical administration were to remain largely unsuccessful.[39]

The administrative level beneath the diocese and/or the vicariate general was that of the deaneries. The Diocese of Brixen initially had 26 deaneries, and the 1850s saw the two largest ones – both of which lay west of Innsbruck – divided: the new deaneries of Silz and Prutz were spun off from the deaneries of Flaurling and Zams, respectively, to make 28 deaneries in total. Each of these areas was overseen by its own dean, who served as a point of contact for the clergy of the local parishes, curacies and branches (*Expondituren*) and as an intermediate between them and the prince-episcopal consistory. The order in which enquiries, requests and the like were addressed adhered strictly to this hierarchy: local clergy did not communicate directly with the diocesan consistory regarding dispensation matters. In the Diocese of Trento, on the other hand, the direct route from the parishes to the consistory was the norm. The number of parishes that belonged to Brixen's individual deaneries varied. It ranged from the single parish in the Deanery of Ampezzo to 37 in the Deanery of Flaurling prior to its division. On average, there were between 15 and 25.[40]

On the whole and in ways that depended on the administrative context, diocesan ordinariates, district offices and the *Gubernium* represented

---

38 On the territorial development of the Diocese of Brixen cf. sources including Fridolin Dörrer, "Der Wandel der Diözesaneinteilung Tirols und Vorarlbergs", *Beiträge zur Geschichte Tirols. Festgabe des Landes Tirol zum Elften Österreichischen Historikertag in Innsbruck vom 5. bis 8. Oktober 1971* (Innsbruck, 1971), pp. 141–170; Gelmi, *Geschichte der Kirche in Tirol*, pp. 283–289; Josef Fontana, "Von der Restauration bis zur Revolution (1814–1848)", in *Geschichte des Landes Tirol*, vol. 2: Die Zeit von 1490 bis 1848, ed. Fontana et al., 2nd ed. (Bolzano, 1998), pp. 583–737, 613–620; Rainer, *Die Diözese Brixen*, pp. 21–59; Bastgen, *Die Neuerrichtung der Bistümer*.

39 On this cf. Benedikt Bilgeri, *Geschichte Vorarlbergs*, vol. 4: Zwischen Absolutismus und halber Autonomie (Vienna/Cologne/Graz, 1982), pp. 275–282.

40 Cf. for example *Schematismus der Geistlichkeit der Diözese Brixen für das Jahr 1840*, vol. 24 (Brixen, 1840). The relevant tables appear following the descriptions of the respective deaneries.

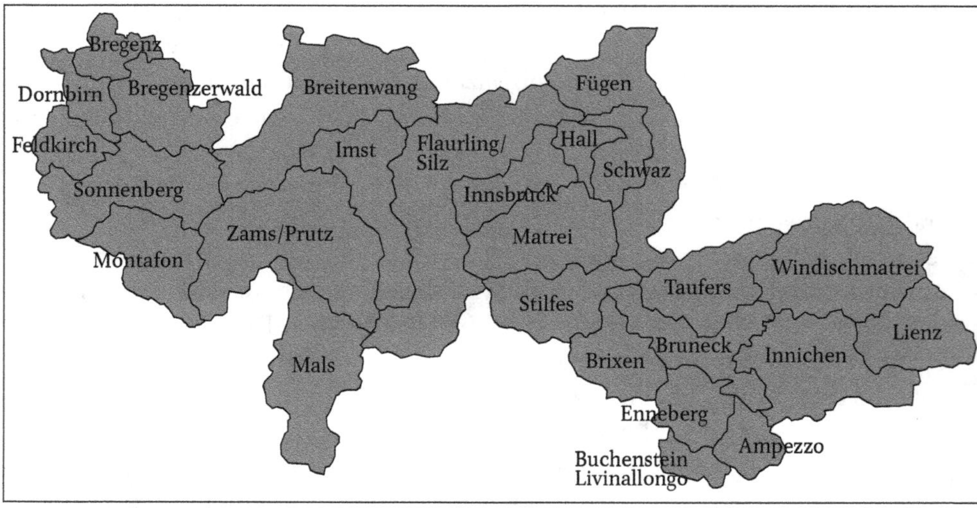

MAP 2 Deaneries of the Diocese of Brixen as reorganised in 1818

SOURCE: DIGITISED BY MARGARETH LANZINGER FROM THE ORIGINAL BY HUGO A. LANZINGER, IN ALEXANDER, "ZUR REGIONALEN HERKUNFT DES PRIESTERNACHWUCHSES", P. 313.

powerful decision-making entities placed before the papal authorities in Rome. Especially in Brixen, the consistory functioned as a bottleneck of sorts due to its representatives' comparative restrictiveness when it came to judging which requests would or would not enjoy good prospects of being answered in the affirmative by Rome, thereafter forwarding or – in a great many cases – rejecting them. On the regional level, therefore, the Church wielded definitional power over which arguments and justifications would be sufficient to receive a marriage dispensation in close degrees of consanguinity or affinity. The share of rejections was hence significantly greater at the diocesan level that it was at the level of the competent Roman authorities: of the 946 requests submitted between 1831 and 1864, 126 (13.3 per cent) were rejected at the diocesan level and 17 (1.8 per cent) were rejected in Rome, while 4 (0.4 per cent) were rejected by the *Gubernium*.[41] Thus approaching this matter via the references to dispensations contained in marriage registers[42] only reveals a certain

41 Not all of the remaining requests were successful: in 65 cases, requests were not pursued further and/or were retracted.

42 Earlier studies were interested in "incest" and hence primarily in dispensations for consanguineous couples, although the information in this respect, as well, is frequently imprecise and therefore of little use for purposes of comparison, insofar as the unequal degrees are not individually specified. Cf. for example Franz Fliri, *Bevölkerungsgeographische*

selection – especially in the stricter dioceses. After all, marriage registers only contain those that were approved. The sometimes arduous bureaucratic processes that were necessary left no traces there. As a consequence, failed marriage projects remain invisible.

2 Knowledge and Perception of Kinship

Knowledge of kinship was situated in various contexts. Formal canonical logics stood vis-à-vis lifeworld logics, as did the written and the spoken.[43] Noble and patrician family books of varied form and content served purposes including intergenerational memory and identity formation while connecting the past with the future.[44] However, they were also often simply "implicit representations concerning open or smouldering conflicts", mostly in relation to property claims.[45] Family trees, for their part, also preserved kinship-related knowledge. Both types of documents hence depicted inclusion as well as exclusion, above

Untersuchungen im Unterinntal (Innsbruck, 1948), pp. 85–86; Gisela Winkler, *Bevölkerungsgeographische Untersuchungen im Martelltal* (*Innsbruck*/Munich, 1973), p. 40. For a critical assessment see Mathieu, "Verwandtschaft als historischer Faktor", pp. 238–241.

43 See Jasmin Hauck, "Le témoignage de la parenté: la mémoire généalogique dans les dispenses matrimoniales à Florence (XVe–XVIe siècles)" *Genre & Histoire* 21 (2018), https://journals.openedition.org/genrehistoire/3512 (last access: June 2022). Recourse to orally transmitted knowledge regarding family and kinship has a long history. For the "birth certificates" or "kinship certificates" documenting legitimate birth that, during the eighteenth century, frequently still had to be issued to budding master tradesmen who sought to open a business far off from their communities of origin, for example, it was not the church registers that were consulted but rather three older men who were summoned to the court to provide information concerning the person's parents, legitimate birth, etc. Cf. Margareth Lanzinger, *Das gesicherte Erbe. Heirat in lokalen und familialen Kontexten, Innichen 1700–1900* (Vienna/Cologne/Weimar, 2003), pp. 80–81.

44 Cf. the thematic emphasis "Écritures et mémoire familiale", *Annales HSS* 59, 4 (2004) with contributions by researchers including Raul Mordenti, "Les livres de famille en Italie", ibid., 785–804, esp. 789–799; Claude Cazalé Bérard and Christiane Klapisch-Zuber, "Mémoire de soi et des autres dans les livres de famille italiens", ibid., 805–826; cf. also Giovanni Ciappelli (ed.), *Memoria, famiglia, identità tra Italia e Europa nell'età moderna* (Bologna, 2009); Birgit Studt, "Haus- und Familienbücher", in *Quellenkunde der Habsburgermonarchie (16.–18. Jahrhundert). Ein exemplarisches Handbuch*, ed. Josef Pauser, Martin Scheutz and Thomas Winkelbauer (Vienna/Munich, 2004), pp. 753–766.

45 Simon Teuscher, "Familienerinnerungen, Beziehungsmanagement und politische Sprache in spätmittelalterlichen Städten", *Traverse* 2 (2002), 53–64, 55–56.

all in terms of how they focused on male lines.[46] However, the number of people who possessed family registers, genealogical records or family trees was not particularly high when compared to the overall population. Dispensation requests thus often required laborious research aimed at ascertaining or excluding the possibility of relatedness by blood or by marriage.

Looking at dioceses and dispensation records,[47] one must not succumb to the illusion of being able to apprehend all kin marriages – not even in cases where extensive collections of documents were stored in an intentionally centralised manner. Even where strict requirements existed such as specific questions in the context of a pre-wedding religious examination, and despite the prescribed threefold public announcement of every impending marriage known as the three "banns of marriage" (*Aufgebote*), clergymen, parishioners and the affected couples sometimes overlooked this or that instance of kinship. It happened more frequently in distant degrees than it did in close ones,[48] and more often in cases of affinity than in cases of consanguinity. But since this was to be prevented wherever possible, the pressure felt by local clergymen was commensurately great.

Most nineteenth-century pastoral handbooks provided extensive support for those seeking to reconstruct blood and affinal kinship. They featured schematic illustrations as well as descriptions of all kinds of configurations (see Fig. 2), furthermore providing memory aids such as sayings or translations of complex relationships into riddles.[49] The handbook by Julius Müllendorff

46 Cf. for example James S. Grubb, "I libri di famiglia a Venezia e nel Veneto", in *Memoria, famiglia, identità*, ed. Ciappelli, pp. 133–158, 140–143. For a general overview cf. Christiane Klapisch-Zuber, *Stammbäume. Eine illustrierte Geschichte der Ahnenkunde* (Munich, 2004). One section here includes an illustration of "The Daughters Cut off of the Tree" (ibid., p. 109).

47 It is above all French and Italian studies that have worked with dispensation records: cf. Burguière, "'Cher Cousin'"; Fazio, "Parentela e mercato"; Gouesse, "Parenté, famille et marriage"; Trévisi, "Le mariage entre parents"; Merzario, *Il paese stretto*; Merzario, "Land, Kinship and Consanguineous Marriage".

48 The way in which awareness of kin relationships diminished toward the more distant degrees is pointed out by Jon Mathieu, "'Ein Cousin an jeder Zaunlücke'", p. 64.

49 Cf. Lyndan Warner, "Kinship Riddles", *genealogy* 6, 43 (2022), https://doi.org/10.3390/genealogy6020043 (last access: June 2022); Stapf/Egger, *Vollständiger Pastoralunterricht*, p. 268: It is pointed out how the fact that blood relatives of the husband could marry blood relatives of the wife – in contrast to the husband or wife doing so him or herself – could be "made visible by holding one's two hands together", where the right-hand thumb represented the husband with the fingers being his relatives out to the fourth degree, and the left-hand thumb represented the wife with the fingers being her relatives out to the fourth degree (ibid., p. 269). The affinity riddle is told as an "anecdote": "On an old gravestone onto which is carved two women with children in their arms, one read this inscription: 'These children are our children, / Their fathers our brothers, / All conceived from

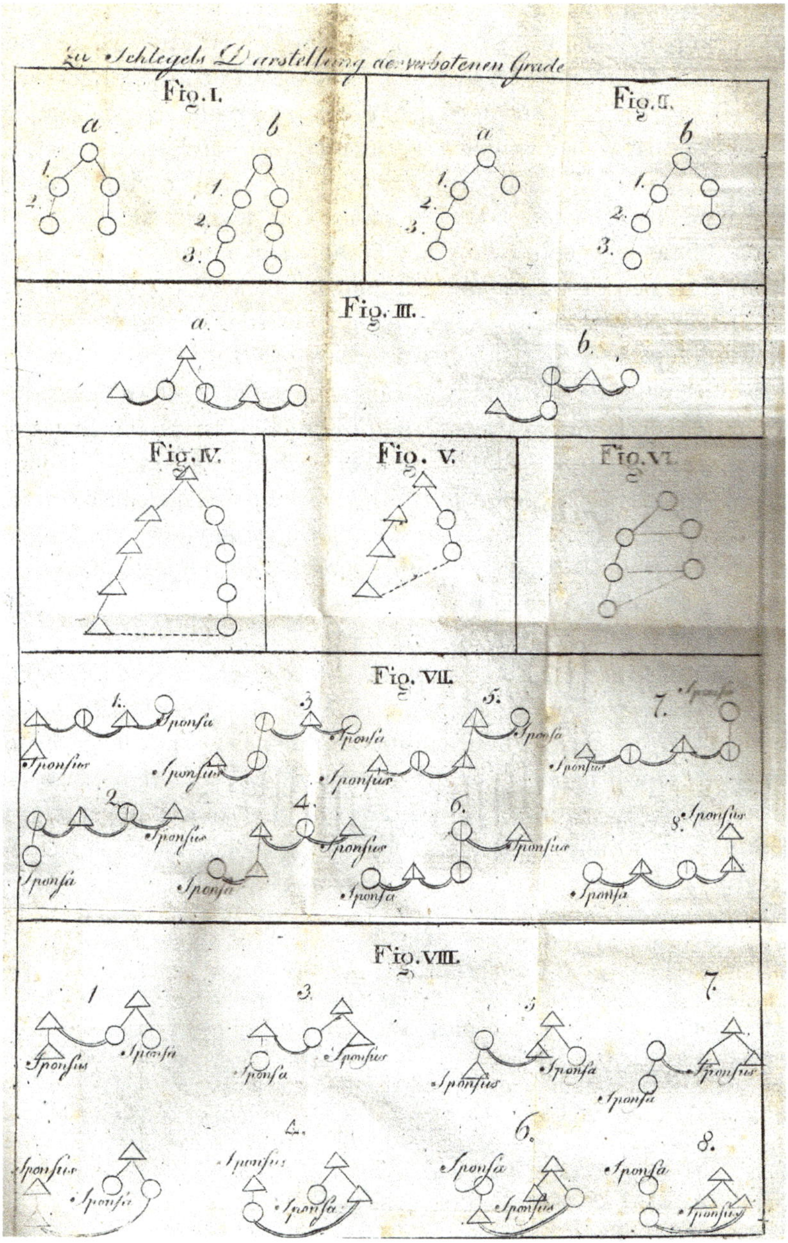

FIGURE 2 Depiction of the prohibited degrees
SOURCE: K.A.M. SCHLEGEL, KRITISCHE UND SYSTEMATISCHE DARSTELLUNG DER VERBOTENEN GRADE DER VERWANDTSCHAFT UND SCHWÄGERSCHAFT, BEY HEURATHEN, NACH DEM MOSAISCHEN GESETZE, DEM RÖMISCHEN UND CANONISCHEN RECHTE, UND DEN PROTESTANTISCHEN KIRCHENORDNUNGEN …(HANNOVER: 1802), APPENDIX.

features a general focus on the detection of marriage impediments.[50] And publishers, for their part, made available pre-printed forms for the four generations of ancestors that needed to be researched.[51] Such illustrative strategies were meant to help ease the reliable detection of unions that required dispensation. But even so, we must always assume a certain number of undetected cases.

As one can ascertain from numerous reports in the dispensation records, local clergymen would first seek to access local knowledge of kinship. Some places were home to people who could recall such things spontaneously. The dean in Innichen called one old man "a living register of kinship in this valley".[52] Certain women also possessed broad knowledge of intricate kinship networks.[53] Clergymen were absolutely dependent on such sources of information, for the clues they succeeded in gleaning provided them with considerable support in their laborious research in the church registers, allowing such research to go forward in a way that was that far better targeted. One local clergyman described his procedure as follows: he would first query the parents of the bridal couple and then "make special enquiries among several old men". Subsequently he would "spend hours upon hours consulting the canonical books" on account of his uncertainty as to whether kinship might not indeed be present.[54]

Several types of structural obstacles could present themselves when searching for possible marriage impediments. Where marriages concluded across parish borders were concerned, opportunities to obtain local knowledge of kinship decreased as the distance between the couples' places of origin increased, and the necessary documentation regarding the ancestors of the bride or the groom was not locally accessible. Clergymen also occasionally lamented church registers whose entries exhibited gaps or that had fallen victim to fire.[55]

---

pure marriages, / Guess what kind of kin they are'". The word for "kin" here, *Sippschaft*, was understood in this context to mean "affinity" (ibid., p. 262).

50 Mühlendorff explains this in his introduction by indicating how it would sometimes pit a priest against "not inconsiderable difficulties" and how it could easily happen "that he will not notice this or that existing marriage impediment. We therefore believe that it will be useful to discuss this matter in depth and present one or more methods whose use will allow one to discover with certainty all existing marriage impediments". Julius Müllendorff, *Methode zur Auffindung der Ehehindernisse bei mehrfacher Blutsverwandtschaft. Ein Beitrag zur Pastoral* (Graz, 1888), p. 5.

51 For such a form cf. ADF, Generalvikariat Matrimonialia (GA), Ehesachen II, 1811–1916, Fasc. 1880, 1884, Hintanhaltung von Ehen in den nächsten Verwandtschaftsgraden betreffend.

52 DIÖAB, Konsistorialakten 1864, Fasc. 22, Bischöfliche Dispensen, no. 247.

53 Cf. DIÖAB, Konsistorialakten 1844, Fasc. 5a, Römische Dispensen, no. 32.

54 DIÖAB, Konsistorialakten 1884, Fasc. 22c, Verschiedenes, no. 20.

55 Cf. DIÖAB, Konsistorialakten 1852, Fasc. 5c, Dispensen in occultis, no. 1.

And above all in small communities, the large numbers of identical names also exacerbated the difficulty of researching kin relationships.[56] Difficulty identifying marriage impediments could be expected particularly in cases where the bride, the groom or one of their ancestors had been born out of wedlock. For such couples, the lines of descent could only be reconstructed in their entirety if the father of the illegitimately born prospective spouse had declared himself to be such in the context of alimony payments or a financial settlement, or if his identity had been known in the corresponding social circle. A parish's baptismal records were likewise not necessarily of help here during the nineteenth century, since fathers of illegitimate children in Austria could only be entered into such records if they themselves requested it. This rule had been established by Joseph II in a 1784 patent that regulated how baptismal registers were to be kept.[57]

If the father of a child born out of wedlock was known neither officially nor informally, clerics had to depend on rumours or coincidence. The Diocese of Brixen's dispensation records document one particularly dramatic case that was ultimately decided before a marriage court: Johann Kaspar Meusburger and the illegitimately born Elisabeth Rüscher from the Bregenz Forest community of Bizau had gone to their rectorate and expressed their desire to be wed. The uncle and godfather of the bride subsequently informed the clergyman responsible for their case that his sister, the bride's mother, had told him "on her death bed" that the man and woman to be wed were half-siblings. The groom was unwilling to accept the categorical refusal that ensued and involved a lawyer in the further proceedings – but to no avail.[58]

Finally, errors could also occur. In principle, the role of supervisory authority was to be fulfilled by the deans, who were the first to see the family trees and

56 In one case, the dean in Schwaz justified the fact that it was "entirely by chance" that he had discovered a case of second degree affinity in addition to the known third degree consanguinity that had been regularly dispensed by the bishop with reference to the difficult familial situation up on the Wattenberg: there had originally been just four family names there. Even though, as the dean emphasised, he possessed "assured familiarity with how people are related here thanks to long practice and study", this had unfortunately still occurred. DIÖAB, Konsistorialakten 1862, Fasc. 22a, Römische Dispensen, no. 10. For an extreme case cf. the family reconstruction by Hans Matschek, *Sippenbuch von Schröcken 1490–1906* (Regensburg, 2007). In the Vorarlberg community of Schröcken, 75 per cent of all pre-1800 inhabitants bore the family name of Jochum.

57 Cf. Peter Becker, *Leben, Lieben, Sterben. Die Analyse von Kirchenbüchern* (St. Katharinen, 1989), p. 29. A comparable stance on this matter was taken up by the French *Code civil* of 1804. Article 340 expressly forbade research for the purpose of identifying fathers: "*La recherche de la paternité est interdite*". Ibid., p. 201.

58 DIÖAB, Konsistorialakten 1861, Fasc. 22a, Römische Dispensen, no. 40.

schematic illustrations drawn by local priests. One dean reported that when the bridal couple of Johann Klieber and Maria Graßl had come to take the matrimonial examination at his office in Flaurling, he had been so "preoccupied" by the opinion that they were blood kin in the third and fourth degree and hence a case for an episcopal dispensation that it had rendered him "entirely blind" and no longer able to count. Only while making a copy of the family tree had he then noticed that this was a case of kinship in the second and third unequal degree, which required a papal dispensation.[59]

Assured information regarding the bride and groom's kinship status was supposed to come primarily from the mandatory two witnesses involved in the matrimonial examination. The consistory in Brixen repeatedly urged that only "well-informed" witnesses be used. And around 1856, amidst a period that saw the handling of dispensation cases grow altogether more severe, witnesses' suitability began receiving special attention. Several letters concerning this were sent to various deaneries.[60] Suspicions tended to crop up especially whenever a witness's community of residence was also the seat of the deanery where the examination had been protocolled while the bridal couple resided somewhere else entirely. The fact was that summoning a second witness on location saved time and the expense of a long journey there, which made it a practical solution.[61] The letters from the diocese were targeted attempts to address this "grievous state of affairs". They referred to the "church rule" according to which witnesses had to "be selected from the dispensation applicant's place of residence". The only exception permissible was if "the witnesses from elsewhere" were among "the supplicants' closest kin".[62]

---

59 DIÖAB, Konsistorialakten 1856, Fasc. 5a, Römische Dispensen, no. 27.

60 Cf. DIÖAB, Konsistorialakten 1856, Fasc. 5c, Verschiedenes über Ehe, no. 7, no. 26, no. 27 and no. 28; occasionally, there were orders to provide additional information on witnesses. Cf. DIÖAB, Konsistorialakten 1856, Fasc. 5a, Römische Dispensen, no. 24.

61 Cf. DIÖAB, Konsistorialakten 1856, Fasc. 5c, Verschiedenes über Ehe, no. 14. Here, the Dean of Innichen requested permission – albeit to no avail – to delegate the protocolling of the required examinations to the local priest in the case of Obertilliach. This community was a six-hour journey from the seat of the deanery, and it was impossible for bridal couples and their witnesses to make the journey in both directions within the space of one day – a situation that entailed considerable expense. He also reported that "particularly in Tilliach, the importance of marriage impediments in the minds of the people has declined so far that they view dispensation as naught but an unnecessary plague and an opportunity to extract fees"; and he quoted a "commonly heard statement": "[T]hey love each other, and that should be enough". The latter passage is underlined in the original.

62 DIÖAB, Konsistorialakten 1856, Fasc. 5c, Verschiedenes über Ehe, no. 27. These criteria for witnesses were also portrayed in this way to the dean of the newly established Deanery of Silz with reference to the 1855 edition of the *Manuale Sacrum*, a handbook for the clergy of the diocese. An initial edition of the *Manuale Sacrum ad usum sacerdotum Dioecesis*

Despite all efforts, there were some instances where marriage impediments came to light too late, which triggered a specific procedure aimed to solve the resulting problem of an invalid marriage. In the case of the prospective spouses Gottlieb Vith from Laterns in the Deanery of Feldkirch and Seraphina Zech, their double marriage impediment of affinity – in the first and second unequal degree as well as in the third equal degree – only became apparent on the eve of their wedding, for which all preparations had already been made. In light of the this and by virtue of his authorities to act in such urgent circumstances, the dean felt entitled to issue an emergency dispensation of sorts – "due to *gravem et urgentem necessitatem*". It was required that he report this action to Brixen. In Brixen, however, there existed uncertainty as to whether the dean's authority had actually been valid in such a close degree of affinity. The consistory therefore forwarded this matter to Rome, where the Apostolic Penitentiary proceeded to invalidate the already concluded marriage.[63]

Most of the time, however, it was only after couples had been wed that priests would catch wind of such hidden cases of affinity or blood kinship: in Luttach in present-day South Tyrol's Ahr Valley, which belonged to the Deanery of Taufers, Anna Auer appeared before the parish priest ten days after a wedding had taken place to report that "her aged mother had discovered by chance, in a conversation only a couple of days ago, that the aforementioned newlyweds are blood relatives". The priest then set about investigating these claims of kinship, a task that required him to procure information from the church registries of three neighbouring parishes. "The certainty" of blood kinship in the fourth degree, he wrote, could now no longer be doubted.[64] Jakob Neumair and Agnes Fischnaller of St. Lorenzen in the Puster Valley were also already married when a "woman related to the groom" came to their parish priest and declared that she was "left no peace by her fear that the two newlyweds are related". Following a lengthy bit of research, it in fact did turn out that the groom and the bride had two great-grandfathers who had been brothers.[65]

Only once do the Brixen records reveal an overlooked marriage impediment in the second consanguineous degree, one discovered only after five years of marriage. Konrad Berkmann, who had been 43 years old and previously unmarried at the time of the wedding, and the 66-year-old widow Barbara Friß of Riefensberg were first cousins and had been wed without a dispensation. According to the dean's report, they had voiced their own suspicion of

---

Brixinensis had been published in Brixen in 1838, and editions were also published in 1886 and 1906. Cf. also DIÖAB, Konsistorialakten 1859, Fasc. 5a, Römische Dispensen, no. 12.

63 DIÖAB, Konsistorialakten 1858, Fasc. 5a, Römische Dispensen, no. 20.

64 DIÖAB, Konsistorialakten 1872, Fasc. 22b, Verschiedenes, no. 17.

65 DIÖAB, Konsistorialakten 1885, Fasc. 22a, Römische Dispensen, no. 46.

possibly being related prior to their marriage in 1854. The parish priest had then asked around in the community – but at that time, nobody had known anything about "the ancestry of the bride's mother". "Only recently", after the two had already been married for five years, wrote the dean to the consistory in Brixen, had their parish priest – "in a pertinent discourse with the retired teacher Berkmann" – realised that this couple was related by blood in the second canonical degree. Questions put to the husband, who was immediately summoned, permitted the inference that the couple honestly believed that they were not related. The new knowledge was thereupon revealed to him with the request that he "keep silent" about it. He was also instructed to "voice no demands for conjugal duties" until the necessary papal dispensation had been granted. In a postscript, the dean explained that the teacher Berkmann had in fact known of their kinship prior to the wedding but "refrained from reporting this impediment for fear of making enemies of the bride's relatives, who had been pushing for this marriage *par force*". The clerics of the consistory had a stern reprimand issued to the competent parish priest, since they found themselves unable to comprehend how this marriage impediment could have escaped him.[66]

Kin relationships that were overlooked and only discovered after the fact made necessary "revalidation" of the affected marriages. If, moreover, such a relationship was in degrees that fell within the purview of Rome, a dispensation had to be applied for there. In the Diocese of Brixen, this happened an average of once every ten years. Revalidation was typically handled in a way that kept secret the problem that had arisen. As soon as the dispensation had arrived from Rome, the couple was summoned to the parsonage and had to renew their consent to the union, the vows of 'I do' that had already been given. From the perspective of the Church, such a situation entailed a certain degree of risk. The supposed spouses could, after all, use the invalidity of their marriage as an excuse to separate and seek its annulment. Clergymen for the most part refrained from addressing the risk of such a scenario in explicit terms. This approach is exemplified by the interim parish priest Alois Pichler of Burgeis in connection with an overlooked case of fourth-degree consanguine kinship: he emphasised that the invalidly wed spouses were "of a good Christian disposition" and lived together "well and peacefully". For this reason, "no difficulty on their part that would run counter to marriage consent renewal need be feared".[67] It was typically two members of the clergy who functioned

66 DIÖAB, Konsistorialakten 1859, Fasc. 5a, Römische Dispensen, no. 10.

67 DIÖAB, Konsistorialakten 1852, Fasc. 5c, Dispensen in occultis, no. 1.

as witnesses to the marriage in order to finalise revalidation in the most discreet way possible and unbeknownst to the local public.

In order to avoid a flood of revalidations, and probably also in order to minimise and best conceal the problem of the sheer impossibility of discovering and duly dispensing all marriage impediments in the more distant degrees of consanguinity and affinity, the nineteenth century saw the Church employ the instrument of *sanatio in radice*, or "radical sanation", on a broad basis.[68] *Sanatio in radice* rendered a marriage that had been concluded despite the existence of a marriage impediment fundamentally valid, entailing that the act of consent – meaning the couple's mutual assent – did not need to be repeated.[69] In a normative sense, the employment of this option required that at least one member of an affected marriage know nothing of that marriage's invalidity. This instrument was employed primarily in so-called mission areas,[70] but increasingly also – as the practice of Brixen's consistory shows – in European dioceses in cases involving more distant degrees of consanguinity or affinity that had been discovered after the fact.[71]

The effectiveness of this form of control has to be taken into account not least whenever the frequency of kin marriage is at issue. In his analysis of the church registers of Vouvry in the Swiss canton of Valais between 1720 and 1840, Sandro Guzz-Heeb attributes such marriages' steadily rising numbers in part to closer ecclesiastical scrutiny. During the eighteenth century's second half, multiple consanguineous marriages had not been registered as such by the parishes. In Guzz-Heeb's view, this may have been owed to a lack of genealogical knowledge but also possibly to an interest in keeping existing relational ties secret[72] – as was also implied in the aforementioned case of Konrad Berkner

68 This process had begun in 1803 with instructions issued by Cardinal Caprara in the form of dispensation authorities that French bishops had received as a consequence of the Concordat of 1801 between Pius VII and Napoleon.

69 Cf. Peter Fabritz, *Sanatio in radice. Historie eines Rechtsinstituts und seine Beziehung zum sakralen Eheverständnis der katholischen Kirche* (Frankfurt a. M. et al., 2010), p. 201.

70 Cf. Fabritz, *Sanatio in radice*, pp. 204–211, 225.

71 Cf. for example DIÖAB, Konsistorialakten 1861, Fasc. 22 II, Ad matrimonium spectantia, no. 20. This letter was also signed by Johann Duille, then consistorial chancellor. Cf. also DIÖAB, Konsistorialakten 1857, Fasc. 5b, Ehedispensen in occultis, no. 5 and no. 7. For a general look at this practice cf. Baura, *La dispensa canonica*, pp. 181–183.

72 Guzzi-Heeb, *Donne, uomini, parentela*, pp. 222–223. Marion Trévisi, starting from the fact that requests in the third degree were considerably more common than those in the fourth during the eighteenth century in the area that she was studying, draws similar conclusions. This, she writes, could indicate that genealogical memory did not extend that far, meaning that knowledge of fourth-degree relationships among the populace was less common, though it could also be owed to deliberate concealment. Trévisi, "Le mariage entre parents", pp. 248–249; cf. also the corresponding findings of Nina Stren,

and Barbara Friß. Guy Tassin, also looking at the eighteenth century, ascertained that one third of those 53 couples from Haveluy in the north of France who would have needed a dispensation according to his genealogical reconstructions never applied for one.[73] Just how consistently or inconsistently dispensations were sought and granted would hence appear to have depended on the competent clerics' zeal, the accessibility of the relevant knowledge and on the willingness of the couples' close social circles to provide information on existing consanguine and affinal relationships.[74]

Where questions of social perception are concerned, it is necessary to distinguish between close and distant degrees. After all, dispensations in the third and fourth degrees were far more common than those granted in the close degrees, and their history also extended further back. Among the requests received by the Diocese of Brixen, the share of those in the close degrees that required papal dispensations amounted to but a few small percentage points.[75] Such requests would occasionally proliferate in local clusters, however, and indeed increased noticeably – if not explosively – over the course of the nineteenth century. Yet their number alone is not sufficient to illustrate the contemporary social presence of this phenomenon. Marriage projects in the close degrees, especially when they occurred but rarely or were accompanied by dramatic situations, did not remain concealed from the local public in the village, the neighbourhood, the section of town or sometimes even

---

Verbotene Beziehungen: Frühneuzeitliche Verwandtschafts- und Beziehungskonzepte in Ehedispensansuchen vor dem Passauer Konsistorium, diploma thesis, University of Vienna, 2014, p. 78.

73 Guy Tassin, *Qui épouser et comment. Alliances récurrentes à Haveluy de 1701 à 1870* (Paris, 2007), p. 124. David Sabean likewise points out that by employing family reconstitution, one arrives at a far higher number of kin marriages than the number of dispensations indicated by church registers. Sabean, *Kinship in Neckarhausen*, pp. 431–432.

74 Martine Segalen, in her study, speaks of a "certain ambiguity about the depth of people's genealogical memory". Segalen, *Fifteen Generations*, pp. 125–128 (quote 125).

75 On numbers and percentages for the Diocese of Brixen see chapter six. In thematically related studies, the corresponding values have not always been indicated in a way that distinguishes between degrees, which would be necessary to facilitate comparison. Typically, it is granted dispensations – rather than dispensation requests – that have been evaluated. In the study conducted by Jon Mathieu in 14 Swiss Catholic communities, the shares of dispensations granted in close degrees of kinship ranged from 0 to 14 per cent, with the first and second halves of the nineteenth century seeing 9 per cent exceeded by only one community during each half. The increase in dispensed marriages beginning in the second half of the eighteenth century can be clearly discerned: if we look at the share of kin marriages extending all the way out to the fourth degree, the percentages exhibit a noticeable increase – in some cases reaching 40, 50 and nearly 60 per cent. Cf. Mathieu, "Verwandtschaft als historischer Faktor", p. 239.

the entire district. They were objects of public communication and judgment. The offered fodder for disputes, occasionally even for scandals. Last but not least, consanguine and affine couples repeatedly referred to other dispensations that had been granted and used these as references in support of their own marriage projects. Fundamentally, the perceived or expected reaction of the local public to a dispensation did represent a relevant factor in the associated decision-making process. Beginning in the mid-1850s, local priests in the Diocese of Brixen were required to provide their own personal assessments regarding the marriage projects for which a dispensation in the close degrees had been requested as a matter of course – though there are several comments that point in this direction earlier on, as well. The priests were now explicitly called upon to indicate whether a planned marriage in their community might make a negative impression or even cause a 'scandal'. Here, the horror at such unions that had been spread and inculcated over the centuries must not be underestimated, particularly in localities where it was comparatively rare for dispensations in the close degrees to be applied for and granted.

Assessments as to the likelihood of public sensations exhibit a broad range. Some priests felt incapable of providing a clear answer to this question, since the marriage project at issue had not yet been made public. Others responded by saying that it was improbable, not uncommonly indicating that everyone in their communities was related by blood and by marriage to begin with, for which reason the lion's share of marriages were possible only with a dispensation. One dean, concerning a request that had been made by the widowed peasant Paul Krug and his sister-in-law, Kriseldis Kranebitter of Miemingen in the Deanery of Silz, emphatically advocated approval and prognosticated "that among the populace in the broader surroundings, it would result in very bad blood if the *well-justified* request of these good supplicants, universally recognised as upstanding, should be rejected". After all, he continued, "priests, confessors and even professors who themselves author works on canon law" gave the impression that dispensations were easy to obtain.[76]

In other cases, however, there were reports of great outrage among the local populace. At nearly the same time, in December 1860, the priest of Anras in the Deanery of Lienz in present-day East Tyrol addressed an identical couple configuration by writing: "Should this marriage actually come to pass, it will make an *utterly wicked impression upon the community*, in part because no marriage such as this one has been concluded here in living memory, in part because there have quite recently been *three examples of such marriages*

76 DIÖAB, Konsistorialakten 1861, Fasc. 22a, Römische Dispensen, no. 9; emphasis underlined in the original.

in the surrounding area *that took a truly unfavourable turn*, and certainly also because, as in so many other places, the people here, too, *are becoming ever more convinced that with enough money, anything becomes possible*".[77] In contrast, the former dean of Lienz had indicated three decades prior in a very extensive December 1832 report on a dispensation request in the second and third unequal degree of affinity that, should the dispensation be granted, "absolutely no outrage must be feared", since a certain Anton Libiseller from a neighbouring village had received a dispensation in the first degree of affinity a few years prior, which was commonly known. What is more, "his marriage turned out to be very happy".[78] Consultation of the dispensation register reveals that the dispensation to which the dean was referring had been granted on 2 July 1816, which was 16 years prior.[79]

The extent to which assessments of this sort reflected the general attitude of the local populace or much rather the position of their priest regarding marriages in close degrees of consanguinity and affinity is difficult to discern. Such marriages' frequency or rarity certainly did play a role here, as did the matter of who the respective couples were, what kind of esteem and reputation they enjoyed and what social position they occupied within their communities. Asked as to the moral impression that a marriage in the second and third unequal degree as well as in the fourth equal degree of consanguinity would make in his community, the curate of a village in the Deanery of Taufers indicated that it would seem to be not a good one. He had heard only "disapproving statements" on this, almost all of them made in a fairly rough tone. One of the statements that he quoted was to the effect that it used to be that nobody had "dared seek marriage in such a configuration". But the sons of Franz Auer lacked any regard for "time-honoured good traditions" to begin with, it was said: "As long as they can advance themselves, nothing at all matters."[80] In connection with the planned marriage, property had already been passed back and forth between Franz Auer's sons.[81]

Regarding the question of how marriage projects between close blood and affinal kin might have struck the local public, and of whether we can assume a certain "normalcy" and disappearance of taboos, the various reactions would indicate that the attitude was not generally indifferent. Therefore, kin marriages cannot be viewed as having enjoyed broad social acceptance during the nineteenth century. Instead, there were probably locally and regionally

---

77 DIÖAB, Konsistorialakten 1860, Fasc. 5a, Römische Dispensen, no. 58; emphasis underlined in red in the original.

78 DIÖAB, Konsistorialakten 1833, Fasc. 5a, Römische Dispensen, no. 16.

79 Cf. DIÖAB, Dispensationes matrimoniales ab anno 1795 usque ad annum 1829 inclusive.

80 DIÖAB, Konsistorialakten 1862, Fasc. 22a, Römische Dispensen, no. 33.

81 Cf. DIÖAB, Konsistorialakten 1862, Fasc. 22a, Römische Dispensen, no. 33.

distinct assessments, though these are rarely documented in so drastic a fashion as they are in the case of a couple from Elbigenalp in the North Tyrolean Deanery of Breitenwang who were related by affinity in the first degree. Their local priest was near-horrified upon learning that they had been granted a dispensation. It was not for him, he conceded, "to object to this decision by the highest church authority". He was also comforted by the fact that responsibility for this lay with the church leadership, but "the bitter fruit" would be enjoyed "solely by their priest". He stressed that "in these parts", a dispensation in such a close degree was "unknown and unheard of". The request at issue had been viewed "around here as being about nothing more than money changing hands", for which reason "the entirely unexpected news of their successfully achieved aim ripped through the entire valley like foul-smelling lightning". The "most vexing talk", including as to the "bribability of the most reverend clergy", had been heard immediately thereafter at three inns.[82] The inn was not only a central location where information was disseminated but also a place of public debate and comment.[83]

3 Resistance and Obstacles

In discussing the frequency of kin marriage, one must also take into account that it was the particular responsibility of local priests[84] in the Diocese of Brixen to fend off marriage wishes of prospective spouses who were closely related by blood or by marriage whenever possible. The rule was that the priests, if approached with such marriage projects, had to reject them three times before they were permitted to take further steps and send a letter to the dean.[85] Often, priests referred to the official argument of decency advanced by

82 DIÖAB, Konsistorialakten 1846, Fasc. 5a, Römische Dispensen, no. 2.

83 This aspect has so far received greater attention by researchers as it pertains to the late Middle Ages and the early modern period. Cf. Beat Kümin, *Drinking Matters: Public Houses and Social Exchange in Early Modern Central Europe* (Basingstoke, 2007); Susanne Rau and Gerd Schwerhoff (eds.), *Zwischen Gotteshaus und Taverne. Öffentliche Räume in Spätmittelalter und Früher Neuzeit* (Cologne et al., 2004); Martin Scheutz, "'hab ichs auch im würthshauß da und dort gehört […]'. Gaststätten als multifunktionale öffentliche Orte im 18. Jahrhundert", in *Orte des Wissens*, ed. Martin Scheutz, Wolfgang Schmale and Dana Štefanova (Bochum, 2004), pp. 169–203.

84 On local priests as central figures in the process of dispensation-granting cf. also Pelaja, "Marriage by Exception", pp. 229–230. They functioned as the outermost connecting links in the Catholic Church's post-Tridentine network of control.

85 The fact that this was not a universal practice can be inferred from examples such as set of instructions intended for clergymen in Linz. If a marriage impediment became apparent, the bridal couple was to be lectured and instructed to "adhere to the law with all due

theologians and jurisprudents, without elaborating these references in detail. Dispensation records also indicate local clerics frequently employed the claim that both Church and state frowned upon such marriages as their fundamental argument when it came to fending off couples in such situations. In individual cases, it was ascertained – and hence simultaneously predicted – that such marriages would turn out to be unhappy ones. "The Office of the Dean made repeated efforts to dissuade the dispensation supplicant and especially his intended bride from their plans by listing several extremely unhappy marriages in such close degrees of kinship and by introducing to them the lack of conjugal love that typically comes to plague such marriages and the horrific consequences that arise therefrom, but all efforts were in vain."[86]

In some cases, couples allowed themselves to be swayed, though there are only scattered and rather coincidental traces of them in the dispensation records. Reports to this effect, such as one submitted by the dean of Breitenwang, reveal how the effectiveness of priests' efforts to thwart such marriages even prior to initiating written communication must not be underestimated. In 1843, this dean wrote to the consistory in Brixen that he had been contacted by five widowers, all of them intending to request dispensations in the first degree of affinity. Two, he wrote, were "not to be dissuaded from their intentions by anything that could be told to them" and were insisting on moving forward with their plans. The three others, he reported with evident satisfaction, he had been able to successfully convince otherwise.[87] One of the two couples mentioned in his letter received the necessary dispensation on their second attempt. From the second couple, however, there is no request in the records, which implies that this couple also eventually backed down from their original intent. It is hence fundamentally impossible to know how many couples who were closely related by blood or marriage planned to marry and articulated these plans before a competent authority only to be thwarted upon this initial enquiry. It also cannot be verified whether the quasi-ritualistic

obedience and, as a consequence, to abandon their initiated marriage plans and avoid all suspicious or dangerous contact with each other. If they then declare their intent to apply for a dispensation and ask the priest for their support, he shall hear their motivations [...] and then judge carefully whether he can recognise the stated reasons as important and dispensation as being advisable". No mention is made here of three refusals. "Ueber das Verfahren bey anzusuchenden Ehedispensen in dem Hinderniße der Verwandtschaft nach dem Sinne des k. k. Ehepatents", *Theologisch-praktische Linzer-Monathschrift zunächst für Seelsorger* 1, 1 (1809), 304–316, 308.

86 DIÖAB, Konsistorialakten 1841, Fasc. 5a, Römische Dispensen, no. 38.

87 DIÖAB, Konsistorialakten 1852, Fasc. 5a, Römische Dispensen, no. 11. This case is filed under a later year because the bridal couple only submitted a renewed – and, this time, successful – application long after their initial request had been rejected in Rome in 1844.

character of the aforementioned three admonishments was generally known.[88] But especially in places where dispensation requests began to cluster locally or regionally, it is fair to assume that information to this effect had indeed been exchanged.

Particularly in the case of strongly taboo unions such as between stepparents and stepchildren or between uncle and niece,[89] it may also be the case that differing administrative contexts also had their effects on marriage projects' documentation. In Vienna and Lower Austria at the end of the eighteenth and the beginning of the nineteenth century, for example, we could find up to three requests per year that were submitted by stepmothers and stepsons or stepfathers and stepdaughters – novel "couple configurations" that would have been "neither imaginable nor capable of being articulated insofar as marriage was concerned" prior to the late eighteenth century.[90] But for Catholics, neither the state nor the Church viewed this first degree of affinity in the direct line of descent as being dispensable.

In Brixen, beginning in 1831 and throughout the period examined here, the records contain one single request in such a configuration. Either the taboo in this regard was actually stronger in this diocese, with the result that virtually no one considered such possibilities, or the local priests – to whom initial requests had to be directed – rejected requests of this type on account of their utter futility, for which reason not even enquiries ended up reaching the consistory. Brixen's only such request documents the desire to marry expressed by a stepmother and her stepson: Ursula Valazza was 33 years old and a widow, and Joseph Crepaz was 30 years old. They resided in Livinallongo, in the Deanery of Buchenstein. In June 1833, it became known that Ursula Valazza was pregnant. The dean thereupon requested instructions from the prince-episcopal consistory and activated the regional court, which was supposed to separate the couple but refrained from doing so.[91] With the dean then being out of ideas as to how he could separate the two, he requested multiple times that they appear at the rectory in order to initiate a dispensation request, "so that this evil may be ameliorated either through merciful forbearance or through the separation of these people". A rejection, after all, would enable enforcement of

88 On distinctions between law and ritual cf. Heinz Duchhardt and Gert Melville, "Vorwort", in *Im Spannungsfeld von Recht und Ritual. Soziale Kommunikation in Mittelalter und Früher Neuzeit*, ed. Duchhardt and Melville (Cologne, 1997), p. v.

89 On this see chapter six.

90 Cf. Saurer, "Stiefmütter und Stiefsöhne", p. 360.

91 This correspondence is not included in the record; it is referred to in a later report by the dean submitted in 1834. DIÖAB, Konsistorialakten 1834, Fasc. 5a, Römische Dispensen, no. 10.

the civil ordinance according to which rejected dispensation-seekers could no longer reside beneath the same roof.[92]

The dean therefore protocolled the matrimonial examination, which was kept rather brief, in early 1834. The most extensive justification for the request was provided by the first witness, Pietro Antonio De Lazer, who was a relative of the bridal couple. The main reason, he stated, was the most passionate love – "*amore appassionatissimo*" – that existed between the two hopefuls, which stemmed from the fact that they had already had carnal knowledge of each other for quite some time. A further reason was that their marriage would put an end to the gossip among the people as well as the public scandal evoked by this prospective couple's cohabitation. And as a third reason, he mentioned significant economic advantages.[93] The fact that passion was mentioned first, which was relatively unusual, may have been due to the bride's pregnancy or been meant to serve as justification of this "unheard-of" ardour. It was with this expression, namely, that Brixen's consistorial secretary characterised their intent. The request, as could hardly have been expected otherwise, was rejected.

Joseph Crepaz was undeterred, however, and soon proceeded to make a second attempt in the form of a personally signed letter of supplication. In it, he portrayed the preceding events: quite some time prior, he had had a two-year love affair – "*Amourschaft*" – with Ursula Valazza. He had desired to marry her but been unable to realise his intent. For his father, who was widowed by that point, then himself took Ursula Valazza as his second wife. Following his father's death in 1832, he had continued "the earlier acquaintance with the stepmother even more devotedly, and mutual love" had "reached such a degree that the oft-mentioned stepmother became pregnant by the most obediently undersigned". The consistory thereupon reiterated its rejection of his request. This couple, however, does reappear one more time in the dispensation records – in a document dated June 1835 and filed in the "miscellaneous" fascicule entitled *Verschiedenes über Ehe*. The consistory in Brixen had sent the district office in Bruneck a complaint "regarding the troublesome cohabitation of Joseph Crepaz and his stepmother". The dean of Buchenstein – who was simultaneously its parish priest – had then requested "effective intervention"

92 Reference was made here to the provincial government decree of 12 September 1823, Z. 20.536.

93 "La causa principale si è un amore *appassionatissimo* tra i suddetti Sposi il quale ebbe origine dall'aversi i medesimi carnalmente conosciuto per largo tempo. Un'altra si è il porre fine alle mormorazioni del popolo ed allo scandalo di tutto il comune a motivo della coabitazione dei due Sposi. La terza sono rilevanti vantaggi economici." Emphasis double underlined in the original.

by the district office "in order to remove the concubine Valazza". The consistory subsequently endorsed this request with an accompanying note in which it once again pointed out that "repeated intervention by the Imperial-Royal Regional Court" had been "fruitless thus far" but that "elimination of the existing scandal" was "most highly necessary".[94] The employment of church and state power evidently had its limitations. Here, clerics' legally and morally founded horror stood vis-à-vis a tragic love story, that of two lovers who had no hope of seeing their relationship legitimised.

Edith Saurer has shown how such couples did have a chance if they converted to Protestantism. Ludwig Galler and his stepdaughter Franziska Delser moved to Pressburg, today's Bratislava, in 1847 after their dispensation request had been rejected by the archepiscopal consistory in Vienna. Galler purchased a house there and acquired the status of a citizen. Both of them then converted, whereupon they received their dispensation from the emperor.[95] At the end of the eighteenth century, another Viennese couple – Joseph and Katharina Arthaber – married in Hungary after both had also converted to Protestantism. This relationship had grown out of the same initial drama that characterised the aforementioned relationship in Livinallongo: the groom's father, a wealthy merchant, had taken as his second wife a far younger woman with whom his son was in love, thus rendering their marriage a near-impossibility following his death.[96]

One such request that did not make it to Brixen – or at least did not make it into the archive there – can be found in the records of the Vicariate-General of Feldkirch. This request – by Rosa Gasser and Josef Sieber, a stepmother and stepson from Bildstein – can be found neither in the diocese's Roman dispensation records nor in the accompanying fascicule "Pertaining to Marriage".[97] The dispensation records from the Diocese of Salzburg that were looked at turned up two requests in step-configurations.[98] Here, reference was also made to the

---

94 DIÖAB, Konsistorialakten 1835, Fasc. 5c, Verschiedenes über Ehe, no. 4.

95 Cf. Saurer, "Formen von Verwandtschaft und Liebe", pp. 269–270.

96 Cf. Edith Saurer, "Belles-mères et beaux-fils. Au sujet du choix du partenaire en Autriche vers 1800", *Annales de démographie historique* (1998), 59–71, 63–64.

97 Cf. ADF, Generalvikariat Matrimonialia (GA), Ehesachen III, Präsidialakten 1830–1900 and Römische Dispensen I, 1853–1858, Fasc. 1862–1865, Präsidial behandelte Ehedispensfälle, 1863, no. 35.

98 Due to the unsystematic way in which records were filed here, the possibility cannot be excluded that still more requests in step-configurations may be preserved in other fascicules. AES, Kasten 22/38, Päpstliche Ehedispensen 1867–1934. This fascicule contains 15 records concerning papal dispensations in the usual degrees from 1868 followed by two cases in the stepfather-stepdaughter configuration from entirely different years: 1866 and 1887.

apostolic injunction that defined this type of affinity as an impediment "that the Church never" dispensed.[99]

The dispensation requests from Vienna and Lower Austria analysed by Edith Saurer were submitted to the provincial government and hence not prefiltered by the Church. But there, as well, all such requests were refused.[100] Apparently, the maxim according to which stepparents and stepchildren were never to be dispensed was generally applicable. In this regard, Wolfgang Dannerbauer ascertained the following in a footnote to his *Praktisches Geschäftsbuch für den Curat-Clerus Oesterreichs*, published in 1893: "It is less rarely than one would believe that stepparents and stepchildren attempt to marry. Such an attempt must be rejected as entirely futile accompanied by serious admonishment and rebuke." Couples contemplating such marriage projects, he continued, should therefore "at once be informed of the utter fruitlessness of the step they intend to take".[101] In some places, nonetheless, the intent and desire to form such unions did still end up being documented, perhaps due not least to the civil administration's greater permeability.

Alongside such absolute marriage prohibitions, economically defined requirements pitted some marriage projects against formidable hurdles. The instrument employed in this respect – to demonstrably quite powerful effect in German-speaking Tyrol and in parts of Vorarlberg – was that of "political marriage consent".[102] Enacted by way of a court decree dated 12 May 1820 and promulgated in the provinces of the Habsburg monarchy in a government circular of 17 June 1820, it made consent on the part of municipal representatives

99 AES, Kasten 22/38 Päpstliche Ehedispensen 1867–1934, dispensation requests of Nikolaus Rußegger and Anna Holzer and of Georg Resel and his stepdaughter.

100 Cf. Saurer, "Stiefmütter und Stiefsöhne", p. 360. On this cf. the court resolution of 18 September 1795, which determined that His Majesty would "regarding the marriage of a stepmother by no means grant dispensation for a civil marriage contract in any case where a deceased father's inability to conceive cannot be legally ascertained". Schwerdling, *Praktische Anwendung*, § 146–151, p. 366. According to this, dispensation of a marriage between stepson and stepmother was only possible in cases where the marriage between the father and the stepmother could not have been consummated.

101 Dannerbauer, *Praktisches Geschäftsbuch*, p. 183, FN.

102 This instrument was also employed in Switzerland and in southern German territories. Ehmer, *Heiratsverhalten*, pp. 45–61, 71–74; Head-König, "Forced Marriages and Forbidden Marriages"; Klaus-Jürgen Matz, *Pauperismus und Bevölkerung. Die gesetzlichen Ehebeschränkungen in den süddeutschen Staaten während des 19. Jahrhunderts* (Stuttgart, 1980); Raffaella Sarti, "Nubili e celibi tra scelta e costrizione. I percorsi di Clio (Europa occidentale, secoli XVI–XX)", in *Nubili e celibi tra scelta e costrizione. (secoli XVI–XX)*, ed. Margareth Lanzinger and Raffaela Sarti (Udine, 2006), pp. 145–318, 182–196.

a prerequisite for marriage.[103] Such marriage consent was granted or refused based on an assessment as to whether the prospective couple commanded sufficient economic resources to sustain a family. While marriage consent was abolished in most provinces of the monarchy in 1869,[104] it existed until 1883 in Salzburg and even longer – until 1921 – in Tyrol. 1869 saw decision-making competency in these two provinces transferred more or less successfully to the district captaincies. This change was made due to the state's desire to effect the more liberal handling of marriage consent issuance.[105]

In some parts of Tyrol, the marriage consent policy was applied with significantly greater severity than the lawgiver had intended. This fact must be viewed here in light of how this policy was wielded with an eye to upholding and solidifying the existing socioeconomic structures. This finding, in combination with the underlying intent, applies primarily to the German-speaking part of Tyrol. In both Trentino and Vorarlberg, "prospects for marriage were far more balanced than in northern and southern Tyrol", ascertained Elisabeth Mantl in her comparative study.[106] While it was initially the case that the obligation to obtain marriage consent officially applied "only" to servants, journeymen, day labourers, lodgers and inhabitants without local citizenship (*Inwohner*), 1850 saw this marriage restriction expanded to cover everyone whose "livelihood" was "not assured over the long term".[107] A look at actual practice does not, however, permit the conclusion that the marriage consent policy only had a "limited effect" prior to the mid-nineteenth century.[108]

Dispensation requests from the Archdiocese of Salzburg contain scattered indications that the supplicants' communities had already issued their consent

---

103 For Austria cf. Elisabeth Mantl, *Heirat als Privileg. Obrigkeitliche Heiratsbeschränkungen in Tirol und Vorarlberg 1820–1920* (Vienna/Munich, 1997); Elisabeth Mantl, "Legal Restrictions on Marriage: Marriage and Inequality in the Austrian Tyrol during the Nineteenth Century", *The History of the Family* 4, 2 (1999), 185–207; Christa Pelikan, *Aspekte der Geschichte des Eherechts in Österreich*, PhD thesis, University of Vienna, 1981, pp. 53–172; Edith Saurer, "Reglementierte Liebe. Staatliche Ehehindernisse in der vormärzlichen Habsburgermonarchie", *Sozialwissenschaftliche Information* 24 (1995), 245–252; Hubert Weitensfelder, "Zu arm zum Heiraten? Ehekonsense in Vorarlberg als Mittel konservativer Sozialpolitik (1850–1914)", *Montfort. Vierteljahresschrift für Geschichte und Gegenwart Vorarlbergs* 57, 1 (2005), 18–40; Lanzinger, "Landlessness and Marriage Restrictions".

104 For an extensive look at related debates cf. Pelikan, *Aspekte der Geschichte des Eherechts*, pp. 72–172.

105 At least in some cases, however, it turned out that municipalities continued to claim decision-making competency. Cf. Lanzinger, *Das gesicherte Erbe*, pp. 131–133.

106 Mantl, *Heirat als Privileg*, p. 73.

107 Ibid., pp. 9–10. The corresponding rule can be found in Tiroler Landesarchiv (TLA), *Landesregierungsgesetzblatt* 1849/50, no. 87, p. 151.

108 Weitensfelder, "Zu arm zum Heiraten", p. 18.

to the couples' marriage.[109] There is no clear indication, however, that this was systematically checked for. In the Diocese of Brixen the situation was different. 1838 witnessed the creation of a legal precedent: the municipality of Lech had refused a bridal couple, Franz Joseph Walch and his cousin Creszenz Gassner, its consent to their marriage due to their lack of wealth while the church dispensation proceedings were already underway. In response, the prince-episcopal ordinariate in Brixen suggested to the provincial government in Innsbruck that all bridal couples, "in order to simplify this business and save time", should be instructed to present preliminary marriage consent at the outset of any dispensation-requesting process.[110] And so it subsequently occurred, almost without exception. Requesting marriage consent would hence appear to have by no means been limited just to that circle of persons – "servants, journeymen, day labourers, lodgers or inhabitants without local citizenship" – specified by law.

It was rarely the case that those applying for dispensations declared that they enjoyed a secure existence and hence did not need to present marriage consent – and those who did tended to be civil servants. Karl Frank, "imperial-royal police commissioner in Milan", pointed to his salary in declaring that he "was bound to no other permission",[111] and Franz Schweiger, an "imperial-royal customs assistant", also insisted that he needed no consent: "Any definitively employed civil servant can marry without obtaining political consent."[112] The 1845 dispensation request of the peasant Joseph Jud from Olang in the Puster Valley, owner of a large farm, was also submitted without marriage consent – for which reason the prince-episcopal consistory demanded that it be supplied. When questioned on this in the matrimonial

109 In the request of Barlmä Rieser, a corporal in the *Kaiserjägerregiment*, and his widowed sister-in-law Maria Kröll, a smallholder and mother to five very young children, for example, the argument was that the widow and her children would become a burden to the municipality if no suitable man could be found. That is why the municipality "did not hesitate" to "grant these marriage supplicants preliminary political marriage consent". AES 22/38 Päpstliche Dispensen 1856–1867, 1858, no. 10.

110 DIÖAB, Konsistorialakten 1838, Fasc. 5a, Römische Dispensen, no. 17. On their second attempt, the couple received both consent and their dispensation.

111 DIÖAB, Konsistorialakten 1847, Fasc. 5a, Römische Dispensen, no. 3.

112 DIÖAB, Konsistorialakten 1849, Fasc. 5a, Römische Dispensen, no. 20. Cf. also ibid., 1854, no. 15, the request of Franz Brandl, chancellery clerk at the Imperial-Royal Postal Directorate in Innsbruck and a "house owner" in the parish of St. Nikolaus, as well as ibid., 1850, no. 1, the request of the shoemaker and small farmer Johann Zach and the farmer's daughter Kreszenz Kallinger, whom the consistory called upon several times to present marriage consent, whereupon the imperial-royal district office in Innsbruck attested "that this bridal couple has, withal, no need of marriage consent".

examination, the groom declared that in keeping with applicable law, "every farm owner is entitled to marry without political consent" – but that in order to "obtain still greater assurance", he had now applied for it.[113]

The instrument of marriage consent needs to be viewed within the general context of the anti-liberal climate that prevailed in Tyrol and Vorarlberg. It was supported by the highest church authorities – in particular by Prince-Bishop Vinzenz Gasser, who vehemently championed the marriage consent policy during his time as a representative in the provincial parliament from 1861 to 1879. Church representatives who were of different mind on this matter seldom voiced their opinions in the context of dispensation requests. One documented case where this did occur is that of the devoted efforts put forth by Franz Höfel, the dean in Hohenems, on behalf of a couple who were related in the first degree of affinity: the widow Elisabeth Klien, who had three small children from her first marriage, and her brother-in-law Anton Mathis, with whom Klien already had a fourth. Both were classified as poor. According to a statement by the Vicariate-General in Feldkirch, the dean had done "everything he was able both vis-à-vis the municipal committee and at the local Commission for the Poor, in particular with an eye to achieving wholesome change and order for the children – but unfortunately, all of his efforts have been in vain". The municipality did ultimately grant marriage consent, but the consistory felt that this dispensation request lacked sufficient justification to be forwarded to Rome.[114]

Even though individual members of the clergy voiced criticism of the marriage consent policy and lobbied local political authorities on certain couples' behalf, municipal and ecclesiastical interests concerning this matter largely overlapped. And especially in rural areas, municipal and church representatives repeatedly formed a united and powerful front whenever they sought to use the marriage consent policy to enforce notions of social order.[115]

4 Roman Dispensations: An Administrative Obstacle Course

The closer a related couple's degree of consanguinity or affinity was, the more laborious the administrative process they faced and the better justified their

113 DIÖAB, Konsistorialakten 1845, Fasc. 5a, Römische Dispensen, no. 9.

114 DIÖAB, Konsistorialakten 1862, Fasc. 5a, Römische Dispensen, no. 20.

115 In this regard, Elisabeth Mantl speaks of "the ultramontane clergy" having provided "the ideological underpinnings for provincial policies that were restorational in both a social and an economic sense". Mantl, *Heirat als Privileg*, p. 152.

dispensation request needed to be. The necessary bureaucratic procedures involved numerous persons and institutions. In the Diocese of Brixen, letters and official notifications circulated between local priests and their deans, between the deans and representatives of the prince-episcopal consistory, and between the consistory and the provincial government in Innsbruck, the dispensation-relevant papal institutions of the Datary and the Penitentiary[116] and the imperial-royal agent in Rome. Furthermore, various documents and certifications were required that had to be issued by parish priests and representatives of a couple's municipality: baptismal certificates, death certificates, certificates of good conduct, evaluations, political marriage consent and last but not least a family tree drawn up by the competent priest. These materials were accompanied by multiple letters of supplication, put to paper mostly by members of the cloth and only in rare cases written by the bridal couples themselves. The latter occurred most often among rural and urban elites. But even then, certain suggestions and formulations may have been contributed by third parties. As a rule, the lines of argument that were employed suggest that those writing were well informed with regard to dispensation-granting logics.

The amounts of material and information contained in the individual requests vary greatly. This can be ascribed in part to the deans' personal ways of discharging their offices, but it could also be tied to the esteem in which the respective supplicants were held. Furthermore, the records not only contain complete dispensation cases but also enquiries that were not pursued further than an initial letter or that the consistory summarily rejected due to insufficient prospects for success. It is about such couples that we learn least because they made no further attempts that reached the prince-episcopal ordinariate.

If the competent local priest was willing to support the request, he would begin with a characterisation of the existing circumstances. Subsequently, the dean – or, in Vorarlberg, the vicariate general in Feldkirch[117] – would forward this initial portrayal together with an accompanying letter or a portrayal of his own to the prince-episcopal consistory in Brixen. The consistory in Brixen would then ideally – that is if prospects for the request appeared good – grant permission to administer the matrimonial examination under oath; such protocols are largely missing in the other dioceses. It was in this phase that the

116 Requests by ruling princes were handled by the *Secretaria brevium ad Principes*.

117 Regarding the dispensation requests from Vorarlberg, it should be noted that it was the vicariate general in Feldkirch that gave permission to protocol the matrimonial examination, and it was initially the case that all correspondence prior to the matrimonial examination remained in Vorarlberg. This was only sent to Brixen along with the examination following a late 1850s request by then Bishop Vinzenz Gasser, for which reason it can be found in Brixen from that point onward.

couple also had to deposit with the competent deanery the sum of money that would have to be paid if their dispensation were granted, with the amount due being estimated in advance. The "matrimonial examination" itself represents more or less the core of each dispensation record. It protocolled the "examination" of two witnesses, without exception male, as well as an interrogation of the bridegroom and the bride according to an official catalogue of questions. While the fornication trials studied by Ulrike Gleixner placed the woman's testimony first, thus providing the foil for the testimony of the man and the witnesses,[118] the order of questioning in the matrimonial examination was reversed: the two witnesses first provided their version of things, followed by the bridegroom and finally the bride. The witnesses' placement at the beginning may indicate the degree to which couples' own circles as well as the broader public took an interest in such marriages.

The matrimonial examination contains general information on the bridal couple such as their names, ages and respective family status, whether they had reached the age of majority and in what degree they were related, and whether they had been aware of their kinship when he proposed and/or she assented. From the mid-1850s onward, deans also had to provide information regarding their wealth. The witnesses were asked whether they were aware of the couple's consanguinity or affinity and, if so, how they had learned of it. Further questions concerned moral qualities. The couple had to provide information, for example, on whether they had "lived a life that was honourable and unobjectionable before God and the world" up to that point, whether "illicit relations" and/or "sins of the flesh" had already occurred and whether any that had occurred had been for the purpose of obtaining a dispensation more easily. This question had to be answered in the negative, for such an intention rendered dispensation fundamentally impossible. The dean in Matrei had written to the consistory in 1837 because "no template whatsoever for a matrimonial examination in order to obtain dispensations on account of kinship" was to be found in his chancery, which is why he requested a copy of such a form. The "remarks" included with the materials he duly received included the instruction to pose "Question VI" – this was the question as to "*copula et raptu*", whether the couple had had sexual contact or the groom had kidnapped the bride – in the most careful possible way, *quam cautissime*, and only ever one-on-one.[119]

118 Ulrike Gleixner, *'Das Mensch' und 'der Kerl'. Die Konstruktion von Geschlecht in Unzuchtsverfahren der Frühen Neuzeit, 1700–1760* (Frankfurt a. M./New York, 1994), p. 80.

119 DIÖAB, Konsistorialakten 1837, Fasc. 5c, Verschiedenes über Ehe, no. 1. The numbering of the questions was inconsistent; there were evidently different forms in circulation in the individual deaneries. Correspondence with the question indicated here was checked on the basis of the next dispensation request from the Deanery of Matrei following the

And of central importance was the question, to be answered by both bride and groom, as to the reasons why the couple wished to marry despite the existence of a marriage impediment.

The dean – or, in exceptional cases, an authorised parish priest – was responsible for posing questions while an "actuary" (*Actuar*) put the resulting testimony to paper. Deans generally played a crucial role as a node of communication between the church hierarchy's various levels: they both forwarded the enquiries and supplications they received from the parishes to the consistory and mediated between the local perspective and that of the diocese. They were personally familiar with the situations at hand, were knowledgeable about church dispensation logics[120] and ideally also possessed experience having to do with effective strategies of argumentation. For a marriage project between close kin, how the couple's situation was portrayed in the initial letter to Brixen could play a decisive role in their chances of receiving a positive response, and the dean's cleverness was the crucial factor behind how promising the reasons formulated in the matrimonial examination were.

The protocolled responses were read aloud to all participants at the end of the examination, and the witnesses as well as the bridal couple had to swear an oath as to the truth of the statements they had made. In the many hundreds of dispensation requests, it was only once that a local priest complained of the exaggerated character of the situation and conditions described by the bridal couple, hastening to put their dramatic quality into perspective. The 52-year-old widower Joseph Lerchegger had indicated in his matrimonial examination that he was already getting on in years and could not leave the "tenancy that he had held for so long" without being "thrown into manifest poverty". He therefore required a wife. The curate characterised his claims as "exaggerated", holding that it was untrue that the groom would be forced to leave his tenancy and become impoverished should his desired marriage not come to be, since he had full-grown daughters. He concluded by adding that this was fortunately not the decisive reason for dispensation, the "*causa finalis*" – for the dispensation request would have otherwise been fraudulent.[121]

In Salzburg, it was not an *examen matrimoniale* that was protocolled, but an *examen informative* – which, however, is rarely to be found in such records

date of the consistory's response. DIÖAB, Konsistorialakten 1838, Fasc. 5a, Römische Dispensen, no. 2.

120 Vinzenz Gasser used the publication *Brixner Diözesan-Blatt*, which he had founded in 1857, to circulate sermons, ordinances and instructions – including ones concerning dispensation practice – as well as current reading tips for the diocesan clergy. The extant correspondence with the deans includes frequent lectures and admonishments.

121 DIÖAB, Konsistorialakten 1852, Fasc. 5a, Römische Dispensen, no. 7.

and was far less detailed. The basis for the further progress of dispensation proceedings here was a portrayal of the situation at hand in the form of a letter from the couple requesting the dispensation and possibly an accompanying letter written by the local priest or dean. A consistorial official would then produce a detailed commentary on the case in question, and his opinion was most probably then presented to the consistory at large. This official's opinion was not, however, the deciding factor in terms of whether or not to forward a case to Rome. Even in cases where his opinion had been negative in character, it did still sometimes happen that the request was forwarded. For the purpose of procuring the *placetum regium*, it would seem that the entire record was sent to the provincial government – which, in the Diocese of Salzburg, played a more prominent role in dispensation proceedings than it did in the Diocese of Brixen. Especially couples who lived in or near towns in the Diocese of Salzburg would quite often submit their requests directly to the civil authorities.[122] A further indication of the Salzburg consistory's fundamentally cooperative stance and attitude toward civil law and state institutions is the fact that the official there, in evaluating the weight of the reasons for dispensation brought forth by a couple, would make reference to the discussions of marital law by Thomas Dolliner, the commentator of the Austrian Civil Code.[123] This was not the case in the Diocese of Brixen.

In Brixen, it was accordingly quite inadvisable to submit one's dispensation request to the provincial government. Gerhard Riedmüller and Gertraud Nockerin, who were related by marriage in the first and second unequal degree, had received a negative response to their initial request in 1819. Eleven years later, they involved the imperial-royal district office for the Lower Inn and Wipp Valleys, which sent a note to the consistory in order to reactivate the dispensation proceedings. The widower Gerhard Riedmüller had by then reached the age of 60 and was in need of nursing care.[124] Gertraud Nockerin, a niece of his deceased wife, had spent eleven years working as his servant. Brixen's response to the district office's inquiry was that there was no prospect of obtaining a dispensation in Rome. The couple turned to the Deanery of Innsbruck, which forwarded their supplication to the consistory after approximately one year. This time, the consistory granted its permission to conduct the matrimonial examination without further ado, and they ultimately received

122 In contrast to the court decree of 16 October 1800, which determined that dispensation supplicants were to "always approach the religious ordinariate first", the ABGB (part one, chapter two, § 84, section 2) had by this point designated the district captaincies as the proper places to submit dispensation requests.

123 Dolliner, *Handbuch*.

124 One of the two witnesses in this matrimonial examination was the groom's physician.

their dispensation.[125] The bride and groom lived in Hall, and it was hence the dean's office there that was officially responsible for them. But Hall's dean had become resigned due to the failure of other dispensation requests and is said to have told them he no longer dealt with Roman dispensations "because he is unable to obtain anything".[126] This had likely also been the reason for the likewise unsuccessful involvement of the district office.

Salzburg's significantly different positioning was associated with the enlightened political stance – not dissimilar to that of Josephinism in its general outlines – taken up by Archbishop Count Hieronymus von Colloredo (1772–1803) during the late eighteenth century.[127] "Practiced religion should first and foremost benefit the state" was the maxim to which his policies adhered.[128] His successor Augustin Gruber (1823–1835), though he did advocate for the renewal of the Church, combined this cause with a moderate position vis-à-vis Josephine church reforms.[129] Friedrich, Prince of Schwarzenberg (1836–1885) also took up an intermediate position in that he favoured stronger orientation of the Austrian Church toward Rome but was not considered ultramontane.[130] In contrast, the bishops of the Diocese of Brixen – primarily Vinzenz Gasser (1856–1879), but also his forerunners – were representatives of a political and Rome-oriented Catholicism.[131] Altogether, the climate in the Diocese of Salzburg was markedly more conciliatory and positive toward the men and women who applied for dispensations. In cases where Rome rejected an application, for example, the ordinariate would immediately take the initiative to begin a renewed attempt, stating – in a way that would have been unthinkable in Brixen. "Nonetheless, in view of the urgency of the circumstances, the ordinariate has seen fit to renew this request."[132]

---

125 DIÖAB, Konsistorialakten 1832, Fasc. 5a, Römische Dispensen, no. 8.

126 Ibid.

127 Cf. Franz Ortner, *Salzburgs Bischöfe in der Geschichte des Landes, 696–2005* (Frankfurt a. M. et al., 2005), pp. 266–270; Weiß, "Dem Pabste brach darüber das Herz".

128 Weiß, "Josephinismus in Salzburg", p. 95; cf. also Ortner, *Salzburgs Bischöfe*, pp. 265–273.

129 Cf. Ortner, *Salzburgs Bischöfe*, p. 282. Peter Unkelbach refers to his "work as a civil servant in state church service from 1802 to 1816". Peter Unkelbach, "Die Päpste und die Bedeutsamkeit des Papsttums dokumentiert am Wirken des Salzburger Fürsterzbischofs Augustin Gruber", in *Salzburg und der Heilige Stuhl*, ed. Paarhammer and Rinnerthaler, pp. 379–432, 379.

130 Cf. Ortner, *Salzburgs Bischöfe*, p. 288.

131 For a general impression of the situation in Tyrol cf. Fontana, *Der Kulturkampf*; as well as more recently Pfeifer/Nössing, *Kulturkampf in Tirol*; on Ultramontanism as a broader context cf. Gisela Fleckenstein and Joachim Schmiedl, "Ultramontanismus in der Diskussion. Zur Neupositionierung eines Forschungsbegriffs", in *Ultramontanismus. Tendenzen der Forschung*, ed. Fleckenstein and Schmiedl (Paderborn, 2005), pp. 7–19.

132 AES, Kasten 22/38, Päpstliche Dispensen 1856–1867, 1856, Dispensansuchen von Sebastian Lederer und Maria Huber.

The consistory in Brixen examined the testimony in matrimonial examinations and use this as a basis to decide whether the stated reasons were sufficient in order to submit the corresponding requests to Rome. Up to the mid-nineteenth century, however, it was first necessary to obtain permission to do so from the provincial government, which still had to be done in Innsbruck. The consistory in Brixen also applied for such permission in the case of couple configurations that did not require dispensations according to civil law. This pertained to dispensations in the second and third unequal degree of consanguinity and affinity as well as to those needed due to affinity *ex copula illicita*. In the case of one such request, the vicar general in Feldkirch attempted to lodge the objection that, for him, the "*Placetum regium*, which so hampers church governance and hopefully stands on shaky ground in our parts anyhow", seemed "entirely superfluous" in the case of a "solely canonical marriage impediment".[133] The consistory in Brixen, however, would not be deterred from its actions in this respect. In actual fact, the *placetum regium* was soon abolished by an ordinance of 18 April 1850. With this, "communication between the popes and the bishops" was officially liberated from state control.[134] The Brixen consistory, however, continued applying for it at the district offices for years, only ending this practice upon the advent of the Concordat of 1855.[135]

Various instances of irritation occurred in the course of dispensation-related communication between the clergy and state officials during the 1840s. In individual cases, the provincial government demanded that the according documents be presented – such as in an extremely protracted case in which the groom, Johann Georg Kropf, had gone so far as to direct a letter of supplication to the emperor himself in 1844. Upon learning that he had done so, the *Gubernium* requested to see the documents. The consistory refused, pointing out that the orally stated reasons for dispensation were considered secret

133 DIÖAB, Konsistorialakten 1848, Fasc. 5a, Römische Dispensen, no. 5.

134 RGBl. 1850, no. 156, 157. On the events leading up to its abolishment cf. Weinzierl-Fischer, *Die österreichischen Konkordate*, pp. 52–59; cf. also Michel, *Beiträge zur Geschichte*, pp. 8, 37.

135 Article 2 of the Concordat states: "Since the Roman pope, in accordance with divine law, possesses primacy of honour as well as jurisdiction over the entire Church as far as it extends, the correspondence between the bishops, the clergy, the people and the Holy See in sacred and ecclesiastical matters is not subject to provincial government permission but entirely free." Quoted in Weinzierl-Fischer, *Die österreichischen Konkordate*, pp. 250–251. On this cf. also Reinalter, "Liberalismus und Kirche", p. 157. With this, Catholics were once again subject to the canonical marriage prohibitions. Cf. "Kaiserliches Patent vom 8. Oktober 1856, Anhang II: Anweisung für die geistlichen Gerichte des Kaiserthumes Oesterreich in Betreff der Ehesachen", in *Reichs-Gesetz-Blatt für das Kaiserthum Oesterreich*, 1856, no. 185, 622–658, §§ 26 and 30.

and could only be used "*pro foro interno*", which is to say: by the Church and its clergy.[136] The Brixen consistory's practice for each case was to send only a specially prepared abbreviated report to the provincial government that contained no more than general information on the couple in question and their situation in life. These reports did not communicate details of a more sensitive nature, such as a bride's pregnancy. In late 1841, the *Gubernium* in Innsbruck – with an eye to the Diocese of Trento – called upon Brixen's consistory to involve the competent district offices as intermediate entities.[137] This admonishment, however, would seem to have been for naught.

The letters to Rome were highly standardised and written in Latin. In 1859, Bishop Vinzenz Gasser introduced his own type of form with rubrics for the necessary information on the dispensation supplicants and in which to list reasons for dispensation (see Fig. 3). For this, he received praise from Rome – specifically from Simon de Dompieri, who was at that point serving as an intermediary:[138] "I cannot help but express to you my satisfaction regarding the forms that you have adopted", he wrote. "While the other Austrian dispensations often necessitate a great deal of informational back and forth, you accomplish everything in one fell swoop. But I am now working on introducing these forms everywhere."[139] In Salzburg, in any case, his efforts were to be unsuccessful. The consistory there continued doing without preprinted materials in their communications with Rome. Furthermore, Salzburg sent both standardised and exceptional letters of recommendation in the supplicants' favour, also formulated in Latin, to the imperial-royal agent in Rome simultaneously with the letters that it sent to the pope. Some of these were sent together with correspondence that addressed financial issues associated with the coverage of dispensation fees and contained information regarding account balances and the transfer of funds.[140]

The dispensation records in Brixen, in contrast to those in Salzburg, contain no documents of this sort. It proved possible to find part of this correspondence in separate holdings of the Diocesan Archive – namely those containing the responses from Rome, which refer to endorsements of dispensation requests alongside various other topics.[141] Until the nineteenth century, Brixen

---

136 DIÖAB, Konsistorialakten 1847, Fasc. 5a, Römische Dispensen, no. 6; this record contains correspondence beginning in 1841. Regarding public and secret marriage impediments see Jemolo, *Il matrimonio*, pp. 208–210.

137 Cf. DIÖAB, Konsistorialakten 1841, Fasc. 5a, Römische Dispensen, no. 35.

138 More details on such intermediation are contained in chapter five.

139 DIÖAB, Konsistorialakten 1859, Fasc. 5a, Römische Dispensen, no. 16.

140 Cf. AES, Kasten 22/38, Päpstliche Dispensen 1856–1867.

141 Cf. DIÖAB, Konsistorialakten, Agentie, box oA. This material covers the period running from 1798 to 1832.

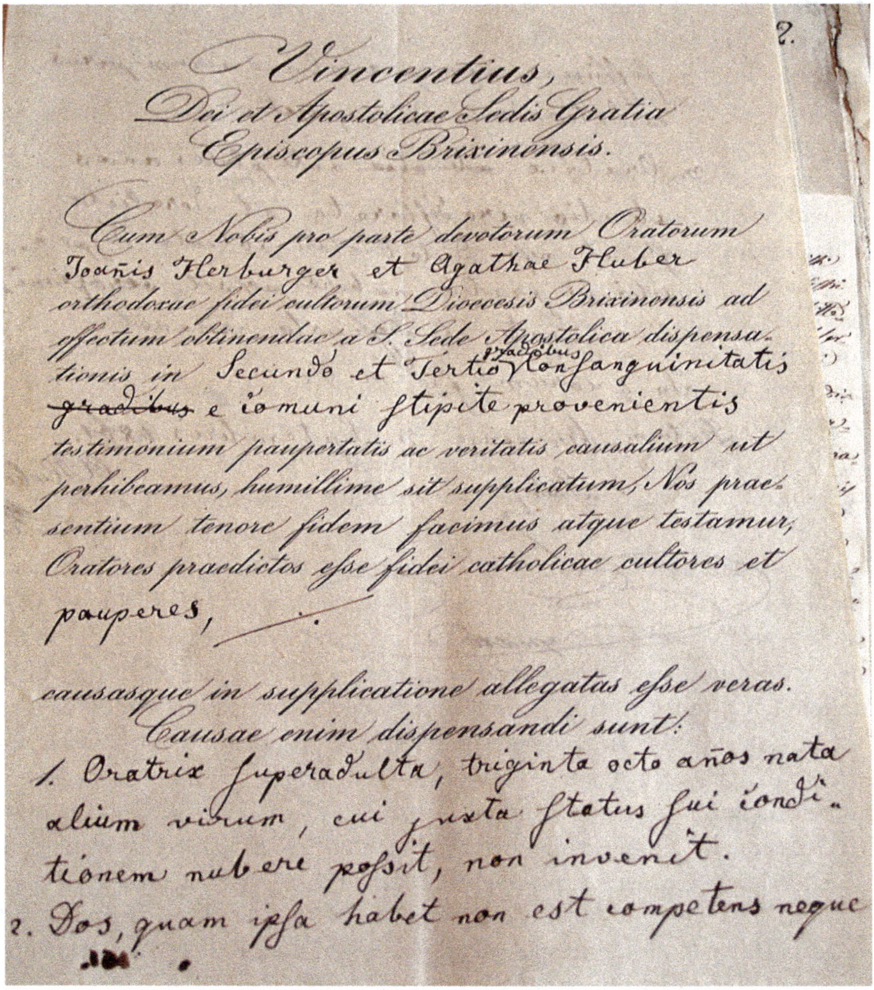

FIGURE 3 Vinzenz Gasser's form for dispensation requests that were to be forwarded to Rome
SOURCE: DIÖAB, KONSISTORIALAKTEN 1861, FASC. 5A, RÖMISCHE DISPENSEN, NO. 51.

had its own Italian secretary, who maintained regular written correspondence with Rome.[142] Afterwards Consistorial Councillor and future Consistorial

142 Cf. for example DIÖAB, Konsistorialakten, Agentie, box 0A, Corrispondenze Agente. In this small-format book, which is an account book of sorts, the 1797 entries are interrupted by the note that the Prince-Bishop of Brixen had charged the note's author, Gianbatt[ist]a Giulliani, with assuming the Italian secretariat – "*Segrettario italiano*" – following the death of "*Segrettario italiano*" Antonio Cibbini. It further states that, in this

Chancellor Georg Prünster and his successor Kaspar Rauter wrote these letters, which they addressed to the imperial-royal agency in Rome as the intermediary and continued to formulate in Italian.[143]

Up to 1850, the so-called dispensation briefs or dispensation mandates received by Brixen initially had to be sent to Innsbruck for provincial government confirmation. In the process, the provincial government also granted its own dispensation that lifted the corresponding "civil marriage impediment".[144] This dispensation brief and/or its contents passed through several offices in the hierarchically graduated postal and communication channels, in urgent cases even being transmitted as a telegram: from Rome to the consistory and on to the deanery – with the vicariate general as an additional intermediate station in Vorarlberg – and from the deanery to the competent parish. At the same time, the fee to cover "agency costs", which had been deposited with the deanery at the beginning of the matrimonial examination, had to be sent to Brixen, from where it was forwarded to Rome. Beginning in 1854, Rome required the production of a verification protocol involving both matrimonial examination witnesses and the bridal couple before the dispensation was handed over. Two questions were central here: whether the previously indicated reasons for dispensation still obtained, and whether "sins of the flesh" had indeed not been committed since submission of the application. If the couple had "sinned" in this regard, a renewed letter to Rome – addressed to the Apostolic Penitentiary – was required for the purpose of the dispensation's "sanation". This incurred an additional – albeit small – fee and entailed even more time lost prior to the wedding.

Occasionally, facts withheld during the verification process would only reach the parish priest's ears after quite some time – typically by way of confession. The cousins Josef and Maria Erath from Au in the Bregenz Forest had received their requested dispensation and married in 1863.[145] After 21 years, it came to light that the dispensation mandate and hence the marriage were invalid, since the couple had engaged in sexual contact between the protocolling

function, he would now reach agreement with the agent Merenda in Rome on the following debts, etc.

143 This correspondence is held by the Austrian State Archives in Vienna. ÖSTA, HHStA, Agentie-Archiv Rom, II Agentie Akten 1817–1832, K. 32–40; ibid., II Agentie Akten 1833–1855, K. 75–76; ibid., II Agentie Akten 1856–1891, K. 163–181 (1871). Some of these holdings exhibit serious moisture damage. From Box 169 (1859) onward, almost nothing more from Brixen appears. These holdings were examined up to box 181 (1871).

144 In doing so, it counted degrees according to civil law. The second canonical degree of consanguinity corresponded to the fourth civil degree.

145 Cf. DIÖAB, Konsistorialakten 1863, Fasc. 22a, Römische Dispensen, no. 24.

of the matrimonial examination and its verification. "This offence", as it was termed in the initial report referring to the pseudonymous Camillus and Afra that was sent to the consistory, had been "withheld from the verification protocol". The consistory applied for an after-the-fact *sanatio* in Rome.[146] Cases such as this one make clear how the arm of the Church, bolstered by the machinery of conscience, could indeed be very long.

The moralising and intensified monitoring of premarital sexuality as manifested by the introduction of the verification process brought with it more adamant insistence on humility, contrition and prostration that was expressed through the assignment of "penance" in connection with the aforementioned "sanation". Moreover, from now on those couples who had admitted to a sexual relationship or for whom such could be assumed due to the bride's pregnancy or the presence of children had to go through multiple months of probation in the run-up to a dispensation request. During such a period, they had to lead morally unassailable lives as proof of their willingness to mend their ways. Only then would the diocesan consistory initiate the decisive steps in the dispensation-requesting process. It is fair to assume a relatively high degree of moral pressure during the second half of the nineteenth century, predominantly in the smaller parishes.

The Church and its clergy were not the only ones who monitored and policed people's lifestyles and moral conduct, with mayors, municipal committee members and other "honourable men" making their own contributions. Indeed, they had already been passing judgment on couples applying for dispensations as those who were charged with deciding on the issuance of political marriage consent, which tied marriageability to economic resources. This was now joined by their involvement in the moralising offensive that got underway beginning in the mid-1850s. Men of the cloth requested their opinions on the "decency" of certain dispensation supplicants, and clerics also assigned neighbours to monitor supplicant couples who had been given periods of probation, which could last half a year or, in extreme cases, even an entire year. While completing such a period, the men and women under observation were to avoid encountering each other whenever possible and – above all at night – scrupulously avoid being beneath the same roof. Due to the diversity of mutual support arrangements, dependencies and obligations between kin, and particularly in the context of difficult familial situations, this was not always manageable with ease.

The request submitted by the widower Franz Schnetzer from Rankweil in the Deanery of Feldkirch and his sister-in-law Regina Henni, who had taken

146 DIÖAB, Konsistorialakten 1884, Fasc. 22a, Römische Dispensen, no. 16.

care of his three children and the household since Schnetzer's wife had fallen ill, was rejected by the consistory in Brixen in October 1858. The reasons given were their "notoriously licentious interactions", the fact that they had "not yet separated or submitted to a test of true penance and reform" and a lack of canonical reasons for dispensation. Regina Henni was pregnant by her prospective groom, and their child was born in December 1858. Following the rejection of their dispensation request, she had been forced to leave the house of her brother-in-law – which was actually also her house that she had inherited together with her sister, so that she not only possessed rights of residency but also rights of ownership to it. Almost a year later, in September 1859, the parish priest reported that he had not neglected to "make strict and diligent enquiries as to whether the dispensation supplicants have, in the interim, striven to adhere to the rules of behaviour imposed upon them". Since he could confirm that they had, he renewed their dispensation request. As Franz Schnetzer, who was a bricklayer, frequently worked away from home, Regina Henni had occasionally returned to the house – where she ultimately remained during the final six weeks prior to the arrival of their dispensation, even though her brother-in-law and groom was also spending his nights there. However, they successfully claimed that they had "mended their ways". In the verification protocol, all those who were questioned affirmed that they had not repeated their sins. They received their dispensation in early 1860.[147]

During the nineteenth century, church and state bodies would sometimes interfere massively in the domestic sphere and family matters.[148] It is hence by no means possible to assume a linear decrease in the significance and strength of the Church's exercise of regulatory power. In cases of publicly known "incest" (*Blutschande*), the prescribed "penance programme" included an obligation for the bride and groom to "humbly beg forgiveness" for the "scandal" they had caused in the community in the presence of the witnesses to their matrimonial examination. It was probably not by chance that the onset of this moralising policy coincided with the declaration of the Immaculate Conception as dogma in 1854.[149]

Nineteenth-century dispensation proceedings always took multiple months following initial contact with the prince-episcopal consistory in Brixen, with

---

147 DIÖAB, Konsistorialakten 1860, Fasc. 5a, Römische Dispensen, no. 23.

148 For a multiperspective approach see Joachim Eibach and Margareth Lanzinger (eds.), *The Routledge History of the Domestic Sphere in Europe Sixteenth to Nineteenth Century* (London, 2020).

149 On this as well as on the related theological concepts and discussions during the early modern period cf. Luisa Accati, *Das Monster und die Schöne. Vater- und Mutterbilder in der katholischen Erziehung der Gefühle* (Berlin, 2006), pp. 50–54, 71–99.

two-and-a-half months being the minimum. But depending on the momentarily valid maxims of dispensation policy and weighting of the different degrees of affinity and consanguinity, the path to a dispensation could also last more than a year – and, in certain situations, even longer. Overly long waits were sometimes owed to external circumstances. If an important piece of writing had got lost on the way to its addressee, it could take some time for the matter to be cleared up. Misunderstandings arose frequently. A typical situation was for Brixen to await notification that the required sum of money for the dispensation fees had been deposited with the deanery before sending its letter to Rome while the competent dean had overlooked the fact that his explicit confirmation of such was required for further processing.

A pope's death and the consequent vacancy of his office also tended to cause considerable delays in the processing of dispensation requests. Following the death of Gregory XVI on 1 June 1846, the first directive to be handed down by Brixen expressed the ordinariate's "great desire" that supplicants with active dispensation cases be convinced to give up.[150] However, this appeal by the consistory met with little success. Dispensation proceedings in Rome indeed came to a standstill for a certain time, since "official duties" of this sort remained undischarged pending election of the new pope.[151] In September 1846, when Pope Pius IX took office, the diocese resent all open requests to Rome – but the granting of dispensations was once again delayed. Johann Schiffer and his sister-in-law Maria Rienzler had received permission to take their matrimonial examination in September 1845, and their request was forwarded to Rome in late February of 1846. Just shy of one year later, on 20 January 1847, Brixen received a letter signed by the groom requesting that "his business" continue to go forward, since it had "gone unresolved forever and a day".[152] For requests submitted in 1846, proceedings generally lasted over a year – with even two years sometimes passing before the requested dispensation arrived from Rome.

It was true that in exceptional circumstances, just like in urgent cases, bishops were authorised to grant dispensations on their own authority in the close degrees – but Brixen's bishops made use of this option only very sparingly. Prince-Bishop Bernhard Galura, in office from 1829 to 1856, granted five dispensations in close degrees during each of the two decades between 1830 and 1850. The 1850s, however, saw such dispensations granted neither under his auspices nor under those of his successor. Exceptional circumstances occurred

---

150 DIÖAB, Konsistorialakten 1846, Fasc. 5a, Römische Dispensen, no. 1.

151 Ibid. Also mentioned here are a number of further dispensation requests from Vorarlberg that were blocked due to the pope's death.

152 DIÖAB, Konsistorialakten 1846, Fasc. 5a, Römische Dispensen, no. 2.

especially during 1848 and 1849 due to the First Italian War of Independence. The various rebellions and battles led to temporary interruptions of communication with Rome, with answers unable to get through by regular mail. The pope had then fled Rome in 1849 – and amidst this situation, Brixen's prince-bishop indeed used his authorisation to dispense. He granted four of the five 1840s dispensations in 1848.[153] Other requests, however, he rejected.[154]

During this period, the vicar general in Feldkirch sought to move the prince-bishop to utilise this competency in a more assertive manner by explicitly presenting a number of supplications as being well suited to being handled in this way.[155] In a letter accompanying two simultaneously submitted requests, for example, he applied for dispensations for both couples "from the impediments preventing their marriage *auctoritate ordinaria*" and, a few lines below, opined that the bishop was unquestionably authorised to do so "in these times and in light of such piteous circumstances as affect the supplicants".[156] Here, it was not only the times that were exceptional but also the cases themselves: the first request spoke of "concubinage". This couple had already produced six children together and were threatening to remove themselves to an "entirely Calvinist" community in Grisons in neighbouring Switzerland instead of, as the letter criticised, showing humility. The other couple had also already produced several children together. The bride and groom were related in the first degree of affinity as well as in the second degree of consanguinity – meaning that they were brother and sister-in-law as well as cousins – and had already submitted a dispensation request in 1844 that had been rejected. This couple also threatened to emigrate. In view of this situation, the bishop declared himself incapable of dispensing – not least in consideration of the fact that these requests would have had little chance of success in Rome. The vicar general, for his part, appears to have been motivated by a desire to bring these two families back into good order and possibly sought to take advantage of an exceptional situation. He therefore wrote a new letter, once again encouraging the prince-bishop to dispense on his own in these cases – and this time, he was indeed successful.

153 Cf. DIÖAB, Konsistorialakten 1848, Fasc. 5a, Römische Dispensen, no. 5, no. 6, no. 7 and no. 23.

154 Cf. DIÖAB, Konsistorialakten 1848, Fasc. 5a, Römische Dispensen, no. 26.

155 For a full four cases, a letter from the vicariate general dated 10 June 1849 requested dispensations *auctoritate ordinaria*, which – in its estimation – would have to be considered permissible "according to old Roman Catholic Church law". This letter is included in the record DIÖAB, Konsistorialakten 1851, Fasc. 5a, Römische Dispensen.

156 DIÖAB, Konsistorialakten 1848, Fasc. 5a, Römische Dispensen, no. 6 and no. 7.

In dispensation matters, the nunciature in Vienna had long served as a tried and true alternative to the papal authorities in Rome. It first reappears as a point of contact during 1849 and 1850. Repeated and urgent "recourse to Rome" concerning several dispensation requests had gone unanswered. In reaction to this, "Ordinarius Huber" – who had been chosen to represent the prince-bishop at the meeting of the Episcopal Conference in Vienna in June 1849 – was charged with bringing up these dispensation cases there. Afterwards, the prince-bishop felt vindicated in his careful approach to the wielding of his dispensatory authority: not a single bishop there had been of the opinion that he had the right to dispense on his own in the cases in question. The papal nuncio also rejected this idea.[157] The ordinariate therefore, in December 1849, requested the nunciature's "gracious intermediation", since the prince-bishop – contrary to his own consistory's recommendation – did not dare dispense on his own. But the nunciature – in stark contrast to its swift handling of yore – took its time with a response.[158] It eventually stated that it would take supportive action in Rome only once the pope had returned there. For the two requests that were open at the time, it would be another half-year and three quarters of a year, respectively, before the dispensations finally arrived.[159]

The following years saw eight requests granted by the nunciature. These concerned cases in which the bride was pregnant,[160] pregnancy was suspected,[161] the bridal couple already had children together,[162] and/or the couple's financial situation seemed quite precarious.[163] In 1856, however, this practice came to an end – concurrent with the tenure of the Apostolic Nuncio Michele Viale Prelà in Vienna[164] and that of Prince-Bishop Bernhard Galura in Brixen. As it had

---

157 This letter is dated 2 July 1849. DIÖAB, Konsistorialakten 1851, Fasc. 5a, Römische Dispensen, no. 18.

158 DIÖAB, Konsistorialakten 1851, Fasc. 5a, Römische Dispensen, no. 18.

159 The second case in DIÖAB, Konsistorialakten 1851, Fasc. 5a, Römische Dispensen, no. 17.

160 Cf. DIÖAB, Konsistorialakten 1854, Fasc. 5a, Römische Dispensen, no. 5; ibid., 1855, no. 8; ibid., 1856, no. 6.

161 Cf. DIÖAB, Konsistorialakten 1854, Fasc. 5a, Römische Dispensen, no. 6.

162 Ibid., no. 33; ibid., 1856, no. 16; ibid., 1856, no. 29.

163 Cf. DIÖAB, Konsistorialakten 1856, Fasc. 5a, Römische Dispensen, no. 31. In this case, a few further special facts pertained: both had been born out of wedlock and had therefore not reckoned with the marriage impediment of kinship even though they knew that his mother and her father were siblings. She had already lived with him as his housekeeper for six years, but – as the groom insisted when asked later on – she was a "very decent and shy, pious and contemplative maiden who knows nothing at all of sexual matters". He was 32 and she was 45 years old.

164 Regarding his person cf. for example Squicciarini, *Die Apostolischen Nuntien*, pp. 256–260.

been during other periods, the advantages of having a dispensation granted by the prince-bishop or the nunciature during the nineteenth century stemmed from the fact that less bureaucracy was involved. Dispensations granted by the nunciature, compared with those from Rome, tended to arrive far more quickly. What is more, there were no dispensation fees – which, especially in the first degree of affinity, were typically quite high. Couples only had to compensate the consistory in Brixen for stamp duties and postage and make a charitable donation of several gulden to the nunciature for the support of missionary efforts.

5 Canonical Reasons for Dispensation: Logics of Status and Gender

A prerequisite for a dispensation to be granted was the presence of officially recognised "canonical reasons". These underpinned the legitimacy of dispensation-granting and the validity of a granted dispensation along with the marriage concluded as a result. The individual canonical reasons for dispensation differed in their importance. As a general rule: the closer the degree of consanguinity or affinity, the weightier the applicable reasons had to be. Canonical reasons were divided into two groups, encompassing "honourable" and "dishonourable" reasons. Just what exactly was deemed worthy of recognition as a canonical reason for dispensation varied, at least at the level of nuance, over the centuries as well as between the various theological handbooks that circulated during the nineteenth century. During the High Middle Ages, the decretalists put forth competing opinions as to whether dispensation should be done for the good of the Church or "*pro persona*", with some viewing the well-being of the individual as synonymous with the well-being of the Church while others insisted on direct benefit to the common good, which was later to be stipulated by the *Decretum Tametsi* adopted at the Council of Trent.[165] The tension between personal and public implications was also to influence dispensation practice of the late eighteenth and the nineteenth centuries.

Six reasons specified as early as the twelfth century by Gratian served as reference for how the canonical reasons for dispensation were configured particularly by the canonists of the sixteenth and seventeenth centuries.[166] Typical

165 On these differing views cf. for example William A. O'Mara, *Canonical Causes for Matrimonial Dispensation. An Historical Synopsis and Commentary* (Washington, 1935), pp. 26–29; treated in detail by A[dhémar] Esmein, *Le mariage en droit canonique*, vol. 2 (Paris, 1891), pp. 314–368.

166 Dictum Gratiani, C. 5, C. 1, q. 7: "Nisi rigor disciplinae quandoque relaxetur ex dispensatione misericordiae. Multorum enim crimina sunt damnabilia, quae tamen Ecclesia

reasons for dispensation during the early modern period included narrowness of place (*angustia loci*), super-adult age (*aetas superadulta sponsae*), lack of a proper dowry (*deficientia aut incompetentia dotis*), conflict over property or wealth (*lites de bonis*), advantage of peace (*bonum pacis*), copula and pregnancy (*copula et praegnantia*), evil repute of the woman (*infamia mulieris*), revalidation of an invalid marriage (*revalidatio matrimonii*), removal of scandals (*remotio gravium scandalorum*) and excellence of merits (*excellentia meritorium*).[167] On 9 May 1877, the Sacred Congregation for the Propagation of the Faith[168] issued instructions on marriage dispensation requests that included a list of 16 reasons for dispensation.[169] The new additions above and beyond the aforementioned reasons were poverty of the widow (point 5), excessive familiarity (point 7), danger of an interconfessional marriage (point 11), danger of incestuous concubinage (point 12), danger of a civil marriage (point 13) and the cessation of notorious concubinage (point 15). The *Brixner Diözesan-Blatt* published these in 1878[170] along with a comment to the effect that this instruction was not intended to represent a "complete enumeration" of all canonical reasons for

---

tolerat pro tempore, pro persona, intuitu pietatis, vel necessitatis, sive utilitatis, et pro eventu rei." Quoted in O'Mara, *Canonical Causes*, pp. 28–29. As the definitive canonists in this regard, O'Mara mentions Vincentius de Justis (*De Dispensationibus Matrimonialibus*, 1726), Pyrrhus Corradus (*Praxis Dispensationum Apostolicarum pro utroque foro*, 1697) and Thomas S.J. Sanchez (*De Sancto Matrimonii Sacramento Disputationum*, 1669), ibid., p. 29, note 19. Somewhat broader is the list provided by Kutschker, *Das Eherecht der katholischen Kirche*, vol. 5, pp. 112–126; on this cf. also Pelaja, "Marriage by Exception", pp. 224–225.

167 Cf. O'Mara, *Canonical Causes*, pp. 31–36.

168 This is the "mission congregation", which was divided into two areas: one for the Latin Rite and one for the Eastern Rite. It had been founded in 1622. Cf. Giovanni Pizzorusso, "La congregazione pontifica *de Propaganda Fide* nel XVII secolo: missioni, geopolitica, colonialism", in *Papato e politica internazionale nella prima età moderna*, ed. Maria Antonietta Visceglia (Rome, 2013), pp. 149–172.

169 The full list was: 1. *angustia loci* 2. *aetas foeminae superadulta*, 3. *deficientia aut incompetentia dotis*, 4. *lites super successione bonorum*, 5. *paupertas viduae*, 6. *bonum pacis*, 7. *nimia, suspecta, periculosa familiaritatis*, 8. *copula iam praehabita et praegnantia, ideoque legitimatio prolis*, 9. *infamia mulieris*, 10. *revalidatio matrimonii*, 11. *periculum matrimonii mixti vel coram acattolico ministro celebrandi*, 12. *periculum incestuosi concubinantes*, 13. *periculum matrimonii civilis*, 14. *remotio gravium scandalorum*, 15. *cessatio publici concubinatus* and 16. *excellentia meritorum*.

170 In slightly different formulations, these can also be found in Dannerbauer, *Praktisches Geschäftsbuch*, pp. 234–240. Under "point five, On Widows" ("*Punkt fünf, Witwen betreffend*"), the burden of numerous children is added: "Paupertas viduae, quae numerosa prole sit onerata"; "point eight" outlines the relevant circle of relatives, but does not mention pregnancy: "Copula cum consanguinea vel affini vel alia persona impedimento laborante praehabita." The tenth reason, on the revalidation of marriages, is missing, but Dannerbauer adds the danger of heresy: "Periculum haeresis".

dispensation, and that readers should refer to tried-and-true authors "for the purpose of precise orientation".[171] 1901 saw the Apostolic Datary issue an even more detailed list that had been expanded to encompass a full 28 reasons.[172]

Among the honourable reasons commonly considered in dispensation practice were the "narrowness of place", which referred to the bride's birthplace or place of residence; super-adult age of the bride at and above age 24; and lack of a proper dowry. These three reasons are encountered primarily in requests in the more distant degrees and typically did suffice in order to receive such a dispensation. In the close degrees, they carried less weight but were still taken into account. Another circumstance recognised as an honourable reason for dispensation was that of poverty of the widow burdened with children (*pro oratrice filiis gravata*). Honourable were also the danger of an interconfessional marriage and the related danger of "being led away" from one's own faith (*periculum seductionis*); the advantage of peace (*bonum pacis*); and the protection of property and wealth. It was the norm, however, for this final reason to be reserved for the nobility and "families distinguished by exceptional service" (*conservatio bonorum in eadem illustri familia*). Moreover, "excellence of merits", defined as major service rendered to the Church, was itself an honourable reason for dispensation.[173]

Typically, endowments that benefited the Church were recognised as service, as were financial and/or logistical support for the restoration and repair of church buildings. The weight accorded to this reason in dispensation in practice makes dispensation logic's inherent social hierarchisation of supplicants all the clearer. Peter Zangerl from Nauders in the Deanery of Mals was the only person in all of the examined dispensation records to successfully thwart this logic: he sought to wed his sister-in-law Theres Zirnföld, a widow who lived on a "lonely, remote mountain". His initial request, which the records show to have been submitted in 1855, was rejected. However, the two chose to live together in spite of this and conceived two children. A later report indicates that the district office then received an August 1856 request that the couple, who were living "in open concubinage", be separated. The autumn of 1858 witnessed their next attempt – initiated via the district office in Nauders – to obtain a dispensation. Its refusal, they argued, would serve to punish "only the innocent children" and the community. The district office held Zangerl to be

171 "Neueste offizielle Instruktion über Ehedispensgesuche", *Brixner Diözesanblatt* 22 (1878), 33–38; on this cf. also O'Mara, *Canonical Causes*, pp. 72–130. The author comments on the above-mentioned canonical reasons in great detail and also describes their application in practice.

172 Cf. O'Mara, *Canonical Causes*, pp. 29, 131–135.

173 On this cf. Knopp, *Vollständiges katholisches Eherecht*, 1854, p. 444.

a "somewhat rough-hewn but by no means disreputable person". The mayor (*Ortsvorsteher*) of Nauders, however, who was subsequently asked to provide his assessment in December 1858, stated that Zangerl led a "disorderly and dissolute life" as one who "gives himself over to drink and excess", haunting various inns for days on end and wasting both "money and time". His assessment of Theres Zirnfeld was no more flattering: her neighbours, he wrote, described her as "a careless person, improvident and unclean". With recommendations like these, this couple's prospects were anything but good. The letter from the district office had indicated that Peter Zangerl had "moved abroad pending a decision on this request". Early 1861 saw things begin moving toward resolution. In the interim, the two had complied with the obligations placed upon them to separate and better themselves. Peter Zangerl was "away at work" in the neighbouring Engadin and was also able to present a "reference from a local priest" in the Pinzgau region, where he had most recently spent seven months working as a day labourer. He had arrived there – and this was the decisive point – from Italy. In Italy, he had performed "volunteer" service as a "soldier in the papal military" in the fight against the Italian unification movement before ultimately being taken captive near Pescara. He believed, as was then duly noted in the protocol of his matrimonial examination, that he had "thereby been of service to the Church" and was "hence now in a position to permit himself to hope for the Church's mercy". The two ultimately received their dispensation in the summer of 1861.[174]

Dishonourable reasons for dispensation included an endangered reputation as well as pregnancy of the bride and the associated "public scandal", a marriage invalidly concluded in ignorance of a marriage impediment and the danger of "defection" from the true faith.[175] Moreover, in cases deserving of special mercy but lacking sufficient officially recognised reasons for dispensation, it was also possible to indicate the existence of special circumstances. The reasons for dispensation were an altogether complex body of material, since they needed to be employed with an eye to the degrees of kinship in play as well as to the categories according to which dispensation fees were calculated – especially in the close degrees. These fees were calculated according to supplicants' social situations: the *forma pauperum* applied to everyone who could not be considered wealthy and lived from their own labours, the

174 DIÖAB, Konsistorialakten 1861, Fasc. 22a, Römische Dispensen, no. 23. Documents from the entire case are present here – while the initial reference to it is in ibid., 1855, Fasc. 5a, Römische Dispensen, no. 21. The characterisations of the two in the protocol of their matrimonial examination of 1861, on the other hand, sound very positive.

175 Cf. Knopp, *Vollständiges katholisches Eherecht*, 1854, pp. 457–461.

forma communi was for wealthier couples and the *forma nobelium* applied to members of the nobility.[176] This meant that fees could vary within one and the same degree of kinship depending on couples' financial situations and moral aspects of the circumstances portrayed.

In processing requests, local parish priests and deans frequently interpreted canonical reasons for dispensation rather freely: they would employ *angustia loci* as a dispensation reason for men or they would list the preservation of property or inheritance as a reason for dispensation-seekers from peasant or artisanal and trade circles. In one instance, the dean of Zams even attempted to employ the age of the groom – who was 39 years old – in the matrimonial examination in the sense of *aetas superadulta*.[177] Repeatedly the consistory had to point out that the reason of advanced age only applied to unmarried prospective brides and could not be taken into account in the case of widows. The overall body of correspondence contains no comments to the effect that exceeding age 24, which was the usual age of marriage as defined by Rome, was in fact fairly irrelevant when it came to women from the Diocese of Brixen. This was a Roman perspective that was applied to the entire Catholic world without accounting for differences between regions. Women in Tyrol and Vorarlberg, however, typically married for the first time between the ages of 28.6 (1828–1836) and 30.2 (1855–1863)[178] – with the average tending to rise towards the end of the century. The dispensation records from Salzburg, on the other hand, contain isolated cases where the idea of dramatically dwindling chances of marriage past age 24 was downplayed. In one case, for example, the official charged with requests' evaluation wrote that the supplicant was 28 years old and thus "certainly in *aetate superadulta* according to canon law, but in fact still at a good age at which the hope for another accommodation [synonymous with marriage, ML] need by no means be viewed as already dwindling".[179] This statement represents a rare counterpoint to the otherwise purely formalistic and pragmatic use of this reason.

Even though it was not, in principle, considered particularly weighty in close degrees of kinship, the reason of *angustia loci* is indeed present in the requests. 300 "hearths" served as a standard point of reference for determining whether the "place" was "narrow", as can be seen in the notes and comments written in

176 Cf. for example the dispensation fees valid in the Austrian dioceses beginning in 1850, listed in Kutschker, *Das Eherecht der katholischen Kirche*, vol. 5, 290–291.

177 Cf. DIÖAB, Konsistorialakten 1835, Fasc. 5a, Römische Dispensen, no. 12. Letter of the prince-episcopal ordinariate of 9 February 1835, signed by Chancellor Georg Prünster.

178 Cf. Mantl, *Heirat als Privileg*, p. 33.

179 AES, Kasten 22/35 Ehe-Dispensen 1841–1846 and 1883–1890, 1842, dispensation request of Jakob Schindler and Ludovika Gordon.

the margins of the dispensation requests from Brixen. *Angustia loci* applied wherever the number of houses in a community was lower. The consistory put some effort into formalising this criterion to the greatest possible extent, conducting a targeted survey in order to have a basis for decision-making.[180] Even so, "narrowness" remained a flexible term and evidently represented an invitation to attempt definitional slights of hand – such as by counting only the houses in a certain hamlet or treating parish and municipality as interchangeable, depending on which of the two was smaller.[181] The dean of Bregenz attempted a different variant by indicating that narrowness of place did not apply to Bregenz, where the widow in question had already been living for 14 years, but to her home village of Hard – "a place that comes nowhere close to numbering 300 hearths".[182]

As illustrated by this reason's description, numerous canonical reasons for dispensation were gender-oriented in that they applied exclusively to women. The intent was to protect women's decency and morals: according to church logic, women were supposed to be able to find their purpose and sustenance in marriage if at all possible.[183] This foundational principle most certainly applied to that most inflationary of all reasons for dispensation, *angustia loci*: if a parish was so small that a woman was unable to find a suitable husband, she was to be permitted to marry a kinsman in order to avoid remaining single. It was also fundamentally to be assumed that the circumstances of "super-adult" age and/or an absent or very low dowry worsened a woman's chances of being able to marry, which could also be compensated for by the option of marrying a kinsman. These reasons for dispensation exhibit a second significant characteristic of dispensation logic: where insufficient selection or poor chances were at issue, the point was not that *absolutely no* marriageable man but that *no suitable* man could be found – with "suitable" being defined according to the socio-economic criteria of a marriage befitting one's social position. In the

---

180 In December 1833, the prince-episcopal consistory in Brixen had called upon all deaneries to survey the "hearths, meaning families, in every pastoral care station of the deanery" in order to provide well-founded indications of their sizes to Rome. These numbers were referred to frequently, often being noted in the margins of matrimonial examination protocols in red or blue ink. DIÖAB, Konsistorialakten 1833, Fasc. 5c, Verschiedenes über Ehe, no. 4: Zahl der Feuerstätten, Familien in jeder Seelsorgs-Station.

181 1876 saw an effort made at the highest level to clarify this. Cf. Petrus Gasparri (ed.), *Codicis Iuris Canonici Fontes*, vol. 6: Curia Romana (Rome, 1932), pp. 593–597, 593, with the conclusion: "Item in literis dispensationum, tum Sacrae Datariae tum etiam Poenitentiariae numquam mentio fit de exiguitate paroeciae, semper autem loquitur de angustia loci." Cf. also ibid., pp. 872–875.

182 DIÖAB Konsistorialakten 1839, Fasc. 5a, Römische Ehedispensen, no. 5.

183 On this cf. also Saurer, "Stiefmütter und Stiefsöhne", pp. 356–357.

context of *angustia loci*, therefore, this logic entails that purely arithmetical calculations regarding potentially available husbands who were related neither by blood or by marriage simply fall short.[184] From the perspective of the Church, the risk of losing one's social status was more important than the prohibition of kin marriage – and this was a regulatory and socio-political function of dispensation practice.

The focus of the reasons for dispensation, oriented as they were toward specific qualities and roles attributed to women, frequently conflicted with the concrete life situations of men – many of whom did, in actual fact, need help and support. This was a context in which institutional and everyday logics drifted impossibly far apart. In many cases, for example, a widower with small children and only a meagre basis for existence would apply for a dispensation because he was unable to pay for household help and could feel lucky if a blood or affinal relative of his were willing to marry him under such difficult circumstances. This configuration was typical, even if the details varied. Widowers were also far more strongly represented in the context of dispensations than were widows: in the Diocese of Brixen, the period from 1831 to 1864 featured three times as many, with 42 per cent of the male supplicants being widowers while only 14 per cent of the female supplicants were widows.[185]

However, there was no reason for dispensation intended specifically for widowers.[186] At best, a widower could express concern for the well-being of

184 David Sabean attempted to extrapolate how probable it was in smaller communities that unions with close consanguineous or affine relatives could be avoided. Sabean, *Kinship in Neckarhausen*, p. 101, note 3: "If one reckons that each parent and grandparent has two siblings and takes the prohibition against marriage with consanguineal relatives out to second cousins, than in a village of about 350 people [...] about 80 percent of the households are 'nonrelated'. Each successive marriage cuts off another 20 percent, the relatives of the deceased wife. In a village of 500, about 84 percent of the households are open for a first marriage, and in a village of 1,000 [...], about 92 percent."

185 Explaining differing remarriage rates of widowers and widows demographically with reference to gender ratios would fall far short of being explanatory – something that Barbara Todd has most unambiguously pointed out. Todd advocates a nuanced view, specifying three interacting factors behind remarriage: opportunity, necessity and preference. The decision to enter into a second marriage should hence be regarded as a considered one. Cf. Barbara J. Todd, "Demographic Determinism and Female Agency: the Remarrying Widow Reconsidered ... Again", *Continuity and Change* 9 (1994), 421–450, 422 and 426–431. As a recent publication see Beatrice Moring and Richard Wall, *Widows in European Economy and Society 1600–1920* (Woodbridge, 2017). In terms of historical research and gender history, widowers have been paid attention far too seldomly. An admirable contribution in this regard is the volume by Sandra Cavallo and Lyndan Warner (eds.), *Widowhood in Medieval and Early Modern Europe* (Halow, 1999).

186 As part of its aforementioned 1901 addition to the list of recognised reasons for dispensation, the Datary did, however, add that of the preservation and/or betterment of a

his children (*bonum prolis*), but this did not count for all that much. There were no equivalents to the other reasons for dispensation that were available to widows. The same went for unmarried men, for whom the official catalogue of reasons for dispensation included none that could have been applied in difficult life situations. During phases when dispensation practice was strict, requests that argued mainly from the perspective of the men could be that much more easily rejected due to a lack of canonical reasons for dispensation. Therefore, a certain amount of abstraction was required in cases where the clerics at the consistory did, in fact, desire to support such a dispensation request. The letters sent to Rome occasionally read as if they had nothing to do with the circumstances that the witnesses and the bridal couple had actually portrayed.

Joseph Singer, an unmarried 45-year-old sexton from Grammais in the Deanery of Imst, had found himself in an unfortunate situation: For "his householding", he needed a "tidy person" – not least because he was responsible for the "church laundry" and the "care of the church linens". He had previously been assisted by two older, likewise-unmarried sisters who had since become unable to continue helping him on account of ill health. Singer also bore responsibility for the care of his mentally impaired brother, who was incapable of working and likewise lived in his household. He could not rely on his two other sisters. One of them had married into a rather sizeable farm and was herself now in need of help with her large brood of small children. The other had already been serving for many years as the housekeeper of a curate, a "good job" that she would hardly be willing to give up for his sake. He was also unable to afford a maidservant. So, if he could not marry his cousin Maria Anna Wechner, who seemed to him to be the only suitable woman in the community, he would perhaps be forced to sell the house that he had inherited from his parents. This was the scenario portrayed in the letter of supplication, which was signed by both marital hopefuls. About the prospective bride, however, one hears no more than that she fulfilled the specified expectations and requirements.[187]

It would probably have been difficult to simply brush off this request by a sexton who, like his father, had performed this "low-paying" job "loyally and earnestly, with tireless industriousness". But what reasons for dispensation could be communicated to Rome? Reading the letter addressed "*ad Sedem Apostolicam*", we will hardly recognise the original story: the bride, according to this letter, lacked a sufficient dowry, she had already exceeded

family – which could be employed by both women and men. Cf. Jemolo, *Il matrimonio*, p. 254.

187 DIÖAB, Konsistorialakten 1843, Fasc. 5a, Römische Dispensen, no. 12.

her twenty-fourth year, and the narrow confines of the community entailed that there was no selection of men "*paris conditionis*" – of the same social status – whom she might marry who were related with her neither by blood nor by affinity. Furthermore, there existed "*affectio*" between the supplicants, who had also already shared a long and dangerous acquaintance. If this dispensation were denied and the marriage prevented from going forward, the letter argues, the bride would surely have to remain unmarried and lose her reputation – "*certe innupta et diffamata remanere deberet*" – which could touch off a considerable scandal. The passage with the words "*innupta*" and "*diffamata*" adhered to Catholic marriage logic, centred as it was on women, and the dispensation context often saw it employed in a manner that was similarly disconnected from the supplicants' actual testimony. In this document, not a word was wasted on the altogether rather grim situation of the groom, whose household included three family members who were in need of care. The motivation behind this marriage project that had at first been formulated primarily from his perspective finds no portrayal whatsoever in this letter to Rome. In this case, the translation-like act that was performed stands out quite drastically – as does the discrepancy between the situation portrayed at the diocesan level and the official dispensation request that was addressed to the Apostolic Datary in Rome. Fundamentally, albeit in most cases more moderately, this mode of translation can be viewed as paradigmatic of communication with Rome.

As a rule, it was advisable to portray supplicants' life circumstances in a way that was oriented as much as possible toward the canonical reasons – an orientation that prestructured the content of both the letters of supplication and the accompanying letters as well as the reports and matrimonial examinations. But as the material examined here shows, it by no means always stopped at that. André Burguière, who has examined eighteenth-century French sources, ascertains a predominantly stereotypical mode of argumentation that was closely tied to the predetermined official canonical reasons. In contrast to the records from Brixen, these hardly make it possible to go beyond quantitative enumeration of the aspects put forth to offer qualitative evaluations that would allow broader inferences.[188] The conclusion drawn by Marion Trévisi is similar,[189] and the fact that formulaically distilled reasons for dispensation can be viewed as being of only limited significance even in quantitative analyses is exemplified by the aforementioned dispensation request of Joseph Singer and Anna Maria Wechner.

188 Cf. Burguière, "'Cher Cousin'", pp. 1346–1347.
189 Cf. Trévisi, "Le mariage entre parents", pp. 252–257.

It is precisely these detailed justifications and situational portrayals that make the material from Brixen especially valuable. At the same time, however, we must bear in mind that the relevant text types and passages represent communication of a strategic character. The arguments put forward are oriented toward the expectations of their addressees. The meaning of that which is communicated can therefore only be understood before the backdrop of the logics of those institutions for which the portrayals were intended – which is to say that the content thus conveyed is inextricably linked with the "how" of communication as guided by the institutionally established reasons for dispensation. What was being asked for was mercy – and therefore, these were supplications of a specific type that always signalled "unequal power relations".[190]

6 Public and Secret, 'Worthy' and 'Unworthy'

The criterion of publicity represented a factor that guided action within dispensation practice. One context in which it became relevant was when "public scandal" was a concern, or when cases involved "acquaintances" between women and men related closely by blood or by marriage that were deemed too familiar by those in their social environments. The opposite criterion, that of secrecy, also had its effect. A marriage rendered invalid by an overlooked marriage impediment that consequently had to be revalidated was, as previously mentioned, a matter that was to be kept as secret as possible. Under certain circumstances, the existence of a pregnancy not yet known to the community could significantly speed the dispensation-granting procedure. Marriage impediments were therefore classified according to this distinction between public and secret. Secret marriage impediments fell within the purview not of the Datary,[191] but of the Penitentiary. One of the responsibilities of this

190 Cf. Cecilia Nubola and Andreas Würgler, "Einführung", in *Bittschriften und Gravamina*, ed. Nubola and Würgler, pp. 7–16, 9. Letters of supplication were also shot through with tropes – such as that of the "poor widow" – that could function as situational gestures of submission in the interest of fulfilling institutional expectations.

191 In Johann Heinrich Bangen's 1854 volume on the Roman Curia, which the title page states that he has "portrayed following several years of my own observation", the topics covered include the practice of the Datary: "But indeed, the current procedures of the Datary show, just as it is clear from the nature of this matter as such, that the person who prepared the supplications for decision and ultimately even brought them to the audience also spoke regarding their content and advised the pope to grant or not to grant – at least insofar as he was requested to do so." Johann Heinrich Bangen, *Die Römische Kurie, ihre gegenwärtige Zusammensetzung und ihr Geschäftsgang* (Münster, 1854), p. 397.

ecclesiastical court of law, which was equipped with extensive authorities to dispense, was for the realm of conscience – *pro foro interno*.[192]

Three types of marriage impediment could be lifted only by means of secret dispensations, namely dispensations *ex voto castitatis*, *inhonestis* and *ex copula illicita*. The first type lifted a vow of chastity to allow a planned marriage to go forward and distinguished between a temporary vow, for which a bishop could grant dispensations, and a vow taken for life, for which only a papal dispensation would suffice. A dispensation *inhonestis* became necessary when a promise of marriage not been known publicly had been dissolved and the groom or bride instead sought to marry a first-degree relative of the formerly intended bride or groom. A dispensation *ex copula illicita* became necessary if a man or a woman had engaged in premarital sexual contact with a close relative of the future bride or groom that had remained concealed from public knowledge.

Matters that were secret or thought to be secret were to be dealt with in a discreet way, without causing a sensation, in order that they remain so. However, a civil ordinance of 1778 attempted to decouple such dispensations from Rome by placing the responsibility for obtaining this type of dispensation solely in the hands of the ordinariates,[193] an attempt that was reinforced by an April 1783 court decree specifically regarding secret dispensations *ex copula illicita*.[194] A July 1783 ordinance walked back this move by declaring that for secret dispensations, the way to Rome remained open: regarding *impedimenta occulta*, the "reverend ordinaries" were free to turn to the Roman Penitentiary

---

192 Regarding the Penitentiary, in existence since the twelfth century as one of the oldest institutions of the Roman Curia cf. Tamburini, "Le dispense matrimoniali". It was subordinate to the major penitentiary, who was equipped with comprehensive authorities. Cf. also the overview by Erwin Ruck, *Die Organisation der Römischen Kurie* (Tübingen, 1913). As authorities of the Penitentiary, he enumerates: "the granting of all mercies, absolutions from all sins and censures, dispensations, condonations, commutations, sanations and decisions on all manner of moral issues" (ibid., pp. 31–32). On the practice of the Penitentiary cf. Schmugge, *Ehen vor Gericht*, pp. 11–15. During the Middle Ages, the Penitentiary had "a quasi-monopoly on the granting of marriage dispensations" (ibid., p. 33). During the nineteenth century, cases where the supplicants were capable of paying only minimal fees saw the Penitentiary repeatedly brought into play as an authority capable of granting mercies. Cf. also Pelaja, "Marriage by Exception", pp. 230–232.

193 Cf. ordinance of 23 January 1778, in *Sammlung in Publico-Ecclesiasticis vom Jahre 1767 bis Ende 1782*, p. 105. In January 1783, this ordinance was sent out again together with two others and an explanation stating that it seemed "the following three supreme ordinances have likely not been publicised or fittingly announced". TLA Innsbruck, Jüngeres Gubernium, Gubernialratsprotokolle, Ecclesiastica, Fasc. 212, 1783 (Jan.–Feb.), Ein- und Auslauf, vol. 5, no. 76 ½.

194 Cf. court decree of 13 April 1783 as quoted in Kropatschek, *Handbuch*, vol. 2, p. 171; cf. also *Sammlung in Publico-Ecclesiasticis vom Jahre 1782 bis 1783*, p. 67.

on behalf of the supplicant parties with no need for approval by the secular power.[195] Requests for dispensations *in occultis* differed primarily in a formal sense. They had to be anonymised, to which end a specific repertoire of names was employed. Titus and Livia from Außervillgraten in East Tyrol, for example, applied for a secret dispensation. The groom admitted "that he is related in the first degree of affinity with the widowed bride Livia due to illicit relations, which is entirely unknown, however, and which he believes shall forever remain unknown".[196] It was the norm that requests in this category had be formulated in Latin – a requirement that members of the clergy did not always uphold, however, such as in the example cited here.[197]

The question of whether a secret marriage impediment might be present was included in the matrimonial examination as well as in the pre-wedding religious examination (*Brautexamen*) that had to be taken prior to every marriage. The protocols do not clearly indicate its exact formulation. The answers allow for the conclusion that in some cases secret marriage impediments were probably gone through individually. Nonetheless, it did happen that a secret marriage impediment was only realised or became known after the wedding. One woman, dubbed Tranquillina in her request and already married to Pubblio for several weeks, had slept with his brothers some time prior but refrained from admitting this in the pre-wedding religious examination. She later explained that she had been sure this "sin" would not affect her nuptials, since it had occurred long before.[198]

A couple's prospects for receiving the mercy of a dispensation not only depended on the presence of canonical reasons but also on the overall impression that they made. In the official church view, only "worthy" bridal couples – people who were known to have been living Christian lives that were beyond

---

195 Ordinance of 10 July 1783, in *Sammlung in Publico-Ecclesiasticis vom Jahre 1782 bis 1783*, p. 90. Exceptions to this were dispensations of *impedimenta occulta ex crimine* – the impediments that arose from having committed adultery – which, from autumn 1781, could no longer be sought via the Penitentiary for a fee, nor from parish priests or confessors; the bishops were expected to dispense *jure proprio*. Ordinance of 25 October 1781, *Sammlung in Publico-Ecclesiasticis vom Jahre 1767 bis Ende 1782*, pp. 143–144, 143.

196 DIÖAB, Konsistorialakten 1893, Fasc. 22c, Varia über Eheangelegenheiten, unnumbered.

197 September 1833 saw the Deanery of Zams, for example, send a supplication for the annulment of a vow of chastity to the prince-episcopal ordinariate in Brixen that was anonymised – "Bertha" being its classic placeholder – but not formulated in Latin. In response to the admonishment that ensued, a new version of the request arrived two weeks later, in October 1833 – this time properly Latinised. Cf. DIÖAB, Konsistorialakten 1833, Fasc. 5b, Ehedispensen in occultis et inhonestis, no. 9.

198 Cf. for example DIÖAB, Konsistorialakten 1891, Fasc. 22b, Casus occulti ex impedimento matrimonii, unnumbered.

reproach with respect to morality and decency – were fundamentally eligible for dispensations. But in practice, at least until the mid-1850s, it was relatively promising – albeit not without risk – if a couple had engaged in all-too-familiar relations, if they had engaged in *copula incestuosa* or if a pregnancy was suspected or actually underway. This gave rise to a certain pressure, felt above all by the local clergy and less so by the higher ranking clerics of the consistory, to create an 'orderly' situation. It was fundamentally in the Church's interest to 'repair' moral transgressions to the greatest possible extent, and marriage was an ideal way to do so. Prospective couples could not count on this, however. Especially during the 1830s and 1840s, the deans of the Diocese of Brixen frequently addressed this ambivalence that was structurally inherent in dispensation practice.[199] Since the most efficient way of avoiding "public scandal" was via marriage, out-of-wedlock pregnancy was in fact quite frequently beneficial to a dispensation request. This could put members of the clergy in an awkward position, however, particularly when forced to refuse requests by couples of sterling reputation. When such couples pointed to dispensations that they knew had been granted under entirely different moral circumstances, clerics found it difficult to argue their positions since, strictly speaking, it was only couples who had lived lives beyond reproach who were worthy of receiving dispensations.

As a phase of moralisation began setting in around the mid-1850s, attention shifted to the period *prior* to the initiation of dispensation proceedings. An 1860 ecclesiastical ordinance required local priests as well as deans to turn away dispensation supplicants when the prospective bride was pregnant until both exhibited clear signs of regret and atonement. Moreover, it soon became typical for diocesan consistories to refrain from dealing with dispensation requests in cases where pregnancy was involved until childbirth had taken place. With this, marriage had been stripped of a function that had been important for centuries – that of avoiding public 'disgrace'. As previously mentioned, a several-month probationary period was required during which the couple had to avoid all contact and, if possible, all encounters. A 'penitential programme' was also imposed upon them in accordance with the seriousness and frequency of their "sins of the flesh". Such programmes entailed regular confession, saying the rosary on one's knees, diligent church attendance on

199 The altogether 735 requests submitted up to 1864 include 93 (12.7 per cent) where the women were pregnant; 81 (11 per cent) already had at least one illegitimate child. The number of pregnant women rose slowly but consistently over multiple decades before then decreasing slightly during the late 1850s followed by a clear rise thereafter. Moreover, nearly 40 per cent of the couples overall had admitted at their matrimonial examinations that they had already engaged in sexual intercourse.

Sundays and holidays, fasting, devotions at the stations of the cross and sometimes even religious instruction by the priest. If a couple had already produced children together at the point in time when they submitted their request, the requirements of recognisable improvement and compensation for the "scandal" caused were even more extensive and frequently near-impossible to fulfil. It seems as if this more severe practice was intended to make examples of people in order to escape the ambivalence and double-tracking associated with the dispensation of 'unworthy' couples. And indeed, it was a certainty in small parishes that the required penance and atonement would not go unnoticed, due not least to the involvement of neighbours as monitors and the summoning of witnesses.

In Salzburg's dispensation records, the tone of the language used is far less moralising – even during the period that began in the mid-1850s. The 'penitential programmes' here were more moderate. They typically mandated going to confession, with anything additional left up to the discretion of the competent priest. The couple's "expiation under oath" took place not as a public act before witnesses but rather in written form. Cases in which an already granted dispensation's "sanation" was mandated due to sexual contact during the intervening period are not documented in the examined material. However, the archepiscopal consistory in Salzburg – though consistently more conciliatory in how it dealt with related couples – allowed no room for manoeuvre when the prospective bride was pregnant, not even in the nineteenth century's first half. Whenever a letter from a priest or a couple's letter of supplication mentioned pregnancy or "sinful relations" as a reason for dispensation, the associated request had no prospects of receiving a positive answer. The recognition of this type of justification was refused not just on a case-by-case basis but as a matter of principle. There was no willingness to allow ambivalences to arise. Clear words to this effect can be found in the reaction to a July 1830 request where the bride was four months pregnant: in his report, the priest listed "a few more detailed circumstances that he characterises as reasons for dispensation, but these reasons are owed solely to the supplicant's own transgression, and I do not think that decency would be served if close kin needed merely to sin with each other in order to immediately have hope of a dispensation's being granted".[200]

The Church even viewed the exchange of information between dispensation supplicants as morally 'perilous'. With the practice of verification protocols that was instituted beginning in the second half of the 1850s, the sworn

200 AES, Kasten 22/34, Ehedispensen I. u. II. Grades 1821–1830, 1830, dispensation request of Jakob Struber and Maria Anna Zink.

statement that "incestuous sin" had not been committed with the intent of more easily procuring a dispensation – which was typically required of all supplicant couples – was augmented by a further passage: they had to swear, under pain of being denied any further dispensation that they might seek in the future they would never "commit such a sin" and additionally swear to never "falsely instruct others" to the effect that a dispensation might be more easily received via this route. They also had to swear that they would refrain from "providing assistance" to others regarding matters of dispensation "in the form of advice or in any other way". But despite all efforts, the opinion that prior sexual relations could positively influence the response to a dispensation request persisted stubbornly among the general public, even giving rise to the occasional case where a couple was said to have 'confessed' to sins that had not actually occurred.

Regarding Severin Hämmerle of Lustenau, a local priest reported the following in June 1863: "He was persuaded to make this false claim by somebody who had told him that dispensations are granted reliably and without delay in cases of sins of the flesh." Upon hearing this, the Bishop of Brixen ordered an investigation that was led by the vicariate council with Canon Fidel Häusle as its commissioner. This investigation pinpointed four men, including the father of the bride, as the originators of this rumour.[201] One of the four referred to a Lustenau dispensation case of 1854, nearly ten years prior, in which the bride had been pregnant and the couple had received a dispensation.[202] The establishment of an investigative commission makes clear that the Church spared no expense during this period in its effort to combat an ambiguity that it had itself long upheld.

•••

The main purpose of this chapter has been to outline the wholly altered premises from which the nineteenth century began in the wake of the late eighteenth

201 DIÖAB, Konsistorialakten 1863, Fasc. 22a, Römische Dispense, no. 57. The groom and bride rescued themselves from the problem resulting from the fact that the matrimonial examination's protocol was defined as under oath by insisting that they had not been made to take such an oath, having only been told that an oath might have to be taken.

202 This was the request of Ludwig Hofer and his sister-in-law Theres Egle. In this case, it was conversely the bride who, out of "shame and fear that she might consequently have no hope of receiving a dispensation", had failed to divulge her "incestuous behaviour" in the matrimonial examination. The fact that the dispensation brief had already been issued and had arrived at the consistory prior to her admission had then made necessary a "sanation", which was taken care of via the nunciature in Vienna. DIÖAB, Konsistorialakten 1854, Fasc. 22a, Römische Dispense, no. 4.

century's conflicts: following secularisation of the Prince-Bishoprics of Brixen, Salzburg and Trento plus the reorganisation of the dioceses, and above all in a post-Josephine era in which little remained of the ambitious programme to reform the practice of dispensation-granting. In the Austrian dioceses, the centralisation of dispensation-related proceedings and the obligatory *placetum regium* persisted. In other respects, however, procedures were anything but homogeneous. The character and extent of the civil authorities' involvement in dispensation-granting varied greatly from diocese to diocese. In Brixen, they played a role that was fairly secondary and for the most part merely formal, while their presence was far greater in Salzburg, and in Trento, all indications point to their having functioned as the central protagonists. In the Swiss diocese of Chur, on the other hand, procedures were organised in an entirely different way. A similar degree of diversity is evident in the way in which dispensation-specific documentation is formulated and archived – which, in turn, entails commensurate differences in terms of such documentation's usefulness as the basis for systematic analysis. The dispensation requests to be found in the Diocese of Brixen proved best suited to this purpose. These were recorded in a database that came to encompass nearly 2,150 cases, with detailed information being entered for slightly less than 1,000 from the 1831–1864 period. This basic source material was supplemented by sampling the material from the other three dioceses. Subsequent analysis indicated considerable divergences – not only in the organisation of procedures but also in how prospective couples and their requests were dealt with.

Further sections of this chapter have dealt with fundamental problem areas and logics of dispensation practice. In order to ascertain kinship and prohibited degrees of kinship, local knowledge proved essential. But some marriage impediments were overlooked even so, necessitating the revalidation of marriages that would have required dispensation but had already been concluded without it; such cases were to be prevented wherever possible. For this reason, clerics were subject to quite some pressure in their research on family relationships. It repeatedly became apparent that kin marriages were topics of public discourse, such as around the table at inns. It was in villages that the reactions to marriage projects in close degrees of consanguinity and affinity seem to have been especially diverse, ranging from perception as something normal to the most extreme scandalisation. We certainly cannot assume general acceptance: each individual case needs to be viewed as part of a specific local and social context.

Fundamentally, as few dispensations as possible were to be granted to couples where close degrees of kinship were in play. Local clergyman were called upon to turn away such couples three times before permitting themselves to put pen to paper for the next step. Moreover, a final bastion of dispensation denial was that of proposed unions between stepmothers and stepsons or vice versa. During the 60 years between 1831 and 1890, the Diocese of Brixen logged but two requests of this type – in contrast to the region of Vienna and Lower Austria, where requests were received primarily by the provincial government. Were there really no such marriage projects in the Diocese of Brixen apart from these two, or was it typical for such plans to only be articulated orally followed by successful deterrence on the local or regional levels by the competent priests, hence leaving no traces in the dispensation records? To the impression regarding contemplated and planned marriage projects between close kin – an impression that, in principle, can never be considered complete – we must not only add those projects that were rejected but also those that never made it into the records.

A further – and not insignificant – obstacle that could stand in the way of couples who desired to marry was that of the economic prerequisites for marriage, whose fulfilment had to be confirmed by municipalities via so-called political marriage consent. Particularly in the German-speaking part of Tyrol municipalities were comparatively rigid when it came to its granting or denial – but marriage consent policy also figured into marriage dispensation practice in Vorarlberg in Salzburg. In the Diocese of Brixen, the presentation of marriage consent became mandatory in 1838 – in response to a specific case. The multi-level procedure along with numerous documents that had to be presented, information that had to be procured, associated costs and numerous rejections make it more than clear that Catholic dispensation-granting in the nineteenth century was by no means a merely formal act. An extremely compressed Latin version, reduced to those reasons for dispensation that were officially recognised by the Church and accompanied by letters of recommendation, ultimately reached Rome. In the best-case scenario, it took months – or, in politically turbulent times, even longer – for a dispensation brief to reach the supplicants' diocese. The 1850s saw the introduction of a requirement to reconfirm the presence of the reasons for dispensation and the moral integrity of the bridal couple in the form of an additional verification protocol. If sexual transgression had occurred during the period since the matrimonial examination, so-called sanation became necessary.

The catalogue-like list of reasons for dispensation adhered to an ecclesiastical logic that was oriented toward social status and the 'protection' of women – in the sense that it was to be made possible for them to marry. For men, the range of available reasons proved limited by comparison – which was not without its effects on how the arguments in dispensation requests were structured. Some administrative procedures had to account for the distinction between public and secret. Another set of opposites, the distinction between 'worthy' and 'unworthy' dispensation supplicants based on sexual morality, frequently led to ambivalences and a lack of good explanations, leaving above all local priests with the following dilemma: as a rule, they were interested in making it possible for extramarital relationships – especially those where the woman was pregnant or the couple already had children – to be put in 'order' and legitimised via marriage. Officially, however, only couples who led morally upstanding lives were considered worthy. This matter shows yet again how the dioceses took differing approaches and how such approaches grew more severe over time. Concerning the wave of moralisation that set in around the mid-1850s, its temporal coincidence with the dogma of the "Immaculate Conception" in 1854 makes a connection seem quite plausible – a finding that would also serve to refute any all-too-linear impression of increasing liberation from church control.

CHAPTER 5

Marriages in Close Degrees of Affinity – Contested Unions

The couple configuration of brother- and sister-in-law had long been a focal point of theological and legal discussion. Especially treatises of the sixteenth and seventeenth centuries had dealt extensively with this type of union,[1] mainly out of concern for the positioning of married women between their families of origin and the families they had married into. This affected the arrangements that were made as part of the practice surrounding inheritance and marital property. Though the Catholic Church insisted that blood and affinal kinship were to be considered equal in weight independent of gender as far as marriage impediments were concerned, the sister-in-law had nonetheless come to occupy a special position from a legal standpoint during the early modern period. As Michaela Hohkamp has pointed out, marriage made a woman part of the "*communio reverentiae sanguinis*" of her husband and his family – something that did not apply the other way around. It was from this that prohibition of marriage to the widow of a brother or uncle had been derived.[2] The Old Testament, by contrast, had explicitly permitted a widower's marriage to his sister-in-law, or sororate marriage – because hers was a different "flesh", while the marriage of a widow to a brother-in-law was forbidden since this involved one and the same "flesh". This ban ceased to have effect, however, if the husband had died without leaving behind any children. In such a case, the widow was obligated to marry the brother-in-law. The children of such a levirate marriage were regarded as children of the deceased brother.[3]

---

1 Cf. Sabean, "Inzestdiskurse", pp. 15–16.

2 Michaela Hohkamp, "Do Sisters Have Brothers? The Search for the 'rechte Schwester'. Brothers and Sisters in Aristocratic Society at the Turn of the Sixteenth Century", in *Sibling Relations*, ed. Johnson/Sabean, pp. 65–83, 70. She refers here to Samuel de Cocceji, *Jus controversum civile: ubi illustriores juris controversiae breviter et succincte deciduntur, difficiliores materiae explicantur, objectiones solide solvuntur, et legum dissensus nova saepe ratione, ubi hactenus satisfactum non videntur, conciliantur* (Frankfurt a.M./Leipzig, 1713–1718), pp. 150–152.

3 On this cf. Klein, "Allein nach dem 'Gesetz Mosis'", pp. 89–94. The widow and her brother-in-law could, however, avoid the obligation to enter into such a union by way of a certain ritual (cf. ibid.).

DOI:10.1163/9789004539877_006

As far as the realisation of marriages between brother- and sister-in-law among Catholic commoners went, Gérard Delille has ascertained that hardly any such unions had been concluded prior to 1770.[4] Towards the end of the eighteenth century, unions with the sister of one's deceased wife began cropping up "un peu partout" and proceeded to steadily increase in number.[5] We can also infer a rise in such marriage projects during this period from a comment attributed to Pius VII (1800–1823): "It would seem that in Germany, widowers are no longer capable of finding any brides other than their sisters-in-law."[6] A critical undertone can be heard in this statement, which touches on two further aspects that were anything but insignificant: first, German-speaking territories seem to have been a hotspot of sorts for this type of couple configuration and, second, it featured an imbalance between the sexes. The perception centred on the configuration of widower and sister-in-law, which by far overshadowed the inverse configuration of widow and brother-in-law.[7] Furthermore, precisely such an imbalance in terms of gender and family status is also clearly evident in the affinal marriage projects to be found among the dispensation records analysed in this study. This impression leads us to expect that the

---

4 It must be asked whether this configuration's vehement rejection should to a certain extent be viewed as an expression of differentiation from the previously mentioned Jewish levirate marriage. Another fact to be considered in connection with the prohibition of marriages in the first degree of affinity is that there were notions regarding the alikeness of siblings that could even entail conceiving of them as being entirely the same. Cf. Gérard Delille, "La fratrie: des frères ou des individus?", *European Review of History – Revue européenne d'histoire* 17, 5 (2010), 705–718, 708–709.

5 Gérard Delille, "Réflexions sur le 'systeme' européen de la parenté et de l'alliance. Note critique", *Annales HSS* 56, 2 (2001), 369–380, 378–379, quote 372.

6 DIÖAB, Konsistorialakten 1847, Fasc. 5a, Römische Dispensen, no. 20. Here, Pius VII is quoted in this form by the parish priest of Tisis in connection with an 1847 dispensation request in the first degree of affinity in which the priest saw nothing more than "cobbled-together reasons". A decision was reached by way of consensus between the ordinariate, the district office, the local priest and "honourable and judicious men in the community" that this request would not be forwarded to Rome, effectively entailing its rejection. On this papal quotation cf. also Kutschker, *Das Eherecht der katholischen Kirche*, vol. 5, pp. 82–83. Kutschker writes: "For it is precisely because it used to be that there were many in these parts who took these things too lightly, leading to the proliferation of such reasons for dispensation, that the blessed Pope Pius VII found himself compelled even on his deathbed to instruct the Cardinal Major Penitentiary to henceforth be hard in the granting of such dispensations since the appearance had arisen that, in Germany, there were no women for brothers-in-law other than sisters-in-law."

7 Such a situation can also be seen in the region of Vienna and Lower Austria researched by Edith Saurer, cf. Saurer, "Stiefmütter und Stiefsöhne", p. 363; see also Lanzinger, "The Relativity of Kinship".

couple configuration of widower and sister-in-law was based on certain interests and needs[8] – and it is in this context that the house shifts into the foreground as a kinship space.[9] Dionigi Albera has emphasised the significance of the question as to "organisation domestique" – household organisation – in kinship research;[10] Joachim Eibach and Raffaella Sarti have developed the concept of the "open house".[11]

To be sure, the presence of marriages in close degrees of affinity was not limited to the German-speaking region. Margherita Pelaja ascertained with regard to her sample of 1850s dispensation requests from the city of Rome that the majority of them involved affinal couples.[12] Martine Segalen, studying the

---

8 Cf. Margareth Lanzinger, "Widowers and their Sisters-in-Law: Family Crises, Horizontally Organised Relationships and Affinal Relatives in the Nineteenth Century", *The History of the Family* 23, 2 (2018), 175–195. In research on the history of the family, the expression "family role completion" (*Rollenergänzungszwang*) came to denote the necessity of filling the vacant position of husband or wife as soon as possible. Michael Mitterauer ascribed special characteristics to the completion of roles in agricultural family economies, in contrast to how things were in other economic sectors. He identified particularly great pressure in the case of widowhood on small farms, which were associated "with incomes from wage labour and commercial activities". Michael Mitterauer, "Formen ländlicher Familienwirtschaft. Historische Ökotypen und familiale Arbeitsorganisation im österreichischen Raum", in *Familienstruktur und Arbeitsorganisation in ländlichen Gesellschaften*, ed. Josef Ehmer and Michael Mitterauer (Vienna, 1985), pp. 185–323, 261–262.

9 That the "term *house* had and has a variety of meanings" and that the "house was a locus for work, and life secured by social and legal norms, and at the same time an integral element of a structure of lordship" has been emphasised by Claudia Ulbrich, *Shulamit und Margarete. Power, Gender, and Religion in a Rural Society in Eighteenth-Century Europe* (Boston, 2004), p. 8. On the differing social forms, the interior and the material culture of the house cf. Raffaella Sarti, *Europe at Home: Family and Material Culture, 1500–1800* (New Haven/London, 2002 [1999]); Eibach/Lanzinger, *The Routledge History of the Domestic Sphere*; Joachim Eibach and Inken Schmidt-Voges (eds.) with Simone Derix, Philip Hahn, Elizabeth Harding and Margareth Lanzinger, *Das Haus in der Geschichte Europas. Ein Handbuch* (Berlin/Boston, 2015).

10 Dionigi Albera, *Au fil des générations. Terre, pouvoir et parenté dans l'Europe alpine, XIVe–XXe siècles* (Grenoble, 2011), p. 7, 47–48. In doing so, his intent was to once again bring together the strands that, in recent historical kinship studies, have led far beyond the household and decoupled from it as part of the concentration on networks. An overview of research involving network studies and approaches is provided by Simone Derix, "Vom Leben in Netzen. Neue geschichts- und sozialwissenschaftliche Perspektiven auf soziale Beziehungen", *Neue Politische Literatur* 56, 2 (2011), 185–206.

11 Joachim Eibach, "Das offene Haus. Kommunikative Praxis im sozialen Nahraum der europäischen Frühen Neuzeit", *Zeitschrift für Historische Forschung* 38, 4 (2011), 621–664; Raffaella Sarti, Margareth Lanzinger and Joachim Eibach (eds.), "Open House", special issue, *European History Quarterly* 51, 4 (2021).

12 Pelaja, "Marriage by Exception", p. 238.

southern Bigouden Country in Brittany, found the rate of marriages between blood relatives to have been quite low, with most of them in more distant degrees. However, this region did witness numerous marriages in close degrees of affinity. Segalen reasoned that this rural society was characterised by high mobility and that the land was worked by people with neither property nor claims to the inheritance thereof.[13] Regarding nineteenth-century France, Jean-Marie Gouesse ascertained a declining number of remarriages but a continual rise in the number of marriages between sister- and brother-in-law.[14] In order to assess these figures, knowledge of the dispensation policies and practices relevant to the respective contexts is essential. The fact that Rome frowned upon the rise in such unions becomes evident even at the outset of the nineteenth century, and this view was to grow even more severe during the 1830s and 1840s. As a consequence of the markedly more challenging bureaucratic procedures, the significance of mediation and recommendations increased noticeably. This begs the question as to which options were available in this regard.

Behind the configuration of widower and sister-in-law stood the relationship between two sisters[15] – and this "sibling archipelago" could also include the widowed brother-in-law. As Mary Jean Corbett has shown, the social and political debate over the prohibition of unions between widower and sister-in-law was echoed broadly in British literature.[16] The both legal and literary discourse that she sketches out starts from the perception of the sister-in-law as a "virtual sister" who was indeed viewed as a sister in actual practice.[17] This coupling of sister-in-law and sister as a single figure had a long tradition in the Anglo-Saxon realm, of which *Hamlet* would be one example. In this play's second scene, Shakespeare has the king, who is Hamlet's uncle and now also his stepfather, state that he married his former sister – by which he means his sister-in-law, the wife of his deceased brother. "Therefore our sometime

---

13 Segalen, *Fifteen Generations*, pp. 114–123; Martine Segalen and Philippe Richard, "Marrying Kinsmen in Pays Bigouden Sud, Brittany", *Journal of Family History* 11 (1986), 109–130.

14 The latter rose from 11.7 per mil during the period between 1836 and 1840 to 20.7 per mil between 1861 and 1865 and ultimately to 30.2 per mil between 1881 and 1885. Gouesse, "Mariages de proches parents", p. 52.

15 On this cf. also Margareth Lanzinger, "Schwestern-Beziehungen und Schwager-Ehen. Formen familialer Krisenbewältigung im 19. Jahrhundert", in *Schwestern und Freundinnen. Zur Kulturgeschichte weiblicher Kommunikation*, ed. Eva Labouvie (Cologne/Weimar/Vienna, 2009), pp. 263–282.

16 Mary Jean Corbett, "Husband, Wife, and Sister: Making and Remaking the Early Victorian Family", in *Sibling Relations*, ed. Johnson/Sabean, pp. 263–287; cf. also Gulette, "The Puzzling Case".

17 Corbett, "Husband, Wife, and Sister", pp. 265–267.

sister, now our queen / Th'imperial jointress to this war-like state / Have we [...] Taken to wife."[18] Corbett furthermore points out how similarity between two sisters – which allowed the sister-in-law to represent the widower's ideal consolation – was a popular literary motif.[19] It would hence also appear necessary to examine how the proximity inherent to the constellation of widower and sister-in-law was contextualised in the dispensation requests.

1 Harsher Dispensation Policies

The widower Joseph Khuen, an Imperial-Royal *Tabak- und Stempel-Magazins-Verwalter* in Innsbruck, applied for a dispensation in 1831.[20] He desired to marry his sister-in-law Karolina Esterle. The consistory in Brixen forwarded his request to Salzburg, since the bride resided in this diocese. The reasoning behind this was that Rome typically designated the ordinariate responsible for the bride as the executive body in dispensation matters.[21] The bride's age – she was 29 at the time – and her meagre fortune were the – typical – reasons for dispensation that were indicated. However, they seemed hardly sufficient to obtain a dispensation in the first degree of affinity. In its letter to accompany the materials' transfer to Salzburg, the consistory in Brixen hence mused as to "whether Rome should be turned to at all", since this was "an uncertain and problematic matter". The consistory in Salzburg also deemed this request "difficult and debatable". In an extensive evaluation of the sort that was typical there, the official Ignaz von Schurmann referred to the rule established at the Council of Trent according to which dispensations were never to be granted in the second degree except to high-ranking princes or in cases of public interest. From this, he concluded that such considerations likely applied all the more to the first degree of affinity. For this reason, a dispensation could be granted "only with difficulty and for very important reasons". He continued, however, by mentioning how it was widely known that "Rome has long since departed from such former strictness".[22]

18 William Shakespeare, *The Tragedy of Hamlet, Prince of Denmark*. Act 1, Scene 2.

19 Corbett, "Husband, Wife, and Sister", p. 268.

20 Cf. DIÖAB, Konsistorialakten 1831, Fasc. 5a, Römische Dispensen, no. 1.

21 Cf. the letter sent by the ordinariate in Brixen of 3 January 1831. They stated that they were turning over this dispensation request to Salzburg "to deal with as is seen fit because the Holy See, which would have to grant this dispensation, always appoints the Reverend Ordinary of the bride as executor of such dispensations". TLA Innsbruck, Jüngeres Gubernium, Hauptgruppe 64 Ehesachen, 1822–1836, Fasc. no. 321, 1831, no. 614.

22 AES, Kasten 22/35, Ehe-Dispensen 1828–1840, 1831, dispensation request of Joseph Khuen and Carolina Esterle. The case records here actually begin in 1831 and are unnumbered.

Further considerations ultimately spoke in favour of forwarding this dispensation request despite all reservations: "Should it prove impossible to fulfil their most fervent wish, this might easily lead to still worse consequences that could then perhaps even be declared the fault of this ecclesiastical entity. Or it could, at the very least, provoke accusations of being unaccommodating, hard-hearted, etc." The Salzburg official also argued that the stance of the new pope, his "degree of mildness or strictness" in such dispensation cases, was as yet unknown. He did believe that a cleverly written supplication would have a chance at success. But at the same time, he also considered "pushing back" this request to the Diocese of Brixen, since it was there that the couple would be settling if they were to marry. And with that, he reasoned, his consistory would be liberated from having to deal with "such an awkward matter".

In the case of Khuen and Esterle, such careful weighing of pros and cons was surely owed to the bridal couple's social status, which can be inferred not least from the identities of their request's supporters: a brother of the groom – the "imperial-royal auditing secretary in the production management office of the salt works directorate in Tyrol" – as well as one of his cousins – a "chancery clerk at the *Tirolisch-ständische Aktivität*", a body representing the Tyrolean estates – served as witnesses at the matrimonial examination of the groom at the deanery office in Innsbruck. Furthermore, the imperial-royal provincial councillors (*Landräte*) Johann Nepomuk von Gilm zu Rosenegg and Leopold von Lichtenthurn, the latter of whom was also the imperial-royal provincial government submissions protocol director, also supported the granting of this dispensation. Their endorsements need to be viewed as quite weighty, for they represent an occurrence that was exceptional in this form. Regarding the bride, the Salzburg consistory official's discussion emphasised the circumstance that she was the daughter of an imperial-royal district engineer who had lost his life "in service to the state", and that she had "been raised and educated since earliest childhood by the honourable City and Provincial Court President Baron von Auer in Salzburg", in whose household she was also residing at the time.[23]

This evaluation's several pages of pros and cons ultimately concluded with an endorsement, which the consistory followed in its own decision. The dispensation request was thus sent on to Rome in May 1831. One month later, a message arrived that henceforth the only dispensations to be granted in the first degree of affinity would be those where "*periculum defectionis a fide Catholica*", the danger of defection from the Catholic faith, was present. But if the request were to be resubmitted with such a reason, one could indeed

23 Cf. DIÖAB, Konsistorialakten 1831, Fasc. 5a, Römische Dispensen, no. 1; AES, Kasten 22/35, Ehe Dispensen 1828–1840, 1831, dispensation request of Joseph Khuen and Carolina Esterle.

hope for a dispensation.[24] The consistory in Salzburg forwarded the negative decision to the deanery office in Innsbruck that was responsible for the groom. The dean explained to the groom that more weighty reasons had to pertain in order for there to be hope for a dispensation. He, however, refrained from mentioning that the threat of conversion was from now on absolutely required as a reason in the first degree of affinity. The renewed justification from the groom's end therefore only contained a physician's attestation that confirmed his fragile health and deemed it possible that he might be plunged into insanity should his marriage project be rejected. This letter also expressed concern about the raising and education of Khuen's eight-year-old son from his first marriage, who was at that point "left over to the careless supervision of his uneducated maidservant". Finally, the letter continued, it had been the wish of his deceased wife that he marry her sister. Khuen claimed that she had made him promise her this shortly prior to her death.

It is thus unsurprising that in his new evaluation produced in August 1831, the official at the Salzburg consistory described all this as being insufficient from his perspective. He expressed his astonishment that the content of the letter from Rome had not been forwarded to Khuen in all of its points. One could, he noted in closing, simply reject Khuen's renewed supplication, but doing so would only serve to "drag out" this matter endlessly should the supplicant persist in his efforts. And if such action "were to appear excessively hard and strict", he continued, one could infer from the information received that the man's mentally distraught state might result in acts of despair, "including defection from the Catholic faith". This possibility could perhaps be rendered plausible, he reasoned, by referring to the ongoing Protestant "machinations" in the Ziller Valley, which was not far off.[25] In view of this daring construction, he was plagued by doubts as to whether the impression of "a contrived argument" could be avoided. But a few days later, in early September 1831, the Salzburg consistory indeed sent a letter to Rome. In addition to a long-winded introduction and a characterisation of state of the groom's health, this letter actually did contain *the* required reason for dispensation: the threat of conversion. The consistory argued this point with reference to how there were

24 This is indicated in a letter from the Datary in Rome to the Archdiocese of Salzburg dated 11 June 1831. AES, Kasten 22/35, Ehe-Dispensen 1828–1840, 1831, dispensation request of Joseph Khuen and Carolina Esterle.

25 The reference was to the Protestants in the Ziller Valley who found no acceptance despite the Josephine Patent of Toleration and were ultimately expelled as late as 1837. On this cf. Hans Heiss and Thomas Götz, *Am Rand der Revolution. Tirol 1848/49* (Vienna/Bolzano, 1998), p. 34; Fontana, *Der Kulturkampf*, pp. 21–22; concisely summarised in Owen Chadwick, *A History of the Popes 1830–1914* (Oxford, 1998), pp. 406–408.

numerous Protestants on Austrian territory who could quite easily receive dispensations in the degree at issue. The danger they portrayed was linked with the scenario of the mental confusion that might possibly ensue as a consequence of renewed rejection.[26] The dispensation was promptly granted in November of 1831.

Now, however, one thing was certain: by no means did the newly elected pope, Gregory XVI (1831–1846), intend to be lenient in cases where a widower sought to marry his sister-in-law. Pope Gregory much rather advocated a return to the "earlier stringency" that was generally thought to be a thing of the past. In this, he referred back to Pope Benedict XIV,[27] as he explained in a "chirograph" – a papal decree – and as was mentioned quite often in correspondence regarding such dispensation requests.[28] In general, Gregory XVI is characterised as a "man of the Counter-Reformation". It was immediately following his election that revolution broke out in Bologna, coinciding with the revolutions already underway in France and other countries. Contemporary assessments of his person state that in ascending to office, he had not become "a prince" but rather remained "a simple monk, oblivious to the ways of the world", who was indeed familiar with the scholastic and real sciences but wished to know nothing "of the new times". Everything "that smacked even slightly of progress" was "proscribed" in the Papal States. This included "the railways, the chain bridges, the gas lamps". However, as Franz Xaver Seppelt

---

26 "[…] *si in debilitatem caderet intellectus, incidat quoque in cogitationem infaustam deficiendi a S[ancta] fide catholica, cum in terris austriacis multi sunt haeretici protestantes, qui licentiam matrimonium in hoc gradu affinitatis ineundo quam facillime impetrant.*" Letter from the Salzburg consistory to the Roman agent, Baron von Genotte, dated 5 September 1831, ÖSTA, HHStA, Agentie-Archiv Rom, II Agentie Akten 1817–1832, K. 39, Salzburg 1831.

27 On this cf. *Chirografo della santità di nostro signore Papa Gregorio XVI sulle dispense matrimoniali in primo grado di affinità e in primo misto col secundo di consanguinità o affinità* (Roma, 1836), BAC, 111.02.04, Päpstliche Erlasse, Bestände 19. Jahrhundert.

28 In such cases, reference was made to Benedict's document "Ad Apostolicae"; cf. *Chirografo della santità*, p. 5, in: BAC, 111.02.04, Päpstliche Erlasse, Bestände 19. Jahrhundert. Johann Kutschker likewise refers to Benedict XIV in connection with *periculum apostasiae*, the danger of conversion, which Benedict had already specified as the only acceptable reason for dispensation in the configuration of brother- and sister-in-law. Kutschker, *Das Eherecht der katholischen Kirche*, vol. 5, p. 122. Benedict XIV is regarded as having been one of the strictest popes were marital law was concerned. Cf. Pelaja, "Marriage by Exception", p. 227. On the ambivalent historiographic assessment of this pope, who held office from 1740 to 1758, cf. Elisabeth Garms-Cornides, "Benedikt XIV. – ein Papst zwischen Reaktion und Aufklärung", in *Ambivalenzen und Aufklärung. Festschrift für Ernst Wangermann*, ed. Gerhard Ammerer and Hanns Haas (Vienna/Munich, 1997), pp. 168–186.

comments further in his history of the papacy: "Gregory's leadership of the Church exhibited no trace of such diffidence or such a feeling of weakness."[29]

Word that only the "threat of departure from the faith" would now suffice to merit a dispensation in the first degree got around relatively fast in the individual dioceses – including in Salzburg and Brixen – on the occasion of such dispensation requests. Likewise affected by this greater stringency in dispensation-granting was the first and second unequal degree of affinity – when a widower sought to marry a niece of his deceased wife or a widow sought to marry a nephew of her deceased husband. Requests in this configuration, however, arrived less frequently than those between brother- and sister-in-law. And finally, this rule also applied to the first and second unequal degree of consanguinity, meaning marriages between blood-related uncles and nieces or aunts and nephews[30] – though the examined materials reveal hardly any marriage projects of this type.[31]

The outcome of the dispensation request of Joseph Khuen and Karolina Esterle shows nonetheless that a certain degree of leeway remained despite the stricter handling prescribed by Rome – leeway that, in this case, the Salzburg official Ignaz von Schurmann had exploited in his generous interpretation of the reasons for dispensation indicated by Joseph Khuen. In doing so, Schurmann appears to have cared far more about the eventuality that this couple might react by accusing the Church of being "unaccommodating" or hard-hearted than he did about adhering to a Roman directive. By contrast, the tone of the letters sent by Brixen's consistory during the 1830s – more often than not written and signed by Pro-Chancellor Georg Prünster – was for the most part comparatively harsh and uncompromising. One typical answer to requests from widowers who sought to marry their sisters-in-law was that the stated reasons for dispensation were "actually not such" that hope for a dispensation could be held, why the supplicants were to be sternly rejected "once more and for all time".[32] Or that in the case at hand, "the stated reasons" were

---

29 Seppelt, *Papstgeschichte*, p. 301, 303–304; for more details cf. Giacomo Martina, "Giorgio XVI.", in *Enciclopedia dei papi*, vol. 3: Innocenzo – VIII Giovanni Paolo II (Rome, 2000), pp. 546–560, as well as the first chapter of Chadwick, *A History of the Popes*. As far as marriage is concerned, this source focuses solely on issues relating to civil and interconfessional marriage.

30 On this cf. the above-quoted letter from Gregory XVI. *Chirografo della santità*, in: BAC, III.02.04, Päpstliche Erlasse, Bestände 19. Jahrhundert. This letter is also referenced now and then in the correspondence of the other dioceses examined here.

31 For a quite spectacular case see chapter 6.

32 DIÖAB, Konsistorialakten 1831, Fasc. 5a, Römische Dispensen, no. 6.

"insufficient by far".[33] Under Alois Rabanser, who succeeded Georg Prünster as consistorial chancellor, the basic tone of communication became markedly friendlier and more supportive but still moved within far narrower limits in terms of active support for requests when compared with Salzburg.

It was not only in the context of Roman dispensation policy, however, that unions between brother-in-law and sister-in-law were on the agenda during the early 1830s. In France, 1832 witnessed the promulgation of a law that empowered the sovereign to grant dispensations "entre beaux-frères et belles-soeurs", a privilege of which copious use was made.[34] This reform's introduction shortly after Gregory XVI had taken office as pope[35] was surely no coincidence. And compared with the situations in other countries, the affected couples here enjoyed a significant degree of relief that, after all, could build upon the instrument of civil marriage that had been introduced at the close of the eighteenth century.

Austria's embassy in Rome, for its part, indeed negotiated in an attempt to obtain more favourable conditions for such couples – but to no avail. The Austrian Envoy von Lützow accordingly filed a May 1834 report concerning the difficulties under the new pontificate when it came to obtaining marriage dispensations in the above-mentioned degrees of affinity and consanguinity in cases where the "required canonical reasons" were "not explicitly specified". For the Italian dioceses, he stated that "certain or probable danger to life, threatened by a third party" was necessary, while for the non-Italian dioceses it was "the certain or at least highly probable danger of defection from the Catholic faith".[36] Lützow indicated that after several such dispensations

33 Ibid., no. 5. Requests from consanguineous bridal couples, as well, frequently evoked responses where the request was said to be "in no way justified" (ibid., 1831, no. 9), the "absolutely necessary reasons" were said to be entirely absent (ibid., 1831, no. 10), or there was said to exist "no prospect whatsoever" (ibid., 1831, no. 20). The list of such rejection variants goes on and on.

34 Delille, "Réflexions", pp. 376–377. Civil dispensation request figures show that unions between brothers- and sisters-in-law rose to total more than 1,000 per year between 1832 and 1914, peaking around 1870. At that time, marriages between uncle and niece and/or aunt and nephew likewise increased markedly to total around 200 per year.

35 Nikolaus Knopp quotes a rescript of Gregory XVI dated November 1836 and addressed to Pro-Datary Bartolomeo Pacca in which, in light of the "multitude of requests" in close degrees of affinity and consanguinity, he called for stringency and instructed that only reasons for dispensation that were in conformance with canon law be recognised. Knopp, *Vollständiges katholisches Eherecht*, 1854, p. 230, note 67.

36 The validity of differing reasons for dispensation in Italian and non-Italian dioceses is noteworthy. The territory of the Diocese of Trento in present-day southern South Tyrol and Trentino was home to both German-speakers and Italian-speakers. The records of the district office in Bozen contain a letter from the late imperial-royal agent in Rome, Baron

had been refused in the autumn of 1833, he had officially taken the matter in hand particularly for those dioceses that were "non-Italian and bordering on Protestant countries and populations". In this context he requested that, due to the "geographic situation" as well as "the presence of non-Catholics amidst the populations of most of the dioceses in question", the danger of a conversion be viewed as fundamentally given even in requests where it was not explicitly listed among the reasons for dispensation – hoping that this would make it easier for dispensations to be obtained. But it was only just shy of almost four months after this initiative, he reported, that he had received an official answer, which was in the negative.[37] On 22 May 1834, this matter featured on the agenda of the meeting of the United Imperial-Royal Court Chancellery.[38] This body subsequently had a message expressing regret regarding the pope's rigid stance sent to the provincial governments, from where it was distributed to the district offices.[39] However, the imperial-royal agent in Rome, Baron von Genotte, had remarked that exceptions were sometimes made "on *especially important grounds*" in the absence of the one required reason, but only as a special type of mercy that could not be claimed in other cases: "*ex speciali gratia in exemplum non adducenda*".[40]

In the wake of these developments, the consistory in Brixen oriented itself on the stringency prescribed by Rome. The process of requesting a dispensation in the first degree of affinity was therefore quite difficult during the papacy of Gregory XVI, that is throughout the 1830s and until after the mid-1840s. In this situation, mediation by high-ranking members of the clergy or other people close to the papal offices via the usual letters of recommendation played an important role above and beyond the activities of the Imperial-Royal Agency in Rome. Their intervention was capable of improving the success rate – for as research by Angiolina Arru has shown, negotiation, mediation and recommendation were integral components of institutional processes in nineteenth-century Rome.[41]

---

von Genotte, indicating that both reasons had been recognised in the case of a dispensation request made by a brother- and sister-in-law. ASBz/SABo, Kreisamt Bozen, Bündel 346, 1832, Geistlich, Ehe II, no. 191.

37 ÖSTA, AVA, Alter Cultus, K. 1, Ehesachen und Taufen, 1807–1834, no. 12.562/1.839.

38 Ibid.

39 ASBz/SABo, Kreisamt Bozen, Bündel 373, 1 and 2, 1834, Geistlich, Ehe, no. 300.

40 ASBz/SABo, Kreisamt Bozen, Bündel 346, 1832, Geistlich, Ehe II, no. 191; emphasis underlined in the original. The quoted letter is appended here.

41 Angiolina Arru, "Die Ermordung eines Richters – ein Delikt aus Liebe. Das Gericht als Ort der Vermittlung und Einflussnahme, brüchiger Allianzen und wechselnder Strategien (Rom 1795)", in *Liebe und Widerstand*, ed. Bauer/Hämmerle/Hauch, pp. 229–242.

2 Mediation and Recommendations

Communicating the new pope's strict dispensation policy to the diocesan consistories and informing them of rejected requests but also of potentially promising ways forward fell within the purview of the Imperial-Royal Agency in Rome. This was simultaneously the institution that, in keeping with the norm that prevailed during the period examined here, possessed exclusive authority to act as an intermediary where dispensation requests from the Habsburg monarchy were concerned. Richard Blaas explains how the phenomenon of agencies and agents arose in light of the growing volume of official communication with the Roman Curia and the related "complication of bureaucratic pathways". "The involved administrative channels and routines moved parties engaged in ongoing proceedings with the papal authorities to consider it advisable to call upon the help of a man who was capable of shepherding their cases through these channels, one who – accredited by the papal authorities – could advance their business on location."[42] Such intermediaries, initially employed ad hoc, eventually gave rise to the office of agent[43] and, in time, to national agencies – which were first set up by Spain, France, Sardinia and Venice. The imperial-royal agents are documented from 1730 onward.[44] Their responsibilities, which gradually expanded, included submitting documents they had received to the competent offices of the Roman Curia, monitoring the issuance of briefs, bulls and official decisions, expediting mail as well as collecting and forwarding fees – of which they were entitled to keep a certain percentage as a commission. The greater the number of requests that were submitted to the Roman Curia, the more money the agents made.[45]

Several attempts were needed to ensure the imperial-royal agents' central positioning as intermediaries. To this end, Maria Theresia issued a brief and concisely formulated court rescript in December 1759 – which, however, encountered resistance and had to be "indirectly retracted". It stipulated: "The clergy are forbidden to use the private agents in Rome."[46] The modified

42 Richard Blaas, "Die k. k. Agentie für geistliche Angelegenheiten", *Mitteilungen des österreichischen Staatsarchivs*, vol. 7 (Vienna, 1954), 47–89, 47.

43 On the earliest among the permanent agents, who are documented back to the thirteenth century, cf. Horst Herrmann, "Die römische Agenzie für kirchliche Angelegenheiten Deutschlands und Österreichs", *Römische Historische Mitteilungen* 11 (1969), 182–205, 186–187.

44 Cf. Blaas, "Die k. k. Agentie", p. 49; For a list of Austrian agents, cf. ibid., p. 89; Herrmann, "Die römische Agenzie", pp. 188–189.

45 Cf. Blaas, "Die k. k. Agentie", p. 47, 49.

46 *Sammlung aller k. k. Verordnungen und Gesetze vom Jahre 1740 bis 1780* (Gesetze unter Maria Theresia), vol. 3 (Vienna, 1786), p. 572, no. 534.

formulation of this rule, promulgated in 1767, stated that "all business with the exception of the *forum internum* may henceforth only be conducted via the state agency", failing which the necessary provincial government permission would be denied.[47] Regarding marriage dispensations, a court decree of 2 May 1785 provided that bishops who sought to have a dispensation granted in Rome had to deal exclusively with the imperial-royal agent, at the time Francesco Brunati,[48] "and refrain from attempting to have any other agent initiate further proceedings in such a case".[49]

In this way, the Imperial-Royal Agency represented an important part of the effort to centralise dispensation proceedings. If a dispensation brief had not been obtained via the imperial-royal agent, die *Placetum regium* could be denied. Blaas concludes: "This rendered the Agency for Spiritual Affairs an instrument of state churchism."[50] 1817 saw the Imperial-Royal Agency reorganised.[51] It henceforth served as a permanent "accredited representation at the Holy See" in church affairs and was connected with the Imperial-Royal Embassy via the person of the imperial-royal agent, who was simultaneously first embassy councillor.[52] It was headquartered at the Palazzo Venezia. Embassy Councillor Wilhelm Ferdinand von Genotte assumed its leadership on 1 March 1817, at first in a provisional capacity.[53] In his organisational plan, and in order to protect state interests, Genotte called for the ordinariates to

47 Herrmann, "Die römische Agenzie", 189–190.

48 Francesco Brunati from Rovereto, who served as imperial-royal agent from 1751 to 1806, was a nephew – a son of a sister – of his predecessor Johann Baptist Ruele, for whom he had worked from 1746. Cf. Blaas, "Die k. k. Agentie", p. 55. The phenomenon of nephews 'inheriting' offices from their uncles, which was common within the Roman Curia, included the appropriate socialisation and introduction to their work, as has been studied by Marina D'Amelia, "Trasmissioni di offici e competenze nelle famiglie curiali tra Cinquecento e Seicento", in *Famiglie*, ed. Ago/Borello, pp. 47–81. Cf. dazu auch Herrmann, "Die römische Agenzie", p. 186.

49 TLA Innsbruck, Protocolla cum Indice in Geistlichen Co[mmissi]ons-Sachen vom 1. Jänner bis Ende Juni 1785, Sitzung vom 14. Mai 1785, fol. 813, no. 1.005. The decree concerned here was renewed on 30 April 1807.

50 Blaas, "Die k. k. Agentie", pp. 48–50.

51 Cf. Blaas, "Die k. k. Agentie", pp. 65–75.

52 Josef Karl Mayr, "Gesandtschaftsarchive", in *Gesamtinventar des Wiener Haus-, Hof- und Staatsarchivs*, vol. 1: Entwicklung des archivalischen Besitzstandes und der Einrichtungen des Archivs, Biographien der Archivbeamten, Fundbehelfe, Geschichte und Inventare der Reichsarchive, des Archivs der Staatskanzlei (des Ministeriums des Äußeren), der Gesandtschaftsarchive und der Staatenabteilungen, ed. Ludwig Bittner (Vienna, 1936), pp. 469–508, 501.

53 From this point in time onward, there also exist records that were independently kept and organised by the Agency's own archive, which is now at the Haus-, Hof-, und Staatsarchiv of the Austrian State Archives in Vienna.

be prevented from employing their own agents, with all recourse to Rome having to take place via the Agency. The only exception was to be "matters of conscience", which lay within the domain of the *forum internum* and could be addressed directly to the Apostolic Penitentiary. In return, Genotte made the following guarantee: "The Agency assumes an obligation toward parties to ensure swift and secure handling of their requests and to work for the most uniform and lowest possible assessment of fees."[54] An Imperial Court Chancellery decree of 25 December 1817 ultimately reinforced the Agency's position in this sense.[55]

Genotte, who had been ennobled as a baron (*Freiherr*) in 1827, was initially succeeded by Embassy Secretary Ferdinand von Ohms on an interim basis and, in 1833, by Carl von Binder-Kriegelstein, who served as imperial-royal agent until 1849.[56] With the abolishment of the *placetum regium* in 1850, the Agency lost its "basis in state law" but did continue to operate – now in the Church's interest and, in a reversal of the former situation, "dependent upon the goodwill of the ordinariates".[57] In a May 1851 note from Brixen's Consistorial Chancellor Alois Rabanser to the Vorarlberg district office, in which he explained the various components of dispensation fees in great detail and justified their differing amounts,[58] reference was made to the "not insignificant agency fees" that were

---

54 Blaas, "Die k. k. Agentie", p. 66.

55 It contains three points: "1. That it is generally mandated that the Imperial-Royal Agency be called upon for all rescripts to be obtained from the Holy See; 2. that this applies in particular and most decidedly in all matters pertaining to marriage dispensations; and 3. that only the bishops and cathedral chapters, in the course of their business, are permitted to employ the services of a private agent in conjunction with intervention by the imperial-royal agent in Rome." *Franz des Ersten politische Gesetze und Verordnungen für die Oesterreichischen, Böhmischen und Galizischen Erbländer*, vol. 45 (Vienna, 1819), no. 165. Joseph Linden's volume on family law in Austria, characterised as a "guide" in its foreword, describes the situation as follows: "The ordinary, however, must always do this business in Rome mediated by the imperial-royal agent installed there, and it is he or the Imperial-Royal Embassy there that must append to the papal dispensation briefs a *Vidit* [official acknowledgement thereof] insofar as no doubts obtain as to the existence of provincial government permission to request a dispensation." Joseph Linden, *Darstellung der in Oesterreich über die Rechtsverhältnisse der Ehegatten, Eltern, Kinder, Waisen und Pflegebefohlenen bestehenden Vorschriften nebst den auf das Hausgesinde bezüglichen Anordnungen*, 2nd ed. (Vienna, 1839 [1834]), p. 93.

56 On this cf. Blaas, "Die k. k. Agentie", pp. 72–74.

57 Herrmann, "Die römische Agenzie", p. 198.

58 Opaque calculation of fees was a problem that made frequent appearances. On this cf. also the Brixen consistory's explanation of the valid fee schedule in response to a complaint regarding discrepancies between fees assessed for the same degree of kinship. Konsistorialakten 1860, Fasc. 5c, Verschiedenes über Ehe, no. 14.

still being invoiced in order to support the "functioning agency" in Rome that continued to operate at the behest of the Imperial-Royal Ministry.[59]

The "agency fees" he mentioned were part of the overall costs that had to be covered in order to obtain a dispensation.[60] The necessary financial expenditures were comprised of four items: the charges for dispensation-granting as such, those for the dispensation's formal issuance, the agency fee and postage. The ratios can be roughly estimated. While detailed monthly and annual accounting records from the Austrian dioceses that break down the expenses into these categories do exist,[61] such tables typically also include after-the-fact entries for which the total amounts are included in the final sum instead of being attributed to the four categories. Even so, these accounting records can indeed serve to provide an impression of the costs incurred for the individual items. For 1855, for example, the Austrian dioceses recorded total dispensation costs of nearly 24,870 scudi – of which 18,340, a good two thirds, are itemised in the table: 57.3 per cent of the latter sum went for the dispensation fees in the narrow sense collected by the Roman Curia,[62] 20 per cent was likewise paid to the Roman Curia for the actual issuance of dispensations, 21.5 per cent was accounted for by agency fees and 1.2 per cent was postage.[63] For 1870, the total sum amounted to 39,720 scudi – thus substantially more.[64] Converted into gulden, this would amount to approximately two-and-a-half times as much. In terms of the individual Roman dispensations, one can deduce that the costs incurred in the Diocese of Brixen in 1855, for example, amounted to just shy of 10, 15, 20, 45 and 50 gulden for dispensations in the second degree as well as in the second and third unequal degree of consanguinity, and around 160, 170 and 190 gulden for dispensations in the first degree of affinity. These were most expensive of all, which was owed to the fee schedule's being based on the closeness of the degree in question but was also meant to have a deterrent effect.

---

59 DIÖAB, Konsistorialakten 1851, Fasc. 5a, Römische Dispensen, no. 21.

60 In his description of the Roman Curia as it existed around 1900, Paul M. Baumgarten mentions how the call for reforms pertained especially to the various fees. This, however, stood in conflict with how "the individual authorities were quite possibly intended to support themselves on the basis of these fees", and he went on to remark that the Curia indeed seemed incapable "of sustaining the large bureaucracy that was necessary with its own resources". Baumgarten, "Die Geschäftsführung", p. 95.

61 In part, the records of the Agency also contain double-entry accounts for the individual dioceses.

62 On the general administration of papal funds cf. John F. Pollard, *Money and the Rise of the Modern Papacy. Financing the Vatican, 1850–1950* (Cambridge, 2005).

63 Cf. ÖSTA, HHStA, Agentie-Archiv Rom, III Agentie Akten 1833–1855, Agentierechnungen, K. 65.

64 Cf. ÖSTA, HHStA, Agentie-Archiv Rom, IV Agentie Akten 1856–1891, Rechnungen, K. 149.

In the interest of keeping the Agency in business, its advocates contrasted the services it provided with the "extortionary methods of the Roman private agents". They also pointed out the Agency's protection by the Imperial-Royal Embassy, which was valid for all business with the Holy See, and last but not least the Agency's proven and efficient organisation.[65] During this phase, however, it was increasingly viewed as disadvantageous that the agent, as the central intermediary in dealing with the papal authorities, was not a man of the cloth – and in fact had to, in accordance with the earlier state church-oriented concept, be a layman in order to not be subject to papal jurisdiction. As a consequence, the German national church in Rome, Santa Maria dell'Anima,[66] employed its own agents from the monarchy's dioceses and eventually developed into a veritable competitor.[67] The Anima's chaplain, Simon de Dompieri from the Diocese of Trento, even styled himself "Agente generale dei vescovi tedeschi" – General Agent of the German Bishops – to the Imperial-Royal Agency's great displeasure.[68] The initiative to involve the Anima in mediation was said to have been birthed by the consistory in Brixen. In 1849, the consistory suggested via a canon whom it sent to the Epicscopal Conference in Vienna that a Rome-based priest by employed as an agent for the German-speaking bishops or at least for the Austrian bishops. The mid-1850s saw agency activities assigned to the Anima's rector, Anton Flir, in 1863 to his successor Michael Gaßner.[69]

---

65 Blaas, "Die k. k. Agentie", p. 78. Columban von Schnitzer, who had taken over the Agency in 1849, argued by conjuring up a scenario suggestive of the damage to the Church's reputation that might result from unchecked competition by the private agents: "La concorrenza sfrenata degli Agenti particolari porterebbe inevitabilmente ad un mercimonio vergognoso colle grazie del Sommo Pontefice, mercimonio in cui l'arbitrio si farebbe strada senza rossore e senza riguardo alcuno, sia per il decoro, sia per il rispetto dovuto alla S. Chiesa ed ai suoi Ministri." Circular sent out by Schnitzer on 15 May 1850, quoted in: Blaas, ibid., p. 81, note 9.

66 On its history cf. Joseph Schmidlin, *Geschichte der deutschen Nationalkirche in Rom S. Maria dell'Anima* (Freiburg i. B./Vienna, 1906); Anton Kerschbaumer, *Geschichte des deutschen Nationalhospizes Anima in Rom* (Vienna, 1968).

67 Cf. Blaas, "Die k. k. Agentie", p. 79 (quote), 82; Herrmann, "Die römische Agenzie", pp. 197–200.

68 Blaas, "Die k. k. Agentie", p. 83. Dompieri is mentioned briefly in Schmidlin, *Geschichte der deutschen Nationalkirche*: he is described as "a 'true asset' on account of his comportment, his ambition, his education and his knowledge of the Italian and German languages" (ibid., p. 728, note 2). When Rector Alois Flir fell ill, writes Schmidlin, Dompieri continued "doing business with the Agency" until being forced to yield to "his enemies" in 1860 (ibid., p. 768).

69 Cf. Schmidlin, *Geschichte der deutschen Nationalkirche*, p. 734, 751–752, 770. The Church of Santa Maria dell'Anima has its own archive. On this cf. Hans Spatzenegger, "Das Archiv von Santa Maria dell'Anima in Rom", *Römische Historische Mitteilungen* 25 (1983), 109–163.

In connection with 1859's political turmoil due to the Second Italian War of Independence, the Imperial-Royal Agency shone once more for its ability to uphold secure communication channels with the dioceses via diplomatic couriers.[70] Adverse effects on dispensation proceedings such as those seen in 1848 and 1849[71] are hardly in evidence for this period. But Dompieri, too, had his channels and resources: in September 1859, he sent a telegram – the first to be found in the Brixen dispensation records – indicating that the request of Hermann Spieler, who was mayor in Hohenems, and Anna Maria Rhomberg had to be resubmitted since it was missing "sufficient reasons" as well as the supplicants' ages.[72] This new technology, which would thereafter be used repeatedly in dispensation proceedings for swift information and notifications, was capable of bridging the logistical gaps opened up by the war at least in cases where brief messages sufficed. In the long run, the Imperial-Royal Agency proved unable to hold its own against the competing intermediaries. The Prince-Archbishop of Salzburg, for example, praised the agents of the Anima because they always offered advice and assistance in various matters, while the imperial-royal agent was nothing but a "wickedly expensive postman".[73] The Agency's range of activities and significance thus shrank considerably during the second half of the nineteenth century, though its *de jure* existence continued until 1918.

As the dispensation proceedings of the 1830s and 1840s show, the imperial-royal agents' internal radius of action was limited even this early when it came to requests in close degrees of affinity. Conversely, interventions by third parties – organised in concert with state authorities including the Agency and even using the Agency for communications – did prove successful and/or necessary in individual cases. In response to the dispensation request submitted by the Innsbruck merchant Karl Mörz and his sister-in-law, the widow Josepha Kircher, a recommendation was received from Rome to send "a new attestation of the ordinariate containing the indicated reason for dispensation", since a dispensation in the first degree of affinity would otherwise – that is, without

70 Cf. Blaas, "Die k. k. Agentie", p. 84.

71 On this see chapter 4.

72 DIÖAB, Konsistorialakten 1859, Fasc. 5a, Römische Dispensen, no. 27. The omission of the supplicants' ages may have actually been intentional – the bride was just 20 years old.

73 Letter of 23 July 1874, quoted in Herrmann, "Die römische Agenzie", p. 200. For a more detailed analysis of this case see Margareth Lanzinger, "Liebe, Ehe, Ökonomie. Materielle und immaterielle Ressourcen im Kontext von Verwandtenheiraten", in *Die Ökonomie sozialer Beziehungen: Ressourcenbewirtschaftung als Geben, Nehmen, Investieren, Verschwenden, Haushalten, Horten, Vererben, Schulden*, ed. Gabriele Jancke and Daniel Schläppi (Stuttgart, 2015), pp. 157–176.

reference to "possibly impending defection from the faith" – not be possible. But the imperial-royal agent Baron von Genotte also went on to suggest an alternative: if the reason of possible defection "would not suit", one could also attempt a "special recommendation" – which the supreme Imperial-Royal Provincial Government in Innsbruck was encouraged to apply for with His Excellency, the Imperial-Royal Envoy in Rome.[74] The Provincial Governor of Tyrol, Count Friedrich von Wilczek, indeed proved willing to write to the Imperial-Royal Embassy in Rome and request its recommendation in favour of Mörz's marriage project.[75] The couple's dispensation arrived in early March of 1832 – "finally obtained only thanks to the special employment of His Excellency, Imperial-Royal Envoy Count von Luzow [Lützow]", as the accompanying note stated. The costs amounted to nearly 500 gulden, the highest sum documented in the examined records. It was not, however, only high-ranking political and diplomatic protagonists who had contributed to this request's successful outcome.

Karl Mörz had already needed to make several attempts before his request was finally forwarded to Rome. After all, the consistory in Brixen had begun categorically rejecting marriage projects between brothers- and sisters-in-law even upon the very first enquiry in light of their slim chances of success. Alongside his declared willingness to pay high dispensation fees and his steadfast "importunateness", the crucial factor that had eventually enabled Mörz's request to advance to the next level was recommendations from his friends: the municipal councillor Carl Carnelli, who came from a patrician Innsbruck family and stated that he had known Mörz since childhood, had served as one of his matrimonial examination witnesses.[76] There also existed a line of contact

---

74 DIÖAB, Konsistorialakten 1832, Fasc. 5a, Römische Dispensen, no. 5.

75 This letter can be found in ÖSTA, HHStA, Agentie-Archiv Rom, II Agentie Akten 1817–1832, K. 39, Bressanone 1831, letter of 26 January 1832, with an appended note in French signed by Lützow and dated 7 February 1832. Wilczek's letter states, among other things, that "both the supplicant and the intended widow enjoy a good reputation and are very upstanding and decent people; he is already of a somewhat advanced age and will therefore have need of her support. Since his business includes fashion items, she takes care of any related work, which could be entrusted to strange hands only to the disadvantage of the business. In both these respects, the supplicant must desire to marry *precisely this* upstanding person, a desire that is guided neither by impure intentions nor by reprehensible passions. In my view, the conditions that pertain here are such that this request deserves *all* possible consideration, for which reason I do not hesitate to most sincerely commend this matter to Your Excellency's esteemed support. I remain, with the most consummate respect." The emphases in this text are circled in the original.

76 In autumn 1801, a certain Karl Carnelli, merchant and widower, had requested permission from the provincial government in Innsbruck to turn to the ecclesiastical authorities "about marrying his sister-in-law", Claudia von Dinkl, which was granted. TLA Innsbruck,

between Mörz and the papal authorities via the banker Giovanni Carnelli, likewise from Innsbruck, who frequently took care of dispensation-related payment transactions with Rome for the prince-episcopal consistory in Brixen and did the same for Mörz.[77] Regarding this, Carnelli gave advance notice of the soon-to-arrive request of his friend, "Sig[no]r Mörz mio amico" in a letter to the Imperial-Royal Agency, expressed his own recommendation of him and assured that he would promptly transfer the costs incurred by the dispensation.[78] Giovanni Carnelli addressed the Imperial-Royal Agency a second time to give notice of the Innsbruck governor's impending letter and request that the agent make a personal effort on Mörz's behalf.[79] All in all, the success of this particular dispensation request came thanks to a network that included multiple people whose reach extended to Rome, a network based on their social status and occupations as well as their acquaintances and

---

Jüngeres Gubernium, Hauptgruppe 64 Ehesachen, 1801–1802, Fasc. no. 316, 1801, no. 129. In the provincial government's internal report of July 1802, it is written that Carnelli received his papal dispensation via Brixen. TLA Innsbruck, Jüngeres Gubernium, Hauptgruppe 64 Ehesachen, 1801–1802, Fasc. no. 316, 1802, no. 107. In the dispensation register there, it is noted that Carnelli had applied for the dispensation in Rome himself: "*dispensati sunt a Sede Rom[ana] per Breve ab oratore ipso impetratu*". The record also does not fail to note that he had obtained the *placetum regium* required for this purpose. DIÖAB, Dispensationes matrimoniales ab anno 1795 usque ad annum 1829 inclusive, 115. It is possible that this refers to the above-mentioned municipal councillor Carnelli.

77 Furthermore, it was probably above all merchants who were entrusted with the transfer of Brixen's dispensation fees to Rome. It is accordingly that Consistorial Pro-Chancellor Georg Prünster wrote to the Agency in September 1835 that he had instructed the Innsbruck merchant Franz Josef Habtmann to pay the Agency 400 scudi. "Adunque ho dato ordine al Sig[no]re Habtmann, mercante in Innsbruck, di pagarle a mio Conto una rimessa di Scudi quattrocento." Letter dated 7 September 1835, ÖSTA, HHStA, Agentie-Archiv Rom, III Agentie Akten 1833–1855, K. 75, Bressanone 1835. A bill of exchange totalling 200 scudi to be delivered by "*mercante*" Habmann is mentioned in a letter to the Agency dated September 1846. ÖSTA, HHStA, Agentie-Archiv Rom, III Agentie Akten 1833–1855, K. 77, Bressanone 1846. Isolated difficulties did arise, since bills of exchange worth more than 150 scudi were not accepted all that gladly. The merchant house of Habtmann numbered among Tyrol's most prominent during the early nineteenth century; Habtmann was a business associate of Carnelli's. Regarding the concrete process, Brixen's consistory explained in 1860 that the agent procured the accumulated fees on a semi-annual basis from a "certain banker in Rome" who was then reimbursed via a bill of exchange with monies "paid (by the consistory) to a merchant house here". For this, the banker received a commission of one per cent. DIÖAB, Konsistorialakten 1860, Fasc. 5c, Verschiedenes über Ehe, no. 14.

78 ÖSTA, HHStA, Agentie-Archiv Rom, II Agentie Akten 1817–1832, K. 39, Bressanone 1831, letter dated 8 December 1831.

79 Cf. ÖSTA, HHStA, Agentie-Archiv Rom, II Agentie Akten 1817–1832, K. 40, Bressanone 1832, letter dated 30 January 1832.

friendships. By looking more closely, it becomes apparent how the combination of intermediary and banker revealed in this case was anything but unusual; it was much rather a pattern, insofar as "bankers resident in Rome" had been "entrusted with agency functions" ever from the early fourteenth century. The sixteenth century even saw French kings establish "these official functions of the bankers" as a permanent institution, making them "the official intermediaries between France and Rome where spiritual affairs were concerned".[80]

In the context of some successful requests for dispensations in the first degree of affinity during these years, high-ranking members of monastic orders had intervened. The consistory in Brixen, for example, in response to one particular second attempt where a dramatic situation was in play, strove to secure a "special recommendation" from Albuin Patscheider, general procurator of the Servite Order in Rome. Anton Nigg and Theres Fallstein, brother- and sister-in-law from the Deanery of Zams, had already had a child together – and the bride was once again pregnant. She had leased a farm and was in urgent need of a male labourer. The letter signed by Consistorial Chancellor Alois Rabanser depicted a wretched scenario that included the prospective bride's possible suicide as well as the threat that the prospective groom might convert to another faith. In this way, it proved possible to have a dispensation granted to the couple after two-and-a-half years.[81] They were charged a fee of 56 scudi.[82]

Karl Columban Schnitzer from Bregenz, who was a knight of the Tuscan Order of Saint Joseph, Imperial-Royal chargé d'affaires and legation councillor, intervened to the benefit of the widower Joseph Egg, a butcher and innkeeper from Bregenz with three children who were still quite small, and his sister-in-law Katharina Rauth. Regarding this couple, the objection had been raised that they could "only" point to economic reasons – reasons that the vicariate general had said could be found "in a hundred similar cases". The line of argument behind the vicariate general's initial rejection had been dominated by the omnipresent worry that a precedent might be set. "If Egg were to be

80 Herrmann, "Die römische Agenzie", pp. 186–187. Cf. also D'Amelia, "Trasmissioni di offici e competenze", pp. 63–65.

81 DIÖAB, Konsistorialakten 1843, Fasc. 5a, Römische Dispensen, no. 28. The rejection of their autumn 1842 request can be found as part of ibid., 1841, no. 23.

82 For their second attempt, the couple was once again supposed to deposit 200 or at least 180 gulden – the estimated total sum for fees – with the deanery in advance. The degree to which such outlays burdened household economies is shown by the arrangement made in this case: Anton Nigg appeared at the deanery office in early September 1843, "declaring that they most deeply desired, needed and therefore most humbly requested this mercy", and deposited 100 gulden "with the request that the 80 gulden be left in his hands for three weeks since the markets in Landeck, Kauns and Ried take place during precisely this period, which was also conceded" to him. Letter from the dean dated 27 September 1843.

dispensed, this obsession with similar sorts of unobtainable dispensations that has been suppressed for quite some time now would intensify in earnest."[83] In a lengthy letter addressed to the Bishop of Brixen in December 1843, Karl Columban Schnitzer portrayed the details of the situation surrounding the involvement of his person in this dispensation case. He wrote that he had enquired with the Imperial-Royal Agency as to the possibility of a dispensation and been assured that the Agency would provide all necessary support – seeing as, in Rome, "such cases are anything but rare". However, his efforts to help initially bore no fruit.[84] At the end of August 1844, the Imperial-Royal Embassy in Rome wrote that the request had been refused, but that a further attempt could be made following the autumn break; doing so would require a new attestation or letter of recommendation by the bishop, who would need to explicitly state that he held the marriage at issue to be necessary.[85] This renewed attempt was ultimately successful: in early 1845, the hoped-for dispensation was granted in Rome as a "special mercy".

From the late eighteenth century onward and as a result of the state's centralisation of dispensation-related activities, mediation – as a regular element of dispensation-related practices – was officially the sole responsibility of the Imperial-Royal Agency that had been established in Rome. However, it was actually the case that this institution by no means enjoyed a monopoly. In the 1830s and 1840s, before the backdrop of stricter dispensation policies with respect to the close degrees, there is evidence of interventions by prominent sacred and secular figures who, like the Innsbruck banker Giovanni Carnelli, either worked within the orbit of the Roman Curia or possessed contacts who did. The desire to keep such recommendations' success from becoming the rule was signalled by the addition of the term 'special', with the consequent characterisation of dispensations thus classified as double acts of mercy. By and large, however, activating powerful circles in support of one's request was

---

83 DIÖAB, Konsistorialakten 1845, Fasc. 5a, Römische Dispensen, no. 11.

84 On 18 June of the following year, Schnitzer sent warning of the expected negative answer: he had received "from the Imperial-Royal Agency the confidential message that His Holiness does not deign to grant this dispensation, a refusal that, according to the Agency, can only be explained by the fact that the dispensation was requested by the Reverend Ordinariate *in forma pauperum*, namely as a *causa infamante*, even though such is not the case." He therefore advised using a different formulation – which, however, was no more successful. DIÖAB, Konsistorialakten 1845, Fasc. 5a, Römische Dispensen, no. 11.

85 "Debbo prevenirla che la Dispensa in 1mo grado implorata a favore Egg è stata nuovamente ricusata da Sua Santità; dopo le prossime ferie autumnali si potrebbero fare nuove premure onde indurre il S[anto] Padre ad accordare questa grazia, quante volte S[ua] A[ltezza] Rev[erendissi]ma Monsignore Vescovo rilasciasse un nuovo attestato, ovvero una lettera comendatizia con la precisa indicatione, che giudica neccessario un tal matrimonio." DIÖAB, Konsistorialakten 1845, Fasc. 5a, Römische Dispensen, no. 11.

an option open to only very few people, since the ability to do so was contingent upon the range and power of one's personal networks. Other couples had to employ other strategies.

3 Fighting for Dispensations – by "Means Hitherto Unheard Of"

The discretionary margin concerning the "threat of defection from the faith", which the Salzburg official Schurmann had employed to the benefit of Joseph Khuen and Karolina Esterle, in no way conformed to the officially prescribed procedures. It was much rather the case that handbook authors called upon local priests to "refrain from succumbing to vain deceptions" whenever dispensation requests listed this reason. "Casually made threats by supplicants" were by no means sufficient.[86] The Brixen consistory's high clergy frequently became suspicious when this reason for dispensation was mentioned, and they were quite generally interested in making sure that knowledge of its efficacy did not become all that widespread. Upon a request's refusal, they therefore occasionally reported back to the competent dean that precisely this promising reason had been missing, but would hasten to add that they were revealing this only for the purpose of "*internal official knowledge*" and with the understanding that the affected couple was not to be thus informed.[87]

One feature of the broader regional context was that in nineteenth-century Tyrol, non-Catholics were made out to be enemies – and their presence in or migration to the province was opposed just as staunchly as were interconfessional marriages.[88] The Church, for its part, repeatedly invoked the Catholic unity of the province and called for confirmation of this by the imperial authorities.[89] The Josephine Patent of Toleration of 1781, which had permitted

86 Knopp, *Vollständiges katholisches Eherecht*, 1854, p. 460. Wolfgang Dannerbauer quotes the theologist Michael Haringer as having stated that "Pope Gregory XVI always steadfastly refused to dispense for those who threatened to defect from the faith in the event of refusal, as he found such people undeserving of special mercy". Dannerbauer, *Praktisches Geschäftsbuch*, p. 240.

87 DIÖAB, Konsistorialakten 1836, Fasc. 5a, Römische Dispensen, no. 1, emphasis underlined in the original.

88 On this cf. Stefan Schima, "Die 'Tiroler Glaubenseinheit' vor dem Hintergrund der österreichischen Rechts- und Verfassungsentwicklung im 19. Jahrhundert", *Jahrbuch für die Geschichte des Protestantismus in Österreich* 123 (2007), 65–119; and in general: Stefan Schima, "Glaubenswechsel in Österreich in der staatlichen Gesetzgebung von Joseph II. bis heute", *Wiener Zeitschrift zur Geschichte der Neuzeit* 7, 2 (2007), 79–99.

89 In 1794, Emperor Francis I did still move to affirm the confessional unity of this crown land with its "Tyrolean freedoms". Cf. Gelmi, "Bistum Bozen-Brixen", p. 143. For further details see Fontana, *Kulturkampf*, pp. 18–23.

"the Augsburg and Helvetic religious compatriots and then the non-united Greek Church to worship privately in keeping with their religion",[90] had not been promulgated in Tyrol.[91] The banishment of a congregation of Protestants from the Ziller Valley in 1837 marked a drastic "transition to an aggressive stance of political Catholicism",[92] and Prince-Bishop Vinzenz Gasser, who took office in the Diocese of Brixen in 1856, proceeded to act as a vehement champion of Catholic religious unity.[93] The consistory's alarmed reactions whenever couples "threatened to defect from the faith" in connection with dispensations must be viewed before this backdrop. Strictness and suspicion were the order of the day.

Within the Diocese of Brixen, the couples who could most credibly argue with the possibility of their conversion were those from areas of Vorarlberg and western Tyrol that bordered on Switzerland.[94] Elsewhere, only a very few such threats appear to have been made.[95] It was above all vis-à-vis the vicariate general in Feldkirch and the deaneries in Vorarlberg that the consistory had to defend its strict posture, in light of how efforts to obtain dispensations seemed

---

90 Printed in Peter F. Barton, "Das Toleranzpatent von 1781. Edition der wichtigsten Fassungen", in *Im Lichte der Toleranz. Aufsätze zur Toleranzgesetzgebung des 18. Jahrhunderts in den Reichen Joseph II., ihren Voraussetzungen und ihren Folgen*, ed. Barton (Vienna, 1981), pp. 152–202, 199.

91 Brixen's then-bishop Josef von Spaur, upon been pressed by the *Gubernium* to make the Patent known, did so only among the clergy. It likewise remained unpublicised in Trento. Cf. Fontana, *Kulturkampf*, p. 16.

92 Heiss/Götz, *Am Rand der Revolution*, p. 34; cf. also Fontana, *Kulturkampf*, pp. 21–22.

93 Gasser viewed the establishment of Protestant congregations in Innsbruck and Merano in 1876 as a personal defeat and offered his resignation. Cf. Josef Gelmi, *Die Brixner Bischöfe in der Geschichte Tirols* (Bolzano, 1984), p. 239. In this regard, the author – writing from an explicitly ecclesiastical point of view – speaks of the "bitterest blow". Cf. also the sections "Der Kampf um die Glaubenseinheit" [The Battle for Confessional Unity] and "Das Ende der Glaubenseinheit" [The End of Confessional Unity], in: Josef Fontana, *Geschichte des Landes Tirol*, vol. 3: Vom Neubau bis zum Untergang der Habsburgermonarchie, 1848–1918 (Bolzano, 1987), pp. 85–93 and 160–163. Out of protest against the corresponding ministerial decree, the clerical and conservative deputies to the Tyrolean Territorial Diet – who represented the majority – walked out of the Diet meeting in Innsbruck (ibid., p. 161).

94 On this topic cf. also Margareth Lanzinger, "Kirchliche Macht, antiliberale Tendenzen und ziviles Aufbegehren mit Grenzen. Zur Ehedispenspraxis in Tirol und Vorarlberg im 19. Jahrhundert", *Histoire des Alpes – Storia delle Alpi – Geschichte der Alpen* 12 (2007), 49–68, 58–62.

95 One incidence of which was in the eastern Puster Valley: the widow Anna Viertler from Toblach said that if her dispensation request were to be refused, she would be tempted "to move to Carinthia or to Switzerland" in order to "be married by a priest of another faith". DIÖAB, Konsistorialakten 1832, Fasc. 5a, Römische Dispensen, no. 7.

not to encounter such severe difficulties "in neighbouring lands". By way of explanation, the consistory pointed to the special authorities that the nunciatures and/or ordinariates there had obtained from Rome, thereby also justifying their own strict policies.[96]

Even in the case of the widower Andreas Haunis from Strengen in the Deanery of Zams in western Tyrol, who spent part of the year running an iron dealing business in Ilanz in Switzerland, the consistory deemed conversion implausible. In the letters sent to the consistory concerning his case, various threatening scenarios had been communicated. It was the mayor of the prospective groom's home municipality, serving as his designated representative, who was responsible for the drastically formulated lines referring to what might happen in response to a negative decision from Brixen. Among other things, he wrote that the supplicant – "should his request be refused" – was determined "to leave the fatherland" and moved to Switzerland, where it could easily happen that he might marry a Protestant and convert, thereby becoming "a disgrace to his relatives as well as to the community".[97] Three weeks prior, Haunis himself – writing to the mayor from Switzerland – had stated simply that he intended and was in fact being forced to take his son "out" to him and to leave the fatherland. He did, however, also mention a missionary and a lawyer whom he had likewise enlisted to help with his dispensation case.

The word "lawyer" was, in any case, most probably fit to raise the ordinariate's ire. Lawyers, as representatives of civil law, were per se potential adversaries of the Church. And even if this did not apply to every single one of them, members of their profession were generally regarded as a "pioneering group within bourgeois culture" with a strong "affinity for liberalism's individualistic understanding of politics" in nineteenth-century German-speaking Tyrol, dominated as it was by Catholic and conservative forces.[98] A request was guaranteed to draw suspicion as soon as a lawyer was mentioned. Regarding Haunis's case, Consistorial Pro-Chancellor Georg Prünster assumed that "defection from the faith" as a reason for dispensation had "simply been appropriated" under his lawyer's influence. Therefore, it was imperative "to go to work on this with a most necessary degree of caution" and clarify the situation via "secret interrogation" of the bride. She duly reported that her groom, before departing for Switzerland, had promised to procure for her Swiss citizenship, should he fail to obtain a dispensation in Tyrol, since it would be easier to do so

96 Cf. DIÖAB, Konsistorialakten 1845, Fasc. 5a, Römische Dispensen, no. 11.
97 DIÖAB, Konsistorialakten 1833, Fasc. 5a, Römische Dispensen, no. 13.
98 Götz, *Bürgertum und Liberalismus*, p. 92.

there.[99] Her testimony had its effect: the dispensation request was forwarded to Rome, where it received a positive response.

It was with an 1844 letter of supplication addressed to the emperor that the widower Johann Georg Kropf, a teamster and merchant from Elbigenalp in the Deanery of Breitenwang in western Tyrol who dealt in "wine, brandy and edibles", attempted to achieve his objective after two of his dispensation requests had already been turned down.[100] Kropf was 40 years old and had been widowed in 1839. His deceased wife had left behind four children who were being cared for by her sister Katharina Lumper, who also ran the household. Georg Kropf had sought to marry this sister-in-law in February 1841. The prince-episcopal consistory in Brixen had rejected his dispensation request as hopeless and demanded that the sister-in-law be removed from his house. Accomplishing this, however, had turned out to be anything but a simple matter – for as it was stated later on in greater detail, the two owned the property jointly. It was one month later that Kropf's second request arrived in Brixen – once again in vain. He refused to give up, however – and in late 1841, the consistory in Brixen finally relented and made to forward his dispensation request to Rome, even though it had little chance of success. Rome, as expected, refused this request.

Johann Georg Kropf, however, continued in his adamance – in his "molestation", as it was written – and in the autumn of 1842, the consistory signalled its willingness to initiate a renewed attempt in Rome, this time with its urgent recommendation. It was declared that this would be the final attempt. The ordinariate had been caught utterly off guard by the previous response from Rome since that request had also contained the "danger of defection from the faith", duly confirmed by witnesses. The ordinariate once again pointed out that the affected persons resided near the border of the diocese, in close proximity to "people of another faith", for which reason they were indeed subject to the

99 A court decree of 27 May 1840 tightened civil policy by declaring that a marriage impediment could not be eliminated by converting to a "tolerated non-Catholic confession". A civil dispensation would still be needed and would be denied in such a case. *Sr. k. k. Majestät Ferdinand des Ersten politische Gesetze und Verordnungen für sämmtliche Provinzen des Oesterreichischen Kaiserstaates, mit Ausnahme von Ungarn und Siebenbürgen*, vol. 68: Verordnungen vom 1. Januar bis Ende December 1840 (Vienna, 1842), pp. 236–237. This rule – the enforcement of which Johann Kutschker believed would "blunt the danger of apostasy" as a reason for dispensation – would seem to have been without effect in the regions examined here insofar as threats of conversion typically alluded to the possibility of being wed abroad. Kutschker, *Das Eherecht der katholischen Kirche*, vol. 5, p. 122.

100 DIÖAB, Konsistorialakten 1847, Fasc. 5a, Römische Dispensen, no. 6 (this record contains the correspondence since 1841) and ibid., 1848, no. 13.

temptation and danger of leaving the Catholic Church.[101] The prince-bishop also commended this matter to the attention of Abbot Tizziani, procurator general of the Canons Regular of the Lateran, who happened to be present in Brixen and promised him that he would approach the Austrian embassy as well as intercede vis-à-vis the Holy See upon his return.[102]

All these efforts, however, had been for naught. Johann Georg Kropf now placed his hopes in support from the emperor, requesting in a letter of supplication submitted in 1844 that he first "be permitted to conclude" a valid civil "marriage contract" with the sister of his deceased wife in order to more easily obtain "church forbearance" for his marriage impediment of affinity – a bizarre construction that could not be realised under the laws in force. The consistory in Brixen, to which his letter of supplication had been sent by the *Gubernium* in Innsbruck on its way back, characterised this as a "most outlandish request of His Majesty" with which the dispensation was "meant to be obtained through sheer obstinacy and by means hitherto unheard of in these lands". Consistorial Chancellor Rabanser instantly suspected that Kropf's action was owed to the "insinuations" of third parties who needed to be tracked down. The talk was once again of lawyers and of agents, who they assumed had provided him with poor advice. The outrage at said "means hitherto unheard of in these lands" was owed primarily to the fact that this dispensation-seeker had directed a supplication to the emperor. Across the entire body of material that was examined, this represents an isolated case. 1847 saw Johann Georg Kropf make yet another attempt – once again in vain – to obtain his objective. He had written that he would be willing, "if it would more easily serve the purpose", to himself "venture a journey to Brixen or to Rome". He ultimately made one

---

101 The consistory subsequently ordered more detailed study as to the actual presence of a "danger" stemming from contact with "non-Catholics". The findings from these enquiries, however, indicated that Kropf's merchant activities were only "domestic" in scope – confined to the region between Bozen and Meran, where he procured wine, and the Lech Valley in northern Tyrol, where he sold it – and hence within an area that was fairly "innocuous" with regard to confessional matters.

102 ÖStA, HHStA, Agentie-Archiv Rom, III Agentie Akten 1833–1855, K. 76, Bressanone 1842, letter dated 8 November 1842, signed by L.R. – probably Luigi Rabanser, who served as consistorial chancellor during that period. "Dietro i pregiatissimi rescritti di Vossignoria Illustrissima die 14 Maggio e 27 Agosto p. p. la S. Sede non si è determinata di dare la dispensazione nel primo grado d'affinità a favore Giovanni Kropf e Caterina Lumper ed a favore Giulio Zobl e Maria Anna Woeber. La notizia di questa negativa v'era tanto più inaspettata, essendo ambe due le suppliche corredate di motivi ed attestati tali, che d'un favorevole successo non si poteva dubitare. Principalmente vi è provata colle asserzioni giurate dei supplicanti e dei testimonj la circostanza, che vi sia periculum defectionis a fide, e questo motivo è sempre stato stimato valentissimo."

more attempt, under the new pope in 1848, which finally met with success: he received a dispensation out of "special mercy" – seven and a half years after his marriage project had left its first traces in the records.

This period's most dramatic case from the Diocese of Brixen was that of Martin Gmeiner of Hard and his sister-in-law, the widow Franziska Pfleghart of Bregenz, who was a fashion retailer and modiste. Between 1827 and 1833, they made a total of eight unsuccessful attempts to obtain a dispensation. When they ultimately threatened "to separate themselves from the communion of the Catholic Church in order to seek citizenship in a Reformed community abroad", as the vicariate general put it, this was furiously characterised as "malicious intent" and interpreted as "reprehensible disparagement of the good fortune to be members of the true Catholic Church". The consistory accordingly declared itself "by no means in a position" to seek dispensation in Rome.[103] Martin Gmeiner and Franziska Pfleghart did not move away; six years later, they submitted a new dispensation request. They admitted to having been badly advised back then "by a respected man" – adding in parentheses: "by a lawyer here" – to make their statements regarding conversion, and they averred that such a thought would have otherwise never entered their minds. They had "only passively permitted this to be written down because he had ensured them that it would most certainly enable them to receive their desired dispensation at once".[104] This renewed attempt was then not pursued any further for reasons that the extant documents fail to indicate, even though – and this is singular among the analysed dispensation records – evaluations as to whether a new matrimonial examination should be protocolled and the case forwarded to Rome had been solicited from all ten consistorial councillors. The majority had spoken in favour of doing so. But at any rate, this turn of events had led the consistory to feel confirmed in its assumption that threats of conversion were in fact pretextual, strategically employed, justifications.

In Vienna and Lower Austria, it was quite typical for "backroom legal advisors, lawyers and educated notables" to author letters for dispensation-seekers.[105] In Salzburg, especially in connection with requests from cities and larger towns, the dispensation records likewise contain such documents in the form of letters of supplication but include nothing to indicate that these elicited any

103 DIÖAB, Konsistorialakten 1833, Fasc. 5a, Römische Dispensen, no. 19.
104 DIÖAB, Konsistorialakten 1839, Fasc. 5a, Römische Dispensen, no. 5.
105 Saurer, "Stiefmütter und Stiefsöhne", p. 355.

special reactions.[106] In the Diocese of Brixen, on the other hand, lawyers were mistrusted as a matter of principle. This is inseparably linked with the political stance pursued by the diocese from the eighteenth century – according to which secular institutions were to be excluded to the greatest possible extent from dispensation proceedings. Assistance from a lawyer was usually dismissed as an unsuitable strategy or even viewed with indignation as an outright affront:[107] the Dean of Zams once complained of being stormed "without let-up" by a supplicant despite clear refusals and admonishments, with matters having recently been aggravated when he "even brought a letter of supplication authored by a backroom lawyer", whereupon the dean had turned him away once more.[108] Dispensation-seekers, went the accusation in another case, were being "incited by unbidden agents" who sought to force "the mercy of dispensation".[109] In reaction to a case where conversion was threatened, the vicariate general spoke of a "scandalous supplication" in an "unbecoming style of writing", one that had "probably once again been whispered in their ears by a backroom lawyer".[110] It was with according disgust that the consistory in

---

106 It must be said, however, that few of these letters are signed with the name of a lawyer. And in rural communities, comparison of handwriting with that found in other letters indicates that here, as well, it tended to be local priests who penned such letters. The bride and groom merely signed them.

107 In only one dispensation request from these years in which a lawyer was involved did the consistory in Brixen refrain from a negative assessment. Gabriel Egger and his widowed sister-in-law Agnes Volderauer from the Stubai Valley, which belonged to the Deanery of Matrei south of Innsbruck, had had a lengthy letter of supplication addressed to the Imperial-Royal Provincial Government written "by Dr. Haselwanter", as the dean reported to Brixen. The letter itself, which is over nine pages long, contains no indication of its author. It describes the economic situation of the widow and her property at great length. The bride was pregnant, for which reason the economic justification was followed by an equally detailed description of the advantages of a marriage in this situation for the widow and the child. This letter contains no passages that could be construed as being critical of the Church. DIÖAB, Konsistorialakten 1842, Fasc. 5a, Römische Dispensen, no. 27; TLA Innsbruck, Jüngeres Gubernium, Hauptgruppe 64 Ehesachen, 1840–1842, Fasc. no. 323, 1842, no. 18.899. The author mentioned here may have been the lawyer Johann Haßlwanter, a prominent conservative and future "leader of the Conservatives on the Innsbruck city council". On this cf. Götz, *Bürgertum und Liberalismus*, p. 151. This request was nonetheless rejected in Rome.

108 DIÖAB, Konsistorialakten 1855, Fasc. 5a, Römische Dispensen, no. 22.

109 DIÖAB, Konsistorialakten 1844, Fasc. 5a, Römische Dispensen, no. 6.

110 In this case, the author was known by name: he is said to have been Franz Friedrich von Froschauer, a former theologian.

Brixen reacted to this, calling for humility in place of such brash advances.[111] The consistory was quick to regard all-too-open resistance or obstinate statements in the face of a negative dispensation decision as "threats" or interpret them as defiance, even if it had previously supported the request in question. The "mercy of a dispensation" was to be granted only to those "who behave as obedient children of the Church" – a sentiment on which the clergy frequently fell back.[112]

Alltogether, dispensation requests that document couples' efforts to figure out their own detours and strategies or procure various forms of extra-ecclesiastical support are not particularly numerous. Such attempts came at great cost, and all efforts might ultimately be in vain and even end up exacerbating the situation. It is conspicuous how the majority of supplicants who made attempts of this sort came from the Diocese of Brixen's western reaches. Willingness to take the initiative above and beyond what was provided for and accepted by the Church was hence distributed in an uneven manner not only socially but also regionally. On this basis, one could assume that a political culture of standing up to institutions clear across all social milieus was more strongly present in the west of the diocese than in its eastern areas.[113] Here, political culture is understood as the specific distribution of attitudes, stances and repertoires of action employed in dealing with secular and ecclesiastical authorities, in interacting with institutions and bureaucratic machineries.[114]

In Vorarlberg, the difficulties involved in obtaining dispensations in close degrees of affinity stirred fond memories of having belonged to another

111 The consistory issued the official instruction to "lecture the highly ignorant and impudent dispensation supplicants that with attitudes and statements as hostile to the Church and as defiant as these, not even the attempt to obtain the mercy of dispensation from the Holy See can be made, to say nothing of there being any actual hope of receiving one, as mercy and forbearance can be granted only to those whose requests are made in all humility". DIÖAB, Konsistorialakten 1848, Fasc. 5a, Römische Dispensen, no. 13. The quoted letters are from 1842, the year in which these dispensation proceedings began. The entire body of correspondence was transferred from 1842 (no. 27) to 1848. In 1848, this couple ultimately did receive their desired dispensation "out of special consideration and special mercy".

112 Dannerbauer, *Praktisches Geschäftsbuch*, p. 240. This formulation also makes repeated appearances in the dispensation requests.

113 A certain parallel can be seen in the reactions to refused political marriage consent, the economically based permission to marry required of poorer couples that was applied with particular rigidity on a municipal level in nineteenth-century Tyrol and Vorarlberg.

114 On this cf. Sylvia Greiffenhagen, "Theorie(n) der Politischen Kultur", in *Politische Kultur*, ed. Samuel Salzborn (Frankfurt a. M. et al., 2009), pp. 11–29.

diocese. Johann Baptist Sinz, dean in the Bregenz Forest, mourned the times when Constance had still been responsible for his geographic area and dispensations had been "*quite easy*" to obtain within three to four days. "People remain unwilling to submit to the present circumstances", he wrote in 1832, "and they believe that this is because of the dean – who, on account of a rejection, becomes an object of hate for entire families with whom he must deal day in, day out".[115] Christoph Walser, who served as the dean and city parish priest of Bregenz, concluded a several page letter in support of the aforementioned hapless supplicants Martin Gmeiner and Franziska Pfleghart by remarking that not only "persons of low estate" but also "many of higher rank" had already pressed him for an answer to the question of "why obtaining marriage dispensations now poses such difficulties, whereas it was previously the case – as several still-existing marriages between persons related in the first degree of affinity here in Bregenz and elsewhere indeed prove – that they were so easy to obtain." The words "so easy" are underlined in red, and inserted above them – likewise in red – are the words: "*leider*", unfortunately, and "*tempi passati*" – *those times are over*.[116] However, the situation for couples closely related by marriage was soon to improve with the election of Pope Pius IX in 1847.

In December 1847, the widower Julius Zobel, who had unsuccessfully requested a dispensation to marry his sister-in-law Maria Anna Weber several times from 1841, appeared once more at the deanery office in Breitenwang with a letter of recommendation from his parish priest. This letter contained the urgent request to make a renewed attempt at obtaining the dispensation he desired. The parish priest explained this by relating how he had been "filled with hope" by the "praised benevolence and grace" of the new head of the Church.[117] Pius IX (1846–1878) had become pope the year before.[118] He is regarded as a "liberal" pope and is said to have asserted on the day he was announced that, in contrast to his predecessor, he would even allow the construction of railways in addition to granting amnesty to political prisoners.[119]

---

115 DIÖAB, Konsistorialakten 1832, Fasc. 5a, Römische Dispensen, no. 11, emphases underlined in red in the original.

116 DIÖAB, Konsistorialakten 1839, Fasc. 5a, Römische Dispensen, no. 5.

117 All documents from this case can be found in DIÖAB, Konsistorialakten 1848, Fasc. 5a, Römische Dispensen, no. 13.

118 For a detailed impression of his pontificate cf. Friedrich Engel-Janosi, *Österreich und der Vatikan 1846–1918* (Graz/Vienna/Cologne, 1958), pp. 4–197; Seppelt, *Papstgeschichte*, pp. 312–336.

119 Engel-Janosi, *Österreich und der Vatikan*, pp. 18–19.

His inauguration was celebrated euphorically as the dawn of a new era; in his encyclopaedia article, Giacomo Martina spoke of a "collective delirium".[120]

The news that couples who had previously been refused would now have a chance at realising their marriage projects under the aegis of the new pope evidently spread fast. But initially, as was the case in the Diocese of Trento, not everyone shared this assumption. Stefano C. and his sister Margarita M. from Castello in Fiemme and/or their priest had likewise thought that their desired dispensation request might finally be granted when, in December 1846, they addressed a letter of supplication to the competent regional court in Cavalese. Their request had already been refused once before – nearly ten years before, in fact, in March of 1837. The letter was to renew their request, for it was said of the newly elected pope that, in contrast to Gregory XVI, he was quite willing and inclined – "molto propenso e procline" – to grant dispensations in the first degree of affinity.[121] They received a negative answer, however, from Trento's competent vicar general Jakob Freinadimetz, who saw no prospects for success in Rome. For in this regard, he held, the ecclesiastical laws had seen no changes whatsoever under the new pope.[122] The ordinariate in Trento also ruled similarly in comparable cases, declaring its unwillingness to renew such requests.[123]

In the Diocese of Brixen, several dispensation requests in the first degree of affinity were successful in 1848. In several of these cases, however, difficult or even blocked postal communications due to the war in Italy had moved Brixen's prince-bishop to use his own authorities to dispense, which were

120 Giacomo Martina, "Pio IX", *Enciclopedia dei papi*, vol. 3, pp. 560–575, 561.

121 ASTn, Capitanato Circolare di Trento, busta 213, 1847, Ehe – matrimoni, no. 4.630 Eccl./2.099. Since this letter was addressed to the regional court as a civil institution, the wording of this letter actually refers to the second degree of affinity in keeping with the civil method of counting degrees. It was the first degree according to the canonical method.

122 "[…] che non trova il minimo fondamento per poter raccomandare alla S[anta] Sede con qualche speranza di buon successo l'istanza per ottenere la dispensa dall' impedimento di affinità in primo grado." ASTn, Capitanato Cicolare di Trento, busta 213, 1847, Ehe – matrimoni, no. 3.073 Eccl./1.352.

123 Such futility was attributed to the request submitted by the brother- and sister-in-law Giuseppe Z. and Antonia P. with the following words: "[…] mentre ha tutto il fondamento di credere che rimarrebbero senza effetto". ASTn, Capitanato Circolare di Trento, busta 213, 1847, Ehe – matrimoni, no. 1.852 Eccl./806. It was in the same way that the ordinariate, referring to applicable laws and instructions, had denied its support to the physician Dr. Sp., who wished to marry his sister-in-law Rosina S., in September 1847. ASTn, Capitanato Circolare di Trento, busta 213, 1847, Ehe – matrimoni, no. 4.111.

considered church-legitimised in precisely such situations.[124] The comparison of the number of dispensation requests that were turned down either by Rome or already by the consistory in Brixen in view of Rome's stricter dispensation policy (see Table 1) makes clear that the ratio of granted dispensations to refusals in the first degree of affinity improved significantly under the aegis of Pius IX (see Table 2) in contrast to what it had been during the papacy of Gregory XVI between 1831 and 1846. It is also fair to assume that the great difficulties and the wave of refusals had probably discouraged some couples closely related by affinity from submitting requests at all during this period – and that some such marriage projects were abandoned for good in the face of bureaucratic obstacles.

TABLE 1 Papal dispensation requests in the Diocese of Brixen, 1831–1846
Total: 369 cases, in percentages

Degree	Granted in Rome	Rejected in Brixen	Refused in Rome	Not pursued further	Others	Total
2nd cons.	16.0	2.4	0.0	1.6	0.3	20.3
2nd & 3rd cons.	27.4	1.1	0.0	1.4	0.8	30.6
1st affin.	4.1	7.9	3.0	1.1	0.9	16.8
1st & 2nd affin.	1.9	0.5	0.0	0.3	0.0	2.7
2nd affin.	10.9	3.5	0.8	1.4	0.0	16.5
2nd & 3rd affin.	7.0	0.3	0.0	0.8	0.8	8.9
Others	2.0	0.9	0.0	1.1	0.0	4.2
Total	69.3	16.5	3.8	7.5	2.8	100.0

"Cons." stands for consanguinity, "affin." for affinity.[125]

124 In this regard see the requests contained in DIÖAB, Konsistorialakten 1848, Fasc. 5a, Römische Dispensen, no. 5, no. 6, no. 7 and no. 23.

125 In both tables, the variable "Others" refers to administrative situations in which a case was ceded to another diocese, resolved with a dispensation *auctoritate ordinaria* or from the nunciature, or rejected by the provincial government, as well as to cases in which the supplicant(s) died during the proceedings and to rejected requests in which the degree of kinship had not been indicated. In terms of degrees, "Other" contains the requests *ex copula illicita* as well as a small number of requests involving multiple degrees that cannot be clearly categorised.

TABLE 2 Papal dispensation requests in the Diocese of Brixen, 1847–1862
Total: 493 cases, in percentages

Degree	Granted in Rome	Rejected in Brixen	Refused in Rome	Not pursued further	Others	Total
2nd cons.	16.0	2.2	0.2	1.4	0.8	20.7
2nd & 3rd cons.	22.5	1.0	0.0	0.8	1.2	25.6
1st affin.	13.6	5.3	0.4	1.6	0.8	21.7
1st & 2nd affin.	4.5	0.2	0.0	0.6	0.2	5.5
2nd affin.	9.7	1.2	0.0	1.2	1.0	13.2
2nd & 3rd affin.	4.5	0.4	0.0	0.6	0.0	5.5
Others	4.8	1.0	0.0	0.4	0.6	6.8
Total	76.6	11.4	0.6	6.7	4.6	100.0

"Cons." stands for consanguinity, "affin." for affinity.

The new pope's initially praised "benevolence and grace" was not to last, however. Dispensation policy once again grew successively more severe, not least due to a resurgence of moralisation beginning in the mid-1850s. Moreover, it would seem that the pope in some cases even involved himself directly in dispensation-related decisions. In connection with a complaint about the inordinately long wait in one case, the consistory in Brixen explained that dispensation requests touching the first degree had to be presented personally to the pope. Reserved for this purpose was only one audience day per week – which not infrequently fell victim to a church celebration or another "emergent cause".[126] Some couples had, at least, been able to benefit from the milder phase at the outset of this papacy, but protracted proceedings had nonetheless continued to occur. One affinal couple, Anton Prantl and Anna Angerer, were granted a dispensation in 1869. In this case, 17 years had gone by since their first documented request.[127]

126 DIÖAB, Konsistorialakten 1856, Fasc. 5a, Römische Dispensen, no. 13.

127 Cf. DIÖAB, Konsistorialakten 1852, Fasc. 5a, Römische Dispensen, no. 24; ibid., 1855, no. 19; ibid., 1869, Fasc. 22a, no. 1.

4 Aunt versus Stepmother

How justified was the statement by Pius VII, quoted at the beginning of this chapter, that "widowers are no longer capable of finding any brides other than their sisters-in-law"? Quantitative analysis of dispensation requests from the Diocese of Brixen shows that in the close degrees of affinity, there was generally a more than clear abundance of widowers who wanted to marry either their sisters-in-law or cousins or nieces of their deceased wives in comparison to the number of widows in the accordingly reversed configurations. The ratio was slightly in excess of three to one: 80 per cent of men who submitted a request in such affinal configurations were widowers; among the women, it was 26.5 per cent. Among configurations in the first degree of affinity, 84 per cent of the men were widowers while only 19 per cent of the women were widows. Unlike the far rarer first and second unequal degree affinal configuration with a niece of a deceased wife or the second degree affinal configuration with a deceased wife's cousin, the latter of which was subject to far fewer reservations and difficulties, marriage projects with a deceased wife's sister were a focal point of both discourse and dispensation policy.

This begs the question as to the actual contexts in which these can be found and the specific notions with which they were associated. Historically, men's remarriage rates were significantly higher than those of women and the time spent by men between their spouses' deaths and remarriage was significantly shorter, an observation that researchers such as Antoinette Fauve Chamoux have summarised as follows: "remarriage was much quicker and easier for men, a point on which all statistics are concordant".[128] Moreover, what Lyndan Warner formulated with regard to the early modern period – namely, that a number of aspects have been examined in connection with being widowed while hardly any attention has been paid to the consequences of remarriage – also goes for the nineteenth century.[129] In this regard, dispensation requests do bring into view at least related expectations and fears, as well as stepfamily

128 Antoinette Fauve-Chamoux, "Revisiting the Decline of Remarriage in Early-Modern Europe: the Case of Rheims in France", *The History of the Family* 15, 3 (2010), 283–297, 291; cf. also Koen Matthijs, "Frequency, Timing and Intensity of Remarriage in 19th Century Flanders", *The History of the Family* 8, 1 (2003), 135–162; Sylvie Perrier, "La marâtre dans la France d'Ancien Régime: intégration ou marginalité?", *Annales de démographie historique* 2 (2006), 171–187, 176–178.

129 Lyndan Warner, "Remembering the Mother, Presenting the Stepmother: Portraits of the Early Modern Family in Northern Europe", *Early Modern Women. An Interdisciplinary Journal* 6 (2011), 93–125, 99.

configurations that were lived de facto even if the couples concerned were not (yet) married. A closer look reveals that the lion's share of widowers who requested dispensations were living in situations of spatial and social proximity. Household configurations in which the sister-in-law worked as a maidservant or, much more commonly, in the more responsible position of housekeeper – referred to as a *Wirtschafterin* in the region studied here – predominated. This implies that alongside domestic activities, women also did farm work, contributed business-related skills such as bookkeeping and oversaw other workers.[130] Moreover, they were often quite familiar with the household and its needs thanks to many years' worth of practical involvement.

Spatial and social proximity can be attributed to various patterns that adhered in part to a paradigm of obligation while also being partly associated with legal claims.[131] At the latest, sisters-in-law tended to move into their sisters' households at a time close to when the latter passed away. It was frequently the case that they had already been caring for their ailing sisters for weeks, months or even years, and that they had also assumed the necessary everyday household responsibilities. Some women had already entered a housemaid-like position upon their sisters' being wed or giving birth for the first time, though they also joined the households of their sisters- and brothers-in-law as familiar confidants. If the house or farm came from the wife's family, it could also be that the single sister had simply remained in the house to support her now-married sister. She may also have enjoyed right of residence based on her parents' wills or a contract, or even had a claim to partial ownership. It is for all these reasons that Leonore Davidoff emphasises how single sisters and/or sisters in law could serve as a "crucial resource in running the household or, among the less well off, as an aid in the family enterprise".[132]

It was not at all rare for the sister-in-law to be both the aunt and the godmother of one or even several children of her widowed brother-in-law. Since this so-called spiritual kinship represented a marriage impediment in its own right, it had to be declared when requesting a dispensation. Various studies have revealed that an increasing number of siblings of parents served as godparents and confirmation sponsors over the course of the nineteenth century, while the early modern period had seen such sponsorship used principally to

130 With the temporal focus on the last decades of the eighteenth century and the spatial focus on Salzburg, Vienna and Lower Austria see Margareth Lanzinger, "Emotional Bonds and the Everyday Logic of Living Arrangements: Stepfamilies in Dispensation Records of Late Eighteenth-Century Austria", *in Stepfamilies in Europe, 1400–1800*, ed. Lyndan Warner (Abingdon/New York, 2018), pp. 168–186.

131 On this cf. also Pelaja, "Marriage by Exception", pp. 238–240.

132 Davidoff, *Thicker than Water*, p. 154.

form new and strengthen existing social networks outside one's own circle of blood and affinal kin.[133] This tendency to combine the positions of aunt and godmother can be interpreted as part of the nineteenth century's further densification and familialisation of social relations.

Sisters-in-law knew the everyday household and business routines and had also interacted closely with the widows and their children, meaning that they were not only quite familiar with the work that needed to be done around the house but also with those who lived there: both sides therefore knew who they were dealing with in terms of personal characteristics. Taken altogether, a sister-in-law who possessed the appropriate qualities and competencies and was also emotionally close may well have seemed like the very person who was best suited to become one's new wife, especially considering how her years of presence will have caused her to be viewed as indispensable – or at least easy to credibly portray as being so – in a great many cases.[134] In households that struggled to get by at the very margin of subsistence, such unions were often regarded as the only feasible way in which to organise a family's everyday life and care – for the marriage chances of a widower with small children living in precarious economic circumstances were just as bleak as were the prospects of finding and being able to afford a responsible maidservant or housekeeper.

---

133 Cf. Alfani, *Fathers and Godfathers*; Guido Alfani, "Geistige Allianzen: Patenschaft als Instrument sozialer Beziehung in Italien und Europa (15. bis 20. Jahrhundert)", in *Politiken der Verwandtschaft*, ed. Lanzinger/Saurer, pp. 25–54. The most extreme example described by Alfani is a case from Ivrea: a girl who was baptised as Maria on 20 March 1502 was sponsored by 17 godfathers and 10 godmothers (ibid., p. 29, note 14). For the Catholic world, the Council of Trent reduced the permissible number of godfathers and godmothers to a maximum of one each. In Protestant contexts, a larger number continued to be permissible and typical. Cf. for example Joachim Rüffer and Carsten Vorwig, "Kulturelle Wandlungen am östlichen Hellweg. Die Taufnamengebung in den Kirchspielen Sassendorf und Dinker vom Anfang des 18. bis zum Ende des 20. Jahrhunderts", in *Historisch-demographische Forschungen*, ed. Frank Göttmann and Peter Respondek (Cologne, 2001), pp. 138–165. In the parishes examined by these two authors, the number of godparents ranged between four and five during the nineteenth century. And for the Westphalian community of Borgeln, Christine Fertig ascertains a rise in the number of godparents from an average of three during the 1770s to five over the following decades up to 1850. In Löhne, on the other hand, up to 3 godparents continued to be a typical maximum. Christine Fertig, *Familie, verwandtschaftliche Netzwerke und Klassenbildung im ländlichen Westfalen, 1750–1874* (Stuttgart, 2012), pp. 105–104. On the significance of good parenthood in political networks cf. Sandro Guzzi-Heeb, "Spiritual Kinship, Political Mobilization and Social Cooperation: a Swiss Alpine Valley in 18th and 19th Century", in *Spiritual Kinship in Europe, 1500–1900*, ed. Guido Alfani and Vincent Gourdon (Basingstoke, 2012), pp. 183–203.

134 Polly Morris also views the death of a parent and the resulting need for support in providing and caring for the children as having been a significant context within which affinal marriages took place. Morris, "Incest or Survival Strategy", p. 236.

Accordingly, studies of England have ascertained that poorer households suffered most under the prohibition of marriages between widowers and their sisters-in-law.[135]

In order to underline their indispensability – and unlike in other types of sources that render women's work invisible or subsume it under vague categories such as "maidservant" – the dispensation records highlight and emphasise the significance of women's abilities and achievements, frequently in areas of activity that lay outside the range of responsibilities classically attributed to women.[136] The widower Lorenz Zwickle, for instance, a timber merchant from Hard in the Deanery of Bregenz, insisted on his marriage project by explaining that he did not himself possess the writing and arithmetic skills necessary in his business while his intended bride and sister-in-law – who had already been managing his business for years, ever since she had been asked to by his ailing and since-deceased wife – did.[137]

A sister-in-law typically assumed multiple roles. One highly significant aspect of the context of social proximity was her relationship with the children of her sister and her brother-in-law. Supplicant couples, their witnesses and local priests frequently emphasised the mutuality of the love in question: that of the aunt for the children and of the children for their aunt. In the household of a widowed brother-in-law, the aunt functioned as a replacement of the lost mother and could thereby become an important – if not *the* most important – person of reference for the children. Mutual "attachment" is mentioned repeatedly and how the aunt loved the children as if they were her own – and, the other way around, how she was loved "like a mother" by the children. The sisters, even when one of the two was no longer living, formed the central figuration behind the couple configuration of widower and sister-in-law.

The widower Leopold Rissinger, a master furrier in Innsbruck who had earned himself a considerable fortune, included the following words in his lengthy, seven point letter of supplication: "The most humble undersigned believes himself to be wholly convinced that he has found just such a spouse

---

135 Cf. Gulette, "The Puzzling Case", p. 145; Anderson, "The Marriage", pp. 80–81. As already sketched out in chapter 1, it was roughly concurrent with Pope Gregory XVI's institution of more severe dispensation policies in the first degree of affinity for Catholics that Victorian England witnessed the beginning of a debate across society and the media over unions between widowers and their sisters-in-law that was to continue until the according marriage prohibition was ultimately abolished in 1907.

136 For a more detailed analysis see Margareth Lanzinger, "The Visibility of Women's Work: Logics and Contexts of Documents' Production", in *What is Work? Gender at the Crossroads of Home, Family, and Business from the Early Modern Era to the Present*, ed. Raffaella Sarti, Anna Bellavitis and Manuela Martini (New York/Oxford, 2018), pp. 243–264.

137 DIÖAB, Konsistorialakten 1853, Fasc. 5a, Römische Dispensen, no. 5.

and mother in Karolina Red, his deceased spouse's sister, since she is thoroughly initiated into his business by virtue of having already been in his home *for eight years*, and since the children acknowledge her as their mother due to her having filled the position of a mother to the children with noble sacrifice and out of faithful affection for her deceased sister. After all, the dying mother had entrusted to her, as the beloved sister, the children and the entire household, imploring her not to abandon her spouse and her children and to always remain with them."[138] There is no question that this narrative exhibits strategic features in that it valorises the sister-in-law, thereby simultaneously devaluing and fending off any other possible bride. But even so, this does nothing to weaken the argumentation's lifeworld logic.

The prospects of many women who were open to such a marriage were not exactly attractive: when the children were still small and their number great, when the economic backdrop looked anything but rosy and when the groom's old and sickly parents or parents-in-law – who were sometimes quite unabashedly described as sullen and cantankerous – also lived in the house.[139] When sisters-in-law declared themselves willing to run the households of their widowed brothers-in-law despite such difficult circumstances, it was mostly love for the children of their deceased sisters that they pointed to as their motivation. The detailed letter of supplication submitted by Johann Klauzner, a woodward and bird-catcher who lived in a remote hut perched high above the community of Wilten, now part of Innsbruck, portrays the difficulties he faced and the persuasion that was necessary in order to sway his prospective bride. Following the death of his wife, who had left behind two daughters aged five and one, "not a single person" could be found who would have been willing to move into his "dreary hut, where need and misery reigned". He had, however, at long last succeeded in convincing his sister-in-law. She had taken pity on his children, given up her good employment as a servant and moved in with him as a housekeeper. This dispensation request, submitted only after years of cohabitation and mutual work, was rejected twice as one that had no chance of success.[140]

Women characterised such commitment as a selfless act, as a "sacrifice" that they desired to make out of pity for the children and out of a feeling of obligation toward their deceased sisters. Such perspectives and arguments were founded upon a Christian worldview and the virtues and obligations derived

---

138 DIÖAB, Konsistorialakten 1859, Fasc. 5a, Römische Dispensen, no. 5, emphasis underlined in the original.

139 On this cf. Lanzinger, "Widowers and their Sisters-in-Law".

140 DIÖAB, Konsistorialakten 1836, Fasc. 5a, Römische Dispensen, no. 20; ibid., 1842, no. 25.

therefrom. However, alluding to this religious referential cosmos was also a way to reorient the perspective. It shifted the emotional bond and trajectory from the brother-in-law to the nieces and nephews and hence to a selfless, 'innocent' and morally inoffensive sort of love. This could ultimately help justify years of cohabitation beneath the same roof. Repeatedly, and with particular frequency beginning in the mid-nineteenth century, women emphasised how their sisters had charged them on their deathbeds with assuming care of their children. Other deceased spouses had even explicitly begged their husbands to take their sisters to wife so that they could rest assured their husbands and children would be well cared for.

This required there to be single sisters in the first place who could come to the rescue in a situation of family crisis and become desired marriage partners. Particularly in the German-speaking areas of Tyrol, the nineteenth century featured a relatively high rate of unmarried persons – in extreme cases reaching 50 per cent in the age group of 41- to 50-year-olds. The situation in the Italian districts as well as in Vorarlberg differed quite starkly.[141] Assuming a direct correlation between high rates of unmarried persons and the frequency of marriages in close degrees of affinity would certainly fall short of being explanatory due to the diverse aspects involved in such decisions, but this factor does indeed constitute a context that likely made such marriage projects more probable. Affinal marriages could offer unmarried men and women an opportunity to live their lives in a more independent position – compared with employment as a maidservant or farmhand, seasonal migrant work or dependence on the households of their parents. In dispensation requests, men emphasised above all the value of having their own "accommodations" thanks to their planned marriages while women, for their part, often portrayed their hard lives – which grew harder with increasing age – as servants "to strange people" that they would be able to escape via the desired marital union. In the context of her research on Victorian England, Nancy Anderson points out a common pattern in the bourgeois milieu in which unmarried women, who made up 40 per cent of those between 21 and 44 years of age, lived in the

---

141 According to the census of 1880, the highest share of unmarried women in this age group – at 50.1 per cent – was to be found in the District of Lienz, which lay in the eastern reaches of the Diocese of Brixen, and the lowest share – at 12.6 per cent – was to be found in the Italian District of Trento (which did not include the city itself); among the German-speaking districts, Vorarlberg's District of Feldkirch had the lowest share at 28.7 per cent. Cf. Mantl, *Heirat als Privileg*, pp. 45–46. Cf. also the high age-specific unmarried rates among 45-to-49-year-old men in some districts of the Alpine region, which Josef Ehmer has placed in a broader comparative context, Ehmer, *Heiratsverhalten*, pp. 86–88, 122.

household of a married sister and took care of the children upon the sister's death.[142]

The opposite pole of one's own sister – the children's aunt – who appeared as an ideal second mother[143] was the figure of the "strange" stepmother. Consistently portrayed in a negative light and synonymous with the "wicked" stepmother, she was described as a "possibly evil and barbaric", "hard", "raw", "odious", "careless" or "cruel" person under whose care the children, being treated in a "stepmotherly" – *stiefmütterlich* – fashion, would most certainly be deserving of pity. As the expression itself suggests, and as "experience teaches", one could expect nothing other than a "tense relationship".[144] The stepmother was even stylised as "a misfortune" from which the children had to be protected. In numerous cases, widowers, witnesses and priests emphasised that a "strange" stepmother could not be expected to ensure that the children would be well-raised and cared for.

Depictions of the step-mother only rarely refrained from deprecating vocabulary – and even then, they gave voice to an unambiguously defensive attitude. Martin Huber, a Dornbirn native who served as district captain in Schwaz and sought to marry his sister-in-law, stated the following in a very long self-penned letter of supplication: "Marriage to another female person is something that I would not view as advantageous for my children; they would, at any rate, receive only a stepmother, a fate from which my spouse, as she lay on her deathbed, wished to have them be protected." A similar formulation returns in their matrimonial examination.[145] In another request, it is written that a good stepmother is a "great and rare treasure".[146] Various cases also saw supplicants undergird the negative expectations of a stepmother with examples from their own experience.[147] In the request of the above-mentioned district captain in Schwaz, the bride Anna Maria Haagen stated the following: "The poor children would receive a stepmother, and I would pity them all the more since I was myself forced to experience the greatest possible bitterness of such. The children, whose godmother I also am, love me as their second

142 Anderson, "The Marriage", p. 73.

143 A motif that can also be found in literary portrayals; cf. Corbett, "Husband, Wife, and Sister", p. 278.

144 DIÖAB, Konsistorialakten 1845, Fasc. 5a, Römische Dispensen, no. 11; ibid., 1831, no. 6; ibid., 1847, no. 13; ibid., 1852, no. 26; ibid., 1850, no. 12; ibid., 1856, no. 45; ibid., 1859, no. 16; ibid., 1856, no. 45; ibid., 1841, no. 22; ibid., 1856, no. 33; ibid., 1859, no. 22; ibid., 1848, no. 12; ibid., 1844, no. 4; ibid., 1856, no. 45; ibid., 1856, no. 43; ibid., 1859, no. 20.

145 DIÖAB, Konsistorialakten 1859, Fasc. 5a, Römische Dispensen, no. 22.

146 DIÖAB, Konsistorialakten 1859, Fasc. 5a, Römische Dispensen, no. 13.

147 Cf. DIÖAB, Konsistorialakten 1837, Fasc. 5a, Römische Dispensen, no. 19; ibid., 1857, no. 17.

mother, and their well-being and upbringing are my heart's foremost concerns; furthermore, my father likewise desires this marital union in the interest of his grandchildren."[148]

A sister-in-law and aunt was hardly ever referred to as a "stepmother", meaning that her delineation from a "strange" person was also linguistic. Instead, the children received in her a "true mother" – or "a second mother", as it were. The arguments used to back up a sister-in-law's claim to special suitability in terms of the children's care and raising were also sometimes bolstered with explicit reference to their "common blood". In the Diocese of Brixen, traces of such argumentation can be found from the very beginning of the time period from which dispensation records were examined. An 1831 request, for example, indicates the groom's perception of the "children's natural affection" for their aunt as being a significant factor behind their particularly good relationship with one another.[149] However, references to this linkage grew more frequent – as did negative depictions of the "strange" stepmother – around the middle of the nineteenth century. Here, common blood served generally as a synonym for trustworthy familiarity and reliability.

It was with just such recourse that a parish priest, in a detailed letter accompanying the second, once again unsuccessful dispensation request of the widowed peasant Jakob Schobel, attempted to highlight the chosen bride Elisabeth Küng's special suitability for the groom: "The experiences had by others, as well, have convinced him that it is a mother's sister who strives to raise her sister's children in the least stepmotherly way possible. Even just due to blood."[150] In another case, a matrimonial examination witness assumed, in light of the reasons for dispensation, that "the groom seeks to marry this sister-in-law of his because he has three children by his first marriage and hence thinks a blood relative better and more suitable".[151] Bonds of blood were pointed to as guarantors of a relationship's quality and of good, reliable childcare. Moreover, this type of argumentation allows one to discern a process: the emotional bond between the sister-in-law and the widower's children leads via the image of common blood to the maternal role's naturalisation. This continues in the naturalisation of differences between the sexes,[152] in the attribution and

148 DIÖAB, Konsistorialakten 1859, Fasc. 5a, Römische Dispensen, no. 22.

149 DIÖAB, Konsistorialakten 1831, Fasc. 5a, Römische Dispensen, no. 2.

150 DIÖAB, Konsistorialakten 1856, Fasc. 5a, Römische Dispensen, no. 13.

151 DIÖAB, Konsistorialakten 1858, Fasc. 5a, Römische Dispensen, no. 38.

152 In the construction of social, ethnic and gender distinctions in the nineteenth century, Joanna de Groot perceives different sides of a process: sociological studies conducted at that time, she writes, emphasised class differences while biological, anthropological and medical theories pertaining to "race and sex", for their part, set up differences on

inscription on the body of 'natural' characteristics and abilities of women and men as well as 'natural' endeavours and responsibilities derived from them.[153]

Considering stepmothers' presence in everyday life, it is striking how little attention historical research has paid this apparently ambivalent figure.[154] It was in comedies, tragedies and novels that stepmothers were featured most prominently – and the discursive shift in this figure's nineteenth-century image can be retraced by taking a closer look at the stepmother's role as a stock character in fairy tales, a character that would appear to have only become truly classic as the nineteenth century progressed. A comparison of various versions of the fairy tales authored by the Brothers Grimm turned up some notable findings in this regard.[155] One highly conspicuous phenomenon here is that the stepmother's appearance or characterisation as an evil figure only ever took place in the later versions. She is still entirely absent, for instance, from the 1819 version of the fairy tale *The Riddle* (*Das Rätsel*); in the version of 1857, however, it was she who touched off the "fateful plot"[156] by replacing the parents as the one who gave the prince a poisonous drink. In the 1815 version of *The White Bride and the Black One* (*Die weiße und die schwarze Braut*), the stepmother replaced the foster mother who had featured in the 1810 version. This newly cast figure initially seems rather neutrally connoted, but over the course of the story she reveals herself to be a witch.[157] In the initial version of *Hansel and Gretel* (*Hänsel und Gretel*), published in 1810, it was the mother who had wanted her children out of the house and therefore sent them into

a physical basis that were viewed as "inevitable". Cf. Joanna de Groot, "'Sex' and 'Race': the Construction of Language and Image in the Nineteenth Century", in *Sexuality and Subordination. Interdisciplinary Studies of Gender in the Nineteenth Century*, ed. Susan Mendus and Jane Rendall (London/New York, 1989), pp. 89–128, 92–93; on this cf. also Martin Zwilling, "Mutterstämme – Die Biologisierung des genealogischen Denkens und die Stellung der Frau in Familie und Gesellschaft von 1900 bis zur NS-Zeit", *Tel Aviver Jahrbuch für deutsche Geschichte* 34 (2008), 29–47; on concepts of motherhood see Julia Heinemann, *Verwandtsein und Herrschen. Die Königinmutter Catherine de Médicis und ihre Kinder in Briefen, 1560–1589* (Heidelberg, 2020).

153 Cf. Hausen, "Family and Role-Division"; Brigitte Studer, "Familialisierung und Individualisierung. Zur Struktur der Geschlechterordnung in der bürgerlichen Gesellschaft", *L'Homme. Z.F.G.* 11, 1 (2000), 83–104, 88–93.

154 Notable exceptions include Perrier, "La marâtre", as well as the article focusing on visual depictions authored by Warner, "Remembering the Mother, Presenting the Stepmother" and more recently Lyndan Warner (ed.), *Stepfamilies in Europe, 1400–1800* (Abingdon/New York, 2018).

155 Cf. Ursula Wodiczka, *Das Motiv der Stiefmutter in den Kinder- und Hausmärchen der Brüder Grimm*, diploma thesis, University of Vienna, 1992.

156 Wodiczka, *Das Motiv der Stiefmutter*, p. 32.

157 Cf. ibid, pp. 43–44.

the dark forest with nary a chance of return. The mother was initially replaced by a character referred to simply as "the woman" in the version that followed, after which this evil role ultimately passed to the stepmother in the version that is widely known today.[158] A similar change of motifs can be seen in *Snow White* (*Schneewittchen*): originally, the mother had not died but rather herself committed "those atrocities" that were "attributed to the stepmother" in the versions from 1819 onward.[159]

In cases where the figure of the stepmother had already been present in a fairy tale's initial version, her wickedness proceeded to grow ever greater – such as in *The Three Little Men in the Wood* of 1812, 1819 and 1857[160] – or various characters' evil qualities were shifted more strongly to the stepmother, as was the case in *Cinderella*. This fairy tale's 1812 version – in contrast to later versions published from 1819 onward – had featured the stepsisters as the wicked ones.[161] Hand in hand with the attribution of negative qualities to the stepmother went the idealisation of the mother, in that wickedness was evidently viewed as incompatible with her position and hence removed from her as a character. Even if the "channels of transport" between the horrible stepmother images constructed in Grimm's fairy tales and the statements in dispensation requests cannot be discerned in a concrete way, one can ascertain certain parallels in the chronology of these phenomena. Though it was prior to the nineteenth century that the character of the wicked stepmother had first taken the stage, the role accorded to her before the backdrop of familial relationships' intimisation and naturalisation as a period-specific texture does need to be re-evaluated.

A further feature held in common by Grimm's fairy tales and the dispensation records is the virtual absence of wicked stepfathers.[162] The term "stepfather" itself hardly ever appears in the requests – and when it does, the tone is neutral. The stepfather's position was consistently associated with positive expectations in terms of support in childrearing. In addition, the advantage of a brother-in-law and thus an uncle of the children vis-à-vis another groom was defined strongly in terms of property and wealth, whose upholding and securing was viewed as thus being guaranteed.[163] At the same time, work also

158 Ibid, p. 87.
159 Ibid, p. 93.
160 Cf. ibid., p. 53.
161 Cf. ibid., p. 58, 60.
162 Cf. ibid., p. 102.
163 In one of the most protracted cases of the late 1850s, it was ultimately a promise by the uncle to financially support the business that his then 17-year-old nephew would someday inherit that turned matters decisively in the couple's favour. This promise alone,

played an important role – not only in the sense of the stepfather's investment of his labour but also frequently in the sense of his ability to provide related occupational socialisation. An additional factor, insofar as one or both parents of the deceased husband were still alive and resided beneath the same roof, was a moral claim of sorts on their part to one of their sons being permitted to take the place of the deceased. This was associated with the hope that their sustenance in old age would be guaranteed. If the single brother-in-law's inheritance was still part of the property, marriage to the widow of his brother simultaneously served to ease financial burdens. While the expectations projected upon sisters- and brothers-in-law related to everyday life in differing ways, they all carried exceedingly positive connotations. However, the image of the "strange" and wicked stepmother demonstrates how demarcational stereotypes were employed in a purely one-sided manner even though the father's role – in a way similar to that of the mother – had indeed been a subject of renewed debate from the eighteenth century.[164]

5 "Scandalous Cohabitation"

The lion's share of marriage projects between brothers- and sisters-in-law arose within a context of proximity that was not just social but also spatial in nature. Such couples' submission of a dispensation request frequently concluded a phase of mutual householding that had gone on for years. Such matches made 'beneath the same roof' were based on mutual familiarity and would indeed appear quite logical when viewed from the standpoint of everyday life. Nonetheless, they could easily end up in conflict with prevailing notions of moral order. Even just the fact that dispensation requests had to pass through various ecclesiastical and civil administrative entities – a process that directly or indirectly involved a number of institutions and protagonists who were supposed to and indeed did function as representatives of regulatory

---

however, was insufficient: the uncle-as-groom was then made to submit a legally binding declaration to this effect in court. DIÖAB, Konsistorialakten 1856, Fasc. 5a, Römische Dispensen, no. 35; ibid., 1859, no. 1. On this cf. also Margareth Lanzinger, "'Liebe, Neigung, leider Leidenschaft war es ...'. Kirchliche Heiratsverbote im Spannungsfeld zwischen Ökonomie, Moral und Inzest – eine Fallgeschichte", in *Liebe und Widerstand*, ed. Bauer/Hämmerle/Hauch, pp. 257–273.

164 Cf. Joanne Bailey, "Paternal Power: the Pleasures and Perils of 'Indulgent' Fathering in Britain in the Long Eighteenth Century", *The History of the Family* 17, 3 (2012), 326–342; Claudia Opitz, "Wandel der Vaterrolle in der Aufklärung?", in Opitz, *Aufklärung der Geschlechter, Revolution der Geschlechterordnung. Studien zur Politik- und Kulturgeschichte des 18. Jahrhunderts* (Münster et al., 2002), pp. 21–38.

policies – entailed that a complex structure of surveillance and control was constantly present. Within this context, order was thought of primarily in connection with moral parameters. A marriage would put an end to all suspicion and to the oft-mentioned "public scandal" – but the dispensation needed to accomplish this was by no means always obtainable. Especially for those who were family socially but not legally, being refused a dispensation was a serious problem. After all, the laws in force mandated that this life context be dissolved as a consequence. For this reason, every dispensation request in such a configuration entailed considerable risk.

Particularly in contexts where regulatory policies were in play, we cannot assume a dyadic positioning of ruler and ruled – of institutions and representatives who sought to enforce order vis-à-vis those who were affected by this enforcement. The fabric here was actually more dense. Local clergy, who assumed a central role in conveying the desires and interests of couples who required dispensation, were themselves part of a hierarchy and had to fulfil the obligations of their offices. These obligations included attempting to fend off marriage projects in the close degrees. At the same time, they were also responsible for preventing and/or putting the quickest possible end to "scandalous cohabitation" of unmarried couples who lived in areas these local clerics were responsible for and manifested "disorderly affection" for one another. They were therefore subject to multiple types of pressure, pressure that could be traced back up through the deaneries and diocesan consistories and all the way to Rome. Objections and rebukes travelled in the opposite direction. Local priests frequently exhibited understanding when approached by those desiring a dispensation, even in cases where the bride was pregnant or the couple had already produced children and their lives hence in no way conformed to the Church's moral ideals. Repeatedly, though not in every case, they supported such desires with vigour – while the tendency of higher-ranking clerics in far-off diocesan consistories was to order drastic measures.

The dispensation requests make more than clear how kin represented a significant resource for people who found themselves in difficult familial situations, especially in the wake of deaths that had removed wives and husbands, mothers and fathers from their lives in one fell swoop. However, a circular sent out in 1830 by the diocesan consistory in Brixen decried the resulting tendency to call upon them as "abusive". It would not do, wrote the consistory, "that widowers and widows simply reach for the next-closest relative for help in their household economy following the deaths of their spouses". This, they held, did not deserve to be encouraged and could best be "remedied" by "creating examples" that would "most wholesomely remove" any hopes of marriage that they might have.[165] The deanery offices were told to instruct parish priests to "be watchful of young widowers and impress upon them that they should not take the sister of the deceased or a close relative into their homes (*et vice versa*) on account of the various dangers and difficulties that experience has shown us result therefrom".[166] Passages taken from these instructions were to appear repeatedly in correspondence during the years that followed.[167]

Not only legally and morally motivated positions but also value judgements in relation to a specific situation determined how "scandalous cohabitation" was dealt with. The widower Georg Höllbock, a shoemaker from Höchst in the Deanery of Dornbirn in Vorarlberg who was 27 years old and the father of four small children, desired to marry his sister-in-law Maria Anna Nagel in 1831. In their matrimonial examination, the groom's testimony included the following: "a) Since my first wife, Catharina Nagel, took ill two years ago with such a peculiar attack that it was as if she had lost her mind, I had to turn over my entire household as well as entrust the raising of my still small children to my sister-in-law, who had already been sharing the table of myself and her sister, because no other person desired to care for this disturbed person at any price. b) Following the death of my wife on 14 September of last year, my sister-in-law continued caring for the household and raising my children since they had grown accustomed to her and come to look upon her as their own mother, and she also employed c) her wealth, though small, to the benefit of my household,[168] for which reasons d) she would be completely devastated were I forced to remove her." Somewhat further along in the text, it is mentioned that Höllbock practised his profession as a shoemaker largely outside the home, which made his need of someone to take care of his children all the more urgent.

165 DIÖAB, Konsistorialakten 1832, Fasc. 5a, Römische Dispensen, no. 11.

166 DIÖAB, Protokoll 1830, no. 391, 9 February 1830.

167 Such passages spoke of how it was widely known that *angustia loci* was insufficient in these sorts of cases, and that "the abuse in which Bregenz Forest widowers and widows, following the deaths of their spouses, simply take their closest relatives into their homes to help with their household economies at the very least deserves no encouragement and can best be put to an end by creating examples in light of which the hope of marrying them is most wholesomely removed". DIÖAB, Konsistorialakten 1832, Fasc. 5a, Römische Dispensen, no. 11.

168 In a report sent by the regional court in Dornbirn to the district office in Bregenz, it is said that Maria Anna Nagel possessed "a not insignificant fortune" that would "significantly improve conditions in the household of the widower Joh[ann] Georg Helbock, who is burdened with several children who are still very small". VLA Bregenz, Kreisamt 1, box 48, Domäne, Ehe, Fond, no. 2.386.

The order of the house, here, clashed with the morally defined order as soon as – to quote the widower Leopold Rissinger – "the former love between kin" turned "into sexual affection".[169] The dispensation request of Anna Maria Nagel and Georg Höllbock was subsequently rejected by the consistory in Brixen. The competent local priest wrote that the two were "extremely disconcerted and saddened" at this rejection. He described the consequences in highly dramatic terms and requested that the deanery make a renewed attempt to obtain a dispensation, since great "despair and defection from the true faith" threatened to ensue.[170] Anna Maria Nagel emphasised that her sister, prior to her death, had requested with great urgency that she see to the children's care. This time, it was indicated that a dispensation could indeed be had, though formidable financial obstacles still had to be overcome.[171]

There was a fine line between the respectability of a household that kept itself above water during a difficult period with help from a sister-in-law or other relative and incipient suspicion or even denunciation and "public scandal", entailing situations that were fragile. Anna Maria Bickel, following the death of her sister, had assumed responsibility for the household of her brother-in-law Konrad Amor, a huckster with five children of whom some were still quite young. "Mutual passion", it was said, soon had them "in its grasp". They wanted to marry, but their request for a dispensation was refused and they were subsequently separated multiple times by court order.[172] Though a targeted search for this type of documentation in cases with similar indications of court action turned up nothing, several pertinent pieces of written matter were indeed found concerning this couple. To be sure, they document 'only' one of the attempts that were made to remove Anna Maria Bickel from the house. But they do indeed reveal the complex web of information flows, illustrating the significance of this couple's social environment, which included representatives of the municipality as well as the clergymen who served as intermediaries in the couple's interactions with 'higher' authorities. Such protagonists' moderate reactions and willingness to provide support could tip

169 DIÖAB, Konsistorialakten 1859, Fasc. 5a, Römische Dispensen, no. 5.

170 DIÖAB, Konsistorialakten 1831, Fasc. 5a, Römische Dispensen, no. 6.

171 For this dispensation, the enormous sum of 300 gulden had to be deposited in advance. Georg Höllbock was able to scrape together only 60 gulden, whereupon the consistory in Brixen rejected his request "once and for all", although even the parish priest had offered to contribute 40 gulden of his own. The vicariate general in Feldkirch then raised the spectre of possible "crude public vilification" in the nearby Swiss newspaper *Appenzeller Zeitung* if this marriage were to be prevented from taking place for no reason save for a lack of money. The Roman authorities then granted a reduction of the fees by half and ultimately also waived the still-missing 50 gulden out of "special mercy".

172 DIÖAB, Konsistorialakten 1833, Fasc. 5a, Römische Dispensen, no. 9.

the scales in favour of a positive outcome. In this case, however, we must also take into account the somewhat more distant position of Vorarlberg's deans vis-à-vis the consistory in Brixen, particularly in this initial generation of clergy following the region's integration into the diocese.

In October 1827, the Vorarlberg district office informed the regional and criminal court in Bregenz that the dispensation request of Konrad Amor and Maria Anna Bickel had been rejected by the ordinariate in Brixen and called upon the court to "take official action".[173] After all, their request's rejection triggered a concubinage paragraph that had been introduced in 1807 and was now to be applied in such cases in Vorarlberg, as well.[174] The lawgiver argued as follows: "Since it has occurred that such consanguineous or affinally related parties who had wished to marry one another and been present together in the same dwelling were turned away everywhere with their request to obtain a church marriage dispensation and, despite this, continued living together as before, thereby not only causing sensation and scandal among others who knew about their marriage plans but also permitting the emergence of other vile consequences while going unpunished and unseparated by the authorities whose official duty it is to watch over good order and decency; His Majesty has therefore ordained: that henceforth, in such cases, the cohabiting parties shall immediately be separated from one another as soon as their dispensation and marriage requests have been rejected and shall be forbidden most strictly from engaging in any closer interactions with each other that could raise even the slightest suspicion, and His Majesty has furthermore ordained that the appropriate entities, authorities and pastors shall be made responsible for the timely execution of the supreme volition expressed herewith."[175] This provision also found its way into the Austrian Civil Code of 1811.[176]

It appears that Konrad Amor and Maria Anna Bickel immediately submitted a second dispensation request – and on 25 December 1827, news came from the district office that their "renewed marriage dispensation request" had been "rejected once and for all". This note concluded with a reference to

173 VLA Bregenz, Landgericht Bregenz, box 117: Ehe, Ein- und Auswanderung 1828–1829, Fasc. 10, 1827, no. 2.909/248. The corresponding letter from the vicariate general can be found in VLA Bregenz, Kreisamt 1, box 71, Geistlich 1827, no. 647.

174 Cf. ÖSTA, AVA, Alter Cultus, K. 1, Ehesachen und Taufen, 1807–1834, no. 13.142/1.084, ADF, GA, Ehesachen I, 1820–1850, Fasc. 1821, 2/25, no. 4.902/335 and no. 598, note dated 7 October 1821.

175 Court Chancellery decree of 9 July 1807, *Franz des Ersten politische Gesetze und Verordnungen für die Oesterreichischen, Böhmischen und Galizischen Erbländer*, vol. 29, part 2 (Vienna, 1809), pp. 16–17, no. 6.

176 *ABGB*, Erster Theil, Zweites Hauptstück. §§ 83 and 84, sect. 7.

the regulation cited above.[177] But even so, the couple refused to give up. In July 1828, the district office notified them that they had once again been turned down by the prince-episcopal ordinariate in Brixen, which had furthermore stated that it would refuse to consider any further requests that they might attempt to submit. The passage mentioning suitable "official action", which meant separation, was likewise present here.[178] A letter sent later on by the mayor to the imperial-royal provincial and criminal court indicates that in July 1828, the court had indeed been ordered to notify Maria Anna Bickel that she was to vacate the house of Konrad Amor within three days. Konrad Amor, continues the letter, had declared himself willing to comply, though not in the prescribed form. His suggestion had been for his sister-in-law to no longer stay in the house at night but be permitted to continue caring for his children and household during the daytime because he had nobody else and was frequently absent for days due to his work. The mayor had consulted with the city parish priest of Bregenz, who had indicated his agreement with this solution.[179] And with that, the local authorities were satisfied.

A renewed attempt to obtain a dispensation once again failed, to which effect the district office of Vorarlberg duly notified the provincial and criminal court in May 1829.[180] The next piece of writing in the records of the provincial court is dated December 1832. In the wake of a district office decree, the mayor and a municipal committee member had been summoned before the court – evidently in order to submit an updated report on this couple, who had been so luckless as far as a dispensation was concerned. "This matter of marriage has dragged on for four years already", they stated, mentioning the multiple, repeatedly rejected requests. All this had by now left Konrad Amor nearly bankrupt, so that he was also unable to sustain his meagre business. A "great scandal" had arisen in the community, they said, since he and his sister-in-law had also produced three children of their own by that point. They went on to state that "the entire community now wishes" – and had always wished – that he receive this dispensation. They emphasised the virtues and special suitability of the bride and went on to describe a dark scenario that appears again and again in such requests. If the marriage were not able to go forward, they held,

177 VLA Bregenz, Landgericht Bregenz, box 117: Ehe, Ein- und Auswanderung 1828–1829, Fasc. 10, 1828, no. 3/248. The letter from the vicariate general in Feldkirch can be found in VLA Bregenz, Kreisamt 1, box 71, Geistlich 1827, no. 755.

178 VLA Bregenz, Landgericht Bregenz, box 117: Ehe, Ein- und Auswanderung 1828–1829, Fasc. 10, 1828, no. 2.156/248.

179 Cf. ibid., no. 2.273/248.

180 Cf. ibid., 1829, no. 1898/248. The corresponding letter from Brixen can be found in VLA Bregenz, Kreisamt 1, box 76, Geistlich 1829, no. 3.073.

"Konrad Amor's entire family will be reduced to begging". They concluded by requesting in the name of the municipality that the two finally be granted their dispensation, additionally noting that they were "reputable, industrious, responsible members of the community of whom, save for their conception of three illegitimate children, nothing ill can be spoken".[181]

As early as October of that year, the competent dean Joseph Stadelmann sent the consistory in Brixen a newly protocolled matrimonial examination together with a "certificate" from the mayor's office – with its signatures even certified by the regional court – and an evaluation by the parish office in Bregenz. His accompanying letter was extremely long and detailed. He pulled out all the stops, reporting on events including multiple court-ordered separations. He wrote: "These persons were indeed separated from one another several times; this, however, served only to further inflame their inappropriate affection, and they raised – in part justified – complaints and wailed most penetratingly in the face of every separation, on account of which such separation came to be viewed as an act of shocking cruelty. – The authorities grew tired", he ascertained, concluding: "Why, then, does one not dispense for him?".[182] Financially, Konrad Amor was capable neither of supporting the three small children whom he had had together with his sister-in-law outside of his household nor of employing a maidservant to do the work that his sister-in-law had done. And for that matter, his debts would have long since entailed the loss of his house, had his sister-in-law not held the property together.

The decisive factor that ultimately turned things in their favour was probably the fact that the dean did not exclude the possibility that Konrad Amor might commit suicide or convert to Protestantism – as an act of despair. He was said to be reading the Bible, keeping his distance from other faithful and nursing "within himself a greater and greater aversion" to the Church, in which he – unlike the wealthy and esteemed – found "no motherly pity, no rescue". In order to keep his portrayal of Amor positive nonetheless, Joseph Stadelmann ascribed these "attitudes" to the influence of "bad people" and Amor's forlorn state. He did not neglect to emphasise that in his function as dean he was "of course otherwise entirely averse to dispensations", but he said that in this case, granting one could "still fully rescue" those concerned. Furthermore, "many hundreds of right-thinking people" wished that they be permitted to marry. And finally, the "scandal" that could be kept neither from "the eyes of the youth" nor from those of "the neighbouring Lutherans in Lindau" was also not left unmentioned.

181 VLA Bregenz, Kreisamt 1, box 76, Geistlich 1832, no. 6.865.

182 DIÖAB, Konsistorialakten 1833, Fasc. 5a, Römische Dispensen, no. 9.

The dean's letter was dramaturgically structured. It employed public opinion,[183] his own people's simultaneous lack of understanding and understanding, and observations by adherents of a confession that was portrayed as a competitor. It contained the necessary reason for dispensation of the threat of conversion, and it skilfully compensated for everything that could be construed as negative with justifications and adaptations. Joseph Stadelmann concluded by pointing out once more that kinfolk had already gathered together the 250 gulden in agency fees that would have to be deposited in advance. All this ultimately succeeded in spurring action on this matter, and after five years of uncertainty plus constant threats to their de facto family life, this couple received their dispensation in April of 1833. That same month, Konrad Amor appeared personally at the district office of Bregenz to request a dispensation regarding the banns of marriage so that the wedding would not need to be delayed until after Easter week.[184]

The legal requirement that half of a couple had to leave the household in the wake of an unsuccessful dispensation request posed a huge difficulty in terms of the organisation of work and frequently also in terms of economic aspects, not to mention socially and emotionally. Civil authorities were responsible for effecting such separation if a couple did not separate voluntarily. Removal from the house by force as well as prison sentences could be the result. Local priests frequently complained about such procedures by civil administrative bodies, which they viewed as being insufficiently efficacious, and demanded that they intervene more energetically – after all, "locking people up for several hours" was clearly of little use.[185] However, it was by no means everyone who advocated merciless stringency. Repeated requests for instructions on how to proceed much rather suggest incertitude and ambivalence. In cases where jail time had been imposed, it did not last long, and the woman who had been removed from her brother-in-law's house would return – with the couple having to be separated once more. Courts were for the most part loathe to take such typically ineffective steps, and competent local clerics who insisted had

---

183 Daniela Lombardi has ascertained that in early modern Florence, the tolerance shown by priests was geared toward the tolerance exhibited by the general populace: as long as the latter did not perceive unmarried cohabitation by a couple as scandalous, something that usually only came to pass if and when other bones of contention entered the picture, local clerics did nothing to prevent it. While this assumption may well not be generally transferable to the nineteenth century, it likely did very much hold true in this or that case. Daniela Lombardi, "Giustizia ecclesiastica e composizione dei conflitti matrimoniali (Firenze, secoli XVI–XVIII)", in *I tribunali del matrimonio* (*secoli XV–XVIII*), ed. Silvana Seidel Menchi and Diego Quaglioni (Bologna, 2001), pp. 577–607, 586.

184 Cf. VLA Bregenz, Kreisamt 1, box 76, Geistlich 1833, no. 837.

185 DIÖAB, Konsistorialakten 1840, Fasc. 5a, Römische Dispensen, no. 9.

to fear "becoming objects of hate". For this reason, cohabitation most likely was indeed tolerated in some cases.[186]

Submitting a dispensation request in the close degrees, particularly where affinity was concerned and especially in times when outcomes were extremely uncertain, endangered the established life contexts of bridal couples who already lived beneath the same roof. The fact that numerous couples submitted renewed dispensation requests even after years allows us to infer that a rejected dispensation request often did not mean the end of a couple's relationship. Just how high the share of those who ended up seeking out another spouse was is something that would have to be researched separately on the basis of marriage registers.

6 Property and Wealth – Conflict and Conciliation

Historical kinship studies devote considerable attention to the extent to which marriages were made based on property and wealth-related interests. In marital unions that were economically advantageous in terms of retaining property or acquiring wealth, often not only a given couple's social position but also further-reaching interests of family and kin were in play – especially in social milieus and regional contexts where "family property" represented an important category of thought and value.[187]

Johann Kutschker quotes an official instruction issued to the clergy of the Diocese of Olmütz in 1823, which holds that "wherever several requests for marriage dispensations in the first degree of affinity are submitted, the suspicion arises that preserving wealth undivided is often the hidden motive behind such marriages, a motive that [should] not have any place among the causes for dispensation".[188] Wealth-related interests are implied here as a structural context surrounding affinal marriage projects. Such interests were variously situated depending on what sorts of inheritance practices prevailed and on whether a dowry system, separation of marital property or community of marital property was the norm. The structurally defined fields of conflict

186 Regarding Anna Maria Bickel and Konrad Amor, it is documented that the priest who took over the parish, having been informed of the "hopelessness of receiving a dispensation" and of the fruitless admonishments and equally fruitless jailings, more or less obtained approval of his tolerance of this cohabitation from the consistory. Two years later, however, it did prove possible to obtain a dispensation after all. DIÖAB, Konsistorialakten 1840, Fasc. 5a, Römische Dispensen, no. 9.

187 Cf. Joris, "Kinship and Gender"; Sabean, "Kinship and Class Dynamics".

188 Kutschker, *Das Eherecht der katholischen Kirche*, vol. 5, p. 114.

and axes of competition between the genders and the generations differed accordingly. In both early modern and nineteenth-century Tyrol, separation of marital property prevailed. In Vorarlberg, on the other hand, with several areas where community of property was typical, the legal situation was not quite so clear-cut.[189]

As research has shown, wealth-related arrangements in Tyrol were determined by a strong orientation towards lineage.[190] The transfer of both real estate and money was to adhere as closely as possible to the vertical axis between ancestors and descendants, between parents and children. Separation of goods as a marital property regime had a similar effect. It protected the wealth-related interests of the couple's respective blood relatives especially in the event of childlessness by viewing each group of relatives as entitled to inherit rather than the surviving spouse.[191] If a marriage contract or will favoured a spouse to the relatives' disadvantage, resentment and dispute could be the result.[192] Community of goods, on the other hand, could – in extreme

---

189 For a general impression cf. Wilhelm Brauneder, *Die Entwicklung des Ehegüterrechts in Österreich. Ein Beitrag zur Dogmengeschichte und Rechtstatsachenforschung des Spätmittelalters und der Neuzeit* (Salzburg/Munich, 1973). Regarding the territory of present-day Austria during the nineteenth and early twentieth centuries in particular, Michael Pammer conducted a sample survey. He found that early modern marital property practice persisted in agrarian contexts. Specifically, his analysis of deceased persons' estates showed that 83 per cent of farmers in Lower Austria had agreed to community of property, while this figure was 70 per cent in Upper Austria, 56 per cent in Styria, slightly less than 31 per cent in Salzburg and 25 per cent in Vorarlberg; in this last case, five out of 25 per cent involved agreements that established community of property between siblings. In Carinthia, on the other hand, no such cases appeared in the sample – and in North Tyrol, they amounted to just 1.1 per cent. Michael Pammer, *Entwicklung und Ungleichheit. Österreich im 19. Jahrhundert* (Stuttgart, 2002), p. 77.

190 Cf. Lanzinger, "Von der Macht der Linie zur Gegenseitigkeit"; Margareth Lanzinger, "Paternal Authority and Patrilineal Power: Stem Family Arrangements in Peasant Communities and Eighteenth-Century Tyrolean Marriage Contracts", in *The Power of the Fathers. Historical Perspectives from Ancient Rome to the Nineteenth Century*, ed. Lanzinger (London/New York, 2015), pp. 65–89.

191 Community of goods, on the other hand, benefited the surviving spouse. A combination of both marital property regimes, referred to as community of accrued gains, entailed that wealth acquired prior to marriage remained separate while wealth gained during marriage was evenly divided between the two spouses. On the various models in law and in actual practice cf. Lanzinger/Barth-Scalmani/Forster/Langer-Ostrawsky, *Aushandeln von Ehe*; Margareth Lanzinger et al. (eds.), *Negotiations of Gender and Property through Legal Regimes (14th–19th Century): Stipulating, Litigating, Mediating* (Leiden/Boston, 2021).

192 On this cf. also Margareth Lanzinger, "Tanten, Schwägerinnen und Nichten – Beziehungsgefüge, Vermögenskonflikte und 'Reparaturehen' oder: Linie und Paar in Konkurrenz", *WerkstattGeschichte* 10, 46 (2007), 41–54.

cases, even despite the presence of children – lead to veritable chains of remarriages in which property went through multiple horizontal transfers.[193] In the context of separation of goods, this represented a near-unthinkable practice. Whether or not it was typical in a society for monetary wealth or real estate ownership to jump between lines of descent was something that played a major role in structuring relationships both between the genders and the generations. The systematic interrelation of kinship and marital property logics has so far been neglected in the relevant research. This section therefore aims to highlight various ways in which the favouring of lineage and marriage projects between close affinal kin may have been associated. An argumentative framework here was offered by the officially recognised reason for dispensation of *bonum pacis*, the advantage of peace.

A frequently seen configuration among remarriages between close affinal kin that interlocked quite closely with social and economic considerations was one in which a widowed man or woman lived together in the same household with his or her parents-in-law. If the widower or widow were to enter into a new marriage and bring a "strange" person into the home, there would cease to be a blood relationship between the two generations. Furthermore, generational succession would be interrupted if the previous marriage with an inheriting daughter or son had remained childless or the child or children had died. But if the surviving spouse's choice were to fall on a relative of the deceased spouse, this person could function as a connecting link to the generation of the parents-in-law. Their expectation that they would be treated more considerately by a blood relative and better cared for and looked after in old age or in the event of illness played just as much of a role in dispensation-related argumentation as did the trust placed in relatives regarding one's general sustenance in old age. Above all, if there existed unmarried sisters of the deceased inheriting daughter or unmarried brothers of the deceased inheriting son, the desire on the part of the parents' generation that the closest possible relative of the deceased be chosen was all the stronger. Dispensation requests in such configurations pointed insistently to the preservation of domestic peace, which would thereby best be served: "Domestic peace" would be "entirely

193 For a detailed look at this cf. Gertrude Langer-Ostrawsky, "Vom Verheiraten der Güter. Bäuerliche und kleinbäuerliche Heiratsverträge im Erzherzogtum Österreich unter der Enns", in Lanzinger/Barth-Scalmani/Forster/Langer-Ostrawsky, *Aushandeln von Ehe Aushandeln von Ehe*, pp. 27–76, as well as the chains of remarriages in Schlumbohm, *Lebensläufe, Familien, Höfe*, pp. 475–479; on the conflict potential inherent in horizontal transfers of ownership cf. also Hohkamp, *Herrschaft in der Herrschaft*, pp. 165–172; Iida, "Wiederheiraten und Verwandtschaftsnetze".

disrupted", complained the father-in-law in the dispensation request of Lucius Juen from Galtür, if his son-in-law were to "wed a stranger".[194]

Whether and to what extent the older generation applied targeted pressure in such cases can be inferred but rarely from the extant documents. Sigmund Stainer of Silz, who owned a sizeable property and was an apprentice clerk at the regional court, told a priest attached to his parish – according to a letter from the dean in Imst – that he was requesting a dispensation to marry his sister-in-law primarily "because he was being pushed to do so by the other side, namely by his father-in-law, etc.". The dean counterbalanced this revelation with reassuring words in defence of the groom's father-in-law, who was the regional court judge.[195]

Often, rights of ownership figured into such constellations, as it was in the case of the 25-year-old widower Franz Joseph Mayer from Frastanz. Mayer had purchased – but hardly begun paying for – half a house from the father of his now-deceased wife Katharina Juz, and his father-in-law still owned the other half. In order to pay off his debts, Mayer would have had to work mainly at the local spinning mill and neglect his farming activities, which would have been detrimental to the property. The father-in-law had six unmarried daughters, so that the situation could have been defused by marrying a sister-in-law. To this end, Franz Joseph Mayer sought a dispensation – but his request was denied.[196]

Alongside joint ownership and rights of residence, financial dependencies were another major factor that resulted in complex situations. It was above all debts that could be shifted "inward" to the realm of close kin by marrying a sister- or brother-in-law, which would ideally cause them to disappear upon the collateral's inheritance. After all, any children together with the new

---

194 DIÖAB, Konsistorialakten 1838, Fasc. 5a, Römische Dispensen, no. 4. In another such case, Franz Josef Vonach from Lauterach, a butcher and innkeeper, widower and father to one child, lived together with his parents-in-law – whom he described as "moody" and as "very curious people" – and with his intended bride in the same house, separated by floors. It could be foreseen "with complete certainty" that it would "do no good" for a "strange person" to marry into the house, his dispensation request states. In no case could one expect "that domestic peace could be preserved". DIÖAB, Konsistorialakten 1850, Fasc. 5a, Römische Dispensen, no. 11.

195 DIÖAB, Konsistorialakten 1849, Fasc. 5a, Römische Dispensen, no. 12.

196 DIÖAB, Konsistorialakten 1834, Fasc. 5a, Römische Dispensen, no. 14. Cases of similar character can be found repeatedly in the dispensation records; cf. for example DIÖAB, Konsistorialakten 1842, Fasc. 5a, Römische Dispensen, no. 31: in this request, the widower argued that he had purchased one half of the house from his deceased wife's sister – who was now his prospective bride – and that the stepmother and a further sister had rights of residence in his section of the house.

spouse would have equal claims to inheritance from their father and mother, inheritance that would thereby be combined and have the effect of balancing out debts within the marriage. The dispensation records for example contain several affinal marriage projects in which the new spouse was simultaneously the widow or widower's largest creditor.[197] Where such configurations are concerned, it must be kept in mind that the economic angle may have been viewed as being too obvious, with its revelation entailing a certain risk that the necessary dispensation might be refused – so that this motivation was sometimes only made explicit on the second attempt or may, in some cases, have still remained concealed.

This also applied to large transfers of wealth. The widower Josef Fuchs had been willed the entire fortune – 4,000 gulden – of his deceased wife Anna Maria Huber, who died without having borne children. Had she not left behind a will, her cousin Anna Maria Sonnweber – as her next of kin – would have been designated as her "universal heiress". The widower and his deceased wife's cousin subsequently applied for a dispensation. As the competent chaplain reported in his letter to the diocesan consistory, "the conclusion of this marriage" would mean that "this wealth would at least in large part go to its heir-at-law". For the groom had declared that he would "immediately" sign over 1,500 gulden to her, should their dispensation request go through.[198] A similar story lay behind the marriage project of the widower Hermann Spieler, who was mayor of Hohenems, a factory owner, and the father of two daughters aged ten and eleven, and Anna Maria Rhomberg, a niece of his deceased wife. As the bride explained in the final point of the justification of her planned marriage that she presented at the matrimonial examination, her "cousin, namely the deceased wife" of her prospective groom, had "favoured him exceptionally in

---

197 Anna Tempele was in her early 40s when she became a widow, at which point she had five children aged between nine and 18. Her husband had transferred to her his trade license for the inn that they ran, but this inn was heavily encumbered by debt – as was everything else that they owned. She ended up marrying a widowed cousin of her deceased husband, the 57-year-old mayor, haulier and farmer Josef Jäger, who was her largest creditor. Cf. DIÖAB, Konsistorialakten 1856, Fasc. 5a, Römische Dispensen, no. 7. The widower Josef Senn, postmaster and owner of a large property, likewise faced financial difficulties. His three children, between the ages of two and six, had inherited a property from their mother that was encumbered with considerable debts amounting to a total of 8,000 gulden. This sum, as well as a further 1,000 gulden, was owed by the children to Karolina Flir, the sister of their deceased mother. The widower found himself capable neither of paying his children's debts nor of paying the interest that was due his sister-in-law. A marriage between the two therefore looked like the ideal solution. Cf. DIÖAB, Konsistorialakten 1855, Fasc. 5a, Römische Dispensen, no. 18.

198 DIÖAB, Konsistorialakten 1859, Fasc. 5a, Römische Dispensen, no. 9.

her will", which had caused "great hostility", which continued to persist. Her conclusion: "Through this, our marriage, the former peace that once existed so harmoniously between both families will be restored in full".[199]

One legal innovation that contradicted the logic of both kinship and separation of marital property, namely the intestate succession rule introduced as part of the Josephine Inheritance Patent of 1786, had a perceptible impact on dispensation requests.[200] According to this new rule, the inheritance of a child who had died without issue was to go to both parents equally.[201] All of the children from the marriage of Bonaventura Bader had died, the last of them following the death of his wife. His deceased wife had inherited the house in which the family lived together with her two sisters, of whom one had likewise already died. The half of the house that had been received by the Baders' only surviving child upon the mother's death now fell – in keeping with the intestate succession rule – to the widower. Thus, Bonaventura Bader owned one half, while his unmarried sister-in-law Magdalena Nenning owned the other. This succession and the unavoidable constant "cohabitation" of brother- and sister-in-law ultimately gave rise to "great mutual affection and love" that, were they to be prevented from marrying, threatened to "plunge" them "into sin and vice".[202] This was yet another case where the desired marriage would guide the property back into the lineage from which it had come.

Other marriage projects sounded like ideal arrangements, even if it is impossible to peer behind the scenes and get an impression of the internal dynamics – such as when a nephew, as the intended groom, had inherited shares of a house to which his bride had been granted lifelong rights of use by her deceased husband, who had been the groom's uncle. The groom's two other uncles and "coheirs, brothers of the deceased", had promised to cede their shares to their nephew if this marriage were permitted to go forward. "As a result", reads the conclusion, "this small bit of wealth would remain together within the family."[203] The relevance of common economic interests

---

199 DIÖAB, Konsistorialakten 1859, Fasc. 5a, Römische Dispensen, no. 27.

200 Cf. Joseph Kropatschek, *Handbuch aller unter der Regierung des Kaisers Joseph II. für die k. k. Erbländer ergangenen Verordnungen und Gesetze in einer sistematischen Verbindung*, vol. 11, 1786 (Vienna, 1788), pp. 780–781.

201 Some couples guarded against such an eventuality as early as their wedding via the inclusion of a passage in their marriage contract that excluded this form of intestate succession. Cf. Lanzinger, "Von der Macht der Linie", pp. 304–305.

202 DIÖAB, Konsistorialakten 1851, Fasc. 5a, Römische Dispensen, no. 17.

203 DIÖAB, Konsistorialakten 1849, Fasc. 5a Römische Dispensen, no. 28. On usufruct as a way of compensating for the disadvantageous position in which many widows found themselves in terms of property ownership under a separate marital property regime cf. Margareth Lanzinger, "Women and Property in 18th Century Austria. Separate Property,

shared by a broader family circle beyond the couple, especially where large amounts of wealth were concerned, can be seen not least in the presence of relatives as witnesses at the matrimonial examinations.[204] In some cases, "hard feelings"[205] between families of the surviving and deceased spouses on account of cross-lineage wealth flows had even led to threats of legal action or ongoing lawsuits. The conflict-configurations sketched out here were based on a mode of thought that linked property and lineages and entailed exclusive claims by the latter to the former. Favouring of the vertical line and the resulting disadvantaged position of the couple gave rise to a specific landscape of interests and conflicts.

•••

With its concentration on marriage projects in the close degrees of affinity, this chapter has addressed configurations that made up around half of papal dispensation requests and faced particularly great difficulties during the 1830s and 1840s. To study these is also to analyse the effects of shifting papal dispensation policies on dispensation practice. The often protracted proceedings meant that the records concerning these cases ended up being especially voluminous, detailed and many-voiced. With the onset of Gregory XVI's papacy in 1831, it was exclusively "danger of defection from the faith" – or, in the Italian dioceses, "certain or probable danger to life" – that represented a valid reason for dispensation in cases involving unions between brother- and sister-in-law. Above all in areas that bordered on Switzerland, this led to the former of these

Usufruct and Ownership in Different Family Configurations", in *Female Economic Strategies in the Modern World*, ed. Beatrice Moring (London, 2012), pp. 145–159.

204 DIÖAB, Konsistorialakten 1840, Fasc. 5a, Römische Dispensen, no. 8. In this case, the first witness to appear was a brother of the bride, who indicated that the widowed groom had received approximately 6,000 gulden promised him by his deceased wife – who was a cousin of the bride and the witness. He presented the prospect of protracted disputes and animosity between "the Gaßler and the Spieß families" – but the planned marriage, he said, would keep "everything calm and at peace".

205 This is a topic in the dispensation request of Jakob Schranz, the son of a farmer from Ladis in the Deanery of Zams in Western Tyrol. He was 26 years old and desired to marry Theres Ennemoser. She was 40 years old and the childless widow of his uncle. Her deceased husband had signed over to her his "properties at a price lower by half". He had supposedly done so "with the caveat that he wished for her to take a son of his brother as her new husband" – according to the testimony of the first witness Andrae Schranz, who was a brother of the deceased and simultaneously the father of the groom, while the second witness was likewise a brother of the deceased and thus a further uncle of the groom. The widow contradicted their portrayal. The dispensation was granted. DIÖAB, Konsistorialakten 1838, Fasc. 5a, Römische Dispensen, no. 5.

two reasons (also) being used in a strategic and instrumental manner. In situations where the threat of conversion could not be plausibly argued, couples – repeatedly with help from priests, but also from lawyers and backroom legal advisors – would move heaven and earth to achieve their aims anyway. Here, mediation and recommendations revealed themselves to be possible means of doing so. Austria's Imperial-Royal Agency in Rome, as an official entity charged with mediating between the dioceses and the papal bureaucracy, did act in support of dispensation supplicants, but ultimately enjoyed only a limited radius of action during this era of rigid policies. With a willingness to incur enormous financial expense as well as with evaluations, letters of supplication and all manner of threats, numerous couples tried their luck – mostly over the course of multiple attempts and with huge effort – and quite frequently still failed. Social status along with access to ecclesiastical and/or political networks that could be activated in a targeted manner represented a significant resource in such cases, a resource that improved the chances of ultimately obtaining a dispensation. A comparison of the approval rates for requests from the Diocese of Brixen during the papacy of Gregory XVI (1831–1846) with those during that of his successor, Pius IX (1847–1860), reveals a significantly greater share of rejections during the former period both on the diocesan level as well as in Rome where the close degrees of affinity are concerned, and particularly for the configuration of brother- and sister-in-law.

In terms of the logic of everyday life, however, it was precisely this couple configuration that seemed near-ideal – especially to widowers with small children. Here, after all, the position of the sister-in-law as the children's aunt was not only characterised by kinship – which was positively associated with trustworthiness, reliability, a willingness to sacrifice, etc. – but in most cases also by social proximity and familiarity that had already been lived out over long periods, frequently months and years, within a common household. Sisters-in-law occupied a preferential position within the circle of those people who, in a family crisis sparked by the illness or death of the wife and mother, were willing to jump in and provide assistance even under economically difficult circumstances – helping not only to organise the household and care for the children but also in various areas of work associated with the house or with the profession or occupation of the brother-in-law. In dispensation requests, the stereotype in contrast to such a solid "second mother" was the "strange" stepmother, a figure characterised by all manner of negative qualities. Both this strong distinction, which exhibited a tendency to become even stronger over the course of the period under study, and an emphasis on the "common blood ties" that qualified the aunt as a "second mother" can be read as a process by which the maternal role was increasingly naturalised and biologised.

At the same time, the love of the sister-in-law for her nephews and nieces could distract from an all-too-familiar closeness to and love for the brother-in-law, at least from the standpoint of communication strategy. Dispensation requests were in many cases submitted only after years of cohabitation when, for example, the woman became pregnant or suspicions of excessively familiar relations arose. Submitting such a request entailed quite some risk: in the event of its refusal, civil law mandated that the common household be dissolved. This entailed consequences that were dramatic and also existentially threatening, above all in less wealthy households and in cases where the widower and his sister-in-law had produced children of their own. Court-mandated separations are documented, although it was probably rare for them to have the intended effect. In a society like that of historical Tyrol, where money and property tended to be thought of as tied to familial lineages, affinal marriages could also serve as a way of clawing back wealth that had passed to a surviving wife or husband on the basis of a marriage contract or will and would hence end up in another lineage, that of the in-laws, if the couple had produced no children. And last but not least, this chapter's focus on unions between brothers- and sisters-in-law has made clear how the various couple configurations in close degrees of kinship not only became subject to distinctions in terms of dispensation policy and practice but also allow specific structural logics and interests to be perceived. Altogether, the dispensation requests in affinal configurations covered a broad social arc and were hence surrounded by the most varied justificatory contexts: both in milieus characterised by wealth and among people in economically precarious circumstances, they offered a way in which to reconcile interests – in particular divergent and conflicting interests – and deal with acute situations of need.

CHAPTER 6

Consanguineous Marriages: Contexts and Controversies

In the region examined here, marriage projects between first cousins were not initially a matter of any great salience or urgency, neither in terms of their number nor in terms of the difficulties that the corresponding dispensation requests could face; this was due to the likewise-important affinal configuration of brother- and sister-in-law. Over the course of the nineteenth century's second half, however, cousin marriage projects did begin to receive an increasing amount of attention. Here, the Church – working from the standpoint of its own logic and in light of the ongoing discourse on heredity and health hazards where consanguinity was concerned – felt compelled to ensure that affinity would remain within the spectrum of relevance. The actions of its representatives amidst this changing landscape are what the following chapter seeks to explore. There was hardly any debate, on the other hand, regarding those unions that made up nearly one quarter and hence the largest share of papal dispensation requests – namely those in the second and third unequal degree of consanguinity.

In the microhistorical studies published since the 1980s, consanguineous marriages have classically been conceived of as associated with property-related interests. These studies frequently proposed causal links between the rise in the number of kin marriages and emergent socio-economic patterns as well as changes to inheritance- and property-related law and practices, changing ownership structures and/or (land) markets, ultimately viewing the attendant ways of 'using' relatives as a defensive strategy. Gérard Delille has interpreted the nineteenth-century upsurge in the number of kin marriages in his region of interest, southern Italy, as being in part a reaction to the introduction of new inheritance regulations that stipulated equal inheritance shares for all children as opposed to the previous favouring of sons.[1] Raul Merzario has found that marriages between blood relatives were used to counteract the effects of laws that contradicted the logics of local economies in a society that was partly based on collective ownership.[2] David Warren Sabean, researching the village of Neckarhausen in Württemberg, ascertained a clear increase in

1 Delille, *Famille et propriété*, pp. 369–370.

2 Merzario, "Terra, parentela e matrimoni consanguinei".

 | DOI:10.1163/9789004539877_007

consanguine marriages – above all between first and second cousins – whose number more than doubled during the period between 1750 and 1850.[3] Based on these findings, he asked as to whether endogamy in a society with partible inheritance of land served the purpose of counteracting property's fragmentation but ultimately offered a more nuanced interpretation: Sabean concluded that what he was perceiving was not a direct relationship in the sense of endogamous marriages being intended to preserve stable units of property. Rather, there seemed to have been networks consisting of alliances between kin that guided the flow of property and resources.[4] He held that cooperation between cousins in working the soil, which proved advantageous in light of land's fragmentation and changing agricultural technology, also had the effect of strengthening consanguineous relationships, which themselves could serve to encourage new endogamous unions.[5] Finally, the well-known study *Family Fortunes* by Leonore Davidoff and Catherine Hall came to the conclusion that marital unions resulting in kinship's densification – above all unions between pairs of siblings from two families as well as between cousins – were indeed intended to counteract partible inheritance's centrifugal tendencies.[6]

As the assessments summarised above have made clear, partible inheritance and/or the reform of inheritance laws in the interest of more equal access for all sons and daughters at the transition between the early modern period and the nineteenth century have served to undergird a central context of explanation for the rising rates of kin marriage in the research to date. In the Austrian lands, however, this area of law experienced hardly any change with the introduction of the civil codes of 1786 and 1811, least of all towards a more egalitarian division of inheritance. The sixteenth-century *Tiroler Landesordnung* had not strictly specified who was to succeed to ownership of the house or the farm.[7] Different forms of inheritance practice prevailed in different regions: the eastern part of Tyrol featured the single-heir model, while partible inheritance of real estate[8] was the dominant model in the west as well as in neighbouring Vorarlberg. In contrast to revolutionary France as well as numerous

3 Sabean, *Kinship in Neckarhausen*, pp. 429–430.

4 Ibid., p. 414.

5 Ibid., p. 140, 172; on this cf. also Mathieu, "Ein Cousin an jeder Zaunlücke", pp. 57–58. Here, Jon Mathieu questions and analyses the criteria according to which cooperative arrangements in the rural and agrarian context were organised.

6 Leonore Davidoff and Catherine Hall, *Family Fortunes. Men and Women of the English Middle Class 1780–1850* (London/New York, 2002 [1987]), p. 221.

7 Cf. Rösch, "Lebensläufe und Schicksale".

8 Cf. Palme, "Die Entwicklung des Erbrechtes", pp. 31–32.

areas including nearly all of Italy[9] and also German territories on the Rhine,[10] where the French *Code civil* was either in effect or influential and where equal inheritance for all children – both sons and daughters – was legally enforced, undivided inheritance of property remained untouched in Austria. What is more, the male primogeniture declared for the peasantry by Joseph II initially even privileged the practice of undivided inheritance, thus reinforcing it overall. Due to numerous complaints under Francis II, however, this rule was partially rolled back in a court decree of 9 October 1795: in places where partible inheritance among children or succession of the youngest child had been typical, these practices could be upheld.[11] This is how things then remained during the nineteenth century on the basis of Austria's General Civil Code of 1811.

Ida Fazio characterises kin relations as being influenced by social *and* economic logics in equal measure. In turn, she holds that markets and institutions should not be regarded as depersonalised.[12] Economic logics, viewed from this perspective, are always bound up with social logics and vice versa. The dispensation requests analysed here represent one of the contexts where this becomes apparent. Moreover, the ways in which cousin marriages increased in Neckarhausen, in the southern Italian city of Manduria, in still other places and regions and among the Protestant nobility despite highly divergent socio-economic and socio-political profiles fundamentally calls into question the explanatory power of inheritance practices and ownership structures.[13] Most importantly, it would seem that there is no single 'big' explanation to be found

9 Cf. Manuela Martini, "Neue Rechte, alte Pflichten. Die Rezeption des Code Napoléon zu Beginn des 19. Jahrhunderts in Italien", *L'Homme. Z.F.G.* 14, 1 (2003), 90–96.

10 Cf. Barbara Dölemeyer, Heinz Mohnhaupt and Alessandro Somma (eds.), *Richterliche Anwendung des Code civil in seinen europäischen Geltungsbereichen außerhalb Frankreichs* (Frankfurt a. M., 2006); Elisabeth Fehrenbach, *Traditionale Gesellschaft und revolutionäres Recht. Die Einführung des Code Napoléon in den Rheinbundstaaten* (Göttingen, 1974); Werner Schubert and Mathias Schmoeckel (eds.), *200 Jahre Code civil. Die napoleonische Kodifikation in Deutschland und Europa* (Cologne/Weimar/Vienna, 2005).

11 The rules mentioned here are the content of a patent of 3 April 1787 as well as the Franciscean Inheritance Patent, Justizgesetzsammlung 258. Regarding actual practice cf. Rösch, "Lebensläufe und Schicksale".

12 Fazio, "Parentela e mercato", pp. 141–143, with reference to Bernard Derouet, "Parenté et marché foncier à l'époque modern", *Annales HSS* 2 (2001), 337–368. In this article, Derouet attempts to unite the approaches of those studies that base their analyses on land markets and price formation with the approaches of studies that focus on the dynamics of social reproduction. Kinship, as a variable and a perspective, plays a central role in this context.

13 One of those who calls for reflection in light of this is Gérard Delille, "Evolution within Sibling Groups from One Kinship System to Another (Sixteenth to Nineteenth Century)", in *Sibling Relations*, ed. Johnson/Sabean, pp. 145–163, 159–160.

here. As has already been shown with respect to unions in close degrees of affinity, marriage projects between cousins likewise adhered to situational logics – and in no case were these primarily an elite phenomenon.[14]

Economics and relationships ultimately unite in the theory of kinship's horizontalisation. A significant element of this process, which set in around 1800, was a different mode of interaction within the kinship space that placed horizontal connections – above all relationships between siblings – in the foreground. Intensified sibling relationships, according to this model, led not infrequently to marriages between cousins in the next generation. So far, this is a finding that has emerged mainly from studies of bourgeois milieus based on written correspondence. A 'marriage politics' of this sort can be interpreted as a mode that was a central driving factor behind the societal establishment and consolidation of the bourgeois milieu.[15] The fostering of contact among kin gave rise to a corresponding social environment and hence also a pool from which to select suitable marriage partners. Social proximity and familiarity were viewed as an ideal foundation upon which to make a marriage.[16] This notwithstanding, just how and to what extent horizontalisation went hand in hand with the dissolution of vertical structures still needs to be clarified.

Combining and increasing wealth by way of marriages between cousins was a phenomenon that unquestionably did play a role in the examined dioceses. The interest in doing so was shared by people who farmed mountainous terrain as well as local and urban elites. The dispensation records reveal a conspicuous concentration of cousin marriages that occurred during the late 1830s and 1840s among the Metzlers, a prestigious family and kin network in the Bregenz Forest. This chapter will retrace and contextualise these unions in

14 On this cf. also Guzzi-Heeb, *Donne, uomini, parentela*, pp. 221–222. Regarding the town of Löhne and in contrast to how things looked in the community of Borgeln, Christine Fertig concludes that there were "hardly any differences" between peasants and *Heuerlinge* (cottagers who lived on and worked peasant landlords' land) in terms of the percentages of kin marriages between 1770 and 1870. Fertig, *Familie, verwandtschaftliche Netzwerke*, p. 203.

15 For the nineteenth century cf. Johnson, "Siblinghood and the Emotional Dimensions"; Joris, "Kinship and Gender"; Mathieu, "Verwandtschaft als historischer Faktor", pp. 240, 242 – with a reference to further investigations; Sabean, *Kinship in Neckarhausen*, pp. 59–62, 206, 220; Sabean, "Kinship and Class Dynamics"; Sabean, "Kinship and Prohibited Marriages".

16 Cf. Joris/Witzig, *Brave Frauen, aufmüpfige Weiber*, esp. chapter v; Joris, "Kinship and Gender"; Johnson, "Das 'Geschwister Archipel'", 57–58. Johnson writes: "'Intimate evenings' and Sunday meals, parties and balls, and especially get-togethers of friends and relatives on holidays and at country residences during the summer created a gigantic reservoir of suitable spouses, almost all of whom were connected with each other via the 'sibling archipelago'. All guests were somehow 'cousins', whether blood relatives or not."

order to shed light upon a specific social space. The potency of a certain snowball effect should not be underestimated when considering the general proliferation of marriages between close kin. Knowledge of dispensations that had been granted here and there, often far beyond the confines of one's own village, gave rise to the hope that a request of one's own might also be successful. Previous allowance of a comparably configured marriage provided bridal couples with arguments when the competent parish priest, dean or diocesan consistory sought to reject their dispensation requests as hopeless. Such clusters of requests also, and not insignificantly, had the effect of schooling their authors in the parishes and deaneries: if a certain line of argument had proven successful, its further use was a given. The fact that every new instance of granting a dispensation created a potential precedent came to preoccupy church representatives especially during the second half of the nineteenth century, as did the increase in the number of dispensation requests overall. Furthermore, this period saw the spectrum of possible actions broadened at least theoretically via the introduction of so-called emergency civil marriage. But did couples actually make use of this option for circumventing the Church's administrative bodies? And finally, the realm of consanguineous unions saw those between uncle and niece occasion special controversy.

1 Milieu-Specific Repertoires of Argumentation

The repertoire of arguments used in requests was context-specific. This becomes particularly evident in requests by couples from the agrarian milieu. It was with reference to domestic economic necessities that they argued in support of their desire to marry a certain woman or man. The relevant socialisation and capacity to do work were of special importance here, as was being well practised in certain working techniques. This was all the truer when Alpine farming was at issue.[17] Farming in mountainous terrain was associated with special living and working conditions.[18] In nearly 20 per cent of the

17 On this cf. also Margareth Lanzinger, "Zwischen Anforderungsprofilen und Argumentationsrepertoires. Partner/-innen/-wahl und Arbeitsorganisation im bergbäuerlichen Milieu in Tirol und Vorarlberg im 19. Jahrhundert", *Jahrbuch für Geschichte des ländlichen Raumes* (2008), 86–108; Margareth Lanzinger, "Mountain Farmers' Labour Requirements and the Choice of a Spouse in Nineteenth Century Tyrol and Vorarlberg", in *Agrosystems and Labour Relations in European Societies*, ed. Erich Landsteiner and Ernst Langthaler (Turnhout, 2010), pp. 97–118.

18 For a well-founded impression of Alpine farming and pasturing cf. Mathieu, *History of the Alps*, pp. 44–71; Viazzo, *Upland Communities*.

Diocese of Brixen's requests between the 1830s and the early 1860s, the local priest or bridal couple referred to the mountainous character or remoteness of their place of residence, which they sometimes portrayed at great length.[19] The majority of these requests came from the diocese's western deaneries. This would indicate that such 'local conditions' alone did not preordain marriages in the close degrees – for the eastern part of the diocese featured just as much high elevation farming terrain. What comes to light here is much rather a clear regional distinction.

As a rule, accompanying letters or protocolled testimony would rather generously interpret and attempt to claim the canonical reason of *angustia loci*, or "narrowness of place", which applied when supplicants' residence in small, remote and sometimes difficult to reach communities made selecting a suitable wife or husband who was not of one's kinfolk far more difficult or even impossible. But unlike how it was in the third and fourth degree, this reason usually did not suffice in cases where a papal dispensation was required. A community's disadvantageous Alpine location was typically defined in light of several additional factors that made life there seem highly unattractive. Such factors included long distances to neighbouring communities, the long way to church and a community accessible only by foot or situated in a gorge, near Alpine pastures or glaciers. This was combined with complaints about the raw climate, long winters, excessive amounts of snow and cold. In one letter, the vicariate general in Feldkirch referred to today's cosmopolitan ski resort of Lech am Arlberg as "this Siberia".[20] Such depictions could go so far as to portray hazardous scenarios, such as when avalanches threatened homes or in cases where haymaking on steep slopes seemed dangerous to life and limb. And finally, it was complained all the hard and dangerous work frequently yielded but little reward.

In the request of the widower Thomas Wasl and Maria Singer from Gramais in the Deanery of Imst, it was not the couple themselves but a local representative of the regional court, confirmed by the municipal committee, who portrayed the limitations to which supra-local marital unions were subject in a seemingly timeless way: "Withal, objects from other communities are but rarely suitable in this mountain community, as experience has shown in the

19 A farm's being situated on a mountain also features prominently as an argument in the eighteenth-century dispensation requests from Styria dealt with by Peter Becker, *Leben und Lieben in einem kalten Land. Sexualität im Spannungsfeld von Ökonomie und Demographie. Das Beispiel St. Lamprecht 1600–1850* (Frankfurt a. M./New York, 1990), p. 192.

20 DIÖAB, Konsistorialakten 1843, Fasc. 5a, Römische Dispensen, no. 11.

distant, less-distant and recent past."[21] In the dispensation request of Franz Pfanner from Fluh in the Deanery of Bregenz, one of the two witnesses was of the opinion that the groom could "choose to marry only such a person as is accustomed to laborious and arduous housework and to fieldwork in the mountains". Franz Pfanner himself justified his choice in a similar manner and attributed the according abilities of his prospective bride to her socialisation: "because she is fundamentally a person who was raised in the mountains from her earliest youth" and therefore accustomed to the work that needed to be done there.[22] The "local conditions" in Imsterberg, it is written in the detailed letter of supplication from Joseph Zangerle, were such that "really only women from this community are suited to and capable of the householding and other farming work that need to be done here".[23]

Portrayals of a remote location's drawbacks and its arduous and laborious living conditions grew particularly emphatic whenever the bride was expected to bring money into the marriage. In these cases the argumentation also started from the "local conditions": the groom's own, typically small community would be characterised as having a paltry selection of suitable women. But due to the community's unfavourable conditions, its heavy workloads and the demands that these things entailed, it made little sense to search for a bride further down the valley or "out in the lowlands". Such efforts were, moreover, doomed to failure anyway, for women "from the lowlands neither desire to nor are capable of living in the mountains".[24] The conclusion was that a woman from the lowlands or a lower valley, even if she had but little wealth to her name, would be all the less willing to marry into such a remote community. By the same token, it was likely the case that women from agrarian mountain communities – especially those who would bring a certain amount of wealth into the marriage or who excelled in their ability to work – were in high demand down in the valley. In light of this, the exchange of women between mountain and valley via marriage migration went mainly in one direction: from mountain to valley.[25] In the dispensation requests, we can indeed recognise efforts to keep women and their wealth in the community, and what is more: they and their wealth were to remain among their own kin. With only a few exceptions,

---

21 DIÖAB, Konsistorialakten 1831, Fasc. 5a, Römische Dispensen, no. 5.

22 DIÖAB, Konsistorialakten 1853, Fasc. 5a, Römische Dispensen, no. 23.

23 DIÖAB, Konsistorialakten 1839, Fasc. 5a, Römische Dispensen, no. 11.

24 DIÖAB, Konsistorialakten 1832, Fasc. 5a, Römische Dispensen, no. 19.

25 Marriage patterns as well as kin marriage patterns looked different when the structure of Alpine communities was influenced by a high degree of labour migration and the absence of men. On the implications and dynamics associated with this cf. Luigi Lorenzetti, *Economie et migrations au XIXe siècle: les stratégies de la reproduction familiale au Tessin* (Bern et al., 1999); Merzario, *Il paese stretto*.

the analysed dispensation requests from "remote places" involving situations where the bride would be bringing a sizeable marriage portion or other wealth into the marriage concerned consanguineous unions.

Theresia Matt lived in Hirschegg in the Little Walser Valley, a community that the vicariate general in Feldkirch emphasised was an "*out-of-the-way little* parish in which *most families*" were "closely related".[26] In 1855, she sought to marry her cousin Jakob Ludwig Fritz in neighbouring Mittelberg. At this point in time, both of them were comparatively young: he was 21 years old and owned a farm, while she was 20 and commanded considerable wealth; in the second and more detailed matrimonial examination that was protocolled in this case, one of the witnesses mentioned the sum of 4,500 gulden. Their request had initially been rejected because *angustia loci* was the only reason for dispensation that they could claim. In addition to the fact that this was quite a weak reason, it had also been deemed formally invalid since Theresia Matt would be marrying in the neighbouring parish and was thus a bride who would be escaping the "narrowness" of her place of birth or residence to begin with.

Following the negative decision that ensued and probably not least due to the bridal couple's social status, the local parish priest felt moved to portray their situation in greater detail by way of a renewed request. He reported that Theresia Matt had received a marriage proposal – "not from a valley resident, but rather from a livestock dealer situated elsewhere". She had refused this proposal, since she was attached "to her home valley, which she loves", and since she also believed that she would "not easily" fit into "alien surroundings".[27] In a letter sent to the imperial-royal district office in Bregenz and appended to the dispensation record due to the two hopefuls' status as minors, Brixen's vicar capitular Andrä Huber once again emphasised that the "orphaned supplicant" could not make the decision to marry elsewhere and also pointed to the "peculiar living conditions" in the Little Walser Valley, on account of which it seemed inadvisable for the groom to "seek out a spouse from outside his familiar environs". His line of argument thus led to a juxtaposition of one's "own" and the "alien". Particularly in cases from so-called remote areas, the authors and supporters of dispensation requests had no qualms about adopting an ethnographic perspective in a way that was quite typical of nineteenth-century educated elites.[28]

---

26 DIÖAB, Konsistorialakten 1856, Fasc. 5a, Römische Dispensen, no. 41. Emphasis underlined in the original.

27 Ibid.

28 André Holenstein, referring to Wolfgang Jakobeit, speaks of an "ethnological gaze" that grew sharper during the initial decades of the nineteenth century "prior to the 'idyllically romantic glorification' of the people and their culture". André Holenstein, "'Local-Untersuchung'

Most importantly, however, the local priest – with an eye to supporting this request – counted up the bridal couple's relatives, something that had not yet occurred in this way in any of the diocese's other parishes: the groom was said to have 50 second-degree kin, meaning first cousins, and at least 100 third- and fourth-degree kin; the bride was said to have 40 in the second degree and a great many in the third and fourth degrees. Their second attempt was then allowed to go forward, with the couple's desired dispensation ultimately being granted.[29] Thereafter, the priests of the Little Walser Valley's three parishes – Hirschegg, Mittelberg and Riezlern – retained this strategy of argumentation in such cases, listing the numbers of related persons in dispensation requests with increasing precision[30] until the consistory, in 1860, began objecting due to the absence of canonical reasons.[31]

Marital arrangements befitting of one's class – and the contacts either gained or placed on a permanent footing in the process – ensured the social status of the next generation and made possible continuities in terms of prestige, office and wealth. The networks of the families into which grooms and brides married, a bride's education in a way that was ideally supposed to "convene" (*konvenieren*) with the professional standing of her groom and competencies brought into the marriage by a bride that were fit to help advance her groom's career: all this need to be thought of as types of capital that could be harnessed to acquire further social and cultural capital or converted into economic capital. It is before this backdrop that marriages in the close degrees of consanguinity in the region under study must be viewed, in particular among families of local and regional, economic and political prominence. For centuries, the safeguarding of status-related interests had been a reason for dispensation that was accepted by the Catholic Church. And it was ultimately this that underlay a bride's ability to claim *angustia loci*, narrowness of place. For every wife, in the Catholic conception, was supposed to be able to marry – without being forced to marry a man whose social status was incompatible with her own. It was members of well-regarded and wealthy families who were able to employ this argument with particular success: the higher the social status, the more this justification seems to have weighed.

In several of the consanguineous marriage projects that were examined, moreover, the involvement of paternal, parental and in any case familial

---

und 'Augenschein'. Reflexionen auf die Lokalität im Verwaltungsdenken und -handeln des Ancien Régime", *WerkstattGeschichte* 16 (1997), 19–31, 28–29.

29 DIÖAB, Konsistorialakten 1856, Fasc. 5a, Römische Dispensen, no. 41.

30 Cf. for example DIÖAB, Konsistorialakten 1859, Fasc. 5a, Römische Dispensen, no. 17; ibid., 1860, no. 35.

31 Cf. DIÖAB, Konsistorialakten 1860, Fasc. 5a, Römische Dispensen, no. 31; ibid., 1861, no. 35.

interests can be clearly recognised – such as when property could not be kept within the immediate family and had to be transferred to a relative, instead. If the relative in question were to simultaneously become one's son-in-law, said property and the family would once again be closely linked. Juliana von Wenger, daughter of a merchant from Hall, was to marry the merchant Joseph Christoph Gießenberger, with whom she was related. She was 19 years old, while he was 35. Her only brother was described as incapable of taking over his father's business. This business, however, had been run by the family's ancestors for 200 years, and the intent was therefore to keep it in the family by way of this marriage. In fact, half a year prior to the dispensation request's submission, the father of the bride had already handed over the business to his son and to his nephew, who was the intended future son-in-law. The couple's list of reasons for this marriage included the following: to continue running the merchant business, a man "fit for commercial enterprise" was needed. In this regard, the bride's father had placed his full trust in the groom. It was also held that as a result of the marriage, this "sizeable business" could remain "within the same house". And finally, the bride stated that this marriage would enable her to fulfil "the deepest wish" of her father.[32] The dispensation was granted – and at least as far as the connection between the family and the business was concerned, everything fell into place in an ideal way.

It is quite overtly that the fathers' interests are documented in the marriage of Joseph Malfer from Auer in South Tyrol's Lower Adige Valley.[33] Joseph was his parents' only son, and his cousin Viktoria von Malfer from Innsbruck, who was the daughter of the Imperial-Royal Prefectural Councillor (*Statthaltereirat*) Anton Malfer, Edler von Auerheim and the eldest among four sisters. Both were 28 years old. The fathers Lorenz and Anton Malfer – together with their third brother Peter, who was posted in Venice as a higher regional court councillor (*Oberlandesgerichtsrat*) – owned a large farm in Auer; the talk is of "undivided" and "indivisible" properties and of an associated "*communio bonorum*", which was being managed by the groom's father Lorenz Malfer when the request was submitted and was later to be passed to his son. This marriage between the two, testified the second witness at the matrimonial examination, was desirable since such a marriage would keep everything together. Viktoria von Malfer, for

---

32 DIÖAB, Konsistorialakten 1838, Fasc. 5a, Römische Dispensen, no. 8.

33 His part of the matrimonial examination was protocolled in Auer, which belonged to the Diocese of Trento. There, the mode of questioning and the questions themselves differed from how things were done in Brixen's deaneries. Questions were only put to the two witnesses, whose answers were summarised and passed on. In this case, detailed attention was paid to the status of the couple's wealth. Responsible for overseeing the case as a whole was the diocese to which the bride belonged, which was that of Brixen.

her part, was said to have passed up an outstanding opportunity on account of the suitor's having been "of Greek religion" – here, once again, the "foreign" as a foil. Obtaining a marital partner appropriate to her status and a "marriage similar" to this planned cousin marriage was "an extremely difficult matter", noted the bride's father in a long letter of supplication.[34] For this reason, they claimed *angustia loci* – but also pointed to the bride's father's service to the Church. As proof, he indicated his rank as a "commander" of the Order of St. George, conferred upon him by Pope Pius IX, as well as membership in further orders.[35]

The first cousins Count Alexander von Künigl, a captain in the Kaiser-Jäger-Regiment, and Countess Friederika von Bissingen-Nippenburg, daughter of the provincial governor of Tyrol, needed neither a long letter of supplication – though correspondence regarding a request to have the fees reduced does exist – nor a detailed matrimonial examination. The matrimonial examination protocol contains partly identical testimony by the two witnesses – a Count von Taxis and a Count von Spauer – as well as testimony by the groom, with which the bride concurred: both were from noble houses and families that had been of service to state and Church, the bride was 42 years old and possessed no wealth of her own, and the deposit to be paid by officers upon their marriage had already been paid. The groom furthermore emphasised his bride's "outstanding religious and moral qualities". Even before the matrimonial examination was protocolled, the consistory had signalled its willingness to turn to Rome in order to support this "dispensation, which is desirable in multiple respects". It was then granted with no difficulties.[36]

Among civil servants, professional advancement could be driven forward by a marriage suited to this purpose. For example, the letter of supplication by imperial-royal district office adjunct Andrä Spath and Carolina Clementi, a resident of Innsbruck who had been born in the municipality of Civezzano in Trentino and was the daughter of a regional judge, indicated the following: "The bride possesses all of those characteristics that are necessary for a happy marriage and, in particular, knowledge of the two languages of the land [Tyrol], which places the groom, as a civil servant, in a position to pursue in his career more swiftly and to the advantage of his future family."[37] In such

34 DIÖAB, Konsistorialakten 1860, Fasc. 5a, Römische Dispensen, no. 2.

35 The Order of St. George was a military order whose purpose was knightly service to the Roman Catholic Church in the interest of spreading the faith, defending the Church and supporting the Holy See. A corresponding certificate is included with the dispensation request.

36 DIÖAB, Konsistorialakten 1840, Fasc. 5a, Römische Dispensen, no. 26.

37 DIÖAB, Konsistorialakten 1856, Fasc. 5a, Römische Dispensen, no. 44. On home and work of lower civil servants see Maria Ågren, "Lower State Servants and Home Office Work", in *The Routledge History of Domestic Sphere*, ed. Eibach/Lanzinger, pp. 120–133.

cases where the proposed marital unions were "ideal" in multiple respects the brides' fathers were consistently present as emphatic proponents.[38]

2 Clustered Cousin Marriages: The Metzler Siblings

The analysis of dispensation requests turned up a conspicuous density of cousin marriages during the 1830s and 1840s among the Metzler siblings in the Bregenz Forest community of Schwarzenberg. The same family names appeared again and again – and as it ultimately turned out, the core of this particularly dense network of consanguineous kin consisted of four siblings: one brother and three sisters, each of whom married a first cousin (see Fig. 4):[39] Joseph Anton Metzler (1807–1863) and Anna Katharina Metzler (1814–1876) applied for a dispensation in 1837. Maria Katharina Metzler (1809–1879) and Josef Anton Feurstein (1804–1867) submitted their request the year thereafter, followed by Maria Theresia Metzler (1812–1864) and a further cousin named Josef Anton Feurstein (1811–1877) in 1841 and finally Maria Elisabeth Metzler (1815–1880) and Franz Ignaz Metzler (1816–1885) in 1843. All four dispensation requests were obtained without any difficulty. A further sister, Anna Metzler (1810–1847), married her second cousin Josef Natter, proprietor of the inn "Zum Ochsen" and mayor of Egg. Following her death, Natter entered into his second marriage with Anna's sister Maria (1819–1866), his sister-in-law. The brother Johann Metzler (1821–1876) was the only one of his generation who did not marry a close relative. But he did remain in his accustomed milieu, socioculturally speaking: his wife Maria Anna Fetz was a granddaughter of the regional bailiff (*Landammann*), Franz Xaver Fetz.[40]

The parents of these seven siblings were Maria Anna Feurstein (1782–1853) from Bezau and Joseph Metzler (1776–1851) from Schwarzenberg. They had wed in 1807. In the obligatory marriage consent document, Joseph Metzler had indicated that he and his brothers Anton and Johann had quite some

38 On this cf. the request by the cousins Rudolf Peithner von Lichtenfels, a 28-year-old imperial-royal civil servant at the Imperial-Royal Mine and Salt Works, and "Miss" Amalie Stadler – who was the 25-year-old daughter of Joseph Stadler, a *Hofrat* (court councillor) and director of said mine and salt works. DIÖAB, Konsistorialakten 1838, Fasc. 5a, Römische Dispensen, no. 11 and ibid., 1839, no. 1.

39 For information on the Metzler and Feurstein families, I extend thanks to Helmut Feurstein. The dates of birth and death are taken from his book: Helmut Feurstein, *Die Verwandtschaft Feurstein / Christas-Hensles vom 17. bis ins 19. Jahrhundert* (Bregenz, 2010), pp. 101–111.

40 Carola Lipp refers to the "political virulence of kinship in the political culture of the nineteenth century", though her research indeed extends far beyond the kin networks of local and regional elites. Lipp, "Verwandtschaft – ein negiertes Element", p. 39.

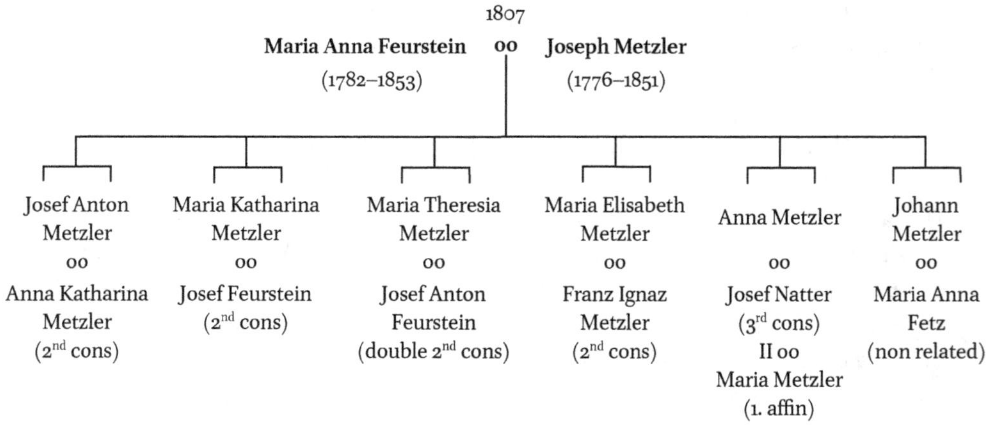

FIGURE 4 The marriages of the Metzler siblings in Schwarzenberg

time – both prior to and since the death of their father, the regional bailiff Metzler, who was also a "wealthy peasant, shopkeeper and merchant dealing in wood, cheese and cattle, as well as a moneylender and a fabricant in one"[41] – done a "considerable" bit of business "in cotton and muslin fabric, and then cheese and lard for other Austrian lands".[42] He and his two siblings had "3 homesteads in the community of Schwarzenberg with significant alp rights"; each "homestead" featured "a house and a barn" and all the other necessities. What is more, they employed fifty weavers and provided cotton spinning work for an equal number of families. "In all of Schwarzenberg", only Johann Georg Metzler paid taxes on more wealth than they. Through their industriousness, Joseph and his brothers had "been of the greatest service to the Bregenz Forest and the entire region".[43] Joseph Metzler himself held political offices: as the regional bailiff, as a representative of his estate for the Inner Bregenz Forest and as a deputy to the territorial assembly of estates (*Landschaft*).[44]

It was in 1837 that his son Joseph Anton Metzler and Anna Katharina Metzler, daughter of the abovementioned wealthiest Schwarzenberg resident Johann Georg, requested their dispensation.[45] In the initial letter sent to the consistory in Brixen, the dean remarked: "Two families, the Metzlers and the

41 Feurstein, *Die Verwandtschaft Feurstein*, p. 103.

42 On this cf. also Weitensfelder, *Industrie-Provinz*, pp. 24–25, 330.

43 VLA Bregenz, Landgericht Bezau box 10, quoted in Feurstein, *Die Verwandtschaft Feurstein*, pp. 101–102.

44 Feurstein, *Die Verwandtschaft Feurstein*, p. 103.

45 Cf. DIÖAB, Konsistorialakten 1837, Fasc. 5a, Römische Dispensen, no. 25.

Feursteins, are the most highly regarded in the entire Bregenz Forest." Their kin network, the dean continued, extended far and wide – meaning that choosing a different groom would surely just mean choosing another cousin, "either a Metzler or a Feurstein". A marriage below the bride's station, on the other hand, would give occasion for unfavourable assumptions concerning her honour.[46] And with this, the social positioning of the bride and the involved families as well as the attendant consequences for partner selection were clearly outlined. Joseph Anton and Anna Katharina Metzler had known each other "since childhood", as they had resided and grown up just a few steps away from each other. The groom's father owned the inn "Zur Krone" and also engaged in a profitable trade in cheese and ran a large farm, while the bride was a daughter of Maria Theresia Feurstein, proprietress of the inn "Zum Hirschen" and also the groom's aunt.[47] The dispensation record describes the bride as a "wealthy innkeeper's daughter".

According to the testimony protocolled in their matrimonial examination, spatial proximity had afforded each of them the chance to become acquainted with and learn to value the "positive traits" of the other. And it was due to this, in a way that was compatible with ecclesiastical models of love and marriage, that their mutual affection had arisen: "The more good traits I discover in her, the stronger my affection and love for her grow [...]. She is possessed of a male intellect and is thrifty, industrious and – most important of all to me – highly religious," declared the groom. The words of the bride struck a similar chord: "I have known the groom since childhood and had the opportunity to observe him in various situations, and I have always found him to be a sober, diligent, hard-working, calm and peaceful person. He is neither a nocturnal reveller, nor is anything indecent heard to escape his lips; he much rather exhibits earnest, masculine behaviour. On account of these good characteristics, I hope to be happy with him in marriage." As their second justification, likewise constructed in parallel and in analogy to the dean's description, they stated that the matter of kinship between the Metzlers and the Feursteins was unavoidable insofar as they intended to marry "in keeping" with their "station". This was followed by arguments against the bride marrying outside of the Bregenz Forest. Experience had shown, it was said, "that such people take just the money and not the girl", and that it was "quite rare for a girl brought up in the

46 ADF, Generalvikariat Matrimonialia (GA), Ehesachen III, Präsidialakten 1830–1900: Schwierige, präsidial behandelte Ehefälle, Zeit Bischof Prünster, 1830–1860, letter from the deanery office in Lingenau dated 22 February 1837.

47 Cf. Feurstein, *Die Verwandtschaft Feurstein*, 108.

country" to be able to "fit into city life". Finally, a closing argument instrumentalised gender roles in order to underline the impossibility of making a match not of one's own rank: "If I truly intended to marry below my station, I would have to approach someone myself; for nobody dares propose to me for fear of receiving a negative answer; I could not, however, myself propose to someone without violating my female modesty."[48]

Responsible for the matrimonial examination was Johann Baptist Sinz, the Bregenz Forest dean in those years, who has already received brief mention in this volume's second chapter. Sinz most probably made his own contributions to these constructions of unavoidability, to the various images and their inherent pathos, and to the exaggerations. And in any case, his interest in these marriages' coming to fruition was quite great – as one can tell from the accompanying letter. Therein, Sinz emphasised the reasons' truth as well as his decades' worth of familiarity with the involved families and their backgrounds. The father of the bride, as an "estates representative", was said to enjoy "such an outstanding degree of respect throughout entire Bregenz Forest that a word from him is viewed as the collective voice of the people". And "in the eyes of the authorities", he enjoyed "outstanding trust" on account of being "known as a clever and honest man". He could therefore do much "for good causes with which priests are typically also" concerned. For these reasons, Sinz – as dean – had to "emphatically wish" that the requested dispensation be granted.

In order to estimate the likely dispensation fees and define the sum of money to be deposited in advance, the prince-episcopal consistory requested more detailed information on the family's financial circumstances. The bride, responded the dean in August 1837, commanded wealth in the amount of at least 40,000 gulden, while the groom had so far "not accrued any wealth" since both of his parents were still alive. He indicated that they would live in part from the wealth of the bride and her hospitality license ("*Tafernwirths-Gerechtigkeit*"), meaning income from the inn. Moreover, the groom's father planned to turn his "considerable cheese business" over to him as he grew older. And regarding expenses for the dispensation, the father of the bride had declared "that what is demanded shall be paid". The vicariate general in Feldkirch, for its part, communicated to the consistory in Brixen that an attempt should be made in *forma communi* in Rome – in other words, in the fee category that was significantly more expensive than the usual *forma pauperum*. "The esteemed agent can also be safely authorised to incur between 300 and 500 scudi of expenses."

48 DIÖAB, Konsistorialakten 1837, Fasc. 5a, Römische Dispensen, no. 25.

In gulden, this will have been around three times the stated figures.[49] The vicar general thought it "a wholesome example for others if these wealthy dispensation supplicants are not allowed through with excessively low fees". Even so, the amount that ultimately ended up being due was 'only' just under 222 gulden.

In 1838, Joseph Anton Metzler's sister, Maria Katharina, and Josef Anton Feurstein submitted a dispensation request.[50] Dean Johann Baptist Sinz began the letter that accompanied their matrimonial examination protocol by pointing out that Josef Anton Feurstein commanded "*significant accrued wealth*",[51] since his parents had already passed away. This included a hospitality license ("*Wirtschaftsgerechtigkeit*") and "a very significant property". For this reason, he required a wife who had "been well raised" and was capable of "governing such a household" – qualities that he would not find in a "daughter from a common peasant household". Bride Maria Katharina Metzler, by contrast, was "from the most esteemed house in the entire Inner Bregenz Forest", and her father was "*wealthy*"[52] – for which reason she would "come into a significant fortune later on". He waxed ebullient on the achievements of her father, not least because the man took "every opportunity to be charitable". And "*that no expense shall be spared*" went "*without saying*".[53]

The first witness was Anton Metzler, proprietor of the inn "Zum Hirschen", who was a cousin of the bridal couple and a brother of the bride from the prior dispensation request mentioned above. The second witness was Jodok Schmied, the innkeeper at "Zum Adler" in Schwarzenberg, who had served as the first witness for the previous dispensation request.[54] The justifications brought forward at the matrimonial examination were variations on the reasons summarised in the letter that accompanied the request. Here, as well, the groom argued how difficult it was to make an appropriate marriage due to the family's extensive kin network: "Furthermore, my kinfolk are so numerous and

---

49 Quite often, the various letters in the dispensation records indicate the sum to be paid to the Agency in Rome in one or the other currency depending on the addressee. For example, the ordinariate informed the *Gubernium* in Innsbruck about the required sum in scudi but expressed the sum to be transferred by the vicariate general in Feldkirch in gulden: in 1837, for instance, 49 gulden and 50 kreuzers were invoiced for 16 scudi and 30 bajocchi. Cf. DIÖAB, Konsistorialakten 1837, Fasc. 5a, Römische Dispensen, no. 20. This meant that the exchange rate was three gulden for one scudo.

50 DIÖAB, Konsistorialakten 1838, Fasc. 5a, Römische Dispensen, no. 15.

51 Emphasis underlined in the original. Such markings were seldom made by the authors but rather by the readers at the prince-episcopal consistory.

52 Emphasis underlined in the original.

53 Emphasis underlined in the original.

54 Cf. Feurstein, *Die Verwandtschaft Feurstein*, p. 98.

widespread that I could hardly find anyone else appropriate to me without it once again becoming necessary to request a most gracious dispensation" – a message that was also echoed in the bride's testimony. His bride, he claimed, had "all the qualities" fit to give him hope of being "happy forever and always". The bride stated that her groom was "very thrifty, very clever in his business dealings and of impeccable behaviour", which is why she hoped that they would "live together in great happiness". Due to the economic circumstances of the groom and the bride's father, the vicariate general viewed turning to Rome in *forma communi* as being the sole option: it would not hurt, after all, if the agent in Rome were "authorised to offer to pay notable fees". The final cost ended up being much like in the previous case, amounting to 221 gulden and 27 kreuzers.

In 1841, Maria Katharina's sister Maria Theresia Metzler and a further cousin named Josef Anton Feurstein requested a dispensation.[55] They were first cousins on their fathers' and their mothers' sides, meaning that they were doubly related in the second canonical degree. The first witness at their matrimonial examination was a certain Joseph Metzler, for whom no age or any other information was listed that would allow to clearly identify him – apart from his statement that the bridal couple were his "closest neighbours". Each of them, he said, came from a "very well-regarded family" and had "a very great number of relatives". Josef Natter, from Egg, was the second witness. Natter was probably that second cousin whom Anna Metzler, a sister of the bride, had married a few years prior.[56] The groom explained that he and his bride had known each other as neighbours since their youth. He characterised his bride as "a highly reputable person" who led "a wholesome life" and was from a "well-regarded house", for which reason "the wish to marry her" had been growing in him "for several years already on account of her good attributes". He indicated that he was a merchant – "running a strong merchant business" – and therefore required a wife who could provide him with "support in writing and other tasks". He had not wanted to "go blind to the market in such an important matter" and hence waited "until having reached my thirtieth year". Now, however, marrying was something he found "advantageous" in every respect. He, too,

55 DIÖAB, Konsistorialakten 1841, Fasc. 5a, Römische Dispensen, no. 17.

56 The future brother-in-law Joseph Natter concluded his first marriage with Anna Metzler on 29 October 1838 with a dispensation in the third degree of consanguinity; she died in 1847. For his marriage to her sister Maria Metzler, he had to request a dispensation in the first degree of affinity. Trauungsbuch der Pfarre Egg 408/3 (1807–1879), 22 (matricula.online); DIÖAB, Konsistorialakten 1850, Fasc. 5a, Römische Dispensen, no. 15. The son from his first marriage who took over the inn "Zum Ochsen", Ignaz Natter, was born in 1845. Cf. Feurstein, *Die Verwandtschaft Feurstein*, p. 108–109.

brought his "widespread" kin network into play. The bride, who was 29 years old, also emphasised their "very extensive" circle of relatives and stated that she had thought long and hard about this "matter". In its accompanying letter to the prince-episcopal consistory, the vicariate general put the groom's wealth at 20,000 gulden – and the bride, for her part, would "be expecting a bountiful inheritance". This request was thus also placed in the higher fee category. The father of the bride pledged to deposit the required prepayment of 300 gulden at the dean's office. The fees ultimately due, however, once again amounted to the same sum as had been paid for the Metzlers' previous two requested dispensations.

Finally, in 1843, Maria Elisabeth Metzler and Franz Ignaz Metzler announced their desire to marry to the competent local priest.[57] The first witness at their matrimonial examination was Josef Anton Feurstein. Due to the concurrent existence of several people thus named, this person cannot be unambiguously identified; he may have been related to the Metzlers by marriage. Franz Ignaz Metzler, said Feurstein, was a merchant and came from a well-regarded family. He held that if this marriage were not to come to pass, one would have to fear that Franz Ignaz might "move away in order to search for a person appropriate to his station". The bride, he said, would likewise have difficulty finding in her place of residence a husband outside her circle of close kin "who would be as appropriate to her station as this one would be". The second witness, Joseph Anton Metzler, concurred. The testimony of the groom then reinforced what had already been said. He knew of no "better place than here to realise" his "happiness". However, he could find not a single person "who, on account of her good reputation, adroitness, lovely deportment and dignity thanks to her own conduct and thanks to the name of her parents (who are most highly respected not only here, but throughout the land), would be more appropriate to my station and situation and possesses such qualities as are fit to provide a foundation for my future well-being". Maria Elisabeth Metzler emphasised their closeness due to their families' being neighbours and indicated that she had loved her prospective groom "ever since childhood – along with his siblings, as close cousins – like children of the same family but always in a way that was honourable before God and man". She could find no other "in this small community" who "would be so appropriate" to her "station, morals, upbringing and accustomed way of life as he". This request, like all of the others, was approved – and once again, the costs were the same.

The Metzlers' wills and probate documents provide a vivid impression of their riches and prestige, showing not only the sums of their own wealth that

57 DIÖAB, Konsistorialakten 1843, Fasc. 5a, Römische Dispensen, no. 13.

were at issue and the sizes of the loans that they had granted to others but also their charitable donations. In cases where the deceased had been childless, it was their relatives – especially siblings, nieces and nephews – who constituted the circles of beneficiaries. The eldest brother, Joseph Anton Metzler, died without issue on 5 March 1863. In his "final testamentary instructions" of August 1862, he appointed his wife Anna Katharina Metzler as the "universal heir" of his real estate holdings.[58] The total value of his assets was indicated as being 166,682 gulden with obligations amounting to 92,488 gulden, making for net wealth of 74,194 gulden. According to the official transfer of the estate (*Einantwortung*) dated 19 October 1864, his siblings had also been designated as heirs. His only brother Johann received 7,000 gulden, while his sisters Maria Katharina, Maria Theresia, Maria Elisabeth and Maria – whose married name was Natter and who lived in Egg – each received 5,250 gulden. This sum was also received by the children of the deceased sister Anna Metzler, who were represented by their father Josef Natter. Furthermore, considerable sums of money – 43,050 gulden, all told – went to foundations and funds, to the Church and to the shooting range in Schwarzenberg.[59]

Josef Anton Metzler's widow Anna Katharina Metzler died in 1876. She left behind three testamentary dispositions, of which one was declared invalid upon the official transfer of the estate, which only took place in January of 1879.[60] Her net worth totalled 267,128 gulden. She was, it was said, "by far the wealthiest person in Schwarzenberg at that time".[61] Bequests in the amount of 1,500 gulden each went to prebends for the parish and chaplaincy in Schwarzenberg, to the parish church there and to the school; 2,000 gulden each went for annual requiem masses as well as a foundation providing scholarships for girls, and 10,000 gulden went to a local institution for the poor ("*Bürgerversorgungsanstalt*"). This type of generosity represented an essential element of status that simultaneously stood for power and wealth and also represented convertible capital – such as whenever a dispensation was needed. The heirs were exclusively her maternal relatives from the Feurstein line: the children of Jodok, Elisabeth, Christian, Josef Gabriel, Maria Anna,

58 In the examined archival materials, no marriage contracts concluded by the couples concerned here were found. This testamentary disposition as well as marriage contracts of other couples allow us to infer that community of marital property was typical in the Bregenz Forest. VLA Bregenz, Bezirksgericht Bezau Verschiedenes, box 1, Testamente 1840–1876; box 2, Testamente 1877–1886.

59 Cf. VLA Bregenz, Verfachbuch Bregenzerwald, 1864, no. 115, fol. 614.

60 Cf. VLA Bregenz, Verfachbuch Bregenzerwald, 1879, no. 153, fol. 79.

61 This assessment can be found in Feurstein, *Die Verwandtschaft Feurstein*, p. 120.

Maria Katharina and Johann Kaspar Feurstein. The listing of their names concluded with the comment that "in the course of the probate process, differences have emerged" in the "interpretation of these testamentary dispositions", whose "legal clarification" had to be awaited. Her properties were sold at a public auction in 1879.[62]

When Josef Anton Feurstein, the widower of Maria Theresia Metzler, died childless in 1877, the estate transfer document (*Einantwortung*) dated 13 February 1878 indicated that he had left behind wealth with a net value of 120,633 gulden.[63] He, too, made bequests to various funds as well as to a farmhand and a maidservant in the amount of one year's pay each. The largest share of the wealth bequeathed to his heirs, in the amount 24,000 gulden, went to the children of Josef Metzler as an "advance bequest" (*Prälegat*). A list of the names of all heirs, positioned further back in the record, makes it possible to clearly identify said children as descendants of his father in law: they were the Metzler siblings featured here in connection with their dispensation requests, his sisters- and brothers-in-law. His father's and mother's siblings – or their respective children in place of those who had already passed away – were declared in the probate proceedings to be his heirs, with equal shares going to the paternal and maternal groups. Since Josef Anton Feurstein and his wife Maria Theresia Metzler had been cousins on both sides and hence doubly related, the Metzler siblings were among both the paternal and maternal heirs: via their mother Maria Anna Feurstein – a paternal aunt of the deceased and the mother of his wife[64] – and via his own mother, who had been a Metzler and an aunt of his wife.[65] They thus inherited thrice altogether.

In the case of the Metzlers, a mode of social positioning becomes visible that ranged significantly beyond the nuclear family and included close relatives – the "cousinfolk".[66] It is in a near-classic way that the portrayal by Maria Elisabeth Metzler in the last-sketched dispensation request, in which she equated her cousins with her own siblings "like children of the same family", fits the hypothesis concerning the greater importance and intensification of horizontal relationships at the turn of the eighteenth to the nineteenth century. This was a configuration of spatial and social proximity, of continually lived and updated kinship that simultaneously represented an environment

62 Cf. Feurstein, *Die Verwandtschaft Feurstein*, p. 121.

63 Cf. VLA Bregenz, Verfachbuch Bregenzerwald, 1878, no. 179, fol. 401.

64 Ibid., under A, point V.

65 Ibid., under B, point II.

66 On this cf. also Delille, "Evolution within Sibling Groups".

for the making of marriages on the basis of a couple configuration that was conceived of as ideal, a configuration defined via familiarity and alikeness that was encoded in multiple ways. It is striking how Christopher Johnson's characterisation of the relationships between the leading bourgeois families he studied in the Breton community of Vannes also applies to Schwarzenberg's Metzlers: "Cousins were little differentiated from siblings, and the two families lived around the corner from each other in the heart of Vannes"[67] – just like the Metzlers and the Feursteins did in Schwarzenberg. In both cases, growing up together from early childhood was thought to promise a happy marriage.[68]

Christopher Johnson and David Sabean view this space of social proximity as a consequence of more frequent endogamy and a tendency toward equal inheritance. This led family interests to consolidate not around a single lineage but rather around a configuration "of loving relatives made as extensive as possible".[69] This new "sibling-based kinship order" is said to have had an effect on intergenerational relationships in the sense of "replacing" the logics of the line of descent. The result, they hold, was a culture in which "parental authority was fading".[70] However, in light of the Metzler, Malfer and other fathers who appeared in the dispensation requests, it would still seem to make sense to keep both axes in view. Among the Metzlers, it was the father who held the reins of the family's extensive economic activities right up to his death. His sons worked alongside him, but it was he who decided when what would be transferred to whom. The authority of Metzler senior was not just economically and socially based but also derived from his political functions. Here, therefore, intensifying horizontal ties between siblings and cousins would seem to have been closely linked with a vertical structure and according positions of power.

Joseph Metzler senior seems to have been a scintillating figure indeed, if the aforementioned self-description prior to his wedding in 1807 is any indication. His palette of activities and responsibilities had been extremely wide-ranging: his father as well as he and his brothers had been merchants on a grand scale as well as textile entrepreneurs, and they had also made numerous loans. They had been part of the region's 'old' economic and political elite and had maintained their elite status. Though the agricultural component of their wealth as well as their landholdings were quite important, they had also opened up new, economically growing and promising areas of activity. The Malfer family's

67 Johnson, "Siblinghood and the Emotional Dimensions", p. 194; Johnson, *Becoming Bourgeois*, chapter four.

68 Ibid., p. 200.

69 Johnson/Sabean, "Introduction", p. 11; Johnson, "Siblinghood and the Emotional Dimensions", p. 194.

70 Johnson/Sabean, "Introduction", pp. 16–17.

circumstances were similar: although two of the three brothers had risen to become high-ranking civil servants and bore noble titles, their mutual landholdings would seem not only to have been a significant component of their wealth but also to have been constituent for their social self-positioning. Elements of bourgeois culture hence joined together here with local anchoring via land, and in view of such multifaceted situatedness, subsuming such families under a class concept would seem difficult.

3 Joseph Feßler's War on Cousin Marriages

Considering the media presence of the discourse on degeneration and health hazards, it was only relatively late that marriage projects in the close degrees of consanguinity – particularly those between first cousins – began to be judged strictly, with dispensations being refused.[71] In the Diocese of Brixen, this can be observed beginning in the mid-1880s. However, there had already been a brief initial phase of rigidity in this respect during the mid-1860s – albeit due mainly to a single person, namely Joseph Feßler (1813–1872), who oversaw the vicariate general in Feldkirch as an auxiliary bishop from 1862 to 1865. Feßler vehemently opposed marriages between first cousins and aimed to prevent such unions entirely in the territory for which he was responsible. It was his firm intent, he announced, "to terminate the possibility of marriage for children of siblings once and for all in order to re-erect the toppled wall, to reintroduce into living practice this notion: that marriage between children of siblings is impossible, unthinkable". In this spirit, there were to be no more exceptions; otherwise, the "appearance of partiality" would repeatedly arise and evoke bitterness among the people or lead them to suspect that "secret reasons" were required, which would entail "the danger of *incestus*".[72]

---

71 The circle of persons viewed by the Church as close blood relations corresponded with those who, in light of recent genetic research, pose a higher risk in terms of danger to the health of mutual children. The attention of the medical field is currently limited to children from configurations comprised of two first cousins. Cf. Martin Langer, "Die konsanguine Ehe – eine medizinische und sozio-kulturelle Herausforderung", *Historische Sozialkunde* 41, 2 (2011), 34–37.

72 Here, he was alluding to the ambivalent attitude toward bridal couples who had already engaged in sexual relations and thus given others cause to assume that it would be easier to obtain a dispensation afterwards – a hope and simultaneously a potential strategy against which the Church constantly fought, albeit ultimately without much success. DIÖAB, Konsistorialakten 1864, Fasc. 22a, Römische Dispensen, no. 34. In this record, three requests are discussed; the quotation is from the correspondence concerning the request of Andreas Mark and Veronika Schwald. A number of other letters from Bishop

The Church, as the supreme administrative authority where marriage prohibitions were concerned, did issue numerous sets of guidelines – that sometimes differed from diocese to diocese – specifying how its representatives were to handle dispensation requests, but only partial success was had in terms of their uniform implementation. A supplicant couple's chances of attaining their goal were in large part dependent on what "mission" the involved clerics were pursuing, whether it was the pope issuing more severe directives or an especially scrupulous and apprehensive – or, conversely, an especially supportive – local parish priest or bishop. The individual administrative protagonists must be viewed as significant switching points within the bureaucratic apparatus at large – in terms of not only their positions and the matters entrusted to them but also their respective personalities. This goes especially for Joseph Feßler, a proponent of conservative Catholic policies.[73]

By comparison, there were only isolated signs of stricter action against marital unions between cousins during the period prior to Feßler's era. The parish priest of Hittisau in the Bregenz Forest, for instance, wrote a very detailed letter to his dean's office in March 1859 portraying the multiple attempts made by one such couple, namely Fidel Riederer, a successful cheese merchant agent working in Vienna for the father of his bride, and Katharina Bader. The priest had "taken great pains to instruct them each time regarding how the Holy Church permits such dispensations to be had only with great difficulty and only for the most compelling reasons, and about how such marriages often lead to unhappiness between the couple or among their progeny, and admonished them each time to give up this acquaintance".[74] Nikolaus Gander, a curate in Afers near Brixen, reported in 1860 that there had been but two marriages "between children of siblings" during his time in office, which had begun in 1852. In the case with which he was dealing at that point, he had spent four years "discouraging the pursuit of this planned marriage in accordance with the instructions in the *Diözensanblatt*".[75]

Feßler regarding cousin marriages can be found in DIÖAB, Konsistorialakten 1864, Fasc. 22c, Verschiedenes, no. 20.

73 On this cf. Gottfried Mayer, *Österreich als katholische Großmacht. Ein Traum zwischen Revolution und liberaler Ära* (Vienna, 1989). This book centres on "three protagonists of the Austrian episcopate" – among them Joseph Feßler – who had devoted themselves to the battle against the liberal forces of their times (ibid., p. 10).

74 DIÖAB, Konsistorialakten 1859, Fasc. 5a, Römische Dispensen, no. 26. Only upon a renewed attempt in 1860, with Fidel Riederer having fallen seriously ill and returned from Vienna, were they granted their dispensation. Cf. ibid., 1860, no. 19.

75 DIÖAB, Konsistorialakten 1861, Fasc. 22a, Römische Dispensen, no. 24.

Joseph Feßler's position was uncompromising – and in his policy of refusal, he was to all appearances more independent in his actions than the vicars general before and after him.[76] Feßler was a native of Vorarlberg, had attended the seminary in Brixen and had taught there as a professor of theology before assuming a professorship in church history and canon law in Vienna. He had been a deputy to the Frankfurt Parliament in 1848.[77] After serving as the Auxiliary Bishop of Brixen and vicar general in Feldkirch, he rose to become bishop of the Lower Austrian Diocese of St. Pölten in 1865. Feßler was also appointed by the Austrian government to head the negotiations with the Roman Curia to revise the concordat in 1862 and 1863, he served as secretary-general of the first Vatican Council, and he wielded considerable influence over church-state policy in Austria.[78]

A long letter to the Bishop of Brixen dated 13 September 1864 paradigmatically represents Joseph Feßler's attitude and position. Feßler opened with a complaint, followed by an admission along with an impressive portrayal of his embattled plight. To hear him tell it, his struggle was in part internal: "It has long been my experience that the handling of marriage dispensations is the matter that weighs upon me most heavily. Today, I am once again having only the most bitter experiences of this sort, which moves me to bring all of the dispensation cases that I have once again received to the attention of Your Prince-Episcopal mercy in order to seek counsel concerning the question of what means could be brought to bear apart from mere rejection. Upon returning here from Brixen in late July with permission to initiate proceedings in three cases involving children of siblings, I was confronted by so many new cases that I lacked the courage to actually do so since I would then have been incapable of resisting the others. For the main reason is always that *others* have also received one, and that it is indeed possible if one will only *pay* and, should

---

76 A biography of a hagiographic and anecdotal character was self-published by its author in 1872 and then by the Brixen-based publisher Verlag Weger in 1874, shortly following Feßler's death: Anton Erdinger, *Dr. Joseph Feßler. Bischof von St. Pölten und Sekretär des vatikanischen Concils. Ein Lebensbild* (Brixen, 1874). The author notes that Brixen's Bishop Vinzenz Gasser had been delighted at Feßler's appointment as auxiliary bishop in Feldkirch, "since, after all, he once more had a friend close by on whose shoulders he could place some of the burdens of his office" (ibid., p. 117). We learn nothing about Feßler's efforts against cousin marriages. The author writes about his appointment and delayed journey to Feldkirch, where he was received by his siblings, and that he undertook a visitation tour of Vorarlberg – which is said to have been one of "affable exchange with the people" (ibid., p. 121) – as early as autumn 1862. The rest of this section deals with his activities in Rome and his transfer to St. Pölten.

77 Cf. Mayer, *Österreich als katholische Großmacht*, p. 157.

78 Cf. on this ibid., p. 11, 184–198.

a pregnancy be involved, also *pray*. If I should give in, I am firmly convinced that everyone, including those who have already been refused, will come to me again; and in most of these cases, I shall have no cogent reasons for turning away the others if I permit even one to go through. People are using all possible means; they entreat, they weep and they threaten, usually coming in person and remaining in my chamber for hours on end, since I cannot, after all, throw them out; they seek to compel my assent."[79]

Feßler continued by listing the requests of 12 couples – nine of them cousins, two of them related by blood in the second and third unequal degree, and one of them a brother- and sister-in-law – and commenting on each of them, in some cases writing "refused multiple times already", "already frequently refused". He closed by asking "urgently for help and counsel", not neglecting to reiterate his uncompromising view: "In all this, you may consider it certain that if leniency is shown in this or that case, all the others shall advance upon us with such force that resistance will no longer be possible." Seven of the brides were pregnant at that point in time, and a further two had already given birth to a child by their prospective grooms. In the dispensation records following Feßler's years in office, nine of these twelve couples reappear – with successful requests, just as he had predicted.[80] During this period, the local priests consistently argued in a different direction than Feßler did – thus confirming the existence of what he was fighting against. They expressed the view that a dispensation for two cousins would "never cause a stir nor make an ugly moral impression in the community", more often than not hastening to explain that "in the neighbourhood, dispensations" had been granted "quite recently in several cases involving the same degrees of kinship". In light of this, they held, a refused dispensation would put "local officials or this parish in a bad light" and

79 DIÖAB, Konsistorialakten 1864, Fasc. 22c, Verschiedenes. no. 20; emphases underlined in the original. In another case, he reported that it had been "a difficult struggle" for him to "determinedly refuse" two couples, for "a mature and, as it seems, otherwise very virtuous man" had stood before him, begging and weeping like a child. If one were to now relent in other cases in the same deanery, he reasoned, this would only awaken "an impression of the most severe injustice". DIÖAB, Konsistorialakten 1864, Fasc. 22a, Römische Dispensen, no. 34 and 1863, no. 8. For a pastoral perspective cf. Anton Hye, *Der vieljährige Seelsorger auf dem Lande in den meisten Verhältnissen seines Amtes lehrend und handelnd dargestellt* … (Vienna, 1831), especially the sections, "Ein Mann, der sich mit dem wiederhohlt abweislichen Bescheid, seine Heirath betreffend, nicht beruhigen will" [A Man Who Remains Implacable Following Repeated Rejections of His Proposed Marriage] and "Vereheligungen, wie sie gewöhnlich Statt haben" [Marriages as They Are Typically Concluded], pp. 252–254. For this reference, I extend thanks to Johann Weißensteiner.

80 Cf. DIÖAB, Konsistorialakten 1865, Fasc. 22a, Römische Dispensen, no. 6, no. 7, no. 8, no. 19, no. 39, no. 40, no. 43, no. 44; ibid.., 1866, no. 9.

nourish suspicions of personal animosity toward the supplicants.[81] This, at the same time, indicates the frequently difficult situation that every single granted dispensation and the knowledge thereof created for parish priests.

The fact that dispensations had indeed been granted for several marriage projects between cousins in the immediate vicinity and within a brief period showed according to Feßler "how common marriages between children of siblings have already become". He went on to mention his constant fear that every further dispensation would "quite naturally" increase "the power of this argument in the eyes of the people". In the event of a refusal, "outrage and ill things" would then have to be "feared". For if a dispensation were to be denied, the dispensation-seekers would be "living together in open incest".[82] What he was doing should, in principal, have appeared hopeless to him. But the various strategies employed by such couples repeatedly evoked his ire – such as when Johann Josef Drisner and his cousin Cäcilia Baldauf from Klösterle, whose requests had been refused a total of four times, presented a physician's attestation as part of a renewed attempt in March 1863. This attestation declared the bride to be suffering from a "melancholic malady" in the wake of her request's rejection and spoke of the danger that she might possibly go mad.[83] This couple knew that physicians' attestations had been successfully employed as part of two other requests by couples whose situations had been comparable. However, they had taken their concern to the wrong person, namely to the local "barber-surgeon and accoucheur" (*Wund- und Geburtsarzt*), a fact that robbed their argument and this attestation of all legitimacy.[84] Joseph Feßler's reaction was accordingly uncompromising: "Apart from the economic reasons that have already been deemed insufficient", the new request put forth "only the reason of health" – but what weight could be accorded a physician's attestation issued by "a mere village surgeon for the benefit of people from his village with an urge to get married"? Feßler thus once again rejected the request of Johann Joseph Drisner and Cäcilia Baldauf due to insufficient justification. "Every new approval of a request for such a dispensation makes resisting that much more tedious, difficult and in fact near impossible in the future", complained Feßler anew in the relevant letter. "If this case is approved, the next

81 DIÖAB, Konsistorialakten 1863, Fasc. 22a, Römische Dispensen, no. 10.

82 Ibid.

83 Ibid.

84 Feßler had the successful dispensation proceedings, which were said to have inspired this couple, verified along with the according physician's attestations: in the first request, a civil servant had been involved; the other had met with success only "after calling upon Professor Vonbank following a long search". These were personages with whom the village surgeon from Klösterle could not compete.

dispensation-seeker will be able to point out three such cases, present a physician's attestation and moreover threaten to otherwise go to Switzerland and marry there."[85]

Alongside physicians' attestations, transfers of wealth and the attendant contracts between unmarried related couples or the mutual construction or purchase of a house also repeatedly put church representatives under pressure. If a marriage did not come to fruition, economic harm or ongoing mutual dependence stemming from debts would have to be feared. Feßler was hence among those who decried such actions as "a means of attempting to force dispensation that has been employed quite often of late",[86] and he demanded radical legal measures. The consistory in Brixen felt pressed to react and sent a letter containing his demands to the *Statthalterei* in Innsbruck (the provincial government apparatus that succeeded the *Gubernium*) in February of 1865. Feßler sought to have district courts officially instructed to enter the mutual purchase of houses by closely related bridal couples into the court's *Verfachbücher* – the books that, in this region, documented all wealth-related matters and thus also transfers of property – only upon presentation of their granted dispensations. This as a way of combating "the evil of marriages in very close degrees of kinship that, especially in Vorarlberg, are getting out of hand in a most lamentable way". The *Statthalterei* in Innsbruck did second the consistory's disapproval by underlining "the concerning, even damaging" nature of such marriages and declaring itself willing to help "guard against such marriages", but it had to simultaneously inform them that decrees fit to institute the recommended preventative strategy were not within its purview: "Such a ban cannot be instituted by the civil administration, and detailed inquiries have indicated that there is absolutely no prospect that such […] might be effected by the legal authorities, as has been shown in a similar case in which a similar request was rejected in no uncertain terms."[87]

During these years, characterised as they were by a policy of discouragement, one couple from Vorarlberg even tried their luck in the French city of Nancy. Vagaries such as this one point yet again to the difficult situation in which the Church found itself, a situation in which couples simply bypassed the officially sanctioned channels when these proved hopeless. However, they also show how the arm of the Church could extend over large areas. Konrad Steurer and his cousin Anna Steurer from Krumbach in the Bregenz Forest

85 DIÖAB, Konsistorialakten 1863, Fasc. 22a, Römische Dispensen, no. 10.

86 Ibid.

87 DIÖAB, Konsistorialakten 1865, Fasc. 22c, Varia über Ehe, no. 1.

Deanery submitted their initial dispensation request in the autumn of 1862; this request got no further than the vicariate general in Feldkirch, where it was blocked by Feßler due to a lack of canonical reasons.[88] As a consequence, the couple made plans to emigrate to Bavaria in early 1863 in hopes of receiving the necessary dispensation more easily there. In order to do so, however, they needed documents, particularly – their baptismal certificates. At the vicariate general's request, the prince-episcopal ordinariate refused to issue these certificates "for the indicated purpose".[89] The local parish priest had assumed that the couple, upon receipt of their dispensation, would "doubtless come right back", for which reason he had interpreted their plans as a "manoeuvre" and asked for advice from the next higher level regarding the issuance of the requested documents. However, as the same priest recounted half a year later in a detailed report, Konrad and Anna Steurer did not give up in the face of the refused issuance, instead travelling to France – specifically, to Nancy – in early December of 1863. They had heard "that marrying goes much more easily there under all circumstances, and that they are not so particular about documents". Rumour had it that their planned undertaking had been well prepared, with them having already registered with the police in Nancy half a year before.

Eastern France, with its borders to Switzerland and southern German territories, was an important destination for migratory labourers from Vorarlberg during the eighteenth century, especially for those who worked in the construction trades, and it remained so during the nineteenth century.[90] During the period between 1840 and 1850, which Markus Hämmerle studied in terms of emigration from Vorarlberg, France was the preferred destination, – accounting for nearly 40 per cent of émigrés.[91] The majority of these people came from the Bregenz Forest and the Montafon, and insofar as their destinations are recorded, they worked mainly in the Franche-Comté in the vicinity

88 This request can be found amongst the Feßler records in ADF, GA, Ehesachen III, Präsidial behandelte Ehedispensfälle (Bischof Feßler) 1862–1865, though the matrimonial examination protocol is not included.

89 DIÖAB, Konsistorialakten 1864, Fasc. 22a, Römische Dispensen, no. 28.

90 The dispensation requests thus contain several submitted by masons who travelled to France every year as seasonal labourers.

91 Markus Hämmerle, *Die Auswanderung aus Vorarlberg von 1815 bis 1914. Dokumentation und Analyse*, PhD thesis, University of Vienna, 1982, pp. 167–168; cf. also Markus Hämmerle, *Glück in der Fremde? Vorarlberger Auswanderer im 19. Jahrhundert* (Feldkirch, 1990). The table containing the figures cited here does not appear in this dissertation's published version.

of Besançon, in Alsace near Colmar in the Département Haut-Rhine and – in considerably lower numbers – in Lorraine, where Nancy is located.[92]

The parish priest, for his part, worried that they might well return "properly married" after just a few weeks, so he immediately wrote to a clergyman in Nancy whom he knew "in order to learn just how such things are handled there". In response, he did indeed receive confirmation that "they really are not so strict where church documents are concerned". Upon learning this, he requested that the couple be sent back immediately and promised to see to their needs, which he then did. He asked the deanery office – and thus also the ordinariate – to lend this request every possible support, arguing above all that Konrad and Anna Steurer would have to rely on Nancy were they to be refused, thereby encouraging others to do likewise. It was in this that he saw the greatest evil – "*malum majus*". In May of 1864, the couple ultimately received their desired dispensation via the 'regular' channels. Present as a subtext here and in Feßler's argumentation was the constant worry that precedents – in terms of granted dispensations as well as successful strategies of circumvention – might be set. Beginning in the 1860s, this view came to determine dispensation practice more pronouncedly than before.

Feßler made his tribulations in connection with dispensation requests quite explicit by addressing to the prince-episcopal ordinariate in Brixen frequent letters consisting of densely written pages.[93] However, he failed to find the hoped-for backing and encouragement there. A comment on the reverse side of one of the lists of related couples that Feßler had compiled reads: "Bishop Feßler tends to be strict where requests for dispensations regarding kin marriage are concerned."[94] The fact that he was alone in his absolutist stance, even

---

92 Cf. Hannelore Berchtold, *Die Arbeitsmigration von Vorarlberg nach Frankreich im 19. Jahrhundert* (Feldkirch, 2003), pp. 36–39, 42–43, 71–73, 83–84, 90–93; Alois Niederstätter, "Arbeit in der Fremde. Bemerkungen zur Vorarlberger Arbeitsmigration vom Spätmittelalter bis zum 19. Jahrhundert", *Montfort. Vierteljahresschrift für Geschichte und Gegenwart Vorarlbergs* 48, 2 (1996), 105–117, 108–110.

93 After having sent off a list of all pending dispensation cases along with a request for counsel and help, he wrote again to Brixen that same day – once more in an urgent tone and demanding a consistent stance: "In this entire matter, I beseech you not to fail to recognise that it is really only about whether all of them or none of them are to be granted dispensations." Regarding his person, he affirmed: "I will be capable of carrying out this general refusal, though I am now being assailed in ever greater degrees of intensity, owed to which my disposition is suffering quite a bit." DIÖAB, Konsistorialakten 1864, Fasc. 22c, Verschiedenes, no. 20. Emphasis underlined in the original. Cf. also DIÖAB, Konsistorialakten 1864, Fasc. 22a, Römische Dispensen, no. 34c and ibid., 1863, no. 8.

94 ADF, GA, Ehesachen III, Präsidialakten 1830–1900, Schwierige, präsidial behandelte Ehefälle, Zeit Bischof Prünster, 1830–1860, no. 92 and 93.

though the Diocese of Brixen did pursue dispensation policies that were altogether rather strict, is shown not least by a letter written in response to one of his numerous complaints and signed personally by Prince-Bishop Vinzenz Gasser. This letter allows us to deduce that Gasser had asked his consistorial councillors whether they thought it expedient to "*reject every such dispensation for a certain period* (for a year or so, naturally) in order that the people gradually realise and become accustomed to the seriousness and importance of this matter, hence combating the evil of incest partly herewith and partly through the disappearance of any hope of marriage". The unanimous opinion of the council's clerics was that they "could *not* advocate such handling of dispensation matters regardless of the very weighty arguments that would favour doing so". This seemed to them "a degree of stringency" that would "overshoot the mark" and ultimately fail to achieve "the intended end". In their view, "stricter handling of ecclesiastical laws" would serve this objective more "than blanket rejection of such dispensation requests".[95]

In his lengthy expositions, which are characterised by mantra-like repetitiveness, Feßler did entirely without physiological and medical justifications. He much rather insisted that both the Catholic Church and "the secular government" had "always strictly forbidden" marriage "between close blood relatives", who included first cousins most prominently of all. In doing so, he suggested that this was a universally valid norm and went on to attribute this to "reasons of decency" that would "contradict such marriages to begin with". And even if one were to ignore said reasons of decency, he concluded, "sad experience" showed that such marriages between all-too-close relatives "usually do not end well".[96] Even if dispensation practice was indeed to become more conciliatory following the departure of Joseph Feßler as auxiliary bishop and vicar general in Feldkirch, complaints about the rising number of dispensation requests in close degrees and especially by cousin couples continued unabated.

4 Consequences of Roman Dispensations: The Survey of 1883

In 1883, Feldkirch's vicar general Simon Aichner had a survey conducted in Vorarlberg's deaneries. His objective was to compile valid "statistics" on the consequences of kin marriages. To his chagrin, this survey failed to produce

95 Reply by Brixen's Prince-Bishop Vinzenz Gasser, ADF, GA, Ehesachen III, Präsidial behandelte Ehedispensfälle (Bischof Feßler) 1862–1865, no. 8.

96 DIÖAB, Konsistorialakten 1864, Fasc. 22a, Römische Dispensen, no. 41.

such statistics on account of the responses' "frequently too general" quality,[97] but its findings were still taken as a basis for a stricter policy of refusal. Aichner's initiative particularly provides insights into the perceptions of the clergy.

This survey had been preceded by a great deal of correspondence that was shot through with an increasing number of complaints by Brixen's ordinariate regarding the dispensation requests from Vorarlberg, which were viewed as being all too numerous. A letter from 1876, for instance, reads: "One cannot lament enough the fact that in Vorarlberg, this business with marriages in the close degrees of kinship has gone so far that parents no longer hesitate to allow their daughters to enter into such marriages at the most callow ages."[98] Surrounding one dispensation request from the following year, a complaint was raised concerning "the tendency, so very virulent in Vorarlberg", to "wed one's closest consanguineous and affinal kin", with the parenthetical remark that this was "certainly most detrimental to general well-being".[99] By its own admission, what the ordinariate feared most was "the examples that are being set, which could cause such marriages in prohibited degrees of kinship to become more and more common in Tyrol as well". For as "experience" had shown, one couple would point to the other in an attempt to "force such dispensations from the Church".[100]

The way in which the 1883 survey was conducted adhered consistently to the canon law notion of kinship in that it addressed marriages between close consanguineous kin and affinal kin indiscriminately. The deans were thus charged with documenting the "consequences of marriages concluded on the basis of Roman dispensations", taking those couples who had been wed between 1860 and 1880 as their sample.[101] Their specific role was to collect the information that arrived from the parishes and forward it to Feldkirch. Once arrived, this information was compiled to produce a comprehensive summary (*Gesamtaufstellung*) rendered as a table. The Deanery of Feldkirch headed up the list. The first two such marriages listed here were between affinal kin. "Only one marriage rather unhappy", reads the accompanying comment. Next to the following three marriages, two of them consanguineous and one affinal, it is

---

97 ADF, GA, Ehesachen II, 1811–1916, An den Hochwürdigen Seelsorgs-Clerus in Vorarlberg [To the Most Reverend Pastoral Clergy in Vorarlberg], printed circular dated 25 June 1884.

98 DIÖAB, Konsistorialakten 1876, Fasc. 22a, Römische Dispensen, no. 34.

99 DIÖAB, Konsistorialakten 1877, Fasc. 22a, Römische Dispensen, no. 24B.

100 DIÖAB, Konsistorialakten 1876, Fasc. 22a, Römische Dispensen, no. 58.

101 ADF, GA, Karton Ehesachen V, Römische Dispensen III, 1877–1885, 1883, Erhebung über die Auswirkungen der mit Römischer Dispens geschlossenen Ehen [Survey on the Consequences of Marriages Concluded on the Basis of Roman Dispensations].

noted: "Nothing conspicuous". In the community of Tosters, one marriage permitted thanks to a Roman dispensation had produced a child "who soon died", as did the mother shortly afterwards – "due to consumption". The one consanguineous marriage in Miemingen was "very happy and blessed with children", and the three Roman dispensation-based marriages concluded in Koblach were also "all very happy". In Mäder, a consanguineous couple was living "in quite some dispeace". Three children had died, etc.

Within the diocese as a whole, the highest concentration of marriages that had required Roman dispensations came from the Deanery of the Bregenz Forest. From its total of 22 parish offices, 18 responses in varying degrees of detail are represented in the final overview that was compiled. A closer look at these makes clear this survey's logic. The evaluations that had been conducted were of the couples as well as of any children they had produced. The spectrum of inquiry regarding the former encompassed information on their further paths in life as well as assessments of their relationships as couples. Regarding the children, the interest was in their mental abilities and physical condition, and the priests reported on abnormalities but also on "normality". Regarding the one consanguine marriage in Lingenau, the parish priest reported "nothing heard so far" to the effect that this marriage had occasioned "any ill consequences" for the children. A considerable number of responses attested that nothing out of the ordinary had been found. The parish priest in Warth, for example, reported on two marriages: on the affinal union concluded in 1872, there was "nothing special to report"; the one from 1881 between blood relatives who were also distant affinal relatives was childless but "otherwise normal". He added that due to the *angustia loci* and the "*sensus communi populi*", the general attitude among the people there, such marriages gave no cause for much of a sensation. The parish priest in Damüls likewise noted "nothing conspicuous" about the two consanguine unions in his parish: marital peace prevailed, and numerous children had been "born in the best of health". One of the two husbands had died, but he had already been "ailing" prior to the marriage. Economic blessings were modest, but this was no wonder, since neither couple had possessed even 100 gulden upon their marriage.

While some priests discussed individual cases at greater length, adding explanations or revealing past histories, others provided only very brief assessments. The chaplain of Egg commented on the three consanguineous marriages in his parish that had been concluded thanks to papal dispensations in a manner that was quite concise: one had remained childless, while the children of another were "rather talentless". He knew of no other "ills" that could be attributed to "close kinship". The nine relevant marriages in Krumbach were also described in only the briefest of terms: two as childless, two as ones about which "nothing special can be noted", one in which the wife had died young twelve years into the marriage and another where the wife had "died young following two years of marriage", one that had not even come to pass due to the bride's death prior to the wedding, and one that was not characterised at all; the ninth, finally, was "happy, though childless", – but the woman in question had already been "blessed richly with children" from her first marriage.

Some couples' lives had taken dramatic turns: the parish priest in Andelsbuch indicated that Johann Jakob Muzel and his cousin Elisabeth Ritter, married in 1875, had been hit by "total economic ruin". They had lost all of their possessions to bankruptcy two years prior and were now "on the street", a "fate" that had already been "prophesied" upon their marriage due to their having acquired a property that was far too expensive. Four of their nine children had died. Disastrous scenarios were likewise dominant in Bezau: a marriage between two cousins had been quite ill-fated – not due to "strife, but because of misfortunes that befell them one after the other". The wife had died at age 35 as a consequence of childbirth after three years of marriage, with the husband following her in death one-and-a-half years later due to tetanus. Their youngest daughter, who had been of fragile constitution from birth onward, had died "of a very peculiar, excruciating malady" at the age of four months. Of the two older boys, he knew nothing special: the older one was healthy "though of weak talents, and the younger one is quite sickly". This family's "household situation" had gone steadily downhill, with the lion's share of their possessions having to be sold off while the husband was still living. The second dispensed marriage in Bezau – this one between a brother- and a sister-in-law – did seem to have been "a rather happy one in terms of mutual affection, but otherwise misfortune upon misfortune": the first child was stillborn, he knew nothing special about the second, and the husband had died at age 50 after just four years of marriage. The parish priest then added a lengthy paragraph "on the ill luck of this man" in his two prior marriages. In doing so, he drew a possible connection to "marriages between quite close blood and affinal kin" that, so he had heard, had taken place among his "forebears": one son from his first marriage suffered from "stuttering so severe as to be incapable of handling more important matters", and a second had "gone missing" – "drowned or otherwise disappeared" – at approximately age seven. In his second marriage, there had been two infelicitous births and one premature death. The only child still alive, he wrote, was "not in a bad way, but of rather weak talents".

From Mittelberg came a report riddled with deaths. A union between affines had produced three children who were "all physically and mentally sound".

The mother, however, had died "of consumption" after five years of marriage. In the other three marriages, which were consanguineous, several children had died: in the first marriage, it was five of eight – four of which were stillborn. Of their three children who still lived, two were "of very good talents, one of them an outstanding student, while the third is of mediocre talents". In the second of these consanguineous marriages, the only child had died at age two with the woman having been "38 years of age already" when she had wed; in the third marriage, one child had died immediately after birth, one was "physically and mentally sound", and one had been stillborn. The mother, in giving birth to this third child, had then followed her child in death due to the physician's late arrival. A couple in Au, who were cousins, had brought forth four children – all of whom had died shortly after being born. On this, the parish priest commented that "happiness and satisfaction" had vanished "despite the fine, lucrative position of the husband and the wealth of the wife". "Lengthy efforts" had preceded the conclusion of this marriage, but it had all been in vain. The groom was said to have claimed that he wanted this bride for her ability to give him clever children, declaring that "in order to conclude his marriage, he ultimately would not need the Church." This letter ends with the words: "God has judged!"[102]

Again and again, the parish priests reported cases of childless marriages: the priest in Mellau indicated concerning one such couple that "otherwise, these spouses" lived "in peace, as is generally known". In Hirschegg, a marriage concluded in the second degree of consanguinity was also "peaceable, but childless". In Schröcken, it was three marriages out of five. In one of these cases, the parish priest opined that this was "presumably irrelevant", since the groom had already been 56 and the bride 46 years old when they had wed. The parish priest in Großdorf reported on one childless couple that had been bereft of domestic peace since the husband had "succumbed to drink". In Schwarzenberg, the parish priest attributed the unhappiness and childlessness of an affinal marriage *ex copula illicita* to the "constitution and behaviour" of the couple, in view of

102 The couples who feature in this report are not named, nor are the years of their dispensations and/or marriages listed. The couple from Au may have been Joseph Erath and Theresia Kaufmann. Their matrimonial examination is unfortunately missing from their dispensation, but the included correspondence indicates that Theresia Kaufmann had inherited a house and some monetary assets from her father – the value of which totalled 10,000 gulden. Groom Joseph Erath, however, is described by the local priest as being "one of the most outstanding boys in the village in terms of his sense of religion, morality, industriousness and physical health". DIÖAB, Konsistorialakten 1874, Fasc. 22a, Römische Dispensen, no. 9.

which "not much else" could have been expected. While some couples were said to be living "quite peaceably", it was said of certain others – such as in Hirschegg and Au – that marital peace was either grossly or somewhat lacking. A couple in Großdorf had spent five years living in an unhappy marriage and had since been separated just as long. Happiness and peace embodied criteria that were viewed as the hallmark of good marital coexistence.

These reports took up perspectives that differed fundamentally: some focused on inconspicuousness or on emphasising positive aspects alongside cases of misfortune, while others started from more negative assumptions. It was this last perspective, for instance, that determined the description of one of the four dispensed marriages from Bizau. Concerning an innkeeper couple, who were cousins, and their four children, the parish priest reported that there existed no "conspicuous misfortune". The second child had died following a difficult birth; among those who still lived, he could "recognise not the least mental or physical degeneracy" (*Entartung*).

Possible consequences of kin marriages were ascertained in a way that adhered strictly to ecclesiastical logic. The interest focused on marital dispeace and unhappy life courses as well as the misfortunes that could befall a family – economic ruin just as much as childlessness and the health and mortality of mothers, fathers and children, without any recognisable prioritisation in terms of the significance and valence attributed thereto. This broad palette seems anachronistic in terms of the set of notions on which it is founded.[103] The parish priests, in their commentaries, took pains to qualify some of their findings by disassociating misfortunes and deaths from the marital context and not directly attributing them to marriage between kin: they wrote that the woman or the man had been sickly prior to the marriage; that fatal illnesses were common in the family and/or had afflicted siblings; that economic ruin had already been visible up ahead prior to the marriage; that childlessness was owed to the couple's age; etc. At the same time, some lamented the difficult position they were in when it came to implementing stricter dispensation policies in terms that were positively drastic. In Hittisau, which was a deanery seat in those days, 15 marriages had required Roman dispensations. At the conclusion of his remarks, which had covered couples affected by death, illness and childlessness as well as couples concerning whom there was "nothing

103 Tirso de Molina, for example, has the character Estefania in his 1636 play *El amor medico* say that marriages between cousins either do none too well or are denied the joy of children: "*que casamientos entre primos,/ o se logran siempre poco,/ o no se alegran con hijos*". Tirso de Molina, El amor médico, third act, scene XIV, verses 3.546–3.548. I am grateful to Wolfram Aichinger for this hint.

conspicuous to be reported", the parish priest emphasised that seven of these marriages – meaning nearly half – had been concluded before he had taken office. He had always "done everything possible to prevent such marriages and thus sometimes downright burdened" himself "with the hate of those families". It was "generally difficult and often simply impossible", he wrote, "to close a door once it has been opened". This was all the more true if one bordered on "German dioceses, where the handling of such matters" was "by no means rigorous for reasons that are well known".

The parish priest in Hirschegg, in his report, added a one-and-a-half page commentary that portrayed his experiences in a similar vein: the "people", he wrote, had "not the least respect for nor a proper idea of [...] the canonical marriage impediments, their causes and their reasons". People maintained "a commonly held notion that marriage impediments are but a means by which the clergy seeks to make money, much like the turnstile at a tollhouse". He continued by stating that priests were only informed of planned marriages once "everything has been concluded". It would then be "demanded" of the priest that he refrain from posing any difficulties, and such demands were accompanied by mentions of other cases in which dispensations had been granted. If a priest voiced objections, he was deemed to be "an outright enemy" – whereupon the supplicants would either seek out another way of obtaining a dispensation or threaten civil marriage. And in the end, they would "triumphally hold up the dispensation received by way of obstinacy or by circumventing the priest" and brag about having obtained it despite the priest's resistance. This, he wrote, was the usual outcome of "such an affair", an outcome that caused "much vexation" for him and other pastors. He consequently held an "episcopal declaration and admonition of the people regarding this matter" to be not only "desirable, but necessary".[104]

The clear findings that had been desired, which would have been harnessed as a well-founded deterrent against pursuing marriages in close degrees, were not produced by this survey. In its final summary, the vicariate general had to admit that marriages between kin could "turn out just as well" or badly as marriages "between non-kin", but it still did attribute to kin marriages a special degree of "damaging impacts" that applied "partially to parents, partially to

104 In his *Praktisches Geschäftbuch* of 1893, which was addressed to "Austria's Curates", Wolfgang Dannerbauer recommended that "marriage impediments, their purpose and reasons for which the Church occasionally grants forbearance be addressed as part of a sermon" at least once a year, such as on the Sunday after Three Kings Day, and that priests should warn especially against marriage to close kin. Dannerbauer, *Praktisches Geschäftsbuch*, p. 233.

children", concluding: "The concern now must be as to suitable means of preventing such marriages whenever possible."[105]

Priests were thus once again called upon to "admonish" against such marriages. They were instructed to pay attention "not just to the petitioners' private well-being but also to the *general* church standpoint". In his circular, Auxiliary Bishop Aichner recommended two "means" by which to deal with the "excessive number" of such marriages: the faithful were to be instructed and enlightened "in public lessons and, where the opportunity presents itself, in private" about Christian marriage and marriage impediments, "about the unfortunate aspects of kin marriages (and especially also mixed marriages)". Furthermore, priests were to "make efforts" to attain early knowledge of possible marriage projects in the prohibited degrees so that "familiarities and relationships between close kin that tend to nurture thoughts of marriage either do not arise or can be nipped in the bud". Parents were to be urged to cooperate rather than abet such marital unions "on account of financial motivations". Unfortunately, he continued, "the natural aversion" to one's kin had been "so dulled already in many areas due to the frequency of such marriages that new cases no longer evoke any sensation at all among the people". This he held to be "an unhealthy state in which public opinion is oblivious to that which goes against healthy nature (*horror sanguinis*)". It was therefore necessary to work towards a "wholesome and healthy reaction" against kin marriages wherever "indifference" had "taken hold".

The circular concluded with a directive concerning what was to be said, literally or in substance, "to the faithful on this matter" – including the reasons why the Church found kin marriages "so displeasing". The aspects featured in the survey appear once more, here: "marital peace and true familial happiness" were not infrequently missing from such marriages; "conspicuous mishaps, dispeace, tragedies and misfortunes of various kinds" were also apparent. It was not rare for these marriages to remain childless, he continued, and one saw among the children "frequent premature mortality, conspicuous physical weakness and degeneracy, mental feebleness, deafness, crippledness, scrofulousness[106] [and] weak nerves", the frequent occurrence of which was also confirmed by statistics from "physicians and students of nature".[107] Finally, Aichner made reference to "morality among close kin" that could "only

105 ADF, GA, Ehesachen II, 1811–1916, An den Hochwürdigen Seelsorgs-Clerus in Vorarlberg, printed circular dated 25 June 1884.

106 This was presumably a reference to scrofula.

107 ADF, GA, Ehesachen II, 1811–1916, An den Hochwürdigen Seelsorgs-Clerus in Vorarlberg, printed circular dated 25 June 1884.

too easily be gravely damaged" through blithe indifference and kin marriage's consequent proliferation. Explicitly addressed were marital unions between first cousins as well as between brothers- and sisters-in-law. To go with the previously mentioned saying, "either an untimely death, no heirs or ruination", this directive provided priests with a second: "Close blood does no good!" (*Nahes Blut thut nicht gut!*) The circular concluded with a plea: "Therefore, you young lads and ladies, all of you who seek to enter married life, take these lessons to heart and do not rashly conclude a marriage that could make you miserable for all time and eternity! And you, dear parents, bring to bear all of your influence so as to best prevent marriages between your children and their closest kin!"

A conspicuous aspect of this survey and how its findings were handled is that not a word was wasted on distinguishing between consanguinity and affinity. References to this distinction were equally absent in the commentaries by the local priests and deans. In this way, it was made implicitly clear that the requirement to obtain a dispensation in cases of affinity was to be consistently upheld as valid and above question. It was in accordance with this logic that the consequences given pride of place in the overall findings had nothing to do with the body, childlessness, excess mortality or endangerment of the children's health, all of which would have been in keeping with the discourse of that era; instead, such observations were subordinated to a focus on marital dispeace, misfortunes and the vicissitudes of life.

In Dornbirn, this survey happened to come right on the heels of a spectacular marriage. City parish priest Gebhard Fink concluded his report by remarking that dispensed marriages "currently do not" cause "much of a stir", since the case of a marriage between uncle and niece had "shown the people" that dispensations could be had even in very close degrees of kinship. It was with three exclamation marks that his remark was rendered in the "comprehensive summary": "With Dr. Waibl having been dispensed, nothing more occasions any notice!!!"[108]

5 "Emergency Civil Marriage" and Difficult Unions: Uncle and Niece

While the Josephine Marriage Patent of 16 January 1783 had defined marriage as a civil contract, this applied mainly to its legal consequences – which made

108 ADF, Generalvikariat Matrimonialia (GA), Karton Ehesachen V, 1877–1885, Römische Dispensen III, 1883, Erhebung über die Auswirkungen der mit Römischer Dispens geschlossenen Ehen. Regarding this dispensation case see the following section on dispensations for the configuration of uncle and niece.

it subject to civil law and the secular justice system – but not to the act of marriage itself, which remained firmly in Church hands. The Concordat of 1855 had then returned jurisdiction over marriage to the Church, entailing that canon law once again applied. An important step in a more politically liberal direction, however, was the December Constitution of 1867, which contained important provisions establishing principles such as the equality of all citizens before the law and complete freedom of worship and conscience.[109] While obligatory civil marriage was also debated, it was not introduced.[110] The May Laws of 1868, for their part, once again made the Austrian monarchy's Catholics subject to state laws on marriage along with the corresponding jurisdiction. And for cases in which the Church refused to marry a couple, the May Laws introduced "emergency civil marriage" (RGBl 47), – which Karl Vocelka has described as "vaguely constructed".[111] On this basis, it had thus become possible to conclude "a marriage valid before the state without observing canon law's requirements".[112] Furthermore, a law passed on 9 April 1870 defined emergency civil marriage as the standard form of marriage for those persons who were not adherents of a particular religion (RGBl 51).[113] So far, there has been no systematic investigation of this practice. However, the dispensation records show that those who took advantage of this newly created option included couples closely related by blood and affinity, though they employed it more often as a threat than as an actual alternative to a church wedding.

In conservative Catholic and ecclesiastical circles, and hence also in the Diocese of Brixen, even the slightest allusion to civil marriage was fit to evoke nightmares. Hubert Weitensfelder portrays one symptomatic case from Vorarlberg: just a few weeks following the introduction of emergency civil

---

109 On this cf. Karl Vocelka, *Verfassung oder Konkordat? Der publizistische und politische Kampf der österreichischen Liberalen um die Religionsgesetze des Jahres 1868* (Vienna, 1978), pp. 46–50; Reinalter, "Liberalismus und Kirche", p. 158.

110 The original intent had been to include a § 17 with the following content: "The validity of a marriage is contingent upon the formal consent of both members of the bridal couple before the authority charged by the state with recording the marriage contract. A church wedding can take place only following conclusion of a civil marriage." Alfred Fischel, *Die Protokolle des Verfassungsausschusses über die Grundrechte. Ein Beitrag zur Geschichte des österreichischen Reichstags vom Jahre 1848* (Vienna/Leipzig, 1912), p. 185, quoted in Vocelka, *Verfassung oder Konkordat*, pp. 48–49.

111 Vocelka, *Verfassung oder Konkordat*, p. 89; on the debates preceding this law's passage cf. ibid. pp. 75–76.

112 Ursula Floßmann, *Österreichische Privatrechtsgeschichte*, 5th ed. (New York, 2005), p. 77.

113 Cf. Ulrike Harmat, "Divorce and Remarriage in Austria-Hungary: the Second Marriage of Franz Konrad von Hötzendorf", *Austrian History Yearbook* 32 (2001), 69–103, 73, note. 17.

marriage, Johann Reiner – a "beer brewer, innkeeper and farm owner" as well as a "municipal councilman in Lochau" – desired to marry the Protestant Maria Friederike Häussler, a teacher's daughter from Württemberg who lived in Bregenz.[114] The competent priest declined to proclaim the banns of marriage, demanding a written declaration that any and all children from this marriage would be raised Catholic and threatening that a Roman dispensation would be required whose arrival might take years. Subsequently, Reiner sent a complaint to the district office and requested that civil banns be proclaimed. He furthermore requested that the *Statthalterei* abbreviate the period of the banns by two weeks. Reiner simultaneously declared his intention to enter into a civil marriage, since the priest had refused to marry him and waiting through church dispensation proceedings would take too long – all the more since the outcome was uncertain.[115]

The claim that a longer wait would endanger the "household" was contested by the priest, who by this point was in open dispute with Rainer. The district office ultimately deemed an emergency civil marriage to be justified. The vicar general protested against the civil banns of marriage and declared that the legally defined prerequisites for a civil marriage had not been fulfilled, "since the priest has refused neither the banns nor the wedding".[116] The Bishop of Brixen then sent a letter to the *Statthalterei*, and this letter had its intended effect: the district office retracted the banns. In response, Reiner turned to the Ministry of the Interior and threatened to emigrate. "Ultimately, the Minister of the Interior acceded to Reiner's complaint and rescinded the decision of the *Statthalterei*." The marriage could go forward. Hubert Weitensfelder ascertains that "for decades", this was to remain "the only" civil marriage in Vorarlberg.[117] Even as late as 1906, Vorarlberg saw 52,039 signatures gathered on a petition opposing planned marriage reforms. With few exceptions, its signatories were mayors and members of municipal committees.[118]

Looking beyond interconfessional contexts, emergency civil marriage also represented a new scenario in the context of kin marriages that church representatives found quite unpleasant. After all, it equipped closely related couples

---

114 Hubert Weitensfelder, *'Römlinge' und 'Preußenseuchler': Konservativ-Christlichsoziale, Liberal-Deutschnationale und der Kulturkampf in Vorarlberg, 1860 bis 1914* (Vienna/Cologne/Weimar, 2008), pp. 164–167.

115 Weitensfelder, *'Römlinge' und 'Preußenseuchler'*, p. 165.

116 Ibid., p. 166.

117 Ibid., p. 167.

118 Ibid., p. 167. He refers to: *Vorarlberger Volksblatt*, 30 March 1906; *Vorarlberger Volksblatt*, 24 April 1906.

whose dispensation requests had been refused with a highly effective threat that they could deploy. In the Diocese of Brixen's dispensation records, the first reference to this legal innovation's consequences – still formulated by the prince-episcopal ordinariate, in this case – appears in 1869. The request submitted by Peter Eberle and the widow Maria Flatz, a mother to four minors from Buch in the Deanery of Bregenz, had been refused in Rome to the Brixen ordinariate's great surprise. The two were first cousins as well as third cousins, and they were also brother- and sister-in-law. This meant that they were subject to a total of three marriage impediments. The ordinariate, in reaction, declared in March 1869 that, "needless to say, this request cannot be resubmitted in Rome without some new motivation", also warning that "this matter must be handled with the greatest possible care so as to avoid giving cause for a civil marriage".[119]

A few years later, it was already the "dispensation seekers" themselves who were bringing civil marriage into play as an overt threat. Joseph Wegmann, an "inn and bathhouse" proprietor who resided in Schluderns in the Vinschgau region's Deanery of Mals, desired to marry Scholastica Wachter, with whom he was related by blood in the second and third unequal degree. The ordinariate forwarded his request to Rome in February of 1875. Wegmann, however, may well have found the whole process too slow or perhaps viewed success as being uncertain – and his bride was pregnant. Whatever the case may have been, it was just a month later – on 13 March 1875 – that he sent a telegram to Brixen containing the following words: "If my plea for a dispensation goes unheard, I will regrettably be forced to realise my plans by way of the civil authorities".[120] The answer is noted on the original telegram itself, and it indicates that handling of the matter was then expedited: "Your dispensation request has been processed by Rome, delivered to the dean in Mals, marriage after White Sunday." And with that, this second case had been resolved – but it was also quite clear by this point that vulnerability to blackmail had become an issue.[121]

119 DIÖAB, Konsistorialakten 1869, Fasc. 22a, Römische Dispensen, no. 30a.

120 DIÖAB, Konsistorialakten 1875, Fasc. 22a, Römische Dispensen, no. 37.

121 It was with similar speed that the request of Gustav Haas, proprietor of the pharmacy Löwenapotheke in Bregenz, and his widowed sister-in-law Helena von Schöppler was handled following the couple's complaint to the district captaincy in Bregenz that the church dispensation was "even now still pending", and that he did not know "how many months might still pass" before he would finally receive the dispensation. He asked the district captaincy to "urge the swift processing" of his dispensation request "by the reverend parish office", and he also remarked that "in the case of a dispensation's denial for no reason by the reverend clergy", he "would proceed to conclude an emergency civil marriage". A good two weeks later, he received a dispensation brief from the nunciature. DIÖAB, Konsistorialakten 1882, Fasc. 22a, Römische Dispensen, no. 30.

In most cases outside of the liberal and intellectual milieus of large cities, however, the step from threatening civil marriage to actually realising it was probably a large one. Even so, a civil marriage nearly did arise between Johann Georg Waibl and Aurelia Waibl. This spectacular dispensation case concerned a union between uncle and niece, a configuration that probed boundaries and spheres of action to a greater extent than any other. Marriage in this degree of kinship was largely taboo and rarely ever appears in the analysed records – and when it does, then only in this configuration.[122] The records document no marriage projects between aunt and nephew. From a canonical perspective, a marriage between uncle and niece was not out of the question but indeed quite controversial. A look at Salzburg indicates clearly that the same standards were not always applied by the bishops of all dioceses. In nineteenth-century Salzburg, a number of couples was granted such dispensations – even if, as the comments on one case indicate, they were granted "quite rarely and not at all gladly".[123] This request, along with seven further requests from the period between 1877 and 1908 concerning uncles and nieces, is contained in its own package within a fascicule. Some of the records documenting successful dispensations are quite thick; two of these dispensations were obtained from the nunciature in Vienna.[124] But it was the case in Salzburg, too, that not every request led to a dispensation, with some already being rejected at the diocesan level.[125]

A dispensation request from 1860 makes especially clear the various spheres of action and options both at the ecclesiastical administration's higher levels and on the part of affected couples. Franz Thury was 37 years old, and Rosina Aßlberger was 33. The age difference between them was a thoroughly inconspicuous four years – but the two were uncle and niece, thus representing the closest possible constellation of blood relatives that was still eligible for a dispensation. The father of the bride was half-brother of the groom; one of these two men was from their mother's first marriage, while the other was from their

122 The dispensation records of the Diocese of Brixen contain a total of nine such cases, the first of which is from 1869. With the exception of two requests, they were filed not in the fascicule "Roman Dispensations" (*Römische Dispensen*) but under "Miscellany Concerning Marriage" (*Verschiedenes über Ehe*) – which clearly shows that there existed no intention to deal with them further.

123 AES, Kasten 22/38, Päpstliche Ehedispensen 1867–1934, fasc. Akt "Dispens. ob impedimento Consanguinitatis II. Grad. tangens Imum", 1895.

124 Ibid.

125 Cf. AES, Kasten 22/40, zurückgewiesene Ehedispensen 1892–1911, 1896. Further cases can be found in AES, Kasten 22/39, Päpstliche Ehe-Dispensen 1868–1877, 1869, namely the request of Franz and Maria Lindner as well as, from the same year, Nikolaus Magreiter and Magdalena Leitner.

mother's second. They officially belonged to the Diocese of Linz, whose bishop reported that they had attempted "everything possible" in order to procure his support for their dispensation request; they had even "had the audacity to threaten defection from the faith". The bishop, however, had "steadfastly" refused them. Faced with this hopeless situation, the couple had then turned to the Apostolic Nunciature in Vienna as well as to the imperial-royal agent in Rome; both had, in turn, done nothing but report back to Linz on Franz Thury and Rosina Aßlberger's actions – whereupon the bishop ascertained with a certain sense of gratification that their request had gone "unheeded". But soon afterwards, something happened that struck him as incomprehensible – for the city parish priest of Linz, who was the groom's parish priest, and the bride's parish priest in Neumarkt near Freistadt received "the announcement" from the city parish of Salzburg at St. Blasius indicating that the couple had "legitimately or fraudulently obtained" a Roman dispensation "even so".[126]

The Bishop of Linz reacted in mid-November of 1860 by requesting an explanation from Salzburg's bishop; he also asked him to investigate whether Salzburg's city parish office had not been "deceived by false testimony" as well as whether this was truly the parish that was responsible for the bride. As a result, the wedding was prevented from going forward as planned. The Bishop of Salzburg then replied to his colleague that the bride actually had been residing in Salzburg since the beginning of the year, as a "governess in an esteemed merchant household". Moreover, he had personally requested that the dispensation be granted. And since the bride had transferred her place of residence to Salzburg, he was now indeed the competent authority. The dispensation had then arrived, "defying all expectations". However, the bishop promised that it would not be acted upon for the moment. There followed a final passage intended to soothe the addressee: "I would be deeply sorry if these events had inadvertently caused Your Excellency any unpleasantness." The consistory then contacted Rome to clarify whether the bride's several months of residence would be sufficient in order for Salzburg to assume total control of matters pertaining to dispensations. By then, the groom had also moved to Salzburg. The couple had obtained a "Certificate of the City Council" confirming this, and they also indicated their intent to continue residing there in the future. Furthermore, they had already received a licence for "the operation of an accessories boutique" and were hence beyond the shadow of a doubt now subject to the Archdiocese of Salzburg. By virtue of this fact, it was no longer necessary to have banns published in Linz. The ordinariate therefore declared

126 AES, Kasten 22/38, Päpstliche Dispensen 1856–1867, 1861, request of Franz Thury and Rosina Aßlberger.

that nothing more prevented the dispensation decree from September of the previous year from being acted upon and that the marriage could thus go forward.

While the Archbishop of Salzburg evidently had no problem granting this dispensation for an uncle and niece, the Bishop of Linz had been categorically opposed. Right at the beginning of the letter quoted above, he had explained that "His Eminence, the most Reverend Cardinal Archbishop of Vienna and I gave our word to each other six years ago that we would never request a dispensation in Rome for the second degree of kinship touching the first." Nonetheless, the wall of opposition erected by this alliance had indeed turned out to have at least one crack in it – which those who possessed the necessary information and means could exploit by changing their place of residence.

In records from the Diocese of Brixen, requests submitted by uncles and nieces are quite rare and only appear during the final decades of the nineteenth century. One such case that attracted broad public attention was the marriage project of Johann Georg Waibl.[127] His case shows how the sphere of action for such couples had expanded thanks to the newly introduced option of emergency civil marriage, and it also embodied a test as to the feasibility of liberal civil lawgiving. It challenged the state and the Church to position themselves. Georg Waibl, born in 1828, trained as a physician in Munich, Berlin and Vienna and was Dornbirn's liberal mayor[128] for 40 years beginning in 1869. Alongside this position, he also served as a deputy in the Imperial Council (*Reichsrat*) and the provincial diet (*Landtag*).[129] Following the death of Waibl's parents, his nieces – first Sophie and later Aurelia Waibl – ran his household. He ultimately desired to wed Aurelia, his half-brother's daughter, with whom it was said – in a stylisation of the bourgeois ideal of marriage – that he could discuss "literature and the fine arts" and who was "familiar with all his needs, his strictly regimented way of life."[130] To this end and in accordance with paragraph 84 of the Austrian Civil Code, as Waibl explained in a January 1883

127 The spelling of his name varies: the dispensation records use the spelling "Waibl", and it is with this spelling that he also signed the documents contained therein; in a biography of his person as well as in the research literature, on the other hand, the spelling "Waibel" is used.

128 As a liberal, it was repeatedly the case that he demonstratively refrained from taking part in the Corpus Christi procession, an event that functioned as something of a representative public staging of Catholic power and significance, and this was also noted by the press. Cf. Weitensfelder, *'Römlinge' und 'Preußenseuchler'*, p. 159; on his doings while in office and on his town's socio-political and sociocultural milieu cf. Karin Schneider, *Dornbirner Bürger 1867–1914. Zwischen Anspruch und Alltag* (Constance, 2005).

129 Cf. also Weitensfelder, *'Römlinge' und 'Preußenseuchler'*, pp. 126–127.

130 Leo Herburger, *Dr. J.G. Waibel, sein Leben und Wirken* (Dornbirn, 1909), p. 38.

letter addressed to the Prince-Bishop of Brixen, they had requested from the provincial government in Innsbruck "forbearance concerning marriage impediments of kinship", which was granted them and transmitted to them by the competent district captaincy on 22 November.[131]

Their wedding ceremony was supposed to take place in Vienna, which was quite far away from home: 500 km linear distance. For this reason, they had written from Vienna to their parish priest in Dornbirn with the request that he proclaim the banns there, in the competent parish, three times before the end of that month. The parish priest in Dornbirn refused to do so, countering that before he would accede to their request, "the church dispensation concerning the existing marriage impediments must be obtained". Waibl then told the priest that his position did not comport with the legal situation "in our Austria", referring to the General Civil Code and to the law of 25 May 1868, which had introduced the option of emergency civil marriage. The law did not contain a mandate "to seek dispensation from marriage impediments from one's confessional authority as well", he held. Therefore, the priest had "no legal basis" upon which to "deny" them the banns. Waibl then turned to the prince-bishop, requesting that he "inform and instruct" the priest to this effect – and he closed his letter with the assurance that he and his betrothed, "as loyal Catholics", would "most willingly submit to the usual rules governing a church wedding".

Waibl was attempting to set a liberal example, as is already indicated by the term "confessional authority" and above all by how he sought to simply ignore and bypass the Church as far as dispensations were concerned by declaring the provincial government's dispensation to be "the only one required by our laws". Brixen's Prince-Bishop at the time, Johann von Leiß, reacted with a letter to the vicariate general in which he noted how it was "apparent that the prospective groom Dr. Waibl cares not a whit about the church marriage impediments", for in this case, one could not assume "ignorance". He told his addressee that Waibl was to be "referred to the nuncio, whom he, as an imperial councillor, should be able to approach quite easily", at the next opportunity. If he were not to follow this advice, the only option would be to direct a request to the pope in which it would be necessary to "put very strong emphasis on the great danger of a civil marriage". The decision would then be left to the pope. Leiß added

131 ADF, GA, Ehesachen III, Präsidialakten 1830–1900 und Römische Dispensen I, 1853–1858, Fasc. 4, 1882–1885 Bischof Aichner, Ehedispenssachen – with the additional note on the cover: "1883 des Bürgermeisters Dr. Waibel – Dornbirn – Ehe mit seiner Nichte" [1883, of Mayor Dr. Waibel – Dornbirn – Marriage to his Niece]; cf. also DIÖAB, Konsistorialakten 1883, Fasc. 22, Verschiedenes, no. 17.

that civil marriage would certainly be the greater evil "in view of his status and his position".

The prince-bishop also sent Waibl himself a long letter dated 22 January 1883 in which he addressed Waibl as "well-born" and adopted a very measured and peaceable tone. He first confirmed that Waibl's turning to the provincial government had been an "entirely correct" course of action. Regarding the refused banns, he explained that there were "two kinds of laws": "ecclesiastical laws and state laws". He then stated that a Catholic Christian, being "simultaneously a member of the Church and a citizen of the state", could conclude a valid marriage only if neither an ecclesiastical impediment nor "an impediment based on state law stands in its way". Therefore, the parish priest's course of action had also been "entirely correct". Even if no marriage impediment at all had been present, the priest would have been capable neither of proclaiming the banns nor of wedding them, since this required a "solemn declaration of consent before one's competent pastor" that, in Waibl's case, had not occurred. He then transitioned to the most sensitive point: the law of May 1868 – he avoided using the term "civil marriage" – would only apply if Rome refused to grant the requested dispensation, and he clarified: "Until then, one cannot speak of a refusal to carry out the wedding." He concluded by taking Waibl at his word: "Now then, show yourself to be a loyal Catholic and turn to the reverend vicar general, who will surely provide you with the best counsel. The shortest way to reach your objective will most likely be that of turning directly to the papal nuncio in Vienna."

Waibl, for his part, found himself willing to relent and followed the advice of the prince-bishop. In a letter to the vicariate general dated 10 March 1883, the prince-bishop indicated having received a telegram from Waibl the previous evening containing the request: "If the nunciature should enquire regarding my dispensation, I beseech you for the love of God to support it. For it is only by way of its approval, I fear, that a disastrous misfortune can be avoided." The prince-bishop interpreted the implied misfortune as being that the bride was pregnant and that this might become public if the marriage were to be delayed further. If the nunciature wanted to hear reasons, continued Leiß, he would be "of course incapable of specifying such", but the great danger of a civil marriage and the danger that the two would fail to be abstinent could be mentioned. He then instructed the vicar general to "research" further possible reasons with the parish priest of Dornbirn and report these to him promptly.

That same day, the prince-bishop wrote a second letter to the vicariate general, evidently following a meeting of the consistory later that morning at which "Waibl's matter" had been part of the agenda. The new turn in this "matter" had cheered him noticeably – for his first sentence reads: "I was greatly delighted by that telegram yesterday." He went on to tell of a conversation with Court Councillor (*Hofrat*) Kirchlehner in Innsbruck a few days prior and concluded: "If the government were to permit civil marriage whenever a bridal couple refuses to obtain a church dispensation, church dispensation law would be rendered illusory, which would amount to an attack on the very essence of the Church itself." He pointed out that the Catholic Church was a recognised confession in Austria and that the government had promised its protection. "It would thus be breaking its word, which would mark the beginning of the separation of Church and state." At this point in time, however, civil marriage was already not only relevant as a reaction to refused church dispensations but also as a possible way of bypassing them entirely.

An article that appeared in the 19 April 1883 issue of the *Österreichische Zeitschrift für Verwaltung* – Austrian Administrative Journal – in a section entitled "News from Actual Practice"[132] portrays an anonymised case history: "On 12 November 1882, N. addressed a request to *Statthalterei* x". The plot that then unfolds instantly brings to mind the case of Johann Georg and Aurelia Waibl. It details the evaluation of an uncle-niece marriage by the *Finanzprokurator* (a legal department of the imperial government). The bride was the daughter of a half-brother, meaning that she was only a half-niece; the "social and political standing" mentioned in connection with aspects including the planned wedding corresponds with that of Waibl, and the portrayed case also coincides temporally. Later on in the article, it becomes clear that Waibl's case is indeed the one being referred to in that documents are mentioned together with dates and reference numbers that correspond to those in the relevant fascicule at the diocesan archive in Feldkirch, namely the notice indicating issuance of the dispensation by the *Statthalterei* on 22 November 1882, the correspondence with the district captaincy and a letter from the Ministry of the Interior.

The journal article is headlined "The Lack of a Church Dispensation From a Marriage Impediment Cannot Prevent Civil Marriage". It explains that paragraph 83 of the Austrian Civil Code specifies the provincial government as the first authority from which "forbearance concerning marriage impediments can be requested for important reasons". In such a case, the provincial government must "take steps to obtain clarity regarding the nature of the circumstances". In this regard, continues the article's author, the question arises as to whether the portrayed case "is such that it requires preliminary examination

132 A.B., "Der Mangel der kirchlichen Dispens vom Ehehindernisse kann die Civil-Eheschließung nicht aufhalten", *Österreichische Zeitschrift für Verwaltung* 16, 16 (19 April 1883), 62–63.

by other authorities". The Austrian Civil Code is said to provide no answer to this question, however, since its treatment of marriage impediments is too general. The author concludes that "forbearance is permissible for those marriage impediments [...] that are based solely on civil law but not on the nature of the marital relationship, on moral principles or on other state laws" – and that the marriage impediment in question here fell into this category.

The author goes on to state that considerations as to whether a state dispensation was justified revolved around weighing various disadvantages, and also that forbearance was to be shown only for important reasons. It was "well known" that the "civil marriage prohibition" in this degree was "based mainly, if not exclusively, on the view that such unions are physically damaging to offspring". In the case at hand, he writes, this was mitigated by the fact that the persons concerned were merely "half"-relatives – an argument that, from a canonical and theological perspective, was irrelevant and hence steadfastly rejected. Far more weighty, on the other hand, were "the interests" associated with a marriage, and these depended on the social and political position of the affected persons. With regard to the decision-making competence of the provincial governments, "consultation with other authorities" was required only in certain circumstances. And in this particular case, the author reasons, it was not required due to the simplicity and clarity of the situation at hand. "Any consultation with the episcopal ordinariate", namely for those cases in which a canonical marriage impediment also pertained, is viewed by the author as no longer being required due to the new legal situation. The conclusion of this disquisition is therefore that the civil authorities would have to approve such a request. Actual practice, however, looked different.

The article continues by portraying the subsequent events in this case, of which one finds only few traces in the diocesan archive: the person in question, following his parish priest's refusal to proclaim the banns, is said to have turned to his district captaincy for the banns' proclamation and the required "solemn declaration" of the two partners' mutual consent. The district captaincy, however, had consulted with the competent parish – and on 7 February, it announced its refusal to perform the "requested official act" and also demanded presentation of a church dispensation. Upon its appeal, this decision was subsequently rescinded by the *Statthalterei* since the absence of a church dispensation did not represent a hindrance as far as the state was concerned. The district captaincy was thereupon ordered to "perform its official duties", which it then duly did, instructing the municipal office to take the necessary steps. But the official there who was responsible for proclaiming the banns (the *Aufgebotswerber*) is said to have reacted by calling the according orders "premature", and the parish priest formally registered "his protest". The

Ministry of the Interior determined that both the decision of the *Statthalterei* and the directive issued by the district captaincy were in conformance with the law.[133] The provincial government was therefore competent to "independently honour" the indicated reasons for dispensation, meaning that the Church's refusal was not binding on its decision. It was just such a distribution of competencies that the Josephine Marriage Patent had, in principle, attempted to create a century earlier, albeit to little success.

In Waibl's biography, this whole process is summarised quite briefly and diverges somewhat from the "official" portrayal: "The state dispensation was obtained, but the Church was initially unwilling to grant its approval. Therefore, he immediately requested state permission for an emergency civil marriage as a precaution. The civil authorities granted their permission without objection, a fact that was announced forthwith by way of an according notice posted in Dornbirn's town hall." This evoked "enormous muttering and scolding among both female and male prayer-sisters" (*Betschwestern*), and the priest was especially strident in his opposition to this "scandalous" marriage.[134] With the nuncio in Vienna then having telegraphically procured a dispensation from Rome, Johann Georg and Aurelia Waibl gave up their original plan of being married in Vienna in order to avoid "nourishing the false suspicion" that they had entered into a civil marriage. It was thus that they were married in Dornbirn's parish of Hatlerdorf on 29 March 1883. And with that, the "uproar among the pious" was laid to rest. The biography describes their marriage as happy and harmonious, free from "discord" and "strife".[135]

What had caused a stir in this case was the prioritisation of state over ecclesiastical competence and not so much the fact that this was a marriage between uncle and niece. The liberal May Laws of 1868 possessed tremendous potential to limit the Church's sphere of action concerning dispensations in close degrees of kinship, even if they had probably not been intended to do so in quite this way. But despite the legal basis thus created, the right to actually take advantage of this new type of opportunity still had to be fought for step by step with the involvement of the Ministry of the Interior. And ultimately,

133 A corresponding official notice from the district captaincy in reaction to the protest of the Dornbirn priest that makes reference to the determination of the Ministry of the Interior can be found in the above-quoted fascicule in the diocesan archive in Feldkirch. ADF, GA, Ehesachen III, Präsidialakten 1830–1900 und Römische Dispensen I, 1853–1858, Fasc. 4, 1882–1885 Bischof Aichner, Ehedispenssachen – with the additional note on the cover: 1883 des Bürgermeisters Dr. Waibel – Dornbirn – Ehe mit seiner Nichte [1883, of Mayor Dr. Waibel – Dornbirn – Marriage to his Niece], letter dated 9 April 1883, Zl. 3344.

134 Herburger, *Dr. J.G. Waibel*, p. 38.

135 Ibid., p. 39.

even though such a course of action's conformance with the law had been confirmed, the Waibls – with an eye to their social environment and social integration – decided to submit to the Church's rules after all.

This case shows yet again how the course taken by dispensation proceedings was inseparable from the status of the groom. As a physician, a mayor and a liberal deputy in both the provincial diet and the Imperial Council, Johann Georg Waibl not only possessed sufficient competencies and knowledge but also contacts and avenues to familiarise himself with the existing legal possibilities. He showed no reluctance to demand institutional support, and he also possessed sufficient fighting spirit and trust in the state to enter an appeal. But despite his political positioning as a liberal, he ultimately stopped halfway and requested a church dispensation after all. He also gave up his original plan to marry in far-off Vienna. These decisions may have been concessions to his situation as a public figure and to the socio-political environment of his hometown.[136] In the final analysis, therefore, proceeding on the basis of civil law would have exposed Johann Georg Waibl to social and political risk. Aurelia Waibl, his bride, played no role in any of these turbulences in terms of what was publicly communicated or documented in the source materials. It hence cannot be assessed whether she felt it important to be in harmony with the Church. In the evaluated source material, it is primarily the battles for dispensations fought by men that become visible – as had already been the case in close degrees of affinity during the 1830s and 1840s. Unsurprisingly, the prince-episcopal consistory in Brixen maintained its fundamental stance and its claim to primacy as an authority in dispensation matters.[137]

The consistory in Salzburg, for its part, was wont to adopt a soothing tone in comparable situations. In response to a parish priest who perceived there to be great danger that the first-degree affines Michael Stadelmann und Theresia Eibl might conclude an emergency civil marriage if their dispensation were refused, the prince-episcopal ordinariate replied: "As much as the inordinately heightened tendency to conclude marriages in the closest degrees of consanguinity and affinity in recent times is to be regretted from a religious and moral standpoint", it was "in fact not averse" to forwarding this request to Rome with its endorsement. And since there had been no refusal of this dispensation by any side, the ordinariate continued, fear of a civil marriage was even less of an

136 Waibl died in October 1909, shortly before what would have been his 80th birthday. In 1912, the town of Dornbirn erected an imposing statue of him on the square in front of the town hall. Cf. Schneider, *Dornbirner Bürger*, pp. 198–199.

137 On this cf. also the protracted but ultimately successful case of Maria and Josef Obholzer, also uncle and niece, DIÖAB, Konsistorialakten 1888, Fasc. 22a, Römische Dispensen, no. 25, and ibid., 1890, no. 11.

issue, seeing as "all other requirements are entirely in keeping with the law" and swift efforts would be made to take care of this matter. The dispensation was granted.[138]

The type of appeasement practiced here can be viewed as a strategy aimed at preventing the threat potential of civil marriage from materialising in the first place, particularly because civil marriage seems to have found little acceptance among the populace in light of the aforementioned petition drive in Vorarlberg. It was with a similar tactic that the ordinariate in Brixen, too, subsequently attempted to escape the vulnerability to blackmail that was associated with civil marriage. A request by two cousins brought forward only *angustia loci* and thus lacked a sufficient reason for dispensation, on top of which the bride was still a minor. Brixen reacted by prioritising the all-too-close kinship and emphasising the contradiction inherent in this request "in that one and the same report, while characterising the dispensation seekers as very Christian and religious people, also expresses fear of a civil marriage being concluded. The ordinariate must repeatedly confess that it views even the *actual* conclusion of an isolated civil marriage, which continues to be regarded as abominable by the people, as a far lesser evil than the epidemic spread of marriages in such close degrees of kinship, which is accompanied by such disadvantageous consequences in moral and physical respects."[139]

Viewed overall, Church and state continued to act within two separate worlds even in the late nineteenth century as long as neither dispensation seekers with an elite bourgeois background nor lawyers were involved. These more sophisticated protagonists were more prone to invoke civil law and occasionally even succeeded in its assertion, thus limiting the power of the Church to a certain extent. Such cases, however, were few and far between – and while the Church did come under pressure as a dispensation granting institution, it was indeed able to retain a position that remained quite powerful.

6 Kin Marriage in Numbers – Political Culture in Context

If knowledge of successfully obtained dispensations motivated others to submit their own dispensation requests, the opposite will also have been true:

138 AES, Kasten 22/39, Päpstliche Ehe-Dispensen 1868–1877, 1875, request of Michael Stadelmann and Theresia Eibl, who was his housekeeper.

139 DIÖAB, Konsistorialakten 1876, Fasc. 22a, Römische Dispensen, no. 23. Emphasis underlined in the original.

knowledge of failed attempts likely discouraged some couples from subjecting themselves to dispensation proceedings. The records document those couples who at least managed to take the initial administrative steps involved in communicating their marriage-related desires: from the local priest to the dean and, from there, to the prince-episcopal consistory in Brixen. The number of couples who were successfully discouraged right at the local level, giving up on their marriage projects before pen had ever been put to paper, cannot be ascertained. As a consequence, it is impossible to know how many marriage wishes among close consanguineous and affinal kin remained unfulfilled. Moreover, kin relationships also ended up being overlooked here and there despite all efforts and despite the pressure to which local clergy were subject. And finally, it is not improbable that some couples moved to places where it was easier to obtain a dispensation without according reports reaching the consistory in Brixen or otherwise entering the records examined here – even though the nineteenth century witnessed relatively frequent communication and rather dense networking between the various civil and ecclesiastical administrative bodies.

Insofar as numbers are to be had, we must take into account not only marriage prohibitions' range and weight but also the respective administrative situations and contexts in order to get a clear impression. This applies especially when comparing the frequency of kin marriage across multiple European regions. After all, the pure numerical evidence paints a very superficial picture, seeing as such figures are abstracted from the contexts in which they were produced – contexts that encompassed divergent legal circumstances as well as differences in the rigidity of dispensation practice. Just how access to a dispensation was organised and what obstacles could arise along the way not only affected the number of documented kin marriages but also the frequency with which certain couple configurations turn up in the records.

1831 is the year in which the examined series of papal dispensation records from the Diocese of Brixen begins. Going by the European kin marriage figures known from other studies, this was already mid-way through the phase during which kin marriages were on the rise. Insights into the previous period are provided by the register volumes *Dispensationes Matrimoniales*, but these list only granted dispensations and contain no records of failed attempts. Systematic comparison of the number of Roman dispensations granted during the eighteenth century with those granted during the nineteenth century would be possible only with great effort due to the shifts in diocesan borders. Moreover, the diverse routes via which dispensations could be obtained prior to the 1770s make it practically impossible to ascertain the extent to which early modern diocesan-level registers are complete. These limitations must be kept in mind. With that said, a random sample of certain years' register entries indicating granted dispensations does suggest a change in the situation over the course of a good hundred years.

At the outset of the eighteenth century, the register contains mostly dispensations in the third and fourth degrees. In 1705 and 1715, these total 114 and 100 granted dispensations, respectively. Out of altogether 132 dispensations in 1725, seven were granted by the nunciature in Vienna for the second and third unequal degree of affinity or consanguinity. In 1755, a total of 179 dispensations was granted, of which eleven arrived from the nunciature and three from Rome. Only two of them were for cousin marriages, while all others were for more distant degrees.[140] In contrast, between 1780 and 1815 particularly the share of approved requests in the second and third unequal degrees of consanguinity and affinity increased. The first degree of affinity occurred only quite rarely and only beginning in the final decades of the eighteenth century.[141] Notwithstanding reservations as to comparability in view of the administrative difficulties that began in the 1780s and the impossibility of ascertaining the records' completeness, the register entries do allow us to infer a gradual shift toward ever closer degrees.

This study's focus is on requests that document *planned* marriages between consanguineous and affinal kin and not on granted dispensations. In relation to the overall number of marriages, the number of documented marriage projects in closely related configurations ranging out to the second and third unequal degree in the Diocese of Brixen averaged between one and two per cent during the nineteenth century. In 1836, for example, a total of 2,023 marriages took place in the diocese.[142] The number of dispensation requests in close degrees submitted during this year was 21,[143] with diocese-level decisions being made on 17 of them plus a further six from the previous year that had

140 Cf. DIÖAB, Registratura Dispensation[um] Matrimonial[ium] inc[o]hoata anno 1690 [until 1730]; ibid., Registratura Dispensation[um] Matrimonial[ium] inc[o]hoata anno 1733 usque ad annum 1752; ibid., Registratura Dispensation[um] Matrimonial[ium] anno 1753 usque ad annum 1768.

141 Cf. DIÖAB, Dispensationes matrimoniales ab anno 1774 usque ad annum 1794 inclusive and ibid., Dispensationes matrimoniales ab anno 1795 usque ad annum 1829 inclusive under the corresponding years.

142 "Conspectus Generalis", *Catalogus Personarum ecclesiasticarum Dioecesis Brixinensis* MDCCCXXXVIII, vol. 23 (Brixen, 1837), without page numbers (at the end of this volume, with figures from 1836).

143 In two requests from Vorarlberg, the matrimonial examinations had already been protocolled in December 1835; Brixen only added the documents to the records in in January,

remained open. Of these altogether 23 requests, 14 were approved.[144] In 1885, by way of comparison, 51 requests in close degrees were submitted and all were approved.[145] The total number of marriages in the diocese came to 2,497.[146] It was therefore a rise from one to two per cent over a period of sixty years that fuelled the perception of a "frightful increase" – as an article in the *Brixner Diözesanblatt* decried in 1878 – of marriages in close degrees of consanguinity and affinity.[147]

There were significantly more dispensations granted in the third and fourth degrees (see Table 3). In these more distant degrees, the number of requests largely corresponds with the number of dispensations that were granted. From the mid-1860s onward, the records of such requests in the diocesan archive in Brixen are present but incomplete, only covering the diocese's Tyrolean part. Certain fluctuations notwithstanding, these requests totalled around 100 per year. Vorarlberg's deaneries of Bregenz, the Bregenz Forest, Dornbirn, Feldkirch, Montafon and Sonnenberg – from which a considerable share of dispensation requests in close degrees came – are missing, however, which means that we must also assume a high number of requests in the more distant degrees. Nonetheless, analysing a few years does show one thing – namely, that dispensations for consanguine unions outnumbered those for affinal unions by a more than clear margin. This was presumably owed to differing economies of attention. Third and fourth degree configurations during the years analysed in this respect accounted for between 5.4 and 8.2 per cent of all marriages (see Table 3).

so that they are filed under 1836: DIÖAB, Konsistorialakten 1836, Fasc. 5a, Römische Dispensen, no. 8 and no. 25.

144 Four of these requests were then either withdrawn or not pursued further for unspecified reasons. One request was refused in Rome while four were rejected in Brixen. In the analysis here, the requests are listed by the year in which the lion's share of the proceedings and either approval or refusal occurred. Renewed attempts following refusals are, insofar as significant steps in dispensation proceedings were taken, counted again. It was according to this logic that the dispensation cases were also entered into the database. For further details see the section on the material's organisation in the Appendix of this volume.

145 Altogether 55 appear in the list: one case was counted twice, two cases concerned revalidations in the fourth degree and one was for a secret dispensation.

146 Cf. *Schematismus der Säkular- und Regular-Geistlichkeit der Diözese Brixen. 1886*, vol. 70 (Brixen, 1886), p. 198.

147 "Neueste offizielle Instruktion über Ehedispensgesuche", *Brixner Diözesanblatt* 22 (1878), 33–38, 38.

TABLE 3 Episcopal dispensations in the Tyrolean deaneries (selected years)[a]

Year	3rd cons.	3rd & 4th cons.	4th cons.	3rd affin.	3rd & 4th affin.	4th affin.	Total dispensations	Total marriages	%
1867	41	21	49	4	0	0	115	1,401[b]	8.20
1872	34	17	38	5	0	0	94	1,742[c]	5.40
1877	41	28	34	0	0	2	104	1,726[d]	6.00
1882	44	19	47	3	3	1	117	1,519[e]	7.70
1887	38	15	46	1	1	0	101	1,678[f]	6.00

a The numbers of episcopal dispensations are calculated on the basis of: DIÖAB, Konsistorialakten under the corresponding year, Fasc. 22. Only the dispensations pertaining to cases of consanguinity or affinity were counted and not the scattered individual dispensations concerning spiritual kinship (*cognationis spiritualis*), prior engagement to a first-degree relative of the prospective spouse (*publicae honestatis*), adultery (*impedimentum criminis ex adulterio*) or the banns of marriage. In cases where multiple degrees of kinship were at issue, the closest degree was counted.

b The schematisms, which were ideally printed at the beginning of the year, contain the figures from the previous year; accordingly, the figures in this table are all shifted earlier by one year. Schematismus der Geistlichkeit der Diözese Brixen für das Jahr 1868, vol. 52, Brixen 1868, 164.

c Schematismus der Geistlichkeit der Diözese Brixen für das Jahr 1873, vol. 57, Brixen 1873, 174.

d Schematismus der Geistlichkeit der Diözese Brixen für das Jahr 1878, vol. 62, Brixen 1878, 192.

e Schematismus der Säkular- und Regular-Geistlichkeit der Diözese Brixen. 1883, vol. 67, Brixen 1883, 196. This schematism's summary table erroneously puts the number of marriages in the Tyrolean deaneries at 540.

f Schematismus der Säkular- und Regular-Geistlichkeit der Diözese Brixen. 1888, vol. 72, Brixen 1888, 210.

Over the course of the nineteenth century, complaints pertained especially to the increase in close consanguineous unions, above all those between first cousins. How realistic was this impression? The overall breakdown by degrees of kinship (see Table 4) shows that the lion's share of requests in the Diocese of Brixen were situated in the second and third unequal degree of consanguinity – a type of union for which a dispensation could be obtained with relatively little trouble during the period under study. The next most common types of requests were marriage projects between brother-in-law and sister-in-law as well as between cousins; these two configurations were represented by equal numbers of cases.

TABLE 4 Close-degree requests in the Diocese of Brixen, 1831–1890

Degrees	Absolute numbers	Percentages
2nd & 3rd unequal cons.[a]	521	24.20
1st affin.	488	22.80
2nd cons.[b]	488	22.80
2nd affin.	267	12.50
2nd & 3rd unequal affin.	120	5.60
1st affin. *ex copula illicita*	82	3.80
1st & 2nd unequal affin.	78	3.60
2nd affin. *ex copula illicita*	47	2.20
1st & 2nd cons.	9	0.40
2nd & 4th affin.	8	0.40
1st & 2nd affin. *ex copula illicita*	7	0.30
2nd & 4th cons.	6	0.30
1st affin. and 2nd cons.	4	0.20
1st affin. and 2nd & 3rd cons.	3	0.10
2nd cons. and 2nd affin.	2	0.10
2nd & 3rd affin. *ex copula illicta*	2	0.10
2nd cons. and 1st & 2nd unequal affin.	2	0.10
2nd cons. and 2nd & 3rd unequal affin.	1	0.05
2nd& 3rd unequal cons. and 2nd affin.	1	0.05
1st & 3rd cons.	1	0.05
1st & 3rd affin.	1	0.05
Not indicated	4	0.20
Total	2,142	99.90

a These include four cases in combination with 1st & 2nd affin. *ex copula illicita*, three cases in combination with 1st affin. *ex copula illicita* and one case in combination with 2nd affin. *ex copula illicita*.

b These include four cases in combination with 1st affin. *ex copula illicita* and two cases in combination with 2nd affin. *ex copula illicita*.

We must therefore ask whether there might have been pronounced changes over time, meaning whether the increase in complaints was correlated with an increasing number of requests in the second degree of consanguinity. In actual fact, the curve rises roughly in parallel with the increase in requests overall but

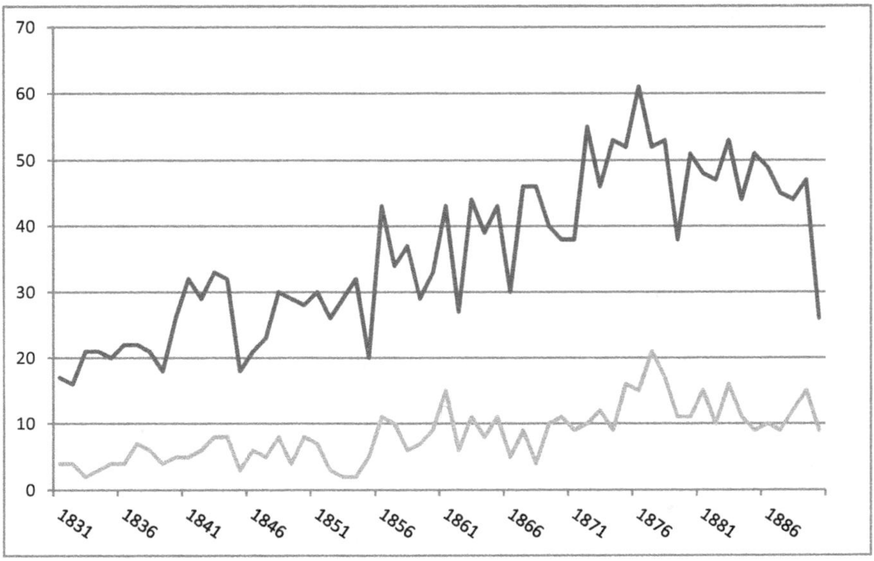

GRAPH 1 Papal dispensation requests in the Diocese of Brixen, 1831–1890 concerning cousin marriages (light) compared with requests overall (dark)

does not exhibit any dramatic leaps (see Graph 1). The high-water mark was reached at the end of the 1870s, followed by a decrease. The repeated directives to admonish and turn away supplicants would seem to have been effective to a certain degree in the parishes and deaneries. But the prospects of receiving a positive response to a request indeed continued to be high in the 1870s, even if the number of cases in which permission to protocol the matrimonial examination was given only upon the second attempt did increase towards the end of that decade.

The fact that attention came to focus increasingly on marriage projects between cousins probably had to do with several aspects: with the emphasis placed on this category by Joseph Feßler, with the successively broader media presence of a discourse concerning possible dangers and last but not least with the perception of a rise in the absolute numbers. In this respect, complaints were aimed above all at Vorarlberg. At the same time, couples from the Diocese of Brixen's western reaches were far more present than those from its eastern areas when it came to exploiting spheres of action and asserting themselves in all manner of contexts and situations such as have been reconstructed so far in this study. This invites us to suppose that the frequency of requests will have been distributed differently between the regions. And indeed: evaluated in terms of absolute numbers, there was a clear concentration of requests in Vorarlberg followed by the western Tyrolean deaneries of Breitenwang, Zams,

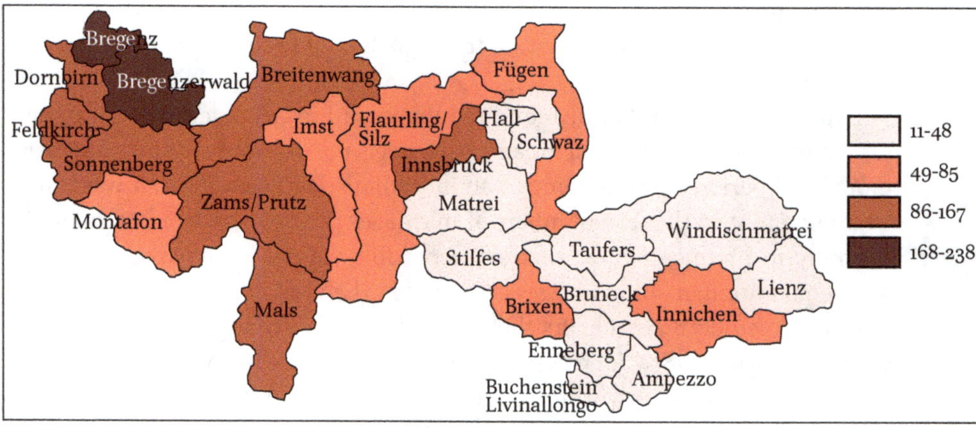

MAP 3 Papal dispensation requests in the Diocese of Brixen by Deanery, 1831–1890, in absolute numbers (total: 2,142 cases)

Imst and Mals (see Map 3).[148] The overall list of deaneries is headed up by the deaneries of Bregenz and the Bregenz Forest.

A look at the spatial distribution of absolute numbers of dispensation requests is relevant insofar as the prince-episcopal ordinariate in Brixen and the vicariate general in Feldkirch were reacting to the concrete numbers of marriage projects and incoming requests. The west-east disparity becomes apparent as early as the 1830s and is quite clear: nearly 75 per cent of the altogether 178 papal dispensation requests from the period between 1831 and 1839 came from the western areas of the diocese, mainly from the deaneries of the Bregenz Forest, Mals, Sonnenberg, Zams and Bregenz. Half of all such requests during this period were distributed among these five out of what were then 26 deaneries. In terms of the individual decades, the Deanery of the Bregenz Forest consistently tops this list. The actions taken by Johann Baptist Sinz, who served as dean there in the 1830s, drew the ire of Dean Joseph Stadelmann in the neighbouring Deanery of Bregenz. In a lengthy letter addressed to the consistory in Brixen, Stadelmann reproached Sinz for what he felt was an all too lax disposition and lamented that couples from Bregenz were "fleeing to him". For in Sinz's view, wrote Stadelmann, a request's success depended "solely upon the deans and the parish priests, upon how they dress things up" – meaning not upon the presence of canonical reasons "but rather upon the portrayal, twisting and bending of appearances". Stadelmann's account,

148 For an introduction to the production of database generated maps, I extend thanks to Annemarie Steidl.

which may serve to partly explain the pathos seen in Sinz's style of writing, also brings up instances of 'dispensation tourism' that he then goes on to describe in greater detail.[149]

Expressing the number of requested dispensations as a percentage of the total number of actually concluded marriages is possible only for a somewhat more brief period without going to an inordinate degree of effort; it was only beginning in 1839 that the numbers of marriages per deanery were calculated centrally to produce figures that are accessible via the schematisms.[150] For 1829, equal numbers of marriages are listed in the west and in the east of the diocese,[151] namely 896 each. But thereafter, the number of marriages rose more clearly in the west: 1839, for example, witnessed 1,034 marriages in the diocese's western region while 951 were concluded in the east. However, the western deaneries were home to only around one third of the diocese's overall population. This indicates that the marriage rate was considerably higher in the west; at the same time, the number of papal dispensation requests expressed as percentages of total concluded marriages in this region's deaneries is also higher. Taking this into account, the west-east disparity in this calculation appears less clear (see Map 4). Moreover, its correlation with the presence or absence of partible inheritance of land is weaker than we might assume. In a few deaneries in the diocese's eastern reaches – such as in Windischmatrei and Lienz as well as in the Ladin-speaking Deanery of Buchenstein/Livinallongo, but also in Vorarlberg's Montafon, the shares of dispensation requests are higher due to the lower numbers of marriages. The opposite situation, namely higher overall numbers of marriages, also weakens this impression in several deaneries in the west and in Innsbruck. In both modes of portrayal, the Bregenz Forest is the deanery with the most dispensation requests. It should be noted that this deanery-based portrayal does not make visible the fact that marriage projects between close kin were often concentrated in a very few parishes within these areas of ecclesiastical administration.[152] What becomes apparent here is the degree of disparity on the regional level.

149 DIÖAB, Konsistorialakten 1832, Fasc. 5c, Verschiedenes über Ehesachen, no. 1.

150 From the 1830s, schematisms with the according information only exist for the years 1831 (providing the figures for 1829) and 1837 (providing the figures for 1836). They appeared on an annual basis beginning in 1840.

151 The attribution of deaneries to the diocese's western or eastern parts corresponds to the borders drawn in the map above: the west includes the Vorarlberg deaneries of Bregenz, Bregenz Forest, Dornbirn, Feldkirch, Montafon and Sonnenberg as well as the western Tyrolean deaneries of Breitenwang, Imst, Mals and Zams including Prutz.

152 This becomes apparent elsewhere, such as in the section on the milieu-specific repertoires of argumentation at the beginning of this chapter that dealt with, among other things, the three parishes of the Little Walser Valley, but also in the highly divergent

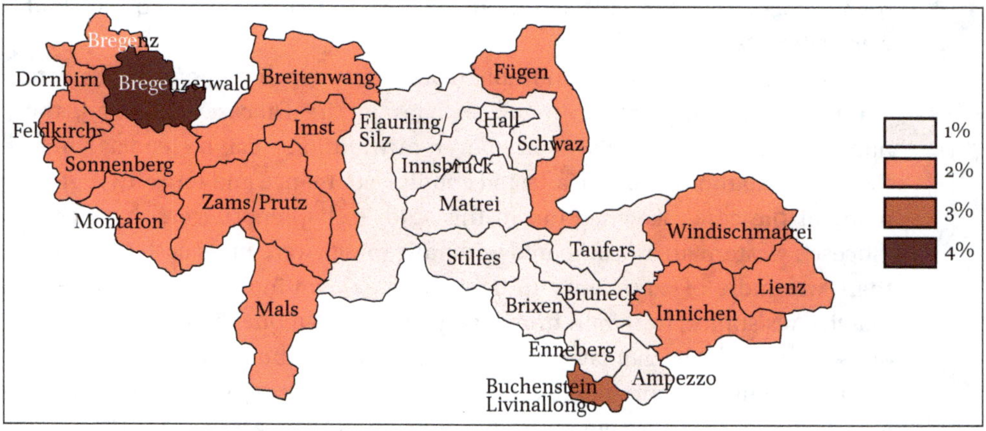

MAP 4 Papal dispensation requests in the Diocese of Brixen, 1839–1890, as a percentage of total concluded marriages in each deanery (total: 1,982 cases)

An uneven distribution can also be seen among the frequencies of requests in affinal and consanguine configurations: in the diocese's eastern deaneries with the sole exception of Windischmatrei, requests in the close degrees of affinity either predominate – with nearly double as many in the Deanery of Innsbruck – or are of equal number. Parts of the west – such as the deaneries of Mals, Breitenwang, Sonnenberg and Montafon, and most clearly the Bregenz Forest – are dominated by consanguine marriage projects. There are two times as many consanguine requests there compared with requests in degrees of affinity. The shares are equal in Feldkirch and Bregenz, while Dornbirn produced a somewhat greater number of requests from affinally related couples.

Failed marriage projects – which is to say, those whose realisation was prevented – represent a significant aspect of the history of kin marriage. Such a perspective shifts administrative practice into focus and with it the respective concrete norms and possible obstacles that marriage among close consanguineous or affinal kin involved. The various numbers and percentages can be the result of vastly differing contexts and circumstances. The confessional differences that existed were considerable, taking into account that some Protestant and Reformed territories and churches curtailed marriage impediments to quite some extent compared with canon law as early as the seventeenth, eighteenth and nineteenth centuries. But even between the Catholic dioceses themselves, the procedures followed and supplicant couples' chances of success most certainly differed. This did have its effects, in terms of not only

numbers of dispensed marriages in the individual parishes evidenced by the commented cases in the survey of 1883.

the numbers of granted dispensations but also the numbers of requests that were submitted.

In contexts where the conditions subject to which dispensations were granted were comparatively rigid, such as in the Diocese of Brixen, the numbers – and in particular their uneven distribution – can be read as something like a barometer of the affected couples' adamance and tenacity. A great many of the cases sketched out in this study's chapters suggest that in the diocese's western areas, compared with how things were in its eastern region, there was more of a tendency to fight for one's own interests in the face of massive resistance, to refrain from giving up easily on one's plans and to seek out ways and means that lay beyond the often narrow boundaries of what the Church deemed acceptable. To some extent, this tendency was probably reinforced by the lingering memories of periods spent as part of other dioceses. Thomas Götz, referring to Tyrol as a political entity, has emphasised that "state, nation building, municipality and confessional ties" across Tyrol's superficially homogeneous *Vormärz*-period territory ranging "from Kufstein to Borghetto" were in fact anything but uniform. From a diocesan perspective, we can add the west-east axis from Feldkirch to Lienz. Götz speaks of "fragmentations" that can be attributed in part to widely divergent "prior histories" and were "still felt by the generations that were politically active around 1850" – and most likely not only by these.[153] The greater openness of marriage policy in Vorarlberg compared with that in Tyrol has been associated by Elisabeth Mantl with proto-industrialisation and early industrialisation – not just as their consequence but also as a pre-existing pattern.[154] This, as well, may have contributed to a fundamental sense of entitlement where marriages were concerned.

It can hence be ascertained as a finding of this study that alongside the interwoven economic and relational logics as well as the contexts of social and spatial proximity, a further relevant factor when it came to close degree marriage

153 In this regard, he mentions the prior "annexation to different territories that underwent extreme consolidation during the Napoleonic Era", "the external interventions of highly differing character in various areas" of Tyrol and the "heritage of centuries-old traditions (especially in the prince-episcopal territories)". Götz, *Bürgertum und Liberalismus*, p. 49; see also Margareth Lanzinger, "Staat, Kirche, Eheagenden: Staatliche Integration in komplexen rechtsräumlichen Gefügen", in *Vormärz. Eine geteilte Geschichte Trentino-Tirols | Una storia condivisa Trentino-Tirolese*, ed. Francesca Brunet and Florian Huber (Innsbruck, 2017), pp. 143–161.

154 Mantl, *Heirat als Privileg*, p. 75; cf. also Ehmer, *Heiratsverhalten*, pp. 133–135. Regarding western Tyrol and Vorarlberg, Ehmer ascertains a "special form of the Alpine marriage pattern" that is not so clearly visible in the demographic data – such as in the rates of lifelong unmarried persons or persons of marrying at an advanced age – but still quite evident in terms of the structural conditions.

projects was political culture – one that attempted to counter the mercy paradigm of dispensation with a paradigm of entitlement. Explicit indications of this, however, can be found only quite rarely in the dispensation records – such as when a parish priest reported that the widowed farmer Johann Josef Zugg from St. Gallenkirch in the Deanery of Montafon was convinced he had "a right to a church dispensation".[155] But implicitly and in light of the spheres of action that were exploited, such a claim was indeed quite often present.[156] It has been possible here to render this type of political culture visible by way of an approach that places bureaucratic procedures in the foreground and views them as a significant aspect of the history of kin marriage.

What remains to be resolved is how this type of interpretation relates to the facticity of the differing structures of ownership in the diocese's west and east due to differing inheritance practices. An establishment census of July 1902 showed that the share of medium sized and larger farming operations covering 10 hectares or more accounted for between just over 40 to nearly 60 per cent in the eastern part of the Diocese of Brixen, similarly to districts in Salzburg and Carinthia – totalling 58 per cent in the District of Lienz, for example, and 44 per cent in the District of Bruneck. In the District of Imst in the diocese's west, on the other hand, such operations made up just six per cent. The situation looked similar further west in Vorarlberg: in the District of Feldkirch, the share was four per cent.[157] But in view of the aforegoing discussions, reconstructions and analyses, the initial hypothesis of a possible link between the prevailing system of partible land inheritance in the west and more frequent kin marriages would seem to be in need of some relativisation. After all, such a direct correlation would seem far too schematic in light of the vastly differing situational logics that underlay kin marriage projects as well as in light of

155 DIÖAB, Konsistorialakten 1861, Fasc. 22a, Römische Dispensen, no. 12.

156 Hubert Weitensfelder portrays a case of marriage consent refusal in which a Vorarlberg factory worker had himself represented by a lawyer. This can be viewed as an analogue to the repertoires of action employed by marriage dispensation seekers. Weitensfelder, *Industrie-Provinz*, p. 284.

157 Cf. *Ergebnisse der landwirtschaftlichen Betriebszählung vom 3. Juni 1902 in den im Reichsrate vertretenen Königreichen und Ländern.* Bearbeitet von dem Bureau der k. k. statistischen Zentralkommission (Vienna, 1909), quoted in Mathieu, *History of the Alps*, table A.5, p. 214–215. In Trentino, the share of medium-sized and larger operations lay between only one and five per cent in all districts. Furthermore, a preponderance of smaller operations also characterised Switzerland and the western Alps as a whole. These differences are shown by a map based on an agricultural census conducted in 1875. *Atlas der Urproduction Österreichs in 35 Blättern mit erläuternden Texten*, verfasst und herausgegeben auf Anordnung des k. k. Ackerbau-Ministeriums, redigirt von Dr. Jos. R. Ritter Lorenz von Liburnau, k. k. Ministerialrath (Vienna, n.y. [c.1875]), Map VIII.

the diverse wealth-related arrangements within a given inheritance model. A linkage between the two could be postulated via the thesis that family configurations resulting from partible inheritance of land may have encouraged disputatiousness as a personality trait and/or a resource. While inheritance did represent the foundation of what was needed for one's existence, it did not suffice for one's livelihood. It was much rather the case, as Andrea Hauser has ascertained, that "the material culture in a community featuring partible inheritance of land" was characterised by "an eternal circular flow involving combination and division. Once one had successively assumed one's inheritance over a period of 20 years or more, it already began to be divided for the next generation."[158] Such processual appropriation required constant attention and the frequent assertion of claims. It would hence be necessary to systematically compare instances of conflict over ownership and wealth in the regions examined here, with their differing inheritance practices, in order to corroborate this postulated linkage.

•••

This chapter has dealt with the salient characteristics of nineteenth-century consanguine marriage projects, which research so far has mainly discussed with regard to the preservation of property and wealth and – viewed as, among other things, a reaction to the introduction of equal claims to inheritance on the part of all children under the influence of the *Code civil*. In Austria, however, a comparable revision and harmonisation of inheritance law did not occur. A possible relationship between the frequency of marriage projects between cousins and differing inheritance models was an initial hypothesis going into this study's examination of the Diocese of Brixen, where impartible inheritance prevailed in the east while partible inheritance predominated in the west. The most important outcome in this regard is a plea for a nuanced view. A primarily economic explanation certainly falls short, even if the overall numbers of dispensation requests did differ in the diocese's two parts, being significantly higher in its western deaneries.

The increase in dispensation requests and dispensations granted in the close degrees served to fundamentally open up a new realm of possibilities that, until far into the eighteenth century, had been the exclusive reserve of nobles.

158 Andrea Hauser, "Erben und Teilen – ein zweiter Blick auf Forschungsergebnisse einer Sachkulturforschung", in *Generationengerechtigkeit? Normen und Praxis im Erb- und Ehegüterrecht 1500–1850*, ed. Stefan Brakensiek, Michael Stolleis and Heide Wunder (Berlin, 2006), pp. 301–315, 308.

Alongside economic logics, the most varied relationship concepts as well as the significance of social and spatial proximity and familiarity were in play. A certain probability of marriage projects between cousins was not least a consequence of denser kinship networks especially among local and regional elites, who were defined by wealth and status. In the reconstruction of the multiple cousin marriages and other unions in the Bregenz Forest's Metzler family, the links between a multitude of aspects become clear. The presence of the fathers in this family structure and in others of similar social situatedness encourages to connect a horizontal conception of kinship with the persistence of power and authority via the vertical axis as two sides of the same coin – and to allow for categorisations and attributions beyond a schematic notion of class in light of broad-based social profiles and economic (pluri)activity.

While the 1830s and 1840s saw marriage projects in close degrees of affinity faced with difficult and often hopeless conditions, the policy of refusal shifted its focus more strongly toward marriage projects between first cousins during the nineteenth century's final decades. It was on moral grounds and with extreme vehemence that such a policy was pursued in the early 1860s by Joseph Feßler in his capacity as vicar general of Vorarlberg. Feßler's doings were ultimately to remain a mere episode, but the attention paid to possible consequences of close degree unions did increase significantly thereafter. A survey conducted in Vorarlberg in 1883 was intended to obtain clarity in this regard but failed to do so on account of its ambivalent results. This survey, which encompassed all marriages concluded on the basis of papal dispensations and hence also affinal unions, once more shows quite impressively how the Church held fast to its conception of kinship that equated consanguinity and affinity and developed specific scenarios with regard to possible consequences. It was thus that danger to children's health, elevated child mortality or the inability of couples to conceive represented only partial aspects of observation while misfortunes of all kinds, economic ruin and marital dispute and dispeace dominated the comments in the final list. In any event, a circular containing an appeal to do everything possible to prevent such marriage projects was subsequently sent to all deaneries.

So-called emergency civil marriage, introduced in 1868, opened up a sphere of action amidst this renewed oppressiveness of dispensation policy that was exploited at least on the level of implication and threat, rendering the Church to a certain extent vulnerable to blackmail. A major sensation was the case of the Dornbirn physician and long-time liberal mayor Georg Waibl, who sought to marry his niece Aurelia Waibl in the early 1880s – and indeed came close to concluding a civil marriage in Vienna. The various stages of this marriage project not only make clear how the probability of a civil marriage weighed more than the largely taboo nature of this union between uncle and niece. They also show the difficulties that state lawgiving encountered as soon as it began interfering in ecclesiastical domains. In this case, church power also proved quite effective at combating innovation on the part of the state, much like it had in the wake of the Josephine reforms.

The number of dispensation requests certainly did rise overall as the nineteenth century progressed, but by no means was there an 'explosion' in the sense of a "kinship 'hot' society".[159] The final section of this chapter aims to create an awareness of the significance attributable to numerical data where such complex material is concerned. Whenever interest in this topic extends beyond the statistical apprehension of approved kin marriages – as they were more or less reliably recorded in marriage or dispensation registers – and "incest coefficients", then the question as to what exactly the compiled figures portray, under what conditions they were compiled and the extent to which regional figures can be compared becomes essential. This study set out to investigate kin marriage as a prominent late-eighteenth- and nineteenth-centuries phenomenon and thus started from dispensation requests, thereby also integrating marriage projects that were rejected and never realised. The numbers are hence the result of both fluctuating dispensation policies and differences in dispensation practice as well as the constantly changing administrative procedures during the period under study. In this, they also reveal significant disparities between the Catholic dioceses. A final important finding of this study is that the supplicant couples' agency consisted mainly in their tenacity and adamance, in the fact that many of them simply refused to give up. And for this reason, political culture must be viewed as having been of major importance in bringing a marriage project to fruition.

159 Sabean, *Kinship in Neckarhausen*, back cover blurb; Sabean/Teuscher/Mathieu, *Kinship in Europe*, back cover blurb.

CHAPTER 7

Conclusion: Demarcations and Spheres of Power

In the Austrian Catholic context of the late eighteenth century, the centuries-old theologically defined marriage prohibitions extending to the fourth degree of kinship encountered competition in the form of liberal civil laws. During the nineteenth century, the theological and legal debate over their moral and social implications was increasingly added by arguments founded on a physiological and medical perspective as well as stemming from the increasingly differentiated natural science disciplines, especially those that dealt with heredity. The justification of marriage prohibitions and the call to respect "natural laws" gave rise to all manner of bricolage. Examining the various lines of argument in a systematic fashion shows clearly how incest boundaries drawn through the kinship space became more permeable beginning in the late eighteenth century. However, this space simultaneously took on new contours due to of the lines that were being drawn between the "strange" and one's "own".

The theological and civil law demand that new members be added to the circle of one's family whenever possible, so that – depending on an author's position – either *caritas* or wealth would be more widely distributed, was opposed particularly by bourgeois concepts of marriage and love with their prioritisation of familiarity and proximity. The Catholic Church's efforts to banish sexuality from contexts of proximity bore less and less fruit: brothers- and sisters-in-law were laying claim to the right to marry, as were first cousins, stepmothers and stepsons, uncles and nieces.

Scholars have discussed the concomitant phenomenon of tendencies toward social closure by way of social endogamy, via marriage among equals and even more via endogamy in the narrower sense: that of marriage between blood kin, primarily between first and second cousins. A marriage appropriate to one's status in this respect was defined in terms of more than just economic criteria: men and women also – as can be seen in the dispensation requests – argued with an eye to their "similarity" of attitudes, education, character and humour. The known and familiar, one's "own", was hypostatised as the ideal prerequisite for marriage. Social homogamy was at the same time 'attitudinal homogamy'. But in light of the dominant position occupied by husbands, it is by no means the case that such unions between 'equals' can be viewed as having been equitable in the sense of gender relations.[1]

1 On this cf. also Hull, *Sexuality, State, and Civil Society*, pp. 223–228.

This phenomenon of homogamy in the comprehensive sense, discernible mainly in bourgeois circles and hence socially situated, was joined by a second, more general and accelerating surge in the significance of one's "own" blood via the naturalisation of "blood ties". One's "own" blood, according to the arguments contained in the dispensation records, was to be preferred over "strange" blood. This elevated the aunt or another close relative of the children, as a "second mother", to a position superior to that of a "strange" stepmother – and, what is more, to that of a "strange" housekeeper or maidservant, if she were charged with looking after the children in addition to running the household. This emphasis was associated primarily with the couple configuration of widower and sister-and-law. And indeed, the theological construction of parallel marriage prohibitions pertaining to consanguineous and affinal kin began to exhibit visible cracks during the nineteenth century, both in terms of how bridal couples forced to request dispensations were perceived and due to the focus of the natural sciences and the medical field on consanguinity. The Catholic Church representatives responsible for dispensation related matters avoided confronting the distinction that resulted, which by that time was no longer to be overlooked or drowned out, and instead continued to act based on an assumption of coequality between consanguineous and affinal marriage prohibitions. Some even undertook explicit transference of the suspected consequences of marriages between close consanguineous kin to affinal unions.

The biological fortification of "blood ties" and the emphasis on preference for "one's own blood" ultimately came to form a basis for racist ideologies. It is thus that medical experts' and heredity theorists' reservations about marrying into "one's own blood" proved subordinate to the fears of mixing that arose before the backdrop of colonialism. Regarding nineteenth-century Great Britain, Nancy Anderson has ascertained that the fear of "miscegenation" was greater than the fear of incest.[2] British studies conducted during the late nineteenth and early twentieth centuries by Francis Galton and Karl Pearson viewed unions between first cousins as possessed of "the most intense purity of blood lines", as Leonore Davidoff has commented. This concept of purity, however, pertained to "superior people" – for in their circles, such unions were believed to prevent moral and physical "degeneration" in the interest of "improving the race".[3] This values matrix of "strange" and "own", oriented on eugenics and racism, was ultimately reflected in the National Socialist "Law for the Protection of German Blood and German Honour". This law forbade marriages between

2 Anderson, "The Marriage", p. 84. She quotes from the article "Kin, The Marriage of the Near", published in: *Westminster Review* CIV (1875), 147–155.

3 Davidoff, *Thicker than Water*, pp. 241–242.

"citizens of German or kindred blood" and Jews, as persons of "alien blood" (RGBl I 1935, p. 1146). Kin marriages, on the other hand, were declared legal.[4] In terms of the distinction drawn vis-à-vis "strange" blood as defined by "race", related blood functioned more or less as the highest form of one's "own".

Beyond their linkage with blood, the topoi of "strange" and one's "own" run throughout the analysed political and social contexts like a golden thread: "strange" as a parameter of demarcation, as a negative foil, and one's "own" as an implicit or explicit countermodel, as a positive connotation and a legitimation of claims. It was around these qualities that the conflicts between Church and state revolved at the close of the eighteenth century. Both sides were at pains to assert their competence when it came to defining kinship-based marriage prohibitions and administrating dispensation related matters. This battle was waged by the state – albeit with little success, viewed from the perspective of the nineteenth century – against the strong position occupied on its own territory by a "foreign" jurisdiction represented by papal power, by the nunciature in Vienna as its proxy and by canon law. Contrary to the intention of the state lawgiver, the more liberal provisions of the Marriage Patent of 1783 – consisting in reduced marriage prohibitions and dispensation proceedings' simplification via the intended sidelining of the authorities in Rome – provided no relief. Instead, they opened up a realm of competition within which couples who were closely related by blood or affinity inevitably became pawns.

Confessions' and religions' efforts in the interest of outward differentiation represent an integral component of their respective histories. The fact that the Catholic Church fought so vehemently against marriages in the first degree of affinity can, in principle, be seen as having been a counterposition to the Jewish practice of levirate marriage, which obligated childless widows to marry their brothers-in-law. During the 1830s and 1840s, Pope Gregory XVI tightened granting dispensations in the close degrees of affinity. His definition of the danger of conversion as the only canonical reason to be recognised in such cases in German-speaking dioceses, a reason that possessed and indeed manifested a certain potential as an instrument of threat especially in the Diocese of Brixen due to neighbouring Switzerland, made the adversarial relationship between the confessions the starting point of argumentation. While this did serve to uphold the demarcational narrative, it simultaneously rendered the

---

4 It was only in the direct line – connecting grandparents, parents, children, grandchildren, etc. – as well as between "full or half-siblings" and between stepparents and stepchildren that marriage remained prohibited. "Gesetz zur Vereinheitlichung des Rechts der Eheschließung und der Ehescheidung im Lande Österreich und im übrigen Reichsgebiet vom 6. Juli 1938", *RGBl I*, no. 106, 8 July 1838, p. 808 as well as *Gesetzblatt für das Land Österreich*, 12 July 1938, issue 75, §§ 6 and 7.

option of conversion at least conceivable for more than a few couples whose dispensation requests had been refused multiple times. Conversion was joined by interconfessional marriages as a second transgression that the Catholic side sought to combat. A look at the confessionally mixed Diocese of Chur revealed that interconfessional marriages were perceived as a problem there during the nineteenth century in a way that clearly overshadowed the issue of kin marriage.

In the dispensation records, "strange" – as a classification applied to unreliable servants, ill-suited caregivers, wicked stepmothers and heirs and heiresses felt to be illegitimate – was contrasted with qualities of relatedness and familiarity as a foil that was riddled with derogatory characteristics across all of the various social milieus. Strangeness was attributed to all those who did not belong to one's own family and kin, and strange was everything 'out there': the city or the valley from the perspective of the village, "strange lands" as a destination of seasonal migration, and also those who came from the outside. The importance of such attributions may well have been a consequence of overall societal changes during those times. However, such a defensive posture vis-à-vis the strange could also be employed as a strategic argument. "Strange" stood for a diffuse conglomerate of fears – regardless of how honest or merely opportune the references to them may have been – and provided the basis for a demarcational rhetoric that pointed beyond the officially recognised reasons for dispensation. It was an argument to which the next higher church representatives repeatedly proved open. And with the increasing discursive glorification of home, hearth and homeliness in the nineteenth century as the sphere of action attributed to women and as a counterworld to the occupational domain and mobility of men, "strangeness" in its entirety was likely accorded a new weight.

Last but not least, the authorship of the analysed documents would suggest that the topos of the "strange" here probably reflected mainly the attitudes of ecclesiastical and conservative circles. Clerics played a key role in developing such images of the "strange" – irrespective of whether they themselves held such a position or were simply reckoning with the positive effect it might have at the prince-episcopal consistory. Rural life, stylised as a cradle of morality, was to be protected from external – which is to say damaging – influences. Such influences were attributed to "so-called liberals and radicals or people indifferent to religion and morality".[5]

The moralistic thrust of such argumentation continued in terms of what went on inside the house. If maidservants would otherwise be required to

5 DIÖAB, Konsistorialakten 1851, Fasc. 5a, Römische Dispensen, no. 12.

replace the deceased wife, the moral danger inherent in their doing so represented an opportune argument in support of a proposed marriage. The farm of Michael Moosbrugger lay in a "very remote location"; a "strange maidservant", it was firmly stated, was not wanted in the house.[6] It was with greater clarity that the widower Johann Michael Nachbauer expressed such negative expectations: the work and conscientiousness of a maidservant, he held, could never equal those of a wife. He could not employ an older maidservant, since she would be incapable of the arduous work required on his hardscrabble farm. Employing a young maidservant, on the other hand, would be morally disadvantageous and damaging above all to his reputation.[7] There were occasional allegations to the effect that a maidservant had deliberately accepted employment from a widower or unmarried man with the ulterior motive of marrying him. And the smaller the household, the more clearly these misgivings were expressed: "Solus cum sola" is "dangerous", noted a local clergyman concerning an unmarried peasant who would have had to seek out a housekeeper as an alternative to marriage.[8] At the same time, filling a deceased wife's position in households with several servants – above all when they were maidservants and farmhands – was considered a particularly urgent priority. Only this was viewed as a guarantor of domestic order in terms of morality and the work to be done.

The fact that dispensation seekers had to prove themselves 'worthy' in a moral sense repeatedly put local clerics in a double bind when a woman was pregnant and marriage at the earliest possible date would be fit to rescue or restore her honour. And beginning the mid-1850s, policies became extremely rigid, – with periods of probation and veritable 'penance programmes' for those couples who had already engaged in sexual contact prior to a dispensation request. If a couple closely related by blood or by affinity lived beneath the same roof, one of the two would be legally obligated to vacate the house, failing which a court could – successfully or unsuccessfully – order their separation, in the worst case scenario effecting such separation by force. It was thus that both Church and state intervened massively in relationships and households again and again via concrete requirements and official acts as well as in the sense of a threat that had to be anticipated.

While matters of domestic organisation and domestic peace featured prominently in the arguments underlying marriage projects between affines, those involving blood kin tended to be associated more frequently with an interest

6 DIÖAB, Konsistorialakten 1837, Fasc. 5a, Römische Dispensen, no. 20.

7 DIÖAB, Konsistorialakten 1833, Fasc. 5a, Römische Dispensen, no. 17.

8 DIÖAB, Konsistorialakten 1847, Fasc. 5a, Römische Dispensen, no. 19.

in preserving wealth – even in less wealthy social contexts. In cases involving urban and rural elites, the concern was also with increasing and preserving status and prestige. Public demeanour, self-portrayal and kin-oriented action in the wealthy families briefly portrayed here – such as the Metzlers – suggest a milieu constituted by specific combinations of continuity and innovation. The dispositif of alliance – defined by Michel Foucault as "a system of marriage, of fixation and development of kinship ties, of transmission of names and possessions" – seems not to have been supplanted by the dispositif of sexuality,[9] but rather to have been interwoven therewith. Beyond conspicuous families and kin networks that belonged to local and regional elites, dispensation records enable access to the marriage plans of related couples situated across a broad social spectrum. With its finding that kin marriage was not an elite phenomenon, this study has broken out of the concentration on bourgeois families that has predominated in the research thus far. Moreover, its simultaneously implemented regionalised perspective on this phenomenon has made it possible to discern a greater degree of nuance in terms of such marriage projects' situational contexts.

Focusing on marriage prohibitions, dispensation practice and dispensation policy places diverse vertical and horizontal relational configurations, their organisation and their interdependencies at the centre of the analysis. Due to the respective state and church claims to both definitional power and administrative competence, the pool of protagonists involved with dispensation requests expanded – as did the relevant spaces of social interaction, forms of mediation and entities. Instances of mutual demarcation as well as intervention were an integral component of this competition for discursive and administrative competence and positions of power. From the perspective of dispensation practice, it was especially in the Diocese of Brixen – in contrast above all to the situation in the dioceses of Trento and Salzburg – that the arm of the Church proved quite long and powerful while that of the state remained comparatively weak. Relying on the latter, claiming a right, could entail making oneself vulnerable and risking both reputation and esteem in one's social environment, and it invariably entailed complex bureaucratic procedures. But if, on the other hand, the focus was on an instrument such as political marriage consent, which served to uphold obsolete socio-political structures, the Church itself would quite enthusiastically resort to the invocation of secular law.

Thanks to the success had by the Church in recovering its position of primacy, the Diocese of Brixen – whose records have represented the lion's share

9 Michel Foucault, *The History of Sexuality*, vol. 1: *An Introduction* (New York, 1978), p. 106.

of those analysed – continued to be dominated by a style of decision-making and communication that was hierarchical and authoritarian, whose logics and lines of argument were not up for discussion and indeed were not allowed to be discussed – at least not by supplicants. All depended upon mercy, since a right to a dispensation did not exist. However, certain latitudes for interpretation and manoeuvring most certainly were exploited by clergymen on various levels of the hierarchy whenever their intent was for a request to have prospects of a positive outcome, for the Church was not exclusively strict but indeed also viewed itself as a "gracious mother". The tighter the moral corset surrounding couples' dispensation worthiness was drawn, the more strongly the consistory in Brixen emphasised such compassion in the rhetoric of its dispensation-related correspondence. Nonetheless, the confines within which possible arguments could move did remain clearly delineated. Those who wished for their dispensation requests to have prospects of success and to surmount the obstacles to further processing that existed on the diocesan level were forced to adapt accordingly.

Even so, the 'system' – in particular the Church and its representatives but also civil entities ranging from municipalities, regional courts and district offices to the Imperial Court Chancellery, the Austrian Embassy in Rome and the Ministry of the Interior – was repeatedly challenged by supplicant couples: through their tenacity and insistence on their marriage plans, their involvement of lawyers, their exploitation of atypical means and channels and their employment of threats and transgression of boundaries that had been drawn in the sexual realm. None of these strategies were in any way guaranteed to make receiving their desired dispensation more likely. Some of these possible actions much rather entailed certain risks and could even end up making dispensation seekers' situations even more hopeless. Couples requesting dispensations were supplicants, after all, and had therefore to present themselves with humility rather than make demands, as the consistory repeatedly declared. They commanded no legally structured power, but they did possess the power of tenacity. And during certain phases, threats could also be wielded – by announcing the intention to convert, marry abroad or enter into a civil marriage. On occasion, these threats most certainly had the intended effect.

It was to be expected that a geographically expansive study would not end up producing the impression of uniform dispensation granting practices and evenly distributed kin marriages. But even so, the ascertained differences in terms of diocesan consistories' and individual bishops' attitudes as well as the actions of bridal couples and the associated number of submitted requests turned out to be more pronounced than originally assumed. Research pertaining to administrative processes can therefore be viewed as essential when it comes to discerning the logics according to which dispensations were granted and refused. Alongside the findings of previous research, the multifarious quality of the source material evaluated in this study and the contexts and logics reconstructed on this basis have made clear that there will ultimately be no single 'grand' explanation. Said contexts and logics indicate that economic considerations, socially proximate relationships and a specific political culture are of equal relevance.

The examined political space was characterised by differing velocities and modes of transition from the 'old' to the 'new' world. It is likely no coincidence that "citizen" does not appear as a category in the records to be found in Brixen, while it does appear repeatedly in dispensation requests submitted in the Diocese of Salzburg. If the presence of this term marks the supersession of a society oriented toward estates and the emergence of a civic self-understanding – in the sense of the *citoyen* – in which actionable rights and clear bureaucratic procedures are constituent elements, its absence enables us to conclude that the supreme representatives of the Church in Tyrol, as an element of society with great definitional power, will have had their difficulties with this transition. Looking at dispensation-related practice hence makes visible a socio-political order in which status and social standing counted for more than the most difficult life circumstances and the most dire need throughout the nineteenth century. Economic and symbolic capital were capable of speeding along dispensation requests even in times of rigid dispensation policies. During the 1780s, the most embittered phase of conflict between competing positions in the wake of the Josephine Marriage Patent, the state's administration of dispensation-related matters had proceeded based upon a provision of the *Decretum Tametsi* formulated by the Council of Trent (1545–1563) that provided for estate-based privileging. This was expressed via the requirement that a marriage should serve the "common good". In the course of this research, it became evident again and again that civil marriage law in Austria was characterised by inconsistency in terms of its independence from ecclesiastical frameworks.

Even though couples requesting dispensations stood as supplicants before powerful church and state hierarchies and bureaucracies, social practice and the diverse realms of interaction that were in play preclude a dichotomous separation into administrators and the administrated. If the decision-making power at each point further 'up' in the church hierarchy grew progressively greater, so did the pressure to which each point further down was subject: local parish priests and deans were charged with discovering marriage impediments sufficiently in advance of a possible marriage, discouraging closely related couples from pursuing their marriage plans whenever possible and only forwarding dispensation requests that would have good prospects. Just like the civil servants who dealt with dispensations, they had to endure repeated rebukes and admonishments. At the same time, they also had the greatest degree of exposure to the supplicant couples. One's own parish priest was easiest to repeatedly badger and besiege, as was perhaps – depending on his geographic location and how close or distant it was – the competent dean. It was considerably rarer for unsuccessful dispensation seekers to personally seek out the clerics of the vicariate general or episcopal consistory and confront them directly with their despair, pleas and entreaties.

In sum, this study has undertaken a first-ever systematic examination of dispensation practices in four dioceses – those of Brixen, Chur, Salzburg and Trento – and related them to church and state dispensation policies, to the myriad administrative and procedural channels that were involved and to the organisation of households and families. An integral aspect of doing so has been retracing the history of competition between ecclesiastical and secular powers that characterised the long transition from the early modern period to a secularised society founded increasingly upon state institutions. While the main thrust of the empirical work concerns the period between 1780 and 1890, the conceptual and legal frame of reference reaches back much further in time. This pertains to the definition of dispensations as mercies to which, even during the nineteenth century, there was no legal claim, hence being something situated outside processes of juridification while also capable of propping up the symbolic and real power of the Church as an "administrant of grace". The marriage prohibitions entailed by kinship extending out to the fourth degree that remained in effect until 1917 in the Catholic context had originally been established by the Fourth Council of the Lateran in 1215. The concepts of incest and "disgrace of the blood" (*Blutschande*), of flesh and blood as kinship-generating substances being applied here were likewise of mediaeval origin. It is thus that this study has delved into that tension-filled space between long-term continuities and those changes that occurred during the modern period and particularly during the late eighteenth and nineteenth centuries. This particularly affected the marriage impediment of affinity, which was based on the notion of "one flesh" – *una caro* – and grew more difficult for the Church to argue before the backdrop of a nineteenth-century discourse that was increasingly informed by heredity theory.

This study has analysed the ways in which structured power functioned and the avenues via which related bridal couples could oppose it by turning a spotlight on the approaches to "administrating kinship" that can be found within a complex melange of church and state institutions and their representatives. It is a view in which institutions come into being through interaction and communication, with their logics being framed by their procedures. The 'cascades' of power ran from the Roman Curia to the curate in a tiny mountain village, from the Imperial Court Chancellery or the Ministry of the Interior in Vienna to the mayors of local municipalities. All of them thus stood in relation to one another and to the hundreds and thousands of consanguineous and affinal couples who requested dispensations. During the period under study, dispensation-related matters were closely intertwined with theological, legal, medical, scientific and societal discourses, with differing conceptualisations of kinship and the organisation of knowledge thereof, with the respective laws and rules, administrative logics and power politics of Church and state, and with the figuration of relations between both genders and generations.

Source material as diverse as it is rich – writings inspired by canon and civil law, medicine and the natural sciences, official correspondence from between the Josephine era and 1850 and nineteenth-century dispensation records (nearly 2,150 from the Diocese of Brixen alone) – formed the basis for this research. Approaches from cultural, political and social history have been employed in this analysis in a way that is closely linked with gender and legal perspectives. The objective has been to shine a light on how kinship embodied a central category in the European modern era, a category that played a crucial role in structuring relations between the genders and the generations and whose efficacy extended into the core of society, thereby unquestionably taking on political significance.

This study has simultaneously been an attempt to produce an organisational, administrative and institutional history of church and state bureaucracies and their protagonists from a cultural historical perspective. Such an approach aims not to describe administrative apparatuses but rather to show them in action within the context of their various procedures. This enables us to capture those moments in which the social occurs, rendering visible diverse and new relationships: it has proven possible to place persons who were situated in their respective contexts – kinship-related, institutional, political, social, etc. – in relation to one another via the most varied pathways. It has thereby also been possible to retrace the logics according to which they acted as well as the transformations of arguments and justifications as documents made their way through the official channels. The multi-relational space of communication and questioning thus conceptualised can be read as an *histoire croisée*.[10]

10 Cf. Michael Werner and Bénédicte Zimmermann, "Vergleich, Transfer, Verflechtung. Der Ansatz der *Histoire croisée* und die Herausforderung des Transnationalen", *Geschichte und Gesellschaft* 28 (2002), 607–636.

Appendix: Organisation of the Material

In order to better manage the great volume of material and be able to access the relevant documents in light of individual questions as well as in order to comprehend structural patterns, it seemed advisable to compile a database encompassing the Diocese of Brixen's series of dispensation records, which begins in 1831. Listed in this database are the competent deanery, the degree of kinship and key data on the persons requesting dispensation – such as family status, age, occupation(s) – as well as information about the characteristics of the individual cases and the courses and outcomes of dispensation proceedings. A number of variables apprehend the concrete situations, arguments and reasons for dispensation in the form of yes/no or numerically coded answers: Was there a context of spatial proximity, such as when the couple lived in the same house or close by? Who spoke of love? What economic and other reasons were brought to bear? Were childrearing or caring for family members topics in the request? Was there talk of "moral danger" or "public scandal"? Was the bride pregnant, and/or were there already children born out of wedlock? How did the couple's situation look in terms of property ownership? What characteristics were mentioned on the woman's side, on the man's side? Was the overall portrayal of the couple in question positive or negative? Any special characteristics of a case were also included, such as if there were problems with financing a dispensation, if the couple employed wayward strategies or if the request travelled via unusual channels. Due to the enormous effort involved, the recording of data in such detail was limited to the years up to 1864; for the following period ending in 1890, only basic data were entered.

In parallel with the compilation of this database, each request along with a brief summary was entered into a table that proved quite useful as a catalogue of sorts, facilitating quick access to certain cases and their details as well as enabling the attribution of additional information concerning the same couples from other archival holdings. Among other things, this type of organisation made it possible to reliably identify those couples who made renewed requests years after failed attempts.

The purpose of undertaking such a formalised, albeit laborious mode of datafication and case documentation was also to allow dispensation requests to be read systematically and comprehended in terms of their content by posing the same questions of all dispensation records. This also made visible matters not addressed in the requests themselves. The database depicts basic information about and specific characteristics of the requests as well as their outcomes, though the processual nature of the dispensation proceedings' various phases does indeed get lost here. The focus of this study has been on the content of the dispensation records, and their quantitative analyses provided an important basis for the questions to be posed as well as for the findings themselves.

Bibliography

Unprinted Sources

Archiv der Diözese Feldkirch (ADF)

ADF, Generalvikariat Matrimonialia (GA), Ehesachen I, 1820–1850.

ADF, Generalvikariat Matrimonialia (GA), Ehesachen II, 1811–1916.

ADF, Generalvikariat Matrimonialia (GA), Ehesachen III, Präsidialakten 1830–1900 und Römische Dispensen I, 1853–1858.

ADF, Generalvikariat Matrimonialia (GA), Ehesachen III, Präsidial behandelte Ehedispensfälle (Bischof Feßler) 1862–1865.

ADF, Generalvikariat Matrimonialia (GA), Ehesachen V, Römische Dispensen III, 1877–1885.

Archiv der Erzdiözese Salzburg (AES)

AES, Kasten 22/34, Ehesdispensen I. u. II. Grades 1813–1880.

AES, Kasten 22/34, Ehedispensen I. u. II. Grades 1821–1830.

AES, Kasten 22/35, Ehe-Dispensen 1828–1840.

AES, Kasten 22/35, Ehe-Dispensen 1841–1846 und 1883–1890.

AES, Kasten 22/38, Päpstliche Dispensen 1856–1867.

AES, Kasten 22/38, Päpstliche Ehedispensen 1867–1934.

AES, Kasten 22/39, Päpstliche Ehe-Dispensen 1868–1877.

AES, Kasten 22/40, zurückgewiesene Ehedispensen 1892–1911.

Archivio Diocesano Tridentino (ADT)

ADT, Dispense matrimoniali, Dispense 1830, Dispense 1831, Dispense 1832, Dispense 1836, Dispense 1842, Dispense 1846, Dispense 1855.

ADT, Protocolli cancelleria. Indice dall'anno 1842 fino al 1845 inclusive.

ADT, Protocolli cancelleria. Indice Eccl[esiastico] 1846–1849.

ADT, Registro delle spese per dispense pontificie, dei relativi depositi, dei pagamenti agli agenti, 1823 [until 1848].

Archivio di Stato Bolzano / Staatsarchiv Bozen (*ASBz / SABo*)

ASBz / SABo, Kreisamt Bozen, Bündel 331, 1 u. 2, 1831, Geistlich, Ehe I.

ASBz / SABo, Kreisamt Bozen, Bündel 332, 1831, Geistlich, Ehe II.

ASBz / SABo, Kreisamt Bozen, Bündel 345, 1832, Geistlich, Ehe I.

ASBz / SABo, Kreisamt Bozen, Bündel 346, 1832, Geistlich, Ehe II.

ASBz / SABo, Kreisamt Bozen, Bündel 353, 1833, Geistlich, Ehe I.

ASBz / SABo, Kreisamt Bozen, Bündel 354, 1833, Geistlich, Ehe II.

ASBz / SABo, Kreisamt Bozen, Bündel 373, 1 u. 2, 1834, Geistlich, Ehe.

ASBz / SABo, Kreisamt Bozen, Bündel 388, 1 u. 2, 1835, Geistlich, Ehe.

ASBz / SABo, Kreisamt Bozen, Bündel 399, 1 u. 2, Miscellanea.

ASBz / SABo, Kreisamt Bozen, Bündel 401, 1 u. 2, 1836, Geistlich, Ehe.

ASBz / SABo, Kreisamt Bozen, Bündel 420, 1 u. 2, 1837, Geistlich, Ehe.

ASBz / SABo, Kreisamt Bozen, Bündel 426, 1838, Geistlich, Ehe, Schul ….

ASBz / SABo, Kreisamt Bozen, Bündel 430, 1, 1839, Geistlich, Kanzl.

Archivio di Stato di Trento (ASTn)

ASTn, Capitanato Circolare di Rovereto, busta 90, 1823, Matrimoni, busta 120, 1825, Matrimoni; busta 143, 1827, Matrimoni; busta 156, 1828, Matrimoni.

ASTn, Capitanato Circolare di Trento, busta 130, 1843, Ehe; busta 195, 1846, matrimoni; busta 213, 1847, Ehe – matrimoni.

Bischöfliches Archiv Chur (BAC)

BAC, Dispensationes matrimoniales, ab anno 1816 de Novem[bris] ad mensem Decembris 1818.

BAC, Dispensationes matrimoniales, 1848–1853.

BAC, Dispensationes matrimoniales expeditae ab Ill[ustrissi]mo et R[everendissi]mo D[omi]no Jos. Mar. Bovieri, S[anctis] Sedis Negotiorum Gestore, ab initio anni 1854 usque ad initium Decembris 1864.

BAC, Dispens[ationes] Matrimoniales, Expeditiones Romanae, Curae Animarum, Confirmatio ad Beneficia, 1859–1933.

BAC, Dispens[ationes] Matrim[oniales], 1877–1892.

BAC, Dispensationes Matrim[oniales] Specialium Facult[atis] Apost[olicae], incipit mense Maji 1892.

BAC, 111.02.04, Päpstliche Erlasse, Bestände 19. Jahrhundert.

BAC, 111.02.04, Päpstliche Erlasse, Bestände 19. Jahrhundert. Chirografo della santità di nostro signore Papa Gregorio XVI sulle dispense matrimoniali in primo grado di affinità e in primo misto col secundo di consanguinità o affinità, Roma 1836.

BAC, Regestum Dispensationum Matrimon[ialium] quae Auctoritate Ap[osto]lica concessae sunt Ab Exc[ellentissi]mo P. Vincentio Macchi Nuntio, Ab Ill[ustrissi]mo P. Aloysio Nevi Internuntio, et ab Exc[ellentissi]mo P. Ignatio ex Comitibus Nasalli Archi-Episcopo Cyri, et Pro Sancta Sede ad Helevtos Nuntio Apostolico 1818–1828.

BAC, Registrum Dispensationum Matrimonialium quae Auctoritate Apostolica concessae sunt a Rev[erendissi]mo D[omi]no Paschale Gizzi Archiepiscopo Thebarum et ad Helvetos Ap[osto]lico Nuntio, 1839 ad 1841 [1848].

Diözesanarchiv Brixen (DIÖAB)

DIÖAB, Dispensationes matrimoniales ab anno 1774 usque ad annum 1794 inclusive.

DIÖAB, Dispensationes matrimoniales ab anno 1795 usque ad annum 1829 inclusive.

DIÖAB, Konsistorialakten, Agentie, Schachtel oA.

DIÖAB, Konsistorialakten 1831 bis 1860, Fasc. 5a, Römische Dispensen.

DIÖAB, Konsistorialakten 1831 bis 1860, Fasc. 5b, Dispensen in occultis.

DIÖAB, Konsistorialakten 1831 bis 1860, Fasc. 5c, Varia de matrimonio / Verschiedenes über Ehesachen.

DIÖAB, Konsistorialakten 1861 bis 1895, Fasc. 22a, Römische Dispensen.

DIÖAB, Konsistorialakten 1861 bis 1895, Fasc. 22b, Dispensen in occultis.

DIÖAB, Konsistorialakten 1861 bis 1895, Fasc. 22b, Varia de matrimonio matrimonio / Verschiedenes über Ehesachen.

DIÖAB, Konsistorialakten 1864 bis 1887, Fasc. 22, Bischöfliche Dispensen.

DIÖAB, Konsistorialakten 1861, Fasc. 22 II, Ad matrimonium spectantia.

DIÖAB, Konsistorialcodices Romana, ab anno 1764 inclusive mense majo usque ad annum 1861.

DIÖAB, Protokoll 1830.

DIÖAB, Registratura Dispensation[um] Matrimonial[ium] inc[o]hoata anno 1690 [until 1730].

DIÖAB, Registratura Dispensation[um] Matrimonial[ium] inc[o]hoata anno 1733 usque ad annum 1752.

DIÖAB, Registratura Dispensation[um] Matrimonial[ium] anno 1753 usque ad annum 1768.

Österreichisches Staatsarchiv (ÖSTA), *Allgemeines Verwaltungsarchiv* (AVA)

ÖSTA, AVA, Alter Cultus, K. 1, Ehesachen und Taufen, 1807–1834.

ÖSTA, AVA, Alter Cultus, K. 9, Ehesachen und Taufen, 1781–1805.

ÖSTA, AVA, Alter Kultus, K. 12, Ehesachen, Taufen, Akatholiken, NÖ, Böhmen, OÖ, Slzb, Stmk, Innerösterr., Vorderösterr., Tirol.

Österreichisches Staatsarchiv (ÖSTA), *Haus-, Hof- und Staatsarchiv* (*HHStA*)

ÖSTA, HHStA, Agentie-Archiv Rom, II Agentie Akten 1817–1832, K. 32–40.

ÖSTA, HHStA, Agentie-Archiv Rom, III Agentie Akten 1833–1855, Agentierechnungen, K. 57–65.

ÖSTA, HHStA, Agentie-Archiv Rom, III Agentie Akten 1833–1855, K. 75–77.

ÖSTA, HHStA, Agentie-Archiv Rom, IV Agentie Akten 1856–1891, Rechnungen, K. 147–153.

ÖSTA, HHStA, Agentie-Archiv Rom, IV Agentie Akten 1856–1891, K. 163–181 [1871].

ÖSTA, HHStA, Rom Varia 1778–1784, K. 58, Ins. 2. Correspondence entre S. Maj. L'Emperéur Joseph II. et S.A.R. L'Electeur de Tréve touchant les édits impériaux en matiere de religion, Philadelphia 1782.

Tiroler Landesarchiv (TLA) Innsbruck

TLA Innsbruck, Hofregistratur, Älteres Gubernium, Reihe L, Publica, Politica, 1783, Fasc. 220, Pos. 29–32, Ein- und Auslauf.

TLA Innsbruck, Protokolle der Geistlichen Commissions-Sachen vom 21. Februar 1782 bis 19. Februar 1783.

TLA Innsbruck, Protocolla in Geistlichen Co[mmissi]ons-Sachen vom 19. Februar bis Ende Dezember 1783.

TLA Innsbruck, Protocolla cum Indice in Geistlichen Co[mmissi]ons-Sachen vom ersten Januar bis Ende Juni 1784.

TLA Innsbruck, Protocolla cum Indice in Geistlichen Co[mmissi]ons-Sachen vom 1. Jänner bis Ende Juni 1785.

TLA Innsbruck, Protocolla cum Indice in Geistlichen Co[mmissi]ons-Sachen vom 1. Juli 1785 bis Ende Juni 1786.

TLA Innsbruck, Jüngeres Gubernium, Gubernialratsprotokolle, Ecclesiastica, Fasc. 212, 1783 (Jan.–Feb.), Ein- und Auslauf.

TLA Innsbruck, Jüngeres Gubernium, Gubernialratsprotokolle, Ecclesiastica, Fasc. 213, 1783 (März–Juli), Ein- und Auslauf.

TLA Innsbruck, Jüngeres Gubernium, Geistliche Sachen, Fasc. 433, 1784, Akten.

TLA Innsbruck, Jüngeres Gubernium, Geistliche Sachen, Fasc. 434, 1785, Akten und Protokolle.

TLA Innsbruck, Jüngeres Gubernium, Hauptgruppe 57 Placetum Regium, 1786–1789, Fasc. No. 1.621.

TLA Innsbruck, Jüngeres Gubernium, Hauptgruppe 57 Placetum Regium, 1790–1793, Fasc. No 1.622.

TLA Innsbruck, Jüngeres Gubernium, Hauptgruppe 64 Ehesachen, 1794–1795, Fasc. No. 312.

TLA Innsbruck, Jüngeres Gubernium, Hauptgruppe 64 Ehesachen, 1796, Fasc. No. 313.

TLA Innsbruck, Jüngeres Gubernium, Hauptgruppe 64 Ehesachen, 1797–1798, Fasc. No. 314.

TLA Innsbruck, Jüngeres Gubernium, Hauptgruppe 64 Ehesachen, 1799–1800, Fasc. No. 315.

TLA Innsbruck, Jüngeres Gubernium, Hauptgruppe 64 Ehesachen, 1801–1802, Fasc. No. 316.

TLA Innsbruck, Jüngeres Gubernium, Hauptgruppe 64 Ehesachen, 1803, Fasc. No. 317.

TLA Innsbruck, Jüngeres Gubernium, Hauptgruppe 64 Ehesachen, 1804, Fasc. No. 318.

TLA Innsbruck, Jüngeres Gubernium, Hauptgruppe 64 Ehesachen, 1805–1808, Fasc. No. 319.

TLA Innsbruck, Jüngeres Gubernium, Hauptgruppe 64 Ehesachen, 1814, Fasc. No. 320.

TLA Innsbruck, Jüngeres Gubernium, Hauptgruppe 64 Ehesachen, 1822–1836, Fasc. No. 321.

TLA Innsbruck, Jüngeres Gubernium, Hauptgruppe 64 Ehesachen, 1840–1842, Fasc. No. 323.

Vorarlberger Landesarchiv (VLA) *Bregenz*

VLA Bregenz, Gemeindearchiv Schwarzenberg, Sch. 3, Gemeinderechnung, Bürgerschaft, No. 3–4/2.

VLA Bregenz, Kreisamt 1, Sch. 48, Domäne, Ehe, Fond.

VLA Bregenz, Kreisamt 1, Sch. 71, Geistlich 1827.

VLA Bregenz, Kreisamt 1, Sch. 76, Geistlich 1829.

VLA Bregenz, Kreisamt 1, Sch. 286, Präsidiale 1814–1848.

VLA Bregenz, Bezirksgericht Bezau Verschiedenes, Sch. 1, Testamente 1840–1876.

VLA Bregenz, Bezirksgericht Bezau Verschiedenes, Sch. 2, Testamente 1877–1886.

VLA Bregenz, Landgericht Bezau Akten, Sch. 35.

VLA Bregenz, Landgericht Bregenz, Sch. 117: Ehe, Ein- und Auswanderung 1828–1829, Fasc. 10.

VLA Bregenz, Verfachbuch Bregenzerwald, 1864, No. 115.

VLA Bregenz, Verfachbuch Bregenzerwald, 1878, No. 149.

VLA Bregenz, Verfachbuch Bregenzerwald, 1879, No. 153.

Printed Sources

Article: "Ehedispense" in Buchberger, M. (ed.), *Lexikon für Theologie und Kirche*, 2nd ed. (Freiburg i. Br.: 1931) col. 174–181.

Article: "Ehedispense", in Hergenröther, J. – Kaulen, F. (eds.), *Wetzer und Welte's Kirchenlexikon oder Encyklopädie der katholischen Theologie und ihrer Hilfswissenschaften*, vol. 4, 2nd ed. (Freiburg i. Br.: 1886) col. 174–181.

Article: "Verwandt", in *Johann Heinrich Zedlers Grosses vollständiges Universallexicon aller Wissenschaften und Künste* …, vol. 48 (Leipzig/Halle: 1746) col. 141–146.

Atlas der Urproduction Österreichs in 35 Blättern mit erläuternden Texten, verfasst und herausgegeben auf Anordnung des k. k. Ackerbau-Ministeriums, redigirt von Dr. Jos. R. Ritter Lorenz von Liburnau, k. k. Ministerialrath (Wien: n.y. [*c.*1875]).

Augustinus, *De Civitate Dei*, online access: http://www.hs-augsburg.de/~harsch/Chronologia/Lspost05/Augustinus/aug_cd00.html (accessed: May 2022).

B., A., "Der Mangel der kirchlichen Dispens vom Ehehindernisse kann die Civil-Eheschließung nicht aufhalten", *Österreichische Zeitschrift für Verwaltung* 16, 16 (19 April 1883) 62–63.

Bangen, J.H., *Die Römische Kurie, ihre gegenwärtige Zusammensetzung und ihr Geschäftsgang* (Münster: 1854).

Baumgarten, P.M., "Die Geschäftsführung an der Kurie", in Weber, C. (ed.), *Die römische Kurie um 1900. Ausgewählte Aufsätze von Paul M. Baumgarten* (Cologne – Vienna: 1986) 90–98.

Bertillon, J., "Mariage", *Dictionnaire encyclopédique des sciences médicales*, série 2, vol. 5 (Paris: 1874) 7–83.

Brandhuber von Etschfeld, H., *Über Dispensation und Dispensationsrecht nach katholischem Kirchenrecht* (Leipzig – Vienna: 1888).

Brixner Diözesan-Blatt, 1 (1857) – 23 (1879).

"Casus x: Ehen zwischen Blutsverwandten", *Brixner Diözesan-Blatt* 8 (1864) 130–136.

Catalogus Cleri Dioecesis Tridentinae ineunte anno MDCCCXCII (Trent: 1892).

Catalogus personarum ecclesiasticarum Dioecesis Brixinensis ad initium anni MCCCCXXXI, vol. 22 (Brixen: 1831).

Catalogus Personarum ecclesiasticarum Dioecesis Brixinensis MDCCCXXXVIII, vol. 23 (Brixen: 1837).

Clerus et Dioecesis Tridentina exeunte anno MDCCCXXVI (Trent: 1826).

Codex Iuris Canonici, 1917, online access: http://www.unilu.ch/files/cic_1917_7810.doc (accessed: April 2022).

Codex Iuris Canonici, 1983, online access: http://www.codex-iuris-canonici.de/index dt. htm.

Combe, G., *The Constitution of Man Considered in Relation to External Objects* (Edinburgh – London: 1828).

Combe, G., *The Constitution of Man and Its Relation to External Objects*, 8th ed. (Edinburgh – London – Dublin: 1847).

Constitutio Criminalis Theresiana, online access http://www.archive.org/details/Cons titutioCriminalisTheresiana-1768 (accessed: April 2022).

Dannerbauer, W., *Praktisches Geschäftsbuch für den Curat-Clerus Oesterreichs* (Vienna: 1893).

Das Bayerische Landrecht vom Jahre 1756 in seiner heutigen Geltung, ed. Max Danzer, (Munich: 1894).

"Das Verbot der Ehen zwischen Verwandten", *Der Katholik. Zeitschrift für katholische Wissenschaft und kirchliches Leben* 43, 1 (1863) 143–160.

de Maistre, J., *Du pape* (Lyon: 1819).

Devay, F., *Du danger des mariages consanguines sous le rapport sanitaire*, 2nd ed. (Paris: 1862 [1857]).

Die Ehe wirdt vornemlich / von wegen der Blutfreuntschafft / Darnach auch von wegen der Schwegerschaft / wie folgend zusehen / verboten (Dresden: 1557).

Dolliner, T., *Ausführliche Erläuterung des zweyten Hauptstückes des allgemeinen bürger(lichen) Gesetzbuches von § 44–77* (Vienna: 1835).

Dolliner, T., "Erläuterung des 83. § des bürgerlichen Gesetzbuches über die Ehe-Dispensen", in, C.J. Pratobevera (ed.), *Materialien für Gesetzkunde und Rechtspflege in den Oesterreichischen Erbstaaten* (Vienna: 1815) 56–99.

Dolliner, T., *Handbuch des in Oesterreich geltenden Eherechts* (Vienna – Trieste: 1813).

Dolliner, T., *Handbuch des oesterreichischen Eherechts, ausführliche Erläuterung des zweiten Hauptstückes des bürgerlichen Gesetzbuches von § 44–77. Neue Ausgabe*, vol. 1, 2nd ed. (Vienna: 1848).

Eichborn, H., *Das Ehehinderniß der Blutsverwandtschaft nach kanonischem Rechte. In seiner geschichtlichen Entwicklung aus den Quellen bearbeitet und übersichtlich dargestellt* (Breslau: 1872).

Ermahnungen an Jünglinge und Jungfrauen, auch an Menschen jeden Alters und Standes von einem Landpfarrer der Diözese Brixen, 6th ed. (Brixen: 1900).

Ernst Valentin Schwaigers rechtliche Abhandlung von dem Rechte und der Pflicht der Bischöfe in allen Fällen zu dispensiren, da der Landesfürst die Dispensreserven abschaffet. Nebst angehängten Lehrsätzen aus der gesammten Rechtsgelehrsamkeit (Vienna: 1784).

Esmein, A., *Le mariage en droit canonique*, vol. 2 (Paris: 1891).

Eybel, J.V., *Nichts Mehreres von Ehedispensen als was Religion, Recht, Nutzen, Klugheit und Pflicht fordert* (Wahrheitsthal: 1782).

First Report of the Commissioners Appointed to Inquire into the State and Operation of the Law of Marriage, As Relating to the Prohibited Degrees of Affinity, and to Marriages Solemnized Abroad or in the British Colonies (London: 1848).

Franz des Ersten politische Gesetze und Verordnungen für die Oesterreichischen, Böhmischen und Galizischen Erbländer, vol. 29, part 2 (Vienna: 1809).

Franz des Ersten politische Gesetze und Verordnungen für die Oesterreichischen, Böhmischen und Galizischen Erbländer, vol. 45 (Vienna: 1819).

Friedberg, E. – Richter, L. (eds.), *Corpus Iuris Canonici. Editio Lipsiensis secunda*, part 2: *Decretalium Collectionis* (Graz: 1955) [unchanged reprint of the edition Leipzig: 1879].

Gasparri, P. (ed.), *Codicis Iuris Canonici Fontes*, vol. 6: *Curia Romana* (Rome: 1932).

Gesetzbuch über Verbrechen (Vienna: 1803).

Gründliche Entwicklung der Emser Dispens- und Nuntiaturstreitigkeiten zur Rechtfertigung des Verfahrens der vier deutschen Erzbischöfe wider die Anmaßungen des römischen Hofes samt einer Prüfung des Fürstbischöflich speyerischen Antwortschreibens an S.e. Kurfürstliche Gnaden zu Mainz in Betref [sic] der Emser Punkte, ([n.p.]: 1788).

Herburger, L., *Dr. J.G. Waibel, sein Leben und Wirken* (Dornbirn: 1909).

[Horten, J.B.], *Ist es wahr, daß die k. k. Verordnungen in Ehesachen dem Sakramente entgegen stehen?* (Vienna: 1785).

Hugo, G. Ritter von, *Lehrbuch des Naturrechts als einer Philosophie des positiven Rechts, 2. umgearb. Versuch* (Berlin: 1799).

Il sacro concilio di Trento con le notizie più precise riguardante la sua intimazione a ciascuna delle sessioni. Nuova traduzione italiana col testo latino a fronte (Venice: 1822).

Joseph des Zweyten Römischen Kaysers Gesetze und Verfassungen im Justiz-Fache. Für Böhmen, Mähren, Schlesien, Oesterreich ob und unter der Enns, Steyermark, Kärnthen, Krain, Görz, Gradisca, Triest, Tyrol und die Vorlande. In dem sechsten Jahre seiner Regierung. Jahrgang von 1786 bis 1786, 2. Fortsetzung 1786 (Vienna: 1817).

Josephinisches Gesetzbuch (eigentlich: Allgemeines bürgerliches Gesetzbuch), Patent vom 1. November 1786, in: Joseph des Zweyten Römischen Kaysers Gesetze und Verfassungen im Justiz-Fache. Für Böhmen, Mähren, Schlesien, Oesterreich ob und unter der Enns, Steyermark, Kärnthen, Krain, Görz, Gradisca, Triest, Tyrol und die Vorlande. In dem sechsten Jahre seiner Regierung. Jahrgang von 1786 bis 1786, 2. Fortsetzung 1786 (Vienna: 1817) No. 591, 71–129.

Knopp, N., *Vollständiges katholisches Eherecht. Mit besonderer Rücksicht auf die practische Seelsorge*, 2nd ed. (Regensburg: 1854).

Knopp, N., *Vollständiges katholisches Eherecht. Mit besonderer Rücksicht auf die practische Seelsorge, vierte vermehrte und verbesserte Auflage* (Regensburg: 1873).

Kropatschek, J., *Handbuch aller unter der Regierung des Kaisers Joseph II. für die k. k. Erbländer ergangenen Verordnungen und Gesetze in einer sistematischen Verbindung*, vol. 2, 1780–1784 (Vienna: 1785). These decrees and laws are also accessable on "Alex – historische Rechts- und Gesetzestexte online", a portal of the Österreichischen Nationalbibliothek, under http://alex.onb.ac.at/ in der Rubrik Justizgesetzsammlung 1780–1848.

Kropatschek, J., *Handbuch aller unter der Regierung des Kaisers Joseph II. für die k. k. Erbländer ergangenen Verordnungen und Gesetze in einer sistematischen Verbindung*, vol. 11, 1786 (Vienna: 1788).

Kutschker, J., *Das Eherecht der katholischen Kirche nach seiner Theorie und Praxis mit besonderer Berücksichtigung der in Österreich zu Recht bestehenden Gesetze*, vol. 3 (Vienna: 1856).

Kutschker, J., *Das Eherecht der katholischen Kirche nach seiner Theorie und Praxis mit besonderer Berücksichtigung der in Österreich zu Recht bestehenden Gesetze*, vol. 5 (Vienna: 1857).

Linden, J., *Darstellung der in Oesterreich über die Rechtsverhältnisse der Ehegatten, Eltern, Kinder, Waisen und Pflegebefohlenen bestehenden Vorschriften nebst den auf das Hausgesinde bezüglichen Anordnungen*, 2nd ed. (Vienna: 1839 [1834]).

Maaß, F., *Der Josephinismus. Quellen zu seiner Geschichte in Österreich 1760–1790. Amtliche Dokumente aus dem Wiener Haus-, Hof- und Staatsarchiv, vol. 2: Entfaltung und Krise des Josephinismus* (Vienna: 1953).

Maaß, F., *Der Josephinismus. Quellen zu seiner Geschichte in Österreich 1760–1790. Amtliche Dokumente aus dem Wiener Haus-, Hof- und Staatsarchiv, dem Allgemeinen Verwaltungsarchiv und dem Archiv des Wiener Schottenstiftes*, vol. 3: *Das Werk des Hofrats Heinke 1768–1790* (Vienna: 1956).

Maaß, F., *Der Josephinismus. Quellen zu seiner Geschichte in Österreich 1760–1850. Amtliche Dokumente aus dem Haus-, Hof- und Staatsarchiv und dem Allgemeinen Verwaltungsarchiv in Wien*, vol. 4: *Der Spätjosephinismus 1790–1820* (Vienna: 1957).

Maaß, F., *Der Josephinismus. Quellen zu seiner Geschichte in Österreich 1760–1850. Amtliche Dokumente aus dem Haus-, Hof- und Staatsarchiv und dem Allgemeinen Verwaltungsarchiv in Wien sowie dem Archivio Segreto Vaticano in Rom*, vol. 5: *Lockerung und Aufhebung des Josephinismus 1820–1850* (Vienna: 1961).

Manuale Sacrum ad usum sacerdotum Dioecesis Brixinensis (Brixen: 1838 [further editions: 1855, 1886 and 1906]).

Mejer, O., *Die Propaganda, ihre Provinzen und ihr Recht. Mit besonderer Rücksicht auf Deutschland*, part 2 (Göttingen – Leipzig: 1853).

Mergentheim, L., *Die Quinquennalfakultäten pro foro externo. Ihre Entstehung und Einführung in deutschen Bistümern*, vol. 2 (Stuttgart: 1908 [reprint Amsterdam: 1965]).

Michaeli, J.D., *Abhandlung von den Ehegesetzen Mosis, welche die Heyrathen in die nahe Freundschaft untersagen, zweite und vermehrte Auflage* (Frankfurt – Leipzig: 1786).

Michel, A.T., *Beiträge zur Geschichte des österreichischen Eherechtes* (Graz: 1870).

Mörsdorf, K., *Lehrbuch des Kirchenrechts auf Grund des Codex Iuris Canonici*, vol. 1: *Einleitung, Allgemeiner Teil und Personenrecht*, 9th ed. (Munich – Paderborn – Vienna: 1959).

Müllendorff, J., *Methode zur Auffindung der Ehehindernisse bei mehrfacher Blutsverwandtschaft. Ein Beitrag zur Pastoral* (Graz: 1888).

"Neueste offizielle Instruktion über Ehedispensgesuche", *Brixner Diözesanblatt* 22 (1878) 33–38.

New reformierte Landesordnung der fürstlichen Grafschaft Tirol (n.p.: [1573]).

O'Mara, W.A., *Canonical Causes for Matrimonial Dispensation. An Historical Synopsis and Commentary* (Washington: 1935).

Orel, H., "Die Verwandtenehen in der Erzdiözese Wien", *Archiv für Rassen- und Gesellschaftsbiologie einschließlich Rassen- und Gesellschaftshygiene* 26 (1932) 249–278.

Pachmann, T., *Lehrbuch des Kirchenrechtes mit Berücksichtigung der auf die kirchlichen Verhältnisse Bezug nehmenden österreichischen Gesetze und Verordnungen*, vol. 2/1 (Vienna: 1851).

Pachmann, T., *Lehrbuch des Kirchenrechtes mit Berücksichtigung der auf die kirchlichen Verhältnisse Bezug nehmenden österreichischen Gesetze und Verordnungen*, vol. 2/1, 2nd revised and added ed. (Vienna: 1853).

Pachmann, T., *Lehrbuch des Kirchenrechtes mit Berücksichtigung der auf die kirchlichen Verhältnisse Bezug nehmenden österreichischen Gesetze und Verordnungen*, vol. 2, 3rd completely revised ed. (Vienna: 1865).

Personalstand der Säkular- und Regular-Geistlichkeit des Erzbisthums Salzburg nebst dem Lehrpersonal-Stande der deutschen Schulen. In dem Jahre 1831 (Salzburg: 1831).

Personalstand der Säcular- und Regulargeistlichkeit des Erzbisthums Salzburg auf das Jahr 1892 (Salzburg: 1892).

Pusey, E.B., *Marriage with a Deceased Wife's Sister Prohibited by Holy Scripture as Understood by the Church for 1500 Years. Evidence given Before the Commission Appointed to Inquire into the State and Operation of the Law of Marriage as Relating to the Prohibited Degrees of Affinity* (Oxford: 1849).

Reichs-Gesetz-Blatt für das Kaiserthum Oesterreich, 1856.

Ruck, E., *Die Organisation der Römischen Kurie* (Tübingen: 1913).

Sammlung aller k. k. Verordnungen und Gesetze vom Jahre 1740 bis 1780 (*Gesetze unter Maria Theresia*), vol. 3 (Vienna: 1786).

Sammlung der Kaiserlich-Königlichen Landesfürstlichen Gesetze und Verordnungen in Publico-Ecclesiasticis vom Jahre 1767 bis Ende 1782 (Vienna: 1782).

Sammlung der Kaiserlich-Königlichen Landesfürstlichen Gesetze und Verordnungen in Publico-Ecclesiasticis vom Jahre 1782 bis 1783, part 2 (Vienna: 1784).

Sattler, Carl Christian, Handbuch des österreichischen Ehe-Rechts nach den darüber erlassenen Gesetzen und Verordnungen, und mit Bemerkungen der Abweichungen des bürgerlichen Gesetzbuchs für Westgalizien. In schematischer Ordnung bearbeitet (Vienna: 1804).

Schematismus der Geistlichkeit der Diözese Brixen für das Jahr 1840, vol. 24 (Brixen: 1840).

Schematismus der Geistlichkeit der Diözese Brixen für das Jahr 1868, vol. 52 (Brixen: 1868).

Schematismus der Geistlichkeit der Diözese Brixen für das Jahr 1870, vol. 54 (Brixen: 1870).

Schematismus der Geistlichkeit der Diözese Brixen für das Jahr 1871, vol. 55 (Brixen: 1871).

Schematismus der Geistlichkeit der Diözese Brixen für das Jahr 1872, vol. 56 (Brixen: 1872).

Schematismus der Geistlichkeit der Diözese Brixen für das Jahr 1873, vol. 57 (Brixen: 1873).

Schematismus der Geistlichkeit der Diözese Brixen für das Jahr 1876, vol. 60 (Brixen: 1876).

Schematismus der Geistlichkeit der Diözese Brixen für das Jahr 1878, vol. 62 (Brixen: 1878).

Schematismus der Säkular- und Regular-Geistlichkeit der Diözese Brixen. 1882, vol. 66 (Brixen: 1882).

Schematismus der Säkular- und Regular-Geistlichkeit der Diözese Brixen. 1883, vol. 67 (Brixen: 1883).

Schematismus der Säkular- und Regular-Geistlichkeit der Diözese Brixen. 1884, vol. 68 (Brixen: 1884).

Schematismus der Säkular- und Regular-Geistlichkeit der Diözese Brixen. 1885, vol. 69 (Brixen: 1885).

Schematismus der Säkular- und Regular-Geistlichkeit der Diözese Brixen. 1886, vol. 70 (Brixen: 1886).

Schematismus der Säkular- und Regular-Geistlichkeit der Diözese Brixen. 1887, vol. 71 (Brixen: 1887).

Schematismus der Säkular- und Regular-Geistlichkeit der Diözese Brixen. 1888, vol. 72 (Brixen: 1888).

Schematismus der Säcular- und Regular-Geistlichkeit der Diözese Brixen. 1892, vol. 76 (Brixen: 1892).

Schlegel, K.A.M., *Kritische und systematische Darstellung der verbotenen Grade der Verwandtschaft und Schwägerschaft, bey Heurathen, nach dem Mosaischen Gesetze, dem Römischen und Canonischen Rechte, und den Protestantischen Kirchenordnungen ...* (Hannover: 1802).

Schmidlin, J., *Geschichte der deutschen Nationalkirche in Rom S. Maria dell'Anima* (Freiburg i. B. – Vienna: 1906).

Schulte, J.F., *Erläuterung des Gesetzes über die Ehen der Katholiken im Kaiserthume Oesterreich vom 8. Oktober 1856 und des kaiserlichen Patentes dazu nebst Darlegung und Begründung der Bestimmungen des Kirchengesetzes* (Prague: 1857).

Schwerdling, J., (ed.), *Praktische Anwendung aller vom Antritte der Regierung Sr. kaiserl. königl. apostol. Majestät Franz II. bis 1. Jäner 1798 für die gesammten Erbländer in geistlichen Sachen* (*Publico ecclesiasticis*) *ergangenen Verordnungen*, 3rd ed. (Krems: 1816).

Shakespeare, W., *Hamlet. Prinz von Dänemark*, transl. by Schlegel, A.W. (Stuttgart: 1980).

Simmel, G., "Die Verwandtenehe", *Vossische Zeitung* (Berlin), Sunday supplement No. 22/23 (3 and 10 June 1894).

Spöndlin, H., Ueber das Eheverboth wegen Verwandtschaft und das Verbrechen des Incestes (Zurich: 1844).

Sr. k. k. Majestät Ferdinand des Ersten politische Gesetze und Verordnungen für sämmtliche Provinzen des Oesterreichischen Kaiserstaates, mit Ausnahme von Ungarn und Siebenbürgen, vol. 68: Verordnungen vom 1. Januar bis Ende December 1840 (Vienna: 1842).

Stapf, F. – Egger, C., *Vollständiger Pastoralunterricht über die Ehe, oder über das gesetz- und pflichtmäßige Verhalten des Pfarrers vor – bei und nach der ehelichen Trauung, nach den Grundsätzen des katholischen Kirchenrechts, mit steter Rücksicht auf Civilgesetze*, 6th ed. (Frankfurt a. M.: 1839).

Steinitz, J., *Dispensationsbegriff und Dispensationsgewalt auf dem Gebiet des deutschen Staatsrechts* (Breslau: 1901).

Stubenrauch, M. v., *Commentar zum allgemeinen österreichischen bürgerlichen Gesetzbuche sammt den dazu erflossenen Nachtrags-Verordnungen*, vol. 1 (Vienna: 1864).

Stutz, U., *Der Geist des Codex juris canonici. Eine Einführung in das auf Geheiß Papst Pius X. verfaßte und von Papst Benedikt XV. erlassene Gesetzbuch der katholischen Kirche* (Stuttgart: 1918).

Thomas Aquinas, *Scriptum super Sententiis*, online access: http://www.corpusthomisticum.org/snp4037.html (accessed: May 2022).

"Ueber das Verfahren bey anzusuchenden Ehedispensen in dem Hinderniße der Verwandtschaft nach dem Sinne des k. k. Ehepatents", *Theologisch-praktische Linzer-Monathschrift zunächst für Seelsorger* 1, 1 (1809) 304–316.

Vasella, O., "Untersuchungen über die Bildungsverhältnisse im Bistum Chur mit besonderer Berücksichtigung des Klerus. Vom Ausgang des 13. Jahrhunderts bis um 1530", *Jahresbericht der Historisch-Antiquarischen Gesellschaft von Graubünden* 62 (1932) 1–211.

"Verordnung über einige bei Eheschließungen zu befolgende Punkte", *Brixner Diözesan-Blatt* 2 (1858) 15–17.

Weber, I., *J.U.D. Prof. Publ. Ordin. eröffnet der studierenden Jugend zu Giessen ein Collegium Theoretico-Practicum über die nothwendige und nützliche Lehre von zugelassenen und verbotenen Graden im Heyrathen* (Giessen: 1714).

Welche canonische Ehehindernisse sollen beibehalten werden, oder näher bestimmt, oder aufgehoben werden? Eine Preisschrift vom Jahre 1811 (Nuremberg: 1859).

Zeiller, F. v., *Commentar über das allgemeine bürgerliche Gesetzbuch für die gesammten Deutschen Erbländer der Oesterreichischen Monarchie*, vol. 1, (Vienna – Trieste: 1811).

Secondary Literature

Ableitinger, A., "Die historische Entwicklung des Liberalismus in Österreich im 19. und beginnenden 20. Jahrhundert", in H. Reinalter – H. Klueting (eds.), *Der deutsche und österreichische Liberalismus. Geschichts- und politikwissenschaftliche Perspektiven im Vergleich*, (Innsbruck: 2010) 121–147.

Accati, L., *Das Monster und die Schöne. Vater- und Mutterbilder in der katholischen Erziehung der Gefühle* (Berlin: 2006).

Ågren, M., "Lower State Servants and Home Office Work", in Eibach, J. – Lanzinger, M. (eds.), *The Routledge History of the Domestic Sphere in Europe Sixteenth to Nineteenth Century* (London: 2020) 120–133.

Alexander H., "Zur regionalen Herkunft des Priesternachwuchses der Diözese Brixen im 19. Jahrhundert", *Histoire des Alpes / Storia delle Alpi / Geschichte der Alpen* 3 (1998) 309–325.

Albani, B., *Sposarsi nel nuovo mondo. Politica, dottina e pratiche della concessione di dispense matrimoniali tra la Nuova Spagna e la Santa Sede (1585–1670)* (PhD. dissertation, University of Rome Tor Vergata: 2008–2009).

Alfani, G., "Geistige Allianzen: Patenschaft als Instrument sozialer Beziehung in Italien und Europa (15. bis 20. Jahrhundert)", in Lanzinger, M. – Saurer, E. (eds.), *Politiken der Verwandtschaft. Beziehungsnetze, Geschlecht und Recht* (Göttingen: 2007) 25–54.

Alfani, G., *Fathers and Godfathers. Spiritual Kinship in Early Modern Italy* (Aldershot: 2009 [2006]).

Alfani, G. – Gourdon, V. (eds.), *Spiritual Kinship in Europe, 1500–1900* (Basingstoke: 2012).

Algazi, G., "Kulturkult und die Rekonstruktion von Handlungsrepertoires", *L'Homme. Z.F.G.* 11, 1 (2000) 105–119.

Anderson, N.F., "The 'Marriage with a Deceased Wife's Sister Bill' Controversy: Incest Anxiety and the Defense of Family Purity in Victorian England", *Journal of British Studies* 21, 2 (1982) 67–86.

Anderson, N.F., "Cousin Marriage in Victorian England", *Journal of Family History* 11, 3 (1986) 285–301.

Ariès, P., *Geschichte der Kindheit* (Munich – Vienna: 1975).

Armenteros, C. – Lebrun, R.A., "Introduction", in: Armenteros, C. – Lebrun, R.A. (eds.), *Joseph du Maistre and his European Readers* (Leiden – Boston: 2011) 1–15.

Ariès, P., *Centuries of Childhood: A Social History of Family Life* (New York: 1962 [1960]).

Arru, A., "Die Ermordung eines Richters – ein Delikt aus Liebe. Das Gericht als Ort der Vermittlung und Einflussnahme, brüchiger Allianzen und wechselnder Strategien (Rom 1795)", in Bauer, I. – Hämmerle, C. – Hauch, G. (eds.), *Liebe und Widerstand. Ambivalenzen historischer Geschlechterbeziehungen* (Vienna – Cologne – Weimar: 2005) 229–242.

Bailey, J., "Paternal Power: the Pleasures and Perils of 'Indulgent' Fathering in Britain in the Long Eighteenth Century", *The History of the Family* 17, 3 (2012) 326–342.

Bake, K., *Spiegel einer Christlichen und friedsamen Haußhaltung. Die Ehe in der populären Druckgraphik des 16. und 17. Jahrhunderts* (Wiesbaden: 2013).

Barth-Scalmani, G., "Ausgewogene Verhältnisse: Eheverträge in der Stadt Salzburg im 18. Jahrhundert", in Lanzinger, M. – Barth-Scalmani, G. – Forster, E. – Langer-Ostrawsky, G. (eds.), *Aushandeln von Ehe. Heiratsverträge der Neuzeit im europäischen Vergleich* (Cologne – Weimar – Vienna: 2010) 121–170.

Barton P.F., "Das Toleranzpatent von 1781. Edition der wichtigsten Fassungen", in Barton P.F. (ed.), *Im Lichte der Toleranz. Aufsätze zur Toleranzgesetzgebung des*

18. Jahrhunderts in den Reichen Joseph II., ihren Voraussetzungen und ihren Folgen (Vienna: 1981) 152–202.

Bastgen, H., *Die Neuerrichtung der Bistümer in Österreich nach der Säkularisation* (Vienna: 1914).

Baura, E., *La dispensa canonica dalla legge* (Milan: 1997).

Beales, D., *Enlightenment and Reform in Eighteenth Century Europe* (London: 2005).

Becker, P., *Leben, Lieben, Sterben. Die Analyse von Kirchenbüchern* (St. Katharinen: 1989).

Becker, P., *Leben und Lieben in einem kalten Land. Sexualität im Spannungsfeld von Ökonomie und Demographie. Das Beispiel St. Lamprecht 1600–1850* (Frankfurt a. M. – New York: 1990).

Becker, P., "Sprachvollzug: Kommunikation und Verwaltung", in Becker, P. (ed.), *Sprachvollzug im Amt. Kommunikation und Verwaltung im Europa des 19. und 20. Jahrhunderts* (Bielefeld: 2011) 9–42.

Bennett, J.M. – Froide, A.M. (eds.), *Single Women in the European Past 1250–1800* (Philadelphia: 1998).

Benthien, C. – Flaig, A. – Kasten, I., "Einleitung", in Benthien, C. – Flaig, A. – Kasten, I. (eds.), *Emotionalität. Zur Geschichte der Gefühle* (Cologne – Weimar – Vienna: 2000) 7–20.

Benvenuti, S., "Le istituzioni ecclesiastiche", in Garberi, M. – Leonardi, A. (eds.), *Storia del Trentino.* vol. 5: *L'età contemporanea 1803–1918* (Bologna: 2000) 275–317.

Berchtold, H., *Die Arbeitsmigration von Vorarlberg nach Frankreich im 19. Jahrhundert* (Feldkirch: 2003).

Berghorn, D., *Verwandtschaft als Streitzusammenhang. Eine Fall-Geschichte in Beziehungen im hohen Adel des Alten Reiches, 16. bis 19. Jahrhundert* (Vienna – Cologne: 2021).

Berkner, L.K., "The Stem Family and the Developmental Cycle of the Peasant Household. An Eighteenth-Century Austrian Example", *American Historical Review* 77 (1972) 398–418.

Bianchi, L., "'Cotidiana miracula', comune corso della natura e dispense al diritto matrimoniale: il miracolo fra Agostino e Tommaso d'Aquino", *Quaderni storici* 131 (2009) 313–328.

Bilgeri, B., *Geschichte Vorarlbergs*, vol. 4: *Zwischen Absolutismus und halber Autonomie* (Vienna – Cologne – Graz: 1982).

Blaas, M., *Der letzte Fürstbischof von Chur und sein Klerus in Tirol. Der Tiroler Anteil der Diözese Chur unter Bischof Karl Rudolf von Buol-Schauenstein (1794–1808 und 1815–1816). Ein Beitrag zur Geschichte des Jahres 1809* (PhD. dissertation, University of Innsbruck: 1983).

Blaas, R., "Die k. k. Agentie für geistliche Angelegenheiten", *Mitteilungen des österreichischen Staatsarchivs*, vol. 7 (Vienna: 1954) 47–89.

Blänkner, R., *'Absolutismus'. Eine begriffsgeschichtliche Studie zur politischen Theorie und zur Geschichtswissenschaft in Deutschland, 1830–1870*, 2nd ed. (Frankfurt a. M. et al.: 2011).

Blasius, D., *Ehescheidung in Deutschland 1794–1945* (Göttingen: 1987).

Blet, P., *Histoire de la représentation diplomatique du Saint Siège des origines a l'aube du XIXe siècle* (Vatican City: 1982).

Blockmans, W. – Holenstein, A. – Mathieu, J. (eds.), *Empowering Interactions. Political Cultures and the Emergence of the State in Europe, 1300–1900* (Farnham et al.: 2009).

Bonfield, L., "Canon Law and Family Law in Medieval Western Christendom", *Continuity and Change* 6, 3 (1991) 361–374.

Borello, B. – Lanzinger, M. "Introduction", *Quaderni storici* 165, 3 (2020), special issue on "Open Kinship" 629–641.

Borscheid, P., "Geld und Liebe. Zu den Auswirkungen des Romantischen auf die Partnerwahl im 19. Jahrhundert", in Borscheid, P. – Teuteberg, H.J. (eds.), *Ehe, Liebe, Tod. Zum Wandel der Familie, der Geschlechts- und Generationsbeziehungen in der Neuzeit* (Münster: 1983) 112–134.

Bourdieu, P., *Die feinen Unterschiede. Kritik der gesellschaftlichen Urteilskraft* (Frankfurt a. M.: 1982).

Bourdieu, P., "The Forms of Capital", in Richardson, J.G. (ed.), *Handbook of Theory and Research for the Sociology of Education* (Westport: 1986) 241–258.

Bourdieu, P., *Entwurf einer Theorie der Praxis auf der ethnologischen Grundlage der kabylischen Gesellschaft*, 2nd. ed. (Frankfurt a. M.: 2009).

Brakensiek, S. – Flügel, A. (eds.), *Regionalgeschichte in Europa. Methoden und Erträge der Forschung zum 16. bis 19. Jahrhundert* (Paderborn: 2000).

Brambilla, E., *La giustizia intollerante. Inquisizione e tribunali confessionali in Europa (secoli IV–XVIII)* (Rome: 2006).

Brauneder, W., *Die Entwicklung des Ehegüterrechts in Österreich. Ein Beitrag zur Dogmengeschichte und Rechtstatsachenforschung des Spätmittelalters und der Neuzeit* (Salzburg – Munich: 1973).

Breit, S., *'Leichtfertigkeit' und ländliche Gesellschaft. Voreheliche Sexualität in der frühen Neuzeit* (Munich: 1991).

Burckhardt, M., "Das Ungeheuer der Vernunft. Joseph de Maistre zur Einführung", in *Joseph de Maistre, Vom Papst. Ausgewählte Texte* (Berlin: 2007) 7–39.

Burghartz, S., "Umordnung statt Unordnung? Ehe, Geschlecht und Reformationsgeschichte", in Puff, H. – Wild, C. (eds.), *Zwischen den Disziplinen? Perspektiven der Frühneuzeitforschung* (Göttingen: 2003) 165–185.

Burghartz, S., *Zeiten der Reinheit. Orte der Unzucht. Ehe und Sexualität in Basel während der Frühen Neuzeit* (Paderborn et al.: 1999).

Burguière, A., "'Cher Cousin': Les usages matrimoniaux de la parenté proche dans la France du 18e siècle", *Annales Histoire, Sciences Sociales* 52, 6 (1997) 1339–1360.

Burschel, P., *Die Erfindung der Reinheit. Eine andere Geschichte der Frühen Neuzeit* (Göttingen: 2014).

Camporesi, P., *Juice of Life: The Symbolic and Magic Significance of Blood* (New York: 1995).

Cancian, F.M., "The Feminization of Love", *Signs. Journal for Women in Culture and Society* 11, 4 (1986) 692–708.

Carlen, L., "Straf- und Sühnewallfahrten nach Rom", in Valentinitsch, H. (ed.), *Recht und Geschichte. Festschrift Hermann Baltl zum 70. Geburtstag* (Graz: 1988) 131–153.

Carsten, J., *After Kinship* (Cambridge: 2004).

Carsten, J., "Introduction: Cultures of Relatedness", in Carsten, J. (ed.), *Cultures of Relatedness. New Approaches to the Study of Kinship* (Cambridge: 2000) 1–36.

Cartron, L., "Degeneration and 'Alienism' in Early Nineteenth-Century France", in Müller-Wille, S. – Rheinberger, H.-J. (eds.), *Heredity Produced. At the Crossroads of Biology, Politics, and Culture, 1500–1870* (Cambridge/Mass. – London: 2007) 155–174.

Casten, I. – Stedman, G. – Zimmermann, M., "Einleitung: Lucien Febvre und die Folgen. Zu einer Geschichte der Gefühle und ihrer Erforschung", *Querelles. Jahrbuch für Frauenforschung* 7 (2002) 9–25.

Cavallo, S., "L'importanza della 'famiglia orizzontale' nella storia della famiglia italiana", in Fazio, I. – Lombardi, D. (eds.), *Generazioni. Legami di parentela tra passato e presente* (Rome: 2006), 69–92.

Cavallo, S. – Warner, L. (eds.), *Widowhood in Medieval and Early Modern Europe* (Halow: 1999).

Cazalé B. – Klapisch-Zuber, C. – Klapisch-Zuber, Ch., "Mémoire de soi et des autres dans les livres de famille italiens", *Annales HSS* 59, 4 (2004) 805–826.

Chadwick, O., *A History of the Popes 1830–1914* (Oxford: 1998).

Ciappelli, G: (ed.), *Memoria, famiglia, identità tra Italia ed Europa nell'età moderna* (Bologna: 2009).

Corbett, M.J., "Husband, Wife, and Sister: Making and Remaking the Early Victorian Family", in Johnson, C.H. – Sabean, D.W. (eds.), *Sibling Relations & the Transformation of European Kinship 1300–1900* (New York – Oxford: 2011) 263–287.

Cristellon, C., "Due fedi in un corpo. Matrimoni misti fra delicta carnis, scandalo, seduzione e sacramento nell'Europa di età moderna", *Quaderni storici* 145 (2014) 41–70.

Cristellon, C., "'Unstable and Weak-Minded' or a Missionary? Catholic Women in Mixed Marriages (1563–1798)", in Gottschalk, K. (ed.), *Gender Difference in European Legal Cultures. Historical Perspectives. Festschrift für Heide Wunder* (Stuttgart: 2013) 83–93.

D'Amelia, M., "Agenti e intermediari tra negozi curiali e merci false (Roma tra Cinque e Seicento)", *Quaderni storici* 124 (2007) 43–78.

D'Amelia, M., "Trasmissioni di offici e competenze nelle famiglie curiali tra Cinquecento e Seicento", in Ago, R. – Borello, B. (eds.), *Famiglie. Circolazione di beni, circuiti di affetti in età moderna* (Rome: 2009) 47–81.

Daum, A.W., *Wissenschaftspopularisierung im 19. Jahrhundert. Bürgerliche Kultur, naturwissenschaftliche Bildung und die deutsche Öffentlichkeit, 1848–1914* (Munich: 1998).

Davidoff, L., "'Eins sein zu zweit'. Geschwisterinzest in der englischen Mittelschicht des späten 18. und frühen 19. Jahrhunderts", *L'Homme. Z.F.G.* 13, 1 (2002) 29–49.

Davidoff, L., *Thicker than Water. Siblings and Their Relations, 1780–1920* (Oxford: 2012).

Davidoff, L. – Hall, C., *Family Fortunes. Men and Women of the English Middle Class 1780–1850* (London – New York: 2002 [1987]).

de Groot, J., "'Sex' and 'Race': the Construction of Language and Image in the Nineteenth Century", in Mendus, S. – Rendall, J. (eds.), *Sexuality and Subordination. Interdisciplinary Studies of Gender in the Nineteenth Century* (London – New York: 1989) 89–128.

Delille, G., "Evolution within Sibling Groups from One Kinship System to Another (Sixteenth to Nineteenth Century)", in Johnson, C.H. – Sabean, D.W. (eds.), *Sibling Relations & the Transformation of European Kinship 1300–1900* (New York – Oxford: 2011) 145–163.

Delille, G., *Famille et propriété dans le Royaume de Naples (XVe–XIXe siècle)* (Rome – Paris: 1985).

Delille, G., "Kinship, Marriage, and Politics", in Sabean, D.W. – Teuscher, S. – Mathieu, J. (eds.), *Kinship in Europe. Approaches to Long-Term Development (1500–1900)* (New York – Oxford: 2007) 163–183.

Delille, G., "La fratrie: des frères ou des individus?", *European Review of History – Revue européenne d'histoire* 17, 5 (2010) 705–718.

Delille, G., *Le maire et le prieur. Pouvoir central et pouvoir local en Méditerranéen occidentale (XVe–XVIIIe siècle)* (Paris – Rome: 2003).

Delille, G., *L'economia di Dio. Famiglia e mercato tra cristianesimo, ebraismo, islam* (Rome: 2013).

Delille, G., "Namen und Linien. Ein süditalienisches Dorf und seinen Genealogen (1572–1739)", *L'Homme. Z.F.G.* 20, 1 (2009) 53–62.

Delille, G., "Parenté et alliance en Europe occidentale. Un essai d'interprétation générale", *L'Homme. Z.F.G.* 193 (2010) 75–135.

Delille, G., "Position und Rolle von Frauen im europäischen System der Heiratsallianzen", in Lanzinger, M. – Saurer, E. (eds.), *Politiken der Verwandtschaft. Beziehungsnetze, Geschlecht und Recht* (Göttingen: 2007) 227–254.

Delille, G., "Réflexions sur le 'systeme' européen de la parenté et de l'alliance. Note critique", *Annales HSS* 56, 2 (2001) 369–380.

Dell'Orto, U., "Die Wiener Nuntiatur im 18. Jahrhundert unter besonderer Berücksichtigung der Nuntiatur von Giuseppe Garampi (1776–1785)," in Koller, A. (ed.), *Kurie und Politik. Stand und Perspektiven der Nuntiaturforschung* (Tübingen: 1998) 175–207.

Dell'Orto, U., *La nunziatura a Vienna di Giuseppe Garampi 1776–1785* (Vatican City: 1995).

Derix, S., "Vom Leben in Netzen. Neue geschichts- und sozialwissenschaftliche Perspektiven auf soziale Beziehungen", *Neue Politische Literatur* 56, 2 (2011) 185–206.

Derouet, B., "Parenté et marché foncier à l'époque modern", *Annales HSS* 2 (2001) 337–368.

Deutsch, C., *Ehegerichtsbarkeit im Bistum Regensburg (1480–1538)* (Cologne – Weimar – Vienna: 2005).

Diaz-Bone, R., *Kulturwelt, Diskurs und Lebensstil. Eine diskurstheoretische Erweiterung der Bourdieuschen Distinktionstheorie*, 2nd ed. (Wiesbaden: 2010).

Dickson, P.G.M., "Monarchy and Bureaucracy in Late Eighteenth-Century Austria", *The English Historical Review* 110, 436 (1995) 323–367.

"Die Liebe der Geschwister", *L'Homme. Z.F.G.* 13, 1 (2002), special issue, ed. by Hausen, K. – Schulte, R.

Dölemeyer, B. – Mohnhaupt, H. – Somma, A. (eds.), *Richterliche Anwendung des Code civil in seinen europäischen Geltungsbereichen außerhalb Frankreichs* (Frankfurt a. M.: 2006).

Döring, J. – Thielmann, T., "Einleitung: Was lesen wir im Raume? Der Spatial Turn und das geheime Wissen der Geographen", in Döring, J. – Thielmann, T. (eds.), *Spatial Turn. Das Raumparadigma in den Kultur- und Sozialwissenschaften* (Bielefeld: 2008) 7–45.

Dörrer, F., "Der Wandel der Diözesaneinteilung Tirols und Vorarlbergs", *Beiträge zur Geschichte Tirols. Festgabe des Landes Tirol zum Elften Österreichischen Historikertag in Innsbruck vom 5. bis 8. Oktober 1971* (Innsbruck: 1971) 141–170.

Duchhardt, H. – Melville, G., "Vorwort", in: Duchhardt, H. – Melville, G. (eds.), *Im Spannungsfeld von Recht und Ritual. Soziale Kommunikation in Mittelalter und Früher Neuzeit* (Cologne: 1997).

Duhamelle, C., *L'heritage collectif. La noblesse d'Église rhenane, 17e–18e siècles* (Paris: 1998).

Duhamelle, C., "The Making of Stability. Kinship, Church and Power among the Rhenish Imperial Knighthood, Seventeenth and Eighteenth Century", in Sabean, D.W. – Teuscher, S. – Mathieu, J. (eds.), *Kinship in Europe. Approaches to Long-Term Development (1500–1900)* (New York – Oxford: 2007) 125–144.

Edeling, T., "Organisationen als Institutionen", in Maurer, A. – Schmid, M. (eds.), *Neuer Institutionalismus. Zur soziologischen Erklärung von Organisation, Moral und Vertrauen* (Frankfurt a. M.: 2002) 219–235.

Ehmer, J., Heiratsverhalten, Sozialstruktur, ökonomischer Wandel. England und Mitteleuropa in der Formationsperiode des Kapitalismus (Göttingen: 1991).

Eibach, J., "Das offene Haus. Kommunikative Praxis im sozialen Nahraum der europäischen Frühen Neuzeit", *Zeitschrift für Historische Forschung* 38, 4 (2011) 621–664.

Eibach, J., *Der Staat vor Ort. Amtmänner und Bürger im 19. Jahrhundert am Beispiels Badens* (Frankfurt a. M.: 1994).

Eibach, J., *Fragile Familien. Ehe und häusliche Lebenswelt in der bürgerlichen Moderne* (Berlin – Boston: 2022).

Eibach, J. – Lanzinger, M. (eds.), *The Routledge History of the Domestic Sphere in Europe Sixteenth to Nineteenth Century* (London: 2020).

Eibach, J. – Schmidt-Voges, I. (eds.) with Derix, S. – Hahn, P. – Harding, E. – Lanzinger, M., *Das Haus in der Geschichte Europas. Ein Handbuch* (Berlin – Boston: 2015).

Eming, J. – Jarzebowski, C. – Ulbrich, C. (eds.), *Historische Inzestdiskurse. Interdisziplinäre Zugänge* (Königstein/Taunus: 2003).

Engel-Janosi, F., *Österreich und der Vatikan 1846–1918* (Graz – Vienna – Cologne: 1958).

Erdinger, A., *Dr. Joseph Feßler. Bischof von St. Pölten und Sekretär des vatikanischen Concils. Ein Lebensbild* (Brixen: 1874).

Fabritz, P., *Sanatio in radice. Historie eines Rechtsinstituts und seine Beziehung zum sakralen Eheverständnis der katholischen Kirche* (Frankfurt a. M. et al.: 2010).

Fauve-Chamoux, A., "Revisiting the Decline of Remarriage In Early-Modern Europe: the Case of Rheims in France", *The History of the Family* 15, 3 (2010) 283–297.

Fazio, I., "Matrimoni, conflitti, istituzioni giudiziarie: le specificità italiane di un percorso di ricercar", *Rivista storica italiana* 2 (2009) 645–672.

Fazio, I., "Parentela e mercato nell'isola di Stromboli nel XIX secolo", in Ago, R. – Borello, B. (eds.), *Famiglie. Circolazione di beni, circuiti di affetti in età moderna* (Rome: 2008) 141–181.

Febvre, L., "Sensibilität und Geschichte. Zugänge zum Gefühlsleben früherer Epochen", in: Honegger, C. (ed.), *M. Bloch, F. Braudel, L. Febvre u. a. Schrift und Materie der Geschichte. Vorschläge zur systematischen Aneignung historischer Prozesse* (Frankfurt a. M.: 1977) 313–334.

Fehrenbach, E., *Traditionale Gesellschaft und revolutionäres Recht. Die Einführung des Code Napoléon in den Rheinbundstaaten* (Göttingen: 1974).

Feldkamp, M.F., "Apostolische Nuntiatur, München", in *Historisches Lexikon Bayerns*, http://www.historisches-lexikon-bayerns.de/artikel/artikel_44502.

Fertig, C., *Familie, verwandtschaftliche Netzwerke und Klassenbildung im ländlichen Westfalen (1750–1874)* (Stuttgart: 2012).

Feurstein, H., *Die Verwandtschaft Feurstein / Christas-Hensles vom 17. bis ins 19. Jahrhundert* (Bregenz: 2010).

Fink, U., *Die Luzerner Nuntiatur 1586–1873. Zur Behördengeschichte und Quellenkunde der päpstlichen Diplomatie in der Schweiz* (Luzern – Stuttgart: 1997).

Fischer, A., "Bistum Chur", in Gatz, E. (ed.), *Die Bistümer der deutschsprachigen Länder von der Säkularisation bis zur Gegenwart* (Freiburg et al.: 2005) 156–174.

Fischer, E., *Die Seelsorge im Generalvikariat Feldkirch von seiner Gründung bis zum Jahr 1848* (PhD. dissertation, University of Innsbruck: 1968).

Fleckenstein, G. – Schmiedl, J., "Ultramontanismus in der Diskussion. Zur Neupositionierung eines Forschungsbegriffs", in Fleckenstein, G. – Schmiedl, J. (eds.), *Ultramontanismus. Tendenzen der Forschung* (Paderborn: 2005) 7–19.

Fliri, F., *Bevölkerungsgeographische Untersuchungen im Unterinntal* (Innsbruck: 1948).

Floßmann, U., *Österreichische Privatrechtsgeschichte*, 5th ed. (New York: 2005).

Flügel, A., "Der Ort der Regionalgeschichte in der neuzeitlichen Geschichte", in Brakensiek, S. et al. (eds.), *Kultur und Staat in der Provinz. Perspektiven und Erträge der Regionalgeschichte* (Bielefeld: 1992) 1–28.

Fontana, J., *Der Kulturkampf in Tirol (1861–1892)* (Bolzano: 1978).

Fontana, J., *Geschichte des Landes Tirol*, vol. 3: *Vom Neubau bis zum Untergang der Habsburgermonarchie (1848–1918)* (Bolzano – Innsbruck – Vienna: 1987).

Fontana, J., "Von der Restauration bis zur Revolution (1814–1848)", in Fontana, J. et al., *Geschichte des Landes Tirol*, vol. 2: *Die Zeit von 1490 bis 1848*, 2nd ed. (Bolzano – Innsbruck – Vienna: 1998) 583–737.

Fontana, J. et al., *Geschichte des Landes Tirol*, vol. 2: *Die Zeit von 1490 bis 1848*, 2nd ed. (Bolzano – Vienna: 1998).

Foucault, M., *Sexualität und Wahrheit*, vol. 1: *Der Wille zum Wissen* (Frankfurt a. M.: 1977).

Freist, D., "'One Body, Two Confessions': Mixed Marriages in Germany", in Rublack, U. (ed.), *Gender in Early Modern German History* (Cambridge: 2002) 275–304.

Frevert, U., "Angst vor Gefühlen? Die Geschichtsmächtigkeit von Emotionen im 20. Jahrhundert", in Nolte, P. et al., (eds.), *Perspektiven der Gesellschaftsgeschichte* (Munich: 2000) 95–111.

Frevert, U., "Ehe und Leidenschaft im 19. und 20. Jahrhundert", in Gestrich, C. (ed.), *Geschlechterverhältnis und Sexualität* (Berlin: 1997) 119–133.

Frevert, U., *Gefühle in der Geschichte* (Göttingen: 2021).

Frevert, U., "Neue Politikgeschichte: Konzepte und Herausforderungen", in Frevert, U. – Haupt, H.-G. (eds.), *Neue Politikgeschichte. Perspektiven einer historischen Politikforschung* (Frankfurt a. M. – New York: 2005) 7–26.

García González, F., "La historia de la familia en el interior castellano. Estado de la cuestión y esbozo bibliográfico (ss. XVI–XIX)", in García González, F. (ed.), *La historia de la familia en la Península Ibérica. Balance regional y perspectivas* (Cuenca: 2008) 277–329.

Garms-Cornides, E., "Benedikt XIV. – ein Papst zwischen Reaktion und Aufklärung", in Ammerer, G. – Haas, H. (eds.), *Ambivalenzen und Aufklärung. Festschrift für Ernst Wangermann* (Vienna – Munich: 1997) 168–186.

Gasser, A., "Kirche, Staat und Gesellschaft", in Verein für Bündner Kulturforschung im Auftrag der Regierung des Kantons Graubünden (ed.), *Handbuch der Bündner Geschichte*, vol. 3: *19. und 20. Jahrhundert*, 2nd ed. (Chur: 2000) 229–247.

Gasser, A., "Vom rätischen Fürstbistum zur schweizerischen Diözese", in Durst, M. (ed.), *Studien zur Geschichte des Bistums Chur (451–2001)* (Freiburg: 2002) 145–174.

Gatz, E. (ed.), *Die Bistümer der deutschsprachigen Länder von der Säkularisation bis zur Gegenwart* (Freiburg et al.: 2005).

Gelmi, J., "Bistum Bozen-Brixen (bis 1964: Brixen)", in Gatz, E. (ed.), *Die Bistümer der deutschsprachigen Länder von der Säkularisation bis zur Gegenwart* (Freiburg et al.: 2005) 141–155.

Gelmi, J., *Die Brixner Bischöfe in der Geschichte Tirols* (Bolzano: 1984).

Gelmi, J., *Geschichte der Kirche in Tirol. Nord-, Ost- und Südtirol* (Innsbruck – Vienna – Bolzano: 2001).

Gerhard, U. (ed.), *Frauen in der Geschichte des Rechts. Von der Frühen Neuzeit bis zur Gegenwart* (Munich: 1997).

Giddens, A., *The Transformation of Intimacy. Sexuality, Love and Eroticism in Modern Societies* (Cambridge: 1992).

Ginzburg, C., *The Cheese and the Worms. The Cosmos of a Sixteenth-Century Miller* (Baltimore: 1980 [1976]).

Gleixner, U., *'Das Mensch' und 'der Kerl'. Die Konstruktion von Geschlecht in Unzuchtsverfahren der Frühen Neuzeit, (1700–1760)* (Frankfurt a. M. – New York: 1994).

Gnant, C., "Der Josephinismus und das Heilige Römische Reich. 'Territorialer Etatismus' und josephinische Reichspolitik", in Schmale, W. – Zedinger, R. – Mondot, J. (eds.), *Josephinismus – eine Bilanz / Échecs et réussites du Joséphisme* (Bochum: 2008) 35–51.

Goody, J., *Die Entwicklung von Ehe und Familie in Europa* (Frankfurt a. M.: 1989) [engl.: *The Development of the Family and Marriage in Europe* (Cambridge: 1983)].

Gottschalk, K., "Herrschaftsvermittlung als kultureller Transfer? Lokalverwaltung und Verwaltungskultur in der Landgrafschaft Hessen-Kassel im 18. Jahrhundert", in North, M. (ed.), *Kultureller Austausch. Bilanz und Perspektiven der Frühneuzeitforschung* (Cologne – Weimar – Vienna: 2009) 175–191.

Götz, T., *Bürgertum und Liberalismus in Tirol 1840–1873. Zwischen Stadt und 'Region', Staat und Nation* (Cologne: 2001).

Gouesse, J.-M., "Mariages de proches parents (XVIe–XXe siècle). Esquisse d'une conjuncture", in *Le modèle familial Européen. Normes, déviances, contrôle du pouvoir. Actes des séminaires organisés par l'École française de Rome et l'Università di Roma* (Rome: 1986) 31–61.

Gouesse, J.-M., "Parenté, famille et mariage en Normandie aux XVIIe et XVIIIe siècles", *Annales ESC* 27, 4–5 (1972) 1139–1154.

Grandner, M. – Harmat, U., "Begrenzt verliebt. Gesetzliche Ehehindernisse und die Grenze zwischen Österreich und Ungarn", in Bauer, I. – Hämmerle, C. – Hauch, G. (eds.), *Liebe und Widerstand. Ambivalenzen historischer Geschlechterbeziehungen* (Vienna – Cologne – Weimar: 2005) 287–304.

Greiffenhagen, S., "Theorie(n) der Politischen Kultur", in Salzborn, S. (ed.), *Politische Kultur* (Frankfurt a. M. et a.: 2009) 11–29.

Grendi, E., "A proposito di 'famiglia e communità': questo fascicolo di Quaderni storici", *Quaderni storici* 33 (1976) 881–891.

Griesebner, A., *Konkurrierende Wahrheiten. Malefizprozesse vor dem Landgericht Perchtoldsdorf im 18. Jahrhundert* (Vienna – Cologne – Weimar: 2000).

Groppi, A., *Il welfare prima del welfare. Assistenza alla vecchiaia e solidarietà tra generazioni a Roma in età moderna* (Rome: 2010).

Grubb, J.S., "I libri di famiglia a Venezia e nel Veneto", in Ciappelli, G. (ed.), *Memoria, famiglia, identità tra Italia ed Europa nell'età moderna* (Bologna: 2009) 133–158.

Guarnieri, P., "Inzest als 'öffentliches Ärgernis'. Gesetzeslage und Moralvorstellungen im vereinten Italien", *L'Homme. Z.F.G.* 13, 1 (2002) 68–94.

Guerreau-Jalabert, A., "Flesh and Blood in Medieval Language about Kinship", in Johnson, C.H. et al. (eds.), *Blood & Kinship. Matter for Metaphor from Ancient Rome to the Present* (New York – Oxford: 2013) 61–82.

Guerreau-Jalabert, A., "*Spiritus* et *Caritas*. Le baptême dans la société médiévale", in Héritier-Augé, F. – Copet-Rougier, E. (eds.), *La parenté spirituelle* (Paris: 1995) 133–203.

Gullette, M.M., "The Puzzling Case of the Deceased Wife's Sister: Nineteenth-Century England Deals with a Second-Chance Plot", *Representations* 31, 2 (1990) 142–166.

Gutierrez, R.A., *Cuando Jesús llegó, las madres del maís se fueron. Matrimonio, sexualidad y poder en Nuevo México, 1500–1846* (Mexico: 1993).

Gutierrez, R.A., "Honor Ideology, Marriage Negotiation, and Class-Gender Domination in New Mexico, 1690–1846", *Latin American Perspectives* 12, 1 (1985) 81–104.

Guzzi-Heeb, S., *Donne, uomini, parentela. Casati alpini nell'Europa preindustriale (1650–1850)* (Turin: 2007).

Guzzi-Heeb, S., "Spiritual Kinship, Political Mobilization and Social Cooperation: a Swiss Alpine Valley in 18th and 19th Century", in Alfani, G. – Gourdon, V. (eds.), *Spiritual Kinship in Europe, 1500–1900* (Basingstoke: 2012) 183–203.

Guzzi-Heeb, S., "Von der Familien- zur Verwandtschaftsgeschichte: Der mikrohistorische Blick. Geschichte von Verwandten im Walliser Dorf Vouvry zwischen 1750 und 1850", *Historical Social Research* 30, 3 (2005) 107–129.

Haas, S., *Die Kultur der Verwaltung. Die Umsetzung der preußischen Reformen 1800–1848* (Frankfurt a. M. – New York: 2005).

Habermas, R., *Frauen und Männer des Bürgertums. Eine Familiengeschichte (1750–1850)* (Göttingen: 2000).

Hacke, D., *Women, Sex and Marriage in Early Modern Venice* (Ashgate: 2004).

Hajnal, J., "European Marriage Patterns in Perspective", in Glass, D.V. – Eversley, D.E.C. (eds.), *Population in History. Essays in Historical Demography* (London: 1965) 101–143.

Hämmerle, M., *Die Auswanderung aus Vorarlberg von 1815 bis 1914. Dokumentation und Analyse*, (PhD. dissertation, University of Vienna: 1982).

Hämmerle, M., *Glück in der Fremde? Vorarlberger Auswanderer im 19. Jahrhundert* (Feldkirch: 1990).

Hammermayer, L., "Die letzte Epoche des Erzstifts Salzburg. Politik und Kirchenpolitik unter Erzbischof Graf Hieronymus Colloredo (1772–1803)", in Dopsch, H. – Spatzenegger, H. (eds.), *Geschichte Salzburgs. Stadt und Land*, vol. II/2 (Salzburg: 1988) 453–535.

Hanisch, E., *Der lange Schatten des Staates. Österreichische Gesellschaftsgeschichte im 20. Jahrhundert (1890–1990)* (Vienna: 1994).

Hansert, A., *Geburtsaristokratie in Frankfurt am Main. Geschichte des reichsstädtischen Patriziats* (Vienna – Cologne – Weimar: 2014).

Hareven, T.K., *Families, History and Social Change. Life-Course and Cross-Cultural Perspectives* (Boulder: 2000).

Harmat, U., "Divorce and Remarriage in Austria-Hungary: the Second Marriage of Franz Konrad von Hötzendorf", *Austrian History Yearbook* 32 (2001) 69–103.

Hauck, J. "Le témoignage de la parenté: la mémoire généalogique dans les dispenses matrimoniales à Florence (XVe–XVIe siècles)" *Genre & Histoire* 21 (2018), https://journals.openedition.org/genrehistoire/3512 (last access: June 2022).

Hausen, K., "Family and Role-Division. The Polarization of Sexual Stereotypes in the Nineteenth Century. An Aspect of Dissociation of Work and Family Life", in Evans, R.J. – Lee, W.R. (eds.), *Social History of the Family in Nineteenth and Twentieth Centuries Germany* (London: 1981) 51–83.

Hausen, K., "Wirtschaften mit der Geschlechterordnung. Ein Essay", in Hausen, K. (ed.), *Geschlechterhierarchie und Arbeitsteilung. Zur Geschichte ungleicher Erwerbschancen von Männern und Frauen* (Göttingen: 1993) 40–67.

Hauser, A., "Erben und Teilen – ein zweiter Blick auf Forschungsergebnisse einer Sachkulturforschung", in Brakensiek, S. – Stolleis, M. – Wunder, H. (eds.), *Generationengerechtigkeit? Normen und Praxis im Erb- und Ehegüterrecht 1500–1850* (Berlin: 2006) 301–315.

Hauser-Schäublin, B., "Blutsverwandtschaft", in Braun, C. v. – Wulf, C. (eds.), *Mythen des Blutes* (Frankfurt a. M. – New York: 2007) 171–183.

Head-König, A.-L., "Forced Marriages and Forbidden Marriages in Switzerland: State Control of the Formation of Marriages in Catholic and Protestant Cantons in the Eighteenth and Nineteenth Centuries", *Continuity and Change* 8 (1993) 441–465.

Hehenberger, S., "Inzest oder 'Hurerey'? Inzest in der gerichtlichen Praxis des 18. Jahrhunderts. Eine Untersuchung am Beispiel Oberösterreichs", in Eming, J. –

Jarzebowski, C. – Ulbrich, C. (eds.), *Historische Inzestdiskurse. Interdisziplinäre Zugänge* (Königstein/Taunus: 2003) 189–213.

Heindl, W., *Gehorsame Rebellen. Bürokratie und Beamte in Österreich 1780 bis 1848*, (Vienna – Cologne – Graz: 1991).

Heindl, W., *Josephinische Mandarine. Bürokratie und Beamte in Österreich* (Vienna – Cologne – Weimar: 2013).

Heinemann, J., *Verwandtsein und Herrschen. Die Königinmutter Catherine de Médicis und ihre Kinder in Briefen, 1560–1589* (Heidelberg: 2020).

Heiss, H. – Götz, T., *Am Rand der Revolution. Tirol 1848/49*, (Vienna – Bolzano: 1998).

Hellbling, E.C., *Grundlegende Strafrechtsquellen der österreichischen Erbländer vom Beginn der Neuzeit bis zur Theresiana. Ein Beitrag zur Geschichte des Strafrechts in Österreich*, revised and edited by Reiter, I. (Vienna – Cologne – Weimar: 1996).

Hering, T. – Sebastián, M., *Rassismus in der Vormoderne. Die 'Reinheit des Blutes' im Spanien der Frühen Neuzeit* (Frankfurt a. M. – New York: 2006).

Héritier, F., *Two Sisters and Their Mother. The Anthropology of Incest* (New York: 1999).

Herrmann, H., "Die römische Agenzie für kirchliche Angelegenheiten Deutschlands und Österreichs", *Römische Historische Mitteilungen* 11 (1969) 182–205.

Hersche, P., *Muße und Verschwendung. Europäische Gesellschaft und Kultur im Barockzeitalter*, (Freiburg – Basel – Vienna: 2006).

Hitzer, B., "Emotionengeschichte – ein Anfang mit Folgen", *H-Soz-u-Kult* 23 Nov. 2011, http://hsozkult.geschichte.hu-berlin.de/forum/2011-11-001 (accessed: May 2022).

Hochenegg, H., "Wallfahrten über die Landesgrenzen. Ein Beitrag zur religiösen Volkskunde", *Tiroler Heimat* 12 (1948) 7–23.

Hohkamp, M., "Do Sisters Have Brothers? The Search for the 'rechte Schwester'. Brothers and Sisters in Aristocratic Society at the Turn of the Sixteenth Century", in Johnson, C.H. – Sabean, D.W. (eds.), *Sibling Relations & the Transformation of European Kinship 1300–1900* (New York – Oxford: 2011) 65–83.

Hohkamp, M., *Herrschaft in der Herrschaft. Die vorderösterreichische Obervogtei Triberg von 1737–1780* (Göttingen: 1998).

Holenstein, A., "'Local-Untersuchung' und 'Augenschein'. Reflexionen auf die Lokalität im Verwaltungsdenken und -handeln des Ancien Régime", *WerkstattGeschichte* 16 (1997) 19–31.

Holzem, A. – Ines Weber, I. (eds.), *Ehe – Familie – Verwandtschaft. Vergesellschaftung in Religion und sozialer Lebenswelt* (Paderborn et al.: 2008).

Hull, I.V., *Sexuality, State, and Civil Society in Germany, 1700–1815* (Ithaca – London: 1996).

Hürlimann, J.-C., *Die Eheschließungsverbote zwischen Verwandten und Verschwägerten* (Bern et al.: 1987).

Iida, T., "Wiederheiraten und Verwandtschaftsnetze auf dem unteilbaren Hof: Bauern, Büdner und Einlieger des brandenburgischen Amtes Alt-Ruppin im 18. Jahrhundert", in Duhamelle, C. – Schlumbohm, J. (eds.), *Eheschließungen im Europa des 18. und 19. Jahrhunderts. Muster und Strategien* (Göttingen: 2003) 125–155.

Illouz, E., "Vermarktung der Leidenschaft: Bedeutungswandel der Liebe im Kapitalismus", *Westend. Neue Zeitschrift für Sozialforschung* 2, 1 (2005) 80–95.

Jarzebowski, C., *Inzest. Verwandtschaft und Sexualität im 18. Jahrhundert* (Cologne – Weimar – Vienna: 2005).

Jemolo, A.C., *Il matrimonio nel diritto canonico. Dal Concilio di Trento al Codice del 1917* (Bologna: 1993).

Johnson, C.H., *Becoming Bourgeois. Love, Kinship, and Power in Provincial France, 1670–1880* (Ithaca – London: 2015).

Johnson, C.H., "Das 'Geschwister Archipel': Bruder-Schwester-Liebe und Klassenformation im Frankreich des 19. Jahrhundert", *L'Homme. Z.F.G.* 13, 1 (2002) 50–67.

Johnson, C.H., "Siblinghood and the Emotional Dimensions of the New Kinship System, 1800–1850: A French Example", in Johnson, C.H. – Sabean, D.W. (eds.), *Sibling Relations & the Transformation of European Kinship 1300–1900* (New York – Oxford: 2011) 189–220.

Johnson, C.H. – Sabean, D.W., "Introduction. From Siblingship to Siblinghood: Kinship in the Shaping of European Society (1300–1900)", in Johnson, C.H. – Sabean, D.W. (eds.), *Sibling Relations & the Transformation of European Kinship 1300–1900* (New York – Oxford: 2011) 1–28.

Joris, E., "Kinship and Gender: Property, Enterprise, and Politics", in Sabean, D.W. – Teuscher, S. – Mathieu, J. (eds.), *Kinship in Europe. Approaches to Long-Term Development (1300–1900)* (New York – Oxford: 2007) 231–257.

Joris, E. – Witzig, H., *Brave Frauen, aufmüpfige Weiber. Wie sich die Industrialisierung auf Alltag und Lebenszusammenhänge von Frauen auswirkte (1820–1940)* (Zurich: 1992).

Judson, P.M., "Early Liberalism in Austrian Society", in Reinalter, H. – Klueting, H. (eds.), *Der deutsche und österreichische Liberalismus. Geschichts- und politikwissenschaftliche Perspektiven im Vergleich* (Innsbruck: 2010) 105–120.

Jussen, B., "Künstliche und natürliche Verwandtschaft? Biologismen in den kulturwissenschaftlichen Konzepten von Verwandtschaft", in Bessmertny, Y.L. – Oexle, O.G. (eds.), *Das Individuum und die Seinen. Individualität in der okzidentalen und der russischen Kultur in Mittelalter und Früher Neuzeit* (Göttingen: 2001) 40–58.

Jussen, B., "Erbe und Verwandtschaft. Kulturen der Übertragung im Mittelalter", in Willer, S., – Weigel, S. – Jussen, B. (eds.), *Erbe. Übertragungskonzepte zwischen Natur und Kultur* (Frankfurt a. M.: 2013) 37–64.

Jussen, B., "Perspektiven der Verwandtschaftsforschung fünfundzwanzig Jahre nach Jack Goodys 'Entwicklung von Ehe und Familie in Europa'", in Spieß, K.H. (ed.), *Die Familie in der Gesellschaft des Mittelalters* (Ostfildern: 2009) 275–324.

Jussen, B., *Spiritual Kinship as Social Practice. Godparenthood and Adoption in the Early Middle Ages* (London – Newark: 2000).

Karlinger, E. – Holböck, C., *Die Vorarlberger Bistumsfrage. Geschichtliche Entwicklung und kirchenrechtliche Beurteilung* (Graz – Vienna – Cologne: 1963).

Kerschbaumer, A., *Geschichte des deutschen Nationalhospizes Anima in Rom* (Vienna: 1968).

Kessel, M., "Das Trauma der Affektkontrolle. Zur Sehnsucht nach Gefühlen im 19. Jahrhundert", in Benthien, C. – Flaig, A – Kasten, I. (eds.), *Emotionalität. Zur Geschichte der Gefühle* (Cologne – Weimar – Vienna: 2000) 156–177.

Klapisch-Zuber, C., *Stammbäume. Eine illustrierte Geschichte der Ahnenkunde* (Munich: 2004).

Klein, B., "Allein nach dem 'Gesetz Mosis'? – Inzestdiskurse über jüdische Heiratspraxis in der Frühen Neuzeit", in Eming, J. – Jarzebowski, C. – Ulbrich, C. (eds.), *Historische Inzestdiskurse. Interdisziplinäre Zugänge* (Königstein/Taunus: 2003) 86–115.

Knodel, J.E., *Demographic Behavior in the Past. A Study of Fourteen German Village Populations in the Eighteenth and Nineteenth Centuries* (Cambridge: 1988).

Kocher, G., "Die Rechtsreformen Joseph II.", in Reinalter, H. (ed.), *Josephinismus als Aufgeklärter Absolutismus* (Vienna – Cologne – Weimar: 2008) 125–161.

Koller, A., "Nuntienalltag. Überlegungen zur Lebenswelt eines kirchlichen Diplomatenhaushalts im 16. und 17. Jahrhundert", in Klieber, R. – Hold, H. (eds.), *Impulse für eine religiöse Alltagsgeschichte des Donau-Alpen-Adria-Raumes* (Vienna – Cologne – Weimar: 2005) 95–108.

Koppetsch, C., "Liebesökonomie. Ambivalenzen moderner Paarbeziehungen", *Westend. Neue Zeitschrift für Sozialforschung* 2, 1 (2005) 96–107.

Kovács, E., "Burgundisches und theresianisch-josephinisches Staatskirchensystem", in Reinalter, H. (ed.), *Der Josephinismus. Bedeutung, Einflüsse und Wirkungen* (Frankfurt a. M. et al.: 1993) 39–62.

Krosigk, R.v., *Bürger in die Verwaltung! Bürokratiekritik und Bürgerbeteiligung in Baden. Zur Geschichte moderner Staatlichkeit im Deutschland des 19. Jahrhundert* (Bielefeld: 2010).

Kümin, B., *Drinking Matters: Public Houses and Social Exchange in Early Modern Central Europe* (Basingstoke: 2007).

Kuper, A., *Incest & Influence. The Private Life of Bourgeois England* (Cambridge/Mass. – London: 2009).

La Rocca, C., *Tra moglie e marito. Matrimoni e separazioni a Livorno nel Settecento* (Bologna: 2009).

Labouvie, E. – Myrrhe, R. (eds.), *Familienbande – Familienschande. Geschlechterverhältnisse in Familie und Verwandtschaft* (Cologne – Weimar – Vienna: 2007).

Landwehr, A., "Diskurs – Macht – Wissen. Perspektiven einer Kulturgeschichte des Politischen", *Archiv für Kulturgeschichte* 85, 1 (2003) 71–117.

Landwehr, A., *Policey im Alltag. Die Implementation frühneuzeitlicher Policeyordnungen in Leonberg* (Frankfurt a. M.: 2000).

Langer, M., "Die konsanguine Ehe – eine medizinische und sozio-kulturelle Herausforderung", *Historische Sozialkunde* 41, 2 (2011) 34–37.

Langer-Ostrawsky, G., "Vom Verheiraten der Güter. Bäuerliche und kleinbäuerliche Heiratsverträge im Erzherzogtum Österreich unter der Enns", in: Lanzinger, M. – Barth-Scalmani, G. – Forster, E. – Langer-Ostrawsky, G. (eds.), *Aushandeln von Ehe. Heiratsverträge der Neuzeit im europäischen Vergleich* (Cologne – Weimar – Vienna: 2010) 27–76.

Lanzinger, M., *Das gesicherte Erbe. Heirat in lokalen und familialen Kontexten, Innichen 1700–1900*, (Vienna – Cologne – Weimar: 2003).

Lanzinger, M., "Emotional Bonds and the Everyday Logic of Living Arrangements: Stepfamilies in Dispensation Records of Late Eighteenth-Century Austria", in Warner, L. (ed.), *Stepfamilies in Europe, 1400–1800* (Abingdon – New York: 2018) 168–186.

Lanzinger, M., "Kirchliche Macht, antiliberale Tendenzen und ziviles Aufbegehren mit Grenzen. Zur Ehedispenspraxis in Tirol und Vorarlberg im 19. Jahrhundert", *Histoire des Alpes – Storia delle Alpi – Geschichte der Alpen* 12 (2007) 49–68.

Lanzinger, M., "Liebe, Ehe, Ökonomie. Materielle und immaterielle Ressourcen im Kontext von Verwandtenheiraten", in Jancke, G. – Schläppi, D. (eds.), *Die Ökonomie sozialer Beziehungen: Ressourcenbewirtschaftung als Geben, Nehmen, Investieren, Verschwenden, Haushalten, Horten, Vererben, Schulden* (Stuttgart: 2015) 157–176.

Lanzinger, M., "La scelta del coniuge. Fra amore romantico e matrimoni proibiti", *Storicamente* 6 (2010), http://www.storicamente.org/07_dossier/famiglia/scelta_del_coniuge.htm (accessed: May 2022).

Lanzinger, M., "Landlessness and Marriage Restrictions: Tyrol and Vorarlberg in the Eighteenth and Nineteenth Centuries", in Fertig, C. – Paping, R. – French, H. (eds.), *Landless Households in Rural Europe 1600–1900* (Suffolk: 2022) 243–269.

Lanzinger, M., "'Liebe, Neigung, leider Leidenschaft war es …'. Kirchliche Heiratsverbote im Spannungsfeld zwischen Ökonomie, Moral und Inzest – eine Fallgeschichte", in Bauer, I. – Hämmerle, C. – Hauch, G. (eds.), *Liebe und Widerstand. Ambivalenzen historischer Geschlechterbeziehungen* (Vienna – Cologne – Weimar: 2005) 257–273.

Lanzinger, M., "Mountain Farmers' Labour Requirements and the Choice of a Spouse in Nineteenth Century Tyrol and Vorarlberg", in Landsteiner, E. – Langthaler, E. (eds.), *Agrosystems and Labour Relations in European Societies* (Turnhout: 2010) 97–118.

Lanzinger, M., "Parenté et genre: des mariages par alliance", in Bellavitis, A. – Edelman, N. (eds.), *Genre, femmes, histoire en Europe. France, Italie, Espagne, Autriche* (Paris: 2011) 233–253.

Lanzinger, M., "Paternal Authority and Patrilineal Power: Stem Family Arrangements in Peasant Communities and Eighteenth-Century Tyrolean Marriage Contracts", in

Lanzinger, M. (ed.), *The Power of the Fathers. Historical Perspectives from Ancient Rome to the Nineteenth Century* (London – New York: 2015) 65–89.

Lanzinger, M., "Schwestern-Beziehungen und Schwager-Ehen. Formen familialer Krisenbewältigung im 19. Jahrhundert", in Labouvie, E. (ed.), *Schwestern und Freundinnen. Zur Kulturgeschichte weiblicher Kommunikation* (Cologne – Weimar – Vienna: 2009) 263–282.

Lanzinger. M., "Spouses and the Competition for Wealth", in Eibach, J. – Lanzinger, M. (eds.), *The Routledge History of the Domestic Sphere in Europe Sixteenth to Nineteenth Century* (London: 2020) 61–78.

Lanzinger, M., "Staat, Kirche, Eheagenden: Staatliche Integration in komplexen rechtsräumlichen Gefügen", in Francesca Brunet, F. – Florian Huber, F. (eds.), *Vormärz. Eine geteilte Geschichte Trentino-Tirols | Una storia condivisa Trentino-Tirolese*, (Innsbruck: 2017) 143–161.

Lanzinger, M., "Staatliches und kirchliches Recht in Konkurrenz. Verwandtenenehen und Dispenspraxis im Tirol des ausgehenden 18. Jahrhunderts", *Geschichte und Region / Storia e Regione* 20, 2 (2011) 73–91.

Lanzinger, M., "Tanten, Schwägerinnen und Nichten – Beziehungsgefüge, Vermögenskonflikte und 'Reparaturehen' oder: Linie und Paar in Konkurrenz", *WerkstattGeschichte* 10, 46 (2007) 41–54.

Lanzinger, M., "The Relativity of Kinship and Gender-Specific Logics in the Context of Marriage Dispensations in the Nineteenth-Century Alps (Diocese of Brixen)", *Genre & Histoire* 21, 1 (2018), online since 1 September 2018, connection on 3 October 2018, http://journals.openedition.org/genrehistoire/3036, 1–19 (accessed: May 2022).

Lanzinger, M., "The Visibility of Women's Work: Logics and Contexts of Documents' Production", in Sarti, R. – Bellavitis, A. – Martini, M. (eds.), *What is Work? Gender at the Crossroads of Home, Family, and Business from the Early Modern Era to the Present* (New York – Oxford: 2018) 243–264.

Lanzinger, M., "Umkämpft, verhandelt und vermittelt. Verwandtenehen in der katholischen Ehedispenspraxis des 19. Jahrhunderts", in Lanzinger, M. – Saurer, E. (eds.), *Politiken der Verwandtschaft. Beziehungsnetze, Geschlecht und Recht* (Göttingen: 2007) 273–296.

Lanzinger, M., "'Und werden sein die zwey ein Fleisch'. Das Eheverbot der Schwägerschaft", *Mitteilungen des Instituts für Wissenschaft und Kunst* 1–2 (2006) 36–42.

Lanzinger, M., "Verwandtenheirat – ein 'aristokratisches' Ehemodell? Debatten um die Goody-Thesen und Dispenspraxis Ende des 18. Jahrhunderts", in Fertig, C. – Lanzinger, M. (eds.), *Beziehungen, Vernetzungen, Konflikte. Perspektiven Historischer Verwandtschaftsforschung* (Vienna – Cologne – Weimar: 2016) 143–166.

Lanzinger, M., "Von der Macht der Linie zur Gegenseitigkeit Heiratskontrakte in den Südtiroler Gerichten Welsberg und Innichen 1750–1850", in Lanzinger, M. – Barth-Scalmani, G. – Forster, E. – Langer-Ostrawsky, G. (eds.), *Aushandeln von Ehe.*

Heiratsverträge der Neuzeit im europäischen Vergleich (Cologne – Weimar – Vienna: 2010) 205–326.

Lanzinger, M., "Widowers and their Sisters-in-Law: Family Crises, Horizontally Organised Relationships and Affinal Relatives in the Nineteenth Century", *The History of the Family* 23, 2 (2018) 175–195.

Lanzinger, M., "Women and Property in 18th Century Austria. Separate Property, Usufruct and Ownership in Different Family Configurations", in Moring, B. (ed.), *Female Economic Strategies in the Modern World* (London: 2012) 145–159.

Lanzinger, M., "Zwischen Anforderungsprofilen und Argumentationsrepertoires. Partner/-innen/-wahl und Arbeitsorganisation im bergbäuerlichen Milieu in Tirol und Vorarlberg im 19. Jahrhundert", *Jahrbuch für Geschichte des ländlichen Raumes* (2008) 86–108.

Lanzinger, M. et al. (eds.), *Negotiations of Gender and Property through Legal Regimes (14th–19th Century): Stipulating, Litigating, Mediating* (Leiden – Boston: 2021).

Lanzinger, M. – Saurer E., "Politiken der Verwandtschaft. Einleitung", in: Lanzinger, M. – Saurer E. (eds.), *Politiken der Verwandtschaft. Beziehungsnetze, Geschlecht und Recht* (Göttingen: 2007) 7–22.

Lanzinger, M. – Saurer, E. (eds.), *Politiken der Verwandtschaft. Beziehungsnetze, Geschlecht und Recht* (Göttingen: 2007).

Laslett, P., "Family and Household as Work Group and Kin Group: Areas of Traditional Europe Compared", in Wall, R. et al. (eds.), *Family Forms in Historic Europe* (Cambridge: 1993) 513–563.

Laslett, P., "Introduction: the History of the Family", in Laslett, P. – Wall, R. (eds.), *Household and Family in Past Time* (Cambridge: 1972) 1–89.

Laslett, P., "Family and Household as Work Group and Kin Group: Areas of Traditional Europe Compared", in Wall, R. – Robin, J. – Laslett, P. (eds.), *Family Forms in Historic Europe*, (Cambridge: 1993) 513–563.

Latour, B., *Reassembling the Social. An Introduction to Actor-Network-Theory* (Oxford: 2005).

Leisching, P., *Die Bischofskonferenz. Beiträge zu ihrer Rechtsgeschichte, mit besonderer Berücksichtigung ihrer Entwicklung in Österreich* (Vienna – Munich: 1963).

Levi, G., *L'eredità immateriale. Carriera di un esorcista nel Piemonte del Seicento* (Turin: 1985).

Levi, G., "On Microhistory", in Burke, P. (ed.), *New Perspectives on Historical Writing* (Cambridge: 1991) 93–113.

Lipp, C., "Kinship Networks, Local Government, and Elections in a Town in Southwest Germany, 1800–1850", *Journal of Family History* 30, 4 (2005) 347–365.

Lipp, C., "Verwandtschaft – ein negiertes Element in der politischen Kultur des 19. Jahrhunderts", *Historische Zeitschrift* 283 (2006) 31–77.

Lombardi, D., "Giustizia ecclesiastica e composizione dei conflitti matrimoniali (Firenze, secoli XVI–XVIII)", in Seidel Menchi, S. – Quaglioni, D. (eds.), *I tribunali del matrimonio (secoli XV–XVIII)* (Bologna: 2001) 577–607.

Lombardi, D., *Matrimoni di antico regime* (Bologna: 2001).

Lönne, K.-E., *Politischer Katholizismus im 19. und 20. Jahrhundert* (Frankfurt a. M.: 1986).

Lorenzetti, L., *Economie et migrations au XIXe siècle: les stratégies de la reproduction familiale au Tessin* (Bern et. al.: 1999).

Lubich, G., *Verwandtsein. Lesarten einer politisch-sozialen Beziehung im Frühmittelalter* (Cologne – Weimar – Vienna: 2008).

Lüdtke, A., "Einleitung. Herrschaft als soziale Praxis", in Lüdtke, A. (ed.), *Herrschaft als soziale Praxis. Historische und sozial-anthropologische Studien* (Göttingen: 1991) 9–63.

Luhmann, N., *Love as Passion. The Codification of Intimacy* (Cambridge/Mass.: 1987 [1982]).

MacFarlane, A., "Review Essay", *History and Theory* 18 (1979) 103–126.

Maleczek, W., "Die päpstlichen Legaten im 14. und 15. Jahrhundert", in Schwinges, R.C. – Wriedt, K. (eds.), *Gesandtschafts- und Botenwesen im spätmittelalterlichen Europa* (Ostfildern: 2003) 33–86.

Mantl, E., *Heirat als Privileg. Obrigkeitliche Heiratsbeschränkungen in Tirol und Vorarlberg 1820–1920* (Vienna – Munich: 1997).

Mantl, E., "Legal Restrictions on Marriage: Marriage and Inequality in the Austrian Tyrol during the Nineteenth Century", *The History of the Family* 4, 2 (1999) 185–207.

Martin, J., "Zur Anthropologie von Heiratsregeln und Besitzübertragung. 10 Jahre nach den Goody-Thesen", *Historische Anthropologie* 1, 1 (1993) 149–162.

Martina, G., "Giorgio XVI", in *Enciclopedia dei papi*, vol. 3: *Innocenzo – VIII Giovanni Paolo II* (Rome: 2000) 546–560.

Martina, G., "Pio IX", in *Enciclopedia dei papi*, vol. 3: *Innocenzo VIII – Giovanni Paolo II* (Rome: 2000) 560–575.

Martini, M., "Neue Rechte, alte Pflichten. Die Rezeption des Code Napoléon zu Beginn des 19. Jahrhunderts in Italien", *L'Homme. Z.F.G.* 14, 1 (2003) 90–96.

Mathieu, J., *Die dritte Dimension. Eine vergleichende Geschichte der Berge in der Neuzeit* (Basel: 2011).

Mathieu, J., "'Ein Cousin an jeder Zaunlücke'. Überlegungen zum Wandel von Verwandtschaft und ländlicher Gemeinde, 1700–1900", in Lanzinger, M. – Saurer, E. (eds.), *Politiken der Verwandtschaft. Beziehungsnetze, Geschlecht und Recht* (Göttingen: 2007) 55–71.

Mathieu, J., *History of the Alps, 1500–1900. Environment, Development, and Society* (Morgantown: 2009 [2001]).

Mathieu, J., "Kin Marriages. Trends and Interpretations from the Swiss Example", in Sabean, D.W. – Teuscher, S. – Mathieu, J. (eds.), *Kinship in Europe. Approaches to Long-Term Development (1300–1900)* (New York – Oxford: 2007) 211–230.

Mathieu, J., "Verwandtschaft als historischer Faktor. Schweizer Fallstudien und Trends, 1500–1900", *Historische Anthropologie* 10, 2 (2002) 225–244.

Mathieu, J., "Von der verstreuten Familie zum 'Ganzen Haus'. Sozialgeschichtliche Übergänge im schweizerisch-österreichischen Alpenraum des 17. bis 19. Jahrhundert", in Loose, R. (ed.), *Der Vinschgau und seine Nachbarräume. Vorträge des landeskundlichen Symposiums Schloß Goldrain 27. bis 30. Juni 1991* (Bolzano: 1993) 245–255.

Matschek, H., Sippenbuch von Schröcken 1490–1906 (Regensburg: 2007).

Matthijs, K., "Frequency, Timing and Intensity of Remarriage in 19th Century Flanders", *The History of the Family* 8, 1, (2003) 135–162.

Matz, K.-J., *Pauperismus und Bevölkerung. Die gesetzlichen Ehebeschränkungen in den süddeutschen Staaten während des 19. Jahrhunderts* (Stuttgart: 1980).

Matzerath, J., "Die Einführung der Ahnenprobe in der kursächsischen Ritterschaft in der zweiten Hälfte des 17. Jahrhunderts", in Harding, E. – Hecht, M. (eds.), *Die Ahnenprobe in der Vormoderne. Selektion – Initiation – Repräsentation* (Münster: 2011) 233–245.

May, G., *Die Auseinandersetzungen zwischen den Mainzer Erzbischöfen und dem Heiligen Stuhl um die Dispensbefugnis im 18. Jahrhundert* (Frankfurt a. M. et al.: 2007).

Mayer, G., *Österreich als katholische Großmacht. Ein Traum zwischen Revolution und liberaler Ära* (Vienna: 1989).

Maynes, M.J. et al., "Introduction: Toward a Comparative History of Gender, Kinship and Power", in Maynes, M.J. et al. (eds.), *Gender, Kinship, Power. A Comparative and Interdisciplinary History* (New York – London: 1996) 1–23.

Mayr, J.K., "Gesandtschaftsarchive", in Bittner, L. (ed.), *Gesamtinventar des Wiener Haus-, Hof- und Staatsarchivs*, vol. 1: *Entwicklung des archivalischen Besitzstandes und der Einrichtungen des Archivs, Biographien der Archivbeamten, Fundbehelfe, Geschichte und Inventare der Reichsarchive, des Archivs der Staatskanzlei (des Ministeriums des Äußeren), der Gesandtschaftsarchive und der Staatenabteilungen* (Vienna: 1936) 469–508.

Mayrhofer, W., *Quellenerläuterungen für Haus- und Familienforschung in Oberösterreich*, 3rd ed. (Linz: 2004).

Medick, H., "Zwischen Mythos und Realität – die historische Erforschung der Familie", in Mayer, S. – Schulte, D. (eds.), *Die Zukunft der Familie* (Munich: 2007) 37–55.

Medick, H. – Sabean, D.W., "Emotionen und materielle Interessen in Familie und Verwandtschaft: Überlegungen zu neuen Wegen und Bereichen einer historischen und sozialanthropologischen Familienforschung", in Medick, H. – Sabean, D.W. (eds.), *Emotionen und materielle Interessen. Sozialanthropologische und historische Beiträge zur Familienforschung* (Göttingen: 1984) 27–54.

Medick, H. – Sabean, D.W. (eds.), *Emotionen und materielle Interessen. Sozialanthropologische und historische Beiträge zur Familienforschung* (Göttingen: 1984).

Meriggi, M., "Il principato vescovile dal 1776 alla secolarizzazione", in Bellabarba, M. – Olmi, G. (eds.), *Storia del Trentino*, vol. 4: *L'età moderna* (Bologna: 2002) 127–156.

Merzario, R., *Il paese stretto. Strategie matrimoniali nella diocesi di Como (secoli XVI–XVIII)* (Turin: 1981).

Merzario, R., "Land, Kinship and Consanguineous Marriage in Italy from the Seventeenth to the Nineteenth Century", *Journal of Family History* 15 (1990) 529–546.

Merzario, R., "Terra, parentela e matrimoni consanguinei in Italia (secoli XVII–XIX)", in Barbagli, M. – Kertzer, D.I. (eds.), *Storia della famiglia italiana 1750–1950* (Bologna: 1992) 253–272.

Mitterauer, M., "Christianity and Endogamy", *Continuity and Change* 6, 3 (1991) 295–333.

Mitterauer, M., "Die 'Sitten der Magier'. Zur Inzestproblematik in historischen Gesellschaften", in Mitterauer, M., (ed.), *Historische Verwandtschaftsforschung*, (Vienna – Cologne – Weimar: 2013) 85–105 [orig.: "The Customs of the Magians. The Problem of Incest in Historical Societies"], in Porter, R. – Teich, M. (eds.), *Sexual Knowledge, Sexual Science. The History of Attitudes to Sexuality* (Cambridge: 1994) 231–250.

Mitterauer, M., "Formen ländlicher Familienwirtschaft. Historische Ökotypen und familiale Arbeitsorganisation im österreichischen Raum", in Ehmer, J. – Mitterauer, M. (eds.), *Familienstruktur und Arbeitsorganisation in ländlichen Gesellschaften* (Vienna: 1985) 185–323.

Mitterauer, M., "Komplexe Familienformen in sozialhistorischer Sicht", in Mitterauer, M., *Historisch-Anthropologische Familienforschung. Fragestellungen und Zugangsweisen* (Vienna – Cologne: 1990) 87–130.

Mitterauer, M., "Kontrastierende Heiratsregeln. Traditionen des Orients und Europas im interkulturellen Vergleich", *Historische Sozialkunde* 41, 2 (2011) 4–16.

Mitterauer, M., "'Spanische Heiraten'. Dynastische Endogamie im Kontext konsanguiner Ehestrategien", in: Mitterauer, M., *Historische Verwandtschaftsforschung* (Vienna – Cologne – Weimar: 2013) 149–212.

Mitterauer, M., *Ledige Mütter. Zur Geschichte unehelicher Geburten in Europa* (Munich: 1983).

Mitterauer, M., *Warum Europa? Mittelalterliche Grundlagen eines Sonderwegs* (Munich: 2003).

Mitterauer, M. – Sieder, R., "The Developmental Process of Domestic Groups: Problems of Reconstruction and Possibilities of Interpretation", *Journal of Family History* 4 (1979) 257–284.

Mordenti, R., "Les livres de famille en Italie", *Annales HSS* 59, 4 (2004) 785–804.

Moring, B., "Land, Labour, and Love: Household Arrangements in Nineteenth Century Eastern Finland – Cultural Heritage or Socio-Economic Structure?", *The History of the Family* 4, 2 (1999) 159–184.

Moring, B. – Wall, R., *Widows in European Economy and Society 1600–1920* (Woodbridge: 2017).

Morris, P., "Incest or Survival Strategy? Plebeian Marriage within the Prohibited Degrees in Somerset, 1730–1835", *Journal of the History of Sexuality* 2, 2 (1991) 235–265.

Mostaza, A., "Forum internum – Forum externum. (En torno a la naturaleza jurídica del fuero interno)", *Revista española de derecho canonico* 23, 65 (1967) 253–331.

Mühlsteiger, J., *Der Geist des Josephinischen Eherechtes* (Vienna – Munich: 1967).

Müller-Wille, S. – Rheinberger, H.-J. (eds.), *Heredity Produced. At the Crossroads of Biology, Politics, and Culture, 1500–1870* (Cambridge/Mass. – London: 2007).

Müller-Wille, S. – Rheinberger, H.-J., "Heredity – The Formation of an Epistemic Space", in: Müller-Wille, S. – Rheinberger, H.-J. (eds.), *Heredity Produced. At the Crossroads of Biology, Politics, and Culture, 1500–1870* (Cambridge/Mass. – London: 2007) 3–34.

Niederstätter, A., "Arbeit in der Fremde. Bemerkungen zur Vorarlberger Arbeitsmigration vom Spätmittelalter bis zum 19. Jahrhundert", *Montfort. Vierteljahresschrift für Geschichte und Gegenwart Vorarlbergs* 48, 2 (1996), 105–117.

North, D.C., *Institutions, Institutional Change and Economic Performance* (Cambridge: 1990).

Nubola, C. – Würgler, A., "Einführung", in: Nubola, C. – Würgler, A. (eds.), *Bittschriften und Gravamina. Politik, Verwaltung und Justiz in Europa (14.–18. Jahrhundert)* (Berlin: 2005) 7–16.

Opitz, C., "Wandel der Vaterrolle in der Aufklärung?", in Opitz, C., *Aufklärung der Geschlechter, Revolution der Geschlechterordnung. Studien zur Politik- und Kulturgeschichte des 18. Jahrhunderts* (Münster et al.: 2002) 21–38.

Ortmayr, N., "Späte Heirat. Ursachen und Folgen des alpinen Heiratsmusters", *Zeitgeschichte* 16 (1988/89) 119–134.

Ortner, F., "Erzbistum Salzburg", in Gatz, E. (ed.), *Die Bistümer der deutschsprachigen Länder von der Säkularisation bis zur Gegenwart* (Freiburg et al.: 2005) 638–653.

Ortner, F., *Salzburgs Bischöfe in der Geschichte des Landes (696–2005)* (Frankfurt a. M. et al.: 2005).

Ostinelli, P., "L'offerta della grazia. Dispense e assoluzioni concesse da vescovi e inviati pontifici in Lombardia nel XV secolo", in Meyer, A. – Rendtel, C. – Wittmer-Butsch, M. (eds.), *Päpste, Pilger, Pönitentiarie. Festschrift für Ludwig Schmugge zum 65. Geburtstag* (Tübingen: 2004) 531–549.

Palme, R., "Die Entwicklung des Erbrechtes im ländlichen Bereich", in Rösch, P. (ed.), *Südtiroler Erbhöfe. Menschen und Geschichten* (Bolzano: 1994) 25–37.

Pammer, M., *Entwicklung und Ungleichheit. Österreich im 19. Jahrhundert* (Stuttgart: 2002).

Parsons, T., "The Kinship System of the Contemporary United States", *American Anthropologist, New Series* 45, 1 (1943) 22–38.

Pelaja, M., "Marriage by Exception: Marriage Dispensations and Ecclesiastical Policies in Nineteenth-Century Rome", *Journal of Modern Italian Studies* 1, 2 (1996) 223–244.

Pelaja, M. – Scaraffia, L., *Due in una carne. Chiesa e sessualità nella storia* (Rome – Bari: 2008).

Pelikan, C., *Aspekte der Geschichte des Eherechts in Österreich* (PhD. dissertation, University of Vienna: 1981).

Perrier, S., "La marâtre dans la France d'Ancien Régime: intégration ou marginalité?", *Annales de démographie historique* 2 (2006) 171–187.

Pesch, R., *Die kirchlich-politische Presse der Katholiken in der Rheinprovinz vor 1848* (Mainz: 1966).

Pflegerl, J. – Geserick, C., *Kinship and Social Security in Austria. A Social History for the 20th Century* (Innsbruck et al.: 2007).

Pfeifer, G. – Nössing, J. (eds.), *Kulturkampf in Tirol und in den Nachbarländern. Akten des Internationalen Kolloquiums des Tiroler Geschichtsvereins (Sektion Bozen) im Kolpinghaus Bozen, 9. November 2012* (Innsbruck: 2013).

Pixton, P.B., *The German Episcopacy and the Implementation of the Decrees of the Fourth Lateran-Council 1216–1245: Watchmen on the Tower* (Leiden – New York – Cologne: 1995).

Pizzorusso, G., "La congregazione pontifica *de Propaganda Fide* nel XVII secolo: missioni, geopolitica, colonialismo", in Visceglia, M.A. (ed.), *Papato e politica internazionale nella prima età moderna* (Rome: 2013) 149–172.

Plakans, A., *Kinship in the Past. Anthropology of European Family Life, 1500–1900* (Oxford: 1984).

Pollard, J.F., *Money and the Rise of the Modern Papacy. Financing the Vatican, 1850–1950* (Cambridge: 2005).

Pomata, G., "Vollkommen oder verdorben? Der männliche Samen im frühneuzeitlichen Europa", *L'Homme. Z.F.G.* 6, 2 (1995) 59–85.

Pranzl, R., "Das Verhältnis von Staat und Kirche/Religion im theresianisch-josephinischen Zeitalter", in Reinalter, H. (ed.), *Josephinismus als Aufgeklärter Absolutismus* (Vienna – Cologne – Weimar: 2008) 17–52.

Prosperi, A., "Fede, giuramento, inquisizione", in Prodi, P. (ed.), *Glaube und Eid. Treueformeln, Glaubensbekenntnisse und Sozialdisziplinierung zwischen Mittelalter und Neuzeit* (Oldenburg: 1993) 157–171.

Prosperi, A., *Tribunali della coscienza. Inquisitori, confessori, missionari* (Turin: 1996) 476–484.

Prost, M., "Evolution comparée de l'apparentement dans les deux paroisses de la vallée de Valloiuse en Briançonnais. (XVIIe et XVIIIe siècles)", in Brunet, G., – Fauve-Chamoux, A. – Oris, M. (eds.), *Le choix du conjoint. Premiers entretiens de la Société de Démographie Historique, Paris 15–16 novembre 1996* (Villeurbanne: 1998) 151–166.

Przyrembel, A., *'Rassenschande'. Reinheitsmythos und Vernichtungslegitimation im Nationalsozialismus* (Göttingen: 2003).

Pulte, M., *Das Missionsrecht ein Vorreiter des universalen Kirchenrechts. Rechtliche Einflüsse aus den Missionen auf die konziliare und nachkonziliare Gesetzgebung der lateinischen Kirche* (Nettetal: 2006).

Rainer, P., *Die Diözese Brixen im Vormärz. Ein Beitrag zur Kirchengeschichte Tirols 1815–1848* (PhD. Dissertation, University of Vienna: 1968).

Rau, S. – Schwerhoff, G. (eds.), *Zwischen Gotteshaus und Taverne. Öffentliche Räume in Spätmittelalter und Früher Neuzeit* (Cologne et al.: 2004).

Reinalter, H. (ed.), *Josephinismus als Aufgeklärter Absolutismus* (Vienna – Cologne – Weimar: 2008).

Reinalter, H., "Josephinismus als Aufgeklärter Absolutismus – ein Forschungsproblem? Gesellschaftlicher Strukturwandel und theresianisch-josephinische Reformen", in Schmale, W. – Zedinger, R. – Mondot, J. (eds.), *Josephinismus – eine Bilanz / Échecs et réussites du Joséphisme* (Bochum: 2008) 19–33.

Reinalter, H., "Liberalismus und Kirche in Österreich im 19. Jahrhundert", in: Reinalter, H. – Klueting, H. (eds.), *Der deutsche und österreichische Liberalismus. Geschichts- und politikwissenschaftliche Perspektiven im Vergleich* (Innsbruck: 2010) 149–160.

Ries, M., "Nasalli, Ignazio", in *Historisches Lexikon der Schweiz* http://www.hls-dhs-dss.ch/textes /d/D26834.php.

Roberg, B., "Verkehrung der Fronten? Bartolomeo Pacca und der Nuntiaturstreit 1785–1794", in Koller, A. (ed.), *Kurie und Politik. Stand und Perspektiven der Nuntiaturforschung* (Tübingen: 1998) 376–394.

Rösch, P., "Lebensläufe und Schicksale. Auswirkungen von zwei unterschiedlichen Erbsitten in Tirol", in: Rösch, P. (ed.), *Südtiroler Erbhöfe. Menschen und Geschichten* (Bolzano: 1994) 61–70.

Rosenbaum, H., *Formen der Familie. Untersuchungen zum Zusammenhang von Familienverhältnissen, Sozialstruktur und sozialem Wandel in der deutschen Gesellschaft des 19. Jahrhunderts*, 5th ed. (Frankfurt a. M.: 1990).

Rosenbaum, H. – Timm, E., *Private Netzwerke im Wohlfahrtsstaat. Familie, Verwandtschaft und soziale Sicherheit im Deutschland des 20. Jahrhunderts* (Constance: 2008).

Rosenwein, B.H., "Controlling Paradigms", in Rosenwein, B.H. (ed.), *Anger's Past. The Social Uses of an Emotion in the Middle Ages* (Ithaca – London: 1998) 233–247.

Rossi, F., *Der Vatikan. Politik und Organisation*, 3rd ed. (Munich: 2005).

Rüffer, J. – Vorwig, C., "Kulturelle Wandlungen am östlichen Hellweg. Die Taufnamengebung in den Kirchspielen Sassendorf und Dinker vom Anfang des 18. bis zum Ende des 20. Jahrhunderts", in Göttmann, F. – Respondek, P. (eds.), *Historisch-demographische Forschungen* (Cologne: 2001) 138–165.

Ruggiu, F.-J., "Histoire de la parenté ou anthropologie historique de la parenté? Autour de Kinship in Europe", *Annales de Démographie Historique* 1 (2010) 223–256.

Sabean, D.W., "Inzestdiskurse vom Barock bis zur Romantik", *L'Homme. Z.F.G.* 13, 1 (2002) 7–28.

Sabean, D.W., "Kinship and Class Dynamics in Nineteenth-Century Europe", in: Sabean, D.W. – Teuscher, S. – Mathieu, J. (eds.), *Kinship in Europe. Approaches to Long-Term Development (1300–1900)* (New York – Oxford: 2007) 301–313.

Sabean, D.W., "Kinship and Issues of the Self in Europe around 1800", in Johnson, C.H. – Sabean, D.W. (eds.), *Sibling Relations & the Transformation of European Kinship 1300–1900* (New York – Oxford: 2011) 221–237.

Sabean, D.W., "Kinship and Prohibited Marriages in Baroque Germany: Divergent Strategies among Jewish and Christian Population", *Leo Baeck Institute Yearbook* 47 (2002) 91–103.

Sabean, D.W., *Kinship in Neckarhausen, 1700–1870* (Cambridge: 1998).

Sabean, D.W., *Transnationale Geschichte. Themen, Tendenzen und Theorien* (Göttingen: 2006) 275–289.

Sabean, D.W. – Teuscher, S., "Kinship in Europe. A New Approach to Long-Term Development", in: Sabean, D.W. – Teuscher, S. – Mathieu, J. (eds.), *Kinship in Europe. Approaches to Long-Term Development (1300–1900)* (New York – Oxford: 2007) 1–32.

Sabean, D.W. – Teuscher, S. – Mathieu, J. (eds.), *Kinship in Europe. Approaches to Long-Term Development (1300–1900)* (New York – Oxford: 2007).

Safley, M.T., "Canon Law and Swiss Reform: Legal Theory and Practice in the Marital Courts of Zurich, Basel, and St. Gall", in Helmholz, R.H. (ed.), *Canon Law in Protestant Lands* (Berlin: 1992) 187–201.

Sarasin, P., *Reizbare Maschinen. Eine Geschichte des Körpers 1765–1914* (Frankfurt a. M.: 2001).

Sarti, R., "Nubili e celibi tra scelta e costrizione. I percorsi di Clio (Europa occidentale, secoli XVI–XX)", in Lanzinger, M. – Sarti, R. (eds.), *Nubili e celibi tra scelta e costrizione (secoli XVI–XX)* (Udine: 2006) 145–318.

Sarti, R., *Europe at Home: Family and Material Culture, 1500–1800* (New Haven – London: 2002 [1999]).

Sarti, R. – Lanzinger, M. – Eibach, J. (eds.), "Open House", special issue, *European History Quarterly* 51, 4 (2021).

Saurer, E., "Belles-mères et beaux-fils. Au sujet du choix du partenaire en Autriche vers 1800", *Annales de démographie historique* (1998) 59–71.

Saurer, E., *Liebe und Arbeit. Geschlechterbeziehungen im 19. und 20. Jahrhundert*, ed. by Lanzinger, M., (Vienna – Cologne – Weimar: 2014).

Saurer, E., "Formen von Verwandtschaft und Liebe – Traditionen und Brüche. Venetien und Niederösterreich im frühen 19. Jahrhundert", in Lanzinger, M. – Saurer, E. (eds.), *Politiken der Verwandtschaft. Beziehungsnetze, Geschlecht und Recht* (Göttingen: 2007) 255–271.

Saurer, E., "Reglementierte Liebe. Staatliche Ehehindernisse in der vormärzlichen Habsburgermonarchie", *Sozialwissenschaftliche Information* 24 (1995) 245–252.

Saurer, E., "Stiefmütter und Stiefsöhne. Endogamieverbote zwischen kanonischem und zivilem Recht am Beispiel Österreichs (1790–1850)", in Gerhard, U. (ed.), *Frauen in der Geschichte des Rechts. Von der Frühen Neuzeit bis zur Gegenwart* (Munich: 1997) 345–366.

Scheutz, M., "'hab ichs auch im würthshauß da und dort gehört [...]'. Gaststätten als multifunktionale öffentliche Orte im 18. Jahrhundert", in Scheutz, M. – Schmale, W. – Štefanova, D. (eds.), *Orte des Wissens* (Bochum: 2004) 169–203.

Schima, S., "Die 'Tiroler Glaubenseinheit' vor dem Hintergrund der österreichischen Rechts- und Verfassungsentwicklung im 19. Jahrhundert", *Jahrbuch für die Geschichte des Protestantismus in Österreich* 123 (2007) 65–119.

Schima, S., "Glaubenswechsel in Österreich in der staatlichen Gesetzgebung von Joseph II. bis heute", *Wiener Zeitschrift zur Geschichte der Neuzeit* 7, 2 (2007) 79–99.

Schlögel, K., *Im Raume lesen wir die Zeit. Über Zivilisationsgeschichte und Geopolitik*, 2nd ed. (Frankfurt a. M.: 2007).

Schlögl, R., "Kommunikation und Vergesellschaftung unter Anwesenden. Formen des Sozialen und ihre Transformation in der Frühen Neuzeit", *Geschichte und Gesellschaft* 34, 2 (2008) 155–224.

Schlumbohm, J., "Gesetze, die nicht durchgesetzt werden – ein Strukturmerkmal des frühneuzeitlichen Staates?", *Geschichte und Gesellschaft* 23 (1997) 647–663.

Schlumbohm, J., *Lebensläufe, Familien, Höfe. Die Bauern und Heuerleute des Osnabrückischen Kirchspiels Belm in proto-industrieller Zeit, 1650–1860* (Göttingen: 1994).

Schmale, W. – Zedinger, R. – Mondot, J. (eds.), *Josephinismus – eine Bilanz / Échecs et réussites du Joséphisme* (Bochum: 2008).

Schmidt, J.F.K. et al. (eds.), *Freundschaft und Verwandtschaft. Zur Unterscheidung und Verflechtung zweier Beziehungssysteme* (Constance: 2007).

Schmolke, M., *Die schlechte Presse. Katholiken und Publizistik zwischen 'Katholik' und 'Publik', 1821–1968* (Münster: 1971).

Schmugge, L., *Ehen vor Gericht. Paare der Renaissance vor dem Papst* (Berlin: 2008).

Schmugge, L. et al. (eds.), *Repertorium poenitentiariae Germanicum. Verzeichnis der in den Supplikenregistern der Pönitentiarie vorkommenden Personen, Kirchen und Orte des Deutschen Reiches*, 5 vols. (Tübingen: 1998–2002).

Schneider, D.M., *A Critique of the Study of Kinship* (Ann Arbor: 1984).

Schneider, J.C. – Schneider, P.T., *Festival of the Poor. Fertility Decline & the Ideology of Class in Sicily, 1860–1980* (Tucson: 1996).

Schneider, K., *Dornbirner Bürger 1867–1914. Zwischen Anspruch und Alltag* (Constance: 2005).

Schraut, S., *Das Haus Schönborn – eine Familienbiographie. Katholischer Reichsadel 1640–1840* (Paderborn: 2005).

Schraut, S., "'Die Ehen werden in dem Himmel gemacht'. Ehe- und Liebeskonzepte der katholischen Reichsritterschaft im 17. und 18. Jahrhundert", in Opitz, C. – Weckel, U. – Kleinau, E. (eds.), *Tugend, Vernunft und Gefühl: Geschlechterdiskurse der Aufklärung und weiblichen Lebenswelten* (Münster: 2000) 15–32.

Schraut, S., "'Doch das bei weitem schwierigste Ehehindernis ist das der Verwandtschaft': Verbotene Ehe zwischen Inzest Tabu und dem Gedeihen der Adelsfamilie (Deutsches Reich 17./18. Jh.)", in *Copenhagen, The Royal Library* 2005: https://www.unibw.de/geschichte/prof/neu/pers/schraut/downloads/a11b_schraut-ger.pdf (accessed: May 2022).

Schraut, S., "Familie ist mehr als die Summe ihrer Mitglieder – Verwandtschaftsbeziehungen im katholischen stiftsfähigen Reichsadels", *WerkstattGeschichte* 46 (2007) 13–24.

Schrör, M., *Metropolitangewalt und papstgeschichtliche Wende* (Husum: 2009).

Schubert, W. – Schmoeckel, M. (eds.), *200 Jahre Code civil. Die napoleonische Kodifikation in Deutschland und Europa* (Cologne – Weimar – Vienna: 2005).

Schwab, D., "Der Zugriff von Staat und Kirche auf die Ehe – eine historische Reflexion", in Kohl, G. – Neschwara, C. – Simon, T. (eds.), *Rechtsgeschichte mit internationalen Perspektiven. Festschrift für Wilhelm Brauneder zum 65. Geburtstag* (Vienna: 2008) 615–633.

Schweitzer, P.P., "Introduction", in: Schweitzer, P.P. (ed.), *Dividends of Kinship. Meanings and Uses of Social Relatedness* (London – New York: 2000) 1–32.

Segalen, M., Fifteen Generations of Bretons. Kinship and Society in Lower Brittany 1720–1980 (Cambridge et al.: 2007).

Segalen, M. – Richard, P., "Marrying Kinsmen in Pays Bigouden Sud, Brittany", *Journal of Family History* 11 (1986) 109–130.

Seidel Menchi, S., "Percorsi variegati, percorsi obbligati. Elogio del matrimonio pretridentino", in Seidel Menchi, S. – Quaglioni, D. (eds.), *Matrimoni in dubbio. Unioni controverse e nozze clandestine in Italia dal XIV al XVIII secolo* (Bologna: 2001) 17–60.

Seidel Menchi, S. – Quaglioni, D. (eds.), *Matrimoni in dubbio. Unioni controverse e nozze clandestine in Italia dal XIV al XVIII secolo* (Bologna: 2001).

Seppelt, F.X., *Papstgeschichte von den Anfängen bis zur Gegenwart*, 5th ed. (Munich: 1949).

Seyferth, G., "Colonização, imigração e a questão racial no Brasil", *Revista USP* 53 (2002) 117–149, https://www.revistas.usp.br/revusp/article/view/33192/35930 (accessed: May 2022).

Sheehan, M.M., "The European Family and Canon Law", *Continuity and Change* 6, 3 (1991) 347–360.

Shorter, E., *The Making of the Modern Family* (London: 1976).

"Siblings – Parents – Grandparants", *Historical Social Research* 30, 3 (2005), special issue, ed. by Fertig, G.

Spatzenegger, H., "Das Archiv von Santa Maria dell'Anima in Rom", *Römische Historische Mitteilungen* 25 (1983), 109–163.

Sperling, J., "Marriage at the Time of the Council of Trent (1560–70): Clandestine Marriages, Kinship Prohibitions and Dowry Exchange in European Comparison", *Journal of Early Modern History* 8, 1–2 (2004) 67–108.

Spörri, M., "Moderne Blutsverwandtschaften. Die 'Blutprobe' und die Biologisierung der Vaterschaft in der Weimarer Republik", *L'Homme. Z.F.G.* 21, 2 (2010), 33–49.

Spörri, M., *Reines und gemischtes Blut. Zur Kulturgeschichte der Blutgruppenforschung, 1900–1933* (Bielefeld: 2013).

Squicciarini, D., *Die apostolischen Nuntien in Wien*, 2nd ed. (Vatian City: 2000).

"Starke Bande. Verwandtschaft, Arbeit und Geschlecht", *Traverse* 3 (1996), special issue, ed. by Sardet, F. – Stubenvoll, M.

Stauber, R., *Der Zentralstaat an seinen Grenzen. Administrative Integration, Herrschaftswechsel und politische Kultur im südlichen Alpenraum 1750–1820* (Göttingen: 2001).

Steeb, C. – Strimitzer, B., "Österreichs diplomatische Vertretung am Heiligen Stuhl im Spiegel der k. (u.) k. Vatikanpolitik im 19. Jahrhundert", in Paarhammer, H. – Rinnerthaler, A. (eds.), *Österreich und der Heilige Stuhl im 19. und 20. Jahrhundert* (Frankfurt a. M. et al.: 2002) 35–63.

Stella, A., "I principati vescovili di Trento e Bressanone", in Marini, L. et al. (eds.), *I Ducati padani Trento e Trieste* (Turin: 1979) 499–606.

Steidl, A., "Verwandtschaft und Freundschaft als soziale Netzwerke transatlantischer MigrantInnen in der Spätphase der Habsburgermonarchie", in Lanzinger, M. – Saurer, E. (eds.), *Politiken der Verwandtschaft. Beziehungsnetze, Geschlecht und Recht* (Göttingen: 2007) 117–144.

Stolberg-Rilinger, B. – Krischer, A. (eds.), *Herstellung und Darstellung von Entscheidungen. Verfahren, Verwalten und Verhandeln in der Vormoderne* (Berlin: 2010).

Stone, L., *The Family, Sex and Marriage in England 1500–1800* (London: 1977).

Strasser, U., *State of Virginity. Gender, Religion, and Politics in an Early Modern Catholic State* (Ann Arbor: 2004).

Stren, N., *Verbotene Beziehungen: Frühneuzeitliche Verwandtschafts- und Beziehungskonzepte in Ehedispensansuchen vor dem Passauer Konsistorium* (Diploma dissertation, University of Vienna: 2014).

Strathern, M., *After Nature: English Kinship in the Late Twentieth Century* (Cambridge: 1992).

Strathern, M., *Relations. An Anthropological Account* (Durham – London: 2020).

Studer, B., "Familialisierung und Individualisierung. Zur Struktur der Geschlechterordnung in der bürgerlichen Gesellschaft", *L'Homme. Z.F.G.* 11, 1 (2000) 83–104.

Studt, B., "Haus- und Familienbücher", in Pauser, J. – Scheutz, M. – Winkelbauer, T. (eds.), *Quellenkunde der Habsburgermonarchie (16.–18. Jahrhundert). Ein exemplarisches Handbuch* (Vienna – Munich: 2004) 753–766.

Tadmor, N., *Family and Friends in Eighteenth-Century England: Household. Kinship, and Patronage* (Cambridge: 2001).

Tamburini, F., "Le dispense matrimoniali come fonte storica nei documenti della Penitenzieria apostolica (sec. XIII–XVI)", in *Le modèle familial Européen. Normes, déviances, contrôle du pouvoir. Actes des séminaires organisés par l'École française de Rome et l'Università di Roma* (Rome: 1986) 9–30.

"Tanten", *WerkstattGeschichte* 46 (2007), special issue, ed. by Hohkamp, M.

Tassin, G., *Qui épouser et comment. Alliances récurrentes à Haveluy de 1701 à 1870* (Paris: 2007).

Teuscher, S., *Bekannte – Klienten – Verwandte. Soziabilität und Politik in der Stadt Bern um 1500* (Cologne – Weimar – Vienna: 1998).

Teuscher, S., "Familienerinnerungen, Beziehungsmanagement und politische Sprache in spätmittelalterlichen Städten", *Traverse* 2 (2002), 53–64.

Teuscher, S., "Flesh and Blood in the Treatises on the *Arbor Consanguinitatis* (Thirteenth to Sixteenth Century)", in Johnson, C.H. et al. (eds.), *Blood & Kinship. Matter for Metaphor from Ancient Rome to the Present* (New York – Oxford: 2013) 83–104.

Teuscher, S., "Verwandtschaft in der Vormoderne. Zur politischen Karriere eines Beziehungskonzepts", in Harding, E. – Hecht, M. (eds.), *Die Ahnenprobe in der Vormoderne. Selektion – Initiation – Repräsentation* (Münster: 2011) 85–106.

Todd, B.J., "Demographic Determinism and Female Agency: the Remarrying Widow Reconsidered ... Again", *Continuity and Change* 9 (1994) 421–450.

Trepp, A.-C., "Gefühl oder kulturelle Konstruktion? Überlegungen zur Geschichte der Emotionen", *Querelles. Jahrbuch für Frauenforschung* 7 (2002) 86–103.

Trepp, A.-C., *Sanfte Männlichkeit und selbständige Weiblichkeit. Frauen und Männer im Hamburger Bürgertum zwischen 1770 und 1840* (Göttingen: 1996).

Trévisi, M., "Le mariage entre parents à La Roche-Guyon (Vexin français) au XVIIIe siècle: une étude de la perception du lien de parenté dans le cras des mariages avec dispense", in Duhamelle, C. – Schlumbohm, J. (eds.), *Eheschließungen im Europa des 18. und 19. Jahrhunderts. Muster und Strategien* (Göttingen: 2003) 241–265.

Trivellato, F., "Is There a Future for Italian Microhistory in the Age of Global History?", *California Italian Studies* 2, 1 (2011), http://escholarship.org/uc/item/0z94n9hq (accessed May 2022).

Ubl, K., *Inzestverbot und Gesetzgebung. Die Konstruktion eines Verbrechens* (300–1100) (Berlin – New York: 2008).

Ulbrich, C., "Artikel 'Ehe'", in *Enzyklopädie der Neuzeit*, vol. 3 (Stuttgart: 2006) col. 38–44.

Ulbrich, C., *Shulamit und Margarete. Power, Gender, and Religion in a Rural Society in Eighteenth-Century Europe* (Boston: 2004).

Unkelbach, P., "Die Päpste und die Bedeutsamkeit des Papsttums dokumentiert am Wirken des Salzburger Fürsterzbischofs Augustin Gruber", in Paarhammer, H. –

Rinnerthaler, A. (eds.), *Salzburg und der Heilige Stuhl im 19. und 20. Jahrhundert. Festgabe zum 75. Geburtstag von Erzbischof Georg Eder* (Frankfurt a. M. et al.: 2003) 379–432.

"Unmarried Lives", *European History Quarterly* 38, 3 (2008), 417–449, special issue, ed. by Evangelisti, S. – Lanzinger, M. – Sarti, R.

Vanysacker, D., *Cardinal Giuseppe Garampi (1725–1792). An Enlightened Ultramonane* (Brussels et al.: 1995).

"Verwandtschaft machen. Reproduktionsmedizin und Adoption in Deutschland und der Türkei", *Berliner Blätter. Ethnographische und ethnologische Beiträge* 42 (2007), special issue, ed. by Knecht, M. et al.

Viazzo, P.P., *Upland Communities. Environment, Population and Social Structure in the Alps Since the Sixteenth Century* (Cambridge: 1989).

Vocelka, K., *Geschichte Österreichs. Kultur – Gesellschaft – Politik*, 3rd ed. (Munich: 2002).

Vocelka, K., *Verfassung oder Konkordat? Der publizistische und politische Kampf der österreichischen Liberalen um die Religionsgesetze des Jahres 1868* (Vienna: 1978).

Wagner, M. – Schütze, Y. (eds.), *Verwandtschaft. Sozialwissenschaftliche Beiträge zu einem vernachlässigten Thema* (Stuttgart: 1998).

Wagner, W., "Die Bestände des Archivio della Nunziatura Vienna bis 1792", *Römische Historische Mitteilungen* 2 (1957/58) 82–203.

Warner, L., "Kinship Riddles", *genealogy* 6, 43 (2022), https://doi.org/10.3390/genealogy6020043 (last access: June 2022).

Warner, L., "Remembering the Mother, Presenting the Stepmother: Portraits of the Early Modern Family in Northern Europe", *Early Modern Women. An Interdisciplinary Journal* 6 (2011) 93–125.

Warner, L. (ed.), *Stepfamilies in Europe, 1400–1800* (Abingdon – New York: 2018).

Weingart, P. – Kroll, J. – Bayertz, K., *Rasse, Blut und Gene. Geschichte der Eugenik und Rassenhygiene in Deutschland* (Frankfurt a. M.: 1992).

Weinzierl-Fischer, E., *Die österreichischen Konkordate von 1855 und 1933* (Vienna: 1960).

Weiß, A.S., "'Dem Pabste brach darüber das Herz …'. Salzburgs Beziehungen zu Rom unter Erzbischof Colloredo – ein gespanntes Verhältnis?", in Paarhammer, H. – Rinnerthaler, A. (eds.), *Salzburg und der Heilige Stuhl im 19. und 20. Jahrhundert. Festgabe zum 75. Geburtstag von Erzbischof Georg Eder* (Frankfurt a. M. et al.: 2003) 433–460.

Weiß, A.S., "Josephinismus in Salzburg? Ein Beispiel der kirchlichen Reformtätigkeit", in Schmale, W. – Zedinger, R. – Mondot, J. (eds.), *Josephinismus – eine Bilanz / Échecs et réussites du Joséphisme* (Bochum: 2008) 93–114.

Weitensfelder, H., *Industrie-Provinz. Vorarlberg in der Frühindustrialisierung 1740–1870* (Frankfurt a. M. – New York: 2001).

Weitensfelder, H., *'Römlinge' und 'Preußenseuchler'. Konservativ-Christlichsoziale, Liberal-Deutschnationale und der Kulturkampf in Vorarlberg, 1860 bis 1914* (Vienna – Cologne – Weimar: 2008).

Weitensfelder, H., "Zu arm zum Heiraten? Ehekonsense in Vorarlberg als Mittel konservativer Sozialpolitik (1850–1914)", *Montfort. Vierteljahresschrift für Geschichte und Gegenwart Vorarlbergs* 57, 1 (2005) 18–40.

Welti, M.E., "Das apostolische Gesandtschaftswesen in der Schweiz", in Bruckner, A. (ed.), *Schweizerische Kardinäle. Das apostolische Gesandtschaftswesen in der Schweiz. Erzbistümer und Bistümer 1* (Bern: 1972) 35–60.

Werner, M. – Zimmermann, B., "Vergleich, Transfer, Verflechtung. Der Ansatz der *Histoire croisée* und die Herausforderung des Transnationalen", *Geschichte und Gesellschaft* 28 (2002) 607–636.

Westphal, S., "Kirchenzucht als Ehe- und Sittenzucht. Die Auswirkungen von lutherischer Konfessionalisierung auf das Geschlechterverhältnis", in Conrad, A. (ed.), *'In Christo ist weder man noch weyb'. Frauen in der Zeit der Reformation und der katholische Reform* (Münster: 1999) 152–171.

Westphal, S. – Schmidt-Voges, I. – Baumann, A., *Venus und Vulcanus. Ehen und ihre Konflikte in der Frühen Neuzeit* (Munich: 2011).

Winkler, G., *Bevölkerungsgeographische Untersuchungen im Martelltal* (Innsbruck – München: 1973).

Wodiczka, U., *Das Motiv der Stiefmutter in den Kinder- und Hausmärchen der Brüder Grimm* (diploma dissertation, University of Vienna: 1992).

Wolfram, S., *In-Laws and Outlaws: Kinship and Marriage in England* (London – Sydney: 1987).

Wunder, H., "Arbeiten, Wirtschaften, Haushalten: Geschlechterverhältnisse und Geschlechterbeziehungen im Wandel der deutschen Agrargesellschaft des 18. und 19. Jahrhunderts", in Prass, R. et al. (eds.), *Ländliche Gesellschaften in Deutschland, Frankreich, 18. und 19. Jahrhundert* (Göttingen: 2003) 187–204.

Wunder, H., *'Er ist die Sonn', sie ist der Mond.' Frauen in der Frühen Neuzeit* (Munich: 1992).

Wunder, H., "'Jede Arbeit ist ihres Lohnes wert.' Zur geschlechtsspezifischen Teilung und Bewertung von Arbeit in der Frühen Neuzeit", in Hausen, K. (ed.), *Geschlechterhierarchie und Arbeitsteilung. Zur Geschichte ungleicher Erwerbschancen von Männern und Frauen* (Göttingen: 1993) 19–39.

Würgler, A., "Bitten und Begehren. Suppliken und Gravamina in der deutschsprachigen Frühneuzeitforschung", in Nubola, C. – Würgler, A. (eds.), *Bittschriften und Gravamina. Politik, Verwaltung und Justiz in Europa (14.–18. Jahrhundert)* (Berlin: 2005) 17–52.

Yanagisako, S. – Collier, J.F., "Toward a Unified Analysis of Gender and Kinship", in Yanagisako, S. – Collier, J.F. (eds.), *Gender and Kinship. Towards a Unified Analysis* (Stanford: 1987) 14–50.

Zarri, G., "Die tridentinische Ehe", in Prodi, P. (ed.), *Das Konzil von Trient und die Moderne* (Berlin: 2001) 343–379.

Zemon Davis, N., *Trickster Travels. A Sixteenth-Century Muslim Between Worlds* (New York: 2006).

Zonabend, F., "Verwandtschaft in der anthropologischen Forschung Frankreichs", in Chiva, I. – Jeggle, U. (eds.), *Deutsche Volkskunde – Französische Ethnologie – Zwei Standortbestimmungen* (Frankfurt a. M.: 1987) 178–193.

Zwilling, M., "Mutterstämme – Die Biologisierung des genealogischen Denkens und die Stellung der Frau in Familie und Gesellschaft von 1900 bis zur NS-Zeit", *Tel Aviver Jahrbuch für deutsche Geschichte* 34 (2008) 29–47.

Index